MULTIMODAL
COMPOSITION

The Bedford/St. Martin's Series in Rhetoric and Composition

Assessing Writing: A Critical Sourcebook, edited by Brian Huot and Peggy O'Neill

Computers in the Composition Classroom: A Critical Sourcebook, edited by Michelle Sidler, Richard Morris, and Elizabeth Overman Smith

Disability and the Teaching of Writing: A Critical Sourcebook, edited by Cynthia Lewiecki-Wilson and Brenda Jo Brueggmann

Feminism and Composition: A Critical Sourcebook, edited by Gesa E. Kirsch, Faye Spencer Maor, Lance Massey, Lee Nickoson-Massey, and Mary P. Sheridan-Rabideau

Literacy: A Critical Sourcebook, edited by Ellen Cushman, Eugene R. Kintgen, Barry M. Kroll, and Mike Rose

An Open Language: Selected Writing in Literacy, Learning, and Opportunity, edited by Mike Rose

Second-Language Writing in the Composition Classroom: A Critical Sourcebook, edited by Paul Kei Matsuda, Michelle Cox, Jay Jordan, and Christina Ortmeier-Hooper

Selected Essays of Robert J. Connors, edited by Lisa Ede and Andrea A. Lunsford

Style in Composition and Rhetoric: A Critical Sourcebook, edited by Paul Butler

Views from the Center: The CCCC Chairs' Addresses 1977–2005, edited by Duane Roen

Visual Rhetoric in a Digital World: A Critical Sourcebook, edited by Carolyn Handa

Writing Across the Curriculum: A Critical Sourcebook, edited by Terry Myers Zawacki and Paul M. Rogers

Writing and Community Engagement: A Critical Sourcebook, edited by Thomas Deans, Barbara Roswell, and Adrian J. Wurr

Writing on the Margins: Essays on Composition and Teaching, edited by David Bartholomae

On Writing Research: The Braddock Essays 1975–1998, edited by Lisa Ede

MULTIMODAL COMPOSITION

A Critical Sourcebook

EDITED BY

Claire Lutkewitte
Nova Southeastern University

BEDFORD / ST. MARTIN'S   Boston • New York

For Bedford/St. Martin's

Senior Executive Editor: Leasa Burton
Developmental Editor: Daniel F. Schafer
Production Supervisor: Victoria Sharoyan
Project Management: DeMasi Design and Publishing Services
Permissions Manager: Kalina K. Ingham
Text Design: Anna Palchik
Cover Design: Donna Lee Dennison
Composition: Jeff Miller Book Design
Printing and Binding: RR Donnelley and Sons

President, Bedford/St. Martin's: Denise B. Wydra
Presidents, Macmillan Higher Education: Joan E. Feinberg and Tom Scotty
Editor in Chief: Karen S. Henry
Director of Marketing: Karen R. Soeltz
Production Director: Susan W. Brown
Associate Production Director: Elise S. Kaiser
Manager, Publishing Services: Andrea Cava

Manufactured in the United States of America.

8 7 6 5 4 3
f e d c b a

ISBN 978-1-4576-1549-8

For information, write: Bedford/St. Martin's, 75 Arlington Street, Boston, MA 02116 (617-399-4000)

Acknowledgments

Acknowledgments and copyrights are continued at the back of the book on pages 526–29, which constitute an extension of the copyright page. It is a violation of the law to reproduce these selections by any means whatsoever without the written permission of the copyright holder.

CONTENTS

MULTIMODAL
COMPOSITION

An Introduction to Multimodal Composition Theory and Practice

Deciding the "what" of our courses is a major part of our task as composition instructors and has been affected by multimodal composition scholarship. This decision encompasses questions such as: What is the point of the composition classroom? Is it to prepare students for writing in academia? in the workforce? in civic life? And what should we teach when we teach composition? If we were to travel across the country and visit composition classrooms at colleges and universities along the way, no doubt we would find diversity in the "what" that composition instructors teach (and the language they use to teach it). While we would find students writing essays in the most traditional sense, we would also find students designing multimodal and multimedia projects.

The field of composition studies has long debated what to call this "what," and much of the confusion over multimodal composition stems from our use of diverse names for this "what." Should we call it multimodal composition, multimedia composition, new media composition, multiwriting, multigenre, or, simply, composition? Additionally, the question of "why" is likely to be at the forefront of any conversation relating to multimodal composition. Why should composition teachers integrate multimodal projects into their courses? Why should instructors care about multimodal scholarship, especially if they have little or no background in it. This sourcebook attempts to address these questions, and interrogate their answers, in the hope of introducing interested readers to multimodal composition, advancing the discussions taking place in the field, and encouraging those who are apprehensive about using modes other than the written word in the composition classroom. Though multimodal composition can appear daunting to teachers and students who lack expertise with multimodal composition and pedagogy, the authors in this book argue it can allow for the rich experiences that engage students in learning and in meaning making.

As a result of an increased interest in multimodal composition, the body of work that explores its nature and value is growing (see for example the program for the 2012 Conference on College Composition and Communication, which was full of presentations devoted to multimodal composition).

Several reasons account for such an increase in this type of scholarship. Multi-modal composition is more popular in composition classrooms than ever before because instructors and students are recognizing that old and new technologies have enabled, and even demanded, the use of more than one mode to communicate, entertain, solve problems, and engage in deliberation. We can likewise point to composition's willingness to draw from other disciplines—like art, for example—that value a range of different modes and media to communicate messages. Combined with a growing body of multi-modal composition scholarship, these factors have greatly impacted the composition field through the shaping of its curricula, practices, and theories, and point to our understanding that rhetorical awareness, which can demand that we create in multiple modes, is essential to any successful communicator.

The term *multimodal composition* was chosen for this book because it speaks to a particular audience. As Claire Lauer contends in Part One, *multimodal* is a term most popular in the composition field and is different from the more popular term *multimedia*. Though this book is titled *Multimodal Composition: A Critical Sourcebook*, there is value in the other terminology mentioned above. In fact, as readers will see, several selections use the terms *multimedia* or *new media*. As Claire Lauer notes, instructors can benefit from using several terms so long as we make clear to our students how we are using them. She explains, for example, that while *multimodal* is a more useful term when helping students understand "the cognitive and socially situated choices students are making in their compositions," the term *multimedia* connects students to the language they will encounter in public spaces outside of the classroom (see p. 23 in this volume).* The task of distinguishing between the terms, though, can be difficult for students—and even instructors—as there is a close relationship between modes and media. For example, drawing from Gunther R. Kress and Theo Van Leeuwen, leading scholars of multimodality, Lauer points out, "Modes and media are independent of and interdependent with each other, meaning that although media and modes are different from each other, the media we use affect the ways in which we can realize meaning through various modes" (p. 25). In everything we teach, as instructors, we need to be careful about how we communicate a terminology to our students to avoid any confusion.

In a broad sense, multimodal composition can be defined as communication using multiple modes that work purposely to create meaning. For a more technical definition, we could turn to Kress and Van Leeuwen who see it "as the use of several semiotic modes in the design of a semiotic product or event, together with the particular way in which these modes are combined" (20). Though this definition mentions a product or event, implying a certain finality, it also highlights the *act* of composing. As readers will see later in the book, Lauer observes that multimodal composition is more about the process, or act of composing, than simply the final product. This sentiment is echoed

---

*Cross-references to material reprinted in this volume are preceded by "p."; references to sections not included in this book carry only the page number.

in Jody Shipka's book *Toward a Composition Made Whole*. Shipka contends that "to label a text multimodal or monomodal based on its final appearance alone discounts, or worse yet, renders invisible the contributions made by a much wider variety of resources, supports, and tools" (52). Therefore, she asserts that it is necessary for students to think critically about the whole process of composing, which involves decisions and reflections on the modes they use. Drawing from Paul Prior's 2009 work, Shipka argues that multimodal composition

> is not some special feature of texts or certain kinds of utterances, but a "routine dimension of language in use" and "has always and every-where been present as representations are propagated across multiple media and as any situated event is indexically fed by all modes present whether they are focalized or backgrounded.... Through composition, different moments of history, different persons, different voices, different addresses may become embedded in the composed utterance." (27)

Shipka's idea of a composition made whole is one that recognizes the multi-modal practices or behaviors that take place throughout the entire composing process and recognizes "the complex ways that texts come to be" (13). Multi-modal composition is situated and thus shaped by context, history, audience, place, time, and other factors. In recognition of those many factors, Shipka supports a workshop approach to teaching, one that allows students to consider a wide range of digital and nondigital modes, materials, and media throughout their composing processes. This process-focused approach encourages students to experiment with multiple modes and rhetorical appeals in a way that broadens their understanding of what effective communication entails. By shifting students' attention away from the finished product and toward the process of composing, we can motivate them to engage in rhetorical aware-ness more deeply than would otherwise be possible.

The history of composition is replete with scholars who value the writing process. This work often privileges the written word and/or reduces the process to a formula that ignores the complicated nature of composing. For example, in the 1970s, process enthusiast Donald Murray wrote:

> What is the process we should teach? It is the process of discovery through language. It is the process of exploration of what we know and what we feel about what we know through language. It is the process of using language to learn about our world, to evaluate what we learn about our world, to communicate what we learn about our world. In-stead of teaching finished writing, we should teach unfinished writing, and glory in its unfinishedness. We work with language in action. We share with our students the continual excitement of choosing one word instead of another, of searching for the one true word....
>
> This process of discovery through language we call writing can be introduced to your classroom as soon as you have a very simple under-standing of that process, and as soon as you accept the full implications of teaching process, not product. (4)

Multimodal composition is not simply an extension of traditional composition, and we can't simply overlay traditional frameworks onto composing with multiple modes. At the same time, though, the entire field of composition exists because of evolving theory and practice—multimodal composition included. Therefore, we can acknowledge Murray-style process theory in order to bridge the past with the present. Murray's quote, for instance, could be referring to multimodal composition if we replaced the word *word* with *mode*, as not all communicative situations involve the search for "the one true word." There are certainly modes beyond the written word through which we can "learn about our world, to evaluate what we learn about our world," and "to communicate what we learn about our world." Instructors shouldn't lead their students to believe otherwise. Further, the process of discovery Murray mentions is more fully realized by thinking about multimodal composition through the composing process. Indeed, embracing multimodality is realizing "the full implications of teaching process, not product."

Shipka and Cynthia L. Selfe believe that multimodal composition gives students the agency they need to reflect on who they are as composers in the world, who their audiences are, what contexts they are writing in, and how to choose the appropriate modes to communicate in this world. Much like Shipka, Selfe suggests that multimodal composition entails more than just the combining of multiple modes. Multimodal composition has as its goal to "[help] students understand the power and affordances of different modalities—and to combine modalities in effective and appropriate ways—multiplying the modalities students can use to communicate effectively with different audiences, and helping students employ modalities to make meaningful change in their own lives and the lives of others" (195). At its heart, Selfe's work argues that rhetorical awareness is key to successful composition. Analyzing one's audience and being able to utilize multiple modes, whether in isolation or combination, allow students to determine the most effective means of communication for any situation.

In addition to Shipka and Selfe, this book highlights scholars whose work points to the enhanced rhetorical awareness that composing in multiple modes, or single modes beyond print when appropriate, provides students and scholars. In drawing from the happenings artists of the 1960s, Geoffrey Sirc, for instance, argues that when compositionists experiment with "new materials and forms," and when they "blur disciplines and boundaries," (p. 58) they frustrate conventions, and therefore, other, perhaps more significant, meanings surface. Similarly, Kathleen Blake Yancey provides a good example of multimodal composition practices at different stages of the composing process in her selection (pp. 62–88) when she talks about her work with graduate students in architecture who use pin-ups on the wall to explore their ideas.

As readers will see in the texts that follow, particularly those in Parts Four and Six, students can engage in a variety of multimodal composition projects in their quest to communicate with their audience as effectively as possible. The pieces highlighted in this book range from digital audio reflections (see Debra Journet et al., pp. 358–59) to quilts or dresses (see Suzanne Kesler Rumsey, pp. 486–96), but what they all have in common is that they exemplify an astute understanding of audience and rhetorical awareness. This work, therefore, nods in agreement with Victor Villanueva's fundamental, significant, and yet often overlooked observation that "composition is complex and diverse," (xiv) and builds upon the theories of traditional composition studies in a quest to help students and scholars communicate and persuade with maximum effectiveness.

From graduate students to senior faculty members, many of the authors in this book come from the forefront of multimodal composition scholarship. Senior faculty have taken it upon themselves to continue to add to the body of knowledge by building upon and challenging composition traditions, while new faculty come to the field with different experiences that help them to see composition from a new perspective. Though these authors could be considered our field's leading experts, they should not be considered the ultimate authorities on multimodal composition as the field would risk conventionalizing what should not be conventionalized (see, for example, Sirc, pp. 42–61, on what is at stake when a field conventionalizes). One of the arguments readers will find in this collection is that multimodal composition allows for many voices—even those new, marginalized, or unpopular voices—to be heard. This is evidenced not only through conventional scholarship, which does play an important role in this work, but also through the kinds of multimodal texts and student examples the authors share with readers.

The book has been divided into six parts, though these parts present only one way, not the only way, of organization. While these readings are brought together by similar discussions about what it means to compose using multiple modes, readers are encouraged to follow their own paths when reading and to discover themes that emerge from those paths. For example, readers might ask themselves how a reading in Part One could be juxtaposed with a reading from Part Three. Texts were chosen for their accessibility and their use of multiple modes and examples, and they should be used as starting points, not as ending points, for discussing and studying multimodal composition. (See the list of additional readings at the end of the book for more multimodal composition scholarship.)

In Part One, "What Counts as Multimodal Composition and Why Does It Matter?" the authors give readers an overview of what multimodal composition is and why those of us who teach composition should care about it. As mentioned earlier, Lauer's piece discusses the differences between multimodal composition and multimedia composition, a distinction that will be helpful to readers as they encounter subsequent works. The rest of the selections in Part One explain the meaning-making capabilities of multimodal composition and call for better support to help students and instructors realize these capabilities.

Part One also looks back at moments in our field's history that have played a role in shaping composition's theories and pedagogy. Specifically, the authors in this section speak about events, particularly fundamental shifts in the field in 1963, that were overshadowed by composition's more traditional practices and canonical texts. In a sense then, Part One serves as an investigation into our field's values, both past and present, and examines more closely what has molded our understanding of what it means to compose and how this meaning has been carried out in the composition classroom. The authors' outlooks on history provide readers with different ways of knowing and approaching the teaching of composition, as well as offer us an opportunity to question conventions set forth by scholarship, administrations, institutions, and other entities.

The work of the New London Group, a group of scholars at the forefront of multimodal composition, begins Part Two, "A Matter of Design," by demanding that we think of literacy in broader terms than traditional perspectives allow. Literacy, according to the New London Group, is not just the ability to read and write the printed word, as such a limiting definition fails to capture our ability to understand and communicate in other modes. Instead, they call upon us to think about all the possibilities for composing because in doing so we can take advantage of ongoing social, cultural, and technological changes that impact our ways of knowing. Like Part One, the works in Part Two challenge the privileged position of the printed word in academia and the practice of critiquing products, countering with ways for putting more emphasis on the process of design in the classroom.

Part Three, "Making Meaning with Multimodal Composition," is designed to encourage readers to think more deeply about composition's role in knowledge creation and how different modes—like sound, image, and gesture—help us to create and understand different meanings. As composers, for example, we must pay attention to a mode's affordances, or capabilities, and how they enable us to communicate a message. The authors in Part Three give readers an opportunity to witness meaning making with multiple modes through their use of different texts as examples. For instance, several of the authors examine web texts that utilize multiple modes and compare them to traditional texts, pointing out differences and similarities. They highlight the rhetorical choices composers/designers must make when creating and reading multimodal texts and how social, cultural, and technological influences impact such choices. As these authors discuss, their leadership and their willingness to try something new or something that has been done outside of the classroom for a long time (and is not necessarily popular) without much support from their institutions, administrations, and fellow faculty has proven beneficial, both to their own understanding and their students' understanding of composition.

Part Four, "Assignments and Assessment," presents practical examples of classroom assignments and activities that enable students to compose using a variety of modes. Backed by research and effective assignment design, the authors contend that multimodal composition allows students more agency in their decision-making processes when they are encouraged to compose multimodally. As well, they introduce a vocabulary for talking about multimodal composition. At the heart of this section are much larger and necessary debates about knowledge creation and the teaching of multimodal composition, specifically whether old ways of teaching can be adapted for such pedagogy. This debate is demonstrated clearly in the section's final two selections, which are devoted to discussing how to assess multimodal composition, an important and often difficult task for instructors.

In order for our pedagogy to succeed, we must be willing to build an environment in which it can thrive. Part Five, "Building a Sustainable Environment for Multimodal Composition," discusses what it takes to build, maintain, and negotiate departmental and institution-wide infrastructures that are supportive of multimodal composition. The authors of this section contend such tasks should not be left to administrators because they lack the perspective instructors cultivate by working in the classroom. They advocate that composition instructors have a responsibility to make sure the environment in which they teach is one that allows students comprehensive opportunities for learning, meaning that merely providing students the opportunity to compose in the dominant mode of writing is severely limiting. While the authors in Part Five are quick to point out the obstacles instructors face when they imbed themselves in decisions concerning infrastructure, they also prepare instructors for these challenges by offering strategies for thinking about sustainable environments, ones that keep students' best interests in mind. The authors show us how we can critically examine the complexities of infrastructures so that we may recognize what is and is not valued by our faculty, departments, administrators, and institutions. The authors maintain that such awareness, coupled with the right actions, can lead to positive changes on our campuses.

For instance, in "Infrastructure and Composing: The *When* of New-Media Writing" (p. 405), Dànielle Nicole DeVoss, Ellen Cushman, and Jeffrey T. Grabill examine the new media composing processes of their students and, in doing so, investigate how a campus's infrastructure helps or hinders those processes. They take on a "productive and activist understanding of infrastructure," one that can help both students and instructors gain a deeper understanding of composing in specific contexts (p. 411). Using Cushman's multimedia writing class as an example, they argue that instructors should be involved in developing and challenging infrastructure on campus, including shaping the policies and standards that govern campuses. Such continual participation on the part of writing faculty can have significant, positive results on pedagogical practices. In Cushman's case, she was able to work with system managers on campus to secure extra space for her students' projects, which went more smoothly after doing so.

The final section of the book, Part Six, "The Dynamic Nature of Literacy and Multimodal Composers," incorporates selections that highlight the many different literacy practices carried out by those who compose multimodally. Specifically, the authors make note of distinct cultures that rely on their abilities to use multiple modes to communicate and to express their identities. These observations can help instructors identify the cultures represented in their classrooms so that they may be better prepared to design assignments and activities that engage all of their students. Finally, the selections in Part Six also serve as examples of the different types of research projects that would greatly benefit our field in terms of investigating multimodal composition. They may lead us to reflect on and question our own research practices and help us to understand ways in which we can improve them.

The purpose of *Multimodal Composition: A Critical Sourcebook* is to help educators and scholars make sense of what has been written about multimodal composition by offering a brief history of it as defined by scholars and practitioners in the field of composition. While this book offers a foundation on which readers can build their own multimodal composition scholarship and pedagogy, the scholarship in this book is not meant to advocate that, when combined, these essays represent *the* Theory or *the* Pedagogy of multimodal composition. Building a Theory or a Pedagogy can be dangerous, because those theories and pedagogies that disagree with *the* Theory or *the* Pedagogy often go ignored. Rather, these selections represent several theories and pedagogies that compliment, contrast, and are in dialogue with one another, and they are also meant to help readers find their own path for engaging in multimodal composition.

WORKS CITED

Kress, Gunther R., and Theo Van Leeuwen. *Multimodal Discourse: The Modes and Media of Contemporary Communication*. London: Arnold, 2001. Print.

Murray, Donald M. "Teach Writing as Process Not Product." *Cross-Talk in Comp Theory*. Ed. Victor Villanueva. 2nd ed. Urbana: NCTE, 2003. 3–6. Print.

Selfe, Cynthia L., ed. *Multimodal Composition: Resources for Teachers*. Cresskill: Hampton, 2007. Print.

Shipka, Jody. *Toward a Composition Made Whole*. Pittsburgh: U of Pittsburgh P, 2011. Print.

Villanueva, Victor, ed. *Cross-Talk in Comp Theory*. 2nd ed. Urbana: NCTE, 2003. Print.

What Counts as Multimodal Composition and Why Does It Matter?

Introduction to Part One

Though many instructors embrace multimodal composition, the authors in this book and in Part One in particular respond to those who do not, contending that it is both useful and necessary for a number of reasons. For example, multimodal composition offers us the opportunity to discover other ways of knowing and communicating ideas besides the ways we know and communicate through traditional print-based writing. Likewise, the acknowledgment of multimodal composition in the classroom can help us reflect on the multimodal practices some of us and our students already participate in outside of academia. The purpose of Part One, then, is to reinforce what scholars in our field have been advocating for, to offer encouragement to those who work within environments that do and do not support multimodal composition, and to bring to light some common misconceptions about multimodal composition. The selections in Part One represent broader discussion threads about multimodal composition (theories, scholarship, technology, pedagogy, and so forth) that will help readers as they approach the remainder of the book.

Part One also serves to define multimodal composition and understand how those definitions help us to think more critically about communicating ideas with the use of multiple modes. Part One begins with the "Position Statement on Multimodal Literacies" adopted by the National Council of Teachers of English (NCTE) in November 2005. Because NCTE plays a significant role in the research and teaching of composition, their position statement influences and supports not only teachers and their students but also the institutions that are responsible for providing educators with the most effective resources for implementing their pedagogies. This particular statement argues that teachers need support on many levels in order to carry out successful multimodal composition pedagogy. The selections that follow speak to the struggles instructors and administrators have encountered and highlight the successes they have had while meeting the precedents set forth by this statement. Reading the statement today allows us to consider what we, as a field, have achieved since 2005 in terms of providing students with the opportunities to develop their multimodal literacy skills. But we might also want to ask: What do texts, like this position statement that is disseminated by a leading authority in composition, mean to our understanding of composition and how do they shape what we know? Such questions are useful because in answering them, we are likely to be critical of the way we make knowledge in our field, and thus, we are forced to work together to consider and appreciate other possible ways of knowing.

NCTE articulates several broad definitions of multimodal literacies in this statement, pointing to the "integration of multiple modes of communication and expression" and the "interplay of meaning-making systems." Such definitions can help us think more critically about how multimodal composition can lead to the types of literacies outlined by NCTE. But we might also look to more specific definitions of multimodal composition, like those offered by the other authors in this book, to help us conceive of ways in which multimodal composition practices are crucial to literacy. Also, more specific definitions of multimodal composition can help us compare and contrast it to traditional composition so that we may better understand its meaning-making capabilities.

In "Contending with Terms: 'Multimodal' and 'Multimedia' in the Academic and Public Spheres," Claire Lauer distinguishes between the terms *multimodal* and *multimedia* to help clarify some common misunderstandings about multimodal composition and to help us understand what the differences are between multimodal and multimedia composition. Lauer notes that *multimodal* is strictly a term used in the composition field and not a term used in nonacademic public contexts where the term *multimedia* is most popular. She sees parallels between the ways these terms are used in different contexts and a much larger discussion that composition has been contending with for decades: the value of process over product. She claims that "[t]here is a greater emphasis on design and process in the classroom, which makes the term multimodal more suitable in that context, and a greater emphasis on production and distribution in non-academic or industry contexts which explains the use of the term multimedia in that context."

Multimedia composition is not the only term often interchanged with multimodal composition. Another such term is *new media composition* (see Cheryl Ball's selection). New media texts combine modes and media without subscribing to the conventions of traditional print texts (i.e., alphabetic linear arguments). Multimedia and multimodal texts can follow traditional print conventions. But when multimedia or multimodal texts break away from traditional conventions, they become (or become like) new media texts, though the multimedia or multimodal texts are often more likely to draw attention to their forms because they appear to be new—they have been refashioned (to borrow from Jay David Bolter and Richard Grusin's *Remediation: Understanding New Media*)—and unlike a traditional text, are not ignored. However one chooses to distinguish between multimedia, multimodal, and new media composition, because of their ability to draw attention to how form and content work together to make meaning, the three are closely linked.

To claim that the field of composition is only now beginning to see value in multimodal composition would be false. Though composition scholarship, theories, and pedagogical practices have privileged the printed word, and thus the book, multiple modes of composing have not been overlooked entirely. Indeed, the authors in this section are not the only scholars who recognize that some of the most canonical texts throughout history have valued modes besides the printed word. For example, Kevin LaGrandeur explicates how several classical and belletristic texts and scholars, like Aristotle, Gorgias, Horace, and Campbell, were clearly aware of the powerful persuasive nature of images. Likewise, Catherine Hobbs traces the importance of the visual throughout history, citing several instances when visualization and images were valued. For example, she writes of the illustrated emblem books of the Renaissance and explains how "[w]ords and pictures worked together as equals" much like the kinds of texts present-day scholars suggest we ask students to compose (60). However, while we can see traces of multimodal composition in those texts that have served as a canon for composition, they are not the only places we can turn to when examining our history and the history of multimodal composition.

Therefore, Part One includes alternative views (or perhaps ones that have been there all along but have been overlooked) of some of the periods in our field's history when scholars, theorists, and pedagogues were interested in the meaning-making capabilities of multimodal composition. Such alternative views allow us an opportunity to question our modern discipline's storied foundations. For example, Stephen North called 1963 "the birth of modern Composition, capital C," because at that time the field replaced practice with research as its dominant mode of inquiry (15). But the following selections suggest that the shift to research in 1963 also marked a shift to text-based academic conventions that have ignored important meaning-making processes and composing practices.

In the third selection, "The Still-Unbuilt Hacienda," Geoffrey Sirc notes the results of composition's established conventions and begins by discussing how composition has become a discipline. In the excerpts included in this book, he claims that by opting for traditional university departments and their long held beliefs about what and how we should teach composition, students and teachers lost out on valuable practices that could shape the way writing is taught. According to Sirc, we lost out on our ability to teach composition as a happening. Drawing from the free spirit of the 1960s movement that fundamentally shifted composition studies to what we know it as today, Sirc believes that composing should involve, among many things, a choice of material "from a vaster field than the disciplined one" (47). We sacrificed what was good about composition (referring to Ken Macrorie's *Uptaught*) for a chance to legitimize ourselves in the eyes of academia. For a straightforward look at our discipline's coming into being, we could turn to James Berlin's *Rhetoric and Reality: Writing Instruction in American Colleges, 1900–1985.* But Sirc prefers that we situate our history in the happenings of the 1960s since they represent work that frustrates conventions and therefore has potential to teach us to take risks, to explore, and to liberate our thinking (32). Weaving his discussion about teaching composition as a happening with his discussion about this visual art movement, he argues that we should find ways to get students to work with multiple modes.

In "Made Not Only in Words: Composition in a New Key," taken from her address at CCCC in 2004, Kathleen Blake Yancey begins by defining what was then the present as a moment in composition's history like none other. It was a moment that recognized the importance of recent technological advancements which have pluralized a very powerful writing public. Her work highlights expanded definitions of what counts as writing as well as the differences between what it means to write inside the academy (traditional words on paper) and outside the academy (collaborative, public, multimodal). She likens this moment to a moment in nineteenth-century Britain when reading became more accessible because of technological advances that, for the first time, made reading materials widely available. Her call for composition in a new key mandates changes. Many of the authors (e.g., Christine Tulley) in this book have attempted to answer her call, while at the same time extending it and making calls of their own. Like Sirc's and the other selections in Part One, Yancey provides us with a view of our discipline's history since the founding of CCCC in 1949 and an understanding of how society views education, and describes the practices of educators who teach literacy.

In *The Rhetoric of Cool: Composition Studies and New Media*, Jeff Rice, like Sirc, paints an alternative history of the 1963 rebirth of composition studies. In a selected chapter from this work, "Imagery," Rice explains what he means by the rhetoric of cool, and in doing so explores events that have been ignored in composition's history, juxtaposing them against canonized events, especially CCCC conventions. The rhetoric of cool, he describes, is a rhetoric of chora, of nonlinearity, of juxtaposition, of appropriation, of commutation, of image, and of performance in new media. Practices such as these are sometimes characteristic of multimodality (and definitely new media) and are needed in the classroom. This is especially so in first-year composition classrooms because we must be capable of flexibility and have an awareness of what each new communicative situation demands, which means we must be able to employ a combination of modes and strategies based on the needs of our audiences, our purposes, our contexts and so forth (Davis and Shadle 123). Not allowing such practices, according to Rice and Davis and Shadle, prohibits us from embracing the rhetoric of cool.

Ultimately, Rice, as well as Davis and Shadle, encourage instructors to think of multiple possibilities for writing that challenge traditional and canonized beliefs about what writing should be and do. Using multiple modes often results in a break from thesis-driven print culture, a culture which prevents us from composing with all meanings and does not adequately prepare students for some of the kinds of creating they will do outside of the academy. Rice does not mean that students must abandon all forms of traditional writing, but rather that they should also consider other possibilities for composing. He asks us to think beyond the narrative by suggesting that we not settle on just one meaning, but to consider all meanings. The question that he poses, then, is: How can multiple meanings combine in order to create a new idea? The answer lies often in multimodal composition.

Writing earlier in *The Rhetoric of Cool*, Rice says that cool belongs in the "tradition of alternatives," drawing inspiration from Winston Weathers's Grammar B (26). He sees the lack of valuing imagery in composition studies as parallel to the lack of valuing the cool, arguing that "working with cool media (visual or not) should not be understood as displacement of our fixation on print culture" (136). Rice also criticizes our obsession with the printed word and uses moments in the 1960s, like the invention of Sketchpad (a computer program that creates images), to find significant links between what counts as writing and imagery. Drawing from Marshall McLuhan, Rice highlights the affordances of electronic visuality to make meaning using a tool like Sketchpad. Such a tool is important to Rice's argument because it counters modern calls to analyze images. Instead, he sees such an invention as an opportunity to produce images, something that Rice points out is missing from writing courses.

In "The Movement of Air, the Breath of Meaning: Aurality and Multimodal Composing," Cynthia L. Selfe sees the field's privileging of the printed word as limiting our understanding of the meaning-making abilities of composing with other modes. Specifically, she usurps the history of the printed word by presenting her own history of aurality. In doing so she challenges us to think more carefully about how we know, share, and create knowledge and how these actions shape our identity. Starting from the nineteenth century when oratory became less of the student's work, and teachers favored working with written texts, she offers us a look at specific moments in history when aural practices were valued as meaningful ways of communicating. During this same period, print literacy became that of privileged white males while other forms of literacy, like those aural in nature, became that of others: women, slaves, Hispanics, and Native Americans.

Like Selfe, Lisa Bickmore and Ron Christiansen make yet another call for multimodal composition pedagogy, though this time, the call is situated specifically in the context of a two-year college, where the fight for more program support often is the toughest. Using Yancey's 2004 *CCCC* article as inspiration, as well as examples of their students' multimodal texts as the basis for their argument, Bickmore and Christiansen discuss the canon of invention in terms of multimodal composition. In " 'Who Will Be the Inventors? Why Not Us?': Multimodal Composition in the Two-Year College Classroom," they contend that instructors should help students "consider how the multimodal documents that emerge from their work and play might function in their lives and in the social settings in which they themselves circulate." They see a move toward multimodal composition as one that expands the boundaries of our discipline, a way of thinking expressed by many of this book's contributors.

Over the past few decades, there has been an increase in scholarship about new media by composition scholars. In the final selection of Part One, "Show, Not Tell: The Value of New Media Scholarship," Cheryl E. Ball explains that "new media" refers exclusively to those texts "that juxtapose semiotic modes in new and aesthetically pleasing ways and, in doing so, break away from print traditions so that written text is not the primary rhetorical means." Using this definition, she argues that scholarship that is digital or online and relies heavily on the written word is not new media scholarship at all. The point she makes is that "[b]eing able to read and understand new media texts as scholarly is integral to the continuation of knowledge making in the field of composition." In other words, multimodal composition matters, and it transcends the mere use of digital technology to create texts. At the same time, she recognizes the difficulty some have when trying to decide the value of new media scholarship because scholars are still learning how to recognize meaning that is made in the design of the text. In other words, interpreting the aesthetic qualities the modes create is difficult. In making this argument, Ball provides an example of what it means to understand that new media, though still contributing to the field, doesn't adhere to traditional composition conventions.

Together, the selections in Part One help to establish the roots of modern multimodal composition and address several key questions: First, how have we as scholars and practitioners defined multimodal composition, and how have these definitions of multimodal composition evolved over time? How do the histories we read, write, and operate under influence what we know about and do in a composition classroom? And, finally, we could also think about how such histories privilege some modes while alienating others. Addressing these questions may serve to further our understanding of what it means to compose and make knowledge.

WORKS CITED

Bolter, David Jay, and Richard Grusin. *Remediation: Understanding New Media.* Cambridge, MA: MIT Press, 2000. Print.

Davis, Robert, and Mark Shadle. *Teaching Multiwriting: Researching and Composing with Multiple Genres, Media, Disciplines, and Cultures.* Carbondale: Southern Illinois UP, 2007. Print.

Hobbs, Catherine L. "Learning from the Past: Verbal and Visual Literacy in Early Modern Rhetoric and Writing Pedagogy." *Language and Image in the Reading-Writing Classroom.* Ed. Kristie Fleckenstein, Linda T. Calendrillo, and Demetrice A. Worley. Mahwah: Lawrence Erlbaum, 2002. 27–44. Print.

LaGrandeur, Kevin. "Digital Images and Classical Persuasion." *Eloquent Images: Word and Image in the Age of New Media.* Ed. Mary E. Hocks and Michelle R. Kendrick. Cambridge, MA: MIT P, 2003. 117–36. Print.

North, Stephen. *The Making of Knowledge in Composition.* Upper Montclair: Boynton/Cook, 1987. Print.

Rice, Jeff. *The Rhetoric of Cool: Composition Studies and New Media.* Carbondale: Southern Illinois UP, 2007. Print.

Sirc, Geoffrey. *English Composition as a Happening.* Logan: Utah State UP, 2002. Print.

1 NCTE Position Statement on Multimodal Literacies

NATIONAL COUNCIL OF TEACHERS OF ENGLISH

"Has there ever been a time when we have not been awash in a remarkable torrent of symbols and opportunities for reading and writing them?"

— WILLIAM KIST

DECLARATIONS CONCERNING THE BROADEST DEFINITIONS OF MULTIMODAL LITERACIES

- Integration of multiple modes of communication and expression can enhance or transform the meaning of the work beyond illustration or decoration.

  What this means for teaching:

  - It is the interplay of meaning-making systems (alphabetic, oral, visual, etc.) that teachers and students should strive to study and produce. "Multiple ways of knowing" (Short & Harste) also include art, music, movement, and drama, which should not be considered curricular luxuries.
  - All modes of communication are codependent. Each affects the nature of the content of the other and the overall rhetorical impact of the communication event itself.

- Young children practice multimodal literacies naturally and spontaneously. They easily combine and move between drama, art, text, music, speech, sound, physical movement, animation/gaming, etc.

  What this means for teaching:

  - Children who grow up in impoverished or repressed literacy environments may not experience this important early literacy foundation.
  - The over-emphasis on testing and teaching to the test may deprive many students of the kinds of multimodal experiences they most need.

A summary statement developed by the Multimodal Literacies Issue Management Team of the NCTE Executive Committee. Approved by the NCTE Executive Committee, November 2005. <http://www.ncte.org/positions/statements/multimodalliteracies>

- An exclusive emphasis on digital literacies is not what most advocates of technology-rich composition advocate. Such an emphasis would limit students' access to other modes of expression.

- The use of different modes of expression in student work should be integrated into the overall literacy goals of the curriculum and appropriate for time and resources invested.

  What this means for teaching:

  - "Students should be able to both read critically and write functionally, no matter what the medium" (William Kist). In personal, civic, and professional discourse, alphabetic, visual, and aural works are not luxuries but essential components of knowing.

- Because of the complexity of multimodal projects and the different levels of skill and sensitivity each individual brings to their execution, such projects often demand high levels of collaboration and teamwork.

  What this means for teaching:

  - Teachers of the English/Language Arts already have models for this type of collaboration, such as those for producing a play. Any dramatic production includes speech, movement, costumes, props, sets, lighting, and, sometimes, music and dance. Beyond the performance itself is the need for producing appealing programs and advertising. And, beyond that are the persuasive verbal skills needed to raise funds to produce the production.

  - Other kinds of more traditional multimodal projects also require this type of collaboration. When students produce brochures, literary magazines, books, videos, or greeting cards, collaboration improves the product and helps all students involved learn more.

- The use of multimodal literacies has expanded the ways we acquire information and understand concepts. Ever since the days of illustrated books and maps texts have included visual elements for the purpose of imparting information. The contemporary difference is the ease with which we can combine words, images, sound, color, animation, video, and styles of print in projects so that they are part of our everyday lives and, at least by our youngest generation, often taken for granted.

  What this means for teaching:

  - Readers in electronic environments are able to gain access immediately to a broad range and great depth of information that not 15 years ago would have required long visits to libraries or days of waiting for mailed replies.

  - The techniques of acquiring, organizing, evaluating, and creatively using multimodal information should become an increasingly important component of the English/Language Arts classroom.

- From an early age, students are very sophisticated readers and producers of multimodal work. They can be helped to understand how these works make meaning, how they are based on conventions, and how they are created for and respond to specific communities or audiences.

What this means for teaching:

- Students should be invited to collaborate with their teachers in the study of new literacies and in the practical aspects of integrating those literacies into the curriculum.

- The additional dimensions of multimodal work add increased complexity to the tasks of teaching, learning, and, therefore, the evaluation of those learning experiences.

What this means for teaching:

- The complexity of multimodal work suggests that an assessment process must be developed and refined collaboratively by students, teachers, administrators, parents, and other stakeholders over time.

- Goals and criteria need to be clear to all from the beginning of the work.

- The difficulty of grading the work using traditional methods may prevent some teachers from attempting this kind of work.

DECLARATIONS CONCERNING THE UNIQUE CAPACITIES AND CHALLENGES OF DIGITAL FORMS

- There are increased cognitive demands on the audience to interpret the intertextuality of communication events that include combinations of print, speech, images, sounds, movement, music, and animation. Products may blur traditional lines of genre, author/audience, and linear sequence.

What this means for teaching:

- Skills, approaches and attitudes toward media literacy, visual and aural rhetorics, and critical literacy should be taught in English/Language Arts classrooms.

- "Unfortunately, while there have been increased calls for a broadened conception of literacy, there do not currently exist resources for the traditional teacher to begin to incorporate new literacies into their classrooms on a continuing basis" (William Kist).

- "We must be able to approach others with generosity, alert to the differences in language use and in assumptions about what constitutes appropriate communication in any context. We need to be good at recognizing the range of strategies others use in communicating, and at figuring out how to open and carry on conversations (in the appropriate medium) with others" (Anne Wysocki).

- Certain conventions of design are more effective than others for visual, aural, or multimodal texts. English/Language Arts teachers will need to become more informed about these conventions because they will influence the rhetorical and aesthetic impact of all multimodal texts.

- In digital forms, students, even very young students, are often more literate in the technical aspects of digital production than many of their teachers. Many students are frequently exposed to popular technologies, have the leisure time to experiment with their own production, develop the social connections that encourage peer teaching and learning, and may have access to more advanced technology than is available at school. The "definitions" of multimodal composing may be written by educators, but they will most likely have first been pioneered by these young people.

What this means for teaching:

- Students may find school instruction increasingly irrelevant (National Educational Technology Plan).

- Educators will have to devise ways of including students who are advanced technology practitioners in the development of curricula, professional development experiences, teacher recruiting, and the setting of relevant policies.

- Implications of the digital divide. Institutions and teachers must create ways to bridge the digital divide, providing access and resources for all students. More specifically, "for students [and teachers] we need to provide adequate, safe, and supported work time" (Dickie Selfe). "We must call on our institutions to provide the necessary support and infrastructural, cultural, and technological adjustments, including access to technology for people with diverse abilities and needs" (BETHA group).

- Creating images, sounds, designs, videos, and other extra-alphanumeric texts is an aesthetic, self-originated, self-sponsored activity for many writers. Digital technologies have increasing capacity for individuals to adapt the tools for their own information and communication purposes. Students have the capability to apply literacy skills to real-world problems and knowledge building. They are able to exercise creativity, work for social justice, and pursue personal passions (CCCC Feb. 2004 position statement). They have the means to publish their work to a global audience.

What this means for teaching:

- Young people are particularly adept at recognizing creative applications for new technologies, but their in-school work should be guided by the wisdom and sophisticated curricular knowledge of their teachers. In addition, they need direct instruction in ethical, critical, and legal considerations.

- Students and teachers will need assistance in the skills of multitasking, accessing "just in time" information, problem solving, and prioritizing tasks and resources to accomplish the goals of their assignments.

- Their work may at times be more like that of the workplace than that of the traditional classroom.

- With more opportunities and greater ease in sending their work out into the world, the quality of the ideas and the effectiveness of the communication media will become more important and more relevant to students.

- With the development of multimodal literacy tools, writers are increasingly expected to be responsible for many aspects of the writing, design, and distribution processes that were formerly apportioned to other experts.

What this means for teaching:

- While digital publishing is often immediate and of an ephemeral nature, the writer loses control over the work and its potential audience in a way that wasn't as true in print publishing. This will blur and complicate ethical issues of ownership, plagiarism, and authenticity.

- Teachers will need to "master technologies enough to guide students in the ethics underlying their use" (Dene Grigar).

2

Contending with Terms: "Multimodal" and "Multimedia" in the Academic and Public Spheres

CLAIRE LAUER

1. INTRODUCTION

In the field of rhetoric and composition, terms such as *new media, multimedia, digital media, multiliteracies,* and *multimodal* are defined by theorists such as Cynthia L. Selfe (2007) and Anne Wysocki (2004), as well as by theorists outside the field whose work is often cited by rhetoric and composition scholars, including Lev Manovich (2001), Bill Cope and Mary Kalantzis (2000), and Gunther Kress (2003). Defining terms is an important and necessary practice in any field, including composition. Edward Schiappa (2003) has argued that definitions "constitute a form of rhetorically induced social knowledge. That is, definitions are the result of a shared understanding of the world and are both the product of past persuasion and a resource for future persuasion" (167). Defining terms is a situated activity that involves determining the collective interests and values of the community for which the definition matters.

In this article I focus primarily on the terms "multimedia" and "multimodal." I examine how each term has been defined and present articles, documents, surveys, web sites, keyword searches, and other examples to show when and how each term is used in both academic and non-academic or industry contexts. Although there are differences between "media" and "modes," which would suggest differences in how each term is defined, in actuality, when each is preceded by the prefix "multi," the terms are defined similarly. And as I show through the examples I present later, though multimodal has become more commonly used in scholarly literature related to the new kinds of texts students are exploring in the composition classroom, it is almost entirely absent from course titles, program names, and more public discussions outside of the academy where the term multimedia takes prevalence. My research also shows that although these terms have been used interchangeably in composition scholarship, the same is not true in more public or industry-oriented discussions, where multimedia is used almost exclusively. This suggests several observations:

From *Computers and Composition* 26 (2009): 225–39.

- Rather than the use of these terms being driven by any difference in their definitions, their use is more contingent upon the context and the audience to whom a particular discussion is being directed.

- These differences can be best explained by understanding the differences in how texts are valued and evaluated in academic versus non-academic or industry contexts. Each term is associated with certain stages of the continuum along which a text evolves from design/process to production/distribution. There is a greater emphasis on design and process in the classroom, which makes the term multimodal more suitable in that context, and a greater emphasis on production and distribution in non-academic or industry contexts which explains the use of the term multimedia in that context.

- Composition instructors need to continue using both terms in their teaching and scholarship because although multimodal is a term that is more theoretically accurate to describe the cognitive and socially situated choices students are making in their compositions, multimedia works as a gateway term for composition instructors to interface in familiar ways with their students and those outside of academia. In addition, by recognizing the more public use of the term multimedia, instructors can prepare students for the kinds of terms they will use more frequently after they graduate.

2. A Brief Look Back

In 1970, Paul Briand wrote a "Staffroom Interchange" piece for *College Composition and Communication* about using multimedia in the classroom. It was called "Turned On: Multi-Media and Advanced Composition," and was one of the first articles to mention the concept of multimedia and its application in the classroom. In this narrative account, Briand described his approach to composition instruction that was inspired by his "failure" to get his students interested in writing. As he put it, "I was ready to try anything" (267). Multimedia, for Briand, was an exciting adventure in which he proposed such innovations as filming and tape-recording himself providing feedback on written essays or having students write essays that they would then tape-record, providing each student access to "a record of his progress, [that he] can replay at will, and hopefully his writing will begin to 'sound' like him now that he can hear it (probably for the first time)" (267). By using such multimedia technologies as the television kinescope, filmstrips, slides, and programmable teaching machines, Briand suggested that instructors would be able to better diagnose the "ills" of student writing and provide new methods to "cure . . . such maladies as strep punctuation, viral grammar, and malodorous spelling" (267). Through innovations such as the transparency and overhead projector, multimedia also became a way for a student "to experiment perhaps with ways of writing he has dared not try before" (268) because it would allow his work to be critiqued anonymously in front of the class. Briand recognized the multi-channeled characteristics of multimedia and its ability to "assault" students "on as many sense levels as possible" (269). He accurately prophesied that the computer console "is where the composition course of the future will be" (Briand, 1970, 269).

In the decades since Briand's experimentations with multimedia in the classroom, our attitudes toward multimedia and our reasons for wanting students to produce such texts have evolved as our culture and technologies have evolved. Today we have sophisticated computers, and instead of audiotapes and filmstrips we have mp3s, digital images and video, 3-D virtual realities, and web sites that support Flash animation, wikis, and blogs. We have hardware and software that will allow us to compose and edit almost any kind of content delivered through any medium we can imagine. With this abundance of technology has arisen an abundance of terms we use to describe the texts we are producing. Briand used the term multimedia, but multimodal is another term that is now regularly included in our discussions of our pedagogies and the composing practices of our students. These terms are used, often interchangeably, to characterize a shift in composition, from a field that focuses exclusively on teaching our students to produce alphabetic print texts to one that acknowledges the changing communicative landscape of our culture and seeks, according to Cynthia L. Selfe and Pamela Takayoshi (2007), to prepare "intelligent citizens who can both create meaning in texts and interpret meaning from texts within a dynamic and increasingly technological world" (8).

3. MODES AND MEDIA

The difference between multimodal and multimedia is largely a difference between "modes" and "media." Modes can be understood as ways of representing information, or the semiotic channels we use to compose a text (Kress & Van Leeuwen, 2001). Examples of modes include words, sounds, still and moving images, animation, and color. Media, on the other hand, are the "tools and material resources" used to produce and disseminate texts (22). Examples of media include books, radio, television, computers, paint brush and canvas, and human voices.

3.1. Defining Multimodal

Multimodal is a term coined by members of the New London Group, including Cope and Kalantzis (2000), Kress (2003; 2005, see p. 283 in this volume), and Kress and Van Leeuwen (2001). These scholars have argued that at this point in history, communication is not limited to one mode (such as text) realized through one medium (such as the page or the book). Rather, as a result of digitization, all modes can now be realized through a single binary code, and the medium of the screen is becoming the primary site where multiple modes can be composed to make meaning in dynamic ways. Essentially, as Kress and Van Leeuwen (2001) put it, all modes "can be operated by one multi-skilled person, using one interface, one mode of physical manipulation, so that he or she can ask, at every point: 'Shall I express this with sound or music? Shall I say this visually or verbally?'" (2). Multimodal texts are characterized by the mixed logics brought together through the combination of modes (such as images, text, color, etc.).[1]

Modes and media are independent of and interdependent with each other, meaning that although media and modes are different from each other, the media we use affect the ways in which we can realize meaning through various modes. For instance, the mode of writing is affected differently by the affordances and limitations of the medium of the book versus the medium of the screen (Kress, 2003). The notion of the author as a single, solitary voice communicating to his or her audience through the finished product of the book has been transformed as communications media have opened up the possibilities for textual production to be non-linear, hypertextual, continuously revisable, and interactive. As writing becomes an increasingly screen-based activity, the ways in which we write (from the grammar we use to the style, tone, appearance, and structure of our words, sentences, paragraphs, and pages) necessarily make more fluid and transitory the role we occupy as "author" of a text. This change in the relationship of author to text, and thus in the way in which meaning can be communicated through text, was facilitated by technological advancement that allowed for a shift from the static medium of the page to the more fluid medium of the screen.

The term multimodal made its way into the field of composition through the work of the New London Group (Cope & Kalantzis 2000) and the influence of Kress (2003; 2005, p. 283). Within the field of composition, Cynthia L. Selfe has been instrumental in popularizing the term by using it frequently in her scholarship and teaching (2005, 2007). As the co-editors of *Computers and Composition*, Gail E. Hawisher and Cynthia L. Selfe (2005) devoted a special issue of the journal to "The Influence of Gunther Kress' Work" following Kress' featured speaker presentation at the Convention on College Composition and Communication (CCCC) in San Antonio in 2004. Further, Selfe and several other scholars secured a grant from the National Council of Teachers of English (NCTE) in which they surveyed composition instructors for how those instructors taught and composed multimodal texts. The article that came out of this study was called "Integrating Multimodality into Composition Curricula" (Anderson, Atkins, Ball, & Millar, 2006a). In it, the authors suggested that multimodal is derived from a theory of semiosis that

> [a]cknowledge[s] the practices of human sign-makers who select from a number of modalities for expression (including sound, image, and animation, for example), depending on rhetorical and material contexts within which the communication was being designed and distributed. (59)

The emphasis on signs (semiotics), materiality, and how communication is designed and distributed borrows from the ways in which the term has been discussed by Kress, Van Leeuwen, and others. For the purposes of their audience of rhetoric and composition scholars, Anderson et al. have also emphasized the "rhetorical" contexts in which meaning is made. This explanation is the most comprehensive and theoretical put forth in rhetoric and composition scholarship, which is not surprising because the article was written to showcase how those who are already familiar with multimodal texts are using and composing such texts.

Definitions of just about everything tend to adapt to the variety of audiences to whom they are being delivered. Daniel Anderson, Anthony Atkins, Cheryl Ball, and Krista Homicz Millar's (2006a) theoretical explanation is useful to those who can understand and apply it but may not be accessible to those who are not familiar with the semiotic theories on which it is based. Those unfamiliar with the theoretical context surrounding multimodal may not see the real-life applicability of a term that refers to "human sign-makers" and "modalities of expression" and thus may not feel ready to introduce it in their classrooms. Such teachers may be curious to explore new ways of composing but wary of such a complicated-sounding term, and thus may benefit from a definition that shows the applicability of the term more immediately. A simpler definition of multimodal was put forth in a textbook edited by Selfe called *Multimodal Composition: Resources for Teachers* (2007). In the first chapter of the book, Selfe and Takayoshi defined multimodal texts as those that "exceed the alphabetic and may include still and moving images, animations, color, words, music and sound" (2007, 1). This definition, as one in which texts simply *exceed the alphabetic*, is much less complex than the explanation put forth in Anderson et al. (2006a,b). It is also more practical in how it avoids theoretical references (i.e., "theory of semiosis," "human sign-makers" and "material contexts") and focuses exclusively on the specific modes that students and instructors can use to compose texts. This more accessible description appeals to a broader audience of teachers who need not be familiar with the nuances provided in the discussions of Kress, Van Leeuwen, Anderson et al., and others to be able to imagine ways of facilitating such textual production in the classroom. This is important because the limited span of a semester or quarter requires that teachers make choices about the composing practices they will help their students pursue. Because there are so many diverse perspectives with which to engage and possible assignments to develop out of those perspectives, the way a perspective is named and discussed can determine whether an instructor feels willing to devote any time to exploring it. Some perspectives, especially those associated with new technologies or non-traditional approaches, may be easily passed over if perceived as being too difficult to understand or implement.

3.2. Defining Multimedia

Previous to multimodal's entrance into the scholarly conversation, multimedia was the term primarily used to describe the expansion of composing practices in composition scholarship and classrooms. Multimedia was used most frequently in the 1990's with the advent of the CD-ROM. It was a term that described texts composed by using a computer to integrate words and visuals as well as sound and video. In a 1991 *MACworld* article (as cited in Hawisher, LeBlanc, Moran, & Selfe, 1996), Jim Heid defined multimedia as "the integration of two or more communications media. It's the use of text and sounds, plus still and moving pictures, to convey ideas, sell products, educate, and/or entertain" (225). Communications media as they are discussed in this definition (e.g., text, sounds, images) might today be considered modes, but the latter half of the definition puts an emphasis on the finished product and the intended uses of the product, which is more characteristic of multimedia and its use in industry than multimodal and its use in the classroom. I'll discuss this comparison in greater depth later in the article.

In composition (more specifically in the subfield of computers and composition), multimedia was preceded by the term "hypermedia," which described texts that assume a non-linear literary hypertext structure (Hawisher et al., 1996). As editing and web technologies became more accessible, the use of the term multimedia became more common. However, as a term it tends to go much more frequently undefined in the scholarly literature, perhaps because it acts as a catch-all term for any text that is not an alphabetic print text.

Fred T. Hofstettler (2000), in his textbook *Multimedia Literacy*, provides one of the most precise definitions of multimedia. Hofstetter defined multimedia as "the use of a computer to present and combine text, graphics, audio, and video with links and tools that let the user navigate, interact, create, and communicate" (2). In this definition there is a greater emphasis on the user and what the text will allow the user to do with it. Emphasis can also be placed on the author and the kinds of texts an author might produce, as definitions of multimedia found on a variety of tech-oriented web sites show. As just one example, TechTerms defines multimedia in this way:

> As the name implies, multimedia is the integration of multiple forms of media. This includes text, graphics, audio, video, etc. For example, a presentation involving audio and video clips would be considered a "multimedia presentation." Educational software that involves animations, sound, and text is called "multimedia software." (Multimedia, n.d.)

In this definition there is no reliance on how a user might consume or interact with a text for it to be considered multimedia. Rather, the definition focuses only on the choices an author makes in composing his or her text (i.e., Does the author include audio and video clips in the text? If so, then it is a multimedia text). Taken together, these definitions show multimedia to be a descriptive term able to support the practices of both authors and users as well as a wide array of technologies and texts. This helps explain its ability to remain a relevant term in both academic and non-academic or industry contexts throughout the multitude of technological changes that have occurred over the past several decades.

But whereas Briand's (1970) notion of multimedia focused primarily on the multiple media he used in the classroom (projectors, recorders, etc.), these more recent definitions seem to suggest that multimedia texts are inherently multimodal texts because rather than being texts that combine various media (such as the book, radio, television, and computer screen), they are texts that combine a variety of modes (such as image, animation, and sound) disseminated through a single medium (such as a computer screen). This change in emphasis has had little discernable effect in non-academic or industry uses of the term because multimedia has proven flexible enough to be adaptable to changes in technology or production that occur. However, in academic contexts, it opened the door for terms like multimodal to come about that more accurately describe the composing practices of students taking place in the classroom today.

4. USING TERMS INTERCHANGEABLY

Both the definitions of multimedia and multimodal are concerned with the combination of modes, which makes them quite similar to one another. In the context of the field of rhetoric and composition, these terms are not only defined similarly, they are often used interchangeably. Considering the relative newness, in composition, of expanding our notions of text and the technologies we use to compose texts, using terms interchangeably reveals how little consensus there seems to be on what these terms should be used to describe. Thus, scholars who want to open up the conversation to as many people as possible may use a variety of different terms to describe the work they and their students produce. One example of this is Jonathan Alexander's call for papers for a special issue of *Computers and Composition* on "Media Convergence" (Figure 2-1).

In his call for papers for this special issue, Alexander (2006) used no fewer than eight different phrases to describe the kinds of texts students are composing. Such phrases include:

- Digital and new media communications technologies
- Multimodal, multimedia texts
- Multimodal experiences
- Array of multimedia
- Media experiences
- Multimodal composing
- Multiple forms of new media
- Multimodal new media texts

The sheer number of different ways that Alexander used to describe the kinds of texts he was looking to address in this special issue suggests that there are a diverse number of terms that can be used to describe "media convergence" and very little consensus on what the terms actually mean. The more terms suggested, the more possibilities for interpretation emerge.

But even when one term is deliberately selected and used, other terms still tend to make their way into the discussion, as is the case in the NCTE-sponsored "Survey of Multimodal Pedagogies in Writing Programs" (Anderson et al., 2006a) mentioned earlier. Although multimodal was the term the survey emphasized, more than one question and response used the term multimedia, especially in the section regarding publication for promotion and tenure. Figure 2-2 illustrates just one example of this.

FIGURE 2-1   CFP email sent to the Writing Program Administration's listserv seeking submissions for a special issue of *Computers and Composition* journal on "Media Convergence."

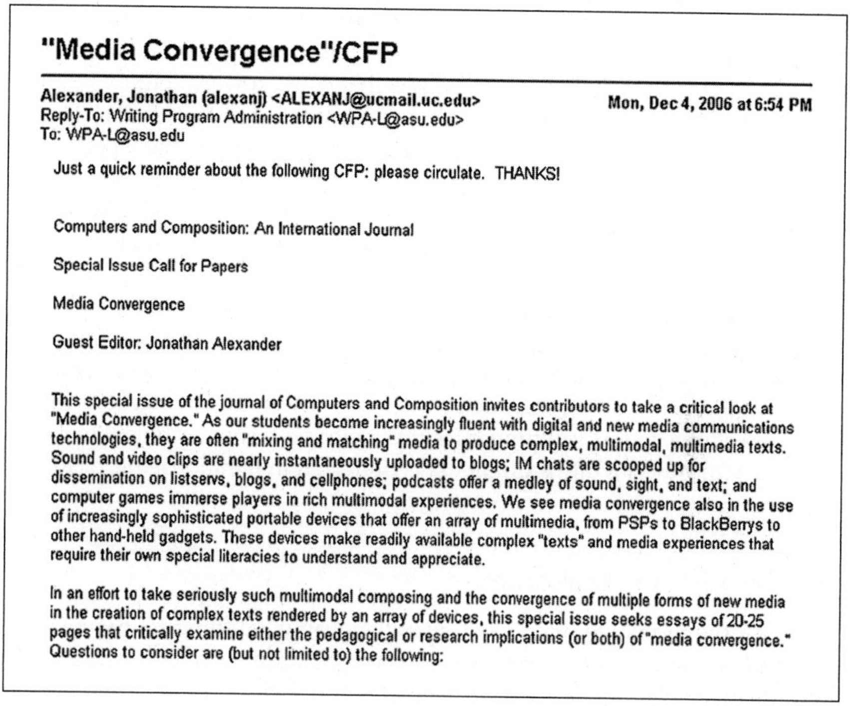

"Media Convergence"/CFP

Alexander, Jonathan (alexanj) <ALEXANJ@ucmail.uc.edu>   **Mon, Dec 4, 2006 at 6:54 PM**
Reply-To: Writing Program Administration <WPA-L@asu.edu>
To: WPA-L@asu.edu

Just a quick reminder about the following CFP: please circulate. THANKS!

Computers and Composition: An International Journal

Special Issue Call for Papers

Media Convergence

Guest Editor: Jonathan Alexander

This special issue of the journal of Computers and Composition invites contributors to take a critical look at "Media Convergence." As our students become increasingly fluent with digital and new media communications technologies, they are often "mixing and matching" media to produce complex, multimodal, multimedia texts. Sound and video clips are nearly instantaneously uploaded to blogs; IM chats are scooped up for dissemination on listservs, blogs, and cellphones; podcasts offer a medley of sound, sight, and text; and computer games immerse players in rich multimodal experiences. We see media convergence also in the use of increasingly sophisticated portable devices that offer an array of multimedia, from PSPs to BlackBerrys to other hand-held gadgets. These devices make readily available complex "texts" and media experiences that require their own special literacies to understand and appreciate.

In an effort to take seriously such multimodal composing and the convergence of multiple forms of new media in the creation of complex texts rendered by an array of devices, this special issue seeks essays of 20-25 pages that critically examine either the pedagogical or research implications (or both) of "media convergence." Questions to consider are (but not limited to) the following:

FIGURE 2-2   Question #114 from "Survey of Multimodal Pedagogies in Writing Programs" asking about the challenges of having multimedia/new media texts count toward tenure.

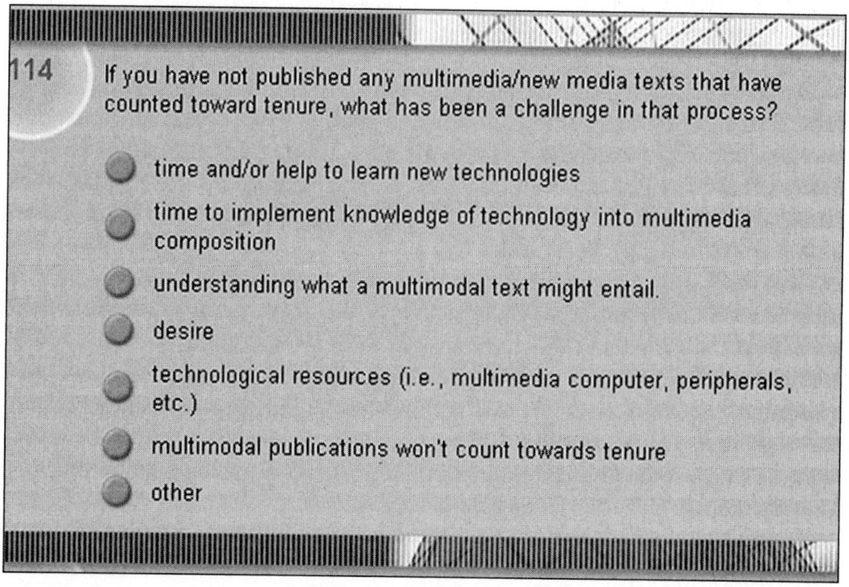

114   If you have not published any multimedia/new media texts that have counted toward tenure, what has been a challenge in that process?

- time and/or help to learn new technologies
- time to implement knowledge of technology into multimedia composition
- understanding what a multimodal text might entail.
- desire
- technological resources (i.e., multimedia computer, peripherals, etc.)
- multimodal publications won't count towards tenure
- other

The question in Figure 2-2 is asking about texts that are described as "multimedia/new media," but the responses include two instances of multimedia and two instances of multimodal. In addition to the texts in question being described in three different ways (multimedia, new media, multimodal), it is significant that multimedia is included in this particular question because it concerns scholarly publications that count toward tenure. Publications toward tenure are valued and evaluated as finished "products." It matters not at all to a tenure committee how long a person has spent on a manuscript or the work they invested in getting it written and published. It only matters that it was published by a reputable press (if a book) or in a peer-reviewed, national journal (if an article) and looked upon favorably by those in a person's field.

In short, the "production" and "distribution" of a text can be considered to be more important than the process it took to get there. This continuum — from process to production and distribution — is one I will discuss later in the article to illuminate why, despite terms being used interchangeably in the examples above, in fact multimodal is the preferred term of scholars in rhetoric and composition while multimedia is preferred in non-academic or industry contexts.

5. MULTIMODAL IN COMPOSITION

Although the terms are often used interchangeably, multimodal has become preferable to multimedia in composition both because it is more theoretically accurate in describing our pedagogies that emphasize the process and design of a text and because it has been championed by leading scholars in our field, including Cynthia L. Selfe. I have already mentioned the NCTE-sponsored survey which asks directly about multimodal composing practices (Anderson et al., 2006a,b), the special issue of *Computers and Composition* dedicated to the work of Gunther Kress (2005, p. 283), and the textbook *Multimodal Composing: Resources for Teachers* (2007) to illustrate the trend toward using multimodal in our field. In addition, a comprehensive search of journals and books from rhetoric and composition (and related subfields like computers and composition and technical writing[2]) reveals that although multimedia was the preferred (and really the only) term used early on in the 1990s, it has since fallen off in usage and been replaced in part by multimodal. The chart shown in Figure 2-3 indicates the trend.

We see in this graph that multimedia hit its peak in 1997, right before the introduction of multimodal to the scholarly literature. Multimodal has since surpassed multimedia in the number of times it is cited in the field of rhetoric and composition, though it has yet to achieve the same frequency of use that multimedia enjoyed at its peak. This is the case in part because multimodal is still a relatively new term and in part because a number of different terms (such as new media and digital media) have also come to be used in place of multimedia.

FIGURE 2-3   Line graph showing the frequency with which the terms "multimedia" and "multimodal" are used in the titles of articles in rhetoric and composition publications from 1992–2007.

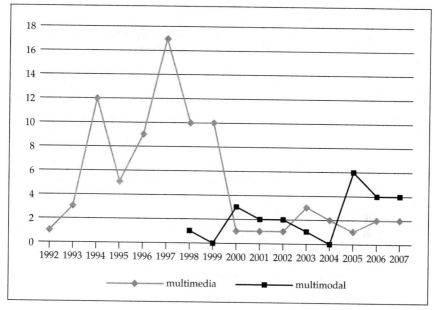

6. MULTIMEDIA IN PUBLIC OR INDUSTRY

But as multimodal has gained popularity in rhetoric and composition, multimedia continues to be the term of choice in non-academic or industry spheres, as well as more "hybrid" sites that interface between the industry and higher education. Such hybrid sites include the following:

- Program or department titles; course titles
- Technical and professional communication publications
- NCTE position statements, which outline stances on issues relevant to English studies and are intended to be read by English educators at all levels (K–graduate level), as well as parents, students, members of the press, and policymakers.
- Partnerships such as EDUCAUSE and the New Media Consortium, which bring together people from business, government, and higher education in an effort to improve student learning.

Non-academic or industry sites include the following:

- National news and media outlets such as the *New York Times, Washington Post, Los Angeles Times*, etc.
- Information technology outlets such as CNET, ZDNet, etc.
- Business and corporate sites, including those offering communication and marketing services

6.1. Hybrid Examples

6.1.1. Program and Course Titles.   A compilation of writing majors, compiled by the CCCCs Committee on the Major in Rhetoric and Composition (2007), showed a variety of courses directed at composing with digital media, technology, and for the Web. One university major (from Arizona State University) and one minor (from University of California Santa Barbara), which is not included in the compilation because it's a minor, use "multimedia writing," in their respective titles, and eight programs require a course called "multimedia writing or "multimedia authoring" (ASU, UCSB, Michigan State, Philadelphia University, Purdue University, University of Texas at Austin, and Washington State University). No programs as of yet had classes that used the term multimodal. There is no doubt, however, that many of the courses listed as multimedia pursue inquiry that would fall under the definition of multimodal provided by Anderson et al. (2006a,b). And yet, multimodal is not used in program and course titles most likely because the audience for such titles are students and community members, many of whom might be unfamiliar with (and suspicious of) a strange-sounding term like multimodal but who would have instant familiarity with a term like multimedia. In addition, because multimedia is a term used so much more often in the public sphere, students can connect courses in "multimedia writing" with the work they may be asked to produce after they graduate.

6.1.2. Technical and Professional Communication Publications.   The more public segments of the field of rhetoric and composition are represented through its technical and professional communication magazines and journals, which regularly publish on workplace studies and preparing students for communications industries beyond their college experience. These publications refer to the work students produce in the classroom as multimedia significantly more so than multimodal. In a keyword search of the most popular magazines and journals in this field (including *Intercom, Technical Communication (TC), Technical Communication Quarterly (TCQ), Business Communication Quarterly (BCQ), IEEE Transactions on Professional Communication (IEEE)*, and *Journal of Technical Writing and Communication (JTWC)*), the term multimedia is cited a total of 243 times and multimodal a total of 3 times. Examples of titles include:

- "How to Incorporate Multimedia in the Business Communication Classroom—Without Learning New Software Packages" (*BCQ*, 1997)
- "Hypermedia, Multimedia, and Reader Cognition: An Empirical Study" (*TC*, 1998)
- "Designing, Developing, and Marketing Multimedia Products" (*JTWC*, 1998)
- "Teaching and Assessing Multimedia-Based Oral Presentations" (*BCQ*, 2001)
- "Toward Accommodating Gender Differences in Multimedia Communication" (*IEEE*, 2004)

- "Tracing Visual Narratives: User-testing Methodology for Developing a Multimedia Museum Show" (*TC*, 2005)
- "Keeping Users at the Center: Developing a Multimedia Interface for Informed Consent" (*TCQ*, 2008)

In this more public subfield of rhetoric and composition, there seems to be greater emphasis on multimedia over multimodal because professional, technical, and business communication programs are often directly linked with organizations and companies where students may engage in internships and eventual employment and where they need to be able to communicate the kinds of work they do and the skills they have acquired to their future employers.

6.1.3. NCTE Position Statements.   NCTE position statements are intended to be read by English educators at all levels (K–graduate level), as well as parents, students, members of the press, and policymakers. In a position statement titled "Toward a Definition of 21st-Century Literacies," approved by the NCTE Executive Council in February of 2008, the committee used the phrase "multi-media texts" exclusively as part of a bulleted list describing the kinds of composing practices writers in the twenty-first century will need to engage in, specifically suggesting students be able to "create, critique, analyze, and evaluate multi-media texts." The choice in using "multi-media" over multimodal to describe the kinds of texts students should be creating, critiquing, analyzing and evaluating is significant considering that in 2005, a rather extended "Position Statement on Multimodal Literacies" was put together by the Multimodal Literacies Issue Management Team of the NCTE Executive Committee (p. 17). The 2005 summary statement seemed especially directed at teachers of English because of the extensive information provided in each section that asked *"what does this mean for teaching?"* And yet, despite this extended statement on the importance of developing "multimodal literacies" in English classrooms, when it came time to take a more general position on "21st-Century Literacies," the committee chose to use the term "multi-media," which signals the need to appeal to diverse audiences in a succinct and familiar way. The committee would be able to assume that all audiences would know what "multi-media" meant and it would thus not need to provide further explanation as might be required if the committee were to use a more obscure, theoretically situated term like "multimodal."

6.1.4. Partnerships.   *EDUCAUSE.* EDUCAUSE (n.d.) is a non-profit organization "whose mission is to advance higher education by promoting the intelligent use of information technology" (n.p.). Ninety-nine percent of all research-extensive universities are members of Educause, as are the majority of other higher education institutions (1864 in all). Sixty-one associations, 24 state agencies, and 252 corporations are also members of Educause. Educause publishes a quarterly journal and magazine as well as a book series and extensive other material on their web site. A keyword search throughout the Educause site and all of its web publications reveals that multimedia is cited 5,540 times while multimodal is cited just 38 times. These numbers are not surprising when we consider that Educause material is written for and read by a wide range of people entering the conversation from a wide range of backgrounds, including education, business, and government. Multimedia is a term that seems able to best accommodate the variety of knowledge bases people bring to the conversation.

New Media Consortium.   The New Media Consortium (NMC) is a non-profit organization "of over 260 learning-focused organizations dedicated to the exploration and use of new media and new technologies" (2005a). Members of the NMC include colleges and universities, community colleges, museums, research centers, foundations, and corporations. In April 2005, the NMC, along with the George Lucas Foundation and Adobe Systems, held a summit to

> identify strategic priorities for what we are calling 21st Century Liter-acy—the set of abilities and skills where aural, visual, and digital liter-acy overlap—and to develop an action list of recommendations to meet those priorities. The summit is intended to catalyze actions globally across five focus sectors: policy, research, media, arts, K–12 education, and higher education. (New Media Consortium, 2005b)

Resulting from the summit was a monograph titled *A Global Imperative: The Report of the 21st Century Literacy Summit* (2005a). A "Visual Record of the Meeting" (2005b) was also produced and published to the NMC web site; it showcased the proceedings of the summit through a variety of illustrated discussion boards and photographs. The monograph used the term multimedia several times, including pull-out stories such as one called "Designing for Multimedia Literacy Across the Curriculum" (NMC, 2005a). But more interesting is the number of times that multimedia is mentioned on the boards included in the "Visual Record of the Meeting." In the poster in Figure 2-4, multimedia is mentioned five times.

Phrases like "We need a TITLE 9 for multi-media," and "multimedia is done in teams" are just a few that accompany some of the visual maps in Figure 2-4, such as the arrow pointing upward along a progression of terms (oral, print, graphic . . . multimedia) and images like the one shown in Figure 2-5, which was located on a previous poster.

The fact that the boards use the term multimedia so frequently is significant because these boards represent the starting points for the discussion that was taking place during the summit. Multimedia in this context is not a term that was arrived upon eventually but one that served as the entry point or gateway term to begin the discussion and bring a diverse group of people (with different knowledge bases and discourses) together on the same page.

FIGURE 2-4   Discussion board put together for the 21st Century Literacy Summit in which presenters and participants reflected on key facets of literacy in the twenty-first century and related topics. Discussion board shows 5 instances of the term "multimedia" being used.

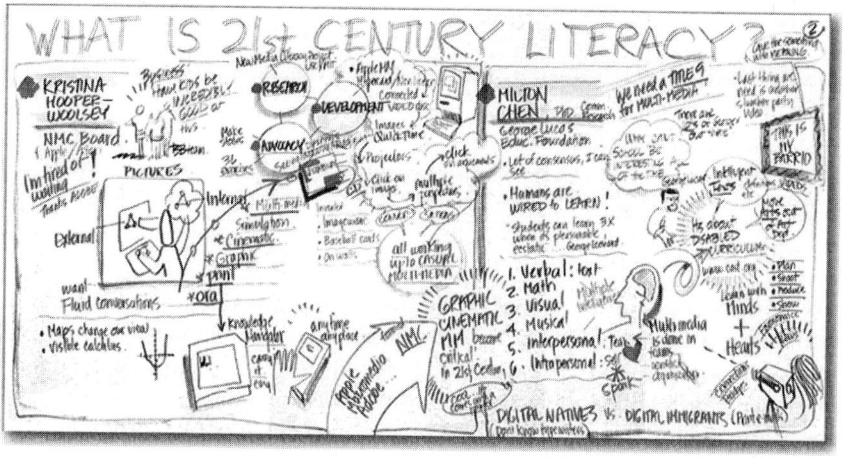

FIGURE 2-5   Segment of a discussion board put together to accompany the "Opening Remarks" of the 21st Century Literacy Summit. This segment uses the term "multi-media" to show the kinds of literacy practices that children are already engaging in.

6.2. Non-academic or Industry Examples

In the hybrid examples discussed above, multimedia is used to interface among a wide variety of audiences. In non-academic or industry examples, it is used to describe non-alphabetic texts as well as texts whose worth is determined not by the processes through which they are composed but by the finished products that are enjoyed or evaluated upon distribution. To characterize non-alphabetic content, many national newspapers have pages devoted to multimedia. For the *New York Times*, multimedia means images and video, not the more customary newspaper alphabetic print.

FIGURE 2-6   Partial screen shot of the "Multimedia Forum" section of the CNET
web site.

In the CNET forum shown in Figure 2-6, multimedia is talked about in
terms of editing and production software and hardware. Users who post to
this forum discuss issues pertaining to video file formats, editing and converting video, Flash animation, DVD recording, and streaming video. Questions
are primarily concerned with the technical manipulation and production of
material used for personal entertainment rather than the organization and
style of content developed for persuasive communication. In the web site for
the Communications Group, multimedia is talked about in terms of "interactive sales presentations," "marketing," and "animations." The Communications Group (n.d.) web site describes how "text, images, music, voice-overs,
video, animation and printed material can all be used to varying degrees in an
attempt to 'move' your audience and effectively communicate your message." We might talk about this as multimodal in a more academic context,
but this group is out to deliver a product, not a way of thinking, which may
contribute to their use of the more generally understood multimedia.

7. MULTIMODAL DESIGN, MULTIMEDIA PRODUCTION

The contexts in which multimedia and multimodal are used become clearer
when we recognize that each term is associated with certain stages of the continuum along which a text evolves from design/process to production/distri-
bution. For instance, The Communications Group develops multimedia
products, and the success of the company depends on how those finished
products are received by clients and how they perform after being distributed
in public. Similar to the previous discussion of tenure materials, multimedia
is used to describe texts whose worth is determined by their successful production and distribution, not by the process an author took to compose them.
Multimodal, on the other hand, is regularly used to characterize the cognitive
and socially-situated choices a student or scholar makes while in the process
of composing a text, before it enters into final production and distribution.

The difference between modes and media can thus be looked at as a difference between design/process (modes) and production/distribution (media).
Kress and Van Leeuwen (2001) introduced their multimodal approach to com-

munication by shaping it around four "domains of practice" or "strata," which include discourse, design, production, and distribution. More simply, these strata distinguish between the content and the expression sides of communication (20).

Design concerns making choices about which modes a person will use and how to develop a concept or content that will eventually be realized or expressed through one or more media. For Kress and Van Leeuwen (2001), design is "a particular way of combining semiotic modes" (21). They elaborated:

> [D]esign is still separate from the actual material production of the semiotic product or the actual material articulation of the semiotic event. . . . The resources on which design draws, the semiotic modes, are still abstract, capable of being realized in different materialities . . . The same design can be realized in different media. (6)

Kress and Van Leeuwen made the distinction that modes are on the "content" side and media are on the "expression" side of meaning-making (21).

Production, then, is associated with the media through which designs can be expressed. Kress and Van Leeuwen defined production as "the material articulation of the semiotic event or . . . artefact" (6). They further elaborate on the relationship between modes and media in this way:

> A whole other set of skills is involved here: technical skills, skills of the hand and the eye, skills related not to semiotic modes, but to semiotic media. We use the term "medium" here in the sense of "medium of execution" (the material substance drawn into culture and worked over cultural time). (2001, 6)

A design necessarily adapts to the medium being used to produce and distribute it; however, many of a design's elements (such as color scheme, language, font, and image choices) extend across various media. So if an instructor were going to have students design a marketing campaign for a new speaker series on her campus, she might ask them, as part of the design process, to determine who they would want to attend the series and how best to appeal to those people and persuade them to attend. The content that the students develop would be multimodal and include decisions they make about language (from a title and description of the event to key words that might especially appeal to their audiences), font style and size, appropriate or catchy images, and appealing color scheme and layout. This content would then be produced or expressed through a number of different media, including flyers, mailers, email announcements, web sites, radio announcements, word of mouth, etc.

To be sure, the evolution from design to production, or from abstract concept to the material realization of that concept, happens along a continuum, and there does not exist a clear line between where one ends and the other begins. However, distinguishing between the two is useful in an effort to explain the prevalence of certain terms being used in certain contexts. Design is important to the composition classroom because it emphasizes the development of ideas (invention) and the engagement with a process by which students make choices, receive feedback, and revise those choices concerning arguments they are making within a particular rhetorical context. Whether developing ideas for a written, visual, aural, or multimodal text, the rhetorical context always includes identifying who the audience for a particular text will be, what the purpose is, and which modes or combination of modes might best suit the communicative event. This process generally precedes any final production that may occur.

Although design encourages students to make appropriate choices within a rhetorical context and is thus a valued practice in composition classrooms, production, or the material expression of design, is not as highly valued. This is the case for several reasons. One may be that instructors don't always have the technical ability to teach production skills to students. Another may be that the production technology—whether that includes computers, hardware (like color printers), or software (like web-design and image editing programs)—may not be available to students or instructors due to funding or lab space shortages. A third may be that there simply isn't time within the short span of a semester to fully execute both the design and production of a text, so an instructor may choose to spend more time with design because the technical skills required to produce a text aren't necessary until after the development of rhetorical invention and decision-making skills that instructors primarily care that students learn. For example, having students produce a "deliverable" web site, as one might do for an actual client, is not necessary for students to generate ideas and make design and content decisions that precede the technical creation of the site.

But more than these reasons, instructors seem to value design over production for the same reasons they moved away from current-traditional models for composing and embraced more process and post-process oriented models that, though complicated in important ways throughout the years, are still valued in classrooms today. Production is often concerned with streamlining style differences and valuing a text for the completeness of its final product. Since the late 60's and 70's, instructors have moved away from an emphasis on grammatical correctness and rigid, formulaic structures for writing that placed too much weight on the correctness of the final product at the expense of creative invention and culturally situated approaches at meaning making. Multimodal is a term that can support an understanding of design-as-process and the situated choices and strategies students need practice developing.

However, outside of the composition classroom, it is production that is most valued because it is only by way of production that companies are able to meet the needs of their clients and stay economically viable. If students were working on an industry project and a final web site was expected to fulfill a contract between a design company and client, the design choices and process by which a designer worked might be used to explain the final product, but in the end it is the final product that is valued and evaluated. As a result, those outside of the academic sphere, in industry and more public environments, may not readily shift from multimedia to multimodal the way composition has because the more important emphasis is on the final product rather than the process that product took to become realized.

8. CONCLUSION

Scholars in the field of rhetoric and composition have begun the practice of defining terms like multimedia, multimodal, digital media, and new media, terms that are used to describe the new kinds of composing practices occurring in our classrooms and scholarship. Coming to more precise definitions and use of these terms must include attention to their histories and the contexts in which they have been used. When faced with a multitude of terms that are often used interchangeably or with little consistency, it may seem desirable to come to more precise definitions of each in an effort to differentiate one from another and better determine when one term (such as multimedia) should be used over another, similar term (such as multimodal). However, any desire for certainty in term choice may not be entirely within the control of the user. Terms like multimedia and multimodal carry with them histories and contexts that already restrict the ways in which they are understood by audiences and thus make it necessary for people to have the flexibility to use terms that are most appropriate for the context and audience to whom they are being directed, regardless of their precise definitions.

Multimedia is a term that has a (relatively) long history within composition, being used in composition scholarship as early as 1970, whereas multimodal is a term that has emerged out of scholarship published in just the last ten years. Both multimedia and multimodal arose in response to the technological advancement that was occurring—in the late 60's and early 90's for multimedia and late 90's for multimodal—but while multimedia emerged out of industry, multimodal arose out of the academic scholarship of the New London Group. As a result, the use of multimedia in industry remains dominant, while the use of multimodal within composition scholarship has grown.

The definition of a term should be driven, in part, by the audience who will encounter and use it. As the different definitions of multimodal that I have discussed in this paper show, scholars can define a term with great detail if they are attempting to illustrate its theoretical nuances, as Anderson et al. (2006a,b) have done. Or, they might determine that a definition should remain more simply defined so that it can connect to the less familiar knowledge base of their audience, as Selfe and Takayoshi (2007) have done.

Multimodal and multimedia are especially interesting terms to examine together because they come from different social, technological, and historical contexts and their definitions are technically different, yet they are often understood similarly. Definitions reflect the shared values of a community. Multimedia used to be the only term available to describe the kind of work students and scholars were producing that included computers, video, audio, and interactivity. Now that we have other terms, such as multimodal, that work better to describe the cognitive and socially situated work students do in the classroom, the rhetoric and composition community has adopted multimodal with increasing frequency. But instructors must be careful to attend to the knowledge bases of the other communities with which rhetoric and composition faculty and students interact and must keep those communities' values in mind as well. If instructors want to make sure they are able to communicate the importance of this work to their students, to others in their departments, to university administrators, to journalists, to grant-finding agencies, and to business and government leaders, they would do well to keep the term multimedia in play as a gateway term because that is the term members of those communities are already familiar with and that describe the kinds of texts they value.

NOTES

1. Although multimodal texts are often discussed as texts realized digitally through a screen, Jody Shipka (2005) showed how they can be non-digital as well.

2. The search was conducted using CompPile (2008), which describes itself as "an inventory of publications in post-secondary composition, rhetoric, technical writing, ESL, and discourse studies" from 1939 to present (Haswell & Blalock, 2008). Additional searches were conducted to supplement missing content, including, for instance, issues of *Computers and Composition* from 1999–present, which are not yet indexed in CompPile.

REFERENCES

Alexander, Jonathan. (2006, December 4). Media convergence: Call for papers. Message posted to WPA listserv, archived at https://lists.asu.edu/cgibin/wa?A2=ind0612&L=WPA-L&T=0&F=&S=&P=8913.

Anderson, Daniel, Atkins, Anthony, Ball, Cheryl, & Millar, Krista Homicz. (2006a). Integrating multimodality into composition curricula: Survey methodology and results from a CCCC research grant. *Composition Studies, 34*(2), 59–84.

Anderson, Daniel, Atkins, Anthony, Ball, Cheryl, Millar, Krista Homicz, Selfe, Cynthia L., & Selfe, Richard. (2006b). Survey of multimodal pedagogies in writing programs. Retrieved from http://www.compositionstudies.tcu.edu/archives/342/cccc-data/index.html

Briand, Paul. (1970). Turned on: Multi-media and advanced composition. *College Composition and Communication, 21*(3), 267–269.

CCCC Committee on the Major in Rhetoric and Composition. (2007). Writing majors at a glance. Retrieved from http://www.ncte.org/cccc/gov/committees/all/123767.htm

Cope, Bill, & Kalantzis, Mary (Eds.). (2000). *Multiliteracies: Literacy learning and the design of social futures.* New York: Routledge.

EDUCAUSE [search of the web site]. (n.d.). *EDUCAUSE.* Retrieved April 1, 2008, from http://www.educause.edu/

Haswell, Rich, and Blalock, Glenn. (2008). *CompPile.* Retrieved from http://comppile.org.

Hawisher, Gail E., LeBlanc, Paul, Moran, Charles, & Selfe, Cynthia L. (1996). *Computers and the teaching of writing in American higher education 1979–1994: A history.* Norwood, NJ: Ablex.

Hawisher, Gail E., & Selfe, Cynthia L. (Eds.). (2005). The influence of Gunther Kress' work (Special issue). *Computers and Composition, 22*(1).

Hofstettler, Fred. (2000). *Multimedia literacy.* New York: McGraw-Hill.

Kress, Gunther. (2005). Gains and losses: New forms of texts, knowledge, and learning. *Computers and Composition, 22*(1), 5–22.

Kress, Gunther. (2003). *Literacy in the new media age.* London: Routledge.

Kress, Gunther, & Van Leeuwen, Theo. (2001). *Multimodal discourse: The modes and media of contemporary communication.* London: Arnold.

Manovich, Lev. (2001). *The language of new media.* Cambridge: MIT Press.

Multimedia. (n.d.). *TechTerms: The text terms computer dictionary.* Retrieved April 1, 2008, from http://www.techterms.com/definition/multimedia

Multimedia forum. (n.d.). *CNet.* Retrieved April 1, 2008, from http://forums.cnet.com/5204-6644 102-0.html?forumID=40&tag=forum.fd.

Multimodal Literacies Issue Management Team of the NCTE Executive Committee. (2005). Position statement on multimodal literacies. Retrieved from http://www.ncte.org/about/over/positions/category/media/123213.htm

NCTE Executive Committee. (2008). Toward a definition of 21st-century literacies. Retrieved from http://www.ncte.org/about/over/positions/category/media/129762.htm

New Media Consortium. (2005a). *A global imperative: The report of the 21st century literacy summit.* Retrieved from http://www.nmc.org/pdf/Global-Imperative.pdf

New Media Consortium. (2005b). *Visual record of the meeting: 21st century literacy summit.* Retrieved from http://archive.nmc. org/summit/summit.pdf

Schiappa, Edward. (2003). *Defining reality: Definitions and the politics of meaning.* Carbondale: Southern Illinois University Press.

Selfe, Cynthia L., & Takayoshi, Pamela. (2007). Thinking about multimodality. In Cynthia L. Selfe (Ed.), *Multimodal composition: Resources for teachers* (pp. 1–12). Cresskill, NJ: Hampton Press.

Selfe, Cynthia L. (Ed.). (2007). *Multimodal composition: Resources for teachers.* Cresskill, NJ: Hampton Press.

Shipka, Jody. (2005). A mutlimodal task-based framework for composing. *College Composition and Communication, 57*(2), 277–306.

The Communications Group—Multimedia. (n.d.). *The communications group.* Retrieved April 1, 2008, from http://www.thecommunicationsgroup.com/multimedia.asp

Wysocki, Anne Frances. (2004). Opening new media to writing: Openings and justifications. In Anne Frances Wysocki, Johndan Johnson-Eilola, Cynthia L. Selfe, & Geoffery Sirc (Eds.), *Writing new media: Theory and applications for expanding the teaching of composition* (pp. 1–41). Logan: Utah State University Press.

3 *The Still-Unbuilt Hacienda*

GEOFFREY SIRC

I suppose the reason none of us burn incense in our writing classes any more is because of the disk drives. Smoke's not supposed to be good for them, right? But what about the sounds, the candlelight, the students on the floor, the dark? What about that *other scene* of writing instruction? Where has that gone, the idea of the writing classroom as blank canvas, ready to be inscribed as a singular compositional space?

> The next class was held in the same room; only this time I made a few alterations in the physical arrangements. There were no neat lines of folding chairs. The students sat, stood, or lay wherever they wished. When everyone was comfortable, I closed the drapes, turned off the lights, lit one candle in the middle of the room and a few sticks of incense, and played the same music as before [Ravel's "Bolero," Strauss's "Zarathustra," some Gregorian chant, selections from the Association, the Doors, Steppenwolf, Jefferson Airplane, Clear Light, Iron Butterfly, Simon and Garfunkel, and others]. The class just listened to music in the dark with the flickering candle and the scent of incense permeating the room. Again, when the period was over, the students were asked to pick up their books and leave. Some of them did not want to. (Lutz, "Making Freshman English" 38)

I begin with this souvenir—from William Lutz's 1969 writing class—because I want to reflect on the novel textures that might be brought to Composition's current course designs, the possibilities that exist for altering the conventional spaces of a writing classroom, allowing the inhabitants a sense of the sublime, making it a space no one wants to leave, a *happening* space.

Because designing spaces, I think, is what it's all about. It's a matter of basic architecture: Robert Venturi has shown that simplified compositional programs, programs that ignore the complexity and contradiction of everyday life, result in bland architecture; and I think the reverse is true as well, and perhaps more relevant for Composition: bland architecture (unless sub-

From *English as a Happening*. Logan: Utah State P, 2002. 1–32.

stantially *detourned,* as Lutz's) evokes simplistic programs. The spaces of our classrooms should offer compelling environments in which to inhabit situations of writing instruction, helping intensify consciousness in the people who use them. Can such intensification happen in a conventional writing classroom? The architectural design for the conventional classroom has become soberly monumental, charged with the heavy burden of preserving the discursive tradition of "our language . . . the peculiar ways of knowing, selecting, evaluating, reporting, concluding, and arguing that define the discourse of our community" (Bartholomae, "Inventing" 134). We erect temples to language, in which we are the priests among initiates (of varying degrees of enthusiasm), where we relive the rites of text-production for the *n*th time, despite the sad truth that the gods have fled so long ago that no one is even sure that they were ever there in the first place (in Composition, the gods are called, variously, *power, authentic voice, discourse, critical consciousness, versatility, style, disciplinarity, purpose,* etc.).

Or better, what we build are Museums, peculiar sorts of cultural temples in which students are "invited" in to sample the best that has been thought and expressed in *our language* and maybe even, like the art students we see poised in galleries with their sketchbooks and charcoals, to learn to reproduce the master's craft. Bartholomae and Petrosky, for example, seem to be only half-joking when they describe what motivated them (and, by extension, what they see as motivating many teachers) to use a canon of readings in their writing classrooms: "We thought (as many teachers have thought) that if we just, finally, gave them something good to read—something rich and meaty—they would change forever their ways of thinking about English" (*Ways of Reading* iii). Once they realized their true purpose—to teach students what to do with the reading material—they resumed the previous task of choosing rich and meaty content ("the sorts of readings we talk about when we talk with our colleagues," "selections . . . that present powerful readings of common experience, that open up the familiar world and make it puzzling, rich, and problematic" [iv]). (Mention must be made of a popular subset of composition reader, the multicultural reader, which presents the same sort of canon, only now more politically correct—like those museums that have re-hung their permanent collections to better reflect America's diversity. So, for example, John Repp selects the pieces for his collection *How We Live Now: Contemporary Multicultural Literature* according to the same tenets as Bartholomae and Petrosky: providing "imaginative literature to excite readers, inspire writers, and enliven classrooms"; readings "deeply satisfying and deeply disturbing at the same time," but overall, "so eloquently multivoiced" [v–vi]. A fine goal, perhaps, but the curated shows always seem to feature the same artists. We await the multicultural reader featuring a Tupac retrospective.) Underlying this trend in the Modern-Composition-Reader-as-Museum is Modernism itself. The Modern student's chief need is an awareness of tradition, which, in itself, comprises a sobering (not to mention Eurocentric) task—as Eliot wrote,

> Tradition is a matter of much wider significance. It cannot be inherited, and if you want it you must obtain it by great labour. It involves, in the first place, the historical sense, . . . and the historical sense involves a perception, not only of the pastness of the past, but of its presence; the historical sense compels a man to write not merely with his own generation in his bones, but with a feeling that the whole of the literature of Europe from Homer and within it the whole of the literature of his own country has a simultaneous existence and composes a simultaneous order. (14)

This consciousness of the past is something that must be nurtured throughout the writer's career; as Eliot phrases it (sounding much like Bartholomae when he speaks of the student's need to learn "the peculiar ways of knowing . . . that define the discourse of our community"), "what happens is a continual surrender of himself as he is at the moment to something which is far more valuable. The progress of an artist is a continual self-sacrifice, a continual extinction of personality" (17). Eliot, we know, tells not quite the whole story, or perhaps he is so clear on what he means himself that he feels no need to qualify the phrase "the whole of literature," because certainly, to the modernists, the whole of literature they're concerned with is not the entire whole. Leavis, for example, makes it clear that only some work is museum-quality; other work can't be bothered with. Indeed, since "the field is so huge and offers such insidious temptations to complacent confusions of judgment and to critical indolence, some challenging discriminations are very much called for" (9). Thus, Leavis offers what can be taken as the selection criteria for the contemporary Composition reader:

> It is necessary to insist, then, that there are important distinctions to be made, and that far from all of the names in the literary histories really belong to the realm of significant creative achievement. And as a recall to a due sense of differences it is well to start by distinguishing the few really great — the major novelists who count in the same way as the major poets [in Composition, we might add "and major essayists"], in the sense that they not only change the possibilities of the art for practitioners and readers, but that they are significant in terms of the human awareness they promote, awareness of the possibilities of life. (10)

If we are unhappy with the dry modernist enterprise of college writing (formal, autonomous, univocal, meaning-driven), we need to remember the way the modernist tradition is reproduced: "those institutions that are the preconditions for and shape the discourse of modernism . . . can be named at the outset: first, the museum; then, art history" (Crimp 108). And we must remember how those institutions consciously fight against exciting possibilities: "it is not in the interests of the institutions of art and the forces they serve to produce knowledge of radical practices" (Crimp 153). Our pedagogical, then, is the curatorial; we teach connoisseurship. Take, for example, the way Richard Rodriguez's reading of Richard Hoggart's *The Uses of Literacy* becomes, for Bartholomae and Petrosky, the masterly style, a manner to be replicated, "a way of reading we like to encourage in our students" (*Ways of Reading* 3). The composition readers themselves, as we have seen, are miniature museums, *bôites-en-valise* without the irony, portable permanent collections or corporate-sponsored temporary exhibits of our Greatest Hits. As instructors, our classroom activities combine the docent's tour (explaining how the great masterpieces are put together) with the hands-on workshop of family day (now that the gallery-goers understand how the masterpieces work, they get to try to make one). The scene of classroom writing is peculiarly overdetermined, then, as Gallery—as physical space in a larger institution (Museum/University), lying on the cusp between the curatorial and the commercial.

But the very *architecture* of the Museum, as some artists and theorists discovered, fights against the possibility of radical meaning in the way it predetermines the art which fits, the art that can be exhibited in (and, hence, created for) its space. Writing instructors, then, feeling constrained by the structural determinants of the spaces (even virtual ones) in which they practice, might do well to recall that moment in the broader cultural field of composition when artists finally abandoned the narrow, predictable constraints of the Gallery's architecture. Like Lutz in our own field, these practitioners felt the need for different, more evocative, spaces. Allan Kaprow, for example, realized the cause-effect relationship between architectural space and the artwork produced to "mean" in that space: "at root paintings, etc. could not possibly exist in their form up to the present without the psychological and physical definition of space given to them by Architecture" (*Assemblages* 153); the design of the gallery room, he reminds us, *"has always been a frame or format too"* (154). Those compositional formats—either the framed picture or the proscenium-delineated stage—are too accreted with associations; performance historian Richard Schechner captured the sentiment: "The single-focus stage and the framed picture are identified with the billboard and the press, and rejected" ("Happenings" 218). Kaprow was one of a group of neo-avant-garde visual and musical artists (including John Cage, Claes Oldenburg, Jim Dine, Robert Whitman, La Monte Young, Ann Halprin, Red Grooms, *et al.*) of the late fifties and early sixties who realized how the received design of the space in which their work appeared resulted in conventional product. And so these artists (compositionists-in-general, we might now name them) realized they would have to reject the architecture of that space, "ignoring the house in which they have for so long been nurtured" (Kaprow, *Assemblages* 153), if they wanted to produce a truly different composition. They practiced an art which interrupted the passivity of the spectator so that, as McLuhan & Fiore put it, "the audience becomes a participant in the total electric drama" (101). It was an art that frustrated conventions in order to allow other meanings to surface. It involved a re-appreciation of everyday material in order to complicate the distinction between art and life. This attempt resulted in new compositional forms: Assemblages, Combines, Neo-Dada works, and, most genre-blurringly, the Happenings.

As we saw with Lutz's attempt to re-style his pedagogical space, compositionists in the field of writing theory and practice in the 1960s were caught in the same frustrating dilemma the Happenings artists were—their desire to do interesting work thwarted by the constraints of conventional forms, spaces, and materials. The radical gestures of the Happenings artists were not lost on writing teachers, and so articles began to appear (by Lutz, Macrorie, and Coles, among a host of others less widely remembered today) which applied these gestures (either directly or, more ambiently, in spirit) to the writing class—initially, and not so remarkably, at the level of architecture:

> The classroom as presently structured does not provide the environment in which anything creative can be taught. Physically the room insists on order and authoritarianism, the enemies of creativity: the teacher as ultimate authority in front of the room and the students as passive receptacles at his feet. The unbridgeable gap (generation and otherwise) is physically emphasized. (Lutz "Making Freshman English" 85)

Such articles rhymed with similar sorts of texts appearing in the larger culture—everything from the situationists' tract "On the Poverty of Student Life" to Jerry Farber's *The Student as Nigger*—which critiqued education for its received nature, its dull curriculum, and its passionless tone. Farber, for example, also begins his critique of school—as the place where "the dying society puts its trip on you" (17)—by questioning the institution's architecture:

> Consider how most classrooms are set up. Everyone is turned toward the teacher and away from his classmates. You can't see the faces of those in front of you; you have to twist your neck to see the persons behind you. Frequently, seats are bolted to the floor or fastened together in rigid rows. This classroom, like the grading system, isolates students from each other and makes them passive receptacles. All the action, it implies, is at the front of the room. . . .
>
> But why those chairs at all? Why forty identical desk-chairs in a bleak, ugly room? Why should school have to remind us of jail or the army? . . . You know, wherever I've seen classrooms, from UCLA to elementary schools in Texas, it's always the same stark chamber. The classrooms we have are a nationwide chain of mortuaries. What on earth are we trying to teach? (24–25)

One of the Composition-specific articles in this genre of radical sixties pedagogy, one which I have never been able to forget since the day I first read it in the dimly-lit stacks of my university's library, was written in 1967 by a young graduate teaching assistant at the University of Oregon, Charles Deemer. His article, "English Composition as a Happening," did what many of these articles did, but did it in a formally compelling way (the article is a collage of brief sound-bite snippets, alternating between Deemer's own poetic reflections-as-manifesto and quotations from Sontag, McLuhan, Dewey, Goodman, and others), and Deemer's ideas seemed to catalyze my own discontent with what passed for Composition during the 1980s. As I read further back into the field, saw the basic questions of language, respect, and student interest these earlier practitioners tried to answer, current books and articles (which were written as if such questions didn't need to be answered every time one planned a course) began to sound increasingly hollow. I began to realize that something questionable happened in our field in the late seventies and early eighties: our insecurity over our status as a valid academic field led us to entrench ourselves firmly in professionalism. To establish Composition as a respectable discipline, we took on all the trappings of traditional academia—canonicity, scientism, empiricism, formalism, high theory, axioms, arrogance, and acceptance of the standard university department-divisions. We purged ourselves of any trace of kookiness, growing first suspicious, then disdainful, of the kind of homemade comp-class-as-Happening that people like Lutz tried to put together:

> At the beginning of the second class of the semester, I gave each student an index card and instructed him not to read it until told to. Then, at a given signal, each student read his card and performed the activity described on it [e.g., Go to the front of the room and face the class. Count to yourself and each time you reach five say, "If I had the wings of an angel." . . . (Or) Be an ice cream cone—change flavor]. At the end of three minutes, a student who had been designated time-keeper called time. I asked the students to sit down and write as much as they could describing what had just occurred in the classroom and their reaction to it. (36–37)

We became Moderns. But I couldn't stop thinking about, for example, Ken Macrorie, and this book of his, *Uptaught*, which read like Kurt Vonnegut's long-lost foray into Composition Theory. How did we go from a book like Macrorie's, urging "that teachers must find ways of getting students to produce (in words, pictures, sounds, diagrams, objects, or landscapes) what students and teachers honestly admire" (186), to meditating on "Texts as Knowledge Claims: The Social Construction of Two Biologists' Articles"? Suddenly, spirit, love, adventure, poetry, incense, kicky language, and rock 'n' roll were gone. The forms and constraints seemed overwhelming, the huge gray University walls had grown tall and imposing, keeping the revelers out. As I read further through this new epistemic, Modernist Composition, I noticed something else—call it Composition's material restraint, the phenomenon by which a *de facto* "Composition Canon" forms, with the same names cropping up not just in anthology tables of contents, but in "Works Cited" lists. As article after article appeared, one could trace the waxing and waning of theoretical trends: Langer, Polanyi, Vygotsky, Odell, Emig, Berthoff, Bruffee, Bartholomae, Berlin, Anzaldúa, Foucault, and Freire. This narrow-banding is curious for a discipline that trumpets the value of linguistic richness. The texts surrounding the Happenings proved richer, more seductive to me, in the way they dealt with the same material and institutional concerns I had as a writing teacher. As I read further into them, I began to read the texts surrounding the artists who prefigured the Happenings—Duchamp and Pollock—as well as the texts of those they prefigured—the Conceptualists, the Minimalists, the Neo-Dadaists. And through it all I continued to listen to popular music (a key thread in the material of Comp '68). The truth of materialism hit home. There was all this wonderful stuff—raising and reflecting on key compositional issues—that wasn't making its way into our journals, and yet an article on how a biologist writes was. Frankly, I don't care how a biologist writes. I assume it's pretty conventional stuff, thoroughly implicated in the traditional departmental divisions that stultify the academy. If the folks in biology want to get together with me and talk about how to re-evaluate the form and subject of biology, I'm there. The way such writing represents the entrenched disciplinarity of academia makes it of dubious value as part of a material sublime. I think of what the idea of composition is: an opportunity to reflect on textuality, its craft, wonder, problems—obviously that should be at the center of any idea of academics; but thanks to the epistemic turn we are simply the eager lapdogs of the big-ticket disciplines. Our self-imposed formal and material subservience marks a sad betrayal of the spirit of verbal risk and writing-as-life that marked the best of our history.

Post-Happenings Composition never ever asks (as Comp '68 did so often) "What's Going On?" To remove any doubt about precisely what was going on, Composition undertook the classical modernist project of self-definition. Bizzell and Bartholomae helped usher in these attempts to articulate exactly what we could claim with certitude about Composition. Lindemann, influenced by these epistemic compositionists, offers perhaps the clearest summative view of the field, one which shows its newly narrowed status of allowing students practice in pre-professional discourse: "Freshman English offers guided practice in reading and writing the discourses of the academy and the professions. That is what our colleagues across the campus want it to do; that is what it should do if we are going to drag every first-year student through the requirement" (312). Composition, then, implicates itself in the contemporary re-figuring of education as training for work rather than intensification of experience. As Frank McCourt realizes, reflecting back with deep sadness on his many years teaching high school in New York City:

> There's no vision. Education's just a branch of industry and commerce. It's about scores, scores, scores—and all of this is designed to supply a workforce. We really don't give a s— about the minds and feelings of the kids. . . . In my eighteen years at Stuyvesant High, only one parent ever asked me, "Is my child enjoying himself?" One. ("What I Learned in School" 60)

Strict boundaries have become maintained in Composition, a separation of (profession-oriented) academy and life, one discipline from another, the specific discourse from a broader lived reality. This is not Freshman English as a Happening, this is Freshman English as a Corporate Seminar. Happenings were all about blurring the boundaries between art and life. They underscored what Cage maintained, which was that "what we are doing is living, and that we are not moving toward a goal, but are, so to speak, at the goal constantly and changing with it, and that art, if it is going to be anything useful, should open our eyes to this fact" (Kirby and Schechner 60). A view such as Cage's marks a de-determination of art, wholly at odds with post-Happenings Composition, which maintains very clear, Leavisesque distinctions between writers, texts, and contexts, so that students can join the Great Tradition. Composition, in this view, styles students to "enter the conversation of the academy and begin to contribute to the making of knowledge . . . guiding students in those uses of language that enable them to become historians, biologists, and mathematicians" (Lindemann 313). A Happenings spirit is more like that laid out by Fluxus founder George Maciunas, in one of his manifestos (the Fluxus artists being as interested as Cage and the Happenings artists in radically rethinking conventional form and content), which implies a Composition centered on amusement, Freshman English as Fluxjoke:

> AMUSEMENT FORGOES DISTINCTION BETWEEN ART AND NONART, FORGOES ARTIST'S INDISPENSIBILITY, EXCLUSIVE-NESS, INDIVIDUALITY, AMBITION, FORGOES ALL PRETENSION TOWARDS SIGNIFIGANCE, RARITY, INSPIRATION, SKILL, COM-PLEXITY, PROFUNDITY, GREATNESS, INSTITUTIONAL AND COMMODITY VALUE. IT STRIVES FOR MONOSTRUCTURAL, NONTHEATRICAL, NONBAROQUE, IMPERSONAL QUALITIES OF A SIMPLE NATURAL EVENT, AN OBJECT, A GAME, A PUZZLE OR GAG. ("FLUXUS" 94)

The reason the teaching of writing is permeated by dissatisfaction (every CCCC presentation seems, at some level, a complaint) is that we—bad enough—don't really know what teaching is, but also—far worse, fatal, in fact—we haven't really evolved an idea of writing that fully reflects the splendor of the medium. (Somewhere out there, for example, is a prof for whom "memo" as a verb is still a big deal.) We have evolved a very limited notion of academic writing (or any genre, really). Our texts are conventional in every sense of the word; they write themselves. They are almost wholly determined by the texts that have gone before; a radical break with the conventions of a form or genre (and I'm not speaking here about the academic convention of the smug, sanctioned transgression, e.g., Jane Tompkins) would perplex—how is *that* history writing? what community group would need *that* for its newsletter? how is *that* going to help you get a job? A Happenings spirit would begin at the point of Elbow's "life is long and college is short" queasiness with academic writing ("Reflections on Academic Discourse" 136).

To de-determine form and content means that the writing can just be; or, as the title of one of the key *CCC* '69 pieces puts it, "this writing is" (Litz). The Happening artists' basic rule was indeterminacy; nothing is previously determined, neither form nor material content; everything is under erasure. The only given, a kind of non-axiom, is the one stated by Rauschenberg, who cared not at all about control or intention, only change: "What's exciting is that we don't know. There is no anticipated result; but we will be changed" (Kostelanetz, *Theatre* 99). Once all the conventions are re-thought, the compositional scene becomes simpler, more an issue of basic being, wonder, the human heart, change. Take Happenings artist Ken Dewey's de-determination of the idea of *theatre*. "The further out one moves, the simpler one's understanding becomes of what theatre is. I now would accept only that theatre is a situation in which people gather to articulate something of mutual concern" (210). Dewey shows a basic, unoccluded desire for communion. That, along with passion, beauty, lyricism . . . why is that *not* our core? Why do we *not* insist on it? Despite all the lip service we give to empowerment in our ideological curricula, we don't really believe in the power of a composition to change the world. We have a concept of audience as construct, not as lived. Which allows us to develop all these step-by-step heuristic-templates to turn the rhetorical situation into a parlor game.

> When you consider the expectations and interests of your readers, you naturally think *strategically*, asking yourself questions such as these:
>
> - To what extent are my readers interested in and knowledgeable about my subject?
> - What formal and stylistic expectations will my readers bring to my essay?
> - What other aspects of my readers' situations might influence how they respond to my essay?
> - How can I use my understanding of my readers' expectations and interests when I make decisions about the content, form, and style of my essay? (Ede 56–57)

When there's really only one heuristic that matters: the person who reads this—and it is one specific person, saturated in lived desire—will that person be changed? We think only in the abstract about how some peculiarly overcrafted college essay or some genre of "real world" writing can change a generic reader. We need to keep in mind how, not in the "real world" but in life, any small fragment has the power to truly change a person, not just (and probably not at all) some heuristic-generated, audience-strategized, oddly-voiced form that results in that weird sort of "prose-lite" essay they publish in those magazines available in the seat backs of airplanes. We need only remember what Salter tells us: "the power to change one's life comes from a paragraph, a lone remark. The lines that penetrate us are slender, like the flukes that live in river water and enter the bodies of swimmers" (161).

Rarefying materials, as Composition does (the middle-brow preciosity or academic aloofness that drives the reading selections we anthologize), only makes the possibilities for Happening Composition more remote, particularly for students. Material access is an issue, and many of the Happenings artists relied on what was available in the trash for their stage properties. It became a theoretical principle for someone like Cage: "I was already interested at that time in avoiding the exclusion of banal elements. . . . I've always been on the side of the things one shouldn't do and searching for ways of bringing the refused elements back into play" (Kirby and Schechner 60). Or take that flower garden Cage writes about: "George Mantor had an iris garden, which he improved each year by throwing out the commoner varieties. One day his attention was called to another very fine iris garden. Jealously he made some inquiries. The garden, it turned out, belonged to the man who collected his garbage" (*Silence* 263). Not only material differences, but formal ones as well, as part of the production necessary for new ideas. La Monte Young offers a simple example of the new text grammar (actually not really new, just basic undetermined juxtaposition) guiding his "Lecture 1960": "The lecture is written in sections. . . . Each section originally was one page or a group of pages stapled together. Any number of them may be read in any order. The order and selections are determined by chance, thereby bringing about new relationships between parts and consequently new meanings" (72). Many of these new genres arise, following the de-conventionalization of the form, from an allegorical reading, seeing one form through the lens of another. According to Dewey, "It should have been made clear that Happenings came about when painters and sculptors crossed into theatre taking with them their way of looking and doing things" (206). So La Monte Young looks at the traditional lecture through the lens of a random generator. Or take Fluxus artist Dick Higgins, who worked out the form for his Happening *The Tart, or Miss America* (1965) by trying to apply the idea of collage to theatre. I like such practices as Young's and Higgins's, as they involve reading texts in (at least) two ways. Is Young's creation a lecture or performance art? Is *The Tart* (with a list of characters including butchers, doctors, steelworkers, electricians, and a chemist) choreography or sociology? Is this book of mine composition, art history, basic writing theory, or cultural studies? Sometimes I'm not sure if the first-year writing course I teach is a course on rap, writing, or technology. Anyway, I like how that blurring messes up a stable reading; it energizes a text or scene, preventing it from becoming fixed.

I would like, then, to return to that point of disenchantment with established spaces and the desire for new forms, a disenchantment and desire that was felt historically in all fields with the idea of *composition* at their center. Much of what I hear in conferences and conversations suggests that we have already returned to a desire for something else (if we've ever really left—Composition Studies as a perpetual scene of disenchantment). Contemporary Composition, as Lindemann shows, is still inflected by that epistemic turn taken in the 1980s, convincing me we need to remember what we've forgotten, namely how impassioned resolves and thrilling discoveries were abandoned and why. I'd like, then, to retrace the road not taken in Composition Studies, to re-read the elision, in order to remember what was missed and to salvage what can still be recovered. This, then, is a negative-space history, one that reverses the conventional figure-ground relations to find the most fruitful avenues of inquiry to be those untouched or abandoned by the disciplinary mainstream. The disruptive/restorative dynamic of my project means both rediscovering the usefulness of some of the materials of Composition that have faded from our conscious screen, and forcing a comparison of our field with the avant-garde tradition in post-WWII American art, running that story through our own traditional, disciplined history—or better, showing our history as already-ruptured, permanently destabilized by our attitude toward (really, ignorance of) the compositional avant-garde. My key compositional theorists—Pollock, Duchamp, the situationists, the Happenings artists, punks—are non-compositionists as our field would define such; and my favorite field-specific theorist-practitioners are those now out of fashion, like Macrorie and Coles, or ones never more than minor figures, like Deemer. My re-reading of the field is really an allegory: reading composition through a particular thread (the Happenings movement, broadly defined) in twentieth century art history. Call it "writing instruction as electric drama," maybe. Of course, what I'm really doing is re-writing Charles Deemer's original 1967 *College English* allegory. Allegorical criticism—in the way allegory tells one story, but tells it as read through (or in) another—is a useful method by which to read our past, particularly for an historical review like mine, which desires to re-affirm the value in an all but forgotten era of Composition Studies, in the hope of finding an alternative to the current tradition. According to Owens, "what is most proper to [allegory is] its capacity to rescue from historical oblivion that which threatens to disappear. Allegory first emerged in response to a . . . sense of estrangement from tradition" (203). Allegory, then, serves as the perfect strategy by which to return to that stirring moment in our history, in the hopes of recapturing its intensity, because, as Owens continues, the "two most fundamental impulses" of allegory are "[a] conviction of the re-moteness of the past, and a desire to redeem it for the present." Seeing the field of writing instruction through the broader compositional allegory of art-in-general connects back to Irmscher, who also suggested an art analogy as an approach to rhetorical theory, urging a focus on those artists who could de-familiarize rhetoric and change perception: "In matters of experimentation with established principles and processes, the other arts are particularly in-structive, for artists continually seek to overcome the limitations and tradi-tional agencies of their medium. . . . We can learn about rhetoric particularly from those artists who have modified our modes of perception, for what each has done is to change, sometimes radically, one or more of the components in the rhetorical paradigm so that interaction no longer occurs in familiar ways" ("Analogy" 354). A field like ours—where articles and monographs and text-books all say basically the same thing, draw materially on the same sources—exists in much the same state as the art world in 1964, described by Harold Rosenberg as "sealed up in itself" ("After Next" 70); an allegorical reading is perfect for such a field, offering immediate fracture. Barthes, as well, affirms the heuristic power gained from the prose/painting allegory: "Why not wipe out the difference between them," he asks, "in order to affirm more power-fully the plurality of 'texts' " (S/Z 56). . . .

It's worth tracing briefly how the history of writing instruction parallels (and where it departs from) that of the visual arts. Assume a composition-in-general, defined as the production of a work that responds to some problem, some exigency. The work itself might be thought of as having a form and con-tent, being made of certain materials to which certain techniques are applied. That work, then, is judged according to certain criteria. In Pre-Modern art, the problem was representation: whether Altamira cave-painters or Renaissance *maîtres*, artists had as their goal the rendering of a realist image (as aesthetics evolved, we might add *beauty* as another part of the problem being worked out in such composition). The content for the image was entirely conventional: the animals the cave-painters wanted to hunt or the religious icons the Renaissance artists wanted to praise. Rendering techniques also became standardized, from two-dimensional art to chiaroscuro and perspective. Materials, too conformed to convention—again, whether we're talking about how cave-painters used burnt wood and blood or how later artists mixed their own pigments (making the studio scene standard, because painters had a difficult time, until pre-mixed tubes of paint became available in the nineteenth century, mixing colors *en plein air*). The paintings were judged mainly on how well they corresponded to the accepted standard. De Kooning captured the thoroughly conventional nature of the art of this era in a comment on Titian: "But he kept on painting Virgins in that luminous light, like he'd just heard about them. Those guys had everything in place, the Virgin and God and the technique, but they kept it up like they were still looking for something" (Kimmelman "Life is Short" 22). Rendering or representation coalesced Pre-Modern writing instruction: the problem being the clear rendering or reproduction of the target language (in our case, Edited American English). Things got especially worrisome when the student couldn't achieve that clarity; so Adams Sherman Hill complains of flawed representation in 1879, of "manuscripts written in an examination room . . . disfigured by bad spelling, confusing punctuation, ungrammatical, obscure, ambiguous, or inelegant expressions . . . blunders which would disgrace a boy twelve years old" (Connors "Basic Writing Textbooks" 260). The materials, besides pen and paper and language, were textbooks, "filled with grammatical and mechanical rules and exercises" (Connors 261), and the technique those materials reinforced was "to atomize writing into small bits and to practice these bits. . . . [The textbooks] break writing down into a set of subskills and assume that conscious mastery of the subskills means mastery of the writing" (262, 265); so copying and drills became standard. The form/content was determined by the expressive, topic-sentence paragraph. And the excellence of the work was judged in large part on the correctness of its correspondence to the standard, on the presence or absence of formal errors.

The Modernist era in art is best described by Clement Greenberg. Briefly, Greenberg associates Modernism with the impulse in Western culture "to turn around and question its own foundations" ("Modernist Painting" 67). Self-reflexivity marked the turn in art, for Greenberg, from the Old Masters to the Moderns: "Realistic, illusionist art had dissembled the medium, using art to conceal art. Modernism used art to call attention to art. The limitations that constitute the medium of painting—the flat surface, the shape of the support, the properties of pigment—were treated by the Old Masters as negative factors that could be acknowledged only implicitly or indirectly. Modernist painting has come to regard these same limitations as positive factors that are to be acknowledged openly" (69). So the Modern painters under the spell of Greenberg worked to identify those properties of painting exclusive to itself. Representation became dispensable, since other arts were also representational; hence, art that was truly Modern had to be abstract. The materials, for the most part, were still oil on canvas (even if radically thinned, as Morris Louis favored). What also made a painting truly a painting (and one had to speak of the Modernist picture *qua* picture: "one sees a Modernist painting as a picture first" [70]) was its flatness on a canvas (anything else became three-dimensional, hence sculptural). Perhaps the only thing that didn't change from the Pre-Modern to the Modern was *excellence* as a criterion—particularly in historical or traditional terms (as beautiful, pleasing, inspirational, well-wrought)—to judge the work; as Greenberg noted, sounding like his fellow-Moderns Eliot and Leavis, "Without the past of art, and without the need and compulsion to maintain past standards of excellence, such a thing as Modernist art would be impossible" (77). Bartholomae, our field's most articulate Modernist, shows how the Modernist program translated into Composition theory and pedagogy. Self-reflexivity ruled: the problem became not so much expressivist representation as analytic criticism; particularly, as in the Greenbergian investigation of the essential elements of painting, this meant a formal inquiry into the medium (academic discourse) and its conventions, finding, for example, "the rules governing the presentation of examples or the development of an argument" ("Inventing" 135). The materials, newly delimited—our flat, abstract, oil canvases—are now what is strictly specific to college writing, the university continually re-invented (as the same traditional thing). So the student must work, technique-wise, on "assembling and mimicking [the university's] language," and the form/content of one's work becomes "the peculiar ways of knowing, selecting, evaluating, reporting, concluding, and arguing that define the discourse of our community" ("Inventing" 135, 134). We can speak now of what is exclusive to Composition, of the field's "historic concern for the space on the page and what it might mean to do work there and not somewhere else . . . composition as a professional commitment to do a certain kind of work with a certain set of materials" ("What is Composition?" 18, 22). Criteria no longer invoke sentence-level correctness; Bartholomae tellingly moves beyond error, as he seemingly abandons representation for criticism—but formalists, of course, never fully abandon representation. The new criterion is a kind of meta-representation: how well the work mimics the original critical text that has interrogated the tradition; how well, that is, the students "take on the role—the voice, the persona—of an authority whose authority is rooted in scholarship, analysis, or research" ("Inventing" 136). What is represented, then, is the newly refigured discourse. So, in *Ways of Reading*, for example, Bartholomae and Petrosky urge the student who has just read a selection from *Mythologies*, "As a way of testing Barthes's method, and of testing the usefulness of his examples, write an essay (or perhaps a series of 'mythologies') that provides a similar reading of an example (or related examples) of American culture—MTV, skateboarding, the Superbowl, Pee Wee Herman, etc. You might ask, 'What would Barthes notice in my examples? What would he say about these significant features?'" (36). This is writing as iterative gesture, typical of Modernist Composition (Lindemann's students, for example, "examine the texts they encounter in the academy [in order to] creat[e] texts like those they read" (314).

Happenings artists reacted to the Modernist program. The problem became not the conventional, but rather how one does something unconventional, sublime, exciting. Any material and technique was allowed, if it could produce something exciting. Form and content were equally open; as Minimalist Donald Judd put it "Any material can be used, as is or painted" (184). The only relevant criteria was one we can also take from Judd: "A work needs only to be interesting" (184). Whether you call this postmodern or (as I prefer) avant-garde, there is very little correspondence for it in Composition Studies. Deemer, an obvious parallel, sees the problem as one of boredom resulting from conventional composition; the aim is for the teacher to "shock the student" (124). It's pedagogy as dare (Composition prefers the truth of resemblance), gambling on the sublime, "the reengagement of the heart, a new tuning of *all* the senses. Taking the first step toward poetry" (125). Materials had to be different, other: "Let [the class] discuss theology to Ray Charles records" (124). Deemer is very purposeful in his article not to describe technique too carefully, because he wants to disrupt the notion of correspondence and reproduction found in the Modernist and Pre-Modernist writing space; he wants to preserve risk: "It is with reason that I have neglected to present a more explicit blueprint for the happening after which to model a reconstruction of English Composition. In the first place, happenings happen; they are not passed down from one to another. Spontaneity is essential. Each 'teacher' must inspire his own happening" (124). Lutz's class, then, described earlier— which also used popular recordings, and had students practice almost meditative techniques while they listened, in order to bring about a sublime state—becomes a record of his own journey (as "teacher") to spontaneity and inspiration. We can consider avant-pop theorist Mark Amerika to see how these ideas might play out in a writing class. Amerika's project starts with tradition itself—particularly the conventional, media-saturated consumerist culture, and how it seems to preclude the sublime—as the problem; for Amerika, the struggle becomes "to rapidly transform our sick, commodity-infested workaday culture into a more sensual, trippy, exotic and networked . . . experience." An avant-garde technique has nothing to do with the formal, replicable, critical methods that serve to represent a discourse or produce a strong reading; rather it is a radically de-determined ambient interaction with cultural information. Text-selection replaces text-production: "Creating a work of art will depend more and more on the ability of the artist to select, organize and present the bits of raw data we have at our disposal" (Amerika). Techniques now include, besides the standard freewriting, listing, drafting, etc., appropriating, sampling, copying, cataloging, scanning, indexing, chatting, and audio/video-streaming (think of these as a new list of gerunds to supercede Bartholomae's *knowing, selecting, evaluating, reporting, concluding,* and *arguing*). If a Happening or Duchamp's *Large Glass* or a Rauschenberg combine-painting or a Beuys multiple or a Koons sculpture are typical example's of avant-garde art, we might think of synchronous/asynchronous conversation transcripts, Story-Space hypertexts, Web pages, emails, or even informal drafts as species of avant-garde composition. Since the compositional arena is now more broadly cultural, which implies post-typographic, the "space on the page" has been ruptured, as well as concomitant standards of evaluation; according to Amerika:

> By actively engaging themselves in the continuous exchange and proliferation of collectively-generated electronic publications, individually-designed creative works, manifestos, live on-line readings, multi-media interactive hypertexts, conferences, etc., Avant-Pop artists and the alternative networks they are a part of will eat away at the conventional relics of a bygone era where the individual artist-author creates their beautifully-crafted, original works of art to be consumed primarily by the elitist art-world and their business-cronies who pass judgment on what is appropriate and what is not.

Notions of correspondence (whether to a representational standard or a discursive tradition) are irrelevant; Arthur C. Danto taught this spirit of the inapplicability of traditional aesthetics to the avant-garde composition when he titled an essay on post-modern art "Whatever Happened to Beauty?" . . .

Childan's gallery is a good starting point from which to allegorically view Composition Studies of the past thirty-odd years because of the implications involved in our field's gradual rejection of that yin world of collapse and decay in its instructional theories, emphasizing instead an ethereal, code-driven, textual re-representation of authenticity and authority. The story told by American Artistic Handcrafts Inc. recurs too frequently in Composition Studies. It's the same story told in every museum's gallery: work is either a classic, desired piece (assuming it's not fake, plagiarized) or it's crude, worthless, fecal—in our galleries, for example, we teach either writers or students (and students' work can be either strong or weak). A re-appreciation of a Happenings aesthetic can reveal what our strictly empyrean formalism misses, the other scene of its vision. What we learn from Childan and Tagomi is the potential effect of a delay in standards: deferring the quick dismissal of aura-less trash, staring a bit longer, watching the light catch, opening ourselves to the new view in our hearts. Work of true beauty and artistic power, it seems, can be crafted in very basic ways from seemingly degraded materials, paying little or no attention to formal or historical tradition. Childan and Tagomi learned a Happenings lesson: to follow a work where it goes; to turn off expectations and be open to meaning, intensity, beauty. I think of Braque, who knew he was finished with a painting when nothing remained of the original idea. Composition's definition of finished writing, on the other hand, is when the original intention is perfectly realized.

And so this [work], which I write out of the lull I feel in contemporary Composition Studies, a disenchantment, which I would locate both in theory and pedagogy. What should be the central space for intellectual inquiry in the academy has become identified as either a service course designed to further the goals of other academic units or a cultural-studies space in which to investigate identity politics. An enthusiasm has been lost, particularly among those entering the profession. Even the newest technologies for composition are rapidly succumbing to this lull—witness collections on what makes writing good in the digital age, taxonomies of email, or standards for evaluating web pages. The cause of our current stasis? Doubtless the major influence has been Composition's professionalization, its self-tormented quest for disciplinary stature. The price we have paid for our increased credibility as an academic field has been a narrowing of the bandwidth of what used to pass for composition. In figuring out our place among the disciplines, we have made the notion of disciplines paramount—what we talk about when we talk about writing is writing-in-the-academy or "real-world" writing that reflects (legitimates) academic departments. This streamlining of the previously disparate narratives of Composition means that less and less do our genres represent a kind of expressivist or art-writing, a writing for non-academic (or non-ideological) goals, that "first step toward poetry." To counter, then, here is my brief journey into the tenets and figures of a group of avant-garde artists who, for want of a better term, I loosely group around the concept "Happenings." It is meant as both disruptive and restorative: to interrupt the uncritical acceptance of Composition as currently institutionalized by recollecting the more open-ended, poetic theories of form and content, congruent with developments in other compositional fields, which remain our forgotten heritage. . . .

It seems odd for an anti-tradition like the Happening to be spoken of in the privileged language of the VIP lounge. There is a will-to-genre there that disturbs; the *complete stranger*'s work should be embraced for its potential, its possibilities: in fact, a stranger would have something important to add to a genre like the Happenings, whose project is, as Robert Whitman defined it, "the story of all those perceptions and awarenesses you get just from being a person" (Kostelanetz *Theatre* 224). Kaprow further reduces the full-blown nature of the Happening's unpredictability by prescribing that those participating in a Happening "have a clear idea what they are to do. This is simply accomplished by writing out the scenario or score for all and discussing it thoroughly with them beforehand." Tellingly, he adds, "In this respect it is not different from the preparations for a parade, a football match, a wedding, or a religious service. It is not even different from a play" (*Assemblages* 197). For one who bemoaned the Cheetah, his compositional grammar is strangely bound by extant realities; instead of trying to build the New Babylon (or even settling for a detournement of the city-space), he simply inserts his compositions into existent theatres (now broadly defined). So, "A Happening could be composed for a jetliner going from New York to Luxembourg with stopovers at Gander, Newfoundland, and Reykjavik, Iceland. Another Happening would take place up and down the elevators of five tall buildings in midtown Chicago" (*Assemblages* 191). The pieces often become derivative of each other, and sometimes seem to include Surrealism for its own sake. On another note, there's a slight queasiness when one thinks of how often the final effect of Kaprow's (and others') Happenings was ecologically distasteful. This, for example, from Kaprow's comments regarding *Self-Service* (1967).

> Other of my Happenings have had far more dramatic and deliberate imagery.
> The majority of events involved doing something and leaving it. For example, we set up a banquet in the Jersey marshes on the side of a busy highway—a complete banquet with food, wine, fruit, flowers, and place-settings, crystal glasses and silver coins in the glasses. And we simply left it, never went back. It was an offering to the world: whoever wants this, take it. So many of the things had just that quality of dropping things in the world and then going on about your business. (Schechner "Extensions" 221)

The world, I feel, is full up already; there's enough intense, natural text to inspire already. This surreal overlay of wasteful excrescence is unnecessary. At least Rauschenberg got his props from the garbage and reused much of them in his Combine paintings and performances.

So, no, this is not wide-eyed, naive nostalgia. My project does not mark a reactionary reverence for old forms, but rather a crucial need to understand the irreverence, the disgust, for old forms, as well as the passion for rethinking forms. I certainly don't want to "make love to the past" as Cage calls it (Kostelanetz *John Cage* 25). What I want is simply to reconsider a group of artists and compositionists who wondered why texts couldn't be new, interesting, and transformative. Why they couldn't experiment with new materials and forms, blur disciplines and boundaries, and subsume the whole with a life-affirming humor. Mostly these artists wondered why their compositions couldn't strive for a sublimity in the participants that might, in some small way, change the world. I locate my interest, then, in the definition of the Happenings put forward by Jean-Jacques Lebel. They weren't meant to recover a lost world, he claimed, but to create a new one, "imperceptibly gaining on reality" (276). Cage speaks of how art can only offer so much, can only be so consumable, and then you need something new. He fails to understand "people attacking the avant-garde on the very notion that the new was something we should not want. But it is a necessity now" (Kostelanetz *John Cage* 25). The forms and techniques of the past are used up, "gone . . . finished. We must have something else to consume. We have now [in 1968], we've agreed, the new techniques. We have a grand power that we're just becoming aware of in our minds" (25). But in Composition, we barely began using that grand power before we abandoned it. I want to see how and why we failed meaningfully to employ those new techniques and what that might say about our current need. It's almost too heartbreaking to read the texts of the Happenings—the scripts, interviews, manifestos—so militant yet joyful, so righteous yet open, so convinced yet innocent. That the world hasn't changed overall in their wake takes nothing from them or their theory. They changed me. And others, too, I bet.

English Composition as a Happening is about the need to address deep, basic humanity in this modern, over-sophisticated age. The Happenings exist as one of the 20th century's periodic attempts to revive a spirit of primitive tribalism in modernity, the aesthetic collective as spiritual cult. Performances of Happenings seemed to occur out of a felt need for new collective spiritual rituals; in staging them, old technologies were renewed just as frequently as newer, more sophisticated ones were used. "Performance art, sometimes hardly distinguishable from a casual gesture, emerges like an artistic regression" (Molderings 176). Macrorie's theory, Coles's classroom work, Deemer's and Lutz's materials . . . reading them is like sitting in a circle and listening to a patient elder gently guide us on the vision-quest, using parables and jokes and truths. It's so retro, it's become avant-garde. Their pedagogy sometimes seems such a part of the fabric of life that it's hardly distinguishable from a casual gesture, much like the student writing they offer as exempla. Mariellen Sandford reflects on the renewed interest in Fluxusart and Happenings in the Preface to her republication of the famous 1963 *Tulane Drama Review* issue devoted to the Happenings. She feels the recuperation of the Happenings in the decade following the 1980s makes spiritual sense; for her, this renewal of attention responds to "a healthy need for inspiration—the inspiration to break free of a decade that in many ways rivaled the conservatism of the years preceding the Fluxus and Happening movements" (xix). Such a project, then, is desublimatory, restoring certain repressed voices to a position of innovative commentary. It was the compositionists of the Happenings era who first felt this tension in our field between deeply humanist goals and the limits of academic conventions. Macrorie's *Uptaught* chronicled "the dead language of the schools . . . [in which] nobody wrote live. Same old academic stuff" (11, 14). And Deemer felt composition to be "the rigid child of a rigid parent" (121); in order to transform that rigidity into a McLuhanesque "electric drama" (123), he urged the "shock and surprise" of the Happening, writing class now conceived of as the theatre of mixed means. The gist of my [work] is nicely expressed by a phrase from Thierry de Duve: "the paradoxical sense of the future that a deliberately retrospective gaze opens up" (*Kant* 86). I offer, then, these backward glances, in fervent hope: to capture the Happenings spirit for our own Composition, shaking off more than a decade of conservative professionalism; to fracture our field's genres open for possibilities, risks, and material exploration, leading to a Composition in which faith and naiveté replace knowingness and expertise; to put pressure on Composition's canon, recalibrating the field according to a general economy of the compositional arts—a destabilized site of various competing schools, undercut by an ongoing, productive tension between the academic and the avant-garde; to liberate thinking in our field from the strictly semantic, re-opening Composition as a site where radical explorations are appreciated, where aesthetic criteria still come into play, but criteria not merely cribbed off an endless, formalist tape-loop. Put simply, to resume building Composition's Hacienda.

REFERENCES

Amerika, Mark. "Avant-Pop Manifesto: Thread Baring Itself in Ten Quick Posts." <http://marketplace.com:70/0/alternative.x/manifestos/avant.po.manifesto.txt.> (20 Sept. 1996).

Barthes, Roland. *S/Z.* Trans. Richard Miller. New York: Hill and Wang, 1974.

Bartholomae, David. "Inventing the University." *When a Writer Can't Write.* Ed. Mike Rose. New York: The Guilford Press, 1985. 134–165.

———. "What is Composition and (if you know what that is) Why Do We Teach It?" *Composition in the Twenty-First Century: Crisis and Change.* Ed. Lynn Z. Bloom, Donald A. Daiker, and Edward M. White. Carbondale: Southern Illinois University Press, 1996. 11–28.

———, and Anthony Petrosky. *Ways of Reading: An Anthology for Writers.* 2nd ed. Boston: Bedford Books of St. Martin's, 1990.

Cage, John. *Silence.* Hanover: Wesleyan University Press, 1973.

Connors, Robert J. "Basic Writing Textbooks: History and Current Avatars." Theresa Enos (ed). *A Sourcebook for Basic Writing Teachers.* New York: Random House, 1987. 259–274.

Crimp, Douglas. *On the Museum's Ruins.* Cambridge: MIT Press, 1993.

Danto, Arthur C. "Whatever Happened to Beauty?" *The Nation* 30 Mar. 1992: 418–421.

de Duve, Thierry. *Kant After Duchamp.* Cambridge, MA: MIT Press, 1996.

Deemer, Charles. "English Composition as a Happening." *College English* 29 (Nov. 1967): 121–126.

Dewey, Ken. "X-ings." In Sandford 206–210.

Dick, Philip K. *The Man in the High Castle.* 1962. New York: Berkley Medallion, 1974.

Duchamp, Marcel. *Salt Seller: The Writings of Marcel Duchamp.* Ed. Michel Sanouillet and Elmer Peterson. New York: Oxford UP, 1973.

Ede, Lisa. *Work in Progress: A Guide to Writing and Revising.* 2nd ed. New York: St. Martin's Press, 1992.

Elbow, Peter. "Reflections on Academic Discourse." *College English* 53 (Feb. 1991): 135–155.

Eliot, T. S. *Selected Essays.* London: Faber and Faber, 1932.

Farber, Jerry. *The Student as Nigger: Essays and Stories.* New York: Pocket Books, 1970.

Greenberg, Clement. "Modernist Painting." *The New Art.* Ed. Gregory Battcock. New York: Dutton, 1973. 66–77.

Higgins, Dick. "Statement on Intermedia." In Armstrong and Rothfuss 172–173.

Irmscher, William F. "Analogy as an Approach to Rhetorical Theory." *College Composition and Communication* 27 (Dec. 1976): 350–354.

Judd, Donald. *Complete Writings 1959–1975.* Halifax: Nova Scotia College of Art and Design, 1995.

Kaprow, Allan. "The Legacy of Jackson Pollock." *ARTnews* October 1958: 24+.

———. " 'Happenings' in the New York Scene." *ARTnews* May 1961: 36+.

———. *Assemblages, Environments and Happenings.* New York: Abrams, 1966.

Kimmelman, Michael. "Life is Short, Art is Long." *The New York Times Magazine* 4 Jan. 1998: 19–23.

Kirby, Michael, and Richard Schechner. "An Interview with John Cage." In Sandford 51–71.

Kostelanetz, Richard. *The Theatre of Mixed Means: An Introduction to Happenings, Kinetic Environments, and Other Mixed-Means Performances.* New York: The Dial Press, 1968.

———, ed. *John Cage.* New York: Praeger, 1970.

Leavis, F. R. *The Great Tradition.* Garden City, NY: Doubleday, 1954.

Lebel, Jean-Jacques. "On the Necessity of Violation." In Sandford 268–284.

Lindemann, Erika. "Freshman Composition: No Place for Literature." *College English* 55 (Mar. 1993): 311–316.

Litz, Robert P. "this writing is: Ralph J. Gleason's Notes on Miles Davis' *Bitches Brew.*" *College Composition and Communication* 22 (Dec. 1971): 343+.

Lutz, William D. "Making Freshman English a Happening." *College Composition and Communication* 22 (Feb. 1971): 35–38.

Maciunas, George. "FLUXUS." In Sandford 94.

Macrorie, Ken. *Uptaught.* Rochelle Park: Hayden, 1970.

McCourt, Frank. "What I Learned in School." *Life* Sept. 1998: 50+.

McLuhan, Marshall and Quentin Fiore. *The Medium is the Massage.* New York: Random House, 1967.

Molderings, Herbert. "Objects of Modern Skepticism." *The Definitively Unfinished Marcel Duchamp.* Ed. Thierry de Duve. Cambridge: MIT Press, 1991. 243–265.

Owens, Craig. "The Allegorical Impulse: Toward a Theory of Postmodernism." *Art After Modernism: Reconsidering Representation.* Ed. Brian Wallis. New York: Museum of Contemporary Art, 1984. 203–235.

Repp, John, ed. *How We Live Now: Contemporary Multicultural Literature.* Boston: Bedford Books of St. Martin's, 1992.

Rodriguez, Richard. "Ganstas." http://www.mojones.com/MOTHER_JONES/JF94/rodriguez .html. 9 Sept. 1996.

Rosenberg, Harold. "After Next, What?" *Art in America* Apr. 1964: 64–73.

Salter, James. *Light Years.* San Francisco: North Point Press, 1982.

Sandford, Mariellen R., ed. *Happenings and Other Acts.* London: Routledge, 1995.

Schechner, Richard. "Happenings." In Sandford 216–218.

———. "Extensions in Time and Space: An Interview with Allan Kaprow." In Sandford 221–229.

Venturi, Robert. *Complexity and Contradiction in Architecture.* 2nd Ed. New York: Museum of Modern Art, 1977.

Young, La Monte. "Lecture 1960." In Sandford 72–81.

4

Made Not Only in Words: Composition in a New Key

KATHLEEN BLAKE YANCEY

On March 22, 2004, I delivered the "Chair's Address." This talk was twenty-six pages, more or less, double-spaced, and composed in Garamond 12. While I talked, two synchronized PowerPoint slide shows ran independently, one to my right, another to my left. Together, the two slide shows included eighty-four slides.[1] There was one spotlight on me; otherwise, the theatre was dark, lit only by that spot and the slide shows. Oddly, I found myself "delivering" the Chair's Address to an audience I could not see. As Chris Farris pointed out to me later, given this setting, the talk was more dramatic performance than address.

Or: what genre was I invoking?

Words strain,
Crack and sometimes break, under the burden,
Under the tension, slip, slide, perish,
Decay with imprecision, will not stay in place,
Will not stay still.

Sometimes, you know, you have a moment.

For us, this is one such moment. In coming together at CCCC, we leave our institutional sites of work; we gather together—we quite literally convene—at a not-quite-ephemeral site of disciplinary and professional work.

At this opening session in particular; inhabited with the echoes of those who came before and anticipating the voices of those who will follow—we pause and we commence.

We have a moment.

> I come to this podium this morning fully conscious of the rather daunting responsibility attached to this occasion—a responsibility heightened by what my distinguished predecessors have said in their Chair's Addresses.
> —Anne Ruggles Gere 1994

These moments: they aren't all alike, nor are they equal. And how we value them is in part a function of how we understand them, how we connect them to other moments, how we anticipate the moments to come. For compositionists, of this time and of this place, this moment—this moment *right* now—is like none other.

This article is a revised version of the Chair's address Kathleen Blake Yancey delivered at the CCCC Convention in San Antonio, Texas, on March 25, 2004. A previous version was published in *CCC*, volume 56, number 2, December 2004.

From *Views from the Center: The CCCC Chairs' Addresses 1977–2005*. New York: Bedford /St. Martin's and NCTE, 2006. 430–54.

Never before has the proliferation of writings outside the academy so counterpointed the compositions inside. Never before have the technologies of writing contributed so quickly to the creation of new genres. The consequence of these two factors is the creation of a writing public that, in development and in linkage to technology, parallels the development of a reading public in the 19th century. And these parallels, they raise good questions, suggest ways that literacy is created across spaces, across time.

Literacy today is in the midst of a tectonic change. Even inside of school, never before have writing and composing generated such diversity in definition. What do our

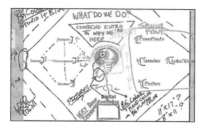

references to writing mean? Do they mean print only? That's definitely what writing is if we look at national assessments, assuming that the assessment includes writing at all and is not strictly a test of grammar and usage. According to these assessments—an alphabet soup of assessments, the SAT, the NEAP, the ACT—writing IS "words on paper," composed on the page with a pen or pencil by students who write words on paper, yes—*but* who *also* compose words and images and create audio files on Web logs (blogs), in word processors, with video editors and Web editors and in e-mail and on presentation software and in instant messaging and on listservs and on bulletin boards—and no doubt in whatever genre will emerge in the next ten minutes.[2]

Note that no one is *making* anyone *do* any of this writing. Don't you wish that the energy and motivation that students bring to some of these other genres they would bring to our assignments? How is it that what we teach and what we test can be so different from what our students know as writing? What *is* writing, really? It includes print: that seems obvious. But: Does it include writing for the screen? How visual is it? Is it the ability to move textual resources among spaces, as suggested by Johndan Johnson-Eilola? Is composing, as James Porter suggests, not only

> **But the main insight I have about my own literacy history is that none of the important or meaningful writing I have ever produced happened as a result of a writing assignment given in a classroom.**
> —Lillian Bridwell Bowles 1995

In planning this address—what some called a script others a transcript—I designed a multi-genred and mediated text that would embody and illustrate the claims of the talk. To accomplish this aim, I developed "stock" of two kinds. I collected verbal material based on readings, some of my own writings, and some of my students' work. Concurrently, I collected images, again from my own work, photographs from places I knew, and images from the public domain. Collecting these different materials and putting them in dialogue with each other was a key part of *this* composing process.

The images, in other words, did not simply punctuate a written text; together words and images were (and are) the materials of composition.[3]

The Chair's Address is, of course, one genre, what Mike Palmquist has called a "call to action" genre. In medium, this address was plural—delivered simultaneously through the human voice and through the PowerPoint slides, both in relation to and also mediated by the twenty-six pages of written text.[5] In response to some requests for the script, I created a version of it in the spirit of an *executive summary*. Another version is being developed for CCC *Online*; its logic is different still. And then there is the text you are reading now, which includes a limited number of slides (reproduced) that are arranged anew. This "Chair's Address" also includes new images and new verbal text—like the meta-text you are reading now.

All of which leads me to ask: how many compositions are in this text?

about medium but also specifically about technology? Suppose I said that basically writing is interfacing? What does that add to our definition of writing? What about the circulation of writing, and the relationship of writing to the various modes of delivery?

And what do these questions mean with respect to another kind of delivery, the curricular and pedagogical delivery of college composition, in classroom to seminar room to online chat room to studio?

Collectively, these questions sound a moment for composition in a new key.

To explain what I mean by this more fully, I'll detail what this moment is, and why and how it matters for us, and what it is that we might want to do about it in a talk I have subtitled Composition in Four Quartets.

QUARTET ONE

In my beginning is my end.

We have a moment.

In some ways our moment is like that in 19th-century Britain when a new reading public composed of middle- and working-class peoples came into being. Technology played a major role in this creation: with a new steam printing press and cheaper paper, reading material became more accessible. There were political and economic reasons as well. Economic changes of the 19th century came in the context of a globalization connected to travel, adventure, colonialism, and a massive demographic shift from farm to city changing the material conditions of work and life.[4] Economically, what has been called the Industrial Age promoted a "rising" middle class, indeed a bourgeoisie, that had the funds to buy print reading material and the leisure in which to read it and that began to have 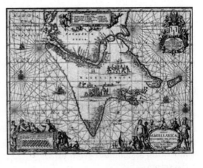 some political rights—and to press for more. From the perspective of literature, the genre receiving the most attention was the novel, which is said to have encouraged readers and in some ways to have created them. As important for our purposes, these novels were often *published in another form first*, typically in serial installments that the public read monthly. In other words, the emergence of this reading public co-occurred with the emergence of a multiply genred and distributed novel. All of Dickens's novels, for instance, were so published, "generally in monthly parts." And the readers were more than consumers; they helped shape the development of the text-in-process. Put differently, the "fluctuations of public demand" influenced the ways that Dickens and other novelists developed future episodes. The British novels of the 19th century were from the very beginning developed and distributed in multiple genres made possible by a new technology, the novelist writing in the context of and for very specific readers who, in turn, provided responses influencing the development of the text in question.

People read together, sometimes in "reading circles," sites of domestic engagement, but also in public places. Technological constraints—bad lighting, eyesight overstrained by working conditions[6]—encouraged such communal readings, since in this setting no single pair of eyes was overly strained. People also gathered frequently to hear authors read their own works in staged readings. For these 19th-century novels, the patterns of circulation thus included both oral and written forums. Or: new forms of writing—the serials, the newspapers, the triple-decker Victorian novel—encouraged new reading publics who read for new purposes.

And all of this happened outside of school.

Today, we are witnessing a parallel creation, that of a *writing* public made plural, and as in the case of the development of a reading public, it's taking place largely outside of school—and this in an age of universal education. Moreover, unlike what happens in our classes, *no one is forcing this public to write.* There are no As here, no Dean's lists, no writing teacher to keep tabs on you. Whatever the exchange value may be for these writers—and there are millions of them, here and around the world—it's certainly not grades. Rather, the writing seems to operate in an economy driven by use value. The context for this writing public, expanded anew, is cause for concern and optimism. On the one hand, a loss in jobs in this country caused (it is said) by globalization is connected to a rise in corporate profits detailed in one accounting report after another,

Modern physics long since made us learn that the world out there has more space than stuff anyway, and it is in the spaces that we find relationships.
—Richard Lloyd Jones 1978

It's worth asking what the principles of all these compositions are. Pages have interfaces, although like much that is ubiquitous, we don't attend to such interfaces as we might. The fact that you have one interface governing the entire text, however, does provide a frame. What is the frame for (and thus the theory governing) a composition in multiple parts? For that matter, how does this text—with call outs, palimpsest notes, and images—cohere?

And: How do we create such a text? How do we read it? How do we value it?

Not least, how will we teach it?

and we are assured by those in Washington that such job loss is actually *good* for us. As one commentator on NPR put it in early March, we've moved from just-in-time jobs to just-in-time people. Such an approach to labor is not news to those of us in composition: we apparently got there first. On the other hand, those committed to another vision of globalization see in it the chance for a (new-found) cooperation and communication among people, one with potential to transform the world and its peoples positively. At best, it could help foster a world peace never known before. At least, as we have seen over the course of the last year, it is (finally) more difficult to conduct any war in secret.

Like 19th-century readers creating their own social contexts for reading in reading circles, writers in the 21st century self-organize into what seem to be overlapping technologically driven writing circles, what we might call a series of newly imagined communities, communities that cross borders of all kinds—nation state, class, gender, ethnicity. Composers gather in Internet chat rooms; they participate in listservs dedicated to both the ridiculous and the sublime; they mobilize for health concerns, for political causes, for research, and for travel advice. Indeed, for Howard Dean's candidacy we saw the first blog for a presidential candidate. Many of the Internet texts are multiply genred and purposed: MoveOn.com sends e-mails, collects money, and hosts a Web site simultaneously. Flash mobs gather for minutes-long social outings; political flash mobs gather for purposes of political reform. And I repeat: like the members of the newly developed reading public, the members of the writing public have learned—in this case, to write, to think together, to organize, and to act within these forums—largely without instruction and, more to the point here, largely without *our* instruction. They need neither self-assessment nor our assessment: they have a rhetorical situation, a purpose, a potentially worldwide audience, a choice of technology and medium—and they write.

The literacies that composers engage in today are multiple. They include print literacy practices (like spelling) that URL's require; they include visual literacy; they include network literacy. As important, these literacies are textured and in relationship to each other. Perhaps most important, these literacies are social in a way that school literacy all too often only pretends to be.

Because we are essentially in partnership with the wider community attempting to share meaningfully in the working out of a community responsibility, we must be in communication with the other parts of the community.
—Vivian Davis 1979

Some of these new Internet genres—e-mail, instant messaging, and so on—divide along lines based in age and in formal schooling. Faculty—the school insiders—use e-mail daily, considering it essential to academic and personal life. In contrast, students use instant messaging at least as often, and unlike most of us, they *like* it. Faculty see blogs—if they see them at all—as (yet) another site for learning, typically in school; students see blogs as a

means of organizing social action, a place for geographically far-flung friends to gather, a site for poets and musicians to plan a jam. But our experiences are the same in one key way: most faculty and students alike *all have learned these genres on our own, outside of school.* Given *this* extracurricular writing curriculum and its success, I have to wonder out loud if in some pretty important ways and within the relatively short space of not quite ten years, we may already have become anachronistic.

Some disturbing data suggest that traditional English departments already are. According to the list of departmental administrators published in the PMLA, over the last twenty years, we have seen a decline in the number of departments called English of about 30%. Let me state this more dramatically: of the number of English departments whose administrators were included on the list in 1985, about one in three has disappeared. Why? They may have simply stopped being represented for any number of reasons: a shortage of funds, a transfer of the listing elsewhere. Naturally, this statistic doesn't mean that En-

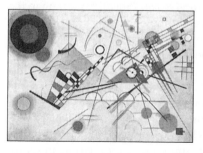

glish is disappearing as an institutional unit. Most obviously, it means that fewer units calling themselves English are listed in the PMLA. And when plotted against another trend line—the *increase* of units called something other than English, like departments of communication and divisions of humanities—it seems more plausible that *something* reductionist in nature is happening to English departments generally. They are being consolidated into other units or disappearing.[8]

Of course, as Anne Gere demonstrated in her own Chair's Address, writing has always been embedded in an extra-curriculum. Public institutions now design for such a curriculum, bringing together what computer game designer Frank Lantz calls a convergence of digital and physical space. Examples include new public libraries, especially those in Salt Lake City and in Seattle. In their designs, both architectural and curricular, these institutions overlap and interplay "domestic spaces" (like Seattle's "living room" inside the library), "conventional" library spaces, and electronic spaces.[7]

Although interpretations of data around the status of English departments vary, here something in English studies is clearly underway. The data points I report plot one trend line, a line that in its downward direction contrasts with the upward swing of the plot line for rhetoric and composition. In the midst of this moment, a new discourse that repositions English and humanities is emerging. The latest evidence: As I write this, literacy scholar Helen Vendler, in her NEH Jefferson Address, has attempted an English-centric redefinition of the humanities that excludes both history and philosophy.

Another data point tells the same story: according to the Association of Departments of English (ADE), if English departments were graduating English majors at the same rate graduated in 1966, we would congratulate 100,000 students this year. Instead, we will offer English degrees to half that number—50,000.[9] And these data points may well explain why the number of tenure-line jobs in English continues its now altogether-too-familiar decline (which makes the continuing increase in tenure-line jobs in rhetoric and composition all the more remarkable). Of course, for many of us, this may be a moot point. We may not be housed in English departments ourselves, and most of us don't teach courses in the major because the major continues to be defined as *territorias literati*, a point to which I will return. Still, enough of us do reside in English to understand that as English goes, so may we.

These shifts: are they minor tremors signifying routine academic seismic activity that makes the world more stable? Alternatively, are they tremors occurring along the fault lines of tectonic plates that will in the not-too-distant future change the very topography of higher education?

These questions assume greater significance as evidence of other tremors within higher education make themselves felt.

In the last two decades, we've seen a shift in the way the country views higher education. According to a 2004 edition of *U.S. News and World Report* (Shea), beginning in the Reagan era, the U.S. began moving away from the view that college is good for the *country*, a view that enfranchises all of us, and began shifting toward the view that higher education is good for the *individual*. Given this shift, perhaps it makes a perverse kind of sense that even though more than half of college students work, they still graduate with debt exceeding $15,000. During this same period, public institutions became state-supported institutions, then state-assisted schools, then state-affiliated schools, and now state-located schools. States haven't abandoned support of education: rather, they have redirected the revenue streams away from the institutions and toward the consumers, the students. In other

Composition is a part of a higher education and the persistent problems in composition are tied to larger issues in the world, in our country, in higher education generally and in each academic institution specifically.
—Miriam Chaplin 1988

words, historically, public funds went to public institutions; today, in many states, including mine, they go directly to the students—chiefly through scholarships titled Hope or Freedom, which one economist has likened to vouchers for K–12. And the worst-case scenario has already been proposed in Colorado: take all funding for public institutions and distribute it not to them but directly to students.[10] Educationally, in the words of Robert Putnam, we are increasingly bowling alone, and apart from the damage it will do to the individual schools, I worry about the damage it will do to the country as a commons.

Relevant to literacy specifically, we can record other tremors, specifically those associated with the screen, and in that focus, they return us to questions around what it means to write. Further, I'd suggest that they constitute a serious challenge to us. As articulated by Elizabeth Daley, dean of the University of Southern California School of Television & Cinema, this view of literacy makes a clear distinction—both in practice and in institutional home—between print literacy and screen literacy. Linking what happens outside of school to what we might do inside, Daley observes that both in metaphorical analogy and in use, the screen has become ubiquitous. "Metaphors from the screen have become common in our daily conversation," she says ("Expanding" 34). Think about these everyday terms: close up, flash back, frame, cut to the chase, segue. Our daily communicative, social, and intellectual practices are screen-permeated. Further, her argument is that *the screen is the language of the vernacular*, that if we

do not include it in the school curriculum, we will become as irrelevant as faculty professing in Latin, "No longer," she declares, "can students be considered truly educated by mastering reading and writing alone. The ability to negotiate through life by combining words with pictures with audio and video to express thoughts will be the mark of the educated student" ("Speaking"). Specifically, she proposes that the literacy of the screen, which she says *parallels* oral literacy and print literacy, become a *third* literacy required of all undergraduates. Not surprisingly, she believes such literacy should

Additional evidence of our unwillingness, as members of a commons, to support higher education is abundant. Again, as I write this, President Bush's plan to maintain the level of funding for Pell Grants goes almost unchallenged. Given that tuition costs have risen and the number of eligible students has likewise risen, what this means is less support for students.

Part of what's at issue with screen literacy is how it too enables the making of stories, a common question we ask of literary texts, a common question we ask of students and of ourselves. As Daley suggests, the screen is very much part of the thinking around narrative. In reviewing *21 Grams*, for instance, film critic Roger Ebert brings the issue into relief (perhaps ironically?) when he says:"Imagining how heartbreaking the conclusion would have been if we had arrived at it in the ordinary way by starting at the beginning, I felt as if an unnecessary screen of technique had been placed between the story and the audience."

be taught not in composition classrooms but in media studies programs. Not least, Daley argues that education needs to get in step with life practices and should endeavor to assist students to negotiate through life.

What do these conceptions of reading and writing publics, these tremors in the world and in higher education and in English have to do with composition?

QUARTET TWO

A people without history
Is not redeemed from time, for history is a pattern
Of timeless moments.

We have a moment.

What we make of this moment is contextualized by our own history as a discipline. Many have noted the role that first-year composition played in the formation of CCCC: it was our raison d'etre—and a worthy cause. We focused then on the gatekeeping moment, the moment when students enter college and in particular on that transition moment between high school and college. It's worth considering, however, how this gatekeeping situation has changed in the last fifty-five years.

Someone has estimated that there are at least nine thousand of us teaching in college courses in composition and communication.
—John Gerber 1950

Early in the decade when CCCC was formed, in 1949, only 30% of students graduated from high school; only 20% of high school graduates even began college, typically at four-year liberal arts institutions; and fewer than 6% graduated. Today, depending on your source, about 89% of students graduate from high school, and some 65% begin college ("America's"). In other words, at various times—in high school in AP classes and dual-enrollment classes, just after high school, years after completing high school—many students—indeed most students—do begin college.[11]

But what happens? They don't finish: only 28% of Americans complete four years of college. It looks bleaker as you go to certain categories: 17% of African Americans have college degrees, 10.6% of Latinos, even fewer Native Americans (Wright). Still, too often we define ourselves as that first-year course. Suppose that if instead of focusing on the gatekeeping year, we saw composition education as a *gateway*? Suppose that we enlarged our focus to include *both* moments, gatekeeping and gateway? And further suppose, to paraphrase Elizabeth Daley, that we designed a curriculum in composition that prepared students to become members of the writing public and to negotiate life. How might that alter what we think and what we do?

Such an agenda is consistent with data that account for successful college experiences. Richard Light, for instance, demonstrates that one of the key factors students and alumni cite in studies of how college can work well is writing. The National Survey of Student Engagement—in both two- and four-year school versions—sounds the same note. We know that writing makes a difference—both at the gatekeeping moment and as students progress through the gateway.

Of course, in this moment in composition's history, I'm making certain assumptions about writing that as a disciplinary community, we are still ambivalent about. What should be the future shape of composition? Questioning the role of technology in composition programs—shall we teach print, digital, composition, communication, or all of the above?—continues to confound us. Do we want to confine our efforts to print literacy only—or, alternatively, to print literacy predominately? Given a dearth of resources—from hardware to professional development, from student access to what Gail Hawisher calls the bandwidth digital divide—many of us continue to focus on print. Given a concern that postmodernism and infobits could undermine a sustained rational discourse that is fundamental to democracy, many of us vote for the known that is, not coincidentally, what our colleagues expect us to deliver in the composition classroom: the print of CCCC—coherence, clarity, consistency, and (not least) correctness.

At the same time, when reviewed, our own practices suggest that we have already committed to a theory of communication that is both/and: print and digital. Given the way we *produce* print—sooner or later inside a word processor—we are digital already, at least in process. Given the course management systems like Blackboard and WebCT, we have committed to the screen for administrative purposes at least. Given the oral communication context of peer review, our teaching requires that students participate in mixed communicative modes. Given the

It's almost impossible to know how many students finish high school. Some finish after four years; some finish after another year or two in an alternative setting; some finish through the GED program. And it is so that some don't finish at all. Where they don't finish, typically in urban settings and in impoverished states, life is harder all the way around. Still, if we in college could graduate the same percentage of students as our colleagues in high school do, we'd nearly triple our graduation rate.

In the Portraits of Composition Research Study, respondents spoke in chorus about the move to digital texts. Nearly all respondents expect students to submit texts composed in a word processor, nearly half of the respondents respond to student texts via e-mail. But very few—less than 30%—use a course management system.[12]

digital portfolios coming into their own, even the move by CCCC to provide LCD's and Internet connects to panelists upon request and for free, we teachers and students seem to have moved already—to communication modes assuming digital literacy. And thinking about our own presentations here: when we consider how these presentations will morph into other talks,

into articles for print and online journals, into books, indeed into our classrooms, it becomes pretty clear that we *already* inhabit a model of communication practices incorporating multiple genres related to each other, those multiple genres remediated across contexts of time and space, linked one to the next, circulating across and around rhetorical situations both inside and outside school.

> That composition has a content at all—other than process—is a radical claim. The CCCCs was founded with a concern about what the content of first-year composition should be, and it is a concern that continues to energize us even today.

This is composition—*and* this is the *content* of composition.

If we cannot go home again to the days when print was the sole medium, what will the new curricular home for composition look like?

QUARTET THREE

Words, after speech, reach
Into the silence. Only by the form, the pattern,
Can words or music reach
The stillness, as a Chinese jar still
Moves perpetually in its stillness.

We have a moment.

At this moment, we need to focus on three changes: Develop a new curriculum; revisit and revise our writing-across-the-curriculum efforts; and develop a major in composition and rhetoric.[13]

> To accept rhetoric and composition . . . as legitimate parts of the graduate curriculum is not a sign of dissolution, dispersion, and decomposition. It is, rather, a sign that we are regaining our composure, taking composure to mean composition in all of its senses.
>
> —Frank D'Angelo 1980

Since the limits of time and space preclude my detailing all three, I will focus on the first, developing *a new curriculum for the 21st century*, a curriculum that carries forward the best of what we have created to date, that brings together the writing outside of school and that inside. This composition is located in a new vocabulary, a new set of practices, and a new set of outcomes; it will focus our research in new and provocative ways; it has as its goal the creation of thoughtful, informed, technologically adept writing publics. This goal entails the other two: extending this new composition curriculum horizontally throughout the academy and extending it vertically through our own major. In other words, it is past time that we fill the glaringly empty spot between first-year composition and graduate education with a composition major.

And in the time and space that's left, I want to sketch briefly what this new curriculum might look like.

To begin thinking about a revised curriculum for composition, we might note the most significant change that has occurred in composition over the last thirty years: the process movement. Although not everyone agrees that the process movement radically altered the teaching of composition (see Crowley; Matsuda), most do think that process—as we defined it in the research of scholars like Janet Emig and Linda Flower and as brought into the classroom by teachers like us—did revolutionize the teaching of writing. We had a new vocabulary, some of it—like invention—ancient, some of it—writing process and re-writing and freewriting—new. We developed pedagogy anew: peer review, redrafting, portfolio assessment. But nothing stays still, and process approaches have given way to other emphases. Recently, we have seen several approaches seeking to update that work, some on the left in the form of cultural studies and post-process; some more interested in psychological approaches like those located in felt sense; others more interested in the connections composition can forge with like-minded educational initiatives such as service learning and first-year experience programs.

Erika Lindemann's work on the bibliographic categories that organize and construct composition reveals the role that process both has and has not played in the discipline. Lindemann notes that while in the 1986 CCCC Bibliography *process* was included in three of twelve categories (or 25%), it is completely absent in the 2001 MLA successor to the Cs bibliography.

What's interesting is that regardless of the changes that are advocated as we attempt to create a post-process compositional curriculum, most (not all but most) attempt this without questioning or altering the late-20th-century basis of composition. To put the point directly, composition in this school context, and in direct contrast to the *world* context, remains chiefly focused on the writer qua writer, sequestered from the means of production. Our model of teaching composing, as generous, varied, and flexible as it is in terms of aims and as innovative as it is in terms of pedagogy—and it is all of these—(still) embodies the narrow and the singular in its emphasis on a primary and single human relationship; the writer in relation to the teacher. In contrast to the reading public nearly two centuries ago, the "real" reading public of school is solitary, the teacher whose reading consists of print text delivered on the teacher's desk. In contrast to the development of a writing public, the classroom writer is not a member of a collaborative group with a common project linked to the world at large and delivered in multiple genres and media, but a singular person writing over and over again—to the teacher.

What no one, including writing teachers, foresaw twenty years ago was the extent to which the creation of wealth would be divorced from labor and redistributed, leaving the United States the most economically polarized among industrialized nations, with the divide between rich and poor continuing to widen.
—Lester Faigley 1997

I am interested in the terms we use to constitute our subject, the terms we take for granted and the degree to which we take them for granted. Today I'll stick to the three terms of our name, composition, communication, conference. These terms are our legacy; we must not betray those who have given them to us. They are also our problem, our burden, since they resist reflection and change.
—David Bartholomae 1989

John Trimbur calls our school model of writing the in loco parentis model: we are the parents who in our practices continue to infantilize our students as we focus their gaze and their energy and their reflection on the moments of creation, on process. I tend to think of it in another, complementary way, as a remediated tutorial model of writing. In other words, it seems to me that in all our efforts to improve the teaching of composition—to reduce class size, for instance, to conference with students, to respond vociferously to each student paper, and to understand that in our students' eyes we are the respondent who matters—we seek to approximate the one-to-one tutorial model. Quite apart from the fact that such an effort is doomed—about a hundred years ago, Edwin Hopkins asked if we could teach composition under the current conditions,[14] which conditions then are the same conditions we work in today, and immediately answered, "NO"—I have to wonder why we want to work this way, wonder why *this* is the neo-Platonic mode to which we continuously aspire. Not that the process model is bad, I hasten to add: students do engage with each other, often do write to the world, and frequently do develop elaborated processes—all to the good. But if we believe that writing is social, shouldn't the system of circulation—the paths that the writing takes—extend beyond and around the single path from student to teacher?

More to the point, the list of what students aren't asked to do in the current model—and what they might—is long:

- consider the issue of intertextual circulation: how what they are composing relates or compares to "real world" genres;

- consider what the best medium and the best delivery for such a communication might be and then create and share those different communication pieces in those different media, to different audiences;

- think explicitly about what they might "transfer" from one medium to the next: what moves forward, what gets left out, what gets added — and what they have learned about composing in this transfer process;

- consider how to transfer what they have learned in one *site* and how that could or could not transfer to another, be that site on campus or off;[15]

- think about how these practices help prepare them to become members of a writing public.

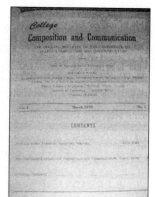

What I'm proposing is that we move to a new model of composing where students are explicitly asked to engage in these considerations, to engage in these activities, to develop as members of a writing public. Such a model of composition is located in three key expressions:

> Circulation of composition
> Canons of rhetoric
> Deicity of technology

Let me begin with circulation: although they are related, I will here outline and exemplify two kinds: (1) the circulation of texts generally, and (2) the circulation of a student's own work within an educational culture. Texts circulate: they move across contexts, between media,

A Boston skyline, the old juxtaposed with the new, old and new interfaced. An architectural intertextuality.

across time. Writers compose in the context of other writers and thinkers and speakers. They imitate them directly and indirectly; they quote them, write in direct reference to them, paraphrase them, and frame their own work in these contexts. This circulation is the one, perhaps, with which we are most familiar: we often talk about it as intertextuality, as a conversation that we invite students to join. The conversation, of course, occurs through genres and is really many conversations, with texts circulating in multiple, interrelated ways.

What I am calling circulation can go by other names: Charles Bazerman and David Russell, for instance, call it

Conceptually, composition itself is in circulation. From music and art, it carries an aesthetic dimension. From chemistry and architecture, it carries an interest in materials. Pedagogically, borrowing from Joe Janangelo and Pablo Picasso, I have talked elsewhere about students as "ongoing compositions." We see such humans-as-compositions in any collected work, summarized minimally in a resume or vita; developed and illustrated more fully and reflectively in a portfolio. Regardless of whether we see such composing or not, it is always in play. In the context of compositionists as professionals, we compose ourselves, both individually, in the words of Elizabeth Flynn, and as participants of a community, in the words of Andrea Lunsford's Chair's Address.

activity theory, but basically it's the same point: As they explain,

> Writing is alive when it is being written, read, remembered, contemplated, followed—when it is part of human activity. . . . The signs on the page serve to mediate between people, activate their thoughts, direct their attention, coordinate their actions, provide the means of relationship. It is in the context of their activities that people consider texts and give meaning to texts. And it is in the organization of activities that people find the needs, stances, interactions, tasks that orient their attention toward texts they write and read. So to study text production, text reception, text meaning, text value apart from their animating activities is to miss the core of text's being.

So: circulation.

With the help of David Russell and Arturo Yañez, let me put a classroom face on what this might look like in terms of curriculum. They tell the story of a student caught in an all-too-familiar dilemma. Beth, the student, is an aspiring journalist convinced of the integrity and objectivity of reportorial accounting; moreover, she believes that good writing is good writing is good writing, regardless of the discipline. Which means, of course, that good writing is the writing she understands and practices. The problem: she's enrolled in an Irish literature class that she needs for graduation, a class where good writing—located in interpretation and exercise of judgment—looks very different. To her, this historical writing feels inexact and duplicitous; and it makes history, which she has understood as an exercise in "Just the facts, ma'am"—as completely alien. What activity theory adds to this mix is a means of making sense of these seemingly disparate texts and ways of knowing.

> Professional historians . . . critically examine and interpret (and reinterpret) primary documents according to the methods (rules, norms) of history. They argue and debate to persuade other experts. And when enough experts (or the enough powerful experts) arrive at consensus, that consensus is put into textbooks for high school students and generally perceived as "fact." And, perhaps, that consensus is eventually put into popular history books, of the kind that journalists review and the rest of us Big Picture People sometimes read—to find the "facts" of history. (Russell and Yañez)

Thinking in terms of circulation, in other words, enables students to understand the epistemology, the conventions, and the integrity of different fields and their genres. Using that as a point of departure allows students to complete the task *and* move closer to the big picture of writing. Trimbur makes an analogous point in outlining a curricular approach where students in health sciences understand how different genres even within the same field function epistemologically: research genres to make scientific knowledge; public health articles deriving from the research genres both diluting and distributing it, each according to its own logic and conventions. His purpose?

> I want students to see that the shift in register and genre between a journal article and a news report amounts to a shift in modality—the relative credibility and authoritativeness invested in written statements—that marks journal articles as "original" contributions and news reports as secondary and derivative. (213)

Media themselves provide another example of circulation. As Jay Bolter and Richard Grusin explain in *Remediation*, and as McLuhan suggested before that, nearly every medium is re/mediated on another medium. In other words, consciously or otherwise, we create the new in the context of the old and based on the model of the old. Television is commonly understood to be remediated on film, for example, and the Web is commonly understood to be remediated on print. Remediation can be back-ended as well, as we see in the most recent CNN interface on TV, which is quite explicitly remediated on the Web. The new,

We look at the present through a rear-view mirror. We march backwards into the future.
—Marshall McLuhan 1964

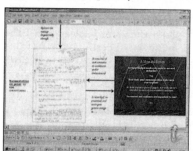

then, repeats what came before, while at the same time remaking that which it models. This isn't a new phenomenon, however, as we remember from the development of that 19th-century novel, which appeared in multiple genres and media: serials, triple-deckers, performances. Fast forward to the 21st century: imagine that in composition classes students, like Victorian novelists before them, focus on remediating their

Who writes the "first draft" of history can change, of course, as can patterns of circulation. Concerns around such issues are not merely academic, as is clear in the following *New York Times* commentary on the relationship between genres and the roles they are currently playing in *this* historical moment: "The sudden outpouring of inside details in books about the Bush administration is all the more remarkable because of the administration's previous success at controlling the flow of information to the press about its workings. It is a phenomenon that is creating an unusual reversal in which books—the musty vessels traditionally used to convey patient reflection into the archives—are superseding newspapers as the first draft of history, leaving the press corps to cover the books themselves as news."

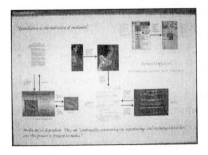

own texts. Beginning with a handout or one pager, they define a key term of the course and revise that on the basis of class response; in addition, they move the material of that handout to a five-slide *PowerPoint* show presented to the class and itself revised. Suppose that they move this material to a poster, then to a presentation, then to a conventional written text. For the conventional written text, they brainstorm in class and on a blog, thinking individually and communally about which of these tasks "counts" as writing—and why. As they move from medium to medium, they consider what they move forward, what they leave out, what they add, and for each of these write a reflection in which they consider how the medium itself shapes what they create. The class culminates with text in which they write a reflective theory about what writing is and how it is influenced or shaped or determined by media and technology. Located in the rhetoric of purpose, audience, genre, this model of circulation is particularly oriented to medium and technology; it permits a student, as Brian Morrison does here, to define composition as "the thoughtful gathering, construction, or reconstruction of a literate act in any given media."

These three related approaches: all oriented to the circulation of texts, to genre, to media, and to ways that writing gets made, both individually and culturally. As important, all three of these approaches, in their analysis of textual relationships and contexts, in their theories and examples of how writing works, and in their situating the student as a maker of knowledge, map the content for new composition. And if you are saying, but I can't do all this in first-year composition, I'm going to reply, "Exactly." First-year composition is a place to begin; carrying this forward is the work of the major in composition and rhetoric.

A second kind of circulation, occurring within the bounds of school and often within the classroom, has to do with the variety of academic texts that students create, with the places in which those texts are created and distributed, and with how *this circulation* contributes to student development in writing. We have some fine research in this sense of circulation that accounts for students moving forward in their writing: research conducted by Lee

Speaking of Remediation . . .

Have you heard Sheryl Crow's version of Rod Stewart's "The First Cut is the Deepest"?

Or how about *Moulin Rouge*?

Ann Carroll, Nancy Sommers and Laura Saltz, Marilyn Sternglass, Richard Haswell, and Elizabeth Chiseri-Strater. Typically, such studies focus on how and what students "transfer" from one site to another; Anne Beaufort's study asks the same question but applied to the site of work. And often we ask students to engage in this activity themselves: in their reflections, students account for the progress (or not) of their texts; of what they have learned in the construction of such texts; in their portfolios—be they digital or print—students comment and demonstrate the circulation of the course.

A vignette composed by Paul Prior and Jody Shipka shows us another way to think about circulation that focused exclusively on a single text.

> A psychology professor reports to us that when she is revising an article for publication she works at home and does the family laundry. She sets the buzzer on the dryer so that approximately every 45 minutes to an hour she is pulled away from the text to tend the laundry downstairs. As she empties the dryer, sorts and folds, reloads, her mind wanders a bit and she begins to recall things she wanted to do with the text, begins to think of new questions or ideas, things that she had not been recalling or thinking of as she focused on the text when she was upstairs minutes before. She perceives this break from the text, this opportunity to reflect, as a very productive part of the process.

What Prior and Shipka point out, of course, is that this text is produced through two activity systems: the domestic and the disciplinary.[16] They raise provocative questions about the role the buzzer plays in the drafting process, about the spaces created here for reflection, about the role reflection plays in composing.

This too is circulation; this too is composition.

As I move into the second expression, the canons of rhetoric—invention, arrangement, style, memory, and delivery—I'm aware that these are hardly new. I wonder about how we understand them, however. Like others before me, I would note that we have separated delivery and memory from invention, arrangement, and style in ways

What is the relationship between and among remediating texts, carrying forward materials, finding new sources, and representing and inventing a self?

One thing that is clear to me as I compose this text for the page is that this remediation feels less like a small morphing of a text from one medium to another than it does like creating a new text. And it's not mere perception: this composition is longer by over 2,000 words, most of which comment on, extend, and complicate the earlier voiced text.

Bill Watterson, the creator of Calvin and Hobbes, talks about how circulation of another kind can influence the development of a creator, in this case of a cartoonist. He notes, "The challenge of any cartoonist is not just to duplicate the achievements of the past, but to build on them as well" (9–10). He argues it is thus necessary for the cartoonist to have access to earlier cartoons, through their collection and republication—in book form.[17]

It's instructive to attempt to map the relationship between and among the canons. As I continue to explore delivery—of text, of instruction, of public extracurricula—delivery seems at the heart of the relationship, but I can see how at other times, other canons take that place.

The revolution, if there is one, is the social one of interconnectivity.
—James Porter 2003

We used to have a stable definition of composing and of the author. These have changed. The freedom to invent, to arrange multiply, can be a wonderful thing. It can also evoke anxiety, somewhat akin to discovering that the tectonic plates underlying the continents are not stable but, in fact, are shifting constantly.

that are counterproductive. Let me further say that too often we treat them as discrete entities when in fact they are interrelated. Let me share with you an image. Don't ask me why, but I have always understood each canon as sitting on a rhetorical shelf, as though a freshly laundered cotton blanket in a laundry closet. I take one canon down—my favorite, if truth be told, is invention—use it, then put neatly back on the shelf. But as my options for delivering texts have widened—from the page to the screen to the networked screen and then back to the page anew—I've begun to see the canons not as discrete entities like those blankets on shelves but, rather, as related to each other in much the same way as the elements of Burke's pentad are related: the canons interact, and through that interaction they contribute to new exigencies for invention, arrangement, representation, and identity. Or: they change what is possible.

Richard Lanham, of course, has argued that with the addition of the digital to the set of media in which we compose, delivery takes on a critical role, and I think that's so. But much more specifically, what a shift in the means of delivery does is bring invention and arrangement into a new relationship with each other. The writer of the page has fundamentally different opportunities than the creator of a hypertext. Anne Wysocki is right about the interface of the page—that is, it has one, and it's worth paying attention to—but even so, as we read the pages of an article, we typically do so line by line, left to right, as you do now: page one before page two. This is the fixed default arrangement. The writer *invented* through such a text is a function of that arrangement. In other words, you can only invent inside what an arrangement permits—and different media permit different arrangements. By contrast, the creator of a hypertext can create a text that, like the page, moves forward. In addition, however, hypertext composers can create other arrangements, almost as in three rather than two dimensions. You can move horizontally, right branching; you can then left branch. The writer invented in a medium permitting these arrangements is quite different—a difference of kind, not degree.

Given my own teaching and research interests, I see such differences, particularly in portfolios. In a print portfolio, remediated on a book, the arrangement is singular. In a digital portfolio, remediated on a gallery, the arrangements are plural. And the students invented in each are quite different. In a print portfolio, the tendency is to tell a single story, one with a single claim and an accumulating body of evidence. In arrangement, a digital portfolio—

again, by contrast— is multiple, is defined by links. Because you can link externally as well as internally and because those links are material, you have more contexts you can link to, more strata you can layer, more "you" to invent, more invention to represent. In sum, the potential of arrangement is a function of delivery, and *what and how you arrange*—which becomes a function of the medium you choose—*is who you invent.*[18] Moreover, I suspect that as multiple means of delivery become more routinized, we will understand *each* of the canons differently, and we will understand and be able to map their interrelationships.

My third and final expression is the deicity of technology. *Deixis*, linguistically, refers to words like *now* and *then*, words whose "meanings change quickly depending on the time or space in which they are uttered" (Leu et al.) or read. The word *Now* when I wrote this text is one time; as I read the word *Now* in San Antonio was a second time; and now, when this talk is published in *CCC* and who knows how many people do (or do not!) read *this* Chair's Address, it will be many, many other times. Literacy is deictic. The speed of technological change has affected literacy, as we know. The particular claim that D. J. Leu, C. K. Kinzer, J. Coiro, and D. Cammack (among others) have made is this: "technological change happens so rapidly that the changes to literacy are limited not by technology but rather by our ability to adapt and acquire of the new literacies that emerge." Deixis, they say, "is a defining quality of the new literacies of the Internet" and other information communication technologies.

According to Leu and his coauthors, there are three sources for this deictic nature of literacy:

1. transformations of literacy because of technological change,

2. the use of increasingly efficient technologies of communication that rapidly spread new literacies, and

3. envisionments of new literacy potentials within new technologies.

The tectonic plate theory of continental drift was "discovered" in 1965. Rohman and Wiecke's stage-model of writing was "discovered" a year earlier; Rohman's *CCC* article detailing prewriting was published the year following, in 1965.

Leu and his colleagues note how our working in a context of deixis changes the way we teach. No longer, they say, can we speak from the podium with the expertise of old. Instead, faculty and students will consider questions and use various technologies to help address them, with the faculty member guiding the work, and in some cases learning along with the students. In composition, we need to learn how to read and write e-texts—synthesizing, questioning, evaluating, and importing from them—databases and catalogues, hyper-texts and archives, Web essays and portfolios.

And this means we all need to learn more about how to use images and sources, how to document them appropriately, how to create our own.

By paying critical attention to lessons about *technology*, we can re-learn important lessons about *literacy*.
—Cindy Selfe 1999

Although deixis might be a new term to many of us, the first two claims are familiar. As we saw in the case of the 19th-century reader, technology changes literacy: that's the kind of transformation we are seeing now with regard to writers. Technology, of course, has always been ubiquitous: as Dennis Baron points out, a pencil is a technology. At the same time, however, *this* digital, networked technology continuously promotes itself and new literacies—through the marketing efforts of the corporations that develop these technologies; through open source and shareware and freeware; through our ability to download new programs and formats that are essentially new engines for a literacy no one can quite predict. The dissemination of this potential capacity is built into this model of technology. Given its worldwide distribution and its democratization of authorship, that's new.

The third source—what Leu calls "envisionments of new literacy potentials within new technologies"—is provocative. Here is what he is referring to: the ability of someone to take a given technology and find a use for it that may be at odds with its design. The example he provides is this. Suppose that you are writing an e-mail but decide to compose the e-mail inside a word processor, which is a different (if related) technology. In this scenario,

Envisionment is a practice most of us engage in, typically without thinking about it as such. Teachers use a spreadsheet for grading purposes. A colleague uses a spreadsheet for a digital portfolio template for her class of 120 students. Elementary teachers use PowerPoint for reluctant writers. High school teachers use textboxes for peer review and links for research hypercards. College teachers invite blocked writers to draft in an e-mail program.

a word processor can be transformed into a tool for composing e-mail messages, a purpose for which it was not designed, but a function it fills admirably. This potential only comes to life when a person *envisions* a new function for a technology and *enacts this envisionment*. In essence, we can say that she envisioned how to repurpose a technology for a new and different function. Envisionments such as this happen regularly as individuals encounter new problems and seek solutions in new and creative uses of existing technologies. (Leu et al.)

And let me provide another example. For the last several years, I have worked with graduate students in architecture, and one of their practices is meeting monthly to talk about how their projects and theses are developing. Now, given that it's architecture, they do more than talk: they *show*—in pinups on the walls, in a one-page handout, and in a set of *PowerPoint* slides. Something that grabbed my attention almost immediately was how those slides were being used: not for *presentation* of a finished idea, as the design of them would have it—and as the name, pre-

> Writing, by its very nature, encourages abstraction, and in the shuttling process from the past to the present, from the particular to the general, from the concrete to the abstract, we seek relationships and find meaning.
> —William Irmscher 1979

sentation software, suggests—but, rather, for a different purpose: for exploration, in fact as a new space for drafting ideas. Since then, in several different classes, I've used *PowerPoint* in just this way, as a site for a rough draft, shared with a real audience. Or: envisionment. What other technologies might be re-envisioned and to what effects? What envisionments have students already created that we don't know about? And how do we build this ability—envisioning—into our curriculum?

A modest proposal: one outcome for all writers is the ability to use many kinds of technologies for their intended purposes and for other purposes, as needed and as imagined.

Or: writers use technology rhetorically.

This new composition includes rhetoric and is about literacy. New composition includes the literacy of print: it adds on to it and brings the notions of practice and activity and circulation and media and screen and networking to our conceptions of process. It will require a new expertise of us as it does of our students. And ultimately, new composition may require a new site for learning for all of us.

Quartet Four

> Time present and time past
> Are both perhaps present in time future,
> And time future contained in time past.

We have a moment.

In her study *Institutionalizing Literacy*, Mary Trachsel makes the argument that when we separate an activity related to curriculum from it, faculty lose control over curriculum to the detriment of students and faculty alike. Trachsel, of course, is speaking of assessment, and how historically it has been cleaved from curriculum, particularly at the gatekeeping moment when students enter college—and she cites the SAT as evidence of the claim. I would make the same observation about technology. If we continue to partition it off as just something technical, or outside the parameters governing composing, or limit it to the screen of the course management system, or think of it in terms of the bells and whistles and templates of the *PowerPoint* screen, students in our classes learn only to *fill up* those templates and *fill in* those electric boxes—which, in their ability to invite intellectual work, are the moral equivalent of the dots on a multiple choice test. Students will not compose and create, making use of all the means of persuasion and all the possible resources thereto; rather, they will complete someone else's software package; they will be the invention of that package.

These spaces—the intertextual, overlapping curricular spaces—between school and the public, including print and screen, are still ours to study, to examine, to work in, and to claim. They are the province of first-year composition but are not limited to it. This curricular change includes renewed attention to WAC. It includes a new major in whatever site: English department, writing studies department, rhetorical studies program. The institutional site is less important than the major itself, which can begin to secure our position in the academy while it makes space for the writing that students do on their own, now, without us.

> It is time to speak for ourselves, in our own interests, in the interest of our own work, and in the interest of our students.
> —Jacqueline Jones Royster 1996

So this talk: yes, it's about change. Change, as we saw in the 19th century, and as we see now, can be very difficult, can be unnerving. I used the metaphor of tremors intentionally. A little more than twenty years ago we talked about "winds of change" (Hairston); today the changes are those of tremors. These are *structural* changes—global, educational, technological. Like seismic tremors, these signal a re-formation in process, and because we exist on the borders of our own tectonic plates—rhetoric, composition and communication, process, activity, service and social justice—we are at the very center of those tremors.

> The metaphors we use to describe also construct. The metaphor of tectonic change, particularly when used in the context of the changes of the 19th century, can help us understand how pervasive our current challenges are, how necessary our efforts to adapt.

Perhaps the most important of the plates on which we stand is advocacy, especially at this moment. As the Dixie Chicks point out, voting is an excellent means of self-expression. In helping create writing publics, we also foster the development of citizens who vote, of citizens whose civic literacy is global in its sensibility and its communicative potential, and whose commitment to humanity is characterized by consistency and generosity as well as the ability to write for purposes that are unconstrained and audiences that are nearly unlimited.

It's an ambitious agenda I laid before you in San Antonio and that I lay before you in these pages today, but yes, this is made not only in words: composition in a new key.

Acknowledgments   Gracious thanks to the CCCC audience in San Antonio and to those who helped me before I arrived there: Kristi and Shawn Apostel, Michael Crawford, Will Dickert, Teddi Fishman, Morgan Gresham, Doug Hesse, Martin Jacobi, Brian Morrison, Michael Neal, Josh Reynolds, Summer Smith Taylor, and Irwin Weiser. For special help in the selection and placement of images and in the overall design of this text, many thanks to Marilyn Cooper.

NOTES

1. The slides were arranged so that duplicates showed up simultaneously at various points in the presentation: two screens showed the same slide. Also, as the performance progressed, some slides were repeated, in part to provide some contour to the performance, in part to provide some coherence. I attempt to explain the logic of this composition in *Composition in a New Key*, forthcoming.

2. In the 1980s, compositionists were excited about the role that process was playing—in our teaching, in the assessment of student work, in our own research. Given the disparity between the out-of-school, often digitally composed genres that students currently work in and the form that current assessments are taking—even the much ballyhooed new SAT "writing test" includes a component on grammar and usage that is allowed *more* time than the pencil-and-paper draft portion—Marshall McLuhan's point about marching backwards into the future sounds all too true. For a compelling analysis of the disjunction between what we teach and what is being assessed, see Miles McCrimmon, "High School Writing Practices in the Age of Standards: Implications for College Composition."

3. Digital compositions include other materials as well: audio files, for instance. For a discussion of such materials in the context of remediation and composition, see Scott Halbritter.

4. The relationship between and among technology, literacy practices, nation states, and centralized control is considerably more complicated than I can pursue here. For an analysis that focuses on the materiality of literacy practices and technology, see Lester Faigley's *Material Literacy and Visual Design*; for a discussion that emphasizes the centralization of the nation state as related to literacy and technology, see Ronald Deibert's *Parchment, Printing, and Hypermedia: Communication in World Order Transformation* and Deborah Brandt's *Literacy in American Lives*.

5. The talk I delivered was not precisely the same as the written text. For historical purposes, CCCC videotapes the talk, and what seemed obvious to me at the time is so in retrospect: the two "talks" differ.

6. How various technologies—from technology producing light to that associated with various printing presses—interact to influence the development of literacy (and whose needs this literacy serves) is a (another) question worth pursuing.

7. You don't have to be present to see them: online, you can see the home pages for the Seattle Public Library and the Salt Lake City Library. For a fuller discussion of the lessons regarding these spaces that libraries have to teach us, see Yancey, "Episodes in the Spaces of the Plural Commons."

8. The idea that English departments are being consolidated into other units was first drawn to my attention by Tina Good, at Suffolk County Community College, who has conducted a study of the SUNY system, verifying the claim in that context.

9. As David Lawrence, the executive director of the Association of Departments of English (ADE), has pointed out to me, there's no reason to regard the number of majors from 1966 as the ideal or the norm, and it is the case that English majors still rank in the top ten of all majors (calculated based on a U.S. government database). Point taken. Still, this seems small comfort to me (as a member of an English department) when I remember that more students go to college and graduate today, in 2004, than did in 1966, so the numbers for the English major, it seems to me, ought to grow, not hold steady. In a population that is increasing, maintaining constitutes a decline, as the numbers attest. One reply to such a view, as explained in the ADE report "The Undergraduate English Major," is to put the numbers in larger historical perspective. In this case, that entails the observation that the "semicaptive" audience of majors that English used to have—that is, women—are now choosing to major in other fields, especially biology, psychology, and business, which given our interest in gender equity is a good thing. *Of course*. Still, the trend lines—number of majors, number of tenure-line hires, number of English departments—plot a narrative that those of us who are aligned with English should not ignore.

10. On May 10, 2004, the Colorado legislature passed this bill, which provides funding vouchers to all college students in the state to be applied to all kinds of postsecondary institutions, including private schools. The implications of this bill are widespread: for an early analysis, see Chris Kampfe and Kyle Endres.

11. As this list indicates, a number of so-called college classes are actually *delivered* in high school: what does this say about college composition? With several others, I attempt to answer this question: see Yancey, *Delivering College Composition: The Fifth Canon*, Heinemann 2004.

12. The respondents included more than 1,800 faculty members from forty-eight states, split about 40/60 between two-year and four-year faculty. In terms of faculty status, 17% identified as graduate students and 23% as adjunct faculty. For a fuller description and analysis of the results, see Yancey et al., "Portraits of Composition: How Writing Gets Taught in the Early Twenty-First Century."

13. The idea for a major in rhetoric and composition is not new. Keith Miller was kind enough to point me toward the George Tade, Gary Tate, and Jim Corder article in *CCC*, "For Sale, Lease, or Rent: A Curriculum for an Undergraduate Program in Rhetoric." And some 25 years later, Robert Connors makes the philosophical argument in his Afterword to *Coming of Age*.

14. For a full account of the influence of Edwin Hopkins, see the article by John Heyda and Randall Popken.

15. As I look over the list of items here, the key word seems to be transfer: from composing site to composing site, from classroom to classroom, from one experience to the next. As I have suggested elsewhere, Donald Schon's notion of "reflective transfer" is crucial to this development. See Yancey, *Reflection in the Writing Classroom*.

16. The activity systems mapped by Paul Prior and Jody Shipka parallel the spaces architects are designing into various kinds of buildings: both conceive of human activity organized into multiple overlapping spaces. Another way to theorize composition of the 21st century is through the overlapping curricular, activity, and physical spaces where it occurs now and where it might occur. In this construct, the circulation of composition takes yet another definition.

17. Bill Watterson has several books that in their commentary on processes, media, and transfer are models for the observation, analysis, and insight we often find in portfolio reflections.

18. For a fuller account of both kinds of portfolios, see Yancey, "Postmodernism, Palimpsest, and Portfolios: Theoretical Issues in the Representation of Student Work" and *Teaching Literature as Reflective Practice*, especially chapter five.

WORKS CITED

ADE. "Report of the Undergraduate English Major. Report of the 2001–2002 ADE Ad Hoc Committee on the English Major. *ADE* (Fall/Winter 2003): 68–91.

"America's Fortunes." Atlantic Online (January/February 2004) 21 Mar 04 <http:www.theatlantic .com/cgi-bin/send.cgi?pae=http%3A//www.theatlantic.com/issues>.

Baron, Dennis. "From Pencils to Pixels." *Passions, Pedagogies, and 21st Century Technologies*. Ed. Gail Hawisher and Cynthia Selfe. Logan: Utah State UP, 1999. 15–34.

Bartholomae, David. "Freshman English, Composition, and CCCC." *College Communication and Composition* 40.1 (1989): 38–50.

Bazerman, Charles, and David Russell, eds. *Writing Selves, Writing Societies: Research from Activity Perspectives*. Fort Collins, CO: The WAC Clearinghouse and Mind, Culture, and Activity. 1 June 2004 <http://wac.colostate.edu/books/selves_societies/intro.cfm>.

Beaufort, Anne. *Writing in the Real World: Making the Transition from School to Work*. New York: Teachers College P, 1999.

Bolter, Jay David, and Richard Grusin. *Remediation: Understanding New Media*. Cambridge: MIT P, 2000.

Brandt, Deborah. *Literacy in American Lives*. New York: Cambridge UP, 2001.

Bridwell-Bowles, Lillian. "Freedom, Form, Function: Varieties of Academic Discourse." *College Communication and Composition* 46.1 (1995): 46–61.

Carroll, Lee Ann. *Rehearsing New Roles: How College Students Develop as Writers*. Carbondale: Southern Illinois UP, 2002.

Chaplin, Miriam T. "Issues, Perspectives, and Possibilities." *College Composition and Communication* 39.1 (1988): 52–62.

Chiseri-Strater, Elizabeth. *Academic Literacies: The Public and Private Discourse of University Students*. Portsmouth, NH: Boynton/Cook, 1991.

Connors, Robert. Afterword. *Coming of Age: The Advanced Writing Curriculum*. Ed. Linda K. Shamoon, Rebecca Moore Howard, Sandra Jamieson, and Robert A. Schwegler. Portsmouth, NH: Boynton/Cook, 2000. 143–49.

Crowley, Sharon. *Composition in the University: Historical and Polemical Essays*. Pittsburgh: U of Pittsburgh, 1998.

D'Angelo, Frank. "Regaining Our Composure." *College Composition and Communication* 31.4 (1980): 420–26.

Daley, Elizabeth. "Expanding the Concept of Literacy." *Educause Review* 38.2 (2003): 33–40.

———. "Speaking the Languages of Literacy." Speech, University of Michigan. April 2003. 9 Aug. 04 <http://web.si.umich.edu/news/news-detail.cfm?NewsItemID=350>.

Davis, Vivian I. "Our Excellence: Where Do We Grow from Here?" *College Composition and Communication* 30.1 (1979): 26–31.

Deibert, Ronald. *Parchment, Printing, and Hypermedia: Communication in World Order Transformation*. New York: Columbia UP, 1997.

Ebert, Roger. Review of *21 Grams. Chicago Sun Times* (2003) 1 June 2004 <http://www.suntimes .com/ebert/ebert_reviews/2003/11/112606.html>.

Emig, Janet. *The Composing Processes of Twelfth Graders.* Urbana, IL: NCTE, 1971.

Faigley, Lester. "Literacy after the Revolution." *College Composition and Communication* 48.1 (1997): 30–43.

———. "Material Literacy and Visual Design." In *Rhetorical Bodies: Toward a Material Rhetoric.* Ed. Jack Selzer and Sharon Crowley. Madison: U of Wisconsin P, 1999. 171–201.

Flower, Linda, and John Hayes. "A Cognitive Process Theory of Writing." *College Composition and Communication* 32.4 (1981): 365–87.

Flynn, Elizabeth. "Composing as a Woman." *College Composition and Communication* 39.4 (1988): 423–35.

Gerber, John C. "The Conference on College Composition and Communication." *College Composition and Communication* 1.1 (1950): 12.

Gere, Anne Ruggles. "Kitchen Tables and Rented Rooms: The Extracurriculum of Composition." *College Composition and Communication* 45.1 (1994): 75–92.

Good, Tina. Personal discussion, 25 April 2003.

Hairston, Maxine. "The Winds of Change: Thomas Kuhn and the Revolution in the Teaching of Writing." *College Composition and Communication* 33.1: 76–88.

Halbritter, Scott. "Sound Arguments: Aural Rhetoric in Multimedia Composition." PhD diss. University of North Carolina, 2004.

Haswell, Richard. *Gaining Ground in College: Tales of Development and Interpretation.* Dallas, TX: Southern Methodist UP, 1991.

Hawisher, Gail. Personal discussion. Feb. 2004.

Heyda, John. "Industrial-Strength Composition and the Impact of Load on Teaching." *More Than 100 Years of Solitude: WPA Work before 1976.* Ed. Barbara L'Eppateur and Lisa Mastrangelo. Forthcoming.

Hopkins, Edwin. "Can Good English Composition Be Done under the Current Conditions?" *English Journal* 1 (1912): 1–8.

Irmscher, William F. "Writing as a Way of Learning and Developing: *College Composition and Communication* 30.3 (1979): 240–44.

Johnson-Eilola, Johndan. "Writing about Writing." Speech, Computers and Writing Town Hall Meeting, 2002, Illinois State University.

Jones, Richard Lloyd. "A View from the Center." *College Composition and Communication* 29.1 (1978): 24–29.

Kampfe, Chris, and Kyle Endres. "Vouchers to Change the Way Higher Ed is Funded." *The Rocky Mountain Collegian.* 10 May 2004. <http://www.collegian.com/vnews/display.v/ART/2004 /05/07/409b21d2bfdee?in_archive= 1>.

Lanham, Richard. *The Electronic Word: Democracy, Technology, and the Arts.* Chicago: U of Chicago P, 1993.

Lawrence, David. E-mail to author. April 2004.

Leu, D. J., C. K. Kinzer, J. Coiro, and D. Cammack. "Toward a Theory of New Literacies Emerging from the Internet and Other ICT." *Theoretical Models and Processes of Reading.* 5th ed. Ed. R. Ruddel and Norman Unrau. D.E. International Reading Association, 2004. 4 Aug. 2004 (Preprint version) <http://www.readingonline.org/newliteracies/leu>.

Light, Richard J. *Making the Most of College: Students Speak Their Minds.* Cambridge: Harvard UP, 2001.

Lindemann, Erika. "Early Bibliographic Work in Composition Studies." *Profession* (2002): 151–58.

Lunsford, Andrea. "Composing Ourselves: Politics, Commitment, and the Teaching of Writing." *College Composition and Communication* 41.1 (1990): 71–82.

McCrimmon, Miles. "High School Writing Practices in the Age of Standards; Implications for College Composition." Forthcoming.

McLuhan, Marshall. *Understanding Media: The Extensions of Man.* 1964. Cambridge: MIT P, 1994.

Matsuda, Paul. "Process and Post Process: A Discursive History." *Journal of Second Language Writing* 12 (2003): 65–83.

Palmquist, Michael. "Review: Made Not Only in Words: Composition in a New Key." 15 April 2004. *Across the Disciplines* at the WAC Clearinghouse. 1 June 2004 <http://wac.colostate.edu /atd/reviews/cccc2004/viewmessage.cfm?messageid=61>.

Popken, Randall. "Edwin Hopkins and the Costly Labor of Composition Teaching." *College Composition and Communication* 55.4 (2004): 618–42.

Porter, James. "Why Technology Matters to Writing: A Cyberwriter's Tale." *Computers and Composition* 20.3 (2003): 375–94.

Prior, Paul, and Jody Shipka. "Chronotopic Laminations: Tracing the Contours of Literate Activity." *Writing Selves, Writing Societies: Research from Activity Perspectives.* Ed. Charles Bazerman and David Russell. Fort Collins, CO: The WAC Clearinghouse, and Mind, Culture, and Activity, 180–238. 1 June 2004 <http://wac.colostate.edu/books/selves_societies/prior>.

Putnam, Robert. *Bowling Alone.* New York: Simon and Schuster, 2000.

Reynolds, Josh. "Writing Process Map." *My English Portfolio.* 1 June 2004 <http://people.clemson.edu/~jsreyno/Process.htm>.

Rohman, D. Gordon. "Prewriting; The Stage of Discovery in the Writing Process." *College Composition and Communication* 16.2 (1965): 106–12.

Rohman, D. Gordon, and Albert O. Wlecke. "Pre-Writing: The Construction and Applications of Models for Concept Formation in Writing." Cooperative Research Project No. 2174. USOE: Washington, DC.

Royster, Jacqueline Jones. "When the First Voice You Hear Is Not Your Own." *College Composition and Communication* 47.1 (1996): 29–40.

Russell, David, and Arturo Yañez. "Big Picture People Rarely Become Historians: Genre Systems and the Contradictions of General Education." *Writing Selves, Writing Societies: Research from Activity Perspectives.* Ed. Charles Bazerman and David Russell. Fort Collins, CO: The WAC Clearinghouse, and Mind, Culture, and Activity. 1 June 2004 <http://wac.colostate.edu/books/selves_societies/russell>.

Selfe, Cynthia L. "Technology and Literacy: A Story about the Perils of Not Paying Attention." *College Composition and Communication* 50.3 (1999): 411–36.

Shea, Rachel Hartigan. "How We Got Here." *U.S. News and World Report,* 9 Aug. 2004: 70–73.

Sommers, Nancy, and Laura Saltz. "The Novice as Expert: Writing the Freshman Year." *College Composition and Communication* 56.1 (2004): 124–49.

Sternglass, Marilyn. *Time to Know Them: A Longitudinal Study of Writing and Learning at the College Level.* Mahwah, NJ: Lawrence Erlbaum Associates, 1997.

Tade, George, Gary Tate, and Jim Corder. "For Sale, Lease, or Rent: A Curriculum for an Undergraduate Program in Rhetoric." *College Composition and Communication* 26.1 (1975): 20–24.

Trachsel, Mary. *Institutionalizing Literacy: The Historical Role of College Entrance Examinations in English.* Carbondale: Southern Illinois UP, 1992.

Trimbur, John. Composition and the Circulation of Writing." *College Composition and Communication* 52.2 (2000): 188–219.

Vendler, Helen. "The Ocean, the Bird, and the Scholar." NEH Jefferson Address, 6 May 2004. 9 Aug. 04 <http://www.neh.gov/whoweare/vendler/lecture.html>.

Watterson, Bill. *Sunday Pages 1985–1995: An Exhibition Catalogue.* Kansas City, MO: Andrews McMeel Publishing, 2000.

John Wright, ed. *New York Times 2004 Almanac.* New York: Penguin, 2003.

Wysocki, Anne, and Julia Jasken, "What Should Be an Unforgettable Face." *Computers and Composition* 21.1 (2004): 29–49.

Yancey, Kathleen Blake. "Episodes in the Spaces of the Plural Commons: Curriculum, Administration, and Design of Composition in the 21st Century." Speech, Writing Program Administration, Delaware, 14 July 2004.

———. "Postmodernism, Palimpsest, and Portfolios: Theoretical Issues in the Representation of Student Work." *College Composition and Communication* 55.4 (2004): 738–61.

———. *Reflection in the Writing Classroom.* Logan: Utah State UP, 1998.

———. *Teaching Literature as Reflective Practice.* Urbana, IL: NCTE, 2004.

Yancey, Kathleen Blake, Teddi Fishman, Morgan Gresham, Michael Neal, and Summer Smith Taylor. Portraits of Composition: How Postsecondary Writing Gets Taught in the Early Twenty-First Century." "Unpublished essay, 2004.

5   *Imagery*

JEFF RICE

"Image Comics Presents: 1963! A Bedazzling Brace of Barnstorming Bargains from the Bower of Brilliance!"

— IMAGE COMICS, *Mystery Incorporated, Book One, 1963*

An accepted trope regarding electronic writing is that writers must learn to work with images. We hear this trope in a number of places, notably in an emerging chorus of contemporary compositionists interested in visuality. "Complicating this scenario," Dean Rader remarks in a 2005 *College English* review essay, "is the realization that our beginning writing students seem to do more sophisticated interpretation with visual texts than written ones" (638). "Rhetoric has always been important in the composition classroom," Carolyn Handa writes in the introduction to Bedford St. Martin's sourcebook on visual rhetoric, "but we are *only now* beginning to understand how it might work as a device to help our students understand and create visually and verbally interwoven texts" (Handa 2, emphasis mine). "A few years ago," Marguerite Helmers and Charles Hill write in the Preface to their collection *Defining Visual Rhetorics*, "we noticed a major shift in the field of rhetoric, one in which an increasing amount of the discipline's attention was becoming focused on visual objects and the visual nature of the rhetorical process. The phrase visual rhetoric was being used more frequently in journal articles, in textbooks, and especially in conference presentations" (ix). The moment he read an airline in-flight emergency brochure comprised only of images, Bruce McComiskey notes in a 2004 *JAC* essay, he "became interested in the rhetorical functions of images; I became interested in 'visual rhetoric'" (187).

The "only now" emphasis largely implicit in Rader, Handa, Helmers, Hill, and McComiskey's observations reflects composition studies' only more recent interest regarding visuality's relationship to writing. Despite a long tradition of rhetorical *and* visual production, composition studies has only

From *The Rhetoric of Cool.* Carbondale: Southern Illinois UP, 2007. 133–57.

recently taken seriously the role visuality plays in meaning making and, in particular, electronic culture. "As we have more and more need to communicate across geographical, linguistic, and cultural boundaries," the editors of the 2004 textbook *Picturing Texts* reflect upon electronic writing, "the use of images will grow in importance" (8). Such use has, in fact, grown. Its growth, however, has been around longer than these writings I quote imply. "There remains much confusion," Diana George notes, "over what is meant by *visual communication, visual rhetoric,* or, more simply, *the visual* and where or whether it belongs in a composition course" (see p. 213 in this volume). George traces the presence of visuality in pedagogy throughout the past sixty years and notes that this presence is often ignored in the recent enthusiasm for the visual. Agreeing with George, I also realize that this confusion is directly connected to the missed 1963 juxtapositions I have utilized to invent the rhetoric of cool. Within the structure of my project, I ask in response to these writings, why is composition studies "only now" interested in the visual?

I ask this question because many of the 1963 texts and writers I've focused on . . . conflate the border between the visual and writing in film (Anger and Smith), culture (Baraka), the computer screen (Nelson, Engelbart, and McLuhan), and even the written page (Burroughs). In these moments, visuality is either explicitly situated within electronic-based rhetorics, or it is implicitly shaped by electronic-based rhetorics. In addition to these figures and texts not being treated in the 1963 composition narrative, they are absent in the current narratives being constructed around visuality as well. There are no nods in these "only nows" to those who engaged with writing and visuality in the early 1960s.

And there were no nods to such writers in the early 1960s either. At the end of *Research in Written Composition*'s chapter "The State of Knowledge about Composition," for instance, the authors outline twenty-four areas of "unexplored territory" relevant to future disciplinary research. None deal with the visual. The absence of visuality in composition studies' rebirth narrative and its consequent delay in reaching our disciplinary vocabulary can be associated with a long-standing tradition in rhetoric and writing of favoring the word over the image, what Jacques Derrida terms *logocentrism.* As Derrida notes, our preference for the word "always assigned the origin of truth in general to the logos" (*Of Grammatology* 3). The connection between the logos and the word demands that "true" meaning derives from the printed text over the visual text. This connection has historical and pedagogical ramifications; it restricts interest in visuality as well as what the discipline is capable of visualizing. As Craig Stroupe writes, the time is long overdue for addressing the forgotten visual history intertwined with expression.

> The discipline needs to decide not only whether to embrace the teaching of visual and information design in addition to verbal production, which some of the more marginalized elements of English Studies have already done, but more fundamentally, whether to confront its customary cultural attitudes toward visual discourses and their insinuation into verbal texts. (Stroupe 608)

More specifically, in the composition studies tradition, the absence of visuality can be understood as the inability to recognize the role of cool in composition in general, both its verbal and visual components. Most importantly, this absence signifies an ideological hesitation to allow imagery a place within composition studies, for most of the "only now" work done in "visual rhetoric" limits not only our understandings of visuality's relevance to composition studies history and new media but also, pedagogically, students' ability to produce their own visual-based writings in new media environments. In much of today's pedagogy, the preference is for writing about images, not with images. The preference is still for the word. Thus, we hear Rader using the word *interpretation* in his review essay of visually oriented textbooks and not the word *production*. Thus, we hear Handa—despite sporadic references to production in her introduction to the sourcebook—stress the idea of "critical thinking" repeatedly, a concept whose origins are in reading, not in producing texts. True writing can only come from reading images, these positions state, not from making images.

The "Seeing" and "Writing" components of Bedford St. Martin's two popular textbooks by that name, for instance, ask students to "see" images as texts and write about them, but never to write with images. As the editors introduce their book to prospective students, they write, "Given the fact that we're asking you to look closely at verbal and visual texts within and beyond this book, we also invite you to turn your attention to the content and design of the pages of the book. What choices have the editors and designers made in presenting the material in this way (McQuade and McQuade lv–lvi). Once that question is answered, however, it is unclear what students are to do with such information. Should they then design their own visual texts? How? Based on the choices they have discovered? Based on other rhetorical ideas? Which? For what reasons would they compose visually even if given the chance? Why isn't any instruction in this example of visual rhetorical pedagogy devoted to actual visual rhetorical production? Why is the visual something one admires but does not perform? These are questions I pose as a conclusion to my breakdown of the rhetoric of cool, for visuality is central to new media writing. Composers of new media texts, Anne Wysocki writes, "design texts that make as overtly visible as possible the values they embody" (15). No better place can this be seen than in cool that makes its meanings possible in a number of media outlets, imagery among them.

The visual, as I note [in another work], is included in my initial juxtaposition of 1963 that showcases Robert Farris Thompson observing visual writing practices in West African Yoruban culture as indicative of the idea of cool: "I recall an incident at Edunabon in the south of Oyo country in the winter of 1963–64, when a man, regarded an ancient, polished blood-red carnelian bead and pronounced it 'cool' (tutu)" (*Flash of the Spirit* 43). The bead incident allows Farris Thompson to generalize to other Yoruban visual practices— sculpting, wood carving, and weaving—and conclude that in absence of alphabetic writing (print culture), Yorubans fashioned a visual language after the belief systems invested in the idea of cool (conciliation, appeasement, restoration, calmness). "The sense of certainty," he writes, "which character and àshe confer, is enriched by mystic coolness (*itutu*), whose emblematic color is often blue or indigo or green" (*Flash of the Spirit* 12). Farris Thompson quotes a Yoruban who states that "coolness or gentleness of character is so important in our lives. Coolness is the correct way you represent yourself to a human being" (qtd. in *Flash of the Spirit* 13). Cool, in this visual discourse, is connected to representation, the ways individuals represent themselves and their thoughts to the outside world. Cool is not so much an emotional appeal (although it embodies that trait) but a visual one as well: "Coolness, then, is a part of character, and character objectifies proper custom. To the degree that we live generously and discreetly, exhibiting grace under pressure, our appearance and our acts gradually assume virtual royal power" (*Flash of the Spirit* 16). Farris Thompson's observation holds significance for a composition pedagogy increasingly interested in the visual. It speaks to the broad desire to express ideas outside of the restrictions of print. The cool, visual traditions of Yoruban culture generate concepts in ways print often cannot accommodate by itself ("appearance and acts" in one compositional gesture, for instance). Farris Thompson's work also teaches that print does not need to be the indigenous practice displaced by some other means. In other words, working with cool media (visual or not) should not be understood as the displacement of our fixation on print culture—a typical response whenever the visual is introduced into writing pedagogy ("does this mean students no longer need to be concerned with grammar?"). Cool has its origins in discourse already; it doesn't replace other concerns. The Yoruban example describes cool as a native practice outside of print, not as a displacement.

SKETCHPAD

My intent is to generalize from Farris Thompson's work to other areas of visual rhetoric within 1963 and thus bring the rhetoric of cool to an expected conclusion's emphasis on visual rhetorical production. Farris Thompson's research signifies only one moment regarding visual writing that went unmentioned by composition scholars in 1963. The distance between the 1963 Los Angeles meeting of CCCC or temporal publications and West Africa cannot be minimized, but it also shouldn't be used to quantify this missed moment as a matter of cultural mis-recognition or unfair critique. In the choral tradition I have established as central to the rhetoric of cool, I am obligated to move chorally from Farris Thompson's studies to other visual moments situated in 1963 but not found in composition's paradigm shift (image motivating my choral moves). These moments connect those practices we typically associate as pertaining to literacy acquisition—as well as the ways literate individuals generate ideas—with imagery.

One notable moment I find is the invention of the personal, graphic manipulation program. Ivan Sutherland's 1963 invention of Sketchpad (and related doctoral dissertation *Sketchpad: A Man-Machine Graphical Communication System*) equated writing with visual expression. With Sketchpad, Sutherland outlined and demonstrated a computer program capable of manipulating user-entered symbols (through a light pen) and then generating visual displays on TV-like monitors. Sketchpad's basic premise is identifiable today as the more contemporary commercial product Adobe Photoshop as well as its numerous clones (for images or for multimedia), tools that have become quotidian in the entertainment and advertising industries. Sketchpad is indicative of a 1963 growing interest in composing with images. "Sketchpad allowed a computer operator to use the computer to create sophisticated visual models on a display screen that resembled a television set. The visual patterns could be stored in the computer memory like any other data, and could be manipulated by the computer's processor" (Rheingold 90). Sutherland's purpose was to allow writers the ability to forge rhetorical gestures via the visual display in front of them. Sutherland recognized the importance of visuality in a world fascinated by film, television, and advertising, and he sought to locate related practices in the computer. By doing so, Sutherland tapped into the rhetorical power of visuality McLuhan described accordingly: "In visual representation of a person or an object, a single phase or moment or aspect is separated from the multitude of known and felt phases, moments and aspects of the person or object" (*Understanding Media* 291).

For McLuhan, visuality, and in particular, electronic visuality, opens up new types of senses and awareness that cannot be accounted for in alphabetic literacy. Because of its cool status (its ability to generate involvement at greater rates than print), electronic visuality has the potential to transform "fragmented and specialist extensions into a seamless Web of experience" (*Understanding Media* 292). In this sense, the question is not just of static image representation (like taking a picture or uploading an image to a Web site) but of imaging in general, of finding visual connections to work among and forge ideas out of. That process is material based (making images) and conceptual (imaging connections). It is a process that reflects Douglas Engelbart's image of connected, computerized writing, what Engelbart called "the symbol manipulator."

> This [symbol manipulator] could be a computer, with which individuals could communicate rapidly and easily, coupled to a three-dimensional color display within which extremely sophisticated images could be constructed, the computer being able to execute a wide variety of processes on parts or all of these images in automatic response to human direction. (14)

Sketchpad's usage of the visual was meant to push writers into a similar rhetorical experience. Sketchpad refigured the writing space from paper to the visual screen. Sutherland introduced his dissertation accordingly:

> The Sketchpad system makes it possible for a man and a computer to converse rapidly through the medium of line drawings. Heretofore, most interaction between men and computers has been slowed down by the need to reduce all communication to written statements that can be typed; in the past, we have been writing letters to rather than conferring

with our computers. For many types of communication, such as describing the shape of a mechanical part of the connections of an electrical circuit, typed statements can prove cumbersome. The Sketchpad system, by eliminating typed statements (except for legends) in favor of line drawings, opens up a new area of man-machine communication. (Sutherland 1)

This extension of the senses Sketchpad generates is more profound today in its contemporary successors like Adobe Photoshop. Photoshop's ability to manipulate, copy, distort, fabricate, and erase visual displays at will ties into McLuhan's understanding of the visual as cool. Through these visual moves, writers extend a variety of ideas and feelings in ways print does not allow for; writers create new kinds of discursive worlds that go beyond the flatness of the page. Whereas Burroughs's cut-up was designed for text, Photoshop (via Sketchpad) puts the logic of cut and paste into visual production, a task that can make connections among images seem, in McLuhan's definition, "seamless." The point is repeated by Lev Manovich, who writes of Photoshop-like techniques in film and visuality, "[T]he problem is no longer how to generate convincing individual images but how to blend them together" (155). In other words, the problem for digital writing is how to write visually in a complex but seamless fashion.

By that, I don't mean to construct a binary between print and the visual (one creates seamless connections, one doesn't) but rather to note how Sketchpad began the process of demonstrating the rhetorical potential of the visual *to all writers* (and not just painters or artists). A writer is asked *to use* Sketchpad, not to analyze its merits or compositional potential. And Sketchpad is meant as a tool for all, not a select, talented few. An early Apple Macintosh promotional film for the Apple II called "Pencil Test" is indicative of this legacy. In the film, the pencil icon for drawing leaves its place in the drawing program, considers itself as a writing instrument by taking the place of a "real" pencil laying on the table, and eventually returns to the computer, the very computer we are to believe created this short film we are watching. In the spirit of Sketchpad, everyday writing with text transforms into everyday writing with images. The interaction between developing an idea and writing that idea now must include the visual, the film claims. "Sketchpad exemplified a new paradigm for interacting with computers," Lev Manovich writes. "By changing something on the screen, the operator changed something in the computer's memory. The real-time screen became interactive" (102). That interactivity, I claim, alters rhetorical expression dramatically, for Manovich's sense of "interaction" is not just pushing buttons or pulling down drop menus on an interface, as I remarked in the previous chapter. It is a reflection of a new dimension of cultural and rhetorical interactivity: connecting a variety of experiences and ideas at once visually, treating "Pencil Test" as a metaphor for an emerging digital practice.

No doubt such thinking regarding visuality and writing would be difficult to understand for those 1963 compositionists translating students into written variables or debating the effectiveness of sentence construction. "If the new grammar is to be brought to bear on composition," Francis Christensen begins his well-known essay in the 1963 October *College Composition and Communication*, "it must be brought to bear on the rhetoric of the sentence" (155). Christensen's concerns with a rhetoric of the sentence reflect the logocentrism Derrida critiques, but Christensen also draws attention to the literate emphasis on learning and meaning making as a print phenomenon despite technological influence already in existence. McLuhan notes, "Our Western values, built on the written word, have already been considerably affected by the electric media of telephone, radio, and TV. Perhaps that is the reason why many highly literate people in our time find it difficult to examine this question without getting into a moral panic" (*Understanding Media* 85). Whether or not Christensen would have entered a "moral panic" over a writing application like Sketchpad is not obvious. But one can assume that the definition of writing as purely text based and alphabetic would lead compositionists like Christensen to reject Sketchpad's premise that writing may be visual as well. How does one teach a rhetoric of the sentence for a compositional text that lacks a sentence or has images in addition to sentences? After all, we see such reactions even today.

Without displacing alphabetic writing entirely, Sketchpad serves the teaching of electronic writing by drawing attention to the additional importance imagery plays in digital communication. This last point is no doubt evident to those compositionists in the twenty-first century who have begun to make visual rhetoric a trope within their pedagogy. That trope, though, still seems to be neglecting the rhetorical issues Sketchpad poses for writing, that sense of "seamless" Web experience McLuhan describes. Mostly, imagery's role in electronic writing is currently reduced to rhetorical analysis and not production. When that is the case, as popular textbooks like *Seeing and Writing* or *Convergences* demonstrate, writing is still a print-directed concept. Students write *about* images, but not with images. Students "see" images but don't use them for generating new experiences. Students observe images but are not asked to find correlations between an image-based experience and their own.

Thus, we are still caught in a bind of print-based literacy assumptions regarding writing. "What will be the new configurations of mechanisms and of literacy," McLuhan concludes *The Gutenberg Galaxy*, "as these older forms of perception and judgment are interpenetrated by the new electric age?" (330). McLuhan's question is a direct challenge not only to the definition of writing as print based but to an entire vision of literacy acquisition. The difference in these two positions (print and electronic) is the continuing motif regarding how each relates to rhetorical production found outside of the classroom. To imagine or engage with a visual rhetoric, one must write as visual writers do outside of the classroom. For 1963 compositionists, that kind of imagination is hard to acquire. Braddock and colleagues, like my other principle composition figures, symbolize a classroom-only attitude, for they work exclusively with the categorization of factors that influence *student* writing and not just writing. A glimpse at their brief mentioning of technology is revealing in this regard for how it shapes a non-imagery-based teaching.

Students in the 1960s write in classrooms with pens and paper, and maybe with the time period's most prominent form of writing technology, typewriters. The typewriter, one would think, would be the most easily adopted technology for writing pedagogy because of its direct relationship to producing alphabetic literacy. However, even this emerging image of writing—writing produced by new technology—was difficult to deal with for the image it evoked of writing. McLuhan recognized this difficulty when he cast doubt on how readily teachers would accept the move toward teaching with typewriters. "In 1882, ads proclaimed that the typewriter could be used as an aid in learning to read, write, spell, and punctuate. Now, eighty years later, the typewriter is used only in experimental classrooms" (*Understanding Media* 227). In terms of composition, McLuhan's critique sounds accurate. This supposedly novel way of writing (via the machine) was still framed by many educators as experimental, and thus, it was not seriously considered as an already conventional practice. The typewriter's "experimental" nature garners a brief mention in *Research in Written Composition*, but not for its ability to change how individuals write or how the very image of writing might be altered by this new device. Instead, in *Research in Written Composition*, the typewriter is still classified as a device devoted to print, and even more so, to typed student essays—an understandable point given that *Research in Written Composition*'s focus is student writing. But even with this point anticipated, Braddock and colleagues convey a limited understanding of technology and writing. The typewriter's influence on student writing, the authors argue, needs to be studied more before the typewriter is used pedagogically on a larger scale (58). The typewriter, in other words, is still too experimental. That the typewriter may already be in use outside of the classroom, that its image as a writing tool may already be in the public imaginary, that almost seventy years earlier—to accept McLuhan's point—advocates called for its inclusion in pedagogy, none of these points are mentioned or considered.

Studying the typewriter more seems an irrelevant point for the kinds of writing 1960s business culture generates using typewriters, but it also shows a lack of recognition of the ways media shapes thought in anticipated and unanticipated ways. One place such recognition surfaced was in 1960s avant-garde practices. Alan Kaprow, for example, found the typewriter to be indicative of visuality and visual-based expression. In his 1963 Happening *Words*, an interactive installation featuring typewritten and handwritten banners to be read or written on, Kaprow turned this print-oriented device into a tool for generating a visual rhetoric.

> Overhead are crudely-lettered signs urging the visitors to roll the rolls, to tear off more word strips from stacks nailed to a center-post, and to staple them over the ones already there; in addition, they are exhorted to play the Victorolas and listen to the records I had made, of talk, lectures, shouts, advertisements, ramblings of nonsense, etc.—either singly or all together. ("Words: An Environment" 446)

One selection in Kaprow's performance read: "Try a record, try a poem. Listen to the word on the Victorolas. Words. Words. Words!" Words, indeed. Words as text and words as image, both occupying the same compositional space. Why call for further study, then, when the typewriter's application was already in circulation in nonclassroom rhetorical moments that posed its usage in complex ways? As Fredric Kittler has more recently demonstrated in *Gramophone, Film, Typewriter*, the tradition of the typewriter cannot easily be disconnected from the overall history of modern writing (and consequently, new media) even if it is not taken seriously by writing pedagogy. "Writing as keystrokes, spacing, and the automatics of discrete block letters bypassed a whole system of education," Kittler notes (193). Kaprow's work marks one effort to teach an emerging model of education (at least in the realm of the plastic arts), a technology-based composition practice. Braddock and colleagues' demand for "further study" of typewriting before approving its usage belongs within the tradition of "bypassing" that Kittler highlights; it is a failure to recognize that outside of the classroom, typewriters were being used extensively.[1]

Moreover, the nonalphabetic usage of typewriters in installations like Kaprow's (or McLuhan's example of poet Charles Olson and his influence on the Visual Poets) shows writing taking place visually as well as typographically. "The typewriter," McLuhan writes, "fuses composition and publication, causing an entirely new attitude to the written and printed word" (*Understanding Media* 228). With this comment, McLuhan makes the broad intellectual jump Braddock and colleagues do not; he connects the typewriter to an even newer invention, the computer. The ability to produce new knowledge via the mechanics of the typewriter—be it typographic or visual—leads to the kinds of visual knowledge computing can allow for via its manipulation of programmed language into alternative kinds of representations. Without this kind of understanding, Sketchpad cannot be invented, and current interest in visual rhetoric cannot develop.

> Especially with the computer, the work effort is applied at the "programming" level, and such effort is one of information and knowledge. In the decision-making and "make happen" aspect of the work operation, the telephone and other such speed-ups of information have ended the divisions of delegated authority in favor of the "authority of knowledge."
> (*Understanding Media* 232)

While Braddock and colleagues are waiting for "further study" that will justify a pedagogy of typing, McLuhan is already looking ahead to the typewriter's successor. As much as typing can allow writers to visualize their work through inventive typographic display or alternative poetic style (McLuhan quotes e. e. cummings extensively), the computer display (though not yet a classroom tool in the early 1960s) will lead to a new kind of visualization of composition. The computer display, McLuhan contends, allows writers to become involved in a visual composing process in ways movable type (which is performed elsewhere, and not by the writer) did not allow. Visuality, McLuhan notes, extends writers' ability to generate knowledge because of how it extends perception. This perception may be reduced to the page or screen (what something physically looks like), but it is also an expansion of an overall ability to understand and connect. My argument . . . has been concerned with that latter point. The connections, commutations, and juxtapositions the rhetoric of cool teaches are meant to produce a type of new media writing while also altering a perception of what composition entails.

Braddock and colleagues' quick rejection of new media tools (in this case, the typewriter) is illuminating, for outright rejection of the new without regard to popular usage demonstrates a lack of perception, or as McLuhan would say, a lack of in-depth involvement. Composition cannot perceive new media's role in writing if the field is not involved in new media innovations. Hence, this rejection has also become a dominant theme in contemporary composition pedagogy. Early rejection of word processing, later dismissal of hypertext, and, even now, the shrugging off of widely popular media like Weblogs or social software is indicative of the attitudes Braddock and colleagues proliferate in their study regarding typewriters (and as I noted earlier, film). The *Research in Written Composition* claim is that the tool is either not applicable or it must be studied in depth empirically before it can be evaluated for pedagogical usage. Its usage must be controlled for its value to be determined. Meanwhile, generations grow up using these tools daily, generations learn their application without controlled study, and, in turn, generations grow up internalizing new kinds of thought processes (the visual functioning by a different logic than the typographic) that affect communicative practices outside of a given classroom situation.[2] The mass proliferation of Weblogs and related applications reflects this point. While Weblogs (as of 2006) are still fairly new and novel, the application's quick and widespread acceptance for composing purposes (food blogs, academic blogs, political blogs, music blogs, personal blogs) has resulted from how the Web alters recognizable writing spaces, how it mixes print literacy with visual literacy. The millions of new writers discovering how to interlink (hyperlinks), visualize (posting of images found or created), and reimagine the writing space (on Blogger, WordPress, or MySpace) are perceiving writing spaces as total in-depth involvement. Each site, as Webloggers often show through quotes, comments, daily posts, and links, is involved with every other writing experience other blogs generate. Popular sites like BoingBoing, Metafilter, and Waxy[3] represent the Web's contents as an always interlinked network of ideas. These sites list (following literacy's tradition of listing) selections from and links to other eclectic, personal, and serious Web sites and, in turn, revisualize the writing space. As if trying out the Web (a picture here, a phrase there), the generic Weblog experience, at times, revisualizes Kaprow's *Words*: "Try a record, try a poem. Listen to the word on the Victorolas. Words. Words. Words!" What television was for McLuhan—"With TV, the viewer is the screen"—the Weblog or social software variant is partly for current electronic discourse (*Understanding Media* 272). And this has all occurred without "further study."

TELEVISION

As McLuhan reminds any investigation into 1963 and composing, television dominated the post-World War II communicative revolution. Regarding technology, and aside from their dismissal of typewriters, the closest Braddock and colleagues come to the visual and the recognition that rhetoric takes place outside of the classroom is their brief mention of television. Without any acknowledgment of theoretical or practical work done regarding television (such as McLuhan's work or the ETV nationwide television systems in place in many universities and colleges),[4] they offer a negative assessment of its value to writing pedagogy: "Despite the fact that much money has been granted by foundations for experiments in the use of television as an instructional aid, little of the research, as published, seems convincing, at least where instruction in written composition is concerned" (47). Despite the skepticism of Braddock, Lloyd-Jones, and Schoer, education had turned to technology's visual component somewhat, and that includes television. In 1962, Walter Ong notes in a republished essay from *College English* that

> [t]elevision is a more feasible means of education than radio. This is not because it can use visual aid devices (figures written on a blackboard on television cannot be seen by any viewer unless the camera is turned on them — they lack the permanent availability of figures on a classroom blackboard). It is because television better implements personal rapport between instructor and student. ("Wired for Sound" 226)

Ong's support for television is actualized in the popularity of ETV (closed-circuit education television) and in 1963 journals like *American School and University*, which are full of advertisements for television and other related media equipment. One would assume that such equipment would be used in various classrooms, including those where composition was taught. These ads include Kodak Pageant Film projectors, Kodak sound recording tapes, the Ampex E-65 tape recorder, 3M tapes, Astatic's Astatiphone headphones, Sony video recorders, and Magnavox TVs. In fact, one advertisement in the *American School and University*'s March 1964 issue asks: "Will the Sony Videocorder Replace Teachers?" "Of course not." the ad comforts.

> Nothing will ever replace the teacher. But the new Sony Videocorder will go a long way toward alleviating the shortage of good teachers, of multiplying the efficiency of the school teaching staff and making the tax dollar go a lot further in this era of increasing costs.

Nothing might replace the teacher, but evidence demonstrates some degree of interest in applying visual-oriented technology to pedagogical usage, and, in particular, to *using* visual-based tools. What exactly teachers were doing with Sony video recorders or Magnavox TVs is not clear. Yet someone was using them; teachers were being solicited to purchase these devices. Increasing attention to the visual in the early 1960s signifies an attempt to split with the typographic centrism central to much of composition's pedagogical practice. There are more significant consequences of typographic centrism than not teaching students how to use cameras or work with television. Like other aspects of cool, those consequences are ideological as well as practical. The decision to study student writers and not *writers* because of such centrism led Braddock and colleagues (and consequently a significant body within composition studies) to not include visuality as part of future work until visual culture became too dominating a force to ignore—as evidenced by the Handa collection. The preponderance of imagery on the Web, on television, in film, in games, on video, and elsewhere is not as much a recent phenomenon as the phrase "visual culture" might lead us to believe. Even though Sketchpad would not have been a common item or known item to composition teachers still concerned with handwritten essays, its emergence in 1963 is a reflection (not a cause) of increasing interest in visuality and expression. Visual writing already had been in circulation in areas composition studies should have noticed and expressed interest in thinking about in terms of writing and writing instruction. In the age of new media, pedagogy cannot remain insular. It must be aware of all media in order to better understand the dynamics of rhetoric within digital culture. Often, such media are objects we encounter daily, like typewriters in the 1960s or Web sites and Weblogs in the twenty-first century. To make my point more explicit, I turn from more obvious, general examples like television to a specific visual example in popular circulation, the record album cover. The record cover identifies the gap between 1963 writing instruction and 1963 writing with images.

BLUE NOTE RECORDS

One place I can develop my initial ideas regarding visual rhetoric (and how writers compose with images) in 1963 is Blue Note Records' influential covers from that year. Even if these examples are not digital texts, they are, as records, intertwined in the emerging electronic apparatus of the 1960s that fused technological innovations with sound recording. "The brief and compressed history of the phonograph," McLuhan comments, "includes all phases of the written, the printed and the mechanized word" (*Understanding Media* 243). By looking at the rhetoric of record covers, I'm trying to expand further the notion of what constitutes writing in the popular sphere. As I have shown, many of the models digital culture draws upon come from nondigital sources and media (film, literature, urban affairs, cultural critique, etc.), especially those familiar to popular spheres of influence. Music, of all forms of composition, is a popularly distributed form of writing. Record covers as well are popular forms of writing, and they circulate in popular vocabularies in complex ways. My interest in studying record covers is similar to what textbook author Robert Atwan instructs writing students to think about when examining visual texts: "In visual texts, composition is often a matter of spatial relations: How has the artist, designer, film director, or photographer first framed a space and then arranged the various elements inside it? How are images grouped? How is your eye drawn to particular features? What do you tend to notice first?" (liii). Blue Note, one of the most prolific producers of jazz in the postwar period, gives me a place to interlink Atwan's questions into a specific way writers can utilize imagery in the rhetoric of cool. Unlike Atwan's textbook *Convergences*, however, which is too fixated on observing images only, I turn to Blue Note to learn how *to teach* its visual methods for electronic writing and not only *to understand* how the images rhetorically function.

Blue Note produced a number of record covers in 1963 distinct in their style: Freddie Roach's *Mo' Greens Please*, Donald Byrd's *A New Perspective*, Jackie McLean's *One Step Beyond*, Hank Mobley's *No Room For Squares*, Blue Mitchell's *Step Lightly*, and Horace Silver's *Silver's Serenade*. Marked by geometric shapes and patterns, tilted angles and sharp recolorations and shadings, these record covers, all designed by Reid Miles, revealed a new aesthetic for jazz and marketing, what Felix Cromey calls "an abstract design hinting at innovations, cool strides for cool notes, the symbolic implications of typeface and tones" (Marsh, Cromey, and Callingham 7). In the tradition of cool rhetorical production (as seen in Beat writings and underground film, for instance), Miles's methods juxtaposed low financial budgets with innovations on previous forms. Speaking about Blue Note's reaction to his work, Miles noted, "Fifty bucks an album . . . they loved it, thought it was modern, they thought it went with the music . . . one or two colours to work with at that time and some outrageous graphics!" (qtd. in Marsh, Cromey, Callingham 72). Blue Note's cover designs commutated the symbols of both urban and pop culture into a cool aesthetic. In addition to the covers' usage of abstract shapes and angles (a marker of pop art influence[5]), Reid's designs often troped the themes of 1950s and 1960s cool: sexy women, cars, and aloof posing. Lou Donaldson's *Good Gracious* comically features Donaldson ogling a passing woman. Herbie Hancock's *Inventions and Dimensions* isolates the pianist's image in the middle of a fairly empty commercial district; his cool look is the recognizable loner in the Baraka sense of political, racial, and economic detachment. Hank Mobley's *No Room for Squares* spotlights Mobley demonstrating the cool look. Wearing dark sunglasses and positioned in an indifferent stance, Mobley inhales nonchalantly on a cigarette, its long ash about to fall. His posture repeats the album's title: There is no room for squares in this cool scene. The circle outline of a trumpet frames Mobley's stance so that the identity of the figure represented and the musical instrument merge. The medium, in this case, distinctly is the message. Another example of Reid's work, Donald Byrd's *A New Perspective*, foregrounds the image of an automobile headlight directing immediate attention; the rest of the vehicle drifts back into the distance, where Byrd stands cross-armed, cool, removed from everything but his car.[6] Similar to the Mobley design, Byrd's identity is formed by the automobile, the urban-ideal media form[7] where utility gives way to aesthetic appeal. The design suggests that driving a car poses less importance than becoming a car; technology and personality, user and design, all juxtapose into one.

These covers construct a variation of what we now often refer to as visual arguments, and they represent what we have come to call visual rhetoric. The visual displays, produced by consumer products, of course, are highly contested for how such designs encourage spending rather than disseminate a given idea. Even Thomas Frank's poignant description of 1960s co-optations of youth values is meant to reveal how consumerist ideology eventually maintains a dominant force on visual communication. It's a point well taken like any other aspect of cool, but one that must be aligned with the overall potential visual writing has for teaching writings *other* than advertising. Blue Note, like other early 1960s producers of consumer goods, uses specific Afrocentric or cool-aesthetic imagery to appeal to record buyers, much in the way, Mina Hamilton and Malcolm Brookes discuss in a 1963 essay, that record packaging is meant to do. "The package must carry some point-of-sale message to inform the prospective purchaser, or to attract him so that he becomes a prospective purchaser" (78). When that place of attraction taps into specific attitudes, as Frank indicates regarding cool and consumer culture, writing (as record packaging) shapes the individual's perception of selfhood (much in the way film or an essay creates similar experiences). Those ads that succeeded in the 1960s, Frank writes, were those that shaped a sense of selfhood. "The basic task of advertising, it seemed in the 1960s, was not to encourage conformity but a never-ending rebellion against whatever it is that everyone else is doing, a forced and exaggerated individualism" (Frank 90). Record covers, of course, are ads as much as they are displays of what a purchaser will discover within the product, and possibly within herself. But it is that question of selfhood that is most important to writing with images. Blue Note shapes selfhood; in particular, its images expand temporal interest in equality, African-American identity, and economics—all complex areas of study that overlap in intriguing ways in the 1960s as well as today. Blue Note Records, then, marks a notable place for me to consider how the label teaches a rhetoric of imagery as well as how such a rhetoric shapes our understandings of writers and writing.

An important writing lesson I find in Blue Note involves the discovery of another method for displaying iconic imagery for rhetorical purposes. Blue Note's visual displays tend to deal with the very explicit, temporal issue of civil rights and black power. Many of the artists recording with Blue Note in the 1960s, like Horace Silver, Herbie Hancock, and Art Blakey's Jazz Messengers, carried these visual arguments into their music, which eventually became known as soul jazz. Soul jazz (or hard bop as it is also called) emphasized the self-proclaimed return to black cultural production. Paralleling the growing influence of the early 1960s civil rights movement, soul jazz highlighted black culture's promise and positive social constructions, even if the iconic markers it chose often bordered on the stereotypical. For example, Freddie Roach's *Mo' Greens Please* record cover features Green ordering soul food, a prominent iconic display of African-American eating habits. Covers like Roach's used iconic display to emphasize black pride and power, stressing the African-American right to choose what to eat as opposed to what white-dominated advertising often tells its audiences to eat through targeted commercials or print ads.

The visual, then, was being used commercially to discuss and respond to difficult subject matter (race relations). Teaching students in 1963 to write about civil rights would seem an obvious pedagogical move for a discipline concerned with treating writing as a "serious intellectual activity that, like all human behavior, has social and ethical consequences," as Kitzhaber writes in his 1963 *College Composition and Communication* essay "4C, Freshman English, and the Future" (134). No better example of social and ethical issues could be found in 1963 than Martin Luther King's 1963 "Letter From Birmingham Jail." . . . King's work has since become a canonical essay in many contemporary first-year rhetoric readers. Both King's essay and Blue Note's covers treat race as a topic of discussion; King does so through the essay, and Blue Note does so visually. The overlap of the two might allow a reborn discipline to think further about the possibilities of both, where each might fit in a newly created composition curriculum, where one might juxtapose with the other. Yet nowhere in a textbook like James McCrimmon's *Writing with a Purpose* do we find writing instruction either promoting visuality to deal with these issues or, at the very least, touching upon the issues that record covers like *Mo' Greens Please* do, or that King's essay fittingly describes.

I make this distinction because the pedagogical decision to not teach students how to work with imagery reflects not only an anti-visual ideological position but also a desire to use print in order to de-emphasize the existence of nonconventional or disruptive subject matter *along with* perceived nonconventional forms of writing (like images). Much in the way that McLuhan's collagist/juxtaposition approach employs a cool rhetoric in order to disrupt the scholarly essay through the fairly nonconventional tactic of collage, Blue Note confronts 1960s conventional attitude toward race through a cool application of images. We see this approach as well on the cover of Dexter Gordon's 1963 *One Flight Up*. Gordon, nicely dressed in a dapper suit, stands in front of a dilapidated, tenement housing project. As an African-American celebrity in the limited-reaching, jazz world, Gordon, the image seems to argue, is only "one step up" from the low-income status most African-Americans living in the inner city experience in the early 1960s. Expressing this point as image and not as text, Blue Note disrupts an accepted manner of discourse in order to, at the very least, begin to form an argument regarding race, economic success, and social status. Who can ascend any kind of flight, this cover seems to argue, when social issues prevent racial success?

For me, or anyone else, to come to that reading (or another), of course, I must interact with the imagery in a way McLuhan defines as cool; I must juxtapose the iconic markers the image displays, and I must create a reading based on association. I cannot read the argument from a series of observations or linear supports in order to understand the cover. And neither, it seems, could 1963 students learning writing from McCrimmon. Instead of confronting and working with complex issues like civil rights (which speak to the very nature of argumentation) through iconography and association, in *Writing with a Purpose,* students learn argumentation from the non-cool method of syllogistic reasoning (a method still dominant in contemporary textbooks). McCrimmon presents the syllogism as a simple and safe exercise in analysis whose linear reasoning keeps subjects under control in terms of comprehension and clearness. Consider the iconic display on *Mo' Greens Please*'s cover, which juxtaposes eating habits with race. Then consider McCrimmon's teaching of argumentative reasoning as a print-based logic.

> She cannot love me and tell lies about me.
> She does tell lies about me.
> She cannot love me.
>
> (McCrimmon 333)

Useful for teaching major and minor premises, McCrimmon's example of the syllogism nevertheless represents a method of writing instruction insistent on leaving difficult issues outside of student writing. In place of civil rights, we find school love. Instead of complexity, we find logical, ordered reasoning ("if she lies, she obviously doesn't love me!"). When McCrimmon does delve into "controversial" topics, such as his example of an argumentative debate entitled "Should Communism Be Studied in Our Schools," his conclusion is that both sides of the debate have done a fair job presenting their case, but both could use more work. In other words, no side wins; no one feels threatened; no beliefs are challenged. "Logic," interpreted as coherence, reins in this kind of pedagogy. Students, the pedagogy calls out to the writers studying this method, always make yourselves logical. "To be reliable, a syllogism must be both true and valid—that is, the information provided in the premises must accord with the facts, and the conclusion must necessarily follow from the premises" (McCrimmon 329). It's a reasonable reflection on how syllogisms work. Yet when questions of "fact" are disputable—such as a government clinging to the validity of segregation—and when conclusions don't always flow from given premises ("all men are created equal" but what to make of segregation? If all "men" are equal, why is Dexter Gordon still in the projects?), how do writers compensate? To read or to write the Blue Note record cover is not to encounter a fact or a reliable conclusion or a logical response to tense social conditions. The Blue Note rhetoric is not a replication of traditional syllogistic argumentation. Its mix of iconic display and juxtaposition propose a more complex construction of ideas. Is *Mo' Greens Please* actually a plea for African-American empowerment as I initially suggested? Or does it comment on how stereotypical African-American habits (like eating soul food) are picked up uncritically by African-American culture itself? Or can both arguments be read off of the cover? Or is the argument something else entirely?

It is the nature of ambiguity that challenges the conventional notion of argumentation demonstrated in a book like McCrimmon's. Students asked to engage with social and cultural issues should encounter such topics not from the point of certainty but from the position of ambiguity, ambiguity regarding what the issues concern as well as how to engage with such issues if at all.

Social conflict is a site of ambiguous meaning; issues must be recognized for their complex histories, makeups, and effects, not for how one premise may be followed by a next in reliable order. By writing with photographs and other images, the Blue Note example pushes writing instruction to locate practices that utilize imagery for such tasks. McLuhan writes, "The logic of the photograph is neither verbal or syntactical, a condition which renders literary culture quite helpless to cope with the photograph" (*Understanding Media* 177). We can say the same about record covers and why the "literate" method of instruction (syllogistic reasoning) does not acknowledge their visual displays.

A PEDAGOGY OF THE IMAGE

What I find in Blue Note record covers is a pedagogy of the image foreign to even those fleeting moments in composition's rebirth that did devote some attention to the visual. In the December 1963 *College Composition and Communication* Staffroom Interchange section, Charlotte Winzeler writes in her brief essay "The Visual Written Image" about her usage of the visual to teach writing. Winzeler describes using an overhead projector in order to "correct" grammar mistakes students typically make. The presentation is meant to teach students what not to do in their own work. Winzeler's short essay stands for a larger trend within composition pedagogy that situates new media only in terms of print culture or the reproduction of existing practices. Like McCrimmon's pedagogy of the syllogism, Winzeler understands the usefulness of visuality in the classroom through the concepts of correctness and simple language structure. What she cannot imagine is the conflicted world visualized in McLuhan's collagist galaxy or Blue Note's imagery, for neither of these options accommodate the print directive for clear and coherent prose. Notice Winzeler describing how she teaches with the overhead: "A grammatical problem, as whether to separate clauses by semicolons or commas, becomes much simpler when I place a red overlay on the independent clauses and a green overlay on the dependent clauses" (Winzeler 265). Even in 1963, the overhead is not the most elaborate form of technology one could employ for writing instruction; yet any application of technology introduced into the classroom should make significant strides toward achieving what may be done differently than if the technology was never used at all. An overhead projector is not needed to demonstrate faulty usage. One could teach the same principles without it. Winzeler's overhead projection of grammar errors is symptomatic of McLuhan's frustration over trying to explain the visual electronic world to those still devoted to a print only world. "A few decades hence it will be easy to describe the revolution in human perception and motivation that resulted from beholding the new mosaic mesh of the TV image. Today it is futile to discuss it at all" (*Gutenberg* 323). Today, forty years after Winzeler, it can feel just as futile to push the visual in a field that still obsesses not over printed words as much as it does over print logic. In a typical contemporary classroom, PowerPoint's slide show of bullet points and static clipart replaces Winzeler's overhead projector because it is the technology that most closely duplicates print logic.[8] Those other logics of visual construction—advertising examples, comic strips, film stills, and Web page displays, which many contemporary textbooks reprint for students, also become places to maintain an already prescribed way of thinking. Textbooks don't ask students to write comic strips, for instance, only to point out the faulty logic or correct reasoning one may embody; in place of identifying incorrect clauses, students are now asked to identify incorrect representations. Even if we are not using overhead transparencies to reveal student error, we are still teaching in manners similar to Winzeler's approach.

The current manifestation of Winzeler's work is the pedagogical directive in many image-oriented textbooks that ask students to decode an image's meaning or analyze its overall rhetorical effect. This kind of exercise offers little more than Winzeler's overhead projector demonstration does; students identify errors in visual logic, note how images and typeface work, respond to faulty visual representations of race, gender, or class, and then offer detailed explanations of these processes in essay form: "What is more effective," Donald and Christine McQuade ask students regarding a Sequoia Citrus Association advertisement, "the image or the language—in ads like these? Choose one such advertisement or commercial—whether the product is an orange, an automobile, or a sneaker—and write an essay in which you explain why you think the ad or commercial does or does not 'work'" (17). "Write an essay" is the prescriptive. Find the errors in the image you are examining (why the ad does or does not work). Construct your response within the logic of print (the essay). One might wonder the purpose of reading an advertisement at all. Why don't these authors ask students to write their own set of images? Could McQuade and McQuade imagine media-oriented prompts like, for example, compose with a series of iconic gestures the way the citrus ad does; critique the ad through your own ad; complicate the ad's pro-citrus message by juxtaposing new images which challenge the ad's stance; further the ad's stance with a new series of ads that promote the same message; or use the ad's logic of juxtaposition to create your own series of ads? None of these assignments are offered, of course, because the logic of McQuade and McQuade's *Seeing and Writing*, despite all its glossy imagery and heavy promotion by its publisher, is still print directed; it is still McCrimmon oriented in its focus.

To compose the Blue Note way, writers assemble iconic imagery into a space like a Web site (though a Photoshop composite, Flash site, or even animated gif would suffice) in order to construct an argument, present a position, express an idea, or perform any other rhetorical act. The iconic, the juxtaposed moment, the cultural signifier are items writers use (among others) to visualize their position. In place of the *Seeing and Writing* assignment, one kind of visual assignment might be to ask students to compose an autobiographical statement only with visual icons. Much in the spirit of *Mo' Greens Please* or any of the other Blue Note covers, the assignment asks writers to contextualize personal positions with cultural issues. Updated for the Web, it would be demonstrated over a series of interlinked Web pages with minimal text (or text that is not narrative but additive to the imagery). Chosen imagery can come from one's area of study, interests, cultural identification, fears, desires, and so forth. Another assignment I suggest is to turn the focus to advertising (a popular trope in texts like *Seeing and Writing*) and ask students to study a particular advertising campaign, like the Absolut Vodka ads whose rhetoric involves the juxtaposition of iconic moments into the repetitive (and appropriated) image of a bottle. These juxtapositions work with familiar icons from popular culture, literature, history, and elsewhere. Instead of analyzing these ads, students use them as models in order to construct a series of iconic self-portraits, advertisements for themselves. What Absolut does with the bottle (how it both appropriates and commutates popular imagery and references), the assignment asks, do with another shape or figure. The challenge of these kinds of visual assignments I contrast with textbook offerings is to invent ways to compose with images, whether to follow the Sketchpad legacy and use a graphic manipulation program or to simply allow for likely and unlikely juxtapositions to motivate the project.

THE COOL WRITER

The bias I draw attention to . . . extends beyond working with images; it also shapes composition studies' *image* of the writer. . . . The courses I have taught entitled Writing about Cool often generate questions from colleagues regarding whether I or the students I work with consider ourselves "cool." These are questions of image, of how we imagine ourselves in writing instruction and how we imagine the individuals we work with as a part of or not a part of digital culture. Even in Alan Liu's lengthy breakdown of electronic culture, the networked society, and what he terms *knowledge work*, the narrative eventually settles on some variation of the troped question of cool, and thus the troped image of cool, which only reflects personality: "I work here, but I'm cool" (*Laws of Cool* 299). Liu writes, "This is why 'cool!' exclaimed about any new toy, dress, high-tech gadget, or Web page always hovers ambiguously between the subjective and objective ('I'm cool/it's cool'). 'Cool!' is the song of a subject robbed of any voice except that of the technological subject" (299–300). Liu's mistake, like composition studies' general error in reducing technology to only the tools of technology, is in ignoring a rich rhetorical tradition associated with cool and digital culture that does not depend on personality. Liu's own vision of technology robs it of the rhetorical possibilities I have drawn attention to . . . and reduces technology and rhetoric to mere catch phrases and latest gadgets. No wonder Liu is overtly fascinated with the declaration "it's cool." His own ability to *imagine* cool is restricted to the popular trope. If the rhetoric of cool succeeds in only producing this kind of image of the new media-oriented writer, the so-called "cool figure," then the project of cool as writing has terribly failed. It has failed because it has maintained a specific image's status quo in our disciplinary vocabulary. It has failed for continuing the dead-end circulation of a trope with limited to little meaning outside of popularity.

When the popular meaning of the word is stressed over the various meanings I have brought together . . . , we foreground the non-digital. When we do that, we find it increasingly difficult to visualize a type of writing or writing situation different from what we currently know and accept as the status quo. The status quo is itself an imagined state. How could the 1963 compositionist imagine the writer any differently than she did, a critique of my own critique . . . might ask? What about the specific apparatus 1963 compositionists worked within? How was that apparatus ideologically constructed? How could she have seen what you, in the twenty-first century and in a different type of apparatus, now see? Indeed, how could she? The images of writing and writers circulating in that time period prevented any kind of image not imagined in the status quo from being entered into the disciplinary discussions taking place. The fault is not with the individual instructor or theorist I draw attention to periodically. The fault is in the ways the discipline itself—as a whole—imagines writing and writers. If the classroom writer, like the cliché cool figure, is the only kind of writer we imagine, then our perception of writing will remain narrow in scope. In 1963 we miss out on cool. Today we miss out on something else. The fault is large scale and ideological, not personal.

While I hope that the complexities cool poses as a rhetoric of electronic writing have made an impact by this point . . . , I also know that by retaining an image of writers who somehow work and live separate from digital culture, composition studies resists the idea of a cool writer being someone outside of personality or status, and it eventually preserves the image of the student as writer as only student writer. In the age of new media, this kind of classification no longer maintains relevance. In his textbook *Internet Invention*, Gregory Ulmer contextualizes the cool writer as a participant in electracy. "'Cool' is a practice of impersonation that accords with the becoming-image that is the emerging subject of electrate people" (309). To be electrate, that is, to compose electronically through the various rhetorical strategies I have described in the preceding chapters, is to be cool. But this version of cool differs drastically from the throwaway term we have culturally grown comfortable using, a comfort expressed in even the most accepted efforts to move into unfamiliar ground, like Gerald Graff's limited vision of "hidden intellectualism." "What is most great criticism, after all," Graff asks, "but an elaborated way of saying in effect, 'It sucks' or 'It's cool'"? (Graff 35). At some point, we must begin the process of imagining intellectualism (of which pedagogy is a part of) to be more than it sucks or it's cool. Cool writing signifies more than sucking or being good; it stands for an electronic rhetoric.

This is a form of coolness that differs from that associated with figures like James Dean or Marlon Brando. In rhetoric, cool does not merely reflect the brooding, male figure; the marginal, African-American; the hipster; the rebel; or any other cliché. The cool writer encompasses what Burroughs calls a "media being," an individual who mixes and is mixed, who composes with media by commutating, appropriating, visualizing, and chorally structuring knowledge. "The basic law of association and juxtaposition," Burroughs writes, "the basic law of association and conditioning is known to college students even in America: Any object, feeling, odor, word, image in juxtaposition with any other object feeling, odor, word, or image will be associated with it" (*Nova Express* 85). The cool writer understands how media shapes her view of the world and her ability to communicate within that world. The composition program, in general, does not yet understand that fact. Even as it hypes media as something to be studied (as its current crop of popular textbooks do), composition studies still does not envision the media shaped writer. It has refused to give up its grasp on the print shaped writer, an image cherished in our profession for so long. Where is the writing student whose juxtapositions, appropriations, commutations, nonlinear thoughts, choral moves, and visual displays mark a significant body of writing production taught and encouraged? Where is the curriculum whose outcomes speak to these rhetorical gestures? Where is the discussion—beyond the fixation on assessing (and, one assumes, controlling)—of this type of digital rhetoric? These are not questions of accusation but genuine inquiries for a field that still struggles to see relevance in such thinking. These are genuine questions for a field still fixated on the topos of writing as controlled experience, on the topos of composition as a single identity, a single locale, for writing. These are questions that remind us of Diane Davis's sharp critique of writing instruction.

> It follows that there is a precious little bit of writing going in comp classes today, where students are commanded to "know" their audience and their (lone) purpose, where they are rewarded for grounding their inscriptions in "common places" (the same), for pretending to have mastered something, and for perpetuating the myths of community and identity via the strategies of clarity and linear presentations. (238–39)

These are genuine inquiries I pose throughout this [work] because the story I am telling challenges such myths but still asks if our research and pedagogies will respond to such challenges and consequently change in this age of new media.

One reason many compositionists are not convinced that such questions are relevant is because composition studies does not fully recognize the image of the media being, or even the influence of media on composition practices. In *Themes, Theories, and Therapy*, Kitzhaber asks, "Suppose that after a course in English composition the student does *not* write better than he did at the beginning. What then?" Kitzhaber proceeds to offer a number of reasons why a student hasn't improved, among them many we might find familiar today:

> It may be that his English teacher's efforts to instill habits of correctness and coherence and precision of statement have been nullified by counter-influences in other courses where teachers tolerate sloppy writing and say that "it's only the ideas that count." The student's friends may exert the same kind of counterinfluence; so may newspapers, radio, television, magazines. (5–6)

This brief excerpt goes a long way toward explaining why composition studies cannot imagine the cool writer as a media being or composition itself as a media being (a media-based body of ideas and practices). Whether it is his preference of form over content (his rejection of the claim that "it's only the ideas that count") or his dismissal of the media's role in shaping writing (newspapers, radio, television, magazines), Kitzhaber encapsulates a disciplinary rejection of those areas I have aligned with the rhetoric of cool. Viewing media as a "counterinfluence" works against imagining the student writer as anything but a *student*. Students don't engage with media, this argument claims. They use only those forms and genres native to the university-accepted curriculum of exams, essays, and other print-related assessment procedures. Thus, when Kitzhaber adds to his diatribe above and claims, "The effects of the English course cannot be isolated from the effects of a myriad of other influences which lie entirely outside the English teacher's control," he is not suggesting that English, or composition, consider these effects for their rhetorical value (6). He is placing these effects within the counterinfluence sphere; as influences to avoid or struggle against.

And here lies composition studies' greatest dilemma regarding media. Are media a counterinfluence, or are they, in fact, *influences*? If we choose the latter, we begin the work necessary to integrate electronic writing into our curricula. If we recognize influence as broader than classroom study, as the 1963 story I am telling dictates we should do, then we can also understand how media is writing. But to make the claim for broad influence, we have to expand the types of writing students do so that they better reflect the kinds of writing media generate. To write to a Weblog is not the same as to write a personal essay; to engage with a wiki is not the same as to write a thesis; to construct a hypertextual project is not the same as to create a print-based research essay. To even conduct research is no longer the same. Media dictate otherwise. Media change us, and media change the nature of our work.

Image is everything, the popular Sprite commercial declares. Image is everything, including how composition studies imagines writing in general. Is writing still the dominance of alphabetic notation, or does writing include imagery as well? Is writing the teaching of thesis-driven representation, is it a rhetoric devoted largely to the concepts of audience and purpose, or is it only logical reasoning? Does a writer really need purpose or a sense of audience each time she sits down to write? Should she be inventing the university or media culture? Or—and possibly in addition to these items—does writing also include those items I note as central to the rhetoric of cool?

These are questions for the future work of composition studies. These are questions 1963 composition studies was unable to address because of the range of its vision regarding writing and writing instruction. These are questions I'm still not confident composition studies today takes seriously. Despite some emerging calls to reconsider the role of media in writing instruction, notably Kathleen Blake Yancey's well received CCCC chair address in 2004, we are not too removed from the very nonmedia outlook embraced in 1963. "Sometimes, you know, you have a moment," Yancey begins her address. "For compositionists, of time and of this place, this moment—this moment *right* now—is like none other" (p. 62). Sometimes disciplines, writers, and texts have moments, and sometimes these items and moments, indeed, are like no others. As I have tried to show, one particular moment, 1963, was in fact like no other moment, but what made it unique has gone unnoticed until now. Our task today is to reimagine our status quos, to reconceptualize writing so that it includes, among other things, the notion of cool. Our task is to live up to the "moment," as Yancey requests. The positive composition studies response to Yancey's address might also remember her call for

> developing *a new curriculum for the 21st century*, a curriculum that carries forward the best of what we have created to date, that brings together the writing outside of school and that inside. This composition is located in a new vocabulary, a new set of practices, and a new set of outcomes; it will focus our research in new and provocative ways; it has as its goal the creation of thoughtful, informed, technologically adept writing publics. (pp. 72–73)

To do all that Yancey requests, and to do all of this in terms of supposedly "provocative" approaches like the one I have outlined in this book, we can more fully realize electronic writing in our work, our teaching, our research, and elsewhere. To do all of this, we can become cool in ways we haven't yet begun to imagine. To do any of this, we must reimagine ourselves and our work entirely.

NOTES

1. A more contemporary example—and one that continues this thought I introduce—can be found in Kid Koala and Money Mark's song "Carpal Tunnel Syndrome," which can be found on the *Funkungfusion* album (Ninja Tune, 1998). The song begins with the sampled sound of a typewriter clicking away. As further samples and music are juxtaposed into the composition, the typing merges with the music. The importance of this example is how it demonstrates that in non-classroom-based writing, tools are often used in a variety of ways to compose. That activity occurs in 1963 as well as 1998. How a writer *imagines* a tool's usage is what is important.

2. Steven Johnson's *Everything Bad Is Good for You* does an excellent job fleshing out the role media play in generating complex thinking, an act that occurs because of how media structures are internalized.

3. See http://www.boingboing.net, http://www.metafilter.com, and http://www.wayxy.org /links.

4. See also Wilbur Schramm, Kack Lyle, and Ithiel de Sola Pool's 1963 *The People Look at Educational Television: A Report of Nine Representative ETV Stations* (Stanford: Stanford UP) a study of television's affects on education. Prior to 1963, NCTE issued its 1961 report *Television and the Teaching of English* (New York: Appleton) an argument for television's pedagogical usage.

5. See the cover of Cecil Taylor's 1966 *Unit Structures* (Blue Note). An almost exact replication of Warhol's 1963 Marilyn paintings, it depicts rows of the same image in different silk screen colors.

6. Blue Note Records 2004 release *Blue Note Revisited* remixes the Byrd cover with new images of an attractive African-American woman leaning on an automobile foregrounded in the frame. The songs on the album are remixes of Blue Note recordings as well, making the album a fine example of cool writing visually and compositionally.

7. Following McLuhan's inclusion of the automobile as a media form in *Understanding Media*, I comment likewise.

8. For a specific contemporary example, see Gerald Graff's interview with the online publication Academic Commons, http://www.academiccommons.org/commons/interview/graff. Asked how he uses technology in his courses, Graff responds: "I love using e-mail for writing instruction. I can get right inside my students' sentences and paragraphs, stop them and ask them 'can you see a problem with this phrase?' or 'can you think of an alternative to this formulation?' or 'please improve on this sentence,' with an immediacy and turnaround speed that handing papers back with comments cannot begin to match." Graff repeats Winzeler's usage of the overhead, replacing it with e-mail.

WORKS CITED AND CONSULTED

Atwan, Robert. *Convergences: Message, Method, Medium.* Boston: Bedford–St. Martin's, 2004.

Braddock, Richard, Richard Lloyd-Jones, and Lowell Schoer. *Research in Written Composition.* Champaign, IL: NCTE, 1963.

Brookes, Malcolm, and Mina Hamilton. "Off the Record." *Industrial Design* (Mar. 1963): 78–81.

Burroughs, William S. *Nova Express.* New York: Grove, 1992 (1964).

Christensen, Francis. "A Generative Rhetoric of the Sentence." *College Composition and Communication* 14.3 (Oct. 1963): 155–61.

Davis, Diane D. *Breaking Up (at) Totality: A Rhetoric of Laughter.* Carbondale: Southern Illinois UP, 2000.

Derrida, Jacques. *Of Grammatology.* Baltimore: Johns Hopkins UP, 1974.

Engelbart, Douglas. "A Conceptual Framework for Augmenting Man's Intellect." *Vistas in Information Handling.* Washington, DC: Spartan, 1963.

Farris Thompson, Robert. *Flash of the Spirit: African and Afro-American Art and Philosophy.* New York: Vintage, 1983.

Frank, Thomas. *The Conquest of Cool: Business Culture, Counterculture, and the Rise of Hip Consumerism.* Chicago: U of Chicago P, 1997.

Graff, Gerald. "Hidden Intellectualism." *Pedagogy* 1.1 (Winter 2001): 21–36.

Handa, Carolyn. *Visual Rhetoric in a Digital World: A Critical Sourcebook.* Boston: Bedford–St. Martin's, 2004.

Hill, Charles, and Marguerite Helmers. *Defining Visual Rhetorics.* Mahwah, NJ: Erlbaum, 2004.

Johnson, Steven. *Everything Bad Is Good for You: How Today's Popular Culture Is Actually Making Us Smarter.* New York: Riverhead, 2005.

Kaprow, Allan. "Words: An Environment." *A Book of the Book: Some Words and Projections about the Book and Writing.* Ed. Jerome Rothenberg and Steven Clay. New York: Granary, 2000.

Kittler, Friedrich A. *Gramophone, Film, Typewriter.* Trans. Geoffrey Winthrop-Young and Michael Wutz. Stanford: Stanford UP, 1999.

Kitzhaber, Albert. "4C, Freshmen English, and the Future." *College Composition and Communication* (Oct. 1963): 129–38.

———. *Themes, Theories, and Therapy: The Teaching of Writing in College.* New York: McGraw, 1963.

Liu, Alan. *The Laws of Cool: Knowledge Work and the Culture of Information.* Chicago: U of Chicago P, 2004.

McComisky, Bruce. "Visual Rhetoric and the New Public Discourse." *JAC* 24.1 (2004): 187–206.

McCrimmon, James. *Writing with a Purpose.* Boston: Houghton, 1963.

McLuhan, Marshall. *The Gutenberg Galaxy.* Toronto: University of Toronto, 1962.

———. *Understanding Media.* New York: Signet, 1964.

McQuade, Donald, and Christine McQuade. *Seeing and Writing.* New York: Bedford–St. Martin's, 2000.

Manovich, Lev. *The Language of New Media.* Cambridge: MIT, 2000.

Marsh, Graham, Felix Cromey, and Glyn Callingham. *Blue Note: The Album Cover Art.* San Francisco: Chronicle, 1991.

Ong, Walter. "Wired for Sound: Teaching, Communications, and Technological Culture." *The Barbarian Within: And Other Fugitive Essays and Studies.* New York: MacMillan, 1962.

Rader, Dean. "Composition, Visual Cultures, and the Problems of Class." *College English* 67.6 (July 2005): 636–50.

Rheingold, Howard. *Virtual Reality.* New York: Touchstone, 1991.

Schramm, Wilbur, Kack Lyle, and Ithiel de Sola Pool. *The People Look at Educational Television: A Report of Nine Representative ETV Stations.* Stanford, CA: Stanford UP, 1963.

Sony. Advertisement. *American School and University* 36 (1964).

Stroupe, Craig. "Visualizing English: Recognizing the Hybrid Literacy of Visual and Verbal Authorship on the Web." *College English* 62.5 (May 2000): 607–32.

Sutherland, Ivan. *Sketchpad: A Man-Machine Graphical Communication System.* Diss. MIT, 1963.

Ulmer, Gregory L. *Internet Invention: From Literacy to Electracy.* New York: Longman, 2003.

Winzeler, Charlotte. "The Visual Written Image." *College Composition and Communication* 14.4 (Dec. 1963): 264–65.

Wysocki, Anne Francis. "Opening New Media to Writing: Openings and Justifications." *Writing New Media: Theory and Applications for Expanding the Teaching of Composition.* Ed. Anne Frances Wysocki, Johndan Johnson-Eilola, Cynthia Selfe, and Geoffrey Sirc. Logan: Utah State UP, 2004.

6

The Movement of Air, the Breath of Meaning: Aurality and Multimodal Composing

CYNTHIA L. SELFE

Participation means being able to speak in one's own voice, and thereby simultaneously to construct and express one's cultural identity through idiom and style.
> — NANCY FRASER, "Rethinking the Public Sphere"

. . . perhaps we can hear things we cannot see.
> — KRISTA RATCLIFFE, "Rhetorical Listening"

A turn to the auditory dimension is . . . more than a simple changing of variables. It begins as a deliberate decentering of a dominant tradition in order to discover what may be missing as a result of the traditional double reduction of vision as the main variable and metaphor.
> — DON IHDE, *Listening and Voice*

Anyone who has spent time on a college or university campus over the past few decades knows how fundamentally important students consider their sonic environments—the songs, music, and podcasts they produce and listen to; the cell phone conversations in which they immerse themselves; the headphones and Nanos that accompany them wherever they go; the thumper cars they use to turn the streets into concert stages; the audio blogs, video soundtracks, and mixes they compose and exchange with each other and share with anyone else who will listen.

Indeed, students' general penchant for listening to and producing sound can be eloquently ironic for English composition teachers faced with the deafening silence of a class invited to engage in an oral discussion about a written text. This phenomenon, however, may reveal as much about our profession's attitudes toward aurality and writing[1]—or the related history of these expressive modalities within our discipline—as it does about students' literacy values and practices. Sound, although it remains of central importance both to

From *College Composition and Communication* 60 (2009): 616-63.

students and to the population at large, is often undervalued as a compositional mode.

My argument in this article is that the history of writing in U.S. composition instruction, as well as its contemporary legacy, functions to limit our professional understanding of composing as a multimodal rhetorical activity and deprive students of valuable semiotic resources for making meaning.[2] As print assumed an increasingly privileged position in composition classrooms during the late nineteenth century and throughout the twentieth century, aurality was both subsumed by, and defined in opposition to, writing (Russell, "Institutionalizing" and *Writing*; Halbritter; B. McCorkle, "Harbingers"; Elbow, "What"), thus establishing and perpetuating a false binary between the two modalities of expression (Biber, "Spoken" and *Variation*; Tannen, "Oral" and *Spoken*), encouraging an overly narrow understanding of language and literacy (Kress, "English"), and allowing collegiate teachers of English composition to lose sight of the integrated nature of language arts. Further, I argue that a single-minded focus on print in composition classrooms ignores the importance of aurality and other composing modalities for making meaning and understanding the world. Finally, I suggest that the almost exclusive dominance of print literacy works against the interests of individuals whose cultures and communities have managed to maintain a value on multiple modalities of expression, multiple and hybrid ways of knowing, communicating, and establishing identity (Gilyard; Dunn, *Learning* and *Talking*; Royster, *Traces* and "First Voice"; Hibbitts; Powell; Lyons).

My ultimate goal in exploring aurality as a case in point is *not* to make an either/or argument—*not* to suggest that we pay attention to aurality *rather than* to writing. Instead, I suggest we need to pay attention to *both* writing *and* aurality, *and* other composing modalities, as well. I hope to encourage teachers to develop an increasingly thoughtful understanding of a whole range of modalities and semiotic resources in their assignments and then to provide students the opportunities of developing expertise with *all available means* of persuasion and expression, so that they can function as literate citizens in a world where communications cross geopolitical, cultural, and linguistic borders and are enriched rather than diminished by semiotic dimensionality.

What is at stake in this endeavor seems significant—both for teachers of English composition and for students. When teachers of composition limit the bandwidth of composing modalities in our classrooms and assignments, when we privilege print as *the only* acceptable way to make or exchange meaning, we not only ignore the history of rhetoric and its intellectual inheritance, but we also limit, unnecessarily, our scholarly understanding of semiotic systems (Kress, "English") and the effectiveness of our instruction for many students.

The stakes for students are no less significant—they involve fundamental issues of rhetorical sovereignty[3]: the rights and responsibilities that students have to identify their own communicative needs and to represent their own identities, to select the right tools for the communicative contexts within which they operate, and to think critically and carefully about the meaning that they and others compose. When we insist on print as *the* primary, and most formally acceptable, modality for composing knowledge, we usurp these rights and responsibilities on several important intellectual and social dimensions, and, unwittingly, limit students' sense of rhetorical agency to the bandwidth of our own interests and imaginations.[4]

By way of making this argument, I begin by recounting a very brief, and necessarily selective, history of aurality, focusing on the role it came to assume in college composition classrooms from the mid-nineteenth century onward. I then discuss some of the ways in which aurality has *persisted* in English composition classrooms in the midst of a culture saturated by the written word. Finally, I suggest how digital communication environments and digital multimodal texts have encouraged some teachers of composition to rediscover aurality as a valuable modality of expression.

The irony of making an argument about aurality in print is not lost on me, nor, I suspect, will it be on most other readers of this article. Indeed, it is very much the point of what I try to say in the following pages. Thus, throughout this article I have included references to four sound essays composed by students at Michigan Tech, the University of Louisville, and The Ohio State University. I consider these pieces a crucial part of my argument about valuing aurality as a composing modality. Hence, I encourage readers to go to <http://people.cohums.ohio-state.edu/selfe2/ccc/>, listen to these sound essays, read what their authors have said about composing them.

Aural Composing: Sample 1, Sonya Borton's *Legacy of Music*

At this point, I ask readers to leave this printed text and go to <http://people .cohums.ohio-state.edu/selfe2/ccc/>, where they can listen to Sonya Borton's autobiographical essay, *Legacy of Music*, in which she tells listeners about the musical talents of various members of her Kentucky family. In relating her narrative, Borton weaves a richly textured fabric of interviews, commentary, instrumental music, and song to support her thesis that a love of music represents an important legacy passed down from parents to children within her family.

A Short History of Aurality in College Composition Classrooms

Theorizing the role of aurality in composition classrooms is not a task that comes easily to most composition teachers. Since the late nineteenth century, writing has assumed such a dominant and central position in our professional thinking that its role as the major instructional focus goes virtually uncontested, accepted as common sense. As Patricia Dunn (*Talking*) writes, it seems absurd even to

> question an over-emphasis on writing in a discipline whose raison d'etre is, like no other discipline, for and about writing. That common-sense assumption, however, may be what makes it so difficult for us in Composition to see word-based pedagogies in any way other than supportive of learning. (150)

Composition teachers, she concludes, have come to believe "writing is not simply *one* way of knowing; it is *the* way" (15). *Doxa*, or common belief, however, always maintains its strongest hold in the absence of multiple historical and cultural perspectives. Although writing has come to occupy a privileged position in composition classrooms—and in the minds of many compositionists—historical accounts by such scholars as David Russell ("Institutionalizing" and *Writing*), James Berlin, Nan Johnson, and Michael Halloran confirm this situation as both relatively recent and contested.

In the first half of the eighteenth century, for example, collegiate education in America was fundamentally shaped by Western classical traditions and was oral in its focus. As Michael Halloran notes, within this curriculum students learned to read, speak, and write both classical language and English through recitation—the standard pedagogical approach for all subjects—as well as through a wide range of oratorical performances, debates, orations, and declamations, both inside formal classes and in extracurricular settings such as literary societies. The goal of these activities was to build students' general skill in public speaking, rather than encouraging specialized inquiry as mediated by the written word.

This old model of oratorical education, David Russell notes ("Institutionalizing" and *Writing*), was linked to the cultural values, power, and practices of privileged families in the colonies who considered facility in oral, face-to-face encounters to be the hallmark of an educated class. The male children of these families were expected to help lead the nation in the role of statesmen, enter the judicial and legal arena, or become ministers. For heirs of these families, as Susan Miller has added, little instruction in writing was needed other than practice in penmanship. Their lives were imbricated with oral communication practices—speeches, debates, sermons—and such individuals had to be able to speak, as gentlemen, in contexts of power. Universities were charged with preparing these future leaders to assume their roles and responsibilities.

During the latter half of the nineteenth century, however, universities began to change in response to the rapid rise of industrial manufacturing, the explosion of scientific discoveries, and the expansion of the new country's international trade. These converging trends accumulated with increasing tendential force and resulted in profound cultural transformations that placed an increasing value on specialization and professionalization, especially within the emerging middle class. Such changes required both new approaches to education and a new kind of secular university, one designed to meet the needs of individuals involved in science, commerce, and manufacturing. It was within this new collegiate context that the first departments of English were able to form, primarily by forging identities for themselves as units that educated a range of citizens occupied with business and professional affairs.[5] In response to these cultural trends, Russell has observed, "the modern project of purification, the drive toward specialization, made old rhetoric impossible" ("Institutionalizing" 40).[6]

Instead, departments of English focused on preparing professionals whose work, after graduation, would increasingly rely on writing, as Russell explains—articles, reports, memoranda and communications, "texts as objects to be silently studied, critiqued, compared, appreciated, and evaluated" (*Writing* 4–5). Supporting this work were technological innovations—improved printing presses, typewriters, and pens, among others—that combined with innovations in business operations, efficient manufacturing techniques, and science to lend added importance to writing as a cultural code, both within the new university and outside it (Russell, "Institutionalizing").

As they emerged in this context, departments of English sought increasingly modern approaches to changing communication practices and values—hoping to distance themselves from the old-school education in oratory, which was considered increasingly less valuable as a preparation for the world of manufacturing, business, and science, and to link their curricula to more pragmatic concerns of professionalism in the modern university. The new departments of English taught their studies in the vernacular—rather than in Greek or Latin—and separated themselves from a continued focus on oratory, religion, and the classics, which became devalued as historical or narrowly defined studies. These newly emergent departments of English focused primarily on their ability to provide instruction in written composition. During this brief period in the latter third of the nineteenth century, writing became one of a very few subjects required for a university course of study (Berlin; Russell, *Writing*).[7] Charles William Eliot, who became president of Harvard in 1869, noted that instruction in writing—distinguished by a natural, uninflated style—was not only desirable for students at the new university but also necessary for the success of a national culture based on economic development, modern industrial processes, and trade (359).[8]

Scholars have described, in various ways, the historic shift that occurred during the last half of the nineteenth century, from an older style of education based on declamation, oratory, forensics, and delivery[9] to a new style of education based primarily on the study and analysis of written texts, both classical and contemporary[10]—and the production of such texts. Perhaps the most succinct statement, however, and the one most directly to the point for this history of aurality in college composition classrooms is Ronald Reid's (1959) comment:

> The most significant change was rhetoric's abandonment of oratory. The advanced courses, commonly known during this period as "themes and forensics," consisted almost exclusively of written work. . . . The beginning course, too, gave much practice in writing, none in public speaking. (253)

Although attention to aurality persisted in various ways into the twentieth century, it was clearly on the wane in English studies.[11] By 1913, one year before teachers of speech seceded from the National Council of Teachers of English, John Clapp was moved to ask in an article published by the *English Journal*,

> Is there a place in College English classes for exercises in reading, or talking, or both? The question has been raised now and then in the past, almost always to receive a negative answer, particularly from English departments. (21)

The general response of the profession to these questions, Clapp noted, was that "for the purposes of the intellectual life, which college graduates are to lead, talking is of little importance, and writing of very great importance" (23).

This brief history of composition as a discipline can be productively viewed within a larger historical frame as well—specifically that of the rise of science (and its progeny, technology) in the West before, during, and immediately after the Enlightenment, from the seventeenth to the nineteenth centuries. At the heart of science as a rational project was the belief that humans could unlock the secrets of nature using systematic observations and precisely recorded written measurements. In a world attuned to the systematic methodologies of science, the recorded word, the visual trace of evidence, provided proof, and observations rendered in the visual medium of print revealed truth—Newton's notes on mathematical proofs, Franklin's written descriptions of experiments, Darwin's Beagle diaries. If the scientific revolution rested on the understanding that seeing was believing, it also depended on writing—and after the mid-fifteenth century—on printing as a primary means of recording, storing, and retrieving important information and discoveries. Later, with the application of scientific methods to a wide range of legal, military, industrial, and manufacturing practices, the complex network of cultural formations that reinforced the privileged role of visual and print information.

From the seventeenth to the nineteenth centuries, then, as the power of vision and print gradually waxed in the context of a university education, the power of aurality gradually waned, although this trend was, at different times and places, far from even or immediate in its effects. U.S. colleges and universities, for instance, lagged slightly behind those in Europe for a time in this regard, but education within the two cultures followed the same general trajectory. As Hibbitts notes, it was during this period that "the social and intellectual status of vision gradually undermined the position still occupied by the other forms of sensory experience in the Western tradition" (2.25).

In educational institutions and, later, departments of English and programs of English composition, the effects of this shift were far reaching. Writing and reading, for example, became separated from speech in educational contexts and became largely silent practices for students in classroom settings. Written literature, although including artifacts of earlier aural forms (Platonic dialogues, Shakespearean monologues, and poetry, for instance), was studied through silent reading and subjected to written analysis, consumed by the eye rather than the ear.[12] The disciplined practices of silent writing, reading, and observation that characterized collegiate education became normalized and, importantly, linked to both class and race. In educational contexts, Hibbitts observes, "[t]he most important meta-lesson became, as it today remains, how to sit, write, and read in contented quiet" (2.25). It was through such changes that writing became the focus of a specialized academic education delivered primarily to, and by, privileged white males.

If print became increasingly important within the new U.S. universities in the nineteenth and early twentieth centuries, however, aurality retained some of its power and reach in other locations, where individuals and groups were forced to acquire both written and aural literacies by a range of informal means or through an educational system that retained a fundamental integration of the language arts. Many women during this period, for instance, were discouraged from pursuing a university education or had less time and money for such a luxury. Blacks, Hispanics and Latinos/as, and American Indians, in addition, were, for prolonged periods, persecuted for learning to read and write (Gere; Royster, *Traces*; Richardson), educated outside the schools that males attended, and denied access to the white colleges and universities.[13] Although individuals from these groups learned—through various means and, often, with great sacrifice—to deploy writing skillfully and in ways that resisted the violence of oppression, many also managed to retain a deep and nuanced appreciation for aural traditions as well: in churches and sacred ceremonies, in storytelling and performance contexts, in poetry and song.

The history of slavery in the United States, for example, shaped the educational opportunities of black citizens, many of whom survived and resisted the violence and oppression in their lives by developing literacy values and practices—often, but certainly not exclusively, aural in nature—that remained invisible to whites and that were, often because of this fact, highly effective. Although many of the legal prohibitions against teaching blacks to read and write were lifted after the Civil War, de facto barriers of racism continued to function. Many black citizens were denied access to schools with adequate resources and others had to abandon their own formal education to help their families survive the economic hardships that continued to characterize the lives of blacks in both the North and the South (Hibbitts). And although black citizens, under adverse conditions, found their own routes for acquiring written literacy—in historically black colleges and universities, in churches, literary societies, homes, segregated public schools—artifacts of this historical period persisted in black communities in verbal games, music, vocal performance, storytelling, and other "vernacular expressive arts" (Richardson 680). These aural traces identify communities of people who have survived and thrived, not only by deploying but also by resisting the literacy practices of a dominant culture that continued to link the printed word and silent reading, so closely to formal education, racism, and the exercise power by whites (Banks; Smitherman, "CCCC"; Richardson; Royster, "First Voice"; Mahiri). "[T]he written word," notes Ashraf Rushdy, in part "represents the processes used by racist white American institutions to proscribe and prescribe African American subjectivity."[14]

Hispanic/Latino communities, too, while valuing a wide range of literacy practices in their cultural, familial, and intellectual lives (Guerra; Guerra and Farr; Kells, Balester, and Villanueva; Gutierrez, Baquedano-Lopez, and Alvarez; Cintron; Villanueva; Trejo; Limon; and Ruiz) also managed to retain, to varying extents and in a range of different ways, an investment in collective storytelling, cuentos, corridos, and other aural practices developed within a long—and continuing—history of linguistic, educational, economic, and cultural discrimination. Contributing to the persistence of these traditions has been the history of U.S. imperialism and discrimination in Texas, California, and other border states; the troubled history of bilingual education in this country; the devaluing of Latin American, Puerto Rican, and Mexican Spanish speakers; and the persistence of the English-Only movements in public education. Given this history of discrimination, as Hibbitts points out, Hispanic citizens often find themselves "drawn and sometimes forced back into the soundscapes of their own ethnic communities" (2.43), while simultaneously deploying a wide range of written discourses—skillfully and, sometimes, in ways that productively resist mainstream discourses (Kells, Balester, and Villanueva; Reyes and Halcon; Cintron).

Many American Indians, too, have managed to sustain a value on aurality—as well as on writing and a range of other modalities of expression—as means of preserving their heritage and identities: in public speaking, ceremonial contexts, shared stories, poetry, and song (Clements; Blaeser; Keeling; Evers and Toelken), although as both Scott Lyons and Malea Powell point out, the diversity of tribal histories and the "discursive intricacies" and complexity of Native American's literacy practices and values remain misunderstood, under-examined in published scholarship, and prone to painful and simplistic stereotypes. The aural literacy practices that many tribal members have valued and continue to value—along with the skillful and critical use of other modalities—serve as complex cultural and community-based responses to the imperialism of the "Euroamerican mainstream" (Powell 398). Such practices form part of the story of survival and resistance that American Indians have composed for themselves during the occupation of their homeland and the continuing denigration of their culture as their battles for sovereignty continue.

In sum, the increasingly limited role of aurality within U.S. English and composition programs during the last half of the nineteenth and the twentieth centuries was intimately tied to the emerging influence of writing as the primary mode of formal academic work, of commercial exchange and record-keeping, and of public and professional expression. This trend, influenced by the rise of manufacturing and science, as well as the growing cultural value on professionalism, was instantiated in various ways and to varying extents in courses and universities around the country and enacted variously by groups and individuals according to their different cultures, literacy values, and practices. The trend was, nevertheless, consistent in its general direction and tendential force. In formal educational contexts, writing and reading increasingly became separated from speech and were understood as activities to be enacted, for the most part, in silence.

In this discussion, I take an important lesson from colleagues like Jacqueline Royster ("First Voice"), Geneva Smitherman (*Talkin'*), Adam Banks, Scott Lyons, and Malea Powell, who point out the serious risks, when discussing the oral traditions and practices of people of color, to cede written English as "somehow the exclusive domain of Whites" (Banks 70). The work of these scholars reminds us in persuasive and powerful terms that people of color have historically deployed a wide range of written discourses in masterful and often powerfully oppositional ways while retaining a value on traditional oral discourses and practices. My goal in this article, then, is not to suggest that teachers focus on *either* writing *or* aurality, but rather that they respect and encourage students to deploy *multiple* modalities in skillful ways—written, aural, visual—and that they model a respect for and understanding of the various roles each modality can play in human expression, the formation of individual and group identity, and meaning making. In this work, the efforts of the scholars such as those cited above as well as attention to historical and contemporary discursive practices of blacks, Native Americans, Hispanics, and other peoples of color can help direct our thinking and lead our profession forward in productive ways.

AUDIO COMPOSING: SAMPLE 2: ELISA NORRIS'S "LITERACY = IDENTITY: CAN YOU SEE ME?"

At this point, please go to <http://people.cohums.ohio-state.edu/selfe2/ccc/> and listen to Elisa Norris's audio poem, "Literacy = Identity: Can You See Me?" which opens with a school bell, a teacher reading a classroom roll, and her own personal call and response, "Elisa Norris, Elisa Norris . . . is she absent today? No. Do you see her? No." In this poetic text, an aural variation on a conventional writing assignment, Norris layers music, voice, and poetic images to create a composition that asks listeners to acknowledge her presence and the complex dimensions of her cultural identity. Through the sonic materiality of her own voice, Norris invites listeners to enter her life, and with her to resist the cultural erasure and racial stereotypes that shape her experience.

ARTIFACTS OF AURALITY

Tracing how aurality became subsumed by print within composition classrooms in the United States during the nineteenth century, however, provides us only one part of a complex historical picture. Another, and perhaps as important, part of the picture involves investigating how and why aurality has *persisted* in English composition classrooms, in the midst of a culture saturated by print.

From one perspective, this process can be understood as a kind of cultural and intellectual *remediation*.[15] Within the specialized cultural location of the college classroom in the United States, aural practices became gradually, but increasingly, subsumed by academic writing, which was presented as the improved medium of formal communication characterizing new U.S. universities. At the same time, academic writing often made its case for superiority by referring backwards to characteristics of aurality, which was never entirely erased. By the end of the nineteenth century, for instance, as scholars such as Ben McCorkle ("Harbingers") has noted, the academic focus on the production and delivery of *aural texts* was increasingly to be mediated by *written textbooks* on delivery and elocution. English studies faculty still lectured and students still engaged in some oral activities, but within the context of the new university, instruction was increasingly mediated by writing and printed materials—published textbooks, in written assignments, collected and printed lectures, written examinations for students.

Throughout the twentieth century, too, English composition faculty continued to talk about oral language, but primarily in comparison with written language. They continued to make reference to the oral qualities of language, but often metaphorically and in the service of writing instruction and in the study of written texts (the *voice* of the writer, the *tone* of an essay, and the *rhythm* of sentences) (Yancey; Elbow, "What"). Similarly, although students continued to have opportunities for oral performance, they were carefully circumscribed and limited to conferences, presentations, and class discussions focused on writing.[16] And although writing assignments in the twentieth century sometimes focused on topics that touched on aurality and oral performances—popular music, for example—students were expected to *write* their analyses of songs, to focus on *written* lyrics, or to use music as a prompt for *written* composition. In scholarly arenas, scholars studied the history of rhetoric but considered orality and the canon of delivery (McCorkle, "Harbingers") to be of interest primarily as a historical artifact. Even rhetoric scholars whose work was designed to focus attention on the discursive practices and "voices" of long-ignored groups—blacks, Latinos/as, Native Americans, women—*wrote* about these oral practices.[17] The majority of English composition scholars who spoke about their work at professional conferences delivered written papers that they wrote first and, only then, read. By the end of the twentieth century, the ideological privileging of writing was so firmly established that it had become almost fully naturalized. The program of the 1998 Watson Conference, for example, included Beverly Moss as a featured speaker. Moss, who had fractured the elbow of her right arm, delivered a talk about oral language practices in black churches. She introduced her presentation by mentioning her own struggle to prepare a talk without being able to write her text first. Moss's presentation and delivery were superb—cogent and insightful—but her framing comments highlighted how difficult and unusual it was for her, and many other scholars, to deliver an oral presentation without a written text.

Writing as Not-Speech

A brief examination of some aural artifacts in English composition classrooms during the twentieth century can be instructive in helping readers understand the ways in which attention to orality has persisted in U.S. composition classrooms.

By the time the Conference on College Composition and Communication was formed in 1949, attention to students' writing in English departments, with a few brief exceptions, had almost completely eclipsed attention to aural composition. Although the professional focus on speech was revived somewhat after scholars like Lev Vygotsky published his groundbreaking work on the developmental relationship between speech and writing in 1962, many composition scholars—concerned with staking out the territory of the new field and identifying the intellectual and professional boundaries of the nascent discipline—chose to focus on the differences between writing and speech, to define the work of composition classrooms (i.e., writing and the teaching of writing) in opposition to talking, speech, and aurality.[18] This scholarly effort continued throughout the 1960s, 1970s, and early 1980s, until informed by the work of linguists like Douglas Biber ("Spoken" and *Variation*) and Deborah Tannen ("Oral" and *Spoken*), many in the profession came to recognize that writing and speaking actually shared many of the same characteristics and did not exist in the essentialized, dichotomous relationship that had been constructed by scholars.

During the 1960s and 1970s, however, many compositionists defined writing primarily in terms of how it differed from speech. Motivating some of this activity, at least in part, were two converging trends. The first, well underway at this point, was the movement away from current-traditional rhetoric (which posited knowledge as pre-existing language, as external, as discoverable, and as verifiable) and toward a social-epistemic understanding of rhetoric (which posited knowledge as socially constructed and created in, and through, the social uses of language) (Berlin). During roughly the same period, teachers of composition were also attempting to digest poststructuralist theories of language, which occasionally proved less than directly accessible. In his 1976 work *Of Grammatology*, for example, Jacques Derrida pointed out the fallacy of immediacy and questioned the notion of coherent, self-presentation of meaning in *spoken* discourse, and he urged close attention to *writing* as the ground for understanding the active play of difference in language and the shifting nature of signification. Although Derrida's aim was *not* to reverse the historical hierarchy of speech over writing, but rather to call into question logocentricity itself, many composition scholars connected his focus to the field's emerging understanding of writing as both social and epistemic. Influenced not only by these scholarly streams of thought, but by the overdetermined forces of specialization that continued to shape the field within the modern university, compositionists turned their scholarly attention and pedagogical efforts, increasingly, away from speech and toward writing, defining the figure of writing against the ground of speech.[19]

In 1984, for instance, Sarah Liggett annotated fifty-one articles on "the relationship between speaking and writing" (354) and suggested another nineteen pieces for "related reading." The majority of these works, not surprisingly, concluded that the aural language practices of talking and speaking were related to writing in various ways and at various levels, but also that they differed significantly from writing in terms of important features (Emig; Barritt and Kroll; Connors, "Differences"; Farrell; Halpern; Hirsch). Further, in a number of cases, scholars claimed that writing posed more intellectual challenges to students than speech or oral composing, that writing was more sophisticated or complex than speech (Sawyer). Many of these works associated speaking and talking with less reflective, more "haphazard" communication

(Snipes) and with popular culture, while writing was considered "inherently more self-reliant" (Emig 353), a "more deliberate mode of expression" and "inherently more intellectual" (Newman and Horowitz 160). In their 1965 article in *College Composition and Communication*, John Newman and Milton Horowitz concluded:

> Writing and speaking clearly represent different strata of the person. Although both functions funnel thought processes, speaking evidences more feeling, more emotive expression and more "first thoughts that come to mind." While writing is more indicative of the intellectualized, rational, and deliberative aspects of the person. (164)

Other scholars (Dyson; Bereiter and Scardemalia; Carroll; Furner; Lopate; Snipes; Zoellner) explored speech and talking as auxiliary activities that could help students during the process of writing. The ultimate goal of these activities, however, was always a written composition or a literate writer. The profession's bias against aural forms of expression was also evident in the work of scholars who implied that students' reliance on the conventions of oral discourse resulted in the presence of problematic features in their written work (Cayer and Sacks; Collins and Williamson; Robinson; Snipes; Shaughnessy). In 1973, for example, Wilson Snipes investigated the hypothesis that "orientation to an oral culture has helped cause a gradual decrease in student ability to handle written English in traditionally acceptable ways" (156), citing "haphazard punctuation," "loose rambling style," and "diminutive vocabulary" (159), writing that is "superficial, devoid of subtle distinctions," and thought that remains "fixed in a larval state" (160).

Despite the scholarly work of linguists (Biber, "Spoken" and *Variation*; Tannen, "Oral" and *Spoken*) who identified a broad range of overlapping elements that writing and speaking shared as composing modalities, the bias toward writing continued to grow in composition studies throughout the twentieth century. By 1994, Peter Elbow sounded a wondering note at the profession's continued efforts to separate voice from writing:

> What interests me is how . . . most of us are unconscious of how deeply our culture's version of literacy has involved as decision to keep voice out of writing, to maximize the difference between speaking and writing—to prevent writers from even using those few crude markers that could capture more of the subtle and not so subtle semiotics of speech. Our version of literacy requires people to distance their writing behavior further from their speaking behavior than the actual modalities require. ("What" 8)

THE SILENCE OF VOICE

Another persistent artifact of aurality in the composition classroom has been the reliance on metaphors of *voice* in writing. In Kathleen Yancey's germinal collection *Voices on Voice*, for instance, the bibliography annotates 102 sources that inform professional thinking about voice. Yet Yancey and Elbow, the authors of this bibliography, describe it as "incomplete" because " 'voice' leads to everything" (315). The treatment of voice in *College Composition and Communication* and *College English* attests to that statement: between 1962 and 1997, in articles or citations to other scholarly works, voice was explored in connection with feminist theory (Finke), rhetorical theory (Shuster); personal expression, identity, and character (Gibson; Faigley, "Judging"; Stoehr); the writing process (Winchester); style and mimesis (P. Brooks); academic writing (Bartholomae); race, gender, and power (Royster, "First Voice"; Smitherman, "CCCC's Role"; Wiget, Hennig); technology (Eldred), political dissent (Murray), advertisements (Sharpe), public and private discourses (Robson), and authenticity and multiplicity (Fulwiler), and evangelical discourse (Hashimoto), among many other subjects. Between 1972 and 1998, ten books with *voice* in their titles were reviewed in *CCC*.[20]

What these works on composition had in common, however, was less an understanding of embodied, physical human *voice* than a persistent use of the metaphorical language that remediated voice *as a characteristic of written prose*. As Kathleen Yancey outlined the scope of work on voice in 1994,

> [W]e use the metaphor of voice to talk generally around issues in writing: about both the act of writing and its agent, the writer, and even about the reader, and occasionally about the presence in the text of the writer.... Sometimes we use voice to talk specifically about what and how a writer knows, about the capacity of a writer through "voice" to reveal (and yet be dictated by) the epistemology of a specific culture. Sometimes we use voice to talk in neo-Romantic terms about the writer discovering an authentic self and then deploying it in text. (vii)

AURALITY IN POPULAR CULTURE

Although aurality continued to take a back seat to writing throughout the twentieth century in collegiate composition classrooms—especially in terms of the texts that students were asked to produce—teachers continued to recognize its importance in the lived experience of young people. In 1968, for instance, Jerry Walker wrote of his concern that English majors were asked to focus almost exclusively on printed works of "literary heritage" (634) that provided youths little help in dealing with the problems of the Cold War era. Given students' concerns about "alienation, war, racial strife, automation, work, and civil disobedience" (635), Walker noted, they often found the texts of television and radio, which involved the aural presentation of information, to resonate more forcefully than the written texts of historical eras. Walker pointed to the successes of teachers who focused on popular culture and who used aural texts and popular music as foci for classroom assignments. Similar suggestions for assignments were put forward in subsequent years—with assignments that examined the music of the Beatles (Carter) and Billie Holiday (Zaluda); popular music in general (Kroeger); and the writing associated with popular music (Lutz)—for instance, the liner notes that accompany albums and CDs.

In general, however, the aural text was not the focus of these scholars. Music and communication in mass media (especially radio, film, newspapers) was considered part of popular culture, and teachers of English composition—influenced by the biases of the belletristic tradition (Trimbur; Paine) that shaped composition as a discipline—distinguished such texts from academic discourse, dismissing them as part of the "philistine culture" outside the walls of the university (George and Trimbur 694).[21] Although most composition teachers in the twentieth century were willing to accept the draw of popular culture, the goal of the composition classroom remained, at some level, as Adams Sherman Hill had described it in the nineteenth century: to "arm" students (Hill, qtd. in Paine 292), to "inoculate" (Paine 282) them against the infectious effects of popular culture and various forms of mass communication, to encourage them to turn to the written texts of geniuses from the past as a means of discovering their "real selves" (Hill, qtd. in Paine, p. 282) and "*resisting* mass culture" (Paine 283). Although it was permissible to lure students into English classes with the promise of focusing on popular culture or music, most composition teachers agreed it was best to approach such texts as objects of study, analysis, interpretation, and, perhaps most importantly, critique (Sirc).

As representative pieces of popular—or low—culture, aural texts were not generally recognized as appropriately intellectual vehicles for composing meaning in composition classrooms. Only writing held that sinecure, and the goal of composition teachers' assignments continued to be excellence in reading and writing. Robert Heilman summarized this view succinctly in 1970, within the context of a discussion about the use of electronic media in composition classrooms:

> the substitution of electronic experience [music, film, radio] in the classroom, for the study of the printed page is open to question. It tends to reduce the amount of reading by creating a thirst for the greater immediate excitement of sound and light. The classroom is for criticism; the critical experience is valuable; and it cannot be wise to attenuate it by the substitution of sensory experience which the age already supplies in excess. (242–43)

Despite this common characterization, some pioneering teachers during the 1960s, 1970s, and 1980s continued to experiment with more contemporary texts and assignments that involved aural components. Lisa Ede and John Lofty, for instance, suggested incorporating oral histories into composition classrooms. Both authors, however, also considered the goal and the final step of such assignments to be written essays that quoted from conversations with interview subjects. Although aurality was acknowledged and deployed as a way of engaging students and even a way of investigating various phenomena, it was generally ignored as a compositional modality.

AURALITY AND PEDAGOGY

A value on aurality—in limited and constrained situations—also persisted in the context of certain classroom practices throughout the twentieth century. One strikingly persistent thread of work, for instance, focused on teachers and using audio recordings to convey their responses to student papers (G. Olson; Sommers; Mellen and Sommers; Anson; Sipple). In such articles, faculty talked about the fact that their taped oral responses to students' written work allowed for a clearer acknowledgment of the "rhetorical nature" of response to a piece of writing, because remarks could be "more detailed and expansive" (Mellen and Sommers 11–12) and unfold across time. As Jeff Sommers noted, the sound of an instructor's voice seemed at once more immediate and more personal; the aural nature of the comments were able to give students a "'walking tour'" through their texts, as if a reader were conversing with them (186). Interestingly, however, none of these authors mentioned some of the more basic affordances of aural feedback—that speech conveys a great deal of meaning through pace, volume, rhythm, emphasis, and tone of voice as well as through words themselves.[22]

Teachers continued to provide other aspects of their instruction orally, as well. Diana George, for example, explored the use of audio taping in the composition classroom as a way of recording the texts of small-group interactions and responding to these texts with her own suggestions, observations, and remarks. George noted that this approach provided her insight about the problems that such groups encountered when discussing each other's written papers, as well as the work that small groups accomplished when a teacher was not present. This scholarship deserves attention because it is one of the relatively rare instances in which students' oral exchanges were considered *as semiotic texts* that were composed and could be studied for the meaning they contained.

As much of this scholarship suggests, however, while students were expected to engage in discussion and oral group work in many composition classrooms, their speaking was located within specific contexts and occasions and was expected, generally, to happen on cue. Such occasions were limited in many classrooms and often were not wholly satisfying to teachers. In 1974, for instance, Gerald Pierre noted that well-meaning teachers who depended on lecturing to convey information often short-circuited their own attempts to generate class discussions, turning them into "oral quizzes, guess-my-conclusion games, or bristling silences" (306).

In an attempt to address such concerns, some teachers turned to oral presentations as venues for student talk within the classroom. Mary Saunders, in a 1985 article in *College Composition and Communication*, described a sequence of assignments in which students were asked to make short oral presentations abstracted from drafts of their written research papers and then to revise their papers based on the feedback they received from classmates. The primary goal of these presentations, of course, was to improve students' *written* work, to help them "write better papers" (358). Similarly the aural work accomplished within teacher-student conferences (Schiff; North; Arbur; A. Rose; Memering) and writing-center appointments (North; Clark) was subordinated almost wholly to the end goal of writing. For students, the primary reason for speaking and listening in composition classrooms was identified as improved writing.

In this context, it is interesting to note that aurality also continued as a key form of *faculty* teaching and testing practices.[23] Lecturing, for instance, remained a relatively popular form of teaching in many composition classrooms through the end of the century and beyond—despite a growing agreement that classrooms should be centered around students' opportunities to practice composing strategies rather than teachers' chances to talk about such strategies (Finkel; Dawe and Dornan; Pierre; Lindemann).[24]

The continued use of the lecture as one method of conducting instruction foregrounds some of the complications and contradictions of the profession's stance toward aurality and writing: although students have been encouraged to focus on the production of *written* texts and such texts have increasingly become the standard of production for composition classes, many teachers have continued to impart information through *oral* lectures, often expending a great deal of time to craft and deliver effective oral texts. In this respect, as every teacher and student understands, power and aurality are closely linked. Indeed, the enactment of authority, power, and status in composition classes is expressed, in part, *through* aurality: how much one is allowed to talk and under what conditions. This phenomenon has been mapped as well in teachers' aural evaluations of both undergraduate and graduate students, which, although not generally considered as important as the evaluation of *written* work, has remained nonetheless persistent. For undergraduates, for instance, such evaluations have continued to be conducted in highly ritualized one-on-one conferences in which students are expected to explain the purposes, audiences, and approaches taken in their written projects (Schiff; North; Arbur; Rose; Memering). For graduate students, oral questioning and disputation has persisted in candidacy exams, as well as in more public defenses of theses and dissertations. To pass such exams, graduate students are expected to succeed both in producing a written text and defending their ideas in disputational aural exchanges, forms rooted historically in verbal argument and display (Ong, *Fighting*; Connors, "Teaching").

Aurality and Silenced Voices

It is important to note that attention to aurality has also persisted in the work of scholars who focused on the rhetorical contributions and histories of marginalized or underrepresented groups. Individual scholars such as Jacqueline Jones Royster (*Traces* and "First Voice") and Beverly Moss, Scott Lyons and Malea Powell, Anne Ruggles Gere and Geneva Smitherman ("CCCC's Role"), among others, for example, brought to bear an understanding of aurality—and its complex relationship to written literacy—informed by the historical richness of their own families, communities, and experiences, and trained it on the complex problems associated with race, class, and gender inequities, and the exercise of power in education and English composition.

This richly textured scholarship—which holds great value for the profession and our larger culture—contributes, in particular, to resisting simplistic binary splits between writing and aurality that have informed instruction in mainstream college composition classrooms during much of the twentieth century, despite linguistic evidence suggesting the erroneous nature of such a division. At the same time, this work acknowledges aurality as an important way of knowing and making meaning for many people in this country— especially those for whom, historically, higher education has often been part of a system of continued domination and oppression. Royster, for example, in her 1996 *College Composition and Communication* article "When the First Voice You Hear Is Not Your Own" and in her later book *Traces in the Stream: Literacy and Social Change among African American Women*, explored the cumulative and multiplied power of her own authentic voice and those of other African American women—and the responses of a racist culture to these voices. In doing this work, Royster outlines a powerful argument for aural discourses (as well as, and in combination with, written discourses and hybrid forms of communication) that take up the challenge of border crossing and political action to confront the insidious "cross-cultural misconduct" (32) so frequently characterizing racism, especially in educational contexts.

The work of Malea Powell and Scott Lyons, too, has helped compositionists complicate the profession's "uncritical acceptance of the oral/literate split" (Powell 397) which helps mask the complexity, range, and depth of Native American texts and discourses, and perpetuate the stereotypes that continue to sustain racism. Native Americans, these authors point out, have employed both oral and written discourses as tactics of "survivance" (Powell 428), while acknowledging the many problems associated with communicating in discursive systems—academic writing, legal writing, treaties, legislative venues—that have been "compromised" (Lyons) as part of a racist, colonial mainstream culture. As Lyons reminds us, because writing for many Native American people is bound so intimately to the project of white colonization and domination, and oral discourse so often supports uncritical and racist stereotyping, "rhetorical sovereignty" (449) is a centrally important feature of Native American self-determination.

AURAL COMPOSING, SAMPLE 3: WENDY WOLTERS HINSHAW'S *YELLING BOY*

At this point, please go to <http://people.cohums.ohio-state.edu/selfe2/ccc/> and listen to Wendy Wolters Hinshaw's *Yelling Boy*, a reflective examination of her interaction with an undergraduate student in a section of first-year composition. The reflection, a painfully frank and honest look at Wolters Hinshaw's own teaching is rendered in stark terms—no music and no soundmarks of the classroom,[25] no chalk sounds on a blackboard, no scraping of chairs as a class session ends, no rustling of papers or announcements of assignments due. This piece, a memory of what took place in a "dirty grey office," is focused on a single exchange that happened across a "small teacher's desk" and takes three minutes for Wolters Hinshaw to recount in its entirety.

AURALITY AND DIGITAL ENVIRONMENTS FOR COMPOSING

As many contemporary scholars have pointed out—among them Graff, Gee, Brandt ("Accumulating" and *Literacy*), Barton and Hamilton, Powell, Royster ("First Voice"), Hawisher and Selfe—we cannot hope to fully understand literacy practices or the values associated with such practices unless, and until, we can also understand the complex cultural ecology that serves as their context. Such ecologies both shape peoples' literacy practices and values and are shaped by them in an ongoing duality of structuration (Giddens). In the United States, then—especially at the end of the twentieth century and the beginning of the twenty-first century—we cannot hope to fully understand aural or written literacy practices and values without also understanding something about digital and networked contexts for communication, among many other factors.

Although digital environments have had many different effects at local, regional, national, and international levels (Castells, *End; Power; Rise*), some of the most profound and far-reaching changes have involved communication forms, practices, values, and patterns. Although the relationship between digital technologies and literacy remains complexly articulated with existing social and cultural formations, and digital environments continue to be unevenly distributed along axes of power, class, and race, it is clear that the speed and extended reach of networked communications have directly affected literacy efforts around the globe (*Human Development Report*). Digital networks, for example, have provided routes for the increasing numbers of communications that now cross geopolitical, cultural, and linguistic borders, and because of this situation, the texts exchanged within such networks often assume hybrid forms that take advantage of multiple semiotic channels. The international versions of the Aljazeera, *Japan Times*, BBC, and the *International Herald Tribune* websites, for example, offer not only traditional alphabetic journalism, but also video and audio interviews. Similarly, the United Nations, Human Rights Watch, and the International Olympic Movement, among many other international organizations, all maintain richly textured websites that offer not only print reports and white papers, but audio, video, and photographic essays as well. These communications—which consist of not only words, but also audio and video transmissions, images, sounds, music, animations, and multimedia presentations—are used by organizations, nongovernmental agencies, multinational corporations, international financial institutions, governments, affinity groups, and individual citizens who form around common interests and projects, and who compose, exchange, and interpret information, and through these efforts and others, these communications help establish the cultural codes of communication in the twenty-first century.

At the same time, new software and hardware applications—video and audio editing systems and conferencing software, electronic white boards, digital video cameras, multimodal composing environments, and digital audio recorders, among many, many more—have provided increasing numbers of people the means of producing and distributing communications that take advantage of multiple expressive modalities.

These two converging trends have had many effects,[26] among them an increasing interest in aurality and modalities of expression other than the printed word—not only in linguistics, literacy, and language studies (Ong, *Orality*; Kleine and Gale; McCorkle, "Harbingers"; Halbritter; Hawisher and Selfe; DeVoss, Hawisher, Jackson, Johansen, Moraski, and Selfe; Tannen, "Oral," and *Spoken*) but also in medicine (Sterne), legal studies (Hibbitts; Gilkerson; Hespanha), cultural studies (Bull and Back), geography (Sui; J. Olson; Carney), architecture (Labelle, Roden, and Migo; C. N. Brooks, *Architectural*; Kahn), film (Altman; O'Brien; Chion), and history (B. Smith; Yow; Richie) among many other areas and disciplines. As Hibbitts sketches the connection:

> The history of Western culture over the past 125 years suggests that the recent turn toward the aural is largely a product of new aural technologies. In essence, cultural aurality has tended to become more pronounced as aural technologies have multiplied and spread. At every stage in this process, the existence of these technologies has radically extended the power and range of aurally communicated information. As technologically transmitted and amplified sound has become able to assume more of the cultural burden, culture itself has turned towards sound for information. (3.12)

In composition studies, then, it is not surprising that some of the impetus for a new turn toward aurality has been contributed by technology scholars focusing on electronic, multimedia, and multimodal composing. This early thread of scholarship resisted, for the most part, simplistic distinctions between orality and writing, and connected digital writing to aurality in *metaphorical* terms. Such work became increasingly important throughout the last decade of the twentieth century as computer systems developed to accommodate new forms of communicative exchanges: online conferences (Bruce, Peyton, and Bertram; Faigley, *Fragments*); listservs (Cubbison; Selfe and Myer); MOOs and MUDs (Haefner; Haynes and Holmevik), and email (Yancey and Spooner), for example.[27]

By the end of the decade and the century, low-cost and portable technologies of digital audio recording, such as minidisc recorders, and simplified open-source audio editing software, such as Audacity, put the material means of digital audio production into the hands of both students and English composition teachers.[28] Many of these teachers were already experimenting with digital video, using Apple's iMovie or Microsoft's Movie Maker,[29] both which contained an audio track and limited audio-editing capabilities, but digital audio-editing programs made it possible for teachers and students to *compose with audio* in ways that they could not do previously: recording and layering environmental and artificial sounds to create a textured sonic context and collection of detail, weaving vocal interview and commentary sources together to provide multiple perspectives on a subject; adding music, silence, and audio effects to ways of changing emphasis, tone, pace, delivery, and content.

Although new software environments expanded the opportunities for experimentation with audio compositions in English classrooms, the intellectual basis of such work was also fueled by the germinal scholarship of the New London Group (see p. 193 in this volume), Gunther Kress and Theo Van Leeuwen, and Cope and Kalantzis—who identified the aural as *one modality among many* on which individuals should be able to call as a rhetorical and creative resource in composing messages and making meaning. These scholars argued for an increasingly robust theory of semiosis that acknowledged the practices of human sign makers who selected from a range of modalities for expression (including sound, image, and animation, for example) depending on rhetorical and material contexts within which the communication was being designed and distributed. They also noted that no one expressive modality, including print, was capable of carrying the full range of meaning in a text, and pointed out that the texts sign makers created both shaped and were shaped by the universe of semiotic resources they accessed.

This expanded semiotic theory brought into sharp relief the hegemony of print as an expressive mode in English composition classrooms—especially for scholars studying emerging forms of communication in digital environments. Many of these scholars had observed the profession's love-hate relationship with these new forms of expression during the last decade of the twentieth century—blogs,[30] home-made digital videos,[31] multimedia sites like MySpace[32] and Facebook,[33] digital audio and podcasting.[34] Although such texts had begun to dominate digital environments and self-sponsored literacy venues, print continued to prevail as *"the* way" of knowing (Dunn, *Talking* 15), *the* primary means of learning and communicating in composition classrooms. Although email, websites, and multimedia texts were accepted as objects for study, critique, and analysis—and while many students were already engaging in the self-sponsored literacy practices of creating digital video and audio texts—composition assignments, for the large part, continued to resemble those of the past hundred years (Takayoshi and Selfe).

In a 1999 chapter, "English at the Crossroads," in *Passions, Pedagogies, and 21st Century Technologies*, for instance, Kress described the cultural changes he saw literacy practices undergoing in an increasingly technological world and compared these to the continued privileging of print by teachers of English. The exclusive focus on print and written language, he noted,

> has meant a neglect, an overlooking, even suppression of the potentials of representation and communicational modes in particular cultures, an often repressive and always systematic neglect of human potentials in many . . . areas; and a neglect equally, as a consequence of the development of theoretical understandings of such modes. . . . Or, to put it provocatively: the single, exclusive and intensive focus on written language has dampened the full development of all kinds of human potential, through all the sensorial possibilities of human bodies, in all kinds of respects, cognitively and affectively. (85)

With the development of the Internet and digital audio and video applications, new depth and scope were added to scholarship around aurality. In 2004, for example, Scott Halbritter, of the University of North Carolina at Chapel Hill, wrote a dissertation that explored sound as a rhetorical resource in multimedia compositions. In 2005, Tara Shankar, in her MIT dissertation, described a project in which young students composed using a "spriting" software that she had developed to take advantage of their oral exchanges; and in a 2005 dissertation completed at Ohio State University, Warren Benson (Ben) McCorkle explored the remediation of aurality by print and writing, as well as the subsequent diminishment of professional attention to the canon of delivery in nineteenth century collegiate instruction.

By 2006, *Computers and Composition: An International Journal* published a special issue on sound, edited by Cheryl Ball and Byron Hawk. In tandem with this collection of print articles, Ball and Hawk also published a related set of online essays and resources in *Computers and Composition Online*, an online version of the journal edited by Kristine Blair. The collection contained not only print essays but also video and audio texts that offered key arguments, illustrations, and examples that could not be rendered in a print environment.

As such scholarly works have emerged during the last decades, compositionists have continued to experiment with assignments that encouraged students to create meaning in and through audio compositions, focusing assignments on podcasting,[35] mashups, voicemail compositions and sound poems,[36] radio essays,[37] audio documentaries and interviews,[38] audio ethnographies,[39] as well as video, multimedia, and other forms of multimodal composition. Other rhetoric and composition scholars, taking their cue from increasingly visible projects in history, folklore, and anthropology, began to involve students in recording and collecting the oral histories of two-year college composition teachers,[40] key figures in rhetoric and composition studies,[41] and pioneers in the writing center movement.[42]

AURAL COMPOSING SAMPLE 4: DANIEL KELLER'S *LORD OF THE MACHINES: READING THE HUMAN COMPUTER RELATIONSHIP*

At this point, please go to <http://people.cohums.ohio-state.edu/selfe2/ccc/> and listen to Daniel Keller's audio essay, *Lord of the Machines: Reading the Human Computer Relationship*. This richly textured composition explores the complex relationship that humans have established with computers through their daily interaction and through media representations.

BY WAY OF CONCLUDING, BUT NOT ENDING . . .

In this essay, I offer some perspective about the way in which U.S. composition studies has subsumed, remediated, and rediscovered aurality during the past 150 years. This story, however, is far from complete, and far from as tidy as I have suggested. The recent attention to, and rethinking of, sound as a composing modality—and the understanding and use of other composing modalities such as video, images, and photographs—remain fragmented and uneven, far from a broadly defined professional trend. Although many teachers who work with digital media in this country recognize the efforts I describe here and have participated in them or helped sustain them, for other teachers the bandwidth of composing resources remains limited to words on a printed page.

Sustaining this situation is a constellation of factors—not all of them technological. Chief among them, for instance, is the profession's continuing bias toward print and ongoing investment in specialization, understandable as historically and culturally informed methods of ensuring our own status and continuity. Given this context, many English composition programs and departments maintain a scholarly culture in which, nonprint forms, genres, and modalities of communication are considered objects of study and critique, but not a set of resources for student authors to deploy themselves. As Gunther Kress observes, "Control over communication and over the means of representation is, as always, a field in which power is exercised" ("English" 67).

It is also true that recording and editing sound—or images or video—in digital environments is still far from a transparent or inexpensive activity, and many composition teachers lack the technology, the professional development training, and the technical support needed to experiment with assignments such as those I have described. Although most schools now have access to computers, and most departments of English and writing programs can count on some kind of computer facility, work with sound and video still requires computers specially equipped for such projects, access to mass storage for student projects, support for teachers who want to learn to work with audio, and sympathetic and knowledgeable technical staff members who understand the importance of such work. These resources are unevenly distributed in small state- and privately funded schools, historically black colleges and universities, and reservation schools, rural schools, and schools that have been hit by devastating events such as Hurricane Katrina. None of this, of course, is helped by the reduction of support for education in the wake of our country's massive expenditures on national security and the wars in Afghanistan and Iraq.

I should be as clear as possible here about exactly what I am advocating, and why. My argument is not *either/or*, but *both/and*. I am *not* arguing against writing, the value we place on writing, or an understanding of what writing—and print—contribute to the human condition that is vitally important. Indeed, it is evident to me that the ability to express oneself in writing will continue to be a hallmark of educated citizens in the United States for some time to come. Nor do I want to contribute to re-inscribing the simplistic terms of a writing/aurality divide, a division that is as limiting as it is false.

I *do* want to argue that teachers of composition need to pay attention to, and come to value, the *multiple* ways in which students compose and communicate meaning, the exciting hybrid, multimodal texts they create—in both nondigital and digital environments—to meet their own needs in a changing world. We need to better understand the importance that students attach to composing, exchanging, and interpreting new and different kinds of texts that help them make sense of their experiences and lives—songs and lyrics, videos, written essays illustrated with images, personal Web pages that include sound clips. We need to learn from their motivated efforts to communicate with each other, for themselves and for others, often in resistance to the world we have created for them. We need to respect the rhetorical sovereignty of young people from different backgrounds, communities, colors, and cultures, to observe and understand the rhetorical choices they are making, and to offer them new ways of making meaning, new choices, new ways of accomplishing their goals.

I *do* want to convince compositionists how crucial it is to acknowledge, value, and draw on a range of composing modalities—among them, images (moving and still), animations, sound, and color—which are *in the process of becoming increasingly important to communicators*, especially within digital networks, now globally extended in their reach and scope. The identities that individuals are forging through such hybrid communicative practices, as Manual Castells (*Power* 360) points out, are key factors in composing the cultural and communicative codes that will characterize coming decades. Students are intuitively aware of these related phenomena, being immersed in them, but they need help understanding the implications of such cultural trends as well as managing their own communicative efforts in ways that are rhetorically effective, critically aware, morally responsible, and personally satisfying. Responsible educators, critically aware scholars of semiotic theory and practice, will not want to ignore these world-order changes or the opportunities they offer.

To understand how literacy practices change, especially in times of rapid transformation, Deborah Brandt ("Accumulating") maintains that both teachers and students need to understand how literacy forms emerge and contend and to study those contexts within which "latent forms of older, residual literacies . . . are at play alongside emerging ones" (665). To undertake such work in classrooms, Brandt suggests, we can talk to students about how both " 'school based' and 'home-based' literacies form and function within larger historical currents" (666). Composition classrooms can provide a context not only for *talking about* different literacies, but also for *practicing* different literacies, learning to create texts that combine a range of modalities as communicative resources: exploring their affordances, the special capabilities they offer to authors; identifying what audiences expect of texts that deploy different modalities and how they respond to such texts.

Within such a classroom, teaching students to make informed, rhetorically based uses of sound as a composing modality—and other expressive modalities such as video, still images, and animation—could help them better understand the particular affordances of written language, and vice versa. Pam Takayoshi and I have outlined this case elsewhere in the following pragmatic terms:

[T]eaching students how to compose and focus a thirty-second public service announcement (PSA) for radio—and select the right details for inclusion in this audio composition—*also helps teach* them specific strategies for focusing a written essay more tightly and effectively, choosing those details most likely to convey meaning in effective ways to a particular audience, for a particular purpose. In addition, as students engage in composing a script for the audio PSA, they are motivated to engage in meaningful, rhetorically-based writing practice. Further, as students work within the rhetorical constraints of such an audio assignment, they learn more about the particular affordances of sound (the ability to convey accent, emotion, music, ambient sounds that characterize a particular location or event) and the constraints of sound (the difficulty of going back to review complex or difficult passages, to convey change not marked by sound, to communicate some organizational markers like paragraphs). Importantly, students also gain the chance to compare the affordances and constraints of audio with those of alphabetic writing—and, thus, improve their ability to make *informed and conscious choices* about the most effective modality for communicating in particular rhetorical contexts. (3)

The challenges and difficulties of such work cannot be underestimated. The time that students spend in composition classrooms is altogether too short—especially during the first two years of college. Indeed, many teachers will argue that they do not have enough instructional time to teach students what they need to know about writing and rhetoric, let alone about composing digital audio texts (or digital videos or photo essays, for instance). A variation of this argument will be familiar to any compositionist who has offered a writing-across-the-curriculum workshop to colleagues who understand their job as involving coverage of a set amount of disciplinary material rather than the task of teaching students how to think through problems using writing. Frequently, these colleagues—who design instruction around the mastery of facts, procedures, or series of historical events—consider writing instruction to be add-on content, material that detracts from the real focus of disciplinary mastery. Like most writing-across-the-curriculum specialists, however, I would argue that the primary work of *any* classroom is to help students use semiotic resources to think critically, to explore, and to solve problems. In composition classes, this means helping students work through communicative problems—analyzing a range of rhetorical tasks and contexts (online, in print contexts, and face to face); deploying a range of assets (both digital and nondigital) effectively and responsibly; and making meaning for a range of purposes, audiences, and information sets.

It is an understandable, if unfortunate, fact, as Patricia Dunn (*Talking* 150) argues, that our profession has come to equate *writing* with *intelligence*. Even more important, she adds, we have allowed ourselves to ignore the "back story" implications of this equation, the unspoken belief that those who *do not privilege writing above all other forms of expression*—those individuals and groups who have "other ways of knowing," learning, and expressing themselves—may somehow lack intelligence. This unacknowledged and often unconscious episteme has particular salience for contemporary literacy practices that are not focused solely on print or alphabetic writing. As teachers of rhetoric and composition, our responsibility is to teach students effective, rhetorically based strategies for taking advantage of *all available means* of communicating effectively and productively as literate citizens.

And so back to what's at stake. As faculty, when we limit our understanding of composing and our teaching of composition to a single modality, when we focus on print alone as the communicative venue for our assignments and for students' responses to those assignments, we ensure that instruction is less accessible to a wide range of learners, and we constrain students' ability to succeed by offering them an unnecessarily narrow choice of semiotic and rhetorical resources. By broadening the choice of composing modalities, I argue, we expand the field of play for students with different learning styles and differing ways of reflecting on the world; we provide the opportunity for them to study, think critically about, and work with new communicative modes. Such a move not only offers us a chance to make instruction increasingly effective for those students from different cultural and linguistic backgrounds, but it also provides an opportunity to make our work increasingly relevant to a changing set of communicative needs in a globalized world. As Gunther Kress ("English") has suggested, it may also make us better scholars of semiotic systems by providing us with additional chances to observe, systematically and at close quarters, how people make meaning in contemporary communication environments when they have a full palette of rhetorical and semiotic resources on which to draw, new opportunities to theorize about emerging representational practices within such environments, and additional chances to study the communicative possibilities and potentials of various modes of expression. It gives us another reason to pay attention to language and to learn.

For students, the stakes are even more significant. Young people need to know that their role as rhetorical agents is open, not artificially foreclosed by the limits of their teachers' imaginations. They need a full quiver of semiotic modes from which to select, role models who can teach them to think critically about a range of communication tools, and multiple ways of reaching their audience. They do not need teachers who insist on *one* tool or *one* way.

Students, in sum, need opportunities to realize that different compositional modalities carry with them different possibilities for representing multiple and shifting patterns of identity, additional potential for expression and resistance, expanded ways of engaging with a changing world—as the four audio essays I reference in this article indicate. As student Elisa Norris put it, "If we can imagine using these types of projects in our writing studios, we can open up that learning space so that *all* students have room to express themselves."

Students need these things because they will join us as part of an increasingly challenging and difficult world—one plagued by destructive wars and great ill will, marked by poverty and disease, scarred by racism and ecological degradation. In this world, we face some wickedly complex communicative tasks. To make our collective way with any hope for success, to create a different set of global and local relations than currently exists, we will need *all available means* of persuasion, all available dimensions, all available approaches, not simply those limited to the two dimensional space of a printed page.

NOTES

1. With the term *aurality*, I refer to a complexly related web of communicative practices that are received or perceived by the ear, including speech, sound, and music. In exploring aurality, I focus on both the *reception* and the *production* of aural communications. I also focus on the purposeful composition of aural texts. One of my goals in exploring the role of aural communication in composition classrooms is to suggest that the written word is not the only way of composing and communicating meaning or understanding, nor should it be *the* sole focus of composition instruction in a world where people make meaning and extend their understanding through the use of multiple semiotic modalities in combination—sound, printed words, spoken words, still and moving images, graphical elements.

In using the term *aurality*, rather than the more common *orality*, I hope to resist models of an oral/literate divide and simplistic characterizations of cultures or groups as either oral or literate in their communicative practices. Humans make and communicate meaning through a combination of modalities—sound, still and moving images, words, among them—and using a variety of media. And they read and interpret texts that combine modalities as well.

2. The term *multimodal* is used by the New London Group to indicate the range of modalities—printed words, still and moving images, sound, speech, and music, color—that authors combine as they design texts.

3. I borrow the term *rhetorical sovereignty* from Scott Lyons (2000), but extend it, advisedly, and in ways that I recognize might not remain faithful to his use of the term. Lyons uses the term to describe the right of indigenous peoples to have "some say about the nature of their textual representations," to determine their own representational needs and identities, their own accounts of the past and present. For Lyons, rhetorical sovereignty is intimately connected to the land; to the history, the present, and the future of native peoples; to culture and community. I use *rhetorical sovereignty* to refer to the rights of students to have "some say" about their own representational needs, identities, and modalities of expression. In making this statement, however, I do *not* want to suggest that all college students are subject to the same systems of domination and cultural violence as native peoples. They are not. Nor do I want to diminish, in any way or to any degree, the importance, of Lyons's insights or our professional responsibility for supporting the sovereignty efforts that native peoples have undertaken. I stand in solidarity and support of these efforts.

4. As I suggest throughout this article, aurality remains a relatively small but valued part of the composition classroom—only, however, in limited and constrained circumstances: in the occasional oral presentation, in classroom discussions, or in one-on-one conferences, for example. In these situations, aurality is valued and even prized. In the vast majority of compositions classrooms, however, the formal expression of knowledge is reserved for writing, and written papers are the product toward which students are taught to work.

5. In 1873, Harvard formed its Department of English. The mission of this unit was to teach written English within the new secular, specialized university. For extended and informative discussions of how rhetorical education was conducted during this period, see Russell ("Institutionalizing"); Halloran; Wright and Halloran; Johnson; Berlin; and Congleton.

6. Within this context, David Russell (*Writing*) notes, writing

> was now embedded in a whole array of complex and highly differentiated social practices carried on without face-to-face communication. The new professions . . . increasingly wrote . . . for specialized audiences of colleagues who were united not primarily by ties of class but by the shared activities, the goals, . . . the unique conventions of a profession or discipline. (4–5)

7. James A. Berlin notes that "Charles William Eliot, Harvard's president from 1869 to 1909 . . . considered writing so central to the new elective curriculum he was shaping that in 1874 the Freshman English course at Harvard was established, by 1894 was the only requirement except for a modern language, and by 1897, was the only required course in the curriculum, consisting of a two-semester sequence" (20). Influenced variously by the belles lettristic tradition, the pressures of increasing collegiate enrollments, the influential move toward graduate education on the German model, and continued moves toward specialized study in the new university, however, writing gave way, in fairly short order, to a focus on the reading and analysis of contemporary and

classical literary texts. And by the first part of the twentieth century, the efforts of most departments of English were focused primarily on literary works. For an extended discussion of this trend, see Halloran; Berlin; and Russell.

8. In the *Atlantic Monthly* of March 1869, Eliot wrote

> No men have greater need of the power of expressing their ideas with clearness, conciseness, and vigor than those whose avocation require them to describe and discuss material resources, industrial processes, public works, mining enterprises, and the complicated problems of trade and finance. In such writings, embellishment may be dispensed with, but the chief merits of style—precision, simplicity, perspicuity, and force are never more necessary. (359)

9. See Ben McCorkle's article "Harbingers of the Printed Page" for an extended explanation of how the canon of delivery fared in nineteenth-century composition classes and how orality became subsumed to, and remediated by, writing in composition classrooms.

10. Ronald Reid describes these changes in terms of the Boyleston Professorship at Harvard—and the occupants of this position—as cases in point.

> In 1806, rhetoric was concerned primarily with persuasive oratory and sunk its roots deeply in the classical tradition. By the time of Hill's retirement [in 1904], what was called "rhetoric" was concerned not with oratory, but with written composition, expository and literary as well as persuasive and made little direct reference to classical authors. And not even these new concerns were those of the Boyleston professorship, which abandoned rhetoric for literature, oratory for poetry. Such a dramatic shift took place not only at Harvard, but in higher education generally. (239)

The Boyleston Professorship of Rhetoric and Oratory, was held by the following individuals from 1806 to 1904: John Quincy Adams (statesman, 1806–1809), Joseph McKean (former minister, mathematician, 1809–1818), Edward T. Channing (attorney, editor of *North American Review*, 1819–1851), Francis James Child (who studied at Gottingen University in Germany and applied many German practices to the revision of U.S. curricula, 1851–1876), and Adams Sherman Hill (1876–1904). For an extended discussion of this professorship and the changes it underwent at the end of the nineteenth century, see Ronald Reid's article "The Boyleston Professorship of Rhetoric and Oratory, 1806–1904."

11. Although oral composition—both scripted and nonscripted—waned relatively rapidly in English composition classrooms during the last half of the nineteenth century, it persisted in other locations. One of these was the extracurricular literary and debate societies that gained popularity in the eighteenth century and persisted throughout the nineteenth century in various collegiate and noncollegiate forms (Gere; Halloran; Royster, *Traces*; Berlin). In colleges, this movement was often initiated and carried on by students, often with little help from faculty, to support practice in public speaking and debating topics of interest. Many such clubs engaged in intercollegiate contests.

Attention to aurality was also sustained by the popular Elocutionary Movement, which began its rise to prominence in the late eighteenth century and continued throughout the nineteenth century. This movement, too, was built on the general interest in systematic and scientific knowledge, identifying elaborately prescriptive texts with "highly encoded notational systems to precisely regulate vocal inflection, gestures of the arms, hands, and legs, and even facial countenances as a means of directly manipulating different faculties in the minds of listeners." (B. McCorkle, "Harbingers" 35). In this movement, oral delivery figured centrally and prescriptively.

12. As Hibbitts (2.25) describes this shift,

> Within the white community, public speech became more dependent on visual, written scripts; old-fashioned oratory was increasingly dismissed as "mere rhetoric." Storytelling survived, but it was largely, if not altogether accurately, associated with children, members of less literate lower classes, and inhabitants of backward rural areas. Most white American authors jettisoned the more obvious aural mannerisms and formats that had characterized so much American literature in the antebellum era. At the same time, white Americans gradually embraced silence as both a social norm and a primary means of social discipline. Increasingly used to sitting quietly in front of texts, white American theater- and concert-goers who had formerly been inclined to spontaneously talk to each other and interact with stage performers became more willing to sit in silent (or at least suspended) judgment on the musicians and actors who appeared before them. In the schoolroom where white American teachers had once taught their students to read by recitation, the most important meta-lesson became, as it today remains, how to sit, write, and read in contented quiet.

13. I write about the complexly articulated effects of race, class, and gender from my subject position as a white female academic. As Marilyn Cooper reminds me, this position limits my work: I can write *about* people of color, but never *as* a person of color. I also recognize the great danger, especially in such a brief article, of glossing over the important differences, cultural complexities, and rich histories of different groups, ignoring the specific ways in which individuals and communities have figured in the history of the United States, the distinctive kinds of oppression and discrimination they have experienced, the ways in which they have been treated within educational, judicial, and legislative arenas. I encourage readers to refer to more extended works by the notable scholars cited in this section who write *as* people of color, as well as *about* people of color.

14. For a rich and insightful discussion of how African Americans have both retained a value on historical oral forms and skillfully deployed written discourses in resistant ways, see Adam Banks's *Race, Rhetoric, and Technology: Searching for Higher Ground*. In this book, Banks notes how black online discourse and spaces such as Black Planet have served as nonmainstream sites for keeping "self-determination, of resistance, of keeping oppositional identities and worldviews alive, refusing to allow melting pot ideologies of language and identity" (70) to prevail.

15. Bolter and Gruisin's term *remediation*—explored in their 1999 book of the same name—refers to the processes by which new media and media forms (for instance, flat-screen television) take up and transform prior media (conventional televisions)—promising to fulfill a particular unmet need or improve on some performance standard. Bolter and Grusin note, however, that new media *never completely supplant or erase prior media* because they must refer to these forms in making the case for their own superiority (54). Their discussion of remediation extends far beyond the simple, limited, and metaphorical use of the term I make in this article.

16. Technical, professional, and business communication courses offer an important exception to the diminishing role of aurality. In these courses, the oral presentation has consistently retained its currency as an important part of the curriculum. In 1994, Heather A. Howard reported that every single one of the authors of the ten leading textbooks in business and professional communication considered "oral communication and public speaking as worthwhile topics" for inclusion in their books, and 70 percent of these authors specifically mentioned "informative and persuasive" speeches (5). And, in 2003, Kelli Cargile Cook noted that oral presentations were the most frequently assigned tasks in 197 technical communication courses identified in a random sampling of ATTW listserv members (54). It is possible that this situation persists because such courses are so responsive to the needs of employers. In 1995, for example, Karen K. Waner noted that "oral communication skills" such as "using appropriate techniques in making oral presentations"; using "appropriate body action in interpersonal and oral communication"; "analyzing the audience before, during, and after an oral report"; and "objectively" presenting information in oral reports" were considered "important" or "very important" by both business faculty and business professionals (55).

17. Contributing to these practices, of course, was the cultural value that the academy placed—and continues to place—on written scholarship published in print journals. This value has been instantiated at numerous levels of university culture and through articulated systems of salaries, raises, hirings, and promotion and tenure guidelines. These related formations have shaped the professional culture of composition studies and continue to do so in fundamental ways.

18. One of the notable exceptions to this trend can be found in the work of Peter Elbow, who has, for years, reminded readers that writing and speech, far from being absolutely distinct activities, are complexly connected through a constellation of cognitive, linguistic, and social relationships. See Elbow's "The Shifting Relationships between Speech and Writing" and "What Do We Mean When We Talk about Voice."

19. I thank Debra Journet, of the University of Louisville, for this insight and for many others.

20. The books with "voice" in their title included: Frank O'Connor's *The Lonely Voice: A Study of the Short Story*; Donald Stewart's *The Authentic Voice: A Pre-Writing Approach to Student Writing*; Otis Winchester's *The Sound of Your Own Voice*; Jill Wilson Cohn's *Writing: The Personal Voice*; Martin Medhurst's *Voice and Writing*; Jim W. Corder's *Finding a Voice*; Kathleen Yancey's *Voices on Voice*; Johnny Payne's *Voice and Style*; Michael Huspek and Gary P. Radford's *Transgressing Discourses: Communication and the Voice of the Other*; and Albert Guerard, Maclin Guerard, John Hawkes, and Claire Rosenfield's *The Personal Voice: A Contemporary Prose Reader*.

21. In this article, and elsewhere, George and Trimbur argue persuasively against this conception, as well as English studies' adherence to the historical distinction between high and low culture.

22. For further explanation of this technique and a bibliography see Susan Sipple's and Jeff Sommers's "A Heterotopic Space: Digitized Audio Commentary and Student Revisions."

23. My thanks to Peter Elbow for pointing out the persistence of aurality and lecturing in both composition classroom settings and testing contexts for graduate students.

24. Increasingly throughout the 1960s to 1990s, lecturing in composition classrooms became supplanted by peer-group and project-based work and the one-on-one conferencing approaches that characterized student-centered pedagogies. This process, however, was slow, often uneven, and certainly never complete.

In a 1965 Conference on College Composition and Communication workshop session ("New Approaches in Teaching Composition") that was attended by James Moffett, for example, William Holmes reported on using "televised lectures" developed by Ohio University as a "solution to teaching ever more freshman with ever more graduate students" (207), W. Grayson Lappert described lecture sessions at Balwin Wallace (208); and Eric Zale described using lectures used to teach composition at Eastern Michigan University (208).

In 1972, James R. Sturdevant—defending lectures as one effective method for teaching large groups of students, especially when such methods were combined with other approaches—described a pilot program at Ohio Wesleyan University. This program was developed to teach large groups of students effectively and efficiently: "Students were exposed to the study of composition through assigned readings in a rhetoric text and an essay anthology, large group lectures, short diagnostic exercises, small group meetings, and coordinating writing assignments" (420).

And even later, in 1997, Martha Sammons, providing readers advice on using Power-Point, noted:

> Electronic presentations tend to make you lecture more quickly than usual, so remember to move slowly from slide to slide. To maintain suspense, you can use the feature of hiding bullets until you are ready. Use traditional lecturing techniques to elaborate on key points. Most important, don't lose your normal teaching style.

Indeed lecturing has never entirely disappeared from college-level writing classrooms, although it has certainly become less popular. In 2000, Donald Finkel wrote in his book *Teaching with Your Mouth Shut*:

> Most people have a set of ready-made assumptions about what a teacher does. A teacher talks, tells, explains, lectures, instructs, professes. Teaching is something you do with your mouth open, your voice intoning. . . . After hearing their stirring lectures, we left their classrooms inspired, moved. But did we learn anything? What was left of this experience five years later? These questions usually don't get asked. (1)

25. *Soundmark* is R. Murray Schafer's (1977) term, derived from the word *landmarks*, to refer to sounds that characterize the life of a particular place, time, or group, sonic markers that "make the acoustic life of a community unique" (10).

26. I do not mean to suggest that digital technologies are the *only* reason for a renewed interest in orality. The cultural ecology of literacy is a complexly rendered landscape and comprises a large number of related factors.

27. It is important to note that one of the very earliest online conferencing systems—ENFI (Electronic Networks for Interaction)—was used as a communicative environment for deaf students. As my colleague Brenda Brueggeman has reminded me, innovations in communicative technologies often begin in communities of people who have different abilities and forms of making and exchanging information, of composing meaning. For more about ENFI, see Bruce, Peyton, and Batson. For more about technology and disability, see Brueggemann and Snyder, Brueggemann, and Garland-Thomson.

28. The minidisc recorder was developed by Sony in 1991–1992 ("Hardware and Software"), providing consumers with a low-cost and highly portable digital audio recording device that is still used today. Audacity, a widely used open-source audio editor, was invented in 1999 by Dominic Mazzoni. As the Audacity manual describes the project's development, Mazzoni was a "graduate student at Carnegie Mellon University in Pittsburgh, PA, USA. He was working on a research project with his advisor, Professor Roger Dannenberg, and they needed a tool that would let them visualize audio analysis algorithms. Over time, this program developed into a general audio editor, and other people started helping out" (Oetzmann). This combination put digital audio recording, editing, and production within the reach of teachers and students in English composition, much like the personal computer put word processing within the reach of such classes in the early 1980s.

29. Apple's iMovie was first released to consumers in 1999 ("Apple Computer"). Microsoft's MovieMaker was released on 14 September 2000 as part of the Windows Millennium Edition ("Windows ME").

30. According to Technorati, by January of 2006, over 75,000 new blogs were being created each day, an average of one new blog every second of every day. In addition, 13.7 million bloggers are still posting three months after their blogs were created. At this point, Technorati tracked 1.2 million new blog posts a day, about 50,000 per hour. For further statistics, see the Technorati website at <http://www.technorati.com/>.

31. In August of 2006, YouTube.com reported more than 100 million video views every day with 65,000 new videos uploaded daily and approximately 20 million unique users per month (<http://www.youtube.com/t/fact_sheet>). Grouper.com, another site that allows users to upload their homemade videos, reported 8 million unique visitors (<http://www.grouper.com/about/press.aspx>).

32. Kevin Poulson reported in 2006 that MySpace has "gathered over 57 million registered users (counting some duplicates and fake profiles). As of last November, it enjoyed a 752-percent growth in web traffic over one year, according to Nielsen//NetRatings."

33. Facebook, the "second most-trafficked PHP site in the world," reports "175 million active (users who have returned to the site in the last 30 days)."

34. The Arbitron/Edison Media Research report, *Internet and Multimedia 2006*, notes that the ownership of MP3 players increased from 14 percent to 22 percent among all age groups in the United States and from 27 percent to 42 percent among 12- to 17-year-olds in 2005–2006 (32), and that more than 27 million people in the United States have listened to audio podcasts (Rose and Lenski 29).

35. See Daniel Anderson, Erin Branch, and Stephanie Morgan's website, *Casting about with Sound: A Podcast Workshop*, offered at the 2006 Computers and Writing conference <http://www.siteslab.org/workshops/podcast/>.

36. See Daniel Anderson's blog, *I am Dan: A Writing Pusher in the Media Age*, at <http://www.thoughtpress.org/daniel/> for innovative uses of sound in the composition classroom.

37. See Jeff Porter's course "Radio Essays" at the University of Iowa at <http://isis5.uiowa.edu/isis/courses/details.page?ddd=08N&ccc=145&sss=001&session=20063> and Jonah Willihnganz's course "The Art of the Audio Essay" at Stanford University at <http://www.stanford.edu/~jonahw/PWR2-W06/Radio-Home.html>.

38. See Lisa Spiro's course "The Documentary Across Media" at Rice University at <http://www.owlnet.rice.edu/~hans320/syllabus.html>.

39. See Katherine Braun's course "Documenting Community Culture" at Ohio State University at <http://people.cohums.ohio-state.edu/Braun43/teaching/10901Au05/index.htm>.

40. See "Oral History Project" (24 March 2005) on the Community College English website at <http://twoyearcomp.blogspot.com/2005/03/oral-history-project.html>.

41. See The Rhetoric and Composition Sound Archives (18 Feb. 2006) at Texas Christian University at <http://www.rcsa.tcu.edu/collection.htm>.

42. See the "Oral History Archive" on the Writing Centers Research Project website at <http://coldfusion.louisville.edu/webs/a-s/wcrp/oral.cfm>.

WORKS CITED

Aljazeera.net news website. 17 Feb. 2007 <http://english.aljazeera.net/News/>.

Altman, Rick. *Silent Film Sound*. New York: Columbia UP, 2004.

Anderson, Daniel. "Mostly Partially Occasional Words." *I am Dan: A Writing Pusher in the Media Age* (blog). 29 March 2009 <http://thoughtpress.org/daniel/>.

Anson, Chris. "Talking about Text: The Use of Recorded Commentary in Response to Student Writing." *A Sourcebook for Responding to Student Writing*. Ed. Richard Straub. Cresskill, NJ: Hampton P, 1999. 165–74.

"Apple Computer: 1998–2005 New Beginnings." *Wikipedia* website. 13 Oct. 2006 <http://en.wikipedia.org/wiki/Apple_Computer>.

Arbur, Rosemarie. "The Student-Teacher Conference." *College Composition and Communication* 28.4 (Dec. 1977): 338–42.

Ball, Cheryl, and Byron Hawk. "Special Issue: Sound in/as Compositional Space: A Next Step in Multiliteracies." *Computers and Composition* 23.3 (2006): 263–65. Online version: *Computers and Composition Online*. 28 Sept. 2008 <http://www.bgsu.edu/cconline/sound/>.

Banks, Adam. *Race, Rhetoric, and Technology: Searching for Higher Ground*. Mahwah, NJ: Lawrence Erlbaum, 2006.

Barritt, Loren S., and Barry Kroll. "Some Implications of Cognitive-Developmental Psychology for Research in Composing." *Research on Composing: Points of Departure*. Ed. Charles R. Cooper and Lee O'Dell. Urbana, IL: National Council of Teachers of English, 1978. 49–57.

Bartholomae, David. "Inventing the University." *When a Writer Can't Write: Research on Writer's Block and other Writing Problems.* Ed. M. Rose. New York: Guilford, 1986. 134–66.

Barton, David, and Mary Hamilton. *Local Literacies: Reading and Writing in One Community.* London: Routledge, 1998.

BBC: International Version. News website. 17 Feb. 2009 <http://www.bbc.co.uk/home/i/index.shtml>.

Berlin, James A. *Rhetoric and Reality: Writing Instruction in American Colleges, 1900–1985.* Carbondale: Southern Illinois UP, 1987.

Bereiter, Carol, and Marlene Scardamalia. "From Conversation to Composition: The Role of Instruction in Developmental Process." *Advances in Instructional Psychology.* Ed. R. Glaser. Hillsdale, NJ: Lawrence Erlbaum, 1982. 1–64.

Biber, Douglas. "Spoken and Written Textual Dimensions in English: Resolving the Contradictory Findings." *Language* 62 (1986): 384–414.

———. *Variation across Speech and Writing.* Cambridge: Cambridge UP, 1988.

Blaeser, Kimberly (Ojibwa). *Gerald Vizenor: Writing in the Oral Tradition.* Norman: U of Oklahoma P, 1996.

Bolter, J. David, and Richard Grusin. *Remediation: Understanding New Media.* Cambridge, MA: MIT, 1999.

Borton, Sonya. "Self-Analysis: A Call for Multimodality in Personal Narrative Composition." *Computers and Composition Online* (Spring 2005). 26 Aug. 2006 <http://www.bgsu.edu/cconline/home.htm>.

Brandt, Deborah. "Accumulating Literacy: Writing and Learning to Write in the Twentieth Century." *College English* 57.6 (1995): 649–68.

———. *Literacy in American Lives.* Cambridge: Cambridge UP, 2001.

Brooks, Christopher N. *Architectural Acoustics.* Jefferson, NC: McFarland, 2002.

Brooks, Phyllis. "Mimesis: Grammar and the Echoing Voice." *College English* 35.2 (Nov. 1973): 161–68.

Bruce, Bertram, Joy Kreeft Peyton, and Trent Batson, eds. *Network-Based Classrooms: Promises and Realities.* New York: Cambridge UP, 1993.

Brueggemann, Brenda Jo. *Lend Me Your Ear: Rhetorical Constructions of Deafness.* Washington DC: Gallaudet UP, 1999.

Bull, Michael, and Les Back, eds. *The Auditory Culture Reader.* Oxford, UK: Berg, 2003.

Carney, George O., ed. *The Sounds of People and Places: A Geography of American Music from Country to Classical and Blues to Bop.* 4th ed. Lanham, MD: Roman & Littlefield, 2003.

Carroll, Joyce Armstrong. "Talking through the Writing Process." *English Journal* 70 (Nov. 1981): 100–02.

Carter, Steven. "The Beatles and Freshman English." *College Composition and Communication* 20 (1969): 228–32.

Castells, Manuel. *End of the Millennium.* Vol. 3 in *The Information Age: Economy, Society, and Culture.* Malden, MA: Blackwell, 1998.

———. *The Power of Identity.* Vol. 2 in *The Information Age: Economy, Society, and Culture.* Malden, MA: Blackwell, 1997.

———. *The Rise of the Network Society.* Vol. 1 in *The Information Age: Economy, Society, and Culture.* Malden, MA: Blackwell.

Cayer, Roger L., and Renee Sacks. "Oral and Written Discourse of Basic Writers: Similarities and Differences." *Research in the Teaching of English* 13 (May 1979): 121–28.

Chion, Michel. *The Voice in Cinema.* Trans. Claudia Gorbman. New York: Columbia UP, 1999.

Cintron, Ralph. *Angels' Town.* Boston: Beacon, 1997.

Clapp, John M. *English Journal* 2.1 (Jan. 1913): 18–33.

Clark, Beverly Lyon. "Tutoring, within Limits." *College Composition and Communication* 35.2 (May 1984): 238–40.

Clements, William M. *Native American Verbal Art: Texts and Contexts.* Tucson: U of Arizona P, 1996.

Cohn, Jill Wilson. *Writing: The Personal Voice.* New York: Harcourt Brace Jovonavich, 1975.

Collins, James L., and Michael M. Williamson. "Spoken Language and Semantic Abbreviations in Writing." *Research in the Teaching of English* 15 (Feb. 1981): 23–35.

Conference of College Composition and Communication. "New Approaches in Teaching Composition: Further toward a New Rhetoric." *College Composition and Communication* 16.3 (Oct. 1965): 207–8.

Congleton, J. E. "Historical Development of the Concept of Rhetorical Perspective." *College Composition and Communication* 5 (1954): 140–49.

Connors, Robert J. "The Differences between Speech and Writing: Ethos, Pathos, and Logos." *College Composition and Communication* 30 (Oct. 1979): 285–90.

———. "Teaching and Learning as a Man." *College English* 58.2 (Feb. 1996): 137–57.

Cook, Kelli Cargile. "How Much Is Enough? The Assessment of Student Work in Technical Communication Courses." *Technical Communication Quarterly* 12.1 (2003): 47–65.

Cope, Bill, and Mary Kalantzis, eds. *Multiliteracies: Literacy Learning and the Design of Social Futures.* London: Routledge, 2000.

Corder, Jim W. *Finding a Voice.* Glenview, IL: Scott Foresman, 1973.

Cubbison, Laurie. Configuring Listserv, Configuring Discourse. *Computers and Composition* 16.3 (1999): 371–82.

Dawe, Charles W., and Edward A. Dornan. *One to One: Resources for Conference-Centered Writing.* Boston: Little, Brown, 1981.

Derrida, Jacques. *Of Grammatology.* Trans. Gayatri Chakravorty Spivak. Baltimore: Johns Hopkins UP, 1976.

DeVoss, Danielle, Gail Hawisher, Charles Jackson, Joseph Johansen, Brittney Moraska, and Cynthia L. Selfe. "The Future of Literacy." *Literate Lives in the Information Age: Stories from the United States.* Ed. Gail E. Hawisher and Cynthia L. Selfe. Mahwah, NJ: Lawrence Erlbaum, 2004. 183–210.

Dunn, Patricia A. *Learning Re-Abled: The Learning Disability Controversy and Composition Studies.* Portsmouth, NH: Boynton/Cook, 1995.

———. *Talking, Sketching, Moving: Multiple Literacies in the Teaching of Writing.* Portsmouth, NH: Boynton/Cook, 2001.

Dyson, Anne Hass. "The Role of Oral Language in Early Writing Processes." *Research in the Teaching of English* 17 (Feb. 1983): 1–30.

Ede, Lisa. "Oral History: One Way out of the Slough of Despond." *College Composition and Communication* 28.4 (Dec. 1977): 380–82.

Elbow, Peter. "The Shifting Relationships between Speech and Writing." *College Composition and Communication* 36.3 (Oct. 1986): 283–303.

———. "What Do We Mean When We Talk about Voice in Texts? *Voices on Voice: Perspectives, Definitions, Inquiry.* Ed. Kathleen Blake Yancey. Urbana, IL: National Council of Teachers of English, 1994. 1–35.

Eldred, Janet C. "The Technology of Voice." *College Composition and Communication* 48.3 (Oct. 1997): 334–47.

Eliot, Charles William. "The New Education, Its Organization—II." *Atlantic Monthly* 23 (March 1869): 359.

Emig, Janet. "Writing as a Mode of Learning." *College Composition and Communication* 28 (May 1977): 122–28.

Evers, Larry, and Barre Toelken, eds. *Native American Oral Traditions: Collaboration and Interpretation.* Logan: Utah State UP, 2001. Originally published as a special issue of *Oral Tradition* 13 (1998).

"Facebook Factsheet." Facebook website. 8 March 2009 <http.www.facebook.com/press/info .php?factsheet>.

Faigley, Lester. *Fragments of Rationality: Postmodernity and the Subject of Composition.* Pittsburgh: U of Pittsburgh P, 1992.

———. "Judging Writing, Judging Selves." *College Composition and Communication* 40.4 (Dec. 1989): 395–412.

Farrell, Thomas, J. "Differentiating Writing from Talking." *College Composition and Communication* 29 (Dec. 1978): 346–50.

Finke, Laurie. "Knowledge as Bait: Feminism, Voice, and the Pedagogical Unconscious." *College English* 55.1 (Jan. 1993): 7–27.

Finkel, Donald. *Teaching with Your Mouth Shut.* Portsmouth, NH: Heinemann Boynton Cook, 2000.

Fraser, Nancy. "Rethinking the Public Sphere: A Contribution to the Critique of Actually Existing Democracy." *Habermas and the Public Sphere.* Ed. Craig Calhoun. Cambridge, MA: MIT Press. 1992. 109–42.

Fulwiler, Toby. "Looking and Listening for My Voice." *College Composition and Communication* 41.2 (1990): 214–20.

Furner, Beatrice A. "An Oral Base for Teaching Letter Writing." *Elementary English* 51 (April 1974): 589–94, 600.

Gee, James Paul. *Social Linguistics and Literacies: Ideology in Discourses.* 2nd ed. London: Taylor and Francis, 1996.

Gere, Anne Ruggles. "Kitchen Tables and Rented Rooms: The Extracurriculum of Composition." *College Composition and Communication* 45.1 (Feb. 1994): 75–92.

George, Diana. "Working with Peer Groups in the Composition Classroom." *College Composition and Communication* 35.3 (Oct. 1984): 320–26.

George, Diana, and John Trimbur. "The 'Communication Battle,' or Whatever Happened to the 4th C?" *College Composition and Communication* 50.4 (June 1999): 682–98.

Gibson, Walker. "The Voice of the Writer." *College Composition and Communication* 13.3 (1962): 10–13.

Giddens, Anthony. *Central Problems in Social Theory: Action, Structure and Contradiction in Social Analysis.* Berkeley: U of California P, 1979.

Gilkerson, Christopher. "Poverty Law Narratives: The Critical Practice and Theory of Receiving and Translating Client Stories." *Hastings Law Journal* 43 (1992): 861.

Gilyard, Keith. "Literacy, Identity, Imagination, Flight." *College Composition and Communication* 52.2 (Dec. 2000): 260–72.

Graff, Harvey J. "The Legacies of Literacy: Continuities and Contradictions in Western Culture and Society." Bloomington: Indiana UP, 1987.

Guerard, Albert J., Maclin B. Guerard, John Hawkes, and Claire Rosenfield. *The Personal Voice: A Contemporary Prose Reader.* Philadelphia: J. B. Lippincott, 1964.

Guerra, Juan C. "Emerging Representations, Situated Literacies, and the Practice of Transcultural Repositioning." *Latino/a Discourses: On Language, Identity, and Literacy Education.* Ed. Michelle Hall Kells, Valerie Balester, and Victor Villanueava. Portsmouth, NH: Boynton/Cook, 2004. 7–23.

Guerra, Juan C., and Marcia Farr. "Writing on the Margins: The Spiritual and Autobiographical Discourse of Two Mexicanas in Chicago." *School's Out: Bridging Out-of-School Literacies with Classroom Practice.* Ed. Glynda A. Hull and Katherine Shultz. New York: Teachers College P, 2002. 96–123.

Gutierrez, Kris D., Patricia Baquedano-Lopez, and Hector H. Alvarez. "Literacy as Hybridity: Moving beyond Bilingualism in Urban Classrooms." *The Best for Our Children: Critical Perspectives on Literacy for Latino Students.* Ed. Maria de la Luz Reyes and John J. Halcon. New York: Teachers College P, 2001, 122–41.

Haefner, Joel. "The Politics of the Code." *Computers and Composition* 16.3 (1999): 319–24.

Halbritter, Scott K. "Sound Arguments: Aural Rhetoric in Multimedia Composition." Diss. U of North Carolina at Chapel Hill, 2004. Ann Arbor, MI: UMI 3140325.

Halloran, Michael. "Rhetoric in the American College Curriculum: The Decline of Public Discourse" *Pre/Text: The First Decade.* Ed. Victor J. Vitanza. Pittsburgh: U of Pittsburgh P, 1993. 93–116.

Halpern, Jeanne W. "Differences between Speaking and Writing and Their Implications for Teaching." *College Composition and Communication* 35.3 (1984): 345–57.

"Hardware and Software Get an Early Start." Sony Corporation website. 21 Feb. 2009 <http://www.sony.net/Fun/SH/1-21/h5.html>.

Hashimoto, I. "Voice as Juice: Some Reservations about Evangelic Composition." *College Composition and Communication* 38.1 (Feb. 1987): 70–80.

Hawisher, Gail E., and Cynthia L. Selfe, eds. *Literate Lives in the Information Age: Stories from the United States.* Mahwah, NJ: Lawrence Erlbaum, 2004.

Haynes, Cynthia, and Jan Rune Holmevik, eds. *High Wired: On the Design, Use, and Theory of Educational MOOs.* Ann Arbor: U of Michigan P, 1998.

Heilman, Robert B. "The Full Men and the Fullness Thereof." *College Composition and Communication* 21.3 (1970): 239–44.

Hennig, Barbara. "The World Was Stone Cold: Basic Writing in an Urban University." *College English* 53.6 (Oct. 1991): 674–85.

Hespanha, Antonio Manuel. "The Everlasting Return of Orality." Paper presented to Readings of Past Legal Texts. International Symposium in Legal History in Tromsø, Norway, 13–14 June 2002. 17 Aug. 2005 <www.hespanha.net/papers/2003_the-everlasting-return-of-orality.pdf>.

Hibbitts, Bernard. "Making Sense of Metaphors: Visuality, Aurality and the Reconfiguration of American Legal Discourse." *Cardozo Law Review* 16 (1994): 229. 24 Sept. 2008 <http://www.law.pitt.edu/hibbitts/meta_int.htm>.

Hinshaw, Wendy Wolters. "Re. CCC Article." Email message to the author. 17 Feb. 2007.

Hirsch, E. D., Jr. "Distinctive Features of Written Speech." *The Philosophy of Composition.* Chicago: U of Chicago P, 1977. 14–32.

Howard, Heather A. "Communication Practices of Yesteryear: A Qualitative Analysis of Business and Professional Communication Textbooks in the Last Ten Years." Paper presented at the Annual Meeting of the Speech Communication Association, New Orleans, Nov. 1994. ED 381820. 16 Feb. 2006 <http://edres.org/eric/ED381820.htm>.

Human Development Report 2001: Making New Technologies Work for Human Development. United Nations Development Programme. New York: Oxford UP, 2001.

Human Rights Watch website. 17 Feb. 2007 <http://www.hrw.org/>.

Huspek, Michael, and Gary P. Radford, eds. *Transgressing Discourses: Communication and the Voice of the Other*. Albany: State U of New York P, 1997.

Ihde, Don. *Listening and Voice: A Phenomenology of Sound*. Athens: Ohio UP, 1976.

International Herald Tribune website. 17 Feb. 2007 <http://www.iht.com/>.

Japan Times. Website. 17 Feb. 2007 <http://www.japantimes.co.jp/>.

Johnson, Nan. *Nineteenth-Century Rhetoric in North America*. Carbondale: Southern Illinois UP, 1991.

Kahn, Douglas. *Noise, Water, Meat: A History of Voice, Sound, and Aurality in the Arts*. Cambridge, MA: MIT, 1999.

Keeling, Richard. *Cry for Luck: Sacred Song and Speech among the Yurok, Hupa, and Karok Indians of Northwestern California*. Berkeley: U of California P, 1992.

Keller, Daniel. "Re. CCC Article." Email to author. 17 Feb. 2007.

Kells, Michelle Hall, Valerie Balester, and Victor Villanueva, eds. *Latino/a Discourses: On Language, Identity, and Literacy Education*. Portsmouth, NH: Boynton/Cook, 2004.

Kleine, Michael, and Fredric G. Gale. "The Elusive Presence of the Word: An Interview with Walter Ong." *Composition FORUM* 7.2 (1996): 65–86.

Kress, Gunther. "'English' at the Crossroads: Rethinking Curricula of Communication in the Context of the Turn to the Visual." *Passions, Pedagogies, and 21st Century Technologies*. Ed. Gail E. Hawisher and Cynthia L. Selfe. Logan: Utah State UP, 1999. 66–88.

Kress, Gunther, and Theo van Leeuwen. *Reading Images: The Grammar of Visual Design*. London: Routledge, 1996.

Kroeger, Fred. "A Freshman Paper Based on the Words of Popular Songs." *College Composition and Communication* 19.5 (1968): 337–40.

Labelle, Brandon, Steve Roden, and Christof Migo. *Site of Sound: Of Architecture and the Ear*. Copenhagen: Errant Bodies P, 2000.

Liggett, Sarah. "The Relationship between Speaking and Writing: An Annotated Bibliography." *College Composition and Communication* 35.3 (1984): 334–44.

Limon, Jose E. "Oral Tradition and Poetic Influence: Two Poets from Greater Mexico. *Redefining American Literary History*. Ed. A. Lavonne Brown Ruoff and Jerry Washington Ward. New York, Modern Language Association, 1990. 124–41.

Lindemann, Erika. *A Rhetoric for Writing Teachers*. New York: Oxford UP, 1995.

Lofty, John. "From Sound to Sign: Using Oral History in the College Composition Class." *College Composition and Communication* 36.3 (Oct. 1985): 349–53.

Lopate, Phillip. "Helping Students Start to Write." *Research on Composing: Points of Departure*. Ed. Charles R. Cooper and Lee O'Dell. Urbana, IL: National Council of Teachers of English, 1978. 135–49.

Lutz, William D. "Making Freshman English a Happening," *College Composition and Communication* 22.1 (Feb. 1971): 35–38.

Lyons, Scott. "Rhetorical Sovereignty: What Do American Indians Want from Writing?" *College Composition and Communication* 51.3 (Feb. 2000): 447–68.

Mahiri, Jabari. *Shooting for Excellence: African American and Youth Culture in New Century Schools*. Urbana, IL: National Council of Teachers of English; New York: Teachers College P, 1998.

McCorkle, Ben. "Harbingers of the Printed Page: Nineteenth Century Theories of Delivery as Remediation." *Rhetoric Society Quarterly* 35.4 (2005): 25–49.

McCorkle, Warren Benson, Jr. "Tongue, Nib, Block, Bit: Rhetorical Delivery and Technologies of Writing." Diss. Ohio State University, 2005.

Medhurst, Martin. *Voice and Writing*. Davis, CA: Hermagoras P, 1994.

Mellen, Cheryl, and Jeff Sommers. "Audio-Taped Response and the Two-Year Campus Writing Classroom: The Two-Sided Desk, the 'Guy with the Ax,' and the Chirping Birds." *Teaching English in the Two-Year College* 31.1 (Sept. 2003): 25–39.

Memering, W. Dean. "Talking to Students: Group Conferences." *College Composition and Communication* 24.3 (Oct. 1973): 306–7.

Miller, Susan. *Rescuing the Subject: A Critical Introduction to Rhetoric and the Writer*. Carbondale: Southern Illinois UP, 1989.

Moss, Beverly J. "Creating a Community: Literacy Events in African-American Churches." *Literacy across Communities*. Ed. Beverly J. Moss. Creskill, NJ: Hampton P, 1994.

Murray, Donald, M. "Finding Your Own Voice: Teaching Composition in an Age of Dissent." *College Composition and Communication* 20.2 (May 1969): 118–23.

Newman, John B., and Milton W. Horowitz. "Writing and Speaking." *College Composition and Communication* 16.2 (Oct. 1965): 160–64.

North, Stephen M. "Training Tutors to Talk about Writing." *College Composition and Communication* 33.4 (Dec. 1982): 434–41.

O'Brien, Charles. *Cinema's Conversion to Sound: Technology and Film Style in France and the U.S.* Bloomington: Indiana UP, 2005.

O'Connor, Frank. *The Lonely Voice: A Study of the Short Story.* Cleveland, OH: World, 1963.

Oetzmann, Anthony. "Who Developed Audacity?" Manual on the Audacity software website. 17 Aug. 2006 <http://audacity.sourceforge.net/manual-1.2/index.html>.

Olson, Gary A. "Beyond Evaluation: The Recorded Response to Essays." *Teaching English in the Two-Year College* 8.2 (Winter 1982): 121–23.

Olson, Judy M. "Multimedia in Geography: Good, Bad, Ugly, or Cool." *Annals of the Association of American Geographers* 87.4 (1997): 571–78.

Olympic Movement website. 2007. 17 Feb. 2007 <http://www.olympic.org/uk/index_uk.asp>.

Ong, Walter, J. *Fighting for Life: Contest, Sexuality, and Consciousness.* Ithaca, NY: Cornell UP, 1981.

———. *Orality and Literacy: The Technologizing of the Word.* London: Methuen, 1982.

Paine, Charles. "The Composition Course and Public Discourse: The Case of Adams Sherman Hill, Popular Culture, and Cultural Inoculation," *Rhetoric Review* 15.2 (Spring 1997): 282–99.

Payne, Johnny. *Voice and Style.* Cincinnati: Writer's Digest Books, 1996.

Pierre, Gerald J. "Generating Discussion: The First Ten Minutes." *College Composition and Communication* 25.4 (Oct. 1974): 305–7.

Poulson, Kevin. "Scenes from the MySpace Backlash," *Wired News,* 27 Feb. 2006. 8 March 2008 <http://www.wired.com/politics/law/news/2006/02/70254>.

Powell, Malea. "Rhetorics of Survivance: How American Indians Use Writing." *College Composition and Communication* 53.3 (Feb. 2002): 396–434.

Ratcliffe, Krista. "Theoretical Listening: A Trope for Interpretive Invention and a 'Code of Cross-Cultural Conduct.'" *College Composition and Communication* 51.2 (Dec. 1999): 195–224.

Reid, Ronald F. "The Boyleston Professorship of Rhetoric and Oratory, 1806–1904: A Case Study in Changing Concepts of Rhetoric and Pedagogy." *Quarterly Journal of Speech* 45.3 (Oct. 1959): 239–57.

Reyes, Maria de la Luz, and John J. Halcon. *The Best for Our Children: Critical Perspectives on Literacy for Latino Students.* New York: Teachers College P, 2001.

Richardson, Elaine. "'To Protect and Serve': African American Female Literacies." *College Composition and Communication* 54.4 (2002): 675–704.

Richie, Donald A. *Doing Oral History.* Oxford: Oxford UP, 2003.

Robinson, Jay L. "Basic Writing and Its Basis in Talk: The Influence of Speech on Writing." *Forum* 4 (Fall 1982): 73–83.

Robson, John. "Mill's 'Autobiography': The Public and the Private Voice." *College Composition and Communication* 16.2 (May 1965): 97–101.

Rose, Alan. "Spoken versus Written Criticism of Student Writing: Some Advantages of the Conference Method." *College Composition and Communication* 33.3 (Oct. 1982): 326–30.

Rose, Bill, and Joe Lenski, presenters. *Internet and Multimedia 2006: On-Demand Media Explodes.* Arbitron/Edison Media Research report. 16 Aug. 2006 <http://www.arbitron.com/downloads/im-2006study.pdf>.

Royster, Jacqueline Jones. *Traces of a Stream: Literacy and Social Change among African American Women.* Pittsburgh: U of Pittsburgh P, 2000.

———. "When the First Voice You Hear Is Not Your Own." *College Composition and Communication* 47.1 (1996): 29–40.

Ruiz, Reynaldo. "The Corrido as a Medium for Cultural Identification." *Imagination, Emblems, and Expressions: Essays on Latin American, Caribbean, and Continental Culture and Identity.* Ed. Helen Ryan-Ranson. Bowling Green, OH: Popular, 1993. 53–64.

Rushdy, Ashraf H. A. "Reading Mammy: The Subject of Relation in Sherley Anne Williams' Dessa Rose." *African American Review* 27 (1993): 365–66.

Russell, David R. "Institutionalizing English: Rhetoric on the Boundaries." *Disciplining English: Alternative Histories, Critical Perspectives.* Ed. David R. Shumway and Craig Dionne. Albany: State U of New York P, 2002. 39–58.

———. *Writing in the Academic Disciplines, 1870–1990: A Curricular History.* Carbondale: Southern Illinois UP, 1991.

Sammons, Martha C. "Using PowerPoint Presentations in Writing Classes." Aug. 1997. Technology Source Archives at the University of North Carolina. 14 Feb. 2007 <http://technologysource.org/article/using_powerpoint_presentations_in_ writing_classes/>.

Saunders, Mary. "Oral Presentations in the Composition Classrooms." *College Composition and Communication* 36.3 (Oct. 1985): 357–60.

Sawyer, Thomas M. "Why Speech Will Not Totally Replace Writing." *College Composition and Communication* 28.1 (Feb. 1977): 43–48.

Schafer, R. Murray. *The Soundscape: Our Sonic Environment and the Tuning of the World*. Rochester, VT: Destiny Books, 1977.

Schiff, Peter M. "Revising the Writing Conference." *College Composition and Communication* 29.3 (Oct. 1978): 294–96.

Selfe, Cynthia L., and Paul R. Meyer "Gender and Electronic Conferences." *Written Communication* 8.2 (1991): 163–92.

Shankar, Tara M. Rosenberger. "Speaking on the Record." Diss. Media Laboratory, MIT, Cambridge, MA, 2005.

Sharpe, Susan G. "The Ad Voice in Student Writing," *College Composition and Communication* 36.4 (Dec. 1985): 488–90.

Shaughnessy, Mina P. *Errors and Expectations: A Guide for the Teacher of Basic Writing*. New York: Oxford UP, 1977.

Shuster, Charles. "Mikhail Bakhtin as Rhetorical Theorist." *College English* 47.6 (Oct. 1985): 594–607.

Sipple, Susan. "Digitized Audio Commentary in First Year Writing Classes." 16 Aug. 2006. Academic Commons website. 25 Aug. 2006 <http://www.academic-commons.org/ctfl/vignette/digitized-audio-commentary-first-year-writing-classes>.

Sipple, Sue, and Jeff Sommers. "A Heterotopic Space: Digitized Audio Commentary and Student Revisions." 16 Nov. 2005. Academic Commons website. 21 Feb. 2009 <http://www.users.muohio.edu/sommerjd/>.

Sirc, Geoffrey. "Never Mind the Tagmemics, Where's the Sex Pistols?" *College Composition and Communication* 48.1 (Feb. 1971): 9–29.

Smith, Bruce R. "Tuning in London c. 1600." *The Auditory Culture Reader*. Ed. Michael Bull and Les Back. Oxford, UK: Berg, 2003. 127–35.

Smitherman, Geneva. "CCCC's Role in the Struggle for Language Rights." *College Composition and Communication* 50.3 (Feb. 1999): 349–76.

———. *Talkin' That Talk: Language, Culture, and Education in African America*. New York: Routledge, 2000.

Snipes, Wilson Currin. "Oral Composing as an Approach to Writing." *College Composition and Communication* 24.2 (May 1973): 200–05.

Snyder, Sharon L., Brenda Jo Brueggemann, and Rosemarie Garland-Thomson, eds. *Disability Studies: Enabling the Humanities*. New York: Modern Language Association, 2002.

Sommers, Jeff. "Spoken Response: Space, Time, and Movies of the Mind." *Writing with Elbow*. Ed. Pat Belanoff, Marcia Dickson, Sheryl I. Fontaine, and Charles Moran. Logan: Utah State P, 2002.

Sterne, Jonathan. "Medicine's Acoustic Culture: Mediate Auscultation, the Stethoscope and the 'Autopsy of the Living.'" *The Auditory Culture Reader*. Ed. Michael Bull and Les Back. Oxford, UK: Berg, 2003. 191–217.

Stewart, Donald. *The Authentic Voice: A Pre-Writing Approach to Student Writing*. Dubuque, IA: Wm. C. Brown, 1972.

Stoehr, Taylor. "Tone and Voice." *College English* 30.2 (Nov. 1968): 150–61.

Sturdevant, James R. "Large Group" Doesn't Have to Be a Dirty Word." *College Composition and Communication* 23.5 (1972): 419–21.

Sui, Daniel Z. "Visuality, Aurality, and Shifting Metaphors of Geographical Thought to the Late Twentieth Century." *Annals of the Association of American Geographers* 90.2 (2000): 322–43.

Sykes, Ingrid. "The Aesthetics of Sonic Diagnosis in Nineteenth Century France." 2005. Website of Café Scientific et Cultural. Retrieved 16 Aug. 2006 at http://www.birminghamcafe.org/view.html?eid=22

Takayoshi, Pamela, and Cynthia L. Selfe. "Thinking about Multimodality." *Multimodal Composition: Resources for Teachers*. Ed. Cynthia L. Selfe. Cresskill, NJ: Hampton P, 2007. 1–12.

Tannen, Deborah. "Oral and Literate Strategies in Spoken and Written Narratives." *Language* 58 (1982): 1–21.

———. ed. *Spoken and Written Language: Exploring Orality and Literacy*. Norwood, NJ: Ablex, 1982.

Trejo, Arnulfo D. "Of Books and Libraries." *The Chicanos: As We See Ourselves*. Ed. Arnulfo Trejo. Tucson: U of Arizona P, 1979. 167, 172–74.

Trimbur, John. "Taking the Social Turn: Teaching Writing Post Process." *College Composition and Communication* 45.1 (1994): 108–18.

United Nations website. 2007. 17 Feb. 2007 <http://www.un.org>.

Villanueva, Victor. *Bootstraps: From an American Academic of Color*. Urbana, IL: National Council of Teachers of English, 1993.

Vygotsky, Lev. *Thought and Language*. Cambridge, MA: MIT P, 1962.

Walker, Jerry L. "Bach, Rembrandt, Milton, and Those Other Cats." *English Journal* 57 (1968): 631–36.

Waner, Karen K. "Business Communication Competencies Needed by Employees as Perceived by Business Faculty and Business Professionals." *Business Communication Quarterly* 58.4 (Dec. 1995): 51–56.

Wiget, Andrew. "Sending a Voice: The Emergence of Contemporary Native American Poetry. *College English* 46.6 (Oct. 1984): 598–608.

Winchester, Otis. *The Sound of Your Own Voice.* Boston: Allyn and Bacon, 1972.

"Windows ME." 14 Oct. 2006. *Wikipedia.* 14 Oct. 2006 <http://en.wikipedia.org/wiki/Windows _Me>.

Wright, Elizabethada A., and S. Michael Halloran. "From Rhetoric to Composition: The Teaching of Writing in America to 1900." *Writing Instructor* Dec. 2001. 8 March 2009 <http://www .writinginstructor.com/haloran-wright.html>.

Yancey, Kathleen B., ed. *Voices on Voice: Perspectives, Definitions, Inquiry.* Urbana, IL: National Council of Teachers of English, 1994.

Yancey, Kathleen, and Michael Spooner. "Postings on a Genre of Email." *College Composition and Communication* 47.2 (May 1996): 252–78.

Yow, Valerie R. *Recording Oral History: A Guide for the Humanities and Social Sciences.* 2nd ed. Lanham, MD: AltaMira P, 2005.

Zaluda, Scott. "Sophisticated Essay: Billie Holiday and the Generation of Form and Idea." *College Composition and Communication* 42.4 (Dec. 1991): 470–83.

Zoellner, Robert. "Talk-Write: A Behavioral Pedagogy for Composition." *College English* 30 (Jan. 1969): 267–320.

7 "Who Will Be the Inventors? Why Not Us?" Multimodal Compositions in the Two-Year College Classroom

LISA BICKMORE AND RON CHRISTIANSEN

"A 'NEW' WAY OF COMPOSING"; OR, WHY WRITE MULTIMODALLY?

Diana George's essay "From Analysis to Design" notes that "there remains much confusion over what is meant by *visual communication, visual rhetoric,* or, more simply, *the visual* and where or whether it belongs in a composition course" (see p. 213 in this volume). She goes on to note that, as practitioners in our field, we haven't really done the work of defining this confusion, or setting it as a disciplinary problem. Rather, we have treated it as "an anomaly, a 'new' way of composing, or, somewhat cynically, as a strategy for adding relevance or interest to a required course" (p. 213). Considering that we are now more than a century into the image revolution, this seems willfully neglectful.

This neglect may stem in part from the very nature of disciplinarity. Gregory Ulmer says that "disciplines are organized around paradigmatic problems and their solutions; . . . the solutions to these problems are important to the society to which the disciplines contribute as a mode of collective intelligence." Because the "emerging predominance of the image as technology and culture is a problem of the society," it becomes, he says, "a proper task for English departments . . . to develop rhetorical and composition practices for citizens to move from consumers to producers of image discourse" (5–6). Ulmer's optimistic habit of mind helps us to think forward, considering what we might now do; despite the neglect George sensibly identifies, and despite the amnesia Ulmer sees our discipline—"like most others"—as having succumbed to regarding the "inventive side of its history," he believes that we have a particular role to play in inventing new practices: "who will be the inventors? Why not us?" he asks (5).

Our students may not be able to afford to wait for us to do this inventing: Daniel Anderson, in defining the student writing in the multiple modes enabled by new media, comes up with a new term, the "prosumer," one who

---

From *TETYC* 37 (2010): 230–42.

engages in productive consumption of new media. This term might help us think about why, as Kathleen Yancey says in "Made Not Only in Words," that "literacy today is in the midst of a tectonic change. Even inside of school, never before have writing and composition generated such diversity in definition" (p. 63). Moreover, the demands of such diverse definitions of literacy are significant—as Kip Strasma says (citing Stuart Selber), "knowledge of computers, networks, and course-management systems," which in turn requires from us as instructors a "complex, diverse assignment design that builds in complexity as students construct and repurpose texts" (254). Strasma concludes, "This is where our students are and where I want (think) my assignments (ought) to be" (254).

Gunther Kress pointedly notes:

> Curriculum is a design for the future. The contents and processes put forward in curriculum, and in its associated pedagogy, are the design for future human dispositions. They provide one set of important means, one important set of resources, for the individual's transformative, shaping action in making him or herself as social humans. (79)

To move in this direction—the direction of invention and transformation rather than conservation, of designing a curriculum for a new kind of social human—runs counter to a powerful tendency of disciplinary activity, which is to maintain its jurisdictional powers, as Anne Freadman notes in her essay "Uptake":

> Speech acts presuppose a jurisdiction, which authorizes them and provides their felicity conditions, and jurisdictions presuppose constitutions, which regulate their boundaries and their relations, the limits on their powers, and so on. We know that it is the institutional parameters of our classroom practice that has this authorizing power for the work of our students; it regulates, it controls, and it is also the condition of the freedoms they invent. (44)

Whatever the work is we put before our students largely creates the conditions for what they might invent from it. Their uptakes of our assignments are regulated by our own vision of the constraints within which they must operate. This places an ethical burden before us: how inventive can we be in conceiving of the widest possible, and the most forward-thinking, parameters for our classroom practice, in order to create the widest possible range of responses?

A note on our curriculum: At our community college, most students take two composition courses. The first of these courses has traditionally focused on academic genres (the essay, involving summary, synthesis, formal argument) and by the end of the course introduces concepts of visual rhetoric, other genres, and nonschool audiences. The second course focuses on public genres and the bridge between academic forms of inquiry, academic genres, and writing for public settings.

COHERENCES AND INVENTIONS:
WHAT DO MULTIMODAL TEXTS LOOK LIKE?

Coming face to face with nonlinear texts—even awkward or strange looking ones—can both rejuvenate our teaching and force us to reshape our notions of assessment. But it's difficult work because we often assess these new compositions using, as Yancey points out in "Looking for Sources of Coherence in a Fragmented World," the familiar "frameworks and processes" of linear text mediums. A narrow view of coherence—one claim/several interconnected supporting points/resolution—can't be strictly applied to multimodal texts. Instead, we must see new ways of achieving coherence such as pattern making, weaving, associational logic, reiteration, and layering, all techniques Yancey identifies.

In *The Practice of Everyday Life*, Michel de Certeau talks about "uses and tactics" that allow people to operate in a variety of social spaces—tactics that "use, manipulate, and divert th[o]se spaces" (30), which may create opportunities for new coherences. Among the tactics of everyday life are

> a *realization* of the linguistic system through a speech act that actualizes some of its potential (language is real only in the act of speaking); (2) an *appropriation* of language by the speaker who uses it; (3) the postulation of an interlocutor (real or fictive) and thus the constitution of a relational *contract* or allocution (one speaks to someone). (33)

De Certeau's schema of tactics makes clearer that in "situating the act [of language use] in relation to its circumstances, 'contexts of use' draw attention to the traits that specify the act of speaking . . . and are its effects" (33). Thus, the writing assignments we design should prompt students to take account of the contexts of use in which their language might "specify" and create its effects—to make use of circumstance, to act upon the contingent.

Yancey alludes to and de Certeau explicitly states that these kinds of moves are not merely transformations of coherence but rather an opening of the space in which students can potentially "[divert THE/our system] without leaving it," tactically using the parameters and rules of the system in ways unrecognizable to the system itself (de Certeau 32). Genre often delineates these parameters and rules, and, as Freadman notes, writers are constantly renegotiating the boundaries of genre, for instance, suggesting that every "'translation,' of whatever kind, is the mediation of a boundary, not its obliteration. . . . I want to say that 'uptake' is the local event of crossing a boundary" (43). In fact, students "repurpose" (a word that both Daniel Anderson and Kip Strasma use) all sorts of things: genres, media, typical rhetorical occasions. Such repurposing and boundary-crossing is one characteristic of multimodal writing that we as instructors must learn to recognize (see Anderson; Strasma, 45). Anderson says, "Let's just go out on a limb and say that repurposing both between and within media constitutes an essential act of new media composition." The student examples that follow illustrate such acts.

EXAMPLE 1: THE GENRE TRANSLATION, "LIFE GUIDE"

The final project in our first course includes a researched argument and a genre translation. The genre translation is literally a translation of the argument being made in the researched argument into a "public genre" (an op-ed, a brochure, a film, a website, etc.). While these individual texts are not necessarily multimodal, the overall final project is multimodal and opens up new spaces as well as potentially new contexts of use.

The genre translation assignment produces student texts that we might initially view as insubstantial on the one hand, or that on the other hand might have very high production value while being rhetorically simplistic. Both kinds of texts present challenges to our evaluative frameworks: we may not be able to see students' efforts to structure an apparently lightweight text (an appropriation of a mundane object, such as a pill bottle or a Chinese take-out container, with minimal textual additions) through design and visual rhetoric, or we may be overwhelmed by a student writer's professional and technical knowledge (a thirty-dollar professionally produced poster or a slick computer-generated ten-minute film), which may shift our attention away from rhetorical knowledge.

D'Ann's genre translation, a "Life Guide," adeptly illustrates nontraditional coherences and new contexts of use. In her researched argument she makes commonplace claims, such as "Television is here to stay, but I recommend that you limit your TV time. Create your own rules for how often it's okay to watch"; in her genre translation she recreates the *TV Guide* in a visual parody called the "Life Guide." Of this piece, D'Ann states: "I like my 'Life Guide' better than I like my researched argument. It's making the argument I really wanted to make" (Squire). She carefully crafts this document to have the same appearance as the *TV Guide*: reddish colors, boxes with bolded categories, times and dates, and a search box for "activities" rather than shows. It combines overt, conventional argument (using the blank grey spot in the regular *TV Guide* for the phrase "What you could be doing instead of watching television") with more subtle, juxtapositional, and associative arguments. For example, each grey box represents a carefully chosen channel name. Several times she redeploys the same name with a shift in meaning—"Home and Garden," "Life," and "Sports" now represent activities rather than programming. She manipulates channel names to make her point: "Discover USA" as a combination of the actual channels "Discovery" and "USA," and "Outdoors" as a play on the now defunct "OLN" (Outdoor Life Network).

D'Ann's work in her "Life Guide" also influenced how she revised her researched argument; as she says, "The researched argument focuses more on why you shouldn't watch hours of television. . . . With each revision, I tried to move more toward the positive. Rather than saying, 'don't do,' I wanted to say, 'Here is what you should do.'" Multimodal possibilities not only offer up alternative coherences but can also open up spaces for different tactics. D'Ann's multimodal text reshaped her invention and forestalled a premature closure of her ideas and claims.

Multimodality became important in D'Ann's writing process by shifting her construction of herself as a writer. She explained to the class that she had become engrossed in her parody for hours, evidence that she was beginning to see herself as a unique agent in the invention process. While students often feel they are only repeating what others have said ("I'm not an expert, what can I say?"), multimodal projects allow students to produce unique work with their own personal stamp. This can lead to a more engaged relationship with the potential circulation of their texts. As D'Ann relates in her self-assessment paper,

> I used station names that would fit areas of life and suggested activities that fit that area. I thought a billboard on your way home would be a good place for this (southbound I-15 out of Salt Lake or northbound I-15 going into Davis County). As people are driving home it gives them something to think about as they decide what to do with their evening.

While her "Life Guide" as a billboard might create challenges (would one be able to read and understand the "Life Guide" at such a distance?), it would be a mistake to dismiss her rhetorical plans as merely naive. She projects future circulation of the text, using the circumstances around her: rarely do students consider lived environments in which such texts might directly intervene in readers' lives, as in this potential billboard. Later, in an email interview, D'Ann mentions other ways in which she envisions the "Life Guide's" circulation: "Coincidentally, my argument and genre translation were finishing up the same time that 'TV-Turnoff Week' was happening (April 23–29). I thought this 'Life Guide' would have been a great way to bring this week to the publics' attention. It makes the argument without belittling the TV viewer."

EXAMPLE 2: A COMMUNITY WRITING CAMPAIGN, "OPERATION DESTROY SUGAR HOUSE"

At our community college, one of the culminating writing projects in the second sequence of composition courses is a collaborative community writing campaign (see Bickmore and Ruffus for a full discussion of this writing project). The assignment asks students to

- identify a community need or an issue of concern to the community;
- and develop pieces of writing which address this community need or issue.

Beyond this, they have a great deal of freedom to choose the pieces of writing they'll do and to shape them as they will. Students select several genres that work together in some way to achieve an effect they've designed on the community. We see a great deal of multimodal work in response to the assignment.

One group decided to respond to the imminent redevelopment of a retail district, the Granite Block, in one of Salt Lake City's historic neighborhoods, Sugar House. The students were already familiar with the issues involved, since several retailers were engaging in vocal talk-back with the city and the developers. The owners of the property planned to raze an existing building and rebuild a mixed-use complex. Rents were expected to be significantly higher, meaning at the least relocation for the mostly local businesses; for many, it would likely mean the end of business.

The students decided to use a MySpace platform to house many of the documents they produced. They also decided to make a short, satiric film they planned to host on the MySpace site. Both these strategies involve de Certeau's idea of the writer using the "vocabularies" and "syntaxes" of "established languages." The students took an existing web platform, with its manifest social networking intent, and appropriated it for uses congruent with their own purposes. For instance, they used MySpace's notoriously busy interface by, essentially, redefining the predefined spaces. Under "blurbs," they wrote brief profiles of businesses. Under "interests," they put links to relevant people and sources, including the city councilman who had championed the local businesses likely to be displaced by the redevelopment; a recent article in an independent newspaper; and an announcement of a local event, a poetry reading at Sugar House Coffee. Under "Who I'd Like to Meet," the group placed the logo for "Buy Local First Utah," connecting their project to a larger social movement.

Their film, scripted by the group and shot on location in the community college parking lot, involved building a loose replica of the Granite Block, made of graham crackers, canned icing, and candy, populated by the businesses and by action figures hanging out there. The film begins with this scene, and the strains of Bob Marley's "Three Little Birds" ("don't worry about a thing/cause every little thing gonna be all right"). A black screen announces "... meanwhile, in a secret lair ... ," with the Darth Vader theme from *Star Wars.* This features a war room (also populated by action figures), where the Red Mountain Retail Group plots the destruction of Sugar House:

> BART: Thank you gentlemen for coming to this meeting on such short notice; the reason you are here is because I'm a little concerned with the hippy dippy counter culture in Sugarhouse. Those free thinking beatniks spend most of their money within the Sugarhouse area, in those little ma and pa retail shops buying clothes and music from privately owned businesses as if they don't need those chain stores like the Gap.

> LIZARD: Oh my gosh! Are you telling me there isn't the Gap in Sugarhouse?

> BART: I'm afraid not, well at least not yet. This is why I have developed a plan that will put an end to there indie music listening, local merchant supporting lifestyle. Gentlemen I would like to call this plan Operation: Destroy Sugar House. As you can see I haven't quite worked out all the quirks, but it mainly consists of myself arriving unannounced to Sugarhouse via army tank. Also dropping in unexpectedly will be classic exploding devices and other harmful weapons utterly destroying the locally owned businesses and also the

nonconforming culture of Sugarhouse! Any questions? Yes you birdbrain.

BIRD: What is that flying toward the house at the end of the drawing?

BART: What? What this? This is a sword . . .

LIZARD: You're going to use a sword to destroy Sugarhouse?

BART: Yes, yes there will be sword, but it will not be just any sword, it will be sword of mass destruction! Okay never mind, I told you I haven't quite worked out all the quirks yet. Any other questions?

E.T.: Well I'm a little concerned with the manner which has been chosen to destroy Sugarhouse. I think, if we play our cards right, we can do just as much damage but make sure it falls within legal jurisdiction. Now I'm just as shocked and appalled as you all are that Sugarhouse doesn't have a Gap or a Wal-Mart, but I believe there is a way we can get them there very soon.

BART: Yes, go on.

E.T.: If we bulldoze the local merchants within what's called The District of Sugarhouse and then replace them with a higher scaled Gateway type of development with a mall and condominiums, then it will be impossible for these privately owned businesses to keep and maintain a shop there because it will be to expensive.

GIZMO: You're a genius! Instead of Orion's music it will be Sam Goody, and instead of Blue Boutique–Victoria Secret and instead of Pib's Exchange it will then be Starbucks Coffee!

LIZARD: Wait, there isn't a Starbucks in Sugarhouse either?

BART: No I'm afraid not. Frankly, I believe it's the last place on earth where Starbucks is not at.

GIZMO: Oh my gosh! It's like it's a third world country down there!

The film uses many existing cultural constructions: the *Star Wars* films are clearly a source, but so are the Iraq War and the culture of secrecy that surrounded it. They also use cultural materials at hand—the Bob Marley song, connoting optimism in the face of difficulty; the R.E.M. song "It's the End of the World as We Know It" as the music for the destruction of the facsimile Sugar House. Do the students create straw men (composite plastic men)? Do they do justice to the claims of the Red Mountain Retail Group? By making an argument-by-other-means, they argue that the imperative of a for-profit commercial operation to maximize possible profits will compete against the idiosyncratic, lived experience of a neighborhood, almost as surely as if the group had come in with weapons. Redevelopment destroys the idiosyncratic texture of a neighborhood, especially if citizens and tenants don't have a voice. Would this argument have been more effectively made in an op-ed piece? In a researched argument? Or does it become a strategy of articulation, to create pieces in multiple modalities, all speaking to a purpose of resistance, critique, and affirmation of an original local environment?

EMERGENT CURRICULUM: DELIVERY, RECEPTION, CONTINGENCY, AND RHETORICAL PRODUCTION

Jody Shipka's "A Multimodal Task-Based Framework for Composing" suggests that "students' uptakes of a much wider, richer repertoire of semiotic resources, coupled with their efforts to purposefully structure the delivery and reception of that work, afford new ways of thinking, acting, and working within and beyond the space of first-year composition" (279). Shipka's examples—a grocery bag of boxes with notes and a repurposed hometown Web page—demonstrate that by simple means students influence the ways in which their work will be received. These examples push us to consider just how inventive we can be. Shipka shows that students can "purposively structure the delivery and reception," of their work—de Certeau's contexts of use—prompting us to re-evaluate the boundaries of the class and of our discipline.

Paul Prior, as well, wants us to examine these boundaries; using the lens of activity theory, he invites us to revisit what he sees as the "synchronic rhetoric," the classical rhetorical canons, in order to compose a more situated, "emergent, laminated" history of the rhetorical occasion. He asks us to consider reception and distribution as critical parts of any rhetorical scene—certainly connected, for us, to the notion of contexts of use. We find this account of rhetoric compelling in light of our students' multimodal work, an account that gives us more to work with as we respond and evaluate (Prior et al.).

However, once "contexts of use" becomes an active category for us as we read and respond to student writing, we confront almost immediately what we don't know about the places where writing circulates, and the intricate rhetorical options writers navigate in those places. De Certeau imagines writers as "unrecognized producers, poets of their own affairs, trailblazers in the jungles of functionalist rationality, consumers [who] produce . . . 'indeterminate trajectories' that are apparently meaningless, since they do not cohere with the constructed, written, and prefabricated space through which they move" (34). He foregrounds for us the always-present inventive possibilities in writing, for the writers who

> use as their *material* the *vocabularies* of established languages (those of television, newspapers, the supermarket or city planning), although they remain within the framework of prescribed *syntaxes* (the temporal modes of schedules, paradigmatic organizations of places, etc.), these "traverses" remain heterogeneous to the systems they infiltrate and in which they sketch out the guileful ruses of *different* interests and desires. (33)

Instead of fitting into the norms of our more established discourses, "they circulate, come and go, overflow and drift over an imposed terrain, like the snowy waves of the sea slipping in among the rocks and defiles of an established order" (33).

De Certeau's sense of writers circulating over and around the parameters of an "imposed terrain"—for instance, a classroom—reminds us again of

Freadman's formulation of the jurisdictional power of classroom parameters, and the need to consider the sorts of writing our assignments allow—understanding and acknowledging how the jurisdictional power we wield makes a material difference in what our students invent in response to the courses we design. Geoffrey Sirc, for example, has made a project of rethinking the apparatus of composition, in particular its most venerable genres and their attendant strategies. In "Box Logic" Sirc identifies "a primary goal" of his writing classes to "show my students how their compositional future is assured if they can take an art stance to the everyday, suffusing the materiality of daily life with an aesthetic" (117). Rather than aiming for the linear, composed argument that edits out the *dérivé*—the drift—Sirc argues for foregrounding other strategies: "Arrangement of materials and notational jottings is a desperately important compositional skill" (123), he urges. Students can bring their aesthetic sense, their artful arrangements, to all sorts of compositions, and the pieces they devise often speak with more rhetorical sharpness to situations we haven't imagined and could not fully expect until we work with and evaluate them.

De Certeau, Freadman, and Sirc all imagine language use as a practice of freedom. Our commitment to this principle as a discipline includes, at the most basic level, the sorts of assignments we develop—the writing we solicit from our students—the design of our courses, and the ways we consider evaluating student work. This means developing assignments and assignment sequences that actively engage students' existing familiar practices, encourage them to develop new ones, and invite them to consider how the multimodal documents that emerge from their work and play might function in their lives and in the social settings in which they themselves circulate. Strasma describes such a curriculum as "emergent"—in which "interactions among content, students, teacher(s), distribution, circulation, technology, and collaboration" allow "the very assignment itself [to emerge and change] through the unfolding of time within a classroom space" (255). But this means some practices we take for granted in the composition classroom may be left behind: "designing with emergence as a goal requires a course system that encourages distributed knowledge (and thus authority) and the development of content over a span of days or weeks" (256). An emergent curriculum is full of surprises, both locally and globally—we don't quite know where our students' work will take us as we attempt to interact with it and ultimately assign it a grade. Our two student examples specifically illustrate this.

RESPECTING STUDENT INVENTION, BECOMING PATHFINDERS

While new media or multimodal genres do not seem as stable as more conventional genres, and may never be (Yancey, "Looking"), we should engage these student texts through rich response. These types of text are certainly not new, but the digitized world is: it does not take specialized knowledge or expertise to parody the textual design of *TV Guide*—a student, a computer, and an hour.

We may not give proper respect to the power of student invention, instead unwittingly using students' inventions to build our own sophisticated critiques that would not be possible without the original student inventions. Here our responses profit from their inventions without acknowledging our reliance on them. This ethical challenge compels us to value these inventions and to mute our own facile criticisms. For example, we originally used the word "subtle" to describe the rhetorical impact of D'Ann's text, demonstrating our difficulties, even while explicitly hoping to do the opposite, to appropriately value these new ways of knowing. D'Ann's "Life Guide" is not making an "explicit argument" about watching less TV; therefore is the coherence of her argument really more *subtle*? In order to assess multimodal texts, we must relinquish some of our text-based authority. In this case the word "subtle" illuminates our biases, specifying a *degree* of coherence—just look harder, you'll recognize the coherence!—while the difference is actually qualitative. Instead it is a coherence that relies on arrangement and context and may be, at first, unrecognizable to the systems of textual norms and student assessment. As Yancey states, "Digital compositions weave words and contexts and images: they are exercises in ordered complexity" ("Looking" 300). The context in D'Ann's "Life Guide" is the original format and design of the *TV Guide*, something not easily and "logically" communicated quickly in words, rather something organized by association and context.

STRATEGIES OF EVALUATION: SITUATED WRITING, LOCAL KNOWLEDGE, AND RHETORICITY

How does a teacher reasonably approach evaluating a project that includes a MySpace page and a video, starring Bart Simpson as a Darth Vader–like mastermind of a council of evildoers (Big Bird, Gizmo, generic Lizard)? In part the answer is design: the design of assignments must allow for greater latitude of student response and encourage a multigenre and multimodal approach. Writing teachers well know that the particular design of an assignment sets up the parameters for response. This means that the teacher must think in terms of the whole project when considering any one piece of writing: the entire evaluation doesn't rest on the degree of sophistication and the excellent execution of a single piece.

In the case of the MySpace project (including the video), because the community writing campaign concludes the semester, most of the feedback is formative and in-person. The student writers presented the video to the class, along with the MySpace frame, in a presentation meant to show work in progress and to address the way the piece fit both into the community writing campaign as a whole as well as how it fit the communicative situation and worked to achieve a communicative aim. The students clearly found great enjoyment and satisfaction in creating this video; the instructor saw it as an accomplished composition, easily "A" work in both rhetorical conception and execution (in its filmed form). Because it was a part of a larger project— the community writing campaign—the overall grade was an "A-," simply because the other parts of the project were less thoroughly developed and not as fully executed. The evaluation of projects like this can be somewhat holistic and require on the part of the instructor a balancing of rhetorical aim and execution, as well as the effect of the various parts on the whole. Like most evaluation, making final judgments about multimodal composition is more an art than a science.

A dilemma with multimodal compositions arises when instructors have little direct knowledge of producing multimedia writing, understandably feeling themselves out of their depths. Situating the production of multimodal pieces in their contexts of use allows an instructor to see them as embodying a communicative aim, rather than as stand-alone assignments, which therefore must merely meet criteria and exhibit features. A more situated approach—which almost certainly entails envisioning the scope and sequence of the entire course and not just of a single assignment—can help to refocus the evaluative gaze, making the entire project of evaluating student writing more rhetorical.

Moreover, trying to see the local knowledge at play in student writing can help us see their savvy responses to the issues and rhetorical practices of a particular communicative scene. The student working on the genre translation project—the "Life Guide"—made a leap into a form of rhetorical production we had not anticipated. One way to look at the project would be to excise the textual elements, to merely assess the ways the textual content succeeded, or did not, as an address to the original assignment, or as an argument. But this would miss what is remarkable about this piece of writing—that the student embodied a fully rhetorical gesture by taking up a genre already situated in a particular scene and using it for a purpose of their own. This act of rhetorical embodiment did not require advanced technical skills; rather, it required a situated and personal knowledge and a small degree of rhetorical daring—the daring to design a billboard for a writing class.

In this particular case the instructor gave in-person formative feedback on the "Life Guide" during a class peer review. This feedback included praise for the elements discussed in the above paragraph, but also specifically asked D'Ann how this genre translation would, if at all, impact her researched argument on the same issue. At the end of the semester D'Ann's portfolio containing both the "Life Guide," researched argument, and self-reflective essay received an "A" grade because, although the work was unconventional, D'Ann still effectively demonstrated the rhetorical knowledge asked for in our outcome goals for English 1010, especially this one: "#1 *Rhetorical Strategies*, including adapting to differences in purpose, audience, and genre." In doing so she engaged the feedback the instructor gave her on a rough draft of her argument: "I think you overstate some of your claims and oversimplify cause and effect. . . . I like your move at the end as it seems more realistic and sensitive but I found myself wanting to see this more balanced view throughout your paper." Not only did D'Ann demonstrate how to adapt her argument from the genre of argument to a visual parody, but she also allowed interplay between the genres to change the overall purpose and framing of her argument piece.

From a broader perspective, then, writing teachers must develop their own rhetorical imaginations—to envision a piece of writing in a setting beyond the classroom and to appreciate what, exactly, the student writer aims to be doing in that setting with the piece of writing he or she has made.

To this end, then, we urge the following:

Design and sequence assignments with an eye toward what Kip Strasma calls "emergence."

Thicken the rhetorical situations framed in your assignments.

Aim to have students define and address potential audiences, to conceive of and execute strategies of delivery and reception.

Ask students to consider the context of use for their productions.

Offer feedback formatively, so that students can try and try again at the above.

Evaluate whether the student's written production succeeds in terms of its own aims within a thick rhetorical situation.

CONCLUSION: (BOTH/AND)

As these reconstructions of students' multimodal productions above illustrate, the boundaries of the classroom and the discipline of composition may be much less rigid than we assume. Yet the maturing discipline of composition often enough still rebuffs such illustrations and the calls for opening up these boundaries. Plenty of us worry about diffusing our disciplinary activities to the point we no longer recognize ourselves, often voiced as a warning call to move "back to the core" of writing and argument. As compositionists we should know better, especially when the debate is crudely cast as an either/or: *either* we shore up the boundaries of our discipline *or* we will be indistinguishable from media studies and communication, and we will lose the focus on teaching students how to write. Henry Jenkins argues in *Convergence Culture* that educators can remain too focused on the "dangers of [media] manipulation rather than the possibilities of participation . . . rather than in expanding skills at deploying media for one's own ends, rewriting the core stories our culture has given us" (259). To accomplish this we must accept the necessary ambiguity of being *both*, as Stuart Moulthrop (cited in Williams) insists, "advocates of an endangered literacy **[and]** . . . pathfinders for new modes of information exchange" (479).

Acknowledgment We offer our thanks to our students D'Ann Squire, Danielle Lail, Jamison Featherstone, Aaron Mann, and Zach Smith for their permission to cite from and represent their work here, work that has inspired and illuminated our own.

WORKS CITED

Anderson, Daniel. "Prosumer Approaches to New Media Composition: Consumption and Production in Continuum." *Kairos* 8.1 (Spring 2003). 10 Dec. 2003. 9 Oct. 2009 <http://www.technorhetoric.net/8.1/index.html>.

Bickmore, Lisa, and Stephen Ruffus. "The Half-Life of the Classroom: Students as Public Agents." *Research Writing Revisited: A Sourcebook for Teachers*. Ed. Pavel Zemliansky and Wendy Bishop. Portsmouth, NH: Boynton/Cook, 2004.

de Certeau, Michel. *The Practice of Everyday Life*. Trans. Steven Rendall. Berkeley: U of California P, 1984.

Freadman, Anne. "Uptake." *The Rhetoric and Ideology of Genre*. Ed. Richard Coe, Lorelei Lingard, and Tatiana Teslenko. Cresskill, NJ: Hampton P, 2002.

Jenkins, Henry. *Convergence Culture*. New York: New York UP, 2006.

Kress, Gunther. "Visual and Verbal Modes of Representation in Electronically Mediated Communication: The Potentials of New Forms of Text." *Page to Screen: Taking Literacy into the Electronic Age*. Ed. Ilana Snyder. London: Routledge, 1998.

Prior, Paul, Janine Solberg, Patrick Berry, Hannah Bellwoar, Bill Chewning, Karen J. Lunsford, Liz Rohan, Kevin Roozen, Mary Sheridan-Rabideau, Jody Shipka, Derek Van Ittersum, and Joyce Walker. "Re-situating and Re-mediating the Canons: A Cultural-historical Remapping of Rhetorical Activity: A Collaborative Webtext." *Kairos* 11.3 (Summer 2007). 16 Mar. 2009. <http://kairos.technorhetoric.net/11.3/binder.html?topoi/prior-et-al/index.html>.

Shipka, Jody. "A Multimodal-Task-Based Framework for Composing." *College Composition and Communication* 57.2 (Dec. 2005): 277–306.

Sidler, Michelle, Richard Morris, and Elizabeth Overman Smith, eds. *Computers in the Composition Classroom*. Boston: St. Martin's, 2008.

Sirc, Geoffrey. "Box Logic." *Writing New Media: Theory and Applications for Expanding the Teaching of Composition*. Ed. Anne Frances Wysocki, Johndan Johnson-Eilola, Cynthia L. Selfe, and Geoffrey Sirc. Logan: Utah State UP, 2004. 111–46.

Squire, D'Ann. Email interview with the author. 7 June 2007.

Strasma, Kip. "Assignments by Design." *Teaching English in the Two-Year College* 34.3 (Mar. 2007): 248–63.

Ulmer, Gregory. *Internet Invention: From Literacy to Electracy*. New York: Pearson Education, 2003.

Williams, Sean. "Part 2: Toward an Integrated Composition Pedagogy in Hypertext." Sidler, Morris, and Smith. 469–84.

Yancey, Kathleen Blake. "Looking for Sources of Coherence in a Fragmented World: Notes toward a New Assessment Design." Sidler, Morris, and Smith. 293–307.

8

Show, Not Tell: The Value of New Media Scholarship

CHERYL E. BALL

1. INTRODUCTION

In the summer of 2002, the major online journals in composition published a collaborative issue on electronic publishing. In that issue, several authors referenced the Conference on College Composition and Communication's (CCCC) position statement on scholarship requirements for tenure and promotion in the field of composition. The dire tone of the statement referred to the poor economy and lack of book publication opportunities, causing tenure-track faculty and department chairs alike to wonder if tenure would still be attainable for folks without a book in hand. This statement suggested that departments reconsider the types of publications needed for tenure or advancement and to update their guidelines to include accepting scholarly works that are "observational and experimental," both of which are deemed "important" in advancing knowledge in the field (CCCC, n.d.). Although electronic or online publication of scholarly works wasn't mentioned directly, many authors in the collaborative issue inferred to this option and spoke of the online publications' value as a viable option for scholarship. Many compositionists see the value of publishing online, whether they do so themselves or read texts that colleagues have published. But, the debate has not fully subsided as to whether online scholarship is as valuable as an article or book published by a major print journal or press. What counts as scholarship is still under the microscope. Steven Krause (2002), in his article "Considering the Values of Self-Published Web Sites," compared the difference between print and online scholarship when he said:

> Prior to the web, it was easy to determine what should or shouldn't count as scholarship: if it appeared as an article in a peer reviewed journal or if it was published as a book by a respectable press, it was definitionally "scholarship" both in the abstract sense of advancing knowledge and in the tangible sense of being worthy to count toward tenure, review, merit, and so forth.

From *Computers and Composition* 21 (2004): 403–25.

Certainly, tenure and advancement issues play a large role in an author's decision to publish texts in an online journal. But is work published online in peer-reviewed journals still considered risky for tenure? A URL instead of a page number doesn't generally make these texts experimental anymore. Krause (2002) concurred, saying "few of us in English studies nowadays would label articles published in these places as 'not scholarship' for the purposes of tenure and review." But, most authors who do publish online in scholarly, peer-reviewed journals publish texts that do not break print-bound conventions and rarely travel into an apparent experimental realm of scholarship. In response to this reliance on print-based traditions within a supposedly experimental realm of publication in online journals, I distinguish between *scholarship about new media*, which uses print conventions such as written text as the main mode of argument, and *new media scholarship*, which uses modes other than only written text to form an argument. I demonstrate the print-bound conventions of current online scholarship in journals such as *Kairos*, and argue that applying the term new media scholarship to digital texts that use print-based conventions is an inappropriate application of the term. Instead, new media scholarship should only be applied to texts that experiment with and break away from linear modes of print traditions.

New media scholarship—online scholarship that uses modes such as audio, video, images, and/or animation in addition to written text to make meaning—is fairly new in composition studies (and other fields), which might cause readers to misinterpret these texts as too artistic to satisfy scholarly conventions. I suggest, however, that new media scholarship has a necessary aesthetic component because of its designed, multimodal elements, and because these multiple modes can be read in conjunction with written text to form the text's meaning. So that authors and readers might come to expand the field's notions of what could be considered and valued as composition scholarship, I analyze a new media text, "Digital Multiliteracies" (Miles, 2002b), to show how its video-editing interface and navigational structure make meaning in ways appropriate for scholarly publication. This new media text uses strategies that could be considered experimental and removed from print traditions, which works to support and inform the author's argument.

In writing this article, I acknowledge with an uncomfortable irony that I have created a paradox—it is my intention for authors to think about and understand new media scholarship as a way to use multiple modes of communication to form persuasive meanings (and subsequently to create their own new media publications) instead of always relying on written, linear text. Yet, I am not enacting the practice I suggest. *Mea culpa*: New media scholarship is so new to humanities fields that I wanted the evidence of this linear article to point toward the exploration of new media texts as directly and conventionally as possible. Had I chosen to discuss this issue through a new media presentation, the evidence for the necessity of moving toward new media would have had less impact. This article, remediated into new media presentation, simply could not convey the same linear, argument-based meanings because the modes in which new media texts are composed are not based in linear, print traditions. *Modes*, here and throughout, refer not to the traditional modes of writing but, rather, the semiotic elements such as video, graphics, written text, audio, and so on that a designer uses to compose multi-modal or new media texts. How audiences make meaning from animated graphics, for example, is different than how they make meaning from a sentence, paragraph, or full-length article. The formation of argument in new media texts, then, becomes not a linear construction linking one sentence — meaning to a consecutive other. It is, instead, a persuasion, a juxtaposition of modal elements from which readers infer meaning. For this reason, when I use *argument* to discuss an author's or designer's intention in a new media work, I am not suggesting that her or his argument is readable in the same ways as print constructions of an argument would be. Instead, I offer argument as a term for the persuasive meaning-making elements in new media texts. In the case of the text I examine later in this article, which signals itself as a scholarly text, using argument helps me refer to the elements through which the text makes scholarly connections and meanings. It is my intention in this linear article, then, not to outline how the forms of rhetorical argument can be applied neatly to new media texts (as I don't believe they easily can), but to help readers understand the possibilities of interpreting new media scholarship so that when they approach a new media text, they can make meaning from it. And, if readers are able to realize the meanings in new media texts, next time I may take advantage of new media techniques to compose meaning in different ways. No doubt, in many cases, this is why other new media scholars choose to present their work in a print-based format. It may be time, however, to begin composing more of the so-called experimental new media texts. In the next sections, I discuss how a re-focused definition of new media scholarship will help readers make meaning from such texts.

2. THE CLICHÉ OF NEW MEDIA SCHOLARSHIP

The current trend in online scholarly publications is to name many of these texts new media scholarship. I believe this is an inaccurate use of the term as it defines new media too broadly to be useful in helping readers approach and interpret the various modes used in scholarship published on the World Wide Web. To make the term new media scholarship more precise and useful, I offer a focused definition of *new media* as texts that juxtapose semiotic modes in new and aesthetically pleasing ways and, in doing so, break away from print traditions so that written text is not the primary rhetorical means. For instance, some of the semiotic modes in a new media text might include sound, graphics, video, animation, and/or written words. These texts are typically distributed in an online context, and because of their use of modes that readers more typically find in aesthetic texts (i.e., film, audio, animation), their argumentative models are not linear, alphabetic, or reminiscent of traditional print-bound models. In this section, I will discuss why using the term new media scholarship to refer to any digitized, online scholarship defines new media too broadly; instead, the terms *online scholarship* or scholarship about new media should be employed when discussing online texts where the written word is most prominent.

Recently,[1] I performed a search for "new media scholarship" on Google, and most of the nearly 200 hits referred to the Electronic Theses and Dissertations (ETD) initiative or the Networked Digital Library of Theses and Dissertations (NDLTD). As far back as 1987, the NDLTD—through the efforts of schools including Virginia Tech, University of Florida, and the University of Michigan—has been encouraging graduate schools across the country and internationally to have students submit their theses and dissertations electronically in portable document format (PDF). This initiative offers unprecedented access to new scholarship in all fields of graduate study. The language of the initiative refers to these digital theses and dissertations as "new media scholarship" (UNESCO, 2001). The ETD initiative has greatly expanded since 1987 to include formats such as hypertext, hypermedia, video, VRML (Virtual Reality Modeling Language), and others.[2] But the primary method of creating an ETD is by using Adobe Acrobat so that students type their dissertations in a word-processing program, then save them as PDFs in Acrobat. A PDF version of their print document keeps the print-based formatting intact for online presentation. Essentially, most ETDs resemble a print dissertation—they can be downloaded and printed just like a document from Microsoft Word. Scholars such as Lev Manovich (2001) would have found no trouble in defining new media scholarship as a print-based text remediated for online distribution, such as an ETD. But I believe that using the term to cover a huge range of online scholarly texts, each with their own set of conventions, will make it difficult for readers and scholars to develop and define specific reading strategies for texts that differ from print-based meaning-making strategies. PDFs and most websites are not experimental scholarship; nearly all follow a long history of print conventions. For this reason, I suggest using the term online scholarship to refer to texts such as ETDs and many kinds of websites where the written text is the main mode of the author's argumentation strategies.

Another inappropriate use of the term new media scholarship arises when it is applied to online scholarship that specifically discusses new media elements or techniques. Over the past several years, the field of computers and composition has seen a sharp rise in the number of published texts that reference areas of study that have led up to new media including visual rhetoric, digital literacies, design, multimedia, and new media—articles and webtexts whose authors argued for the inclusion of reading and creating multimodal texts (texts that incorporate more than a singular mode of communication, more than just the written word) in composition classrooms. There have been multiple special issues on these topics in journals: visual literacy in *Enculturation* 3.2 (Blakesley & Brooke, 2002), digital literacy in *Computers and Composition* 18.1 and 18.2 (Handa, 2001), and new media in the Spring 2003 issue of *Kairos* (for which I must disclose that I was the co-coverweb editor). It seems obvious, based on the increasing abundance of scholarship, that teachers are interested in how to interpret and teach texts that extend beyond the written word. But the look of online scholarship about visual rhetorics, digital literacies, and multimedia that has been published to date appears familiar. With the exception of the *Kairos* special issue, all the articles and webtexts look as if they could just as easily have been published in a print journal as in an online journal. Even Krause (2002), in the online, collaborative issue mentioned earlier, said, "Increasingly, the only significant difference between online journals and their more traditional counterparts is the medium." The problem is that online journals have the ability to cost-effectively publish texts that can technologically push beyond our reading habits associated with the limits of the printed page. But they don't. It is the same, linear story with all the major online journals in computers and composition.[3] Composition and new media scholars write about how readers can make meaning from images, typefaces, videos, animations, and sounds[4] . . . but most scholars don't compose with these media. It is evident from the scholarship available that compositionists are interested in new media. Yet, they do not seem to value creating new media texts for scholarly publications to explore the multimodal capabilities of new technologies. The linear tradition of composition scholars' publications about new media techniques causes me to suggest that this type of scholarship should not be called new media scholarship but should, more accurately, be labeled scholarship about new media. To show how composition scholars overlook the distinction between scholarship about new media and new media scholarship, I want to explore Patricia Webb Peterson's (2002) analysis of a text published in *Kairos*, which has (traditionally?) been the online journal where authors can publish experimental texts.

Peterson (2002) closely analyzed two peer-reviewed composition journals—*Kairos*, published online, and this print-based journal, *Computers and Composition*. In her close reading of these two journals, she remarked that *Kairos* "identifies its purpose as both conforming to while still challenging traditional disciplinary definitions of scholarship and scholars." *Kairos* has, however, also "adopted print-based, traditionally accepted strategies for structuring" certain elements of the journal such as the table of contents. Peterson suggested that this switch from challenging to conventional modes is based on how "we are used to reading." *Kairos* began and continues to offer itself as a place where authors can publish experimental and non-traditional scholarly texts. It is one of the few places online where compositionists can find texts that do not always mimic print conventions by sticking to the written word as the main argumentative mode. *Kairos* attempts to achieve "a balance between tradition and innovation . . . a fact that suggests that the physical (or virtual) medium directly influences the kinds of scholarship that is allowed/encouraged," as Peterson's reading showed. But does *Kairos* follow through on the innovative potentials of publishing online scholarship? (I ask this, too, as a devoted reader-turned-editor of this journal . . .) If a reader finds link-node hypertexts still innovative in 2003, then, yes, *Kairos* does push scholarly boundaries. However, if readers see how quickly new media technologies are changing this field and want scholarship reflective and truly experimental, then *Kairos* has barely made an impact. This is not to say that authors have not yet approached using new media technologies in online journals—just that there is still much to accomplish, as the example below indicates.

In a Fall 2002 *Kairos* webtext, "[Continuing to] Mind the Gap: Teaching Image and Text in New Media Spaces," the authors stated on the first screen that their intention with this text was to "claim academic legitimacy" in multi-media by creating "such a text" (Gossett et al.). The work of new media schol-ars crosses so many disciplinary and departmental boundaries, which makes it necessary for scholars to show colleagues across fields that one can work in new media (and not just write about it); this step is essential to staking claims in the field of new media. "Mind the Gap" takes advantage of new media techniques, including video clips of the authors in a roundtable discussion and still images that add visual interest to the text. These new media elements allow readers to see and hear the authors as they add to their written argu-ments, but these visual elements do not perform the work of the written argu-mentative modes—they act as footnotes to the text, supplemental areas to explore, not necessary paths to follow to fully interpret the argument. It is the written text that readers are asked to rely on. The written text is central to the design of the screen and its prominence requires that readers use the text as the main meaning-making mode in understanding the authors' arguments (see Figure 8-1).

FIGURE 8-1 An example of *scholarship about new media*—an online text that argues for the production and use of new media texts while it maintains print conventions.

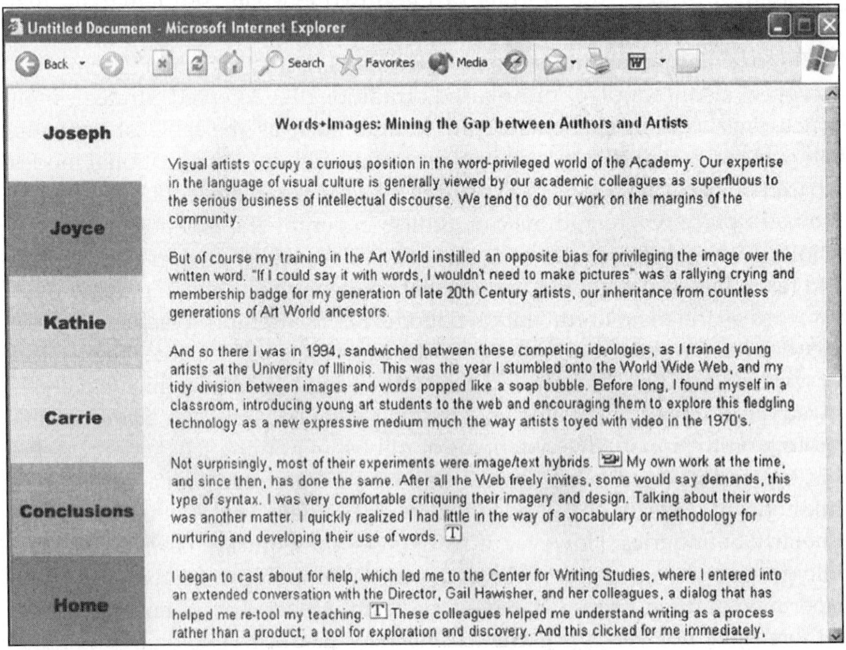

The authors' argument focused on the need to incorporate multimodal literacies with verbal and textual literacies—a notion not new in this field, as evidenced through The New London Group's *Multiliteracies* (2000) and Günther Kress and Theo van Leeuwen's *Multimodal Discourse* (2001) as well as in listserv discussions [see TechRhet's Fall 2002 thread on (web) design]. But, in "Minding the Gap," there is no question that the written text is the main mode of meaning and that the authors' arguments can be found by reading the written text. And there's no question, based on where the text was published (*Kairos*), that the authors intended it to be scholarly. "Minding the Gap" is an example of scholarship about new media and not new media scholarship, as the authors intended.[5] Continuing to write about the potential of multiliteracies rather than acting through those literacies will limit our notion of scholarship for the future. When authors write about new media, they describe the potentials and possibilities of understanding and using multimodal theories. This scholarship is important in order to have a common (or at least contentious) ground on which to stand, teach, and go forward in the field of new media. But the current scholarship about new media makes it evident that what we preach is not what we practice. Our scholarly conventions remain in the realm of old media. Let me turn, then, to new media scholarship as I discuss meaning-making strategies useful to such texts.

3. MAKING MEANING IN NEW MEDIA SCHOLARSHIP

There are few texts to look to as examples of true new media scholarship and many good reasons as to why journals are not publishing new media texts. It is the authors who must create these texts in order for journals to publish them, and without current examples, authors may feel that new media scholarship is not viable. Peterson (2002) said:

> As authors themselves, scholars interpret the journal's purpose and publication requirements through their own ideological, cultural, and political lenses. By pushing the boundaries (in content and form, or what I'll call here, rhetorical presentation), scholars play an integral role in creating a journal's purpose.

The culture of many departments may make it seem like experimental scholarship is not valued. Traditional, written publications are the modes that have been most accepted. Recently, online scholarship has become more accepted, but certainly not to the extent that it is common to find tenure review committees who value an electronic publication equally to a print one. And, then, how many scholars in humanities computing feel as if they can compose new media texts adequate enough to branch out to this experimental, scholarly level and still have enough energy to defend this decision to the review committee? It is not easy, or certain. It is easy (at least, easier) to produce the same kinds of texts—such as this article—we've been taught and are teaching students to produce and value. For authors to find themselves in a routine of producing traditional scholarly texts allows them to concentrate on the argument and not on the overdetermined space and structure of the academic paper. However, in new media texts, the space and structure the arguments are made in can be more immediate and immersive, foregrounded in relation to the structural transparency of the book or link-node hypertext (Bolter & Grusin, 2000, 225). Anthony Giddens (1994) suggested that it was possible to break out of this social "routinisation," to "re-groove" what is expected (p. 128). As of yet, new media scholarship is an underdetermined genre, waiting for authors and readers to "determine the design" of these texts (Feenberg, 1999, 79). Applying Gidden's and Andrew Feenberg's theories to new media scholarship, it is possible to say that authors who wish to take agency with their scholarship to produce new media arguments can lead the way for others.

But, how do readers of new media scholarship—scholarship that relies on modes of communication other than (or in addition to) alphabetic text—approach and interpret that work as being scholarly? According to the CCCC position statement on the standards of scholarly publications, authors of experimental works should be aware that "traditionally valued projects . . . move back and forth between theoretical discussion and practical application" ("Scholarship in Composition," n.d.). New media texts, which are experimental if only because audiences are not used to recognizing their meaning-making strategies, typically move freely between theory and practice through their interactive and animated designs. (In the final section of this article, I will discuss a new media text that explicitly performs its meaning through the audience's understanding of its multimodal elements and interface design.)

Traditionally, it is the argument—the focused meaning of the text—that a reader looks for to determine its scholarly worth. New media texts may not have linear, print-based argumentation models, so how do readers discover the author's main point? The scholarly discussion of the semiotic potential of visual and aural modes with—and extending beyond—written modes has increased over the last few years. Strategies for reading non-traditional, electronic texts have been described for at least a decade (see, e.g., Douglas, 2000; Johnson-Eilola, 1997; Landow, 1994; Lanham, 1993; Murray, 1997; Sloane, 2000). Hypertext theorists have long been describing how structural models of hypertext essays are modeled on traditional interpretational and rhetorical strategies (earlier, e.g., Bolter, 1991; Landow, 1997; recently, e.g., Carter, 2003). I will forego an in-depth argument into the connections between traditional and hypertextual reading strategies as literary hypertext critics and authors have provided much scholarship about this subject over the last decade. Instead, I refer briefly to authors whose arguments turned toward multimodal and new media texts. Jay David Bolter and Richard Grusin (2000) suggested that using new media techniques would extend texts beyond the print-remediated-as-Web standard where the written word has remained the main mode of communication (although they didn't specify how this might be done). The New London Group (2000) described the necessity of including multiliteracy theories and practice in everyday pedagogies. Building on the multiliteracies tradition, Kress and van Leeuwen (2001) described how meaning is assigned to all of the "modes deployed in a multimodal object/phenomenon/text" (28) such that a unified interpretation of the various elements in a designed text makes a cohesive argument. They demonstrated this by providing sample analyses of multimodal texts, but those texts remained strictly in comfortable territory, relying on written text and static image combinations. Static text-and-image combinations are increasingly used as examples for analysis in multiliteracy theories (see, e.g. Kress, 2003; Newman, 2002; Unsworth, 2001), and Diana George (2002) offered reading strategies for visual arguments created by students in composition classes. But, these two, while helpful for teachers new to understanding, let alone assigning, such texts also remain in the realm of print, static media. However, Anne Wysocki, in two articles "Impossibly Distinct" (Wysocki, 2001) and "Seriously Visible" (Wysocki, 2003), moved beyond the text-and-image combo by analyzing the interactive and aesthetic features of several multimedia CD-ROMs, showing how each CD creates meaning through its multimodal design.

The point is this: When readers begin to understand and value the multiple semiotic modes of new media texts, the shape of "what counts as forms of knowledge in 'disciplines' or 'subjects'" will also begin to change (Kress & van Leeuwen, 2001, 43). Peterson (2002) offered a similar explanation of how readers have sway over the value of new media scholarship and whether it will appear in an online journal: "What is at stake here is not simply print versus online work, but, rather, who gets to define what it means to be a scholar in the university." Being able to read and understand new media texts as scholarly is integral to the continuation of knowledge making in the field of composition. However, misinterpretation of the variable modes in a new media text can happen. For readers unfamiliar with understanding how a video, sound, or photograph can function as a way of creating meaning in a scholarly text, new media scholarship may be dismissed as having an unnecessarily fussy "advertising aesthetic" (Glazier, 2001) making it unworthy as a scholarly text in the eyes of the reader.

3.1. Misreading New Media Scholarship

With all the modes available for interpretation in a text, including images, animation, sound, and video—modes more often associated with art than composition studies—how can readers understand the potential of using artistic strategies in new media scholarship? As with Kathie Gossett, Carrie A. Lamanna, Joseph Squier, and Joyce R. Walker's (2002) text described previously, readers understood it to be an academic text because it was published in an academic journal. But, some new media texts blur the lines between scholarship and art so much that readers new to multimodal genres cannot distinguish the argument for the art. For readers expecting a traditional, linear argument, the confusion between generic uses of aesthetic and scholarly modes can cause them to dismiss the text altogether. This situation is not uncommon, and is seen in a range of new media texts. For instance, Megan

Sapnar (2002), co-editor of the new media site Poemsthatgo (<http://www
.poemsthatgo.com/>), which features Flash-based poetic texts, said:

> We have received many comments from "traditional" readers of poetry
> and fiction who express reservations about the New Media format and
> who see images as "visual tricks" that may give poorly thought out writ-
> ing an appealing wrapper. One visitor commented, "Our attention may
> become distracted by the visuals thus making us less critical and more
> acceptant of anything, regardless of quality." But it's my hope that this
> will give us an opportunity to raise the level of critical discourse regard-
> ing textual, aural, and visual literacy. (90–91)

Although Sapnar spoke specifically about poetic texts, the notion that
readers are less critical of a text when images are present is a typical academic
argument against the need to critique, or even consider worthy, any new
media text that employs non-alphabetic modes. Readers who are unfamiliar
with the meaning potentials of such modes usually proffer this argument.
Kress and van Leeuwen (2001) suggested, however, that readers who are familiar with some semiotic modes can adapt to understanding new modes so
that "what is or is not a formally, officially acknowledged mode in a given
domain of practice can change over time" (54). The levels of expertise in reading new media texts varies greatly between composition scholars—even
those who specialize in visual rhetorics, technology studies, and the combinations of web, print, and/or design experience. In the field of composition,
readers simply haven't seen enough examples of new media scholarship to
understand their value.

Until the Spring 2003 special issue on new media in *Kairos*, there had been
only one text published in any of the major online journals that could be
labeled new media scholarship—Wysocki's "A Bookling Monument," which
appeared in *Kairos* Fall 2002 issue. [It was published after our initial call for
new media submissions—at a time when my co-editor and I believed there
were no examples of new media scholarship published in composition and
English studies.] One new media text submitted for this *Kairos* call—the text
which I will discuss below—made us debate whether new media scholarly
texts, those that announced themselves as such, were scholarly in their arguments. This particular text, called *Violence of Text*, was a self-proclaimed "online academic publishing exercise" containing six scholarly texts designed for
new media distribution. It used a combination of sound, video, and written
text (in various forms including visible coding) to make its argument. The editor of the collection, Adrian Miles (2002c), announced in his introduction that
the texts were not art, despite aesthetic uses of sound and video in ways that
broke away from standard presentations of online scholarly texts.

In deciding whether this text was appropriate for publication, the three of
us (two co-editors and an assistant editor) wrangled over its "artful" qualities,
debating whether a text that had been designed to be aesthetically pleasing
and incorporated that aesthetic sense into its meaning had any place in a
scholarly journal. Each of us understood the semiotic modes of sound, video,

and alphabetic text differently, which meant that each of us made meaning from those modes to a lesser or greater extent than what may have been intended by the designer. These varying interpretation strategies seemed to be based on our prior reading habits of online texts. In turn, this meant that the value those elements held for less-experienced readers of such texts was only as artistic additions to a slim, written text. To editors of a peer-reviewed journal who understood the importance of linear, written arguments, the aesthetic components of this piece translated into non-scholarly elements and were, therefore, outside the realm of needing interpretation. This non-recognition of the text's multimodal elements is not singular among the readers I discuss here. Composition scholars and students are used to reading electronic texts based in print conventions and rhetorically interpreting still images. But scholars and students differ in new media reading expertise depending on (a) their individual understandings of non-written modes and (b) their backgrounds in other areas of technology and, more so, the arts. One reader and designer of new media texts, Katherine Parrish (2002), described her reading strategies of such texts as making "visible the strategies we already use, or ones that we could or should use when reading any text" (93). As with viewing avant-garde art for the first time and not knowing how to contextualize it, when I read *Violence of Text*, I placed it within a historical framework and used those intertextual knowledges to relate this text to works of different modes and genres I was already familiar with (see Carroll, 1999; Kress, 1999, 30). It is the combination of understanding the use of aesthetic elements within intellectual meaning-making strategies that will best help readers interpret scholarly new media texts.

3.2. Necessary Aesthetics

Akin to Duchamps' readymades, which critics say are "art" because the pieces appear in museums and not on the street, new media scholarship signals itself as scholarship through its publication context in scholarly online journals. When readers approach a print or hypertext article, they know they are supposed to be reading efferently—for the argument, the "so what" factor. Compositionists are looking for practical and theoretical applications of the author's argument. Yet, with new media texts, the argument isn't necessarily foregrounded as it would be in a print, linear, and/or hypertextual article or webtext. The reader must discover the meaning with the help of the text's multimodal elements. Readers new to new media may overlook the additional layer of meaning created by the combination of these elements in a text's design, causing readers to believe new media texts are too artistic to be serious scholarship. Compositionists are well acquainted with the argumentation strategies of print-based scholarly texts and scholarship about new media. But the added layer of multimodal and non-linear argumentation strategies requires readers to approach these texts with an appreciation of the aesthetic qualities that new media elements can offer toward creating the author's overall meaning. Understanding how video, audio, and other elements

FIGURE 8-2   The initial screen audiences see of Geoffrey Sirc's "Never Mind the Tagmemics," which appeared online in *Pre/Text Electra(lite)* in 1997.

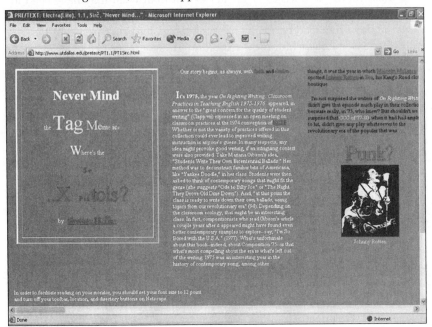

can work with or enact an argument can help readers value new media scholarship as worthy of scholarly pursuit. These texts are not traditionally linear nor alphabetic, which may make readers feel they are more experimental than print-based texts.

Composition scholars have designed experimental, online texts for almost a decade (a long time in relation to the technological and theoretical changes this field has seen in that time). Included in this mode of experimental work is Geoffrey Sirc's "Never Mind the Tagmemics, Where's the Sex Pistols?" (1997), which appeared in the first issue of *Pre/Text: Electra(lite)*. This text is memorable for shocking us out of our print-based complacency with its green background, increasing colorization of words for emphasis, and horizontal scrolling text (see Figure 8-2). It shows a conscious effort to use the technology at hand to make readers aware of and think about the meanings of design through layout, images, colors, and font choices. The bulk of the page (I call it this because it is one web page in total) is written text. It's reminiscent of print and because the article was republished in *Pre/Text* from the original print version in *College Composition and Communication*, readers would not be surprised to find its text-heavy presentation, especially given typical web-design conventions in 1997. However, its purposeful horizontal scrolling and use of color for words that aren't links is counter to webtext traditions. Sirc's purpose in this piece is to remind readers that the value of counter-culture (in this case, the Sex Pistols) can play an extremely useful role in composition classrooms and that students might react more congenially to first-year composition courses if instructors asked them to read and write non-traditional texts.

I agree with Sirc's argument; yet, the design of the site, while mimicking the punk-rock culture of being in-your-face, makes me cringe. Seeing the text is difficult because of the multiple colors, which makes reading and understanding the online version of the text next to impossible for readers who don't want design to get in the way of the scholarship. I don't blame those readers, design should never get in the way, unless that's the intention. With each choice a designer makes, the meaning of the text is affected. The choice of green background and white text makes Sirc's argument stand out in my mind, even if it is still difficult to read. Many readers would not want to approach such a text, and that is a choice that Sirc made through his design. How design contributes (or takes away from) an argument is an issue that authors must confront if they want to continue composing for online distribution.

Since 1997, Sirc has continued to crusade for the use of non-traditional and pop-culture texts in the composition class. In *Writing New Media*, Sirc (2004) called for "aestheticizing the scene of composition in an idiosyncratic, obsessional way" through technology use and new media (116). Experimenting with texts in this way—in the classroom and in our scholarship—will help bring what Fluxus founder George Maciunas called "an art consciousness to daily life" (cited in Sirc, 117). It is through an art consciousness and the valuation of aesthetic elements in our scholarship that the notion of what is acceptable as scholarship will begin to shift. When new media scholarship becomes more prevalent, readers will begin to see in journals such as *Kairos*, as Peterson (2002) said, a shift in "what academic scholarly work on the web will look like." *Kairos* wants to "challenge traditional disciplinary definitions of good scholarship in that already created field by creating a space for unconventional projects—both in terms of topic and presentation" (Peterson, 2002). The *Kairos* new media issue, in particular, was intended to broaden what would be accepted as composition scholarship. Expanding our notion of acceptable scholarship and allowing non-traditional, non-print-based, and aesthetic compositions into our classroom practices will benefit, on a daily basis, our changing communication strategies.

Compositionists, myself included, have much to learn about the role aesthetics can play in composing meanings. We can turn to practitioners of aesthetic new media texts for help. Even though readers have become accustomed to clicking links and reading lexias to determine a text's argument, over the past few years arguments against a traditional link-node structure have begun to emerge in new media studies, specifically in electronic writing circles (Glazier, 2002; Sanford, 2001). Christy Sheffield Sanford (2001), a web-based poet, said in regards to the changing styles and materiality of writing for the web that "the dependence on endless linking has weakened in favor of show hide scripts and scripts that allow a number of documents to open simultaneously or in tandem. . . . The ability to work with space time has grown more sophisticated." Innovations in new media texts typically come from the art and creative writing fields first, and then move into realms such as composition studies. Writers such as Sanford and Loss Glazier have composed new media poetic texts—texts that incorporate Flash animation and that display the materiality of coding and scripting to make meaning—for several years. Composition studies and authors who compose for online publication will need to embrace these changing composition patterns just as teachers have with the inclusion of visuals and web design into their classrooms. To do this, teachers need examples to follow. Thus, in the next section, I provide a reading of one of the few existing examples of a successful scholarly new media text that does move away from link-node structures. I analyze "Digital Multiliteracies," a section from *Violence of Text*, to demonstrate how aesthetic modal elements offer meaning in a new media text.

4. Reading a New Media Text

Readers of new media texts can construct meaning from, among other ways, a text's multimodal elements and navigational design. This method of interpreting the meaning of a new media text is similar to George P. Landow's (1997) notion that readers of hypertext can interpret meaning from individual nodes to form a larger argument (see also Hawk, 2002). In the new media text, "Digital Multiliteracies," Adrian Miles (2002b) argued that teachers should have students compose multimodal texts such as video blogs, or vogs (short, video-based texts), as a way of teaching students to be digitally multiliterate. His text is designed to enact his argument because the reader must choose multimodal clips (still images, audio, and written text)[6] to play back simultaneously on a timeline, creating a vog based on the reader's selections. I strongly encourage readers of this article to visit and interact with "Digital Multiliteracies," which was published in *Kairos'* new media issue (see <http://english.ttu.edu/kairos/8.1>).

Miles' text was designed in collaboration with one of his students, James Taylor, who designed the new media text to resemble the interface of a video-editing program. Miles (2002c) introduced this text to readers with the following road map (keeping in mind that Miles is also the editor of the *Violence of Text* collection, hence his use of the third person):

> With Adrian Miles' "Digital Multiliteracies" the readerly versus writerly text has been turned on its head into the composed versus performed text. Here image, text, and audio need to be dragged from their place holders in the clip selector onto their corresponding timeline. Once assembled the play button in the viewer window can be clicked and this will play what the reader has assembled as a 'roll your own' edit of the paper and presentation. This dramatically appropriates Miles' commentary on the significance of digital multiliteracy and interactive video as a writing practice where the 'what next' remains radically open. As Miles' text only ever happens through the intervention of a reader who appropriates its parts in building, it foregrounds the dissolved authority of reader and author. (4)

With this introduction, readers can situate Miles' argument within the context of reading-reception theory (i.e., "readerly versus writerly," "dissolved authority of reader and author") and hypertext and postmodern theory (i.e., "composed versus performed text"). It also stated Miles' argument: Composing video is similar to "writing practice" in becoming digitally multiliterate. He also referred to the notion of "what next" as a traditional organizational structure of print and web-based texts, which he wanted to broaden akin to transactional theorists' ideas of the open text (see Eco, 1984; Rosenblatt, 1994) and early hypertext theorists' arguments for non-linearity and reader-composed texts (see Landow, 1994, 1997; Murray, 1997). Although Miles' text does not necessarily do away with reader and writer in the grand sense of "the author is dead"—because it offers a specific and limited set of text, audio, and image choices for readers to manipulate—it does provide readers with individual opportunities to (re)construct Miles' argument through the use of multimodal clips and navigational strategies associated with video-editing software. In the next sections, I briefly analyze five of the major design features of "Digital Multiliteracies" to demonstrate how Miles and Taylor used aesthetically based, multimodal elements to create scholarly meaning in their text.

4.1. The Interface

Readers, upon opening "Digital Multiliteracies," see a clip selector, a viewer, and three time-lines (see Figure 8-3). There are three areas in the clip selector—stills, audio, and text—from which readers can choose individual, timed clips.

FIGURE 8-3   The interface of *Violence of Text* mimics interfaces of video-editing software programs like iMovie.

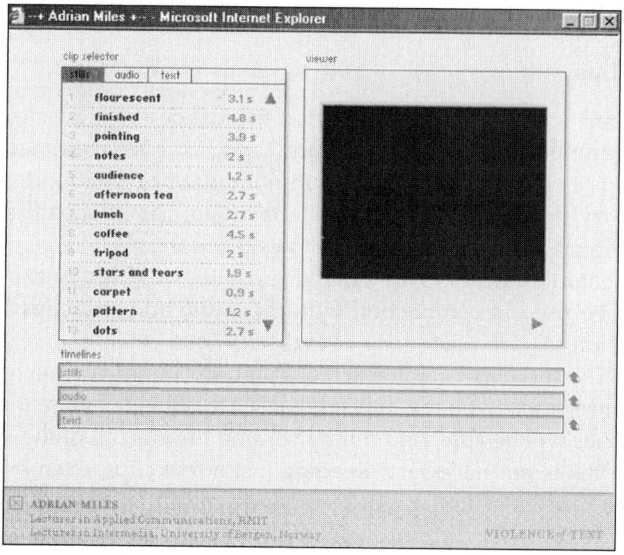

By choosing which clips to drag to the timeline, readers "interpret through implementation," as Miles (2002c) stated in his introduction to the text. Clips can be chosen at random, or readers can click once on each of the clips in the selector to see or hear that individual clip in the viewer.

Because there are three types of clips, a reader can drag any number of each kind into the timeline and play them back to form what Adrian Miles (2002a) called a "mollage"—the combination of montage and collage (10)—from which readers can make meaning. Many hypertext theorists have noted the connection between hypertext writing and collage. Bolter and Grusin (1999) furthered that connection between collage and the reading and composing strategies that authors and readers use with new media texts when they said, "In collage and photomontage as in hypermedia, to create is to rearrange existing forms" (39). By rearranging the clips in Miles' text, the reader gets to create the text, performing its argument in a true non-linear fashion. Without the reader choosing clips to include on the timelines, this new media text would not be able to perform its intended argument. Although, the same could be said of more traditional hypertexts (scholarly and literary)—that the reader must click to make the text move forward (or backward or in any direction the author has prescribed)—with Miles' text, a click will not suffice to move the reader much farther into the text. The reader must participate by dragging the still, audio, or text clips that she wants to the timelines. For the fullest understanding of the text's meaning, all three timelines must be used, and then the reader must click the play button on the viewer to see the composed mollage. No matter which selection and arrangement of clips the reader makes, the argument she constructs will be a smaller version of the whole, perhaps made to lesser or greater strengths depending on the combination of clips chosen. I will now briefly examine the clip selectors to show how new media elements, such as individual multimodal clips, can help readers construct arguments in new media scholarship.

4.2. Text Clips

I want to start with the third clip selector, the text clips, because it will be the mode that compositionists are most familiar with. I believe the designer set the text clips as the last option in this multimodal presentation to encourage readers to try the other two (and perhaps unfamiliar) modes first. The text clips in "Digital Multiliteracies" are quotes taken from Miles' paper[7] version of his presentation. Readers are offered text-bites of Miles' linear argument, which can be used in conjunction with the audio and still clips in the new media version to give readers an overall view and sense of interpreting his argument. The text clips step linearly through the paper version of Miles' argument, and readers who are in need of a sense of his organization of digital multiliteracies will be able to find it by reading through all of the text clips in order. But this is not necessary. Reading just a few clips, even out of order, would give readers a similar clue into Miles' meaning. Keep in mind, however, that the designer did not include all of Miles' linear text. On average, there is about a sentence or less quoted from each paragraph of the ten-page paper. Some paragraphs are skipped altogether. If readers simply browsed through the text clips, they would find written text to support Miles' argument for digital multiliteracies. For example, the second clip, "reading & writing," says, "However, it is apparent that to be literate includes reading and writing, that reading by itself renders us consumers of literacy but that consumption, of itself, is only half of what constitutes a proper literacy." This clip constructs the argument that literacy is more than interpretive skills; it must include production of texts. Another clip, "hard copy," says, "there are some aspects of hard copy [print-based texts] that we have maintained in relation to 'soft' forms such as the World Wide Web." In this quote, Miles argued that the Web is too much in this (print) world and does not take enough advantage of technological capabilities and reading strategies that move away from print standards.

The text clips tend to spell out Miles' argument more specifically and succinctly than the audio and still clips do. But, Miles and Taylor reminded us through the text's design that, in Western reading habits of left-to-right and the Web's typical organizational and hierarchical navigation patterns, the text clips are the least important of the three modes because they are placed third in a line of choices for the reader. The text clips would normally be the last ones readers would encounter, after they have read and made meaning from the still clips and audio clips. Because of the placement of the text clips in the navigational hierarchy, the designer signals to readers that written text is not the most important, nor the only method of making meaning in a new media text. By taking readers' focus away from written text, the designer intended for readers to make meaning through the other multimodal elements, which helps to enact Miles' argument that readers should be digitally multiliterate. From the text clips, I'll move backwards through the navigational choices; next are the audio clips.

4.3. Audio Clips

The audio tracks are listed in the clip selector by key words taken from the clip. These clips are taken from the question-and-answer session after Miles' presentation, as well as from an interview with him. The still clips present readers with a sonic sense of the symposium, providing an immediacy to the text. This voice-of-immediacy helps readers make meaning from the audio clips because, as Bolter and Grusin (2000) suggested, while cyberspace can be categorized as a nonplace because it is "defined by video and audio as pure perceptual experiences, expressions of the enjoyment of media" (179), the designers combated the nonplace feel of the Internet by using elements that offer immediacy to the physical space in which the original presentation occurred. Readers now have a voice with a face. Even though the presentation is long in the past, being able to hear the speaker's voice, as if he were talking to readers now, recreates immediacy for the audience.

The first clip in the audio selector is called "against something." Although this title is vague, the reader soon discovers that part of the audio says "writing is always against something." The full meaning of the text is quite different than what readers might expect from its short title. The same could be said of another clip, "be literate," which, at first, might seem to be a call-to-action: Be Literate! And while this is somewhat the argument Miles made in this clip, the full audio explores multiple possibilities of what literacy means: "OK, there's an awful lot of variables that we can put in there that we actually have to be literate about." Another clip, called "english teacher," helps readers make sense of Miles' argument for digital multiliteracies because it refers to the outdated (and outmoded?) print-based traditions of reading Shakespeare when students should also know how to compose multimodal texts. Not only is the text of this clip somewhat accusatory, but the tone of the speaker's voice, heard through the audio clip, adds to that indignant feeling—Why should Shakespeare be more important than a shopping list? he seemed to be asking. Miles questioned succinctly in this six-second clip a typical skills-based approach to literacy. Miles repeated his argument later in the list of audio clips, as in the "shopping list" clip, when he said, "It's much more significant to a literate culture that you know how to pick up a biro [pen] and an envelope and write a shopping list on the back than it is to read Shakespeare." (Perhaps Miles' argument tends toward the drastic at this point; it might be better to suggest that, in addition to Shakespeare, students should be well-versed in digital multiliteracies.) By clicking through audio clips, even randomly, a reader can make meaning from these sound-bytes in relation to Miles' overall argument. The multiple modes that the designer presents to readers encourages them to perform, or rather, produce Miles' argument for themselves. In this way, the audio clips can be approached with as much meaning-making potential as the text clips provide, if not more because of their immediacy represented through hearing Miles' voice and the tone with which he delivers these audio-based arguments.

4.4. Still Clips

The still clips present a new challenge to readers unfamiliar with reading aesthetic elements in a scholarly text. These clips appear to be photos taken during the symposium; they range in subject matter from images of coffee cups and the carpet to out-of-focus pictures of Miles yawning. The stills don't necessarily stand out as the best examples of the text's argument on first look. The first clip readers might see when opening Miles' text is an upward, angled shot of fluorescent lighting, entitled "flourescent" [sic]. The designer may have taken advantage of many readers' lack of new media knowledge, forcing them away from a strict, print-based reading by presenting photographs seemingly unrelated to Miles' intended argument. Readers may ask why a designer would include photos of the presentation, monitors, audience members, coffee cups, and the carpet—half of them out of focus and hard to see clearly. However, a reader can get a feeling for the conference location by clicking through these images. When I read through these stills, I get a strong sense of the location, place, size, and atmosphere of the conference—not something very easily or even typically conveyed through the Internet in

HTML-based (HyperText Markup Language) sites. The time-space of the conference is presented to readers through the use of physically locating, albeit quirky, photographs. This physicality has meaning and can be related to what Bolter and Grusin (2000) called immediacy in new media texts:

> A photograph may be either an expression of the desire for immediacy or a representation of that desire. The photograph that represents itself to be viewed without irony expresses the desire for immediacy, while a photograph that calls attention to itself as a photograph becomes a representation of that desire. (110)

In this way, the designer's choice for using a mixture of photo types—where some are realistic (like the blurry shots of Miles, see Figure 8-4) that give us immediacy into the symposium space, and some that call attention to themselves as artful representations of the symposium space—work to make the reader feel more connected to the space of the text. It is shots like these that help to personalize this text in a way that breaks it out of a traditional notion of web-based scholarly texts, those conventions that Roland Barthes (1975) referred to as "the institutions of text" (60), and shows the reader what it felt like to be there at the symposium. If these images seem to be bizarre inclusions into this scholarly text—after all, it is rare (if ever) that an academic would choose to include the parts of a presentation that were spontaneous or off-the-cuff remarks into the published version of that speech—the designer uses them to remind readers of the rare, lived moments in which "Digital Multiliteracies" was presented, that it was part of a conversation, that the ideas are informational and informal, even fun.

FIGURE 8-4   The blurry photo of Miles can be read as a realistic interpretation in an of-the-moment symposium space.

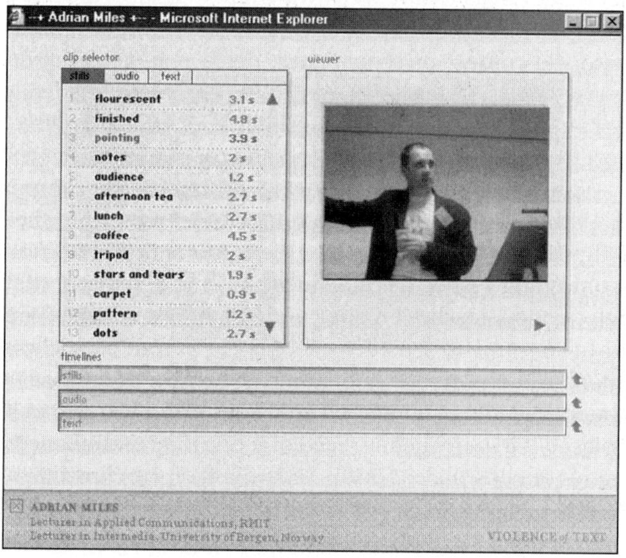

While Bolter and Grusin (2000) suggested that readers "become hyper-conscious of the medium in photomontage, precisely because conventional photography is a medium with such loud historical claims to transparency" (38), the inclusion of a variety of still clips helps readers re-enact Miles' presentation, and in doing so, recreate his argument for using multimodal elements in meaningful ways. Miles and Taylor asked readers to be hyper-conscious of the symposium's setting and the medium of photography and montage as elements not to be overlooked as a meaning-making strategy. The still clips become one more mode through which readers can understand Miles' argument while enacting that argument through their own viewing and interpretation of those stills.

4.5. The Timelines

Sirc (2004) argued that the main challenge of a designer is to invent a uniquely visionary world from carefully chosen fragments of the existing one. Both the designer of "Digital Multiliteracies" and the reader of that text create a "visionary world" of new media scholarship where meaning is made through the reader's choice and arrangement of multimodal fragments. By placing the multimodal clips on the timelines, readers create a video montage (or, as Miles would probably say, the potential to be a vog—based on the shortness of the clips). Through this navigational, meaning-making structure, readers move away from traditional presentations of academic arguments towards new media presentations that take advantage of multimodal techniques to further scholarly argument. The use of these techniques helps readers experience the text as it is being performed.

As I mentioned earlier, Miles' text uses an interface similar to video-editing software. Although the interface of video-editing programs is meant to be transparent even as we are well aware that interfaces are not transparent (see, e.g., Selfe & Selfe, 1994; Wysocki & Jasken, 2004), this assimilated interface, put into the context of scholarship, helps readers construct meaning through its use (Kress & van Leeuwen, 2001, 22). Many readers of this text may not be familiar with video-editing interfaces, which is why Miles provided a short explanation of how to read and/or construct the text in his introduction. Without the timeline, this text's meaning could only be partially interpreted. Although a reader can gain much meaning from the individual playing of clips in the clip selector, it is the combination and arrangement of these clips onto their respective timelines, and the playing of that collection that will help readers reach a broader understanding of Miles' argument. To understand his argument, a reader chooses clips from each clip selector by dragging them to their respective timeline. When she is done selecting clips, she views her collection, playing each still, audio, and text clip in the order in which she placed it in the timeline. Each timeline plays simultaneously so that all three modes of clips play at once. Regardless of the clips that a reader selects for the timelines, Miles' argument is performed in two ways: (a) through the reader's enacting of digital multiliteracies by creating a vog that uses multimodal elements, and (b) through the meaning of the multimodal elements as they are combined and played in the reader's version of a vog.[8] For a reader new to such texts, understanding that the multimodal, extra-alphabetic elements a designer uses are available for meaning making is the first step to recognizing the importance this direction of scholarship can take us.

5. CONCLUSION

"Digital Multiliteracies" offer readers a chance to enact and interpret an author's argument through multimodal elements and navigational strategies. The use of still, audio, and text clips in conjunction with their placement on a timeline that plays the clips back in sequence directly relates to Miles' argument that teachers should help their students become digitally multiliterate by understanding how to "read across" software programs and use technology in ways that break from print traditions (Miles, 2002a, 4). This text demonstrates how multimodal elements and new media strategies such as the enactment of the text through a timeline can help readers interpret meanings made through modes that move beyond linear, print traditions. Similar to reading strategies in hypertext, where readers have to compose an argument based on smaller lexias of meaning, the argument of this text can be gathered through reading and interpreting the smaller sections and multiple modes the designer provided, even if those modes aren't easily recognized as valuable in a scholarly text. While space prevents me from offering specific reading strategies that would help readers new to new media texts interpret the (often experimental) aesthetic and scholarly elements that are usually found in their designs, I hope readers will take away the potential of reading and composing in new media as future avenues for scholarship in and out of the classroom. But in order to value this kind of scholarship readers need more new media texts on which to base a collective understanding of the ways cross-generic modes function. Valuing these texts—and making them less rare, which will increase our analytical and interpretational strategies for them—is important for new media scholarship to move forward. I don't expect authors to jump at creating new media scholarship. There are issues to address including time, technology, and tenure. But, as presses and print journals face growing budgetary constraints that prevent them from accepting as many manuscripts as they have in the past, those authors who are poised at the edge of new media scholarship—scholars in computers and composition and new media studies—should take advantage of their technological talents and creative publication outlets, including *Kairos*, and show the rest of the field that new media texts can be as meaningful as print articles and webtexts. Enacting our scholarship through new media will help us to show, not tell.

NOTES

1. I performed this search in September 2002, January 2003, and November 2003. Hits remained consistent between 200 and 300.

2. There are a few ETDs that don't use PDFs as their distributive mode. Some theses and dissertations are created as HTML documents or use multiple modes (such as audio components) to make meaning, but these texts are rare and still mostly rely on the written word to make their arguments.

3. I reviewed all past issues (up to November 1, 2002) of *Kairos, Enculturation, CCC Online, academic writing,* and *The Writing Instructor,* and based their selection as "major" journals on their participation in a Summer 2002 cross-journal collaboration.

4. Well, no, composition scholars are not writing about sound. Not since *Enculturation*'s special issue [3.1] on it. Why not?

5. It is surprising that the authors chose text-heavy argumentation strategies considering that at least two of them have published texts that took advantage of multimodal elements [See Walker (2001) and Squier (1995)]. It should be noted that Squier's *Urban Diary* heavily influenced my decision to pursue new media as a course of study, which, perhaps, influenced my expectations of how the *Kairos* text was presented. On the other hand, like this print article, it is probable that the authors of "Minding the Gap" wanted readers to see how new media elements could be used to support scholarly arguments while still appealing to readers' expectations of scholarship-as-linear-argument. In fact, the text is quite persuasive in its argument that new media techniques are essential to the growing need for multiliteracies in curricula. My argument here is only that it isn't a new media text.

6. Miles teaches at RMIT University, Melbourne, where in Fall 2002, he asked students in his advanced media course to attend a symposium on digital literacy. Their assignment was to remediate the linear papers of six presenters (including Miles' own text), to conduct interviews of the presenters, and take photographs and audio of the presentations. With these multimodal materials, the students created new media versions of the presenters' arguments—texts that enacted their arguments through their new media presentation. The still, audio, and written clips in Miles' text "Digital Multiliteracies" come directly from that symposium.

7. I must, of course, acknowledge that "Digital Multiliteracies" is a remediation of a conference presentation Miles gave in 2002. I do not dwell, however, on the print-based nature of the original presentation because, in fact, it was not wholly print-based. In remediating the text for new media consumption, the designer used Miles' ten-page written conference paper, but also used—in equal if not greater numbers—photos from the symposium and audio clips taken from the presentation, the question-and-answer session that followed, and from interviews. Thus, while the original argument Miles presented in the paper is present within this new media text, the overwhelming amount of meaning-making strategies relies on non-alphabetic elements.

8. Even though Bolter and Grusin (2000) suggested that new media texts may remediate television moreso than film because films tend to not include written text overlapping the visuals, it is apparent from Miles' text that vogs are the medium he wants to discuss (190). Readers can further relate Miles' text to vogs, rather than television, if they look at other examples of vogs that Miles has created (see his vog website at <http://hypertext.rmit.edu.au/vog/>).

REFERENCES

Barthes, Roland. (1975). Richard Miller (Trans.) *The pleasure of the text.* New York: Hill and Wang.
Blakesley, David, & Brooke, Collin. (Eds.). (2002). *Enculturation* [Special issue: Visual Rhetoric]. Retrieved March 17, 2003, from <http://enculturation.gmu.edu/3 2/>.
Bolter, Jay David. (1991). *Writing space: The computer, hypertext, and the history of writing.* Mahwah, NJ: Erlbaum.
Bolter, Jay David, & Grusin, Richard. (2000). *Remediation: Understanding new media.* Cambridge, MA: MIT Press.
Carroll, Noël. (1999). *The philosophy of art: A contemporary introduction.* New York: Routledge.
Conference on College Composition and Communication. (n.d.). Scholarship in composition: Guidelines for faculty, deans, and department chairs. *CCCC Position Statements.* Retrieved December 28, 2002, from <http://www.ncte.org/ccc/12/sub/state4.html>.
Carter, Locke. (2003). Argument in hypertext: Writing strategies and the problem of order in a nonsequential world. *Computers and Composition, 20,* 3–22.
Douglas, J. Yellowlees. (2000). *The end of books—Or books without end? Reading interactive narratives.* Ann Arbor, MI: University of Michigan Press.
Eco, Umberto. (1984). *The role of the reader: Explorations in the semiotics of texts.* Bloomington, IN: Indiana University Press.
Feenberg, Andrew. (1999). *Questioning technology.* New York: Routledge.
Giddens, Anthony. (1994). *Central problems in social theory: Action, structure, and contradiction in social analysis.* Berkeley, CA: University of California Press.
Glazier, Loss Pequeño. (2001). E-poets on the state of their electronic art. *Currents in Electronic Literacy, 5.* Retrieved April 13, 2002, from <http://www.cwrl.utexas.edu/currents/fall01/survey

/glazier.html>. Glazier, Loss Pequeño. (2002). *Digital poetics: The making of e-poetries.* Tuscaloosa, AL: University of Alabama Press.

Gossett, Kathie, Lamanna, Carrie A., Squier, Joseph, & Walker, Joyce R. (2002). [Continuing to] mind the gap: Teaching image and text in new media spaces. *Kairos: Rhetoric, Technology, Pedagogy, 7*(3) Retrieved January 23, 2003, from <http://english.ttu.edu/kairos/7.3/binder2 .html?coverweb/Gossett/index.html>.

Handa, Carolyn. (Ed.) (2001). *Computers and Composition* [Special double-issue: Digital literacies], *18*(1) & *18*(2).

Hawk, Byron. (2002). Introduction to Facing the future of electronic publishing: Hypertext, form, and scholarly argument. *Enculturation* [Special multi-journal issue: Electronic publication], *4*(1). Retrieved December 12, 2002, from <http://enculturation.gmu.edu/4_1/intro/hawk2 .html>.

Johnson-Eilola, Johndan. (1997). *Nostalgic angels: Rearticulating hypertext writing.* Stamford, CT: Ablex.

Krause, Steven D. (2002). Where do I list this on my CV? Considering the values of self-published web sites. *CCC Online, 54*(1). Retrieved December 12, 2002, from <http://www.ncte.org/ccc /54.1/krause copy.html>.

Kress, Günther. (1999). Multimodality. In Bill Cope & Mary Kalantzis (Eds.), *Multiliteracies: Literacy learning and the design of social futures.* New York: Routledge.

Kress, Günther. (2003). *Literacy in a new media age.* New York: Routledge.

Kress, Günther, & van Leeuwen, Theo. (2001). *Multimodal discourse: The modes and media of contemporary communication.* New York: Oxford University Press.

Landow, George. (Ed.). (1994). *Hyper/Text/Theory.* Baltimore, MD: Johns Hopkins University Press.

Landow, George. (1997). *Hypertext 2.0: The convergence of contemporary critical theory and technology.* Baltimore, MD: Johns Hopkins University Press.

Lanham, Richard A. (1993). *The electronic word: Democracy, technology, and the arts.* Chicago: University of Chicago Press.

Manovich, Lev. (2001). *The language of new media.* Cambridge, MA: The MIT Press.

Miles, Adrian. (2002a). Digital Multiliteracies. Paper presented at *I link therefore I am Symposium,* RMIT University, Melbourne, Australia.

Miles, Adrian. (2002b). Digital Multiliteracies. In *Violence of text: Online academic publishing exercise, Kairos.* Retrieved July 8, 2003, from <http://english.ttu.edu/kairos/8.1/binder2.html? coverweb/vot/index.html>.

Miles, Adrian. (2002c). Introduction. In *Violence of text: Online academic publishing exercise, Kairos.* Retrieved July 8, 2003, from <http://english.ttu.edu/kairos/8.1/binder2.html?coverweb/vot /index.html>.

Murray, Janet H. (1997). *Hamlet on the holodeck: The future of narrative in cyberspace.* New York: The Free Press.

New London Group, The. (2000). *Multiliteracies: Literacy learning and the design of social futures.* New York: Routledge.

Newman, Michael. (2002). *The designs of academic literacy: A multiliteracies examination of academic achievement.* Westport, CT: Bergin & Garvey.

Parrish, Katherine. (2002, Spring/Summer). New media literature: A roundtable discussion on aesthetics, audiences, and histories. Part one. *NC1.*

Peterson, Patricia Webb. (2002). Writing and publishing in the boundaries: Academic writing in/ through the virtual age. The Writing Instructor. Retrieved August 1, 2002, from <http:// flansburgh.english.purdue.edu/twi/essays/webb.html>.

Rosenblatt, Louise M. (1994). *The reader, the text, the poem: The transactional theory of the literary work.* Carbondale, IL: Southern Illinois University Press.

Sanford, Christy Sheffield. (2001). E-poets on the state of their electronic art. *Currents in Electronic Literacy, 5.* Retrieved April 13, 2002, from <http://www.cwrl.utexas.edu/currents /fall01/survey/sanford.html>.

Sapnar, Megan. (2002, Spring/Summer). New media literature: A roundtable discussion on aesthetics, audiences, and histories. Part one. *NC1.*

Selfe, Cynthia, & Selfe, Richard. (1994). The politics of the interface: Power and its exercise in electronic contact zones. *College Composition and Communication, 45,* 480–504.

Sloane, Sarah. (2000). *Digital fictions: Storytelling in a material world.* Stamford, CT: Ablex.

Sirc, Geoffrey. (1997). Never Mind the Tagmemics . . . Where's the Sex Pistols? *Pre/Text: Electra- (lite), 1.* Retrieved January 23, 2003, from <http://www.utdallas.edu/pretext/PT1.1/PT1Sirc .html>.

Sirc, Geoffrey. (2004). Box-Logic. In Anne Frances Wysocki, Cynthia Selfe, Johndan Johnson-Eilola, & Geoffrey Sirc (Eds.), *Writing new media: Theory and applications for expanding the teaching of composition*. Logan, UT: Utah State University Press.

Squier, Joseph. (1995). *Urban diary*. Retrieved March 8, 2003, from <http://theplace.walkerart.org /urban diary/intro.html>.

TechRhet listserv discussion thread. (2002). *Design as whine* [Online]. Archives available at: <http://www.interversity.org/>.

UNESCO. (2001). *ETD models. The guide to electronic theses & dissertations*. Retrieved March 8, 2003, from <http://etdguide.org/models/>.

Unsworth, Len. (2001). *Teaching multiliteracies across the curriculum*. Philadelphia, PA: Open University Press.

Walker, Joyce. (2001). Textural textuality: A personal exploration of critical race theory. *Kairos, 7*(1). Retrieved January 23, 2003, from <http://english.ttu.edu/kairos/7.1/binder.html?features /walker/text/index.html>.

Wysocki, Anne Frances. (2001). Impossibly distinct: On form/content and word/image in two pieces of computer-based interactive multimedia. *Computers and Composition, 18*, 137–162.

Wysocki, Anne Frances. (2002). A bookling monument. *Kairos, 7*(3). Retrieved March 3, 2003, from <http://english.ttu.edu/kairos/7.3/binder2.html?coverweb/wysocki/index.html>.

Wysocki, Anne Frances. (2003). Seriously visible. In Mary Hocks & Michelle Kendrick (Eds.), *Eloquent images*. Cambridge, MA: The MIT Press.

Wysocki, Anne, & Jasken, Julia. (2004). What should be an unforgettable face. *Computers and Composition, 21*(1).

PART TWO

A Matter of Design

Introduction to Part Two

As mentioned at the beginning of this book, the field of composition draws from a number of other disciplines, adapting outside theories and practices to suit its own. Semiotics, the study of signs and sign systems, for instance, has been greatly influential to multimodal composition. The authors in Part Two draw from the field of semiotics to explain the relevancy of design theory. It is obvious to these authors that multimodal composition can be thought of as a matter of design, and as such, a way of thinking that can account for the dynamic nature of literacy. As readers will see from the selections, design is a process in which an author carefully chooses modes and media appropriate for the rhetorical situation. Authors think both globally and locally, examining the impact of cultural, technological, and social changes that necessitate a theory of design. A global understanding is what leads to many scholars seeing our focus on the printed word as limiting our understanding of cultural, technological, and social changes, and prompts them to call for broader definitions of literacy. Such broader definitions allow us more ways of knowing that could be vital in our understanding of the complexities of human communication.

Because they know what is at stake if we don't expand our definitions of literacy and because our understanding of literacy shapes our pedagogical practices, the authors in Part Two also offer a vocabulary for framing the work of multimodal composition, helping us to see multimodal composing for what it really is: composing that involves a careful selection of modes appropriate to the communicative situation at hand. At stake, for instance, are the different ways of knowing and communicating that our students bring with them to the classroom. If we fail to recognize this diversity, then we risk limiting some students while privileging others.

To begin, the New London Group has been instrumental in recognizing the significance of multimodal composition and has actively worked to bring this focus to the forefront in academia. Since 1996, when the New London Group laid out their definitions of multiliteracies, many composition programs have actively followed the group's lead in realizing the value of multimodal composition. In the excerpts from "A Pedagogy of Multiliteracies: Designing

Social Futures" included in this book, the members of the New London Group advocate for a broader definition of literacy that is not based on one mode, the printed word, or on the practices of reading and writing it, as with more traditional definitions of literacy. They see this broader definition as necessary and base their argument on two important principles that account for (1) "the context of our culturally and linguistically diverse and increasingly globalized societies, for the multifarious cultures that interrelate and the plurality of texts that circulate," and (2) "the burgeoning variety of text forms associated with information and multimedia technologies." In other words, the New London Group argues that literacy pedagogy needs to account for all our diversity and how the factors influencing diversity merge, juxtapose, and even oppose one another. Our pedagogy, they contend, should reflect cultural, technological, economical, and social changes, and we should prepare students for the new languages that will develop when these changes occur. Therefore, the move toward pedagogy of multiliteracies is a move toward preparing students for their civic duties, which will most certainly include working with the various languages they will encounter in public spaces. Among the six major areas in which functional grammars are required for a pedagogy of multiliteracies, the New London Group contends that multimodal design is unique and the most significant because it has a dynamic relationship with the other modes of meaning. More specifically, multimodal design "represents the patterns of interconnection among the other modes" that must be recognized and interpreted by the composer (see p. 198 in this volume).

The privileged position of the written word in academia is the subject of Diana George's "From Analysis to Design: Visual Communication in the Teaching of Writing." In this 2002 essay, George notes that written language has long been associated with high culture, while image has long been associated with low culture. As George outlines the history of the written word and the visual, she reveals that the visual has essentially been inferior to the written word in composition because students only ever critiqued visual texts, and never produced them. This privileging of print, then, puts students at a disadvantage because it limits their understanding of the act of producing a text. George addresses the debate over whether the visual has a place in the composition classroom by arguing that students need to both examine and produce visuals because, like the New London Group, she views literacy as more than reading and writing written words. She situates her argument, along with the history of composition, within a larger discussion about how the visual was pitted against the written word and was subjugated to a lower status as a result. This subjugation speaks to the slow embrace of design in the classroom as a serious practice. Moving forward, she sees the field embracing composition as design, and therefore also embracing literacy consisting of both production and analysis.

Like George, Jeff Bezemer and Gunther Kress, in "Writing in Multimodal Texts: A Social Semiotic Account for Learning," examine texts of the past and present, looking at the ways other modes, particularly images, function and how they were treated in the acts of teaching and learning. They note how the traditional role of the image is different than its role at present. In doing so, they look at "representational changes in learning resources between 1930 and 2005" so that they may put "forward conceptual and analytical tools" that can "illuminate principles of designs for representation" (p. 235). Like Claire Lauer in Part One, they situate their argument in social semiotics and give us a vocabulary (along with definitions) to work from. For instance, they distinguish between a mode and a medium, a distinction necessary for the understanding of meaning making in multimodal composition, when they write, "[a] *mode* [such as an image or sound] is a socially and culturally shaped resource for making meaning" (p. 237). On the other hand, they explain a "medium [such as a book] is the substance in and through which meaning is instantiated/realized and through which meaning becomes available to others" (p. 238). They see that as a result of more complex and diverse relationships between modes, rhetors, and environments, we must move from thinking and practicing composition to thinking and practicing design, a process that gives "shape to the interests, purposes, and intentions of the rhetor in relation to the semiotic resources available for realizing/materializing these purposes as apt material, complex signs, texts for the assumed characteristics of a specific audience" (p. 240).

In the last reading of this section, "Embracing Wicked Problems: The Turn to Design in Composition Studies," Richard Marback argues that the move away from critique and analysis is a move toward design, as George contends, which puts the composer's agency into the spotlight. Marking her work as the turning point in composition studies toward multiliteracy, Marback begins by outlining George's argument and calls for production of multimodal texts, rather than mere analysis, in the composition classroom. He sees a progression away from the process that James Berlin describes when we move from critique to design. In doing so he draws from design theorists such as Horst W. J. Rittel and Melvin M. Webber, and defines design as a wicked (ambiguous) problem, one that requires the communicator to approach a communicative situation using design thinking which "begins with the immersion of the designer in responsiveness . . . to artifacts as well as to others as users of artifacts." In other words, composition students should take on the role of designers to build an understanding of designers' thinking.

In approaching the readings in Part Two, we might consider our own knowledge of design theories and how such theories shape the ways we know and learn through multimodal composition. We might also want to consider how such a framework for thinking about multimodal composition as design can translate into what we do in our classrooms. In what ways, for example, can we help our students see multimodal composition as design?

WORK CITED

The New London Group. "A Pedagogy of Multiliteracies: Designing Social Futures." *Harvard Educational Review, 66* (1996): 60–92.

9

From A Pedagogy of Multiliteracies: Designing Social Futures

THE NEW LONDON GROUP

THE "WHAT" OF A PEDAGOGY OF MULTILITERACIES

In relation to the new environment of literacy pedagogy, we need to reopen two fundamental questions: the "what" of literacy pedagogy, or what it is that students need to learn; and the "how" of literacy pedagogy, or the range of appropriate learning relationships.

Designs of Meaning

In addressing the question of the "what" of literacy pedagogy, we propose a metalanguage of multiliteracies based on the concept of "design." Design has become central to workplace innovations, as well as to school reforms for the contemporary world. Teachers and managers are seen as designers of learning processes and environments, not as bosses dictating what those in their charge should think and do. Further, some have argued that educational research should become a design science, studying how different curricular, pedagogical, and classroom designs motivate and achieve different sorts of learning. Similarly, managers have their own design science, studying how management and business theories can be put into practice and continually adjusted and reflected on in practice. The notion of design connects powerfully to the sort of creative intelligence the best practitioners need in order to be able, continually, to redesign their activities in the very act of practice. It connects as well to the idea that learning and productivity are the results of the designs (the structures) of complex systems of people, environments, technology, beliefs, and texts.

We have also decided to use the term "design" to describe the forms of meaning because it is free of the negative associations for teachers of terms such as "grammar." It is a sufficiently rich concept upon which to found a language curriculum and pedagogy. The term also has a felicitous ambiguity: it can identify either the organizational structure (or morphology) of products,

From *Harvard Educational Review* 66 (1996): 60–92.

or the process of designing. Expressions like "the design of the car," or "the design of the text," can have either sense: the way it is—has been—designed, or the process of designing it. We propose to treat any semiotic activity, including using language to produce or consume texts, as a matter of Design involving three elements: Available Designs, Designing, and The Redesigned. Together these three elements emphasize the fact that meaning-making is an active and dynamic process, and not something governed by static rules.

This framework is based upon a particular theory of discourse. It sees semiotic activity as a creative application and combination of conventions (resources—Available Designs) that, in the process of Design, transforms at the same time it reproduces these conventions (Fairclough, 1992a, 1995). That which determines (Available Designs) and the active process of determining (Designing, which creates The Redesigned) are constantly in tension. This theory fits in well with the view of social life and social subjects in fast-changing and culturally diverse societies, which we described earlier.

Available Designs.   Available Designs—the resources for Design—include the "grammars" of various semiotic systems: the grammars of languages, and the grammars of other semiotic systems such as film, photography, or gesture. Available Designs also include "orders of discourse" (Fairclough, 1995). An *order of discourse* is the structured set of conventions associated with semiotic activity (including use of language) in a given social space—a particular society, or a particular institution such as a school or a workplace, or more loosely structured spaces of ordinary life encapsulated in the notion of different lifeworlds. An order of discourse is a socially produced array of discourses, intermeshing and dynamically interacting. It is a particular configuration of Design elements. An order of discourse can be seen as a particular configuration of such elements. It may include a mixture of different semiotic systems—visual and aural semiotic systems in combination with language constitute the order of discourse of TV, for instance. It may involve the grammars of several languages—the orders of discourse of many schools, for example.

Order of discourse is intended to capture the way in which different discourses relate to (speak to) each other. Thus, the discourse of African American gangs in Los Angeles is related to the discourse of L.A. police in historical ways. They and other related discourses shape and are shaped by each other. For another example, consider the historical and institutional relations between the discourse of biology and the discourse of religious fundamentalism. Schools are particularly crucial sites in which a set or order of discourses relate to each other—disciplinary discourses, the discourses of being a teacher (teacher culture), the discourse of being a student of a certain sort, community discourses, ethnic discourses, class discourses, and public sphere discourses involving business and government, for instance. Each discourse involves producing and reproducing and transforming different kinds of people. There are different kinds of African Americans, teachers, children, students, police, and biologists. One and the same person can be different kinds of people at different times and places. Different kinds of people connect through the in-termeshed discourses that constitute orders of discourse.

Within orders of discourse there are particular Design conventions — Available Designs — that take the form of discourses, styles, genres, dialects, and voices, to name a few key variables. A *discourse* is a configuration of knowledge and its habitual forms of expression, which represents a particular set of interests. Over time, for instance, institutions produce discourses — that is, their configurations of knowledge. *Style* is the configuration of all the semi-otic features in a text in which, for example, language may relate to layout and visual images. *Genres* are forms of text or textual organization that arise out of particular social configurations or the particular relationships of the par-ticipants in an interaction. They reflect the purposes of the participants in a specific interaction. In an interview, for example, the interviewer wants some-thing, the interviewee wants something else, and the genre of interview re-flects this. *Dialects* may be region or age related. *Voice* is more individual and personal, including, of course, many discursive and generic factors.

The overarching concept of orders of discourse is needed to emphasize that, in designing texts and interactions, people always draw on systems of sociolinguistic practice as well as grammatical systems. These may not be as clearly or rigidly structured as the word "system" suggests, but there are nev-ertheless always some conventional points of orientation when we act semi-otically. Available Designs also include another element: the linguistic and discoursal experience of those involved in Designing, in which one moment of Designing is continuous with and a continuation of particular histories. We can refer to this as the intertextual context (Fairclough, 1989), which links the text being designed to one or more series ("chains") of past texts.

Designing.   The process of shaping emergent meaning involves re-presentation and recontextualization. This is never simply a repetition of Available De-signs. Every moment of meaning involves the transformation of the avail-able resources of meaning. Reading, seeing, and listening are all instances of Designing.

According to Halliday (1978), a deep organizing principle in the gram-mars of human languages is the distinction among macrofunctions of lan-guage, which are the different functions of Available Designs: ideational, interpersonal, and textual functions. These functions produce distinctive ex-pressions of meaning. The ideational function handles the "knowledge," and the interpersonal function handles the "social relations." As for orders of dis-course, the generative interrelation of discourses in a social context, their con-stituent genres can be partly characterized in terms of the particular social relations and subject positions they articulate, whereas discourses are particu-lar knowledges (constructions of the world) articulated with particular sub-ject positions.

Any semiotic activity — any Designing — simultaneously works on and with these facets of Available Designs. Designing will more or less norma-tively reproduce, or more or less radically transform, given knowledges, social relations, and identities, depending upon the social conditions under which Designing occurs. But it will never simply reproduce Available Designs. Designing transforms knowledge in producing new constructions and representations of reality. Through their co-engagement in Designing, people transform their relations with each other, and so transform themselves. These are not independent processes. Configurations of subjects, social relations, and knowledges are worked upon and transformed (becoming The Redesigned) in the process of Designing. Existing and new configurations are always provisional, though they may achieve a high degree of permanence. Transformation is always a new use of old materials, a re-articulation and recombination of the given resources of Available Designs.

The notion of Design recognizes the iterative nature of meaning-making, drawing on Available Designs to create patterns of meaning that are more or less predictable in their contexts. This is why The Redesigned has a ring of familiarity to it. Yet there is something ineluctably unique to every utterance. Most written paragraphs are unique, never constructed in exactly that way ever before and—bar copying or statistical improbability—never to be constructed that way again. Similarly, there is something irreducibly unique about every person's voice. Designing always involves the transformation of Available Designs; it always involves making new use of old materials.

It is also important to stress that listening as well as speaking, and reading as well as writing, are productive activities, forms of Designing. Listeners and readers encounter texts as Available Designs. They also draw upon their experience of other Available Designs as a resource for making new meanings from the texts they encounter. Their listening and reading is itself a production (a Designing) of texts (though texts-for-themselves, not texts-for-others) based on their own interests and life experiences. And their listening and reading in turn transforms the resources they have received in the form of Available Designs into The Redesigned.

The Redesigned.   The outcome of Designing is a new meaning, something through which meaning-makers remake themselves. It is never a reinstantiation of one Available Design or even a simple recombination of Available Designs. The Redesigned may be variously creative or reproductive in relation to the resources for meaning-making available in Available Designs. But it is neither a simple reproduction (as the myth of standards and transmission pedagogy would have us believe), nor is it simply creative (as the myths of individual originality and personal voice would have us believe). As the play of cultural resources and uniquely positioned subjectivity, The Redesigned is founded on historically and culturally received patterns of meaning. At the same time it is the unique product of human agency: a transformed meaning. And, in its turn, The Redesigned becomes a new Available Design, a new meaning-making resource.

Through these processes of Design, moreover, meaning-makers remake themselves. They reconstruct and renegotiate their identities. Not only has The Redesigned been actively made, but it is also evidence of the ways in which the active intervention in the world that is Designing has transformed the designer.

Designs of Meaning

Available Designs:	Resources for meaning; Available Designs of meaning
Designing:	The work performed on/with Available Designs in the semiotic process
The Redesigned:	The resources that are reproduced and transformed

Dimensions of Meaning

Teachers and students need a language to describe the forms of meaning that are represented in Available Designs and The Redesigned. In other words, they need a *metalanguage*—a language for talking about language, images, texts, and meaning-making interactions.

One objective of the International Multiliteracies Project, as initiated and planned during the New London meeting and as it is now entering a collaborative research and experimental curriculum phase, is to develop an educationally accessible functional grammar; that is, a metalanguage that describes meaning in various realms. These include the textual and the visual, as well as the multimodal relations between the different meaning-making processes that are now so critical in media texts and the texts of electronic multimedia.

Any metalanguage to be used in a school curriculum has to match up to some taxing criteria. It must be capable of supporting sophisticated critical analysis of language and other semiotic systems, yet at the same time not make unrealistic demands on teacher and learner knowledge, and not immediately conjure up teachers' accumulated and often justified antipathies towards formalism. The last point is crucial, because teachers must be motivated to work on and work with the metalanguage.

A metalanguage also needs to be quite flexible and open ended. It should be seen as a tool kit for working on semiotic activities, not a formalism to be applied to them. We should be comfortable with fuzzy-edged, overlapping concepts. Teachers and learners should be able to pick and choose from the tools offered. They should also feel free to fashion their own tools. Flexibility is critical because the relationship between descriptive and analytical categories and actual events is, by its nature, shifting, provisional, unsure, and relative to the contexts and purposes of analysis.

Furthermore, the primary purpose of the metalanguage should be to identify and explain differences between texts, and relate these to the contexts of culture and situation in which they seem to work. The metalanguage is not to impose rules, to set standards of correctness, or to privilege certain discourses in order to "empower" students.

The metalanguage we are suggesting for analyzing the Design of meaning with respect to orders of discourse includes the key terms "genres" and "discourses," and a number of related concepts such as voices, styles, and probably others (Fairclough, 1992a; Kress, 1990; van Leeuwen, 1993). More informally, we might ask of any Designing, What's the game? and What's the angle?

"The game" points us in the direction of purpose, and the notion of genre. Sometimes the game can be specified in terms of a clearly defined and socially labeled genre, like church liturgy; sometimes there is no clear generic category. Semiotic activity and the texts it generates regularly mixes genres (for example, doctor-patient consultations, which are partly like medical examinations and partly like counseling sessions, or even informal conversations).

In trying to characterize game and genre, we should start from the social context, the institutional location, the social relations of texts, and the social practices within which they are embedded. Genre is an intertextual aspect of a text. It shows how the text links to other texts in the intertextual context, and how it might be similar in some respects to other texts used in comparable social contexts, and its connections with text types in the order(s) of discourse. But genre is just one of a number of intertextual aspects of a text, and it needs to be used in conjunction with others, especially discourses.

A *discourse* is a construction of some aspect of reality from a particular point of view, a particular angle, in terms of particular interests. As an abstract noun, discourse draws attention to use of language as a facet of social practice that is shaped by — and shapes — the orders of discourse of the culture, as well as language systems (grammars). As a count noun (discourses in the plural rather than discourse in general), it draws attention to the diversity of constructions (representations) of various domains of life and experience associated with different voices, positions, and interests (subjectivities). Here again, some discourses are clearly demarcated and have conventional names in the culture (for example, feminist, party-political, or religious discourses), whereas others are much more difficult to pinpoint. Intertextual characterizations of texts in terms of genres and discourses are best regarded as provisional approximations, because they are cultural interpretations of texts that depend on the analyst's fuzzy but operationally adequate feel for the culture, as well as for specialist knowledges.

Design Elements

One of the key ideas informing the notion of multiliteracies is the increasing complexity and inter-relationship of different modes of meaning. We have identified six major areas in which functional grammars — the metalanguages that describe and explain patterns of meaning — are required: Linguistic Design, Visual Design, Audio Design, Gestural Design, Spatial Design, and Multimodal Design. Multimodal Design is of a different order to the other five modes of meaning; it represents the patterns of interconnection among the other modes. We are using the word "grammar" here in a positive sense, as a specialized language that describes patterns of representation. In each case, our objective is to come up with no more than approximately ten major Design elements.

Linguistic Design. The metalanguage we propose to use to describe Linguistic Design is intended to focus our attention on the representational resources. This metalanguage is not a category of mechanical skills, as is commonly the case in grammars designed for educational use. Nor is it the basis for detached critique or reflection. Rather, the Design notion emphasizes the productive and innovative potential of language as a meaning-making system. This is an action, a generative description of language as a means of representation. As we have argued earlier in this article, such an orientation to society and text will be an essential requirement of the economies and societies of the present and the future. It will also be essential for the production of particular kinds of democratic and participatory subjectivity. The elements of Linguistic Design that we foreground help describe the representational resources that are available, the various meanings these resources will have if drawn upon in a particular context, and the innovative potential for reshaping these resources in relation to social intentions or aims.

Consider this example: "Lung cancer death rates are clearly associated with increased smoking," and "Smoking causes cancer." The first sentence can mean what the second means, though it can mean many other things as well. The first sentence is more explicit in some ways than the second (e.g., reference to lung cancer), and less explicit in other ways (e.g., "associated with" versus "cause"). Grammar has been recruited to design two different instruments. Each sentence is usable in different discourses. For example, the first is a form typical of much writing in the social sciences and even the hard sciences. The second is a form typical of public health discussion. Grammar needs to be seen as a range of choices one makes in designing communication for specific ends, including greater recruitment of nonverbal features. These choices, however, need to be seen as not just a matter of individual style or intention, but as inherently connected to different discourses with their wider interests and relationships of power.

Our suggested metalanguage for analyzing the designs of language is built around a highly selective checklist of features of texts, which experience has shown to be particularly worth attending to (see also Fowler, Hodge, Kress, & Trent, 1979; Fairclough, 1992a). The following table lists some key terms that might be included as a metalanguage of Linguistic Design. Other potentially significant textual features are likely to be alluded to from time to time, but we think that a facility in using the features on the checklist itself constitutes a substantive, if limited, basis for critical language awareness.

We will examine two of these now in order to illustrate our notion of Linguistic Design: nominalization and transitivity. *Nominalization* involves using a phrase to compact a great deal of information, somewhat like the way a trash compactor compacts trash. After compacting, you cannot always tell what has been compacted. Consider the expression, "Lung cancer death rates." Is this "rates" at which people die of lung cancer, or rates at which lungs die from cancer? You can't know this unless you are privy to what the discussion has been. Nominalizations are used to compact information—

whole conversations—that we assume people (or at least "experts") are up on. They are signals for those "in the game" and thus are also ways to keep people out.

Transitivity indicates how much agency and effect one designs into a sentence. "John struck Mary" has more effect (on Mary) than "John struck out at Mary," and "John struck Mary" has more agency than "Mary was struck." Since we humans connect agency and effect with responsibility and blame in many domains (discourses), these are not just matters of grammar. They are ways of designing language to engage in actions like blaming, avoiding blame, or backgrounding certain things against others.

Some Elements of Linguistic Design

Delivery:	Features of intonation, stress, rhythm, accent, etc.
Vocabulary and Metaphor:	Includes colocation, lexicalization, and word meaning.
Modality:	The nature of the producer's commitment to the message in a clause.
Transitivity:	The types of process and participants in the clause. Vocabulary and metaphor, word choice, positioning, and meaning.
Nominalization of Processes:	Turning actions, qualities, assessments, or logical connections into nouns or states of being (e.g., "assess" becomes "assessment"; "can" becomes "ability").
Information Structures:	How information is presented in clauses and sentences.
Local Coherence Relations:	Cohesion between clauses, and logical relations between clauses (e.g., embedding, subordination).
Global Coherence Relations:	The overall organizational properties of texts (e.g., genres).

Designs for Other Modes of Meaning.   Increasingly important are modes of meaning other than Linguistic, including Visual Meanings (images, page layouts, screen formats); Audio Meanings (music, sound effects); Gestural Meanings (body language, sensuality); Spatial Meanings (the meanings of environmental spaces, architectural spaces); and Multimodal Meanings. Of the modes of meaning, the Multimodal is the most significant, as it relates all the other modes in quite remarkably dynamic relationships. For instance, mass media images relate the linguistic to the visual and to the gestural in intricately designed ways. Reading the mass media for its linguistic meanings alone is not enough. Magazines employ vastly different visual grammars according to their social and cultural content. A script of a sitcom such as *Roseanne*[1] would have none of the qualities of the program if you didn't have a "feel" for its unique gestural, audio, and visual meanings. A script without this knowledge would only allow a very limited reading. Similarly, a visit to a shopping mall involves a lot of written text. However, either a pleasurable or a critical engagement with the mall will involve a multimodal reading that not only includes the design of language, but a spatial reading of the architecture of the mall and the placement and meaning of the written signs, logos, and lighting. McDonalds has hard seats—to keep you moving. Casinos do not have windows or clocks—to remove tangible indicators of time passing. These are profoundly important spatial and architectonic meanings, crucial for reading Available Designs and for Designing social futures.

In a profound sense, all meaning-making is multimodal. All written text is also visually designed. Desktop publishing puts a new premium on visual design and spreads responsibility for the visual much more broadly than was the case when writing and page layout were separate trades. So, a school project can and should properly be evaluated on the basis of visual as well as linguistic design, and their multimodal relationships. To give another example, spoken language is a matter of audio design as much as it is a matter of linguistic design understood as grammatical relationships.

Texts are designed using the range of historically available choices among different modes of meaning. This entails a concern with absences from texts, as well as presences in texts: "Why not that?" as well as "Why this?" (Fairclough, 1992b). The concept of Design emphasizes the relationships between received modes of meaning (Available Designs), the transformation of these modes of meaning in their hybrid and intertextual use (Designing), and their subsequent to-be-received status (The Redesigned). The metalanguage of meaning-making applies to all aspects of this process: how people are positioned by the elements of available modes of meaning (Available Designs), yet how the authors of meanings in some important senses bear the responsibility of being consciously in control of their transformation of meanings (Designing), and how the effects of meaning, the sedimentation of meaning, become a part of the social process (The Redesigned).

Of course, the extent of transformation from Available Designs to The Redesigned as a result of Designing can greatly vary. Sometimes the designers of meaning will reproduce the Available Designs in the form of The Redesigned more closely than at other times—a form letter as opposed to a personal letter, or a classified as opposed to a display advertisement, for instance. Some Designing is more premeditated—planned, deliberate, systematized—than other instances, for example, a conversation as opposed to a poem. At times, Designing is based on clearly articulated, perhaps specialist, metalanguages describing Design elements (the language of the professional editor or the architect), while other Designing may be no more or less transformative, even though the designers may not have an articulated metalanguage to describe the elements of their meaning-making processes (the person who "fixes up" what they have just written or the home renovator). Notwithstanding these different relationships of structure and agency, all meaning-making always involves both.

Two key concepts help us describe multimodal meanings and the relationships of different designs of meaning: hybridity and intertextuality (Fairclough, 1992a, 1992b). The term *hybridity* highlights the mechanisms of creativity and of culture-as-process particularly salient in contemporary society. People create and innovate by hybridizing—that is, articulating in new ways—established practices and conventions within and between different modes of meaning. This includes the hybridization of established ways modes of meaning (of discourses and genres), and multifarious combinations of modes of meaning cutting across boundaries of convention and creating new conventions. Popular music is a perfect example of the process of hybridity. Different cultural forms and traditions are constantly being recombined and restructured—where the musical forms of Africa meet audio electronics and the commercial music industry. And new relations are constantly being created between linguistic meanings and audio meanings (pop versus rap) and between linguistic/audio and visual meanings (live performance versus video clips).

Intertextuality draws attention to the potentially complex ways in which meanings (such as linguistic meanings) are constituted through relationships to other texts (real or imaginary), text types (discourse or genres), narratives, and other modes of meaning (such as visual design, architectonic or geographical positioning). Any text can be viewed historically in terms of the intertextual chains (historical series of texts) it draws upon, and in terms of the transformations it works upon them. For instance, movies are full of cross references, either made explicitly by the movie maker or read into the movie by the viewer-as-Designer: a role, a scene, an ambiance. The viewer takes a good deal of their sense of the meaning of the movie through these kinds of intertextual chains.

THE "HOW" OF A PEDAGOGY OF MULTILITERACIES

A Theory of Pedagogy

Any successful theory of pedagogy must be based on views about how the human mind works in society and classrooms, as well as about the nature of teaching and learning. While we certainly believe that no current theory in psychology, education, or the social sciences has "the answers," and that theories stemming from these domains must always be integrated with the "practical knowledge" of master practitioners, we also believe that those proposing curricular and pedagogical reforms must clearly state their views of mind, society, and learning in virtue of which they believe such reforms would be efficacious.

Our view of mind, society, and learning is based on the assumption that the human mind is embodied, situated, and social. That is, human knowledge is initially developed not as "general and abstract," but as embedded in social, cultural, and material contexts. Further, human knowledge is initially developed as part and parcel of collaborative interactions with others of diverse skills, backgrounds, and perspectives joined together in a particular epistemic community, that is, a community of learners engaged in common practices centered around a specific (historically and socially constituted) domain of knowledge. We believe that "abstractions," "generalities," and "overt theories" come out of this initial ground and must always be returned to it or to a recontextualized version of it.

This view of mind, society, and learning, which we hope to explicate and develop over the next few years as part of our joint international project, leads us to argue that pedagogy is a complex integration of four factors: Situated Practice based on the world of learners' Designed and Designing experiences; Overt Instruction through which students shape for themselves an explicit metalanguage of Design; Critical Framing, which relates meanings to their social contexts and purposes; and Transformed Practice in which students transfer and re-create Designs of meaning from one context to another. We will briefly develop these themes below.

Recent work in cognitive science, social cognition, and sociocultural approaches to language and literacy (Barsalou, 1992; Bereiter & Scardamalia, 1993; Cazden, 1988; Clark, 1993; Gardner, 1991; Gee, 1992; Heath, 1983; Holland, Holyoak, Nisbett, & Thagard, 1986; Lave & Wenger, 1991; Light & Butterworth, 1993; Perkins, 1992; Rogoff, 1990; Scollon & Scollon, 1981; Street, 1984; Wertsch, 1985) argues that if one of our pedagogical goals is a degree of mastery in practice, then immersion in a community of learners engaged in authentic versions of such practice is necessary. We call this Situated Practice. Recent research (Barsalou, 1992; Eiser, 1994; Gee, 1992; Harre & Gillett, 1994; Margolis, 1993; Nolan, 1994) argues that the human mind is not, like a digital computer, a processor of general rules and decontextualized abstractions. Rather, human knowledge, when it is applicable to practice, is primarily situated in sociocultural settings and heavily contextualized in specific knowledge domains and practices. Such knowledge is inextricably tied to the ability to recognize and act on patterns of data and experience, a process that is acquired only through experience, since the requisite patterns are often heavily tied and adjusted to context, and are, very often, subtle and complex enough that no one can fully and usefully describe or explicate them. Humans are, at this level, contextual and sociocultural "pattern recognizors" and actors. Such pattern recognition underlies the ability to act flexibly and adaptably in context—that is, mastery in practice.

However, there are limitations to Situated Practice as the sole basis for pedagogy. First, a concern for the situatedness of learning is both the strength and the weakness of progressivist pedagogies (Kalantzis & Cope, 1993). While such situated learning can lead to mastery in practice, learners immersed in rich and complex practices can vary quite significantly from each other (and from curricular goals), and some can spend a good deal of time pursuing the "wrong" leads, so to speak. Second, much of the "immersion" that we experience as children, such as in acquiring our "native" language, is surely supported by our human biology and the normal course of human maturation and development. Such support is not available in later school immersion in areas such as literacy and academic domains, since these are far too late on the human scene to have garnered any substantive biological or evolutionary support. Thus, whatever help biology and maturation give children in their early primary socialization must be made up for—given more overtly—

when we use "immersion" as a method in school. Third, Situated Practice does not necessarily lead to conscious control and awareness of what one knows and does, which is a core goal of much school-based learning. Fourth, such Situated Practice does not necessarily create learners or communities who can critique what they are learning in terms of historical, cultural, political, ideological, or value-centered relations. And, fifth, there is the question of putting knowledge into action. People may be able to articulate their knowledge in words. They could be consciously aware of relationships, and even able to engage in "critique." Yet they might still be incapable of reflexively enacting their knowledge in practice.

Thus, Situated Practice, where teachers guide a community of learners as "masters" of practice, must be supplemented by several other components (see Cazden, 1992). Beyond mastery in practice, an efficacious pedagogy must seek critical understanding or cultural understanding in two different senses. Critical in the phrase "critical understanding" means conscious awareness and control over the intra-systematic relations of a system. Immersion, notoriously, does not lead to this. For instance, children who have acquired a first language through immersion in the practices of their communities do not thereby, in virtue of that fact, become good linguists. Vygotsky (1978, 1987), who certainly supported collaboration in practice as a foundation of learning, argued also that certain forms of Overt Instruction were needed to supplement immersion (acquisition) if we wanted learners to gain conscious awareness and control of what they acquired.

There is another sense of "critical," as in the ability to critique a system and its relations to other systems on the basis of the workings of power, politics, ideology, and values (Fairclough, 1992b). In this sense, people become aware of, and are able to articulate, the cultural locatedness of practices. Unfortunately, neither immersion in Situated Practices within communities of learners, nor Overt Instruction of the sort Vygotsky (1987) discussed, necessarily gives rise to this sort of critical understanding or cultural understanding. In fact, both immersion and many sorts of Overt Instruction are notorious as socializing agents that can render learners quite uncritical and unconscious of the cultural locatedness of meanings and practices.

The four components of pedagogy we propose here do not constitute a linear hierarchy, nor do they represent stages. Rather, they are components that are related in complex ways. Elements of each may occur simultaneously, while at different times one or the other will predominate, and all of them are repeatedly revisited at different levels.

Situated Practice

This is the part of pedagogy that is constituted by immersion in meaningful practices within a community of learners who are capable of playing multiple and different roles based on their backgrounds and experiences. The community must include experts, people who have mastered certain practices. Minimally, it must include expert novices, people who are experts at learning new domains in some depth. Such experts can guide learners, serving as mentors and designers of their learning processes. This aspect of the curriculum needs to recruit learners' previous and current experiences, as well as their extra-school communities and discourses, as an integral part of the learning experience.

There is ample evidence that people do not learn anything well unless they are both motivated to learn and believe that they will be able to use and function with what they are learning in some way that is in their interest. Thus, the Situated Practice that constitutes the immersion aspect of pedagogy must crucially consider the affective and sociocultural needs and identities of all learners. It must also constitute an arena in which all learners are secure in taking risks and trusting the guidance of others—peers and teachers.

Within this aspect of pedagogy, evaluation, we believe, should never be used to judge, but should be used developmentally, to guide learners to the experiences and the assistance they need to develop further as members of the community capable of drawing on, and ultimately contributing to, the full range of its resources.

Overt Instruction

Overt Instruction does not imply direct transmission, drills, and rote memorization, though unfortunately it often has these connotations. Rather, it includes all those active interventions on the part of the teacher and other experts that scaffold learning activities, that focus the learner on the important features of their experiences and activities within the community of learners, and that allow the learner to gain explicit information at times when it can most usefully organize and guide practice, building on and recruiting what the learner already knows and has accomplished. It includes centrally the sorts of collaborative efforts between teacher and student wherein the student is both allowed to accomplish a task more complex than they can accomplish on their own, and where they come to conscious awareness of the teacher's representation and interpretation of that task and its relations to other aspects of what its being learned. The goal here is conscious awareness and control over what is being learned—over the intra-systematic relations of the domain being practiced.

One defining aspect of Overt Instruction is the use of metalanguages, languages of reflective generalization that describe the form, content, and function of the discourses of practice. In the case of the multiliteracies framework proposed here, this would mean that students develop a metalanguage that describes both the "what" of literacy pedagogy (Design processes and Design elements) and the scaffolds that constitute the "how" of learning (Situated Practice, Overt Instruction, Critical Framing, Transformed Practice).

Much assessment in traditional curriculum required replication of the generalities of Overt Instruction. As in the case of Situated Practice, evaluation in Overt Instruction should be developmental, a guide to further thought and action. It should also be related to the other aspects of the learning process—the connections, for example, between evolving metalanguages as they are negotiated and developed through Overt Instruction, on the one hand, and Situated Practice, Critical Framing, and Transformed Practice, on the other hand.

Critical Framing

The goal of Critical Framing is to help learners frame their growing mastery in practice (from Situated Practice) and conscious control and understanding (from Overt Instruction) in relation to the historical, social, cultural, political, ideological, and value-centered relations of particular systems of knowledge and social practice. Here, crucially, the teacher must help learners to denaturalize and make strange again what they have learned and mastered.

For example, the claim "DNA replicates itself" framed within biology is obvious and "true." Framed within another discourse in the following way, it becomes less natural and less "true": Put some DNA in some water in a glass on a table. It certainly will not replicate itself, it will just sit there. Organisms replicate themselves using DNA as a code, but that code is put into effect by an array of machinery involving proteins. In many of our academic and Western discourses, we have privileged information and mind over materials, practice, and work. The original claim foregrounds information and code and leaves out, or backgrounds, machinery and work. This foregrounding and backgrounding becomes apparent only when we reframe, when we take the sentence out of its "home" discourse and place it in a wider context. Here, the wider context is actual processes and material practices, not just general statements in a disciplinary theory (the DNA example is from Lewontin, 1991).

Through critical framing, learners can gain the necessary personal and theoretical distance from what they have learned, constructively critique it, account for its cultural location, creatively extend and apply it, and eventually innovate on their own, within old communities and in new ones. This is the basis for Transformed Practice. It also represents one sort of transfer of learning, and one area where evaluation can begin to assess learners and, primarily, the learning processes in which they have been operating.

Transformed Practice

It is not enough to be able to articulate one's understanding of intra-systematic relations or to critique extra-systematic relations. We need always to return to where we began, to Situated Practice, but now a re-practice, where theory becomes reflective practice. With their students, teachers need to develop ways in which the students can demonstrate how they can design and carry out, in a reflective manner, new practices embedded in their own goals and values. They should be able to show that they can implement understandings acquired through Overt Instruction and Critical Framing in practices that help them simultaneously to apply and revise what they have learned. In Transformed Practice we are offered a place for situated, contextualized assessment of learners and the learning processes devised for them. Such learning processes, such a pedagogy, needs to be continually reformulated on the basis of these assessments.

In Transformed Practice, in one activity we try to re-create a discourse by engaging in it for our own real purposes. Thus, imagine a student having to act and think like a biologist, and at the same time as a biologist with a vested interest in resisting the depiction of female things—from eggs to organisms—as "passive." The student now has to both juxtapose and integrate (not without tension) two different discourses, or social identities, or "interests" that have historically been at odds. Using another example, how can one be a "real" lawyer and, at the same time, have one's performance influenced by being an African American. In his arguments before the U.S. Supreme Court for desegregating schools, Thurgood Marshall did this in a classic way. And, in mixing the discourse of politics with the discourse of African American religion, Jesse Jackson has transformed the former. The key here is juxtaposition, integration, and living with tension.

> *Situated Practice:* Immersion in experience and the utilization of available discourses, including those from the students' lifeworlds and simulations of the relationships to be found in workplaces and public spaces.
>
> *Overt Instruction:* Systematic, analytic, and conscious understanding. In the case of multiliteracies, this requires the introduction of explicit metalanguages, which describe and interpret the Design elements of different modes of meaning.
>
> *Critical Framing:* Interpreting the social and cultural context of particular Designs of meaning. This involves the students' standing back from what they are studying and viewing it critically in relation to its context.
>
> *Transformed Practice:* Transfer in meaning-making practice, which puts the transformed meaning to work in other contexts or cultural sites.

THE INTERNATIONAL MULTILITERACIES PROJECT

Let us tie the "what" and the "how" of literacy pedagogy back to the large agenda with which we began this article: focusing on Situated Practices in the learning process involves the recognition that differences are critical in workplaces, civic spaces, and multilayered lifeworlds. Classroom teaching and curriculum have to engage with students' own experiences and discourses, which are increasingly defined by cultural and subcultural diversity and the different language backgrounds and practices that come with this diversity. Overt Instruction is not intended to tell—to empower students in relation to the "grammar" of one proper, standard, or powerful language form. It is meant to help students develop a metalanguage that accounts for Design differences. Critical Framing involves linking these Design differences to different cultural purposes. Transformed Practice involves moving from one cultural context to another; for example, redesigning meaning strategies so they can be transferred from one cultural situation to another.

The idea of Design is one that recognizes the different Available Designs of meaning, located as they are in different cultural contexts. The metalanguage of multiliteracies describes the elements of Design, not as rules, but as an heuristic that accounts for the infinite variability of different forms of meaning-making in relation to the cultures, the subcultures, or the layers of an individual's identity that these forms serve. At the same time, Designing restores human agency and cultural dynamism to the process of meaning-making. Every act of meaning both appropriates Available Designs and recreates in the Designing, thus producing new meaning as The Redesigned. In an economy of productive diversity, in civic spaces that value pluralism, and in the flourishing of interrelated, multilayered, complementary yet increasingly divergent lifeworlds, workers, citizens, and community members are ideally creative and responsible makers of meaning. We are, indeed, designers of our social futures.

Of course, the necessary negotiation of differences will be difficult and often painful. The dialogue will encounter chasms of difference in values, grossly unjust inequalities, and difficult but necessary border crossings. The differences are not as neutral, colorful, and benign as a simplistic multiculturalism might want us to believe. Yet as workers, citizens, and community members, we will all need the skills required to negotiate these differences.

This article represents a statement of general principle. It is highly provisional, and something we offer as a basis for public debate. The objective of the International Multiliteracies Project is to test and develop these ideas further, particularly the metalanguage of Design and the pedagogy of Situated Practice, Overt Instruction, Critical Framing, and Transformed Practice. We also want to establish relationships with teachers and researchers, developing and testing curriculum and revising the theoretical propositions of the project.

This article is a provisional statement of intent and a theoretical overview of the connections between the changing social environment and the "what" and the "how" of literacy pedagogy. As the project moves into its next phase, the group that met in New London is writing a book that explores the ideas of multiliteracies further, relating the idea to classrooms and our own educational experiences. We are also beginning to conduct classroom-based research, experimenting with multiliteracies as a notion that might supplement and support literacy curriculum. And we are actively engaged in ongoing public dialogue. In September 1996, the group will be opening the argument up to public discussion once again at the Domains of Literacy Conference at London University, and again in 1997 at the Literacy and Education Research Network Conference in Australia. We want to stress that this is an open-ended process—tentative, exploratory, and welcoming of multiple and divergent collaborations. And above all, our aim is to make some sort of difference for real children in real classrooms.

These activities will be informed by a number of key principles of action. First, the project will supplement, not critique, existing curricula and pedagogical approaches to the teaching of English language and literacy. This will include further developing the conceptual framework of the International

Multiliteracies Project, and mapping this against existing curriculum practices in order to extend teachers' pedagogical and curriculum repertoires. Second, the project team will welcome collaborations with researchers, curriculum developers, teachers, and communities. The project framework represents a complex and difficult dialogue; these complexities and difficulties will be articulated along with an open invitation for all to contribute to the development of a pedagogy that does make some difference. And third, it will strive continually towards reformulations of theory that are of direct use in educational practice.

This article is a tentative starting point for that process.

NOTE

1. An American sitcom (1988–1997) about a working-class Illinois family that starred Roseanne Barr.

REFERENCES

Barsalou, L. W. (1992). *Cognitive psychology: An overview for cognitive scientists*. Hillsdale, NJ: Lawrence Erlbaum.

Bereiter, C., & Scardamalia, M. (1993). *Surpassing ourselves: An inquiry into the nature and implications of expertise*. Chicago: Open Court.

Cazden, C. (1988). *Classroom discourse: The language of teaching and learning*. Portsmouth, NH: Heinemann.

Cazden, C. (1992). *Whole language plus: Essays on literacy in the United States and New Zealand*. New York: Teachers College Press.

Clark, A. (1993). *Associative engines: Connections, concepts, and representational change*. Cambridge, Eng.: Cambridge University Press.

Eiser, J. R. (1994). *Attitudes, chaos, and the connectionist mind*. Oxford, Eng.: Basil Blackwell.

Fairclough, N. (1989). *Language and power*. London: Longmans.

Fairclough, N. (1992a). *Discourse and social power*. London: Polity Press.

Fairclough, N. (1992b). Discourse and text: Linguistic and intertextual analysis within discourse analysis. *Discourse and Society, 3*, 193–217.

Fairclough, N. (1995). *Critical discourse analysis*. London: Longmans.

Fowler, R., Hodge, R., Kress, G., & Trent, T. (1979). *Language and control*. London: Routledge.

Gardner, H. (1991). *The unschooled mind: How children think and how schools should teach*. New York: Basic Books.

Gee, J. P. (1992). *The social mind: Language, ideology, and social practice*. New York: Bergin & Garvey.

Halliday, M. A. K. (1978). *Language as social semiotic*. London: Edward Arnold.

Harre, R., & Gillett, G. (1994). *The discursive mind*. Thousand Oaks, CA: Sage.

Heath, S. B. (1983). *Ways with words: Language, life, and work in communities and classrooms*. Cambridge, Eng.: Cambridge University Press.

Holland, J. H., Holyoak, K. J., Nisbett, R. E., & Thagard, P. R. (1986). In J. H. Holland, K. J. Holyoak, R. E. Nisbett, & P. R. Thagard (Eds.), *Induction: Processes of inference, learning, and discovery*. Cambridge, MA: MIT Press.

Kalantzis, M. (1995). The new citizen and the new state. In W. Hudson (Ed.), *Rethinking Australian citizenship*. Sydney: University of New South Wales Press.

Kalantzis, M., & Cope, B. (1993). Histories of pedagogy, cultures of schooling. In B. Cope & M. Kalantzis (Eds.), *The powers of literacy* (pp. 38–62). London: Falmer Press.

Kress, G. (1990). *Linguistic process and sociocultural change*. Oxford, Eng.: Oxford University Press.

Lave, J., & Wenger, E. (1991). *Situated learning: Legitimate peripheral participation*. Cambridge, Eng.: Cambridge University Press.

Lewontin, R. C. (1991). *Biology as ideology: The doctrine of DNA*. New York: Harper.

Light, P., & Butterworth, G. (Eds.). (1993). *Context and cognition: Ways of learning and knowing*. Hillsdale, NJ: Lawrence Erlbaum.

Margolis, H. (1993). *Paradigms and barriers: How habits of mind govern scientific beliefs*. Chicago: University of Chicago Press.

Nolan, R. (1994). *Cognitive practices: Human language and human knowledge*. Oxford, Eng.: Blackwell.

Perkins, D. (1992). *Smart schools: From training memories to educating minds*. New York: Free Press.

Rogoff, B. (1990). *Apprenticeship in thinking*. New York: Oxford University Press.

Scollon, R., & Scollon, S. B. K. (1981). *Narrative, literacy, and face in interethnic communication*. Norwood, NJ: Ablex.

Street, B. V. (1984). *Literacy in theory and practice*. Cambridge, Eng.: Cambridge University Press.

van Leeuwen, T. (1993). Genre and field in critical discourse analysis. *Discourse and Society, 4,* 193–223.

Vygotsky, L. S. (1978). *Mind in society: The development of higher psychological processes*. Cambridge, MA: Harvard University Press.

Vygotsky, L. S. (1987). *The collected works of L. S. Vygotsky: Vol. 1. Problems of general psychology, including the volume thinking and speech* (R. W. Rieber & A. S. Carton, Eds.; Trans. N. Minick). New York: Plenum.

Wertsch, J. V. (Ed.). (1985). *Culture, communication, and cognition: Vygotskian perspectives*. Cambridge, Eng.: Cambridge University Press.

10   From Analysis to Design: Visual Communication in the Teaching of Writing

DIANA GEORGE

In some respects . . . words cannot compare in effectiveness with pictures. The mere outlines in a Greek vase painting will give you a more immediate appreciation of the grace and beauty of the human form than pages of descriptive writing. A silhouette in black paper will enable you to recognize a stranger more quickly than the most elaborate description in words. *(166)*

— John Hays Gardiner, George Lyman Kittredge,
and Sarah Louise Arnold, 1902

How's this for a visual argument: In response to reading Adam Hochschild's *King Leopold's Ghost*,[1] Boikhutso Jibula, a first-year student from Botswana, reproduces three maps of Africa, each on a transparency. In the first, the continent is empty except for what look like random circles primarily in the sub-Saharan region. The circles outline areas traditionally occupied or claimed by various tribes or communities before colonization. Boikhutso then superimposes a second map—this one of colonized Africa. He points out the English, French, and German names of places that now have well-defined borders, most of which cut through the original circles, splitting traditional regions into new nations, neither named for nor controlled by the people whose places he had identified in the original map. Over that second map, Boikhutso superimposes a third—this one is postcolonial Africa. The names, he points out, are changed. German East Africa is now mainly Tanzania. The Congo Free State is, on this map at any rate, Zaire. Colonization has ended, he tells us, but the boundaries are much the same, the people dispersed or gone, the languages and kingdoms and villages still split or destroyed. It takes very few words for Boikhutso to tell the class what these maps show them: Precolonial Africa cannot be recovered. There is no possibility of going back to what was there before the colonizer. African people must work as nations within the nations now outlined on this third map.

From *College Composition and Communication* 54 (2002): 11–39.

FIGURE 10-1   Original design by Deirdre Johns.

Or picture this: In the same course, Grace VanCamp from lower Michigan creates a dinner place setting, Judy Chicago style. On a place mat, she arranges a plastic plate, knife, fork, spoon, and Coca-Cola© glass. On the face of the plate, Grace has glued a map of the African continent. The place card reads, "King Leopold."

And finally: Deirdre Johns shows the class a remaking of Leopold of Belgium's Congo Free State flag (see Figure 10-1). Like the original, her redesign features a bold yellow star in the center of a deep blue field. She tells the class that in her research she learned of the reasoning for the design: the star was to signify the light of Europe being brought in to the Dark Continent. In Deirdre's flag, the blue field is now covered with images of precolonial African art. The gold star is covered in images of slavery, faces of explorers, photos from the rubber and ivory trade. "This is what Europe really brought to Congo," she tells the class.

There are others I could describe—graphs and oil paintings and Web pages and digital designs and book covers and more—but they would tell much the same story. The work of these students and others like them has convinced me that current discussions of visual communication and writing instruction have only tapped the surface of possibilities for the role of visual communication in the composition class.[2] Or, even more to the point—our students have a much richer imagination for what we might accomplish with the visual than our journals have yet to address.

From W. J. T. Mitchell's claim that the second half of the twentieth century was marked by "the pictorial turn" (11–34) to the New London Group's call for a pedagogy of "multiliteracies," we are experiencing yet another push to incorporate visual language into the composition course.[3] It is, of course, true that an insistence on the importance of visual literacy is an old and perennial one. In fact, it has become common today to talk of multiple literacies, to encourage the uses of visual communication in the teaching of writing, and to argue that writing is itself a form of visual communication.

Even so, there remains much confusion over what is meant by *visual communication, visual rhetoric,* or, more simply, *the visual* and where or whether it belongs in a composition course. What's more, to the extent that this confusion remains unaddressed, visual and written communication continue to be held in a kind of tension—the visual figuring into the teaching of writing as a problematic, something added, an anomaly, a "new" way of composing, or, somewhat cynically, as a strategy for adding relevance or interest to a required course. Only rarely does that call address students as producers as well as consumers or critics of the visual. More rarely does the call acknowledge the visual as much more than attendant to the verbal.

My aim in what follows is not to define visual communication or visual rhetoric in a way that would eliminate that tension. I actually believe that some tug of war between words and images or between writing and design can be productive as it brings into relief the multiple dimensions of all forms of communication. For my purposes here, at any rate, there is little reason to argue that the visual and the verbal are the same, are read or composed in the same way, or have the same status in the tradition of communication instruction.

In place of a resolution, then, I am after a clearer understanding of what can happen when the visual is very consciously brought into the composition classroom as a form of communication worth both examining *and* producing. What, for example, might it mean to ask, as I did of the students whose work opens this paper, for a visual argument? Are we posing a new relationship between composition and communication or resurrecting an older one? How does the visual both promise and threaten to change the composition course?

At this point, I should make an important distinction. I will be examining primarily the places of visual literacy in the *composition* classroom. It is quite true that a concern for visual literacy/ visual communication has been an ongoing one in the teaching of scientific, technical, and professional communication. In

> "Remember that graph-and-chart reading is not one of the three R's" (180).
> —Rudolph Flesch, 1949

fact, for a number of compositionists over the years, the technical writing course was exactly where the visual belonged. (Witness, for example, Rudolph Flesch's rather Gradgrindian declaration that one mainstay of technical writing instruction, understanding the uses of graphs and charts, "is not one of the three R's.") My focus is on arguments that have been made for including the visual in composition courses because these arguments are linked closely to discussions of basic literacy and even to English departments' investments in literary studies rather than to professional communication's emphasis on the functions or uses of visual information. That is not at all to dismiss the extensive work that characterizes professional communication's engagement with the visual. Instead, it is my attempt to bring composition studies into a more thoroughgoing discussion of the place of visual literacy in the writing classroom.

In the end, I argue that the terms of debate typical in our discussions of visual literacy and the teaching of writing have limited the kinds of assignments we might imagine for composition. I do not make a claim that our students have a special talent for the visual or that their knowledge of the visual is necessarily more sophisticated than their teachers' are. Instead, I would argue that if we are ever to move beyond a basic and somewhat vague call for attention to "visual literacy" in the writing class, it is crucial to understand how very complicated and sophisticated is visual communication to students who have grown up in what by all accounts is an aggressively visual culture. Such a move must first address how relationships between visual communication and writing instruction have been typically configured.

In order to get to that argument, however, I find it necessary first to set what I'd call one curricular context through which visual literacy has entered the teaching of writing, at least as it emerges in scholarly journals and textbook assignments for more than fifty years. The history of how visual literacy has entered the teaching of writing, at least as it emerges in scholarly journals and textbook assignments for more than fifty years, is not a smooth or consistent one in which writing instruction and visual literacy move seamlessly from image analysis to design. Instead, it is one that can best be related through major themes that have dominated the English classroom since at least the 1940s. I begin, in fact, at what might seem a far remove from the college writing classroom: examining arguments in elementary and secondary education for including visual instruction alongside lessons more familiar to English language arts. It is here that we see most clearly how visual studies has been perceived as a threat to language and literature instruction.

VISUAL LITERACY IN THE ENGLISH CLASSROOM

In 1946, the instructor's edition of the popular Dick and Jane elementary reader series alerted teachers to the reality that teaching reading demanded attention to more than print literacy. It meant teaching students to read pictures as well as words:

> Skill in interpreting pictures is becoming increasingly important as a means of securing pleasure and information. Adults today are exposed to "picture" magazines, cartoons, advertisements, movies, and many types of diagrammatic schemes for the presentation of facts. Children are surrounded with picture books and "read" the funnies long before they enter school. Regardless of age or situation, the individual who can "read" pictorial material effectively has access to a vast world of new ideas. (Kismaric and Heiferman 88)

Fifty years later, the New London Group issued their report through which they identified the ability both to read and *use* visual information/visual signs as primary among multiliteracies:

> [W]e argue that literacy pedagogy now must account for the burgeoning variety of text forms associated with information and multimedia technologies. *This includes understanding and competent control of representational forms* that are becoming increasingly significant in the overall communications environment, such as visual images and their relationship to the written word—for instance, visual design in desktop publishing or the interface of visual and linguistic meaning in multimedia. (61, emphasis added)*

The two reports sound a common theme about visual communication that might be summed up in this way: Literacy means more than words, and visual literacy means more than play.

Coming as it did at the beginning of a media revolution of sorts, the Dick and Jane statement was repeated in a number of ways for the next thirty years or so. During much of the second half of the twentieth century, mass media became a focus for study or a problem to confront in literacy instruction, and so I turn briefly to school talk about television, the visual medium that, throughout the 1950s and 1960s, threatened (or promised) to change the English classroom permanently.

In 1961, NCTE issued its report from the Commission on the Study of Television, *Television and the Teaching of English*. Neil Postman, who twenty-five years later would publish his own critique of the culture of television (*Amusing Ourselves to Death*), was its primary author. For Postman and the members of his commission, the job at hand was to convince English teachers that television was not only

> "Whatever the future may hold, teachers of English can face it with equanimity if they avoid the temptation to pit television or any other medium against print." (13)
> —Neil Postman, 1961

a proper subject for the English classroom but a necessary one, even though "We do not mean to suggest by its use that television is the equivalent of *belles lettres* but rather that certain kinds of television programs employ language and action in ways that duplicate the functions of traditional literary forms" (39–40). The commission's incentive for bringing the study of television into the English class will likely sound somewhat dated but still very familiar: "To the extent that their responses to television are *informed, discriminating,* and *creative,* we may be assured that our language and literature, as well as the lives of our students, will be enriched by contact with television. *But taste and critical judgment are learned habits of mind*" (1, emphasis added). Here, the points of concern are explicit: Television is what our children are watching. It surrounds them daily. It is their "primary source of literary experience" (1).

---

*Part of the New London Group article has been reprinted in this volume (see p. 193). Cross-references to the material reprinted here are preceded by "p."; references to sections not included in this volume carry only the page number.

The English teacher's job, then, is to foster "taste and critical judgment," two qualities that lift the schooled above the unschooled. This judgment was deemed important because, according to the commission's figures, already in 1961 (only thirteen years after the 1948 postwar boom in television production) 88 percent of American households in the U.S. owned at least one television (30). It was a "literary experience" that threatened to replace those forms more common (and more comfortable) to the English class. "Teachers of English," the report states, "must help the children qualify their enthusiasm with thoughtful criticism" (73).

Though not quite the call for relevance that became common in the 1960s, this report, like the Dick and Jane instructors' manual fifteen years earlier and the New London Group's manifesto thirty-five years later, does acknowledge a changing world in which "a redefinition of 'literacy' is required, one that would extend beyond the printed page" (12). In the end, although the Commission on the Study of Television was not persuaded of the need for a new literacy, its members did accept the challenge to extend the content of the English classroom to include a new literature—television as literary text.

It is here, then, in these early lessons on the uses of visual texts in the reading and writing classroom that literacy instruction and literary studies meet. Visuals (be they paintings, films, comic books, or television narratives) were to be studied in the same way as literary texts, as subjects of close analysis—a use of the visual that continues throughout the history of writing instruction.

In 1962, only one year after the publication of the Postman report, NCTE published William Boutwell's *Using Mass Media in the Schools*, a report from The Committee on the Use of Mass Media. In it, Boutwell writes, "No rain forest in darkest Africa ever confronted men with more unknowns or a stranger mixture of enthusiasm, excitement, fears, and hopes than the tangled strands of communication we call 'mass media'" (v). As Boutwell tells us in his preface to the report, mass media (everything from newspapers and magazines to radio, television, motion pictures, and comic books) "often seems to be a force beyond human control" (vi).

> "Every teacher must, sooner or later, face the fact that television is here to stay." (254)
> —Anita J. Willens, in *Using Mass Media in the Schools*, 1962

An air of resignation over the influence of mass media permeates this collection, even in such writing assignments as Nina T. Fleir's proposal that teachers use students' favorite television shows rather than poetry, drama, or fiction as prompts for writing (150–52). Only rarely do we encounter a suggestion that students might become producers as well as receivers or victims of mass media, especially visual media. As a tool for literacy instruction, then, this collection uses visual media as little more than a prompt for student essays and stories, a substitute for more traditional literary forms, or a subject of scrutiny.

By contrast, the 1996 New London Group report would also direct students' attention toward mass media but not as a subject of scrutiny or an invention prompt alone. Instead, the New London Group adds to the older model of media study the notion of *design* as a way of understanding literacy acquisition. What the New London Group urges, then, is not a closer relationship to media but the use of media to encourage the development of "multimodal designs" that relate

> . . . all the other modes in quite remarkably dynamic relationships. For instance, mass media images relate the linguistic to the visual and to the gestural in intricately designed ways. Reading the mass media for its linguistic meanings alone is not enough. Magazines employ vastly different visual grammars according to their social and cultural content. A script of a sitcom such as *Roseanne* would have none of the qualities of the program if you didn't have a "feel" for its unique gestural, audio, and visual meanings. A script without this knowledge would only allow a very limited reading. Similarly, a visit to a shopping mall involves a lot of written text. However, either a pleasurable or a critical engagement with the mall will involve a multimodal reading that not only includes the design of language, but a spatial reading of the architecture of the mall and the placement and meaning of the written signs, logos, and lighting. (see pp. 200–1 in this volume)

What these scholars urge, then, is not simply the inclusion of mass media as objects of study but the use of media to encourage the development of multimodal designs.

I will return to this issue of design, but for the moment it is important to point out that thinking of composition as *design* shifts attention, if only momentarily, from the product to the act of production. We might say that despite their concern for the influence of television on students' writing and reading abilities, even the 1962 Boutwell collection in some ways prefigured the work of the New London Group. Yet, without a concept like the notion of design, these older media assignments seem to be stuck in a kind of literacy civil war—one that pits poetics against the popular and words against pictures.

VISUAL LITERACY IN THE WRITING CLASS:
THE CASE OF *WRITING WITH A PURPOSE*

The treatment of the visual in postsecondary writing instruction has been a tentative one in many of the same ways as those early attempts to bring mass media into English classrooms. As a case in point, the story of how visual elements were incorporated into successive editions of a single and very popular twentieth-century college writing text (James McCrimmon's *Writing with a Purpose*) can serve to mirror the history of the visual in writing classes, especially as it indicates a clear impulse to include the visual but not always a consistent or stable way of doing that.[4]

Although some visual elements (primarily charts, graphs, and diagrams) were present even in 1950 in the first edition,[5] it wasn't until 1972 when *Writing with a Purpose* introduced a visual assignment, organized around eighteenth-century British artist William Hogarth's prints *Beer Street* and *Gin Lane*, that the textbook used visuals as an integral part of any writing assignment. According to Dean Johnson of Houghton Mifflin,

> The Hogarth pictures were introduced in the fifth edition (cy 1972) and used through the eighth edition (cy 1984). Originally they were the stuff of an exercise to support observation as a means of gathering material. In each edition, however, they were treated differently. In the seventh edition, for example, they were used to illustrate a so-called "three step method of interpretation" (e.g., observe, interpret, infer).[6]

By the eighth edition, the Hogarth prints were linked to lessons in the chapter on planning strategies.

In his discussion of how the 1970s editions of *Writing with a Purpose* reflected the changes in the student population, Robert Connors points to the visual design of the fifth edition as indicating a "lowered evaluation of its audience's abilities" signaled by "wide margins and a two-color format to open up the text's appearance" (107). Later editions, Connors writes, are even more prone to a visual appearance that suggests a dumbing down. The 1976 edition, for example, "goes in deeply for the 'visual observation' invention methods . . . It is filled with photos, cartoons, illustrations, all meant to add spice to the text" (108). And, while I would argue that the visual is not at all a simpler form of communication than the verbal, it seems clear that Connors is very likely correct in his assessment of the editorial motives for changing the visual format of *Writing with a Purpose* and, in particular, for adding visuals like the Hogarth prints.

At the outset, the *Beer Street* and *Gin Lane* prints were meant to teach students the art of observation and develop the skill of creating vivid word images—much in the tradition of *ut pictora poesis*, popularized in literary criticism in the late 1950s and early 1960s, especially by Jean Hagstrum's *The Sister Arts*.[7] According to Johnson, the Hogarth prints remained in McCrimmon's text primarily because teachers liked them. Thus, the prints stayed on for several editions because they were popular with faculty who, no doubt, recognized them as not mere popular culture but popular culture in the literary tradition. Assignments linked to the prints changed with changing composition pedagogy.

This last bit of information is useful to keep in mind in the context of a discussion on the places of visual in the writing classroom. In many respects, the Hogarth prints were absolutely peripheral to whatever writing assignment might be attached to them. Nearly any pair of images might have been used as prompts for the same writing assignments. Within the tradition of verbal/visual communication I am outlining here, only certain kinds of "visual" assignments seem possible for a writing course. Primarily, these would be assignments that use visual images as prompts for essay writing.

Such a tactic was not new with McCrimmon, of course. Lucille Schultz found similar uses of the visual to be common in writing textbooks as far back as the nineteenth century:

> [These texts] rely heavily on illustrations as a teaching tool . . . fairly detailed and complex illustrations were used abundantly in many of the lesser known mid-19th century first books of composition; in addition to common objects, they depicted scenes of home life, school life, and work life, and the illustrations served as writing prompts for young writers who were asked to describe what they saw in the picture. In these books, the illustrations were not simply embellishment or ornament, they were an integral part of the book's instructional practice. (12)

Though these early texts commonly used pictures (often reproductions of paintings) as prompts for student compositions, the aim of each exercise was to bring students to a more vivid or accurate use of written language.[8] Often, the authors made an elaborate case for the advantage or superiority of words over pictures. The Gardiner, Kittredge, and Arnold comment that opens this paper, for example, appears at first to be an argument for the primacy of the visual over the verbal, but the authors go on to say, "what can a picture tell you about wind or heat, about sound or smell, about motion, about the feeling of roughness or moisture? Nothing *directly*; it can only *suggest*" (166, emphasis in original).

Of course, other kinds of assignments involving visuals do occur in college writing pedagogies. Visual analysis (especially advertising analysis) has been commonplace in postsecondary writing instruction for at least fifty years as a part of the post-World War II emphasis on propaganda and semantics characteristic of many composition and communication courses beginning in the 1940s,[9] but that practice did not always or consistently include careful consideration of how images, layout, or graphics actually communicated meaning. Instead, advertising was treated as a subject for critique rather than itself a form of communication that employed both word and image. A 1975 *CCC* article by D. G. Kehl describes an advertising analysis assignment typical for composition in the seventies. Though Kehl does make a brief reference to the images (the pictures) in particular ads, he does so only to suggest that the ad image functions to replicate the "controlling idea" or "central thesis" of a traditional argument essay of the sort students might be assigned to write. Like the McCrimmon assignments, Kehl used advertising as a sort of shadow essay, a form once removed from the actual written essay students would produce. Kehl's stated motive for using advertising at all is one repeated by many of his colleagues throughout this period: He argues that this is a good assignment, especially "For students who are visually but not necessarily verbally sensitive" (135). Running through much of the composition literature of the period, assignments linked to images carried with them a call for relevance, the need to make this dull, required class more interesting, and the suggestion that less verbal students would perhaps succeed with pictures where they could not with words. These were sometimes arguments for using popular culture in the writing class but not always.[10]

> "Drawings are generally more accessible than essays to those college students who are inadequately prepared in reading" (vii).
>
> —Lewis Meyers, 1980

For many instructors during this same period, the use of visuals went hand in hand with expressivist pedagogies. In 1972, for example, Harcourt Brace Jovanovich published Joseph Frank's *You*, a trendy writing text loaded with photos, paintings, ads, drawings, and graphic designs. The basic assumption of this text was that each student was an individual who had something to say and could find a voice with which to say it. The focus is clearly on the self as Frank tells students, "*You* is also concerned with perception, for how and what you perceive determines who you are" (iii). Thus, assignments tied to visuals asked students how a particular image made them feel or of what an image reminded them. One assignment even juxtaposes a Rorschach-like inkblot with an abstract painting to get at how an image can be created "deliberately trying to expand both [the painter's] and the viewer's consciousness" (100). And, of course, Walker Gibson's *Seeing and Writing*, written around this same time, makes much the same argument for using visual media in the writing classroom.

Throughout much of the work mentioned so far, there runs an ongoing suspicion that the visual must somehow be important to writing. It just isn't entirely clear how. Are images strategies for getting students to pay attention to detail? Do they mimic the rhetoric of verbal argument? Are they a dumbing down of writing instruction making visible to nonverbal students what the verbally gifted can conceptualize? Certainly, there is the message in much of this work that images may be useful, even proper stimuli for writing, but they are no substitute for the complexity of language.

"Learning to see well helps students write well."
—Donald and Christine McQuade, 1999

THE TURN TO CULTURAL THEORY

When David Bartholomae and Anthony Petrosky reprinted a portion of John Berger's *Ways of Seeing* in their 1987 composition reader (and named their text *Ways of Reading* in a nod to Berger's work), they connected the visual arts very directly with the world of language. Berger's *Ways of Seeing* initially shook the world of art history with its insistence upon the social production of art. As a text about meaning and culture, *Ways of Seeing* has been even more important to a broader audience.[11] Berger begins his argument simply:

> Seeing comes before words. The child looks and recognizes before it can speak. But there is also another sense in which seeing comes before words. It is seeing which establishes our place in the surrounding world; we explain that world with words, but words can never undo the fact that we are surrounded by it. The relation between what we see and what we know is never settled. . . . The way we see things is affected by what we know or what we believe. In the Middle Ages when men believed in the physical existence of Hell the sight of fire must have meant something different from what it means today. (7–8)

That idea, that images are not a reflection of a fixed reality, that, instead, our ways of understanding the world around us are somehow commingled with how we represent the world visually was a notion that appealed to teachers of writing like Bartholomae and Petrosky who were searching for ways of incorporating cultural theory into the composition classroom.

What was radical about Berger's work was his insistence on breaking down the barriers that separated high culture (in this case art history) from low (advertising). Bartholomae and Petrosky's *Ways of Reading* made that message available to the writing class. In this textbook, not only was meaning no longer restricted to the verbal, the visual was also not used as a gentle step into the "more serious" world of the verbal. As an extract published in a composition reader, *Ways of Seeing* certainly did lead writing teachers to ask students to examine images as culturally informed texts. Yet, the complete written text of Berger's argument was *visually* much farther reaching than any discussion of image analysis might suggest or, at least, than the design of composition readers at the time would allow for.[12]

In a "Note to the Reader" that opens *Ways of Seeing*, Berger writes, "The form of the book is as much to do with our purpose as the arguments contained within it" (5). Berger points particularly to "essays" that consist only of images that "are intended to raise as many questions as the verbal essays" (5). And, yet, he could just as well have been talking about the text's heavy font, the cover design that reproduces the opening remarks of the first essay, or the ragged-right margins that call attention to page design. It would be many years before this very conscious attention to design and its relation to meaning would have much impact at all on college composition courses.

Instead, the push in the eighties was to continue to explore what visuals could teach students about their written compositions. In 1986, for example, William Costanzo, then chair of the NCTE Committee on Film Study, reported in *CCC* on a 1979 NEH project to teach film *as* composition. He lists four arguments for the use of film in teaching writing:

> (1) The basic steps of filmmaking can serve as a working model of the composing process . . . (2) . . . An understanding of the visual code which enables us to "read" a movie can help to clarify the conventions of English diction, syntax, punctuation, and usage. (3) Many of the rhetorical principles of film composition (for organizing inchoate experience into meaningful sequence, for achieving a suitable style, for selling a product or an idea) can be applied directly to specific writing tasks. (4) When students' notions of composition are widened to include these more familiar, visual forms, the writing class seems less remote. (79–80)

This urge to tie the use of images in any way possible to "the composing process" was a common one throughout this period.

Costanzo's report would seem rather ordinary, certainly right in line with attitudes we have already witnessed, if it weren't for an afterword he included as the article was being readied for press. In it, Costanzo acknowledges that his report was written five years earlier and that his understanding of the role of film in writing classes has changed considerably since that time. By 1986, Costanzo is no longer making a simple link between the study of film and the teaching of composing strategies. Instead, he writes: "If I once regarded film study as a path to better writing, I now see film and writing as equal partners traveling along the same road" (86). His concluding remarks signal a significant shift in the way he, at least, had begun to think of the role of visual media in the writing class:

> Much of what once seemed revelatory about the role of visual media in our students' lives is now widely accepted, even taken for granted. Film and television continue to dominate a major portion of their formative years, creating expectations, shaping attitudes, influencing language patterns, and providing a common frame of reference. . . . At the same time, groundbreaking work in semiotics, neurophysiology, and cognitive psychology has made strong connections between visual forms of thought and written language. It now appears that the act of writing involves more visual thinking than we recognized in traditional composition classes. (86)

Here, Costanzo was no longer talking about the visual as a convenient heuristic but, instead, asking that compositionists pay attention to "visual thinking" as one way of understanding the written word. Significantly, Costanzo's report appears in the same issue of *CCC* as Stephen Bernhardt's "Seeing the Text," an article arguing for the importance of teaching not images in the writing classroom but writing-as-image or, at least, of noting that the design of a text as well as the words used in the text conveyed meaning. Bernhardt's work indicated a change in the ways many compositionists began to think of "the visual" as it relates to the teaching of writing. For many, that change was most evident in attention to design.

The Influence of Design

Throughout the history of writing instruction in this country, there has been some attention to the visual nature of written compositions, if only, in the earliest textbooks, to emphasize the importance of handwriting or penmanship as a visual representation of the writer's character.[13] And, of course, even today, the one visual reproduction we can count on in even the most contemporary texts is that snapshot of the research paper, complete with title page and works cited. In these lessons on producing the research paper, such visual marks as margins, page layout, and font size take on the utmost importance, again, in visually representing the seriousness and thoroughness with which the student has approached the assignment. In effect, they become a sign of academic decorum.

For many years, in fact, the research paper section was literally the only place in a composition textbook where we might encounter any reference to page design, layout, or font choices; primarily, we found a reminder to double space, choose a readable font appropriate for serious work (12-point Times, perhaps), and use "normal" margins. That has begun to change, especially since the first edition of John Trimbur's *Call to Write*, which includes a brief chapter on document design as well as attention to visual communication throughout in genres as various as flyers, posters, Web pages, and public service ads.[14]

In his most recent scholarship, Trimbur examines the "materiality of literacy from the perspective that writing is a visible language produced and circulated in material forms" ("Delivering" 188). This attention to the production of text as visible language, emphasizing "the composer's work . . . to make the special signs we call writing" (189) is one that links literacy practice with production and distribution of text and to the history and theory of graphic design (see also Trimbur, "Composition"). Perhaps even more useful for the future of visual communication and writing studies is Trimbur's use of the work of Walter Benjamin who "offers a way to think about how the study and teaching of writing might take up the visual . . . as more than just new texts and topics . . . to write about" ("Delivering" 199–200). As this work suggests, recent emphasis on design history, research, and theory marks a turn in the way scholars and teachers might begin thinking of composition and its relation to graphic design.

Such a turn is, however, very recent. Even as late as 1987, discussion of page design was minimal and often tied to word processing technology or desktop publishing. In March 1987, for example, *College English* ran a Macintosh™ ad entitled "A lesson in English Composition." The ad copy suggests that a Mac can make proofreading, copyediting, and formatting easier. The sample page offered in the ad—"created on a Macintosh"—tells a very different story. This very professional looking page clearly argues that it is the visual dimension of this composition that is most intriguing—layout, graphics, fonts, pull-out quotes. "With a Macintosh your students can prepare compositions that look like classics," the ad reads. "The rest is for posterity to judge."

Perhaps more than any other technology, desktop publishing has moved writing instruction into the world of design, despite, I suspect, our best efforts to contain composition in the essay of the sort familiar in *Harper's* or *Esquire* or *The Atlantic*.[15] To talk of literacy instruction in terms of *design* means to ask writers to draw on available knowledge and, at the same time, transform that knowledge/those forms as we redesign. Design, the New London Group writes, "will never simply reproduce Available Designs. Designing transforms knowledge in producing new constructions and representations of reality" (p. 196; see also Buchanan on the rhetoric of design).[16]

If I have given the impression that the media revolution of the fifties and sixties was a tough one for composition teachers, then I must say here that the world of graphic design, electronic text, and Web technologies certainly will prove even more difficult, though ultimately perhaps more useful for future understandings of composition as design. As with written compositions, Web pages must have an internal coherence; they must, in other words, be navigable. Unlike written compositions, the internal logic of a Web piece is likely to appear first in the visual construction of the page—not only in the images chosen but the colors, the placement of text or links, the font, the use of white space, and other elements linked more closely to the world of graphic design than to composition pedagogy. The work of Anne Wysocki is useful here as she challenges writing teachers to rethink their notions of what composition means—beyond the word and inclusive of the visual. Wysocki writes, "When we ask people in our classes to write for the Web we enlarge what we mean by composition. None of us are unaware of the visuality of the Web, of how that initial default, neutral grey has a different blankness than typing-paper" ("Monitoring Order"). And whether it is true or not that their teachers are aware of the difference between the blank screen and the blank page, our students are certainly aware of this difference. Many already compose for the Web. Many have worked in the realm of the visual (or the *virtual*) as constitutive of composing texts of all sorts years before they get to their first-year college courses.

> "What are we likely to carry with us when we ask that our relationship with all technologies should be like that we have with the technology of printed words?" (349)
> —Anne Wysocki and Johndan Johnson-Eilola, 1999

THE PLACE OF THE VISUAL IN COMPOSITION TODAY

At this point (feeling just a bit like Tristram Shandy telling the story of his life), I must back up once more before I go forward, this time to emphasize how much has changed in the ways we have thought about our students' work in composition over the past twenty-five years or more. In 1975, Harris K. Leonard, writing about his use of *Superman* comics to teach concepts from the classics, expresses concern over his students' request to make their own comics. This is how he describes the situation:

> Once the students realized how influential comic books were, some of them began to inquire why they could not write their own comics, reflecting their own heritage and their own reality. This was a difficult question, but as a teacher of the classics I had only one way to answer it. When they finished the course they would be able to write their own comics. However, the reason they were in college was not to learn comic book writing, but to counter the comic book mentality of our age with a more educated vision. The classics provide that vision. The classics are classics because they represent the finest and most humane statement on the universal human condition. . . . (406)

Nearly twenty-five years later, Lester Faigley in "Material Literacy and Visual Design," describes several Web sites he has encountered that are composed by teens as young as fifteen. "I find these sites remarkable for a number of reasons," Faigley writes, "not the least of which is the considerable design talent of these adolescents" (173). He goes on to compare these teens' thought-provoking and creative uses of image, text, and technology to the dull sameness of official sites created for mainstream companies. At no point in this article does Faigley seem remotely worried that these students are not learning what they should be learning in school. He seems to be asking, instead, why it is that we (their teachers) don't seem to understand how sophisticated these literacy practices actually are.

I don't mean to target Leonard here. His response is one that had a certain currency at the time and is right in line with what I've been describing throughout this discussion. Comics might have seemed like a useful way to get students into the "real" work of the course, but the notion that students should want to create their own comics "reflecting their own heritage and their own reality" would have seemed silly to many good teachers even in the fourth quarter of the last century.

I began by claiming that our students have a much richer imagination for how the visual might enter composition than our journals have yet to address, and so I return here to those students whose work opens this paper. In my assignment (see Appendix), I simply asked for a *visual argument*. The form, medium, and aim of the argument was up to the students. The course was a first-year seminar meant to introduce students to university-level work and to make a passing nod, at any rate, in the direction of oral, written, and visual communication practices. For many faculty across campus, I suspect such a course might represent precisely what Leonard was after in 1975, an intro-duction to the "great works of western culture."

The visual argument is an assignment I have given for at least five years now, but, like Faigley in his encounter with student work, I was struck in the fall of 2000 by how many more students seemed comfortable in the realm of visual design than had in years before and by how very few of them asked what I meant by visual argument. Moreover, these students turned to all sorts of visual design, as the assignment sheet suggested they might, for their proj-ects. Those less comfortable with "art work" chose to create charts, diagrams, or maps. Those like Jake Betzold or Andy Waisanen, more comfortable with digital design and Web technologies, worked with PhotoShop® to make digi-tal "paintings" or set up Web sites devoted to the course. Deirdre's flag was created by using colored construction paper, scissors, glue, and a photocopier. Not one of these students seemed to think that their visual argument was any less complicated or took less research or thought than the typical argument essay that they were also assigned in the course.

When I told other faculty teaching sections of the same course that I would be asking my students to construct a visual argument, many were more than skeptical. They wanted to know if such a genre exists and, if it does, how can it be taught, and for what reason might I use it—except, perhaps, to keep students doing "interesting projects." Primarily, faculty asked how I could evaluate visual arguments since some students, according to these fac-ulty, are just more visual/more visually talented than others. Perhaps the most important of these questions is the first: What is a visual argument?

In 1996, analytic philosopher J. Anthony Blair, writing on "The Possibility and Actuality of Visual Arguments," just barely manages to agree that a vi-sual argument, possessing all of the "salient properties of arguments," could actually be said to exist, and if it could be said to exist, it would have to be quite strictly "non-verbal visual communication" (26). To summarize Blair briefly, an argument must make a claim (an assertion), motivated by reasons for the claim, communicated to an audience in an attempt to convince that audience (the recipient) to accept the claim on the basis of the reasons offered (24). In this definition, drawn from the work of D. J. O'Keefe, claims must be "linguistically explicable" though not necessarily expressed linguistically. In other words, there is room here for the possibility of a nonverbal assertion.

To be faithful to Blair's position, I would have to say that, though he does acknowledge that visual argument is possible and even that visual arguments have been made, he does not hold out much hope for making one that is either propositionally complex or at all unique. Of course, in order to make his own argument, Blair must assert that the visual is open to interpretation in a way that words are not.[17] Such an assertion can only be made if one believes that the verbal and visual both involve communication of meaning. Certainly, parallels between verbal and visual communication do exist, which is why Blair finds himself agreeing, if grudgingly, that visual argument is *possible.*

My own requirements for visual argument are less rigid than Blair's, though I certainly accept his primary description of argument and ask that visual arguments make a claim or assertion and attempt to sway an audience by offering reasons to accept that claim. The simplest way for me to explain visual argument (and one I use with my own students) is to begin with visual parody, especially of the sort familiar to readers of *Adbusters* or the Guerilla Girls. Visual parody, like verbal parody, does make an overt claim, assertion, or proposition that draws particularly on comparison, juxtaposition, and intertextuality to offer the assertion to an audience for acceptance.[18] But visual arguments do not need to be parodic. All sorts of visuals make assertions and develop those assertions with visual information.

Though I would reject Blair's notion that a visual argument must be entirely nonverbal, I would say that a visual argument must make its case primarily through the visual. Deirdre's argument, for example, makes use of the flag as a visual expression of nationhood. Through research, she learned what the original Congo Free State flag was supposed to be saying about that nation. Her assertion, that what Europeans really brought to Africa was not enlightenment but slavery is carried through visually. To make an argument that would convince her audience, she used visuals familiar to that audience, in this case, a class of first-year students in a seminar called Africa in the Popular Imagination. She drew from books the class had read and images the class had seen. In other words, her argument was visually powerful and easily read by her target audience. Though some readers might consider her assertion somewhat sentimental or oversimplified, I do not read it that way at all. The students in this course, including students from Rwanda, Botswana, and Ghana had not heard the history of Leopold's Congo before the course — in particular, the international human rights movement generated by events of the time. The American students began the course recalling stories they had heard or read of African exploration, and most assumed that explorers had opened the Congo, as well as other areas of the continent, up to development of the best sort. Deirdre's decision to turn Leopold's flag back on him, to show it for what it was, represents an attempt on her part to ask her audience to reread the history of Congo exploration and to rethink the state of civilization and art that thrived there before Leopold's Congo Free State.

The same could be said of Boikhutso's map and Grace's place setting. Grace took from the course Leopold's statement that he meant to get for himself "a piece of this magnificent African cake" and extended that to the ludicrous: the king who sees an entire continent as his to feast upon. This, in contrast to the propaganda at the time in which Leopold represented himself as a great philanthropist taking the Congo region under his protection in order to end slavery and ensure international free trade. Her audience knew the background for her argument, and so her piece was shaped for that audience.

Boikhutso's map series aims for a much more difficult position statement. Though his argument might be read as obvious (it is obvious that we can never return to a precolonial Africa), that is not necessarily a position available to everyone involved. Boikhutso began the course by wanting to explain current Zimbabwe land disputes: why some Africans might feel that white settlers should be run off the land no matter the cost. These land disputes, which have become quite bloody, are for some involved an attempt to return Africans to land that was once theirs. As Boikhutso illustrates, theirs is a fruitless attempt if they believe that they can return to precolonial Africa. As he said in his presentation, "African people must learn to deal with what is here; not to try to recover what cannot be recovered." And, though some might see that argument as self-evident or one only useful for a first-year seminar in a small town, it is an argument Boikhutso felt needed to be made to the people involved today in actual violent and ongoing land battles.

The students in these classes were clearly very serious about the arguments they were making. They were also quite serious about how a visual argument should be evaluated. Given an opportunity to design evaluation criteria, students turned to the same criteria we would find common for written arguments: Does the visual make an argument? How well does the visual communicate that argument? Is the argument relevant to the course and to the assignment? Is it interesting? Is it clear or focused?

In other words, these students and others like them took the visual in its broadest sense as a form of communication through which they could make a sophisticated and relevant argument. And, though their evaluation criteria could certainly come under scrutiny within the context of schooling and how schooling elevates certain values/certain ways of thinking over others, I choose to offer them as one way of illustrating how the students saw these assignments fitting into their course work as it is typically evaluated.

COMPOSITION IN A VISUAL AGE

The history I have outlined clearly links words to high culture and the visual to low, words to production and images to consumption. And yet, as Cynthia Selfe has suggested, teachers of English composition have not, until very recently, had the means to produce communication that went very far beyond the word.[19] Many of us still remember producing dittos and stencils. We worked long and tedious hours armed with razor blades, correcting fluid, and as much patience as we could muster given the state of our fingers and hands covered with ink and cracking from printing chemicals. The idea of *producing* anything that went beyond that often blotched or botched handout would have been unthinkable. As well, most English teachers have not been trained in visual thinking beyond the level of *ut pictora poesis* or of media criticism. My own abilities in graphic design are very clearly limited by my willingness to learn software, to the clipart and borders available in that software, and to my barely tutored eye for design and page layout.[20]

Teachers who have been interested in using the visual in writing classes have generally limited their discussions to analysis because there were few ways of doing otherwise. Certainly, more recent access to the Internet and to desktop publishing has given teachers ways of incorporating visual thinking into the writing class, but even that will take time and money and equipment and training. And, again, while some teachers have access to state-of-the-art technology, many others have trouble finding an overhead projector that works or arrives in the classroom on time. My guess is that many of these difficulties will not ease up in yet another age of back-to-basics talk and threats of outcomes-based funding. Yet, our students will continue to work with whatever technology—much of it primarily visual—they can get their hands on.

For those scholars and teachers like Wysocki, Faigley, Trimbur, Johnson-Eilola, and others who are raising new questions about verbal and visual communication, the issue seems to be less one of resources than of emphasis or, rather, relationship. The question for me is not whether, "Learning to see well helps students write well," as Donald and Christine McQuade claim in their 1999 textbook *Seeing and Writing* (vii). Instead, the question is much closer to one Anne Wysocki and Johndan Johnson-Eilola ask: "What are we likely to carry with us when we ask that our relationship with all technologies should be like that we have with the technology of printed words?" (349).

Whether that question will lead us, as the New London Group and others suggest, toward multiliteracies or toward composition as design or simply toward a more complete way of understanding verbal and visual communication practices is not resolved. What such a question, and others like it, does lead to, however, is a new configuration of verbal/visual relationships, one that does allow for more than image analysis, image-as-prompt, or image as dumbed-down language. For students who have grown up in a technology-saturated and an image-rich culture, questions of communication and composition absolutely will include the visual, not as attendant to the verbal but as complex communication intricately related to the world around them.

Acknowledgments   In my world, all scholarship is collaborative, and so I would like to thank the many friends and colleagues who took time to read and advise me on this article as it went through several incarnations. Among them, I particularly thank John Trimbur, Jeanette Harris, Diane Shoos, Cindy Selfe, Anne Wysocki, Julia Jasken, and Robert Johnson. Marilyn Cooper, Jack Selzer, and Joseph Harris provided careful and invaluable commentary in the final shaping of the article. I am especially grateful to MTU students

Boikhutso Jibula, Deirdre Johns, Grace VanCamp, Derrick Siebert, Jake Betzold, and Andy Waisanen for permission to use or refer to their compositions in this article.

APPENDIX

Africa in the Popular Imagination Making a Visual Argument

So far this term, we have talked about how popular ideas and ideals are conveyed in film and in explorers' journals and reports. As well, we have talked about how these ideas can be changed, corrected, enriched by such investigations as Hochschild's *King Leopold's Ghost* or E. D. Morel's reports on the conditions in the Congo at the turn of the century. You have also looked at maps to note how a map can convey a particular argument or idea.

For this next assignment, I want you to make a **visual argument** about Africa and its people. We have been focusing on events in the Congo and on early explorations and reports, so it will be easiest if you focus your work on the issues, people, or ideas you have found in your reading and in the films you have watched.

You'll notice, for example, that even the cover of Hochschild's history makes a visual argument by layering a photo of mutilated African villagers on top of the portrait of Leopold to suggest the two are intricately connected.

A visual argument can take any form you wish. Here are a few suggestions:

1. Make a new cover for one of the books you have read—*Tarzan* or *King Leopold's Ghost* or *Through the Dark Continent* or *Heart of Darkness* or *Travels in West Africa*.

2. Draw a map that conveys an idea of the changing nature of Africa after Leopold—changing populations, exports of raw materials vs. imports, changing political boundaries, changing transportation systems, etc.

3. Design a chart or visually powerful table to convey one or more of these changes.

4. Create a Web page (just the opening page for now) that introduces readers to the issues you think are important.

5. Make a flyer.

6. Create a collage of photos and maps you find that help you convey an argument.

7. Make a painting.

8. Draw a diagram.

You will present your argument to the class. Be sure to tell the class what decisions you made to create your argument and how well you think you got your position across.

The visual can cover any of the material from the beginning of the course through our discussions of *Heart of Darkness*.

NOTES

1. *King Leopold's Ghost* is a history of Leopold of Belgium's colonization of the Congo.

2. I first began assigning visual arguments several years ago at a suggestion from John Trimbur whose work very much informs my own here.

3. The New London Group formed in September 1994 at a meeting in New London, New Hampshire. The ten women and men who make up the group are Courtney B. Cazden, Bill Cope, Norman Fairclough, James Paul Gee, Mary Kalantzis, Gunther Kress, Carmen Luke, Sarah Michaels, Martin Nakata, and Joseph Lo Bianco. Their original manifesto appeared in the *Harvard Educational Review* in 1996 and is cited here under "New London Group" (see note on p. 215). A version of that original piece also appears as the first chapter of the book-length collection *Multiliteracies: Literacy Learning and the Design of Social Futures* cited here under Cope and Kalantzis. For more information on the group, see Trimbur, "Review of *Multiliteracies*."

4. I choose *Writing with a Purpose* here partially because of its popularity and long life but also because Robert Connors (*Composition-Rhetoric*) chose it as a text illustrative of composition pedagogy from the 1950s into the 1970s. Moreover, this was in no way a media-based composition book, and so an examination of McCrimmon's inclusion of the visual for this text can serve to suggest how the visual entered many non-media-based composition classrooms for many years.

5. In Robert Connors's discussion of this text he notes that there were "no illustrations at all in the first three editions, but by the mid-1970s *Writing with a Purpose* contained over thirty pictures and photographs" (106). Actually, there were illustrations in that first edition though no photographs. The illustrations occur in the research paper assignment where McCrimmon has reproduced several graphs and charts.

6. Personal e-mail correspondence with author, April 7, 1996.

7. Jean Hagstrum argues that, though the typical rendering of the phrase came to be "Let a poem be like a painting," there is little warrant for that particular interpretation (9–10).

8. See Lucille Schultz's discussion (18–19) of John Frost's 1839 text, *Easy Exercises in Composition* and A. R. Phippen's 1854 *The Illustrated Composition Book*.

9. See Diana George and John Trimbur ("Communication Battle") for a further discussion of this period in writing instruction.

10. In fact, a brief survey of *CCC* during this period reveals a growing desire to explain how and why we might bring images into the writing class though the assignments are all slightly different, each with different aims. For example, a 1974 "Staffroom Interchange" piece reports on the benefits of assigning a cassette-slide show in required composition as a way to reach what the authors called "non-verbal/right-hemisphere-dominated" students who "find it up-to-date and relevant to their world of movies and TV" (Burnett and Thomason 430). In 1977, Jack Kligerman argued for the use of photography in the composition class to teach students to see objectively, to learn to detail what they see in an image before they try to interpret that image. Here, photography is used as a kind of heuristic aiding the art of selection, planning, arranging, and observing because, Kligerman says of students, "as writers, one of their main problems is to learn to 'capture' a scene in language, to make or re-make part of the world" (174). In his article, Kligerman expressed special concern that students simply weren't ready to interpret what they saw until they could objectively list the details of the world surrounding them: "For unless we can get our students to record what they see in the most unmetaphorical, uninterpretive way," Kligerman writes, "then as teachers we are merely helping them confirm what they already believe. Moreover, we could be reinforcing habits and making it impossible for them to discover a world 'out there' and, perhaps, a basis for inductive reasoning" (176). The picture as evidence of a fixed and knowable outside reality is the lesson here.

11. *Ways of Seeing* was a BBC television series before it came out in book form.

12. Publishers have, off and on, attempted to play with the more traditional design of writing texts. Joseph Frank's *You*, mentioned above, is one example of that. However, it has not been until very recently, perhaps with the publication of Donald McQuade and Christine McQuade's *Seeing and Writing*, that design allowed the visual to take much more than an illustrative role as a supplement to the written text or as a way of making the written text more appealing to the eye.

13. See, for example, Brainard Kellogg's 1891 discussion of letter writing with its emphasis on penmanship in *A Text-Book on Rhetoric Supplementing the Development of the Science with Exhaustive Practice in Composition*.

14. The shift toward normalizing the visual in writing instruction is also one impulse behind many of the assignments in Diana George and John Trimbur's *Reading Culture*, particularly in Visual Culture, Mining the Archive, and Fieldwork sections.

15. In "Delivering the Message," John Trimbur provides a brief bibliographic sketch indicating how design studies is beginning to make itself felt in writing studies.

16. For a further discussion of design and multiliteracies, see Gunther Kress, "Design and Transformation"; Bill Cope and Mary Kalantzis, "Designs for Social Futures"; and Kress, "Multi-modality."

17. See, for example, J. Anthony Blair's assertion that "the conditions of visual expression are indeterminate to a much greater degree than is the case with verbal expression" (27).

18. See Diana George and Diane Shoos for a more thorough discussion of intertextuality and George and Trimbur (*Reading Culture*, 211–15) for assignments based on visual parody.

19. As Cynthia Selfe points out, "I don't think people remain unconvinced that the visual is important, but I don't think they know how to make that turn" from words to the visual. These comments were made during a telephone conversation with the author, December 4, 2000.

20. Add to that the fact that (as we often tell each other about computers in the classroom) technology is unevenly distributed. Ten years ago, it would have been a luxury for many faculty to have consistent access to a video player and inexpensive videos not to mention the capacity for making videotapes of their own. Copyright laws have made some copying, even some video rental for classroom, difficult. Both videotapes and DVDs are now produced without any permission rights for public showing. In the end, just showing an ad or a clip of a film or television program for class discussion can be considered off-limits if some of the most conservative interpretations of copyright laws are observed.

If a classroom is not wired for Internet use, the expense of visuals can be far beyond the reach of most English teachers. Some of the most useful tapes for teaching media analysis, for example, are extremely expensive if individual teachers must purchase them, running from as low as $19.95 to as high as $295 for tapes from such sources as Media Education Foundation. Even cheap rentals are not a wholly satisfying solution to the problem I outline here.

WORKS CITED

Bartholomae, David, and Anthony Petrosky. *Ways of Reading*. Boston: St. Martin's, 1987.

Berger, John. *Ways of Seeing*. London: BBC and Penguin, 1977.

Bernhardt, Stephen. "Seeing the Text." *College Composition and Communication* 37 (1986): 66–78.

Blair, J. Anthony. "The Possibility and Actuality of Visual Arguments." *Argumentation and Advocacy* 33 (1996): 23–39.

Boutwell, William D., ed. *Using Mass Media in the Schools*. New York: Appleton-Century-Crofts, 1962.

Buchanan, Richard. "Declaration by Design: Rhetoric, Argument, and Demonstration in Design Practice." *Design Discourse: History, Theory, Criticism*. Ed. Victor Margolin. Chicago: Chicago UP, 1989. 91–109.

Burnett, Esther, and Sandra Thomason. "The Cassette-Slide Show in Required Composition." *College Composition and Communication* 25 (1974): 426–30.

Connors, Robert J. *Composition-Rhetoric: Backgrounds, Theory, and Pedagogy*. Pittsburgh: Pittsburgh UP, 1997.

Cope, Bill, and Mary Kalantzis. *Multiliteracies: Literacy Learning and the Design of Social Futures*. London: Routledge, 2000.

———. "Designs for Social Futures." Cope and Kalantzis 203–34.

Costanzo, William. "Film As Composition." *College Composition and Communication* 37 (1986): 79–86.

Faigley, Lester. "Material Literacy and Visual Design." *Rhetorical Bodies: Toward a Material Rhetoric*. Ed. Jack Selzer and Sharon Crowley. Madison: U of Wisconsin P, 1999. 171–201.

Flesch, Rudolf. *The Art of Readable Writing*. New York: Harper, 1949.

Frank, Joseph. *You*. New York: Harcourt Brace Jovanovich. 1972.

Gardiner, John Hays, George Lyman Kittredge, and Sarah Louise Arnold. *The Mother Tongue: Elements of English Composition, Book III*. Boston: Ginn & Company, 1902.

George, Diana, and Diane Shoos. "Dropping Breadcrumbs in the Intertextual Forest: or, We Should Have Brought a Compass." Ed. Gail Hawisher and Cynthia Selfe, *Passions, Pedagogies, and Twentieth-First Century Technologies*. Logan: Utah State UP, 1999. 115–26.

George, Diana, and John Trimbur. "The Communication Battle, or, Whatever Happened to the Fourth C?" *College Composition and Communication* 50 (1999): 682–98.

———. *Reading Culture: Contexts for Critical Reading and Writing*, 4th ed. New York: Longman, 2001.

Gibson, Walker. *Seeing and Writing*. 2nd ed. New York: D. McKay Co., 1974.

Hagstrum, Jean H. *The Sister Arts: The Tradition of Literary Pictorialism and English Poetry from Dryden to Gray*. Chicago: Chicago UP, 1958.

Hochschild, Adam. *King Leopold's Ghost*. Boston: Houghton Mifflin, 1998.

Kehl, D. G. "The Electric Carrot: The Rhetoric of Advertisement" *College Composition and Communication* 26 (1975): 134–40.

Kellogg, Brainerd. *A Text-Book on Rhetoric Supplementing the Development of the Science with Exhaustive Practice in Composition.* New York: Effingham Maynard, 1891.

Kismaric, Carole, and Marvin Heiferman. *Growing Up with Dick and Jane.* San Francisco: Collins, 1996.

Kligerman, Jack. "Photography, Perception, and Composition," *College Composition and Communication* 28 (1977): 174–78.

Kress, Gunther. "Design and Transformation: New Theories of Meaning." Cope and Kalantzis 153–61.

——. "Multimodality." Cope and Kalantzis 182–202.

Leonard, Harris K. "The Classics—Alive and Well with Superman," *College English* 37 (1975): 405–07.

McCrimmon, James. *Writing with a Purpose.* Boston: Houghton Mifflin, 1950.

McCrimmon, James, Joseph F. Trimmer, and Nancy Sommers. *Writing with a Purpose.* 8th ed. Boston: Houghton Mifflin, 1984.

McQuade, Donald, and Christine McQuade. *Seeing & Writing.* Boston: Bedford/St. Martin's, 2000.

Meyers, Lewis. *Seeing Writing.* New York: Harcourt Brace Jovanovich, 1980.

Mitchell, W. J. T. *Picture Theory.* Chicago: U of Chicago P, 1994.

New London Group. "A Pedagogy of Multiliteracies: Designing Social Futures." *Harvard Educational Review* 66 (1996): 60–92. [See also p. 193.]

Postman, Neil. *Amusing Ourselves to Death.* New York: Penguin, 1985.

——. *Television and the Teaching of English.* New York: Appleton-Century-Crofts, Inc., 1961.

Schultz, Lucille M. "Elaborating Our History: A Look at Mid-19th Century First Books of Composition." *College Composition and Communication* 45 (1994): 10–30.

Trimbur, John. *The Call to Write.* New York: Longman, 1999.

——. "Composition and the Circulation of Writing." *College Composition and Communication* 52 (2000): 188–219.

——. "Delivering the Message: Typography and the Materiality of Writing." *Composition As Intellectual Work.* Ed. Gary Olson. Carbondale: Southern Illinois UP, 2002. 188–202.

——. "Review of *Multiliteracies: Literacy Learning and the Design of Social Futures.*" *College Composition and Communication* 52 (2001): 659–62.

Willens, Anita. "TV—Lick It or Join It?" Boutwell, 254–56.

Wysocki, Anne Frances. "Monitoring Order: Visual Desire, the Organization of Web Pages, and Teaching the Rules of Design." *Kairos* 3.2 (Fall 1998). 12 Jun. 2002 <http://www.hu.mtu.edu/~awysocki>.

Wysocki, Anne Frances, and Johndan Johnson-Eilola. "Blinded by the Letter: Why Are We Using Literacy As a Metaphor for Everything Else?" *Passions, Pedagogies, and Twenty-First Century Technologies.* Ed. Gail Haiwisher and Cynthia Selfe. Utah State UP, 1999. 349–68.

11 Writing in Multimodal Texts : A Social Semiotic Account of Designs for Learning

JEFF BEZEMER AND GUNTHER KRESS

Frequently writing is now no longer the central mode of representation in learning materials — textbooks, Web-based resources, teacher-produced materials. Still (as well as moving) images are increasingly prominent as carriers of meaning. Uses and forms of writing have undergone profound changes over the last decades, which calls for a social, pedagogical, and semiotic explanation. Two trends mark that history. The digital media, rather than the (text) book, are more and more the site of appearance and distribution of learning resources, and writing is being displaced by image as the central mode for representation. This poses sharp questions about present and future roles and forms of writing. For text, *design* and *principles of composition* move into the foreground. Here we sketch a social semiotic account that aims to elucidate such principles and permits consideration of their epistemological as well as social/pedagogic significance. Linking representation with social factors, we put forward terms to explore two issues: the principles underlying the design of multimodal ensembles and the potential epistemological and pedagogic effects of multimodal designs. Our investigation is set within a research project with a corpus of learning resources for secondary school in Science, Mathematics, and English from the 1930s, the 1980s, and from the first decade of the 21st century, as well as digitally represented and online learning resources from the year 2000 onward.

INTRODUCTION: RETHEORIZING TEXT MAKING AND, IN THE PROCESS, WRITING

For scholars interested in writing, developments in contemporary communication sharply pose questions about the present role and the likely future development of writing. For those interested in contemporary forms of texts, the questions posed are about *design*, that is, *principles of composition*. After a brief introduction, we sketch a framework of explanation to then move to analysis

From *Written Communication* 25 (2008): 166–95.

and discussion of specific examples. Our specific focus in this article is on writing within a broader interest in the relation between social environments and representation.

When we compare a textbook from 1935 with a contemporary one, we note that there tends to be less writing now than there had been, and the writing that there is differs from the writing of 40, 50, or 60 years ago, both syntactically and in its use. Although images were present on the pages of textbooks before, there are more images now; these images look and function differently from those found before. The page is used differently to the way it had been: Writing and image are combined in ways that could not have been conceived of in the 1930s. Curricular content is represented differently, and the manner in which curricular materials are laid out on the page points to a social and epistemological change that cannot be explained by a focus on representational practices alone. If, going one step further, we compare a contemporary textbook with "pages" on the Web dealing with the "same" issues, we see that modes of representation other than image and writing—moving image and speech for instance—have found their way into learning resources, with significant effect.

Divergent, contradictory, confusing views dominate debates on the effects of contemporary practices in representation; they tend to invoke practices of "the past." The views range from cultural pessimism (Postman, 1993; Tuman, 1992) to concerns about economic performance, as witnessed in studies sponsored by the Organisation for Economic Cooperation and Development (OECD), such as the Programme for International Student Assessment (PISA), Trends in International Mathematics and Science Study (TIMSS), and Progress in International Reading Literacy Study (PIRLS). To the pessimists, the increasing use of image threatens literacy skills and must inevitably lead to the "dumbing down" not just of textbooks but of all of culture and, by a further effect, is bound to have deleterious effects on economic performance. Less prominent, if equally firmly expressed, are beliefs in the empowering potential of such changes. In reviewing major contributions to the debate Kaplan (1995) found that rather than engaging in attempts to elucidate the effects of the distinctive affordances of different modes and media, the debate has focused on cultural ideals, while the social production of representation was ignored. We are keen to describe these affordances and to develop such means of elucidation.

There has been considerable research on representation in learning resources from diverse perspectives: Some has focused on comprehension or on the effect of image on students' memory or understanding of concepts (e.g., Martinez Pena & Gil Quilez, 2001; Pintó, 2002). Other studies have focused on the ways in which image is used by designers (Unsworth, 2001). Yet others (Dimopoulos, Koulaidis, & Sklaveniti, 2003; Pozzer & Roth, 2003; Roth, Bowen, & McGinn, 1999) have categorized images and counted occurrences in different textbooks, comparing the results with other media, including scientific journals and newspapers. In other studies, the affordances of electronic media have been the focus (Jewitt, 2003; Lemke, 2000).

Yet what is lacking so far is an account of the relation between the *makeup*, the *shape* of texts—the *designs* of learning resources—and their potentials for learning (Kress, 2005; see p. 283 in this volume). In a current research project, we aim to provide such an account by looking at representational changes in learning resources between about 1930 and 2005. Our frame is a *social semiotic* theory, and we ask, "What exactly is the relation between the semiotic designs of *multimodal* learning resources and their potentials for learning?" We aim to show what changes in principles of designs of texts there have been and how the designers of learning resources—visual artists, editors, writers—have used and now use writing, image, layout, and other semiotic resources to create *potentials for learning*. By potentials for learning we mean the ensemble of semiotic features of a text or of an environment—objects, texts, people—that provides the ground for learning and in that way may shape what learning is and how it may take place. It includes the epistemological as well as the pedagogical significance of representational practice.

Explanations of forms and effects need attention to the social origins of texts as much as to their semiotic effects: attention to the potentials and constraints of modes as well as their interactions in learning resources—image, writing, moving image, speech—as well as attention to the potentials and constraints of media—the printed media, such as the textbook, or the electronic media, such as the Web.

To that end we put forward conceptual and analytical tools that we believe may illuminate principles of designs for representation and help us in understanding the present as much as the developing multimodal representational world. Key concepts are *sign, mode, medium, frame,* and *site of display* (Halliday, 1994; Hodge & Kress, 1988; Jewitt, 2005; Kress et al., 2005; Kress, Jewitt, Ogborn, & Tsatsarelis, 2001; Kress & van Leeuwen, 2001, 2006). In the section titled "Three Examples of Transduction," we focus on two processes of change to representations. One, *transformation,* involves changes within a mode; in the other, *transduction,* semiotic material is moved across modes, from one mode (or set of modes) to another mode (or set of modes). Media— the means for the distribution of messages—also have affordances, so that changes in media have social and epistemological effects. We include these in our discussion and in the theoretical framework we develop here, even though they are outside our focus.

By discussing examples from learning resources we show forms and changes and the epistemological and communicational effects produced in any changes. We ask what might be gained and what might be lost in changes of mode: from artefact and action to image, from image to writing, to speech, or to moving image. Bernstein's (1996) notion of *recontextualization* is useful in two distinct and connected senses, socially and semiotically. The social perspective illuminates how *discourses* that originate outside education are realized in a manner apt for a specific pedagogic site, its audience and its purposes, to constitute the content of school subjects. *Originating* and *pedagogic* sites are defined here in terms of the social positions of the sign makers. Semiotically, this appears in terms of the modes and media typically involved, both in the originating site and in the site of recontextualization. Our examples permit us to show how *meaning material* is moved from social site to social site, from medium to medium, from context to context, in each case requiring social, semiotic remaking and often entailing epistemological change.

The *corpus* consists of multimodal, hyper- or interrelated "texts" (lessons, units, chapters, exercises from textbooks, workbooks, CD-ROMs, DVDs, Web sites) for the lower years (a chronological age of, broadly, 11 to 14 years) of secondary English (Language Arts), Science, and Mathematics in England, published between 1930 and 2005. Each of the subjects is represented via a topic that has been stable enough to remain in the syllabus in one form or another throughout the period we have chosen. The selection of stable topics is meant to allow us to capture some of the potential variability in designs within the subjects and over time. Within English, the focal topic is *simile*, within science, *digestion*, and within mathematics, it is *angles*. In this article we draw on four texts for each topic, one printed text for each "era" and one electronic text for the present era.

REPRESENTATION AS SOCIAL AND SEMIOTIC PRACTICE: SOME CONCEPTS

Sign Makers and Signs

In a social semiotic account of meaning and meaning making, producers as well as users of learning resources—visual artists, editors, writers, teachers, and students—are regarded as meaning makers or *sign makers*. Signs are elements in which meaning and form have been brought together in a relation motivated by the interest of the sign maker. The process of sign making is always subject to the availability of semiotic resources and to the aptness of the resources to the meanings that the sign maker wishes to realize. In principle, limitations apply always and everywhere, even if not with the same severity: In many classrooms around the world there exist the severest constraints on resources both for teachers and children. Yet irrespective of these, the design of a learning resource is treated by us as the sign maker's apt representation of her or his interest.

Interest

The interest of the producer of learning resources is twofold: rhetorical/pedagogical and epistemological. Pedagogical interest responds to the question, "How can I best realize my preferred social relation with the imagined audience?"; epistemological interest to the question, "How is subject content best realized while maximizing the learner's engagement?" The producer's as well as the audience's interests are shaped by the social, cultural, economic, political, and technological environments in which signs are made; the design is the result of the interaction between all of these. At the same time sign makers have to be aware of the media of distribution for their signs and that awareness is factored into the making of the sign.

Meaning and Situated Use

A frequent objection made to this approach is that one cannot analyze representations by focusing on design(ers) and ignoring those who use them. That issue is complex. It asks whether texts carry meaning independent of their situated use—whether texts come "alive" only when they are brought into action and communication, by themselves and in interaction with others (cf. Baker & Freebody, 1989; Maybin & Moss, 1993). A first response on our part is that of course we can analyze representations as a formal exercise; a second response is that here we are not focusing on use—our focus, rather, is on providing means for describing and understanding "what is being used." But to go where the question is actually pointing, that is, whether one can make claims about *readings* and *effects* of representations without a study of their use, we would say, of course one cannot. One can however formulate hypotheses, more or less securely founded. We acknowledge the significance of studies of the situated use of texts and the production of users' accounts of their usages of texts. These help to provide securer foundations. At the same time we consider texts to be *potentials* of a quite specific kind that in their specificity allow an unlimited (in number) yet constrained (in semantic scope) number of readings. These potentials can be understood as the sign makers' shaping of signs such that the text-as-complex-sign fits the purposes of a rhetor (who frequently is also the designer), the designer, and their sense of the audience. The aim of our approach is to draw attention to the potentials and constraints of the "stuff" that is being used, to the agency of sign makers and to the significance of all actions in the process of sign making.

Modes

A *mode* is a socially and culturally shaped resource for making meaning. Image, writing, layout, speech, moving image are examples of modes, all used in learning resources. Meanings are made in a variety of modes and always with more than one mode. Modes have differing *modal resources*. Writing, for instance, has syntactic, grammatical, and lexical resources, graphic resources such as font type, size, and resources for "framing," such as punctuation. Writing might make use of other resources, for instance, the resource of color. Speech and writing share aspects of grammar, syntax, and lexis. Beyond these, speech has intensity (loudness), pitch and pitch variation (intonation), tonal/vocal quality, length, silence. Image has resources such as position of elements in a framed space, size, color, shape, icons of various kinds—lines, circles—as well as resources such as spatial relation, and in the case of moving images, the temporal succession of images, *movement*.

These differences in resources mean that modes can be used to do different kinds of semiotic work or to do broadly similar semiotic work with different resources in different ways. That is, modes have different *affordances*—potentials and constraints for making meaning. This enables sign makers to do different work in relation to their interests and their rhetorical intentions for designs of meaning, which, in modal ensembles, best meet the rhetor's interest and sense of the needs of the audience. That is, by drawing on the specific affordances of different modes in the making of complex signs as modal ensembles, sign makers can meet the complex, often contradictory demands of their own interest, the needs of the matter to be communicated, and the characteristics of the audience.

Mode, community, and convention.   In social semiotics, what is to count as mode is treated as a matter for decision by communities and their social-representational needs. For the "ordinary" user of the mode of writing, *font* is part of that mode. For a typesetter or graphic designer, the meaning potentials—the affordances—of font are such that it can be used as mode; that is, meaning can be made through the affordances of font. What counts as mode depends on sign makers acting within the needs and understanding of a particular community and its more or less conventionalized practices.

Medium

Mode and modal uses have to be considered together with the *medium* of distribution involved in communication. Medium has a material and a social aspect. Materially, medium is the substance in and through which meaning is instantiated/realized and through which meaning becomes available to others (cf. "oil on canvas"). From that perspective, print (as paper-and-print) is medium; by extension, the book is medium, if differently, the screen another; and the "speaker-as-body-and-voice" yet another. The contemporary situation with respect to media may be more complicated than it had been hitherto. In the "new media," the range of different technological devices that operate in a chain of materialization processes are largely invisible to the lay person. So at the end of one chain are, for example, the computer-screen-and-speakers, prior to that are CD-ROM, CD-ROM-player, computer processor, and so on; all play a specific part in the chain of materializing and rematerializing.

Socially, medium is (the result of) semiotic, sociocultural, and technological practices (cf. film, newspaper, billboard, radio, television, theater, a classroom, and so on). From this perspective, textbook is one medium and Web-based learning resources for students are (becoming) another. There are now a range of Web sites funded by public and private organizations—Intel, BBC, Heinemann—that provide resources for primary and secondary school students in England and that, like their textbook counterparts, are organized along the lines of the (English) "National Curriculum." The expansion of Web-based resources, some freely available, may well lead to a decline in the use of the medium of the textbook. The consequences will be far reaching: semiotically, for instance, in changes to the uses, forms, and valuations of the mode of writing, socially through the potentials for semiotic action by sign makers. Such changes in media are always subject to social contestation. As one current example, walls and other surfaces (e.g., [underground] trains) are transformed into medium by graffiti artists.

Site of Display

If we take a sheet of A4 paper, we can write an announcement on it and pin it on a wall; we have created a poster. We can also fold it, write an announcement on the front page, and fill the other three pages with a diverse range of information: We have created a booklet. We can also fold it twice, cut it in four pieces, and write an announcement on all four parts: We have created flyers. In all three instances we have reshaped the material medium of paper to create a *site of display* that is apt for our interests. It is the space that becomes available as medium for the display of text as complex sign.

Frame and Genre

As we were creating different sites of display, we did not change the social *frame*: In all instances we used the same "basic framework[s] of understanding available in our society for making sense" (Goffman, 1986, 10): We made an announcement. Goffman's quote focuses on social frames—*events*. If we replace his social category of event with the semiotic category of *genre*, then kinds of frames in a textbook could be *example, exercise, summary, demonstration*. Genres are the semiotic obverse of the social event. They are realized at the textual level; every text has a generic form. Each of these frames/genres defines text in terms of activity, of social relations of participants in an event, and in terms of the use of modes and media. Frames operate at any level: Whatever the semiotic entity is, it requires a frame.

Frames and sites of display.   In looking at representational changes in learning materials we need to understand how frames relate to sites of display. How does a frame like announcement map onto a site of display? Does an expose map onto a chapter? Does an index map onto the banner of a Web page? The significance of these issues in design become noticeable where they appear to misfire: one announcement using two posters, one expose using two-and-a-half chapters, an index requiring scrolling down to get to the lines beyond the lower edge of the screen. As frames change, new sites of display are created. In the 1930s textbook, for instance, the chapter was the site of display of a coherent, integral unit of knowledge (e.g., an expose on the human digestive system); now, in the contemporary textbook, the double-page spread is used as a site of display for a unit of work (a lesson, a demonstration). Both kinds of sites are afforded by the medium of "the book," but by a notion of book that has changed radically over that 70-year period. As a site of display, a chapter is entirely different from a double page spread: The chapter is organized first and foremost as a conceptual, epistemological site; the double page spread is organized first and foremost as a material and semiotic site.

Site of display and content.   The size of a chapter was determined by the author's sense of the "completeness" and of "justice to the subject matter"; by contrast, it is the space of the double-page spread that shapes what content will appear and how. Of course, both the older and the newer textbook were linked more or less closely into other units and notions: to a curriculum, for instance, and its syllabus, to organization of teaching, such as number and length of lessons. Representation responds to social factors via diverse cultural and semiotic resources. Among others, this raises the question of what the medium of book had been, is, and is likely to become in its interrelation with the rapidly changing "screen." This question applies to all media and to all modes.

Design

Given the complex relation of modal affordance, rhetor's interest and the variability and complexity of social environments, *design* moves into the centre of attention in the making of complex signs-as-texts. The shift, conceptually, from *composition* to *design* mirrors a social shift from competence in a specific practice conceived in terms of understanding of and adherence to convention governing the use of a mode—writing, say—to a focus on the interest and agency of the designer in the making of signs-as-texts. Design is the practice where modes, media, frames, and sites of display on the one hand, and rhetorical purposes, the designer's interests, and the characteristics of the audience on the other are brought into coherence with each other. From the designer's perspective, design is the (intermediary) process of giving shape to the interests, purposes, and intentions of the rhetor in relation to the semiotic resources available for realizing/materializing these purposes as apt material, complex signs, texts for the assumed characteristics of a specific audience.

TRANSDUCTION: CHANGING MODES AND MEDIA

In representing the world, *translations* are constantly made of meanings made in one mode or ensemble of modes to meanings made in another mode or ensembles of modes. Such translations are inevitable because, on the one hand, social environments are changed in recontextualization, and on the other hand, the available modes and media and their affordances are constrained. Our socially/rhetorically oriented theory of meaning (making) suggests that the choices for translation into particular ensembles of modes is motivated by social, pedagogic, and epistemological concerns. An object, such as a protractor, can be drawn into interactions in which participants and material objects are physically copresent, for example in the office of an architect or in a classroom. In both cases the object is present, available as an element in a mode of entities. In a textbook, that object-artefact is not available as a mode. The protractor and its use, involving gesture, body posture, gaze, relations to other material objects, and so on, now has to be "described" (translated) using image, writing, and perhaps other modes, as well as a specific medium. (In our framework we use *translation* as the general semiotic term and *transduction* as the more specific term when we speak of the move of semiotic material from one mode to another.)

Modes have different materiality and it, shaped by the histories of cultural work, has produced the specific affordances of a mode. Given that difference in material and cultural work, there can never be a perfect translation from one mode to another: Image does not have "word," just as writing does not have "depiction"; forms of arrangement (i.e., syntax) differ in modes that are temporally or spatially instantiated. Transduction inevitably brings profound changes in the move from one mode to the other. In such contexts we can ask about gains and losses in the process of modal change.

While transduction describes changes involving a change in mode, *transformation* describes changes in arrangement within one mode. Theoretically, transformations are operations on structures within the one mode in which entities remain the same while structures change. In a transformation, say within the mode of writing, words remain, syntactic/grammatical categories remain those of the mode, as do textual arrangements. What changes is their arrangement. In transduction, the change from one mode to another brings with it a change of entities. There are no words in image, there are depictions; semiotic/semantic relations that, in speech or writing, are expressed in clauses and as verbs are realized through *vectors* or lines. Other semiotic relations between lexical-syntactic elements — prepositions, for instance (on, over, by, etc.) — are realized by spatial means in images, and so on.

As a matter of course, the new media demand facility in design practices of a high level, namely the ability to "move" the *semiotic material* or *content* of a textual entity from one mode or modal ensemble to another. For instance, in translating a novel to a CD-ROM (Jewitt, 2003) a whole range of rhetorical and design decisions have to be made. Characters that, in the novel-as-book, "exist" in the mode of writing can now appear in the mode of image, with all the potentials and constraints — and necessary transductions — involved in that. Assume two characters appeared in the novel-as-book. The author might have given a written description like, "Sitting in the late autumn sunshine, Sam and Bill share a bench in the park." An illustrator or designer might have been asked to "draw across," to *transduct*, the written description into the mode of image. Now the illustrator has to ask "How close to each other were they sitting?"; "Was Bill to the left or to the right of Sam?" The translator/transductor has to become precise, whether she or he wishes to do so or not. In an image-representation the distance between the two characters has to be shown; one cannot do otherwise. Elsewhere (Kress, 2003) this is called *epistemological commitment*. An epistemological commitment is an unavoidable affordance: In the visual mode the designer *has* to show the distance between the two characters. Every mode imposes/demands such commitments as a matter of course, though each such set of commitments is different. That has to be part of the designer's consideration.

Practices of moving semiotic material are not novel, nor are they in any way exclusive to educational environments (cf. Lemke, 2000; Myers, 1990; O'Halloran, 2005, for examples of transduction in science). Transduction is a part of human semiosis and has been as far back as there are records such as sculptures, paintings, carvings in caves, on rock faces, in sites of ancient habitation. But in the time scales of cultural histories of (Western) representation the present may be distinctive through the ubiquity, the "intensity," and the centrality of the process. The new media have made available new kinds of modal ensembles to very many users, offering possibilities of representation that had not existed before, or if so, then rarely (e.g., the opera). The CD-ROM can bring together not just writing and image, as in this example, but writing, moving image, speech, still image, music, sound-track, and so on, and such ensembles offer possibilities for representation that are different from an ensemble of still image and writing or of writing alone. The existence of such wide and diverse representational possibilities, of course, simply demands engagement with and facility in design.

THREE EXAMPLES OF TRANSDUCTION

We will now discuss three examples of transduction: The six modes involved are artefacts/3D objects, still image, writing, action, moving image, speech. The three instances involve transduction from artefact to image and writing, from action to image and writing, and from action to moving image and speech. We begin with transduction from artefact to image and writing.

From Artefact to Image and Writing

In discussing our examples (see Figure 11-1) we draw attention to (some aspects of) significant changes, focusing on what may be gained and what may be lost when moving from artefact to image.

When representing an artefact such as a protractor as an image, there are losses in *specificity*. Certain dimensional and tactile aspects, for instance, cannot be expressed in image, they can only be simulated via perspectival resources. The material substance, its three-dimensional shape and, in many cases, the actual size of the protractor cannot feature in the image. While there is a loss in specificity there is a gain in *generality*: The image depicts a "prototype," not an instance, that is, an "ideal" protractor is shown, not one that is scratchy, used, or odd in some way. Epistemologically there is no commitment that protractors have to be like this. Compared to the 3D object, the image affords a level of generality and idealization apt for the didactic practice involved, a representation that is apt also for the curricular entity that is being constructed. When the artefact is represented in writing there are also losses in specificity, though differently and maybe even more so than with image. Writing does not specify, for instance, whether the centre of the protractor is open, as in the image, or closed, or which colors are used to inscribe marks on it. It affords a yet higher level of generality than that afforded by image.

Another shift occurs in the *arrangement* of the constituents of image and writing. In both the image and in the writing, different entities can be identified. In writing, these appear as lexical entities (e.g., protractor, line) placed in syntactic structures. In "Measure the angle between these lines using the protractor," "the protractor" is in an adverbial clause of manner (i.e., "Using the

FIGURE 11-1 Excerpt from *Impact Maths 1G.*

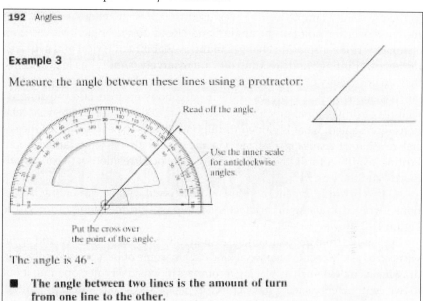

Source: Cole et al. (1999), 192. Reprinted by permission of Harcourt Education.

protractor, measure the angle between these lines"); in that way, it appears as the means or *instrument* in a syntactic element that is subordinated to the main clause ("[You] measure the angle") and placed last. In the written example (spatially realized) sequence is important: The activity is "announced" first, it is foregrounded ("Measure the angle"), with the means for doing so ("using the protractor") placed last. In image, such meanings are realized through structures based on spatial relations of proximity, adjacency, and simultaneity. In the image in Figure 11-1, lines are superimposed onto the protractor (something quite impossible with the original artefact) and an image of the angle qua geometrical entity is "abstracted" away and shown separately.

There are varied relations between writing and image in this representation. In writing there is the "heading" just discussed; there are commands (as imperatives) in captions attached to the main image by lines: "Read off the angle," "Use the inner scale for anticlockwise angles," and so on. There is also the definitional statement at the bottom: "The angle between two lines is the amount of turn from one line to the other." We might generalize the role of writing here—beyond the statements already made—in this way: Image is used to present the core of the information—the protractor and what it is like, the identity between the angle measured by the protractor and the image of the abstracted angle in the top right corner. Writing is used to present actions as commands and to provide a formal definition of angle. This might get close to seeing the functional specialization of image and writing in this aspect of the book at this time.

From Action to Image and Writing

In the previous example writing was used to represent actions such as "Put the cross over the point of the angle," and "Read off the angle." Moves from action to writing also bring changes in the availability of lexical and syntactic resources. "Putting" and "reading off" are relatively "empty" as lexical items; they do not specify exactly what the actions involved are. This may seem trivial, but actions such as gestures, shifts in gaze, body posture, face, are defining features of professional practices (cf. Goodwin, 2000). In terms of social relations represented, what is gained through writing is the expression of the social relation of *command* realized via the syntax of the imperative mood: Writing readily affords the realization of the social relation between an authority and the learner.

Different kinds of gains and losses are at issue when representing the actions involved in using an artefact—a compass—in the mode of image, as Figure 11-2 shows.

The move from action to image also involves loss of specificity, and again we need to ask "Specificity of what kind?" Only some of the actions involved in drawing a circle—such as placing a compass alongside a ruler, opening it out to two centimeters, placing it on a piece of paper, and so on—are represented. The image on the left shows the initial placement of the compass, the image on the right shows the completion of the drawing of the circle. In fact, actions are not represented: What is depicted are points or segments in/of the action, action "frozen" at particular points in time. In terms of an epistemological change, there is the deletion of the actor: The action of drawing a circle is suggested without showing who draws the circle. Again, using a compass becomes less personal or specific and more general. It is a move away from the empirical "real" toward theoretical abstraction. What is to be debated is whether, under what circumstances, and for what purposes that is or is not a gain.

FIGURE 11-2   Excerpt from *Heinemann Mathematics, 7.* (This figure has been reconstructed because reprint rights were not available for the original image.—Bedford Editors)

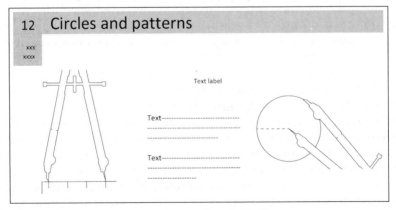

Original source: Scottish Primary Mathematics Group (1991), 12.

From Action to Moving Image and Speech

On the Web, moving image and speech can be used alongside or instead of writing in the transduction of artefacts and actions involved in mathematics, leading to potentially rather complex multimodal configurations. Figure 11-3 [on page 246] is a still from a "scene" on rotational transformations. The scene shows, tells and describes how to rotate an angle.

The text written below the image of the protractor is as follows.

> Put pointer of compass on point "a." Open out compass to length of "ac."
> Draw a curve which passes through "c." This ensures that the length of
> the lines in the image will be the same as in the original triangle. This
> makes sure that the length of "ac" (the image) is the same as "ac" (the
> original) because the size of an object doesn't change during rotation.

In this example there are transductions from artefact to writing with effects similar to those discussed before. All these have effects on changes in specificity and generality as well as in ordering. What is different here is the use of speech for the transduction of artefact and action and the use of moving image for the transduction of action. As we noted before, speech shares certain aspects of grammar, syntax, and lexis with writing. In addition it has intensity (as loudness), pitch and pitch variation, tonal/vocal quality, silence, and other resources. In this example, tone is used in speech as a resource for foregrounding particular lexical items, whereas in the written text foregrounding was realized through syntax. In the transcript below we have marked the boundaries between intonational units using a double slash, and we have italicized the items where the major pitch movement occurs, a *fall*, in this case. The element that receives the major pitch movement is thereby marked as providing *new information*. This creates a contrast of "given" and "new" information within each *information unit* (cf. Halliday, 1967).

> Put pointer of *compass* // on point *a* //. Open *out* // compass to length of
> *a c* //. Draw a *curve* // which passes through *c* //. This *ensures* // that the
> length of the lines in the *image* // will be the same as in the original *tri-*
> *angle* //. This makes *sure* // that the length of *a c* // the *image* // is the
> same as *a c* // the *original* //. Because the *size* // of an *object* // doesn't
> change during *rotation* //.

Comparing the written and spoken text we can see that two specific readings have been provided and with that a specific potential for learning has been created. In the first three sentences of the written text, the readers' attention is drawn to what is mentioned first—the *action* to be performed—and to the imperative mood, thus foregrounding, action as *command*. In the spoken text, the reader's attention is first drawn to the object involved in the action, the compass, and the location where it should be placed, then to the specific *kind of action* of opening—"out"—that should be made and an indication of the extent of the movement, then to the *shape* of the inscription to be made, and so on. What ensues is a contrapuntal organization, with the mode of writing

FIGURE 11-3   Image from lgfl.skoool.co.uk, "Rotational Transformations."

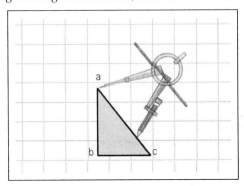

Note: Adapted from http://lgfl.skoool.co.uk/content/keystage3/maths/pc/learningsteps/RSTLC
/launch.html, August 1, 2007.

highlighting action-as-commands—*put, open out, draw*—and the mode of speech highlighting *object, location, shape.*

The paragraph has a three-part structure: Part 2, sentences 4 and 5, provides a reflection on the process just described. Part 3, sentence 6, provides a definitional statement.

This text further uses the mode of moving image. It combines the affordances of still image, spatial organization, with temporal organization: It unfolds in time. That brings distinct increases in semiotic resources. Elements can now appear and disappear, and through that, movement can be suggested. In the scene that we are looking at here, the first element to appear is the triangle. Then the compass appears, placed with its pointer at "a." Then two movements take place: the "opening out" of the compass and the inscription of a curve. Then the compass disappears again. As such, the moving image represents the demonstration of how to use a compass rather differently from the written and spoken text. For instance, it is *specific* about what "opening out" and "drawing a curve" entails. "Drawing a curve" is displayed as a movement of the compass whereby one of its legs retains its position and the other leg, which leaves a trace, makes a gentle, clockwise turn.

The examples show that as we transduct from artefact to a complex of image, writing, speech, and moving image, quite different resources become available for use: resources of lexis or of depiction, with implications for generality and specificity, and syntactic resources with implications for the arrangement of constituents as well as for the social relations of maker of message and "reader"—the relation of command. So for the designer of the learning resource the question becomes one of aptness of the level of specificity-generality and arrangement for the specific occasion. There are also implications for pedagogy: In one mode commands are given, in another actors can be backgrounded; in one mode reading paths are set by the learner, in another by the designer. That in turn will lead to design decisions about use of modes. It also strongly sets the "ground" for engagement and learning.

RECONTEXTUALIZATION: CHANGING SOCIAL SITES

The move from one medium to another has social consequences in changing the possibilities for production: Readers of a book cannot readily alter the text they read—other than in their inner remaking. But inner remaking does not become effective in the social world until it has some outer realization. Readers of a text on the screen can (usually) alter that text along the lines of their interest. In other words, the social potentials of different media in effect mean that the change from one medium to another brings about a change from one social context to another. This makes Bernstein's (1996) notion of *recontextualization* highly suitable for our purposes: Whatever the semiotic—modal and/ or medial—change, it entails a change of social context. Of course changes in social context themselves bring with them changes in the semiotic materialization of meaning. Bernstein had developed the concept of recontextualization in order to describe how "discourses" that originate in one social site—he uses the example of carpentry—are reshaped so as to fit with the social givens of the new site, the school, in the school subject "woodwork." Whatever the school subject, discourses produced in formal and informal sites outside school are transformed along the lines of the social organization of the new site in that process of recontextualization. Discourses are moved from the originating site of production to a pedagogic site.

Sites can be defined along the lines of the social roles of the participants/ sign makers typically involved in the sites, as well as the modes, media, and genres typically used. Carpentry, for instance, is a professional practice engaged in by a community of carpenters—foreman and tradesmen/workers—who work with particular materials, producing objects for another social group, their clients. We can, if we wish, give a semiotic description to this: Carpenters as sign makers use particular materials-as-media (certain kinds of timber), modes (e.g., drawing) in social frames specific to their domain (e.g., shaping timber, assembling objects-as-signs, dismantling). When carpentry is recontextualized to the school, it used to become (in England) the school subject woodwork. Now the participant roles had been student and teacher—not foreman and tradesman/worker. Its sign makers are students and teacher; its material media are still timber; though now there are textbooks, the modes are more frequently image and writing than timber-as-mode and (some of) its genres are demonstration, exercise, examination. The sign-objects produced are very rarely for a client. When the medium of carpentry is not the textbook but the Web, then recontextualization has gone further still and potential modes now include moving image, speech, and writing.

Bernstein's concept of *pedagogic discourse* is a composite of *instructional discourse* (for us, here, broadly, the [content of] a school subject) and *regulative discourse* (for us, here, broadly, the social relations underlying a specific pedagogy). So when Bernstein writes that "pedagogic discourse cannot be identified with the discourses it transmits.... It is the principle by which other discourses are appropriated and brought into a special relationship with each

FIGURE 11-4   Excerpt from *Impact Maths IG*.

Source: Cole et al. (1999), 195. Reprinted by permission of Harcourt Education.

other, for the purpose of their selective transmission and acquisition" (Bernstein, 1996, 46), we agree with the latter part of that statement. As they form one part of the legitimization of the school subject, the discourses that are transmitted have to be acknowledged in the pedagogic site (see Figure 11-4) and their transformations in representation thoroughly understood.

Recontextualization is, literally, moving *meaning material* from one context with its social organization of participants and its modal ensembles to another, with its different social organization and modal ensembles. Meaning material always has a semiotic realization, so recontextualization involves the re-presentation of the meaning materials in a manner apt for the new context in the light of the available modal resources. Pedagogically, recontextualization involves the moving of curricular texts in line with the pedagogic features of the environment of recontextualization.

We see four rhetorical/semiotic principles operating in the process of recontextualisation: selection, arrangement, foregrounding and social repositioning. First, *selection*: What is being recontextualized is meaning material. Not everything in the originating context may be relevant in the new context. Hence there is *selection of meaning materials*. Further, the modal resources of the new context may be different from those of the original one, and the modal ensembles needed for the audience of the new context may require *selection of modes* according to these needs. So meaning materials are selected according to what is pedagogically relevant in the new site, and modes are selected according to what is available and apt for the new site. Selection thus refers to the inevitable and motivated partiality of every representation: What is represented is guided by a complex rhetorical decision. What are the rhetor's interests? What is best for the audience in the new environment? How is the meaning material most aptly represented and what modal resources are available in the new environment?

Second, *arrangement*: In the process of recontextualization a design decision also has to be made about the arrangement of the meaning materials. In what order will they be re-presented, and what kind of semiotic arrangement will be used in their representation? At one level this is an epistemological and pedagogic-didactic decision: What epistemological frame is best for this audience and this purpose, and in what order is it best to present the curricular entities to learners? At a semiotic level this becomes a question of genres — experiment, demonstration, joint construction — but also a question of *layout*: Arrangement is different on the worksheet than in the scientific report or in the acting out of a play, and so on. The elements are ordered, that is, a temporal or spatial order — *a reading path* — is created, an order produced by the designer, in which the learner is expected to engage with the selected elements in the order provided. Of course, a designer may wish to leave the ordering as much as possible to the user.

Third, *foregrounding*: Features of the social environment shape rhetorical/representational decisions. What may be most significant in the originating environment may not be so in the environment of recontextualization. Similarly, modes that may be preferred in the first environment may not be preferred in the second; indeed they may not be available there. Given this, *foregrounding*, the assigning of salience in the context of particular social relations, becomes a principle both at the level of meaning and at the level of representation. Pedagogically, status is accorded to those elements regarded as particularly significant: Some elements are foregrounded and others are backgrounded.

Fourth, *social relations* exist, and are (re-)constructed between teacher and students, between them and the designers of the resource and between them and those who are represented (e.g., the architect in Figure 11-4). This notion of social relations includes but is not limited to *interactivity*, which usually refers to the learner's engagement with and transformation or transduction of the text. In recontextualization there is inevitably a *social repositioning*: A certain pedagogy emerges as the consequence of the re-contextualization.

As modes have different affordances, these four principles are realized differently in different modes. Consider the example in Figure 11-5. The excerpt is taken from a science textbook published in 1935. The chapter is on the digestive system.

Comparing image and writing here shows that in both modes there is selection, arrangement, foregrounding and social (re-)positioning, but with different outcomes in each mode. In writing, for instance, the designer selected the shape of the esophagus to focus (cf. "The oesophagus is a *narrow muscular tube*," Fairbrother et al., 1935, 162, emphasis added), but not on its shape relative to the other organs involved in digestion. In the image, this relative shape *has* to be shown — that is one effect of the epistemological commitment of image — but image does not show the texture of the esophagus (cf.

FIGURE 11-5   Excerpt from *General Science, Part III.*

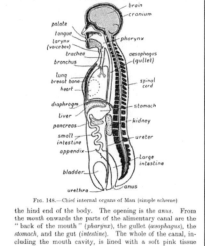

Source: Fairbrother, Nightingale, & Wyeth (1935), 160–161.

"muscular"). In other words, image and writing are not simply copies of each other, nor is image more "simplified" than writing, as the caption of the figure suggests (cf. "Chief internal organs of Man (simple scheme)"). Rather, they each offer distinctive epistemological affordances and commitments.

As far as arrangement goes, writing constructs a reading path that is based on linearity and sequence. The reader is expected to read from top to bottom and from left to right, thus first encountering mention of the pharynx, then of the esophagus, then of the stomach, finally of the gut. The image does not impose such an order; it leaves the reading path open to the learner. Foregrounding, too, is realized in both modes, but with different effects. In writing, foregrounding is realized syntactically, by attaching meaning to what comes first, second, and last: "The oesophagus is a narrow muscular tube" (Fairbrother et al., 1935, p. 162) has a meaning different from "The narrow muscular tube is the oesophagus." In writing, foregrounding is also realized graphically through a bold font. In image, salience is realized through, for example, size: The spinal cord seems disproportionately large. And social relations are created by allowing the learner control over the reading path in the case of image and allowing the textbook designer to set out the reading path for the learner in the case of writing.

The same principles apply to layout, as the examples in Figures 11-6 and 11-7 show.

FIGURE 11-6 Excerpt from *Salters GCSE Science Y11*. (This figure has been reconstructed because reprint rights were not available for the original image. — Bedford Editors)

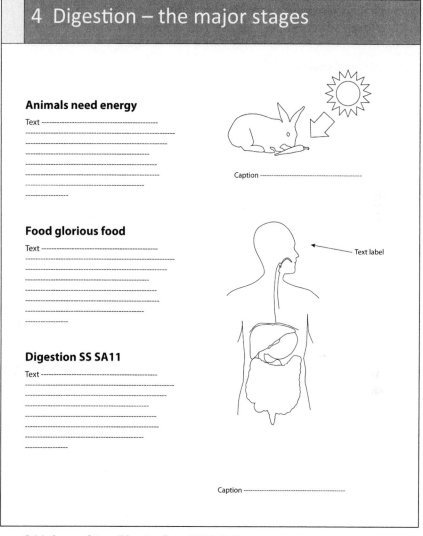

Original source: Science Education Group (2002), 90–91.

FIGURE 11-7   Rearranged Excerpt from *Salters GCSE Science Y11*. (This figure has been reconstructed because reprint rights were not available for the original image. —Bedford Editors)

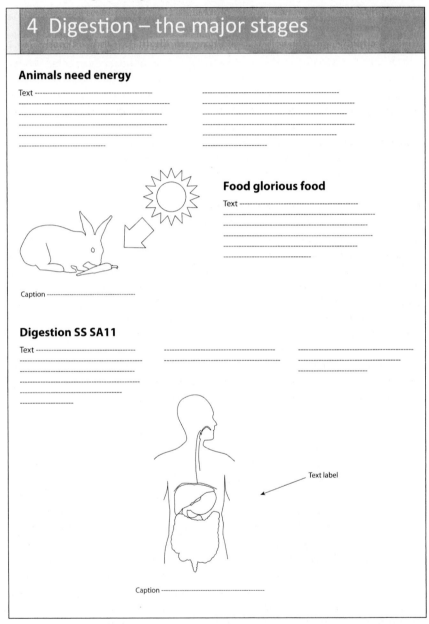

Original source: Science Education Group (2002), 90–91.

At the level of layout, selection can be thought of as the choice of *framing devices* to employ in the placement of (complex) signs (as blocks of image or writing) to make the complete text. Figures 11-6 and 11-7 show two versions of the overall layout/text. The version in Figure 11-6 is the original, the version in Figure 11-7 is one we produced. Comparing the two shows how arrangement can be realized through layout. The original version realizes a *given-new* structure with writing as given and image as new. Salience is implied by placing one set of sign complexes first (i.e., in a left-right reading direction) and another later. Using rearrangement, we *transformed* the original to produce something closer to a *real-ideal* structure (in a semiotic culture where placement at the base of a visual frame implies "the empirical real" and placement at the top suggests an "ideal"), while retaining the sign elements of the original. Now a different arrangement is realized, with different sign complexes being foregrounded. (For *ideal-real* and *given-new* structures see Kress & van Leeuwen, 2006).

The effect of these arrangements on social relations may not be immediately recognizable in this example, but they are also realized through layout. The examples in Figures 11-8 and 11-9 show this neatly. They are different versions of the "same" textbook, used for different "ability tiers." In the version for the "lower tier" (Figure 11-8) layout is much more "spaced out," compared with the "dense" "higher tier" version (Figure 11-9). Spacing is here used as a signifier of ability. That is, this use of layout realizes an ideology of *simplicity of display* that is comparable to what is often said about sans serif fonts: That is, providing less "information" is seen as apt for those regarded to have a lesser capacity to process information.

The same principles also apply to moving image and speech, two modes that are at the disposal of the school Web maker. Both modes share certain resources with their graphic counterparts, image and writing, respectively. In terms of resources, what differentiates moving image from image is movement and what differentiates speech from writing are the different affordances of sound and graphic display. Moving image uses selection not just in the ways that image does, but also in anticipation of the constraints of time in moving image as compared to a still image. That is, moving image is selective in relation to *pace*; the movement of molecules, for instance, has to be slowed down to become visible. Speech is bound by the same constraint of time, and so both are partial at any one moment. In both modes a reading path is established by the sequential unfolding of the semiotic material in (real) time. In moving image, foregrounding can be realized through, for example, lighting (up), in speech, through intonation. In moving image social relations are created through forms of interactivity, for instance, the learner is given control over arrangement, is asked to drag elements in or to tick the right box. That is an affordance of image representation. In speech, social relations/positioning can be realized, for example, through the given-new informational structure, as well as through voice and accent.

FIGURE 11-8   Excerpt from *Catalyst. A Framework for Success, II: Green.*

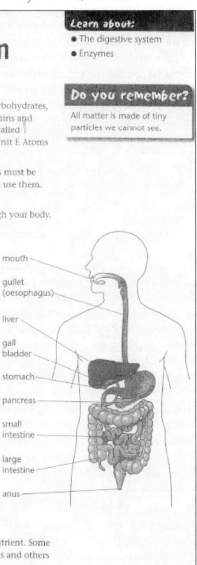

(A4) Total breakdown

Different sized particles

Each nutrient in our food is made up of particles. Carbohydrates, fats and proteins are all made of large particles. Vitamins and minerals are made of small ones. These particles are called **molecules**. You will learn more about molecules in Unit E Atoms and molecules.

Do you remember?

All matter is made of tiny particles we cannot see.

The big molecules in carbohydrates, fats and proteins must be broken down into smaller ones before our bodies can use them. This is called **digestion**.

Digestion happens bit by bit as the food moves through your body.

The long journey

When you chew up and swallow your food, it begins its journey through a long tube from the mouth to the anus. The tube is called the **gut** and it is nine metres long.

The **digestive system** is all the organs that take part in digestion. They are shown in this diagram.

ⓐ Look at the diagram. Name the part of the gut that links your mouth with your stomach.

Breaking it down

As your food goes through the gut it is broken down into smaller molecules by chemicals called **enzymes**. These are added to the food in the mouth, stomach and small intestine.

Enzymes make the digestion of food happen more quickly. Without enzymes it could take a few days instead of a few hours to break down some foods.

ⓑ What are enzymes?

ⓒ Why are enzymes important in digestion?

Each enzyme helps break down a different type of nutrient. Some break down carbohydrates, some break down proteins and others break down fats.

mouth
gullet (oesophagus)
liver
gall bladder
stomach
pancreas
small intestine
large intestine
anus

Source: Chapman (2003a), 8. Reprinted by permission of Harcourt Education.

FIGURE 11-9   Excerpt from *Catalyst. A Framework for Success, II: Red.*

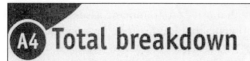

(A4) Total breakdown

Learn about:
- The digestive system
- Enzymes

Different sized particles

Each nutrient in our food is made up of particles. Carbohydrates, fats and proteins are all made of large particles. Vitamins and minerals are made of small ones. These particles are called molecules. You will learn more about **molecules** in Unit E Atoms and molecules.

Do you remember?

All matter is made of tiny particles we cannot see.

The long journey

When you chew up and swallow your food, it begins its journey through a long tube from the mouth to the anus. The tube is called the **gut** and it is nine metres long.

Food contains nutrients. Carbohydrates, fats and proteins are all large molecules. To get these nutrients into our bodies, these large molecules must be broken down into smaller molecules. This is a **chemical process** called **digestion**.

The **digestive system** includes all the organs that take part in digestion. They are shown in the diagram on the right.

The first part of the gut is called the **gullet** or **oesophagus**.

In the **stomach** the food is churned up for a while by its muscular walls. After a few hours the food has become a runny liquid. This leaves the stomach and enters a long tube called the **small intestine**.

As the food passes through the digestive system it is mixed with **digestive juices** that help to break down the different nutrients.

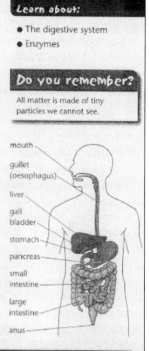

mouth
gullet (oesophagus)
liver
gall bladder
stomach
pancreas
small intestine
large intestine
anus

Breaking it down

The digestive juices contain chemicals called **enzymes**. These help to break the larger molecules into smaller molecules. Enzymes make the digestion of food happen more quickly. Enzymes for digesting food are found in the mouth, stomach and small intestine.

a Why do you think it is important for food to be digested quickly?

Each enzyme speeds up the breakdown of a different type of nutrient. Some break down carbohydrates, some break down proteins and others break down fats.

Did you know?

Some washing powders are described as 'biological', and others are 'non-biological'. **Biological washing powders** contain enzymes that help to clean dirty clothes. They break down stains caused by proteins in foods such as egg or gravy.

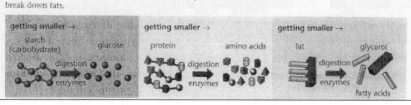

getting smaller →
starch (carbohydrate)   glucose   digestion   enzymes

getting smaller →
protein   amino acids   digestion   enzymes

getting smaller →
fat   glycerol   digestion   enzymes   fatty acids

Source: Chapman (2003b), 8. Reprinted by permission of Harcourt Education.

OUTLOOK: WRITING, REPRESENTATION, GAINS, AND LOSSES

We allow ourselves to conclude with a brief programmatic assessment of issues, directions, and likely developments that follow from our approach.

We regard the framework that we have put forward as a general one; we see its potential as leading to the possibility of an inclusive rhetorical/semiotic framework. We intend to take it toward the articulation of a set of principles of the rhetoric of multimodal communication, in all settings, with any form of technology and all forms of media(tion), in any social environment. In the context of the issue of this journal we have attempted to indicate implications for writing within environments of multimodal representation and the likely impacts of contemporary technologies for communication.

We have exemplified the approach with issues and materials in educational contexts, our present professional environment. We believe that it provides a framework in which urgent questions of pedagogic environments—whether of teaching or of learning, formal or informal—can be addressed within an encompassing theory, allowing some of the most urgent contemporary problems to be addressed. Among these we count issues such as the effect of (features of) learning environments on potentials and possibilities of learning, the question of multimodal representations of knowledge and learning, similarly, the pressing issue of the development of apt forms of assessment for representations in different modes, treated as signs of learning. The approach provides an integration of rhetorical and pedagogic issues and questions, sensitive to environments and conditions of learning, to assessment and evaluation. Practically, it should lead to the articulation of principles applicable in the development of learning materials and environments.

On a semiotic/representational level, the approach provides means for understanding functional issues in multimodal representation, both in production and analysis, such as functional load, functional specialization, functional differentiation, functional (re-)distribution. It provides an account of the relations between social conditions and the take up of potentials of modal and medial affordances, or an explanation of unused affordances of modes and media, which may not be apparent to sign makers.

Socially, culturally, and politically this approach should make it possible to conduct debates on likely impacts of modal choices, of modal changes and modal selection that are better founded theoretically than is the present level of debate around ideologies of simplicity, ability, and the regular panics around "dumbing down" of culture in general.

In brief, we see implications at the most general level of theory of representation as well as in relation to specific disciplinary and professional issues, ranging from general to entirely practical ones.

REFERENCES

Baker, C. D., & Freebody, P. (1989). Talk around text: constructions of texual and teacher authority in classroom discourse. In S. de Castell, A. Luke & C. Luke (Eds.), *Language, authority and criticism: Readings on the school textbook* (pp. 263–283). London: Falmer Press.

Bernstein, B. (1996). *Pedagogy, symbolic control and identity. Theory, research, critique.* London: Taylor and Francis.

Chapman, C. (2003a). *Catalyst. A framework for success. II. Green.* Oxford, England: Heinemann.

Chapman, C. (2003b). *Catalyst. A framework for success. II. Red.* Oxford, England: Heinemann.

Cole, G., Fraser, B., Grantham, K., Hughes, P., Kent, D., et al. (1999). *Impact maths 1G.* Oxford, England: Heinemann.

Dimopoulos, K., Koulaidis, V., & Sklaveniti, S. (2003). Towards an analysis of visual images in school science textbooks and press articles about science and technology. *Research in Science Education, 33*(2), 189–216.

Fairbrother, F., Nightingale, E., & Wyeth, F. J. (1935). *General science. Part III.* London: G. Bell and Sons.

Goffman, E. (1986). *Frame analysis. An essay on the organization of experience.* Boston: Northeastern University Press.

Goodwin, C. (2000). Action and embodiment within situated human interaction. *Journal of Pragmatics, 32,* 1489–1522.

Halliday, M. A. K. (1967). *Intonation and grammar in British English.* The Hague: Mouton.

Halliday, M. A. K. (1994). *An introduction to functional grammar.* London: Edward Arnold.

Hodge, R., & Kress, G. (1988). *Social semiotics.* Cambridge, England: Polity Press.

Jewitt, C. (2003). Computer-mediated learning: The multimodal construction of mathematical entities on screen. In C. Jewitt & G. Kress (Eds.), *Multimodal literacy* (pp. 34–55). New York: Peter Lang.

Jewitt, C. (2005). *Technology, literacy, learning. A multimodal approach.* London: Routledge.

Kaplan, N. (1995). Politexts, hypertexts, and other cultural formations in the late age of print. *Computer-Mediated Communication Magazine, 2,* 3.

Kress, G. (2003). *Literacy in the new media age.* London: Routledge.

Kress, G. (2005). Gains and losses: New forms of texts, knowledge and learning. *Computers and Composition, 22,* 5–22.

Kress, G., Jewitt, C., Franks, A., Bourne, J., Hardcastle, J., Jones, K., & Reid, J. (2005). *English in urban classrooms: A multimodal perspective on teaching and learning.* London: RoutledgeFarmer.

Kress, G., Jewitt, C., Ogborn, J., & Tsatsarelis, C. (2001). *Multimodal teaching and learning. The rhetorics of the science classroom.* London: Continuum.

Kress, G., & van Leeuwen, T. (2001). *Multimodal discourse. The modes and media of contemporary communication.* London: Edward Arnold.

Kress, G., & van Leeuwen, T. (2006). *Reading images. The grammar of visual design.* London: Routledge.

Lemke, J. (2000). Multimedia demands of the scientific curriculum. *Linguistics and Education, 10*(3), 247–271.

Martinez Pena, B., & Gil Quilez, M. J. (2001). The importance of images in astronomy education. *International Journal of Science in Education, 23*(11), 1125–1135.

Maybin, J., & Moss, G. (1993). Talk about texts: reading as a social event. *Journal of Research in Reading, 16*(2), 138–147.

Myers, G. (1990). *Writing biology: Texts in the social construction of science.* Madison, WI: University of Wisconsin Press.

O'Halloran, K. (2005). *Mathematical discourse: Language, symbolism and visual images.* London: Continuum.

Pintó, R. (Ed.). (2002). Visual language in science education [Special issue]. *International Journal of Scientific Education, 24*(3).

Postman, N. (1993). *Technopoly: The surrender of culture to technology.* New York: Vintage Books.

Pozzer, L. L., & Roth, W. M. (2003). Prevalence, function, and structure of photographs in high school biology. *Journal of Research in Science Teaching, 40*(10), 1089–1114.

Roth, W. M., Bowen, M., & McGinn, M. K. (1999). Differences in graph-related practices between high school biology textbooks and scientific ecology journals. *Journal of Research in Science Teaching, 36*(9), 977–1019.

Science Education Group. (2002). *Salters GCSE science Y11.* Oxford, England: Heinemann.

Scottish Primary Mathematics Group. (1991). *Heinemann mathematics 7. Textbook.* Oxford, England: Heinemann.

Tuman, M. (1992). *Word perfect: Literacy in the computer age.* Pittsburgh, PA: Pittsburgh University Press.

Unsworth, L. (2001). *Teaching multiliteracies across the curriculum. Changing contexts of text and image in classroom practice.* Buckingham, England: Open University Press.

12 Embracing Wicked Problems: The Turn to Design in Composition Studies

RICHARD MARBACK

I was in graduate school in composition studies in 1988 when James Berlin's article, "Rhetoric and Ideology in the Writing Classroom," appeared in *College English*. I remember having the impression that Berlin's article changed the landscape of composition studies. Describing the limits inherent in the various assumptions of process pedagogies, Berlin demonstrated a pressing need in composition studies for critical theory and ideological critique. In the 1990s, as many more compositionists turned away from research in process pedagogy toward post-process pedagogy, critical theories or cultural studies of writing, ethnographic researches of writing, poststructuralist accounts of writing, or poststructuralist ethnographies of writing, the field of composition studies became more diffuse and further divided, somehow less capable of accounting for the activity of composing itself. In all fairness, the theoretical turn and emergence of post-process pedagogies did not so much replace the process paradigm as augment it, even if everyone did not always experience it this way. Throughout, students were still being taught some variant of a writing process. They still are. But theories of writing in the classroom largely turned to other, more critical questions, questions of authority (Shor) and authenticity (Petraglia) and relevance (Durst). As Lester Faigley summed up the turn from process, recalling Berlin's 1989 debate with John Schilb, "Postmodern theory offers an ongoing critique of domination, but it does not supply a theory of agency or show how a politics is to arise from that critique" (20). For a field such as composition studies, which is defined around practical issues of agency, such a lack is deeply debilitating.

Today, the centrifugal forces of critique in composition studies are giving way to centripetal interest in design, reinvigorating practical issues of agency. As much as Berlin's article dearticulated our understanding of student production as writing process, my sense of it is that Diana George's article "From Analysis to Design: Visual Communication in the Teaching of Writing" (see p. 211 in this volume) begins the project of rearticulating composition studies

From *College Composition and Communication* 61.2 (2009): W397–W419.

around issues of student production as design. Where Berlin's article gave timely expression to a major turning point in composition studies—from process to critique—George's article initiates the next turning point in composition studies: from critical analysis to design. Taken together, the two articles, Berlin's from 1988 and George's from 2002, mark waypoints along the course of composition's development as a robust field of study that is, as Joseph Harris put it, "a teaching subject" (ix).

My pairing of the articles by Berlin and George may seem arbitrary, my choice of Berlin especially so. Yet it is not. Even though "Ideology in the Writing Classroom" is an important article in the history of composition studies, anthologized and still cited, it appears to have little to do with the emergence of the current design paradigm in composition studies. But it was Berlin among others who not only turned our attention away from process but in doing so also turned our attention away from what might have proven premature articulation with design studies. His persuasive attention to critical theory and cultural studies drew the subsequent attention of compositionists with him away from early interest in design thinking. That attention was momentarily focused on design thinking as a process paradigm is most evident in an article largely forgotten by the majority of compositionists and published in *College Composition and Communication* in 1989, Charles Kostelnick's "Process Paradigms in Design and Composition: Affinities and Directions." Like Berlin, Kostelnick weighed the limits of process paradigms. Unlike Berlin, who privileged ideological critique and eventually cultural studies over process theories, Kostelnick kept his attention focused on the prospects and perils of process itself. He also remained cautiously optimistic about the prospects of process theory, an optimism grounded in his focus on the fate of a process paradigm in design studies—its "quest for a single all-encompassing model, and . . . the loss of credibility resulting from practical application" (275)—a fate, according to Kostelnick, that provides a foil for refining the process paradigm in composition studies. For my purposes, Kostelnick's recommendation, based on his review of design thinking, for a "more flexible [process] paradigm encompassing a plurality of models" (276), serves as sound advice for compositionists today who turn to design as a return to a paradigm for composing.

I believe we can benefit in our quest for a flexible design paradigm for composition studies by following up on Kostelnick's interest in the field of design studies. In particular we can profit by following the move in design studies from a quest for a paradigm of the design process to a focus on designing as an ethical activity, a focus most clearly captured in the idea of design tasks as "wicked problems." Design theorist Horst W. J. Rittel first defined the design process as a wicked problem. In an essay published with Melvin M. Webber, Rittel described the ten characteristics of wicked planning problems. As Rittel and Webber characterize it, the wickedness of design problems derives from the fact that they are not the tame problems solvable through greater command of more information. Wicked problems are wicked because they are never finally solvable; they are contingent problems of deciding what to do that require resolution "over and over again" (160). What makes contingency particularly wicked is the ambiguity created by multiple, potentially competing interests designers and their clients, or composers and their audiences, bring to the design task of creating a specific artifact, whether that artifact is a building, a transportation network, or a text. Never reducible to an unambiguous formulation, wicked design problems are "'vicious' (like a circle) or 'tricky' (like a leprechaun) or 'aggressive' (like a lion, in contrast to the docility of a lamb)" (160). Wicked design problems are problems of deciding what is better when the situation is ambiguous at best.

In what follows I describe and elaborate the wicked problems approach to design thinking. I then use that discussion to highlight the wickedness of design in composition studies. Beginning with Gunther Kress and following the ongoing turn to design through George and then Mary E. Hocks, I propose a fuller turn to design in composition studies. Understanding composition studies as concerned with wicked problems of composing enables us to draw more productively from our appeals to design. The wicked problems approach does not attempt to reduce the unique challenges definitive of any single design task to a comprehensive design paradigm, nor does it mystify the unique creative ability of any designer/composer. Instead it focuses our attention on the ethical dimensions of document designing. It forces us to confront the wickedness in our responses not only to each other but also to the objects we have designed, making us see problems of document designing not as procedural problems of composing but, as Rittel and Webber put it, problems of responsiveness and dilemmas of judgment (164). Document designing is wicked not only because the problem of document designing is not reducible to any single, all-encompassing design paradigm. It is especially wicked because composing in digital media, composing with print and image together, evokes problems of responsiveness that are interpretive as well as affective. Our affective responses and visceral reactions can be elicited and guided, but they remain largely beyond both the conscious awareness of the composer and the rational control available through any design process. This is the wickedness of design in composition studies today.

WICKED PROBLEMS

While a critical turn similar to that taken in composition studies took hold in design studies during the 1990s, the challenge of bridging theory and practice was managed differently and more productively through an appreciation of design as a wicked problem. Rittel and Webber's description of design problems as wicked captures the sense in which every genuine design task is unique and irreducible, a matter of inventing a solution rather than discovering an answer, ultimately less about the constraints of subjectivity and more about the productive interactions of designers and their clientele. Thinking about specific design tasks as wicked problems offers an alternative articulation of (critical) theory and (composing) practice by conceptualizing those tasks, in Herbert Simon's influential formulation, within a science of the artificial. A science of the artificial is a study of productive activity, a study of the individual planning and devising of specific artifacts such as buildings, machines, and texts, things only designed once that could always have been designed otherwise. There are many buildings, many machines, and many texts, all of them singular artifacts. Any building or machine or text that is made, that is artifactual and so artificial, only gets composed or designed once, in response to the demands of the specific situation then and there, and through the immediate purpose brought by a composer or designer to the creation of that artifact in that situation.

According to Rittel and Webber, wickedness rests in the fact that the context-boundedness of planning problems makes those problems value laden, problems of deciding what ought to be done here and now. The question of what artifact it is right to create is never, as Rittel and Webber put it, "exhaustively describable" (164) because it is always contingent on interests that are themselves changeable and always changing. As writing teachers are well aware, the interests of composers/designers and their audiences can and do shift unforeseeably over the course of revising and reworking an artifact's final design, as when an instructor and student decide during a conference to shift the focus of an essay. At the same time, the ambiguity of any wicked design problem does not absolve the designer from responsibility for an ineffective or even dangerous design. Rittel and Webber put it this way: "the aim is not to find the truth, but to improve some characteristic of the world where people live. Planners are liable for the consequences of the actions they generate" (167). Designers concern themselves not with problems of what is, but with problems of what could be, problems of formulating a response to a situation and an audience, which are problems of responsibility for the responses of others. Rittel and Webber continue, "the problems that planners must deal with are wicked and incorrigible ones, for they defy efforts to delineate their boundaries and to identify their causes, and thus to expose their problematic nature. The planner who works with open systems is caught up in the ambiguity of their causal webs. Moreover, his would-be solutions are confounded by a still further set of dilemmas posed by the growing pluralism of the contemporary publics, whose valuations of his proposals are judged against an array of different and contradicting scales" (167).

So the wicked problem in any science of the artificial—whether architecture, engineering, or writing—is first a technical problem, the problem of figuring out how to design an appropriate response to a unique situation. Foremost, the wicked problem of design, as Rittel and Webber make clear, is the problem of being accountable for responses to artifacts such as buildings and Web pages, even though the full range of divergent and potentially conflicting responses to any design can never be exhaustively predicted.

That a designer cannot fully know in advance the responses people will have to any artifact of design is important to a fuller appreciation of the wickedness of designing and has been described by design theorist Richard Buchanan. Buchanan develops Rittel's concept of wicked problems by attending to the artifactuality of designing as well as the responsibility of designing and, in so doing, finds common ground with rhetoric. Design is rhetoric because rhetoric is a study of the most wicked of all problems: making responsible use of the persuasive power inherent in all artifacts. As Buchanan describes it, design studies is the study of rhetoric, "the *rhetoric* of products — the study of how products come to be as vehicles of argument and persuasion about the desirable qualities of private and public life" ("Rhetoric" 26; emphasis in original). Designs make claims on our sense of what is and what is not desirable. Artifacts of design — including all document types from student essays to magazine spreads to Web pages — appeal to our ability for response. Far from passive objects awaiting our responses, artifacts retain as well a kind of capacity to generate responses in us. They are vehicles of meaning. The response ability of a design consists of the argumentative and persuasive features built into the artifact by the designer. As Buchanan suggests, the response ability in a design, something the designer is ultimately responsible for, is also something available in the artifact for response by an audience.

The response ability of a design pivots on erasing the distinction between word and thing, form and content, signifier and signified that relinquishes design to the superficial task of providing style, of merely decorating objects. Design in rhetoric is a responsibility for response because design is the making of a meaningful thing, an artifact that means in the world independently of the meaning created for it by the designer. As Buchanan puts it, "The power of design as deliberation and argument lies in overcoming the limitations of mere verbal or symbolic argument — the separation of words and things, or theory and practice that remains a source of disruption and confusion in contemporary culture. Argument in design thinking moves toward the concrete interplay and interconnection of signs, things, actions, and thoughts. Every designer's sketch, blueprint, flow chart, graph, three-dimensional model, or other product proposal is an example of such argumentation" ("Rhetoric" 18–19). The design process and the artifacts of design are more than mere stylings. Artifacts of design are arguments in and of themselves. We interact with them. They are real things in the world — textual artifacts such as sketches, charts, proposals, as well as the material artifacts built from such designs. They populate our world and as such make real claims on us. We handle them and consider them. They appeal to our sensations and to our emotions. They evoke our ability to respond and we respond with varying degrees of willfulness. Through our interactions as designers with designed artifacts, the problems of designing become even more wicked because we encounter, as Buchanan makes clear, "the array of technical decisions contained in any product" (46). Bruno Latour, as well as Langdon Winner, among others, has argued that the design decisions materialized in any artifact have a significant impact on us, giving physical presence to power and authority by forcing us to turn or stop here and not somewhere else. Because artifacts have consequences on our actions, the wicked problem of design is more than simply the problem of conceptualizing invention; it is the problem of claims artifacts make on our attention.

Competing claims for attention made on us by artifacts, plans, and ambitions create problems for us that are particularly wicked because artifacts introduce values and influence decisions and further confuse information. Sorting through values and information and decisions as we design, we learn not only how wicked it is to make design decisions, we learn also the kind of decision makers we are and what matters to us in making decisions. Here Buchanan is right to claim for design that it is a making that makes us human. Writing about ancient rhetoric, he explains, "To possess that technology or discipline of thinking was to possess the liberal art, to be human, and to be free in seeking one's place in the world" ("Rhetoric" 18). Through the activity of designing we make real both our world of artifacts and our selves as members of that world, people who become who we are through our interactions with the artifacts we place into the world. At the same time Buchanan's claim that design is a making that makes us free underestimates the wickedness of design itself by failing to recognize along with Winner and Latour the breadth of claims our artifacts can have on our attention.

Recent work in new media studies has explored the consequences on experience and perception of our embodied encounters with the artifactual. One such new media critic, Mark Hansen, engages the materialization of text to argue for a more careful articulation of the rhetorical with the technological. Unlike Buchanan, who is less careful in his claims about the rhetoric of artifacts, Hansen argues that something like an integrative aesthetic experience of designed artifacts is an irreducibly embodied experience of the dynamic structures of technologies. We cannot fully capture in words or representations the affective responses of our bodies to machines such as computers, cell phones, or iPods. Neither can we translate our words directly into the designs of these or any other artifacts. Technologies have a structure and a pulse beyond our representations and in this way have an impact so immediately and deeply felt that we cannot express it (even if we were to fully know it). This does not mean we are lost to a vast range of our experience with technologies and their artifacts. But it does push us to enlarge our understanding of the humanity we realize through our design activities.

From even a brief review of design as a wicked problem we become sensitive to the struggle for a vocabulary adequate to discuss intentional interactions with artifacts. That design theorists turn to rhetoric for such a vocabulary should be heartening to compositionists. At the same time, as compositionists appeal to design for a vocabulary, we should be wary of circularity. The problems of design eased by rhetoric and the related problems of composition studies eased by design may not gain critical ground if each only points to the other. As we consider the values of design thinking in composition studies, we have to watch out for exaggerated claims about the potential of design to remove what we might perceive as the underdetermined from what we should accept as the indeterminate wickedness of composing and designing. We also need to be wary of appealing to design as a way of avoiding important issues of response raised by the wicked indeterminacy of composition studies. My preference here is to understand design as disposition toward manipulating tools and producing artifacts that themselves bring into perception issues of human needs and values. Without sensitivity to the persuasive interconnections of "signs, things, actions, and thoughts," design dissolves, privileging motives explicitly expressed by humans while also exposing us to the claims of motiveless technologies.

RETURNING DESIGN TO COMPOSITION STUDIES

Having reviewed the discourse of design as a wicked problem, I now turn to appeals to a vocabulary of design from within composition studies. As will become clear, design enters composition studies most explicitly through the work of the New London Group. At the same time, design enters more pervasively through appeal to the work of Buchanan. While I do point to uses of Buchanan and design studies in composition studies, my goal is to show the degree to which compositionists have and have not fully embraced design thinking in all its wickedness.

In 1989 attention to design studies from within composition studies grew out of shared interest in the process paradigm. After 1989, with interest waning in process as a dominant paradigm in research in composition studies, shared interest with design studies was largely lost. The reintroduction of design thinking to composition studies at least since 2002 has been driven by growing use of computers in first-year writing, an introduction of technology that has expanded understanding of first-year writing as document production requiring of students the integration of (minimally) textual and visual representations. Yet as I have argued so far, design thinking involves more than attention to visual and textual elements during the composing process. In its richest sense design thinking is a nonreductive approach to wicked problems of inventing purposeful artifacts when intentions, circumstances, and outcomes are all ambiguous at best because the designer is immersed in a world of artifacts. If the appeal to design does nothing more than provide a vocabulary for including visual elements in textual production, then the concept of design becomes thinner and, as a result, less significant in composition studies. To decide just how meaningful and so useful the vocabulary of design is and can be in composition studies, I review here some initial discussions.

The genealogy of current uses of design in composition studies follows largely from the 1996 publication of New London Group's "A Pedagogy of Multiliteracies" in which design is a key concept, as when it is described as follows: "we are both inheritors of patterns and conventions of meaning and at the same time active designers of meaning. And, as designers of meaning, we are designers of social futures—workplace futures, public futures, community futures" (65).* This description of design largely follows my discussion above; designers of social futures invent artifacts that evoke responses through which we become who we are. As the authors explain, the broad sweep of their use of the term provides a metalanguage for explaining what

*Part of the New London Group article has been reprinted in this volume (see p. 193). Cross-references to the material reprinted here are preceded by "p."; references to sections not included in this volume carry only the page number.

students learn through a pedagogy of multiliteracies. Justification for the term and the explanation of its use are worth quoting in full:

> We have also decided to use the term "design" to describe the forms of meaning because it is free of the negative associations for teachers of terms such as "grammar." It is a sufficiently rich concept upon which to found a language curriculum and pedagogy. The term also has a felicitous ambiguity: it can identify either the organizational structure (or morphology) of products, or the process of designing. . . . We propose to treat any semiotic activity, including using language to produce or consume texts, as a matter of Design involving three elements: Available Designs, Designing, and The Redesigned. Together these three elements emphasize the fact that meaning-making is an active and dynamic process, and not something governed by static rules. (pp. 193–94)

As a description of design, the New London Group's account is, as they claim, a sufficiently rich concept for grounding language—and writing—pedagogy. Many compositionists have found it so, myself included, although, as I have been tracing the concept of design in my discussion of wicked problems, the richness of the term derives less from design's "felicitous ambiguity" and its capacity to free our thinking from overly burdened terms such as "grammar." After all, "composition" and the attendant concept of composing have a similar exploitable ambiguity. The richness of design derives instead from its capacity to give expression to wicked problems, an involvement of people in their manipulation of words and things—a semiotic and affective conditioning of our responses not entirely translatable into grammars of careful expression or composable into arguments of critical awareness.

Gunther Kress—one of the members of the New London Group—has described the need to use design as something more than a term for identifying and articulating the distinctive features of verbal and visual communication. Immediately Kress discounts the errors inherent in conceptualizing multiple media in vocabularies of print. Not only do vocabularies of print fail to describe the distinguishing features of multiple, nonlanguage media, they also fail to adequately describe the interrelations among different modalities of expression. A theory adequate to the task of accounting for visual and verbal or textual elements "needs to be formulated so as to permit the description both of the specific characteristics of a particular mode *and* of its more general semiotic properties which allow it to be related plausibly to other semiotic modes" ("Design" 153–54; emphasis in original). Design becomes useful to such a theory because it is largely neutral to the media of designing; one can design in image as well as in text, or in any combination of any number of other media. Moving to a more general level at which issues of design in any media are described in terms not drawn from any single media may move past the problem of reductive explanation, but it also introduces the problem of comprehensive explanation. What terms in design allow us to both describe the specific characteristics of print and picture while also allowing us to describe, teach, and then evaluate our responses to the relationship of image and word?

Here Kress makes an important contribution. Following the multiliteracies approach (according to which semiotic systems have been manipulated in the past to produce designs available in the present for manipulation to produce future designs), Kress observes that "Semiotic modes have different potentials, so they afford different kinds of possibilities of human expression and engagement with the world. . . . Or, to put it more provocatively: the single, exclusive and intensive focus on written language has dampened the full development of all kinds of human potentials, through all sensorial possibilities of human bodies, in all kinds of respects, cognitively and affectively, in two- and three-dimensional representation" ("Design" 157). In this passage in particular Kress brings to attention the wicked problem of design, recognition that the artifacts of design appeal affectively as well as cognitively across the entire spectrum of the human sensorium.

Recalling Hansen, the extralinguistic appeal of such things as Web pages—or even advertising in magazines—cannot and should not be reduced to the juxtaposition of print and image because there is more to the experience of "reading" than this. Our experiences of images may seem more immediate, less a matter of decoding or reading, and more a matter of sensing and observing, even though the experience of an image demands our thoughtful attention. Print may seem more conceptual, yet our perception of the printed word is primarily a visual experience. So our habit of dividing a multimedia artifact such as a Web page into the modalities of word and image is just that, a habit, one having less to do with our perceptual experiences of Web pages or the nature of Web pages and more to do with habits of organizing our affective responses to that media. Following such habits uncritically leads us to misconstrue our ability to respond to multimedia artifacts such as Web pages.

Kress steers us away from habits of misconstruing visual media through the privileging of print by directing our attention to the range of sensorial and representational possibilities for communicating meaning in digital media. He does so through the concept of synaesthesia, "the transduction of meaning from one semiotic mode to another semiotic mode, an activity constantly performed by the brain" ("Design" 159). As a synaesthetic activity, design is—to invoke Buchanan—an activity of enlisting our affective sensitivity to engage the persuasive interconnections of signs, things, actions, and thoughts. Kress also invokes Buchanan as demonstrating the claim that design matters because "it requires the orchestration and remaking of these resources in the service of frameworks and models expressive of the maker's intentions in shaping the social and cultural environment" (160). In its thickest sense, Kress's concept of design as orchestrating the range of sensory responses to media artifacts emphasizes the need for greater attention to synaesthetic impact in the teaching of composing in digital media. This is the heart of the wicked problem of composing—the problem of developing and fashioning digitized expression while also responding to and managing digitized perception.

Unfortunately, Kress ultimately evades the wicked problem of composing by concentrating his attention on the affordances of multiple media to represent the meaning or intention of an author. Kress asks a benign version of the wicked question, "In this social and cultural environment, with these demands for communication of these materials, for that audience, with these resources, and given these interests of mine, what is the design that best meets these requirements?" (p. 299). His answer realizes the ambition of his question for a tame solution. For Kress, a designer can comprehend environment, materials, audience, resources, and interests to formulate a satisfactory design, one that meets the requirements. Such comprehension is a function of the designer's agency, the capacity of an "individual who has a social history, a present social location, an understanding of the potentials of the resources for communication, and who acts transformationally on the resources environment and, thereby, on self. . . . Where critique unsettled, design shapes, or has the potential always to shape. It makes individual action central, though always in a field saturated with the past work of others and the present existence of power" (p. 300). Kress has avoided the wickedness of designing by isolating the "individual action" of the designer from the agency of artifacts. The prior designs of others, the artifacts in the world that embody power and with which the designer must interact, are relegated to the background, become nothing more than a field in which and on which the individual designer acts. Prior designs are no more than mere resources for synaesthetic manipulation, while the affordances of multiple media are simply resources for orchestration available for use by the designer. Yet as design theorists from Rittel to Buchanan have realized, the wickedness of design thinking is the unavoidable fact that prior designs in multiple media manipulate and orchestrate the agency of the designer at the same time the designer manipulates and orchestrates them. Kress has it right when he writes, "design shapes." Agency is not the exclusive ability of the designer to fashion a response; agency adheres as well in the ability for response in artifacts. The opposition of critique to design, of agency to field, misconstrues the wickedness of the design problem by isolating us from our responses to our artifacts. Kress returns us to questions of agency that process thinking could not solve without giving us a more sophisticated design perspective with which to resolve those questions.

My brief discussion of Kress shows how difficult it is to balance claims for teaching the agency of designing as a response to the subjectifying force of available designs. Appeal to the concept of design may tempt us into believing we have solved a wicked problem, but as Rittel made clear, wicked problems are never really solved, they are only resolved again and again. What matters here then is that, from Rittel and Buchanan to Kress and the New London Group, composition studies has available to it a robust concept of design, design as a wicked problem, a problem not only of conceptualizing design as a process of invention and creation, but a problem as well of conceptualizing the artifacts of design as the synaesthetic stimuli that make us human. To evaluate the use made so far (as well as the use so far to be made) of design in composition studies, I turn now to Diana George's essay, "From Analysis to Design."

George turns to design in "From Analysis to Design" by tracing in the history of composition studies the opposition of the visual to the verbal. George recalls us to the role visual elements—pictures, television and film, as well as graphic design—have played in the teaching of writing, pointing out that for the duration of composition instruction in American universities, the visual has served primarily as a prompt for writing, or as subject matter for essays—in other words, as a topic for analysis. In this way composition studies has persisted in reasserting the image/word dichotomy, even though that opposition has been long shown to lead us astray of the semiotics of print and pictures. As W. J. T. Mitchell has argued in *Picture Theory: Essays on Verbal and Visual Representation*, struggling with the term "imagetext," "'word and image' is simply the unsatisfactory name for an unstable dialectic that constantly shifts its location in representational practices" (83). Or, in different terms, as Jay David Bolter and Richard Grusin have argued in *Remediation: Understanding New Media*, no medium has privilege of representation over any other. Any medium, whether visual or verbal, is simply "that which remediates. It is that which appropriates the techniques, forms, and social significance of other media and attempts to rival or refashion them in the name of the real" (65).

George offers design as a way of thinking about teaching composition that avoids the theoretically unsound and (in terms of the everyday capacities and experiences of college students) practically unrealistic privileging of the word over the image. In light of Buchanan's argument for design as rhetoric, this move has great appeal. As George puts it, "thinking of composition as *design* shifts attention, if only momentarily, from the product to the act of production" (p. 217; emphasis in original). It is important to be clear here that George's use of design to return the teaching of composition from critique to the act of production is not at the same time a return to the theoretical framework of process pedagogies. Design is not an attempt to finally solve the wicked problems of designing that doomed process theory in the 1990s. Design is a matter of focusing student attention on visual as well as textual elements of documents. Herein lie both the strengths of George's appeal and its weaknesses.

Focusing on design as a matter of attending to extralinguistic argumentation, George proposes that the visual do more than provide opportunity to "bring students to a more vivid or accurate use of written language" (p. 219). Design enables students in composition classrooms to take "the visual in its broadest sense as a form of communication through which they [can] make a sophisticated and relevant argument" (p. 227). In the initial stages of the rediscovery of design by composition studies, this unambitious appeal to the robust concept of design is likely a good thing. Eventually, though, we have to ask ourselves whether this limited use of design takes us far enough into the complex issues of synaesthetic interaction with images and words and things and whether limiting ourselves assiduously avoids the productive wickedness of designing.

I think we can extend George's contribution to design thinking in composition studies by rethinking her paradigm for incorporating the visual into teaching writing, a paradigm constrained by her conceptualization of her primary assignment in a text-based metaphor as a visual "argument." I recognize that George does want to avoid reducing the visual to the verbal. But her formulation of visual elements as resources available for making an argument constrains the reach of her appeal to design thinking in composition studies. The appeal to design asks us to acknowledge the affective impact of visualizations, an impact to some extent beyond our design control. Enlarging the sense of argumentation to encompass the affective and synaesthetic, much as my reading of Buchanan's appeal to argumentation required, resolves the issue of once again privileging text over image, but such resolution also confirms the unavoidable wickedness of design thinking.

George acknowledges that her requirements for a visual argument to be exclusively visual are not philosophically demanding. Along with George, we need not adhere in our teaching, or even in our theorizing, to philosophically rigorous definitions. At the same time we must also admit the extent to which our commitments gloss what are the real limitations of our approaches. As George explains it, a visual argument functions much like a verbal argument. It has a claim, it makes a case, it is convincing, and it can be read. What makes a visual argument "visual" is that it "must make its case primarily through the visual" (p. 226). While this is a thin description, several practical and theoretical consequences do follow from it.

In practical terms, the privileging of visuality as the carrier of an argument ignores the contextualization of the visual argument assignment and its requirements in prior texts, discussions, and readings. It fails to give full account of the synaesthetic bleed of meaning across the senses of sight and sound and tactility. In a first-year writing course, a visual argument is an argument because it is always already "read," framed by the words surrounding its composition and presentation, a framing that—to borrow Bolter and Grusin's term—"remediates" the argument. Or, in the vocabulary of Mitchell, the dynamic of visual and verbal confirms the conundrum of the "image-text." George is not unaware of this. The contribution of a semester's worth of word-grounded context to the features of a visual argument is described in the text of George's assignment to her students (reprinted as an appendix to her essay). A pretext is provided by in-class discussion "about how popular ideas and ideals are conveyed in film and in explorers' journals and reports," and about textual revisions of these ideals "by such investigations as Hochschild's *King Leopold's Ghost* or E. D. Morel's reports" (p. 229). During presentation of the visual projects, students are required to "tell the class what decisions you made to create your argument and how well you think you got your position across" (p. 229). In light of my reading of Buchanan, the point is not to deny the possibility that visual elements can make claims on and appeals to our attention, our perception, or our understanding. Instead, my point is to draw attention to the deep interconnectedness of the experiences of visual and verbal and to keep in the foreground of practice the challenge of nonreductive articulation of visual and verbal responses. Visualizations of argument, while grounded in words, are also something other than words and have an impact on our perception that words cannot adequately replicate. In the end, students cannot comprehensively interrogate either their design decisions or the final successes of their designs because they are so immersed in the discourses of their designs, the designs themselves, and responses to those designs.

In theoretical terms, characterizing visual arguments as making a case and as being read falls short of recognizing the distinct affordances of the visual, and it fails to recognize the synaesthetic activity required to orchestrate those distinctions. By establishing visual argument as a form equivalent to written argument, George misses the opportunity to discuss design of visual artifacts as an activity distinct from the design of textual artifacts. We are left with Kress talking about teaching the design of the visual in terms of the textual, using a vocabulary of claims and evidence that does not speak to the features of the visual that make it a distinctly pervasive and persuasive form of communicating meaning.

Perhaps this criticism is too harsh and the concern is beyond the scope of George's article. After all, her goal is to encourage teachers of writing who have neither "been trained in visual thinking" nor have the "access to state-of-the-art technology" (p. 228) to think of composing as designing. This is an important goal. Nonetheless, we must pick up where George left off. While we can describe visual design as having an "argument" with a "vocabulary" distinct from that of written argument, such description must also account for the synaesthetic articulation of those distinct vocabularies. The articulation of visual and textual vocabularies in a document generates connotations and impressions that have impact beyond the meanings carried in the distinct vocabularies. As the New London Group made clear, use of the term *design* is intended to steer us away from the connotations of text-based terms such as *vocabulary* and *grammar*, terms that not only carry negative connotations but that also do not adequately denote the wickedness of designing. We need to think about the affective, embodied affordances of digital medias in which the wicked problems of designing reside. These are problems of how we might intentionally respond to technologies that have already come to condition the range of our responses. To consider ways we might tackle these problems, I discuss another compositionist who has further contributed to the turn to design in composition studies.

Mary E. Hocks builds on George's appeals to design in her 2003 essay, "Understanding Visual Rhetoric in Digital Writing Environments." Only one year after the publication of George's article, Hocks need not argue for the inclusion of visual rhetoric in the teaching of writing. In her review of research on writing and images, she easily establishes the interdependence and inseparability of image and text in digital media. At the same time, she echoes George's view that teachers of writing do not have a ready understanding of visual rhetoric, a lack that drives them to turn to fields such as design studies, although such a turn is not all bad, according to Hocks. In an endnote identifying the value of appeals to design studies, she observes that Buchanan has shown industrial design discourse to have "a fully demonstrative rhetoric."

She also notes that Ilana Snyder's *Page to Screen* "is a good example of cross-disciplinary scholarship that looks at design processes involved in digital linguistic acts" (653). I point out the endnote to highlight the fact that for Hocks design has taken on a meaning expanded from that of George. Not only does design have a rhetoric, digital linguistic acts—and as she argues visual rhetoric—are end products of a design process teachable to students. The elements of the design process and the teaching of that process are in fact the explicit topics of Hocks's article. At stake in her account is the robustness of a teachable design process in composition studies.

Recognizing that students may have familiarity with the visual elements of digital media, Hocks reminds us that the digital medium of the Internet has a hybrid rhetorical nature; it is minimally both textual and visual. Teaching students to purposefully control the hybrid rhetorical demands of designing for the Web requires that we "help our students pay attention to the rhetorical features of these highly visual digital environments" (631). For Hocks, critical attention to the rhetoric of the Web provides a ground for composing for the Web. As Hocks puts it, "Critiquing and producing writing in digital environments actually offers a welcome return to rhetorical principles and an important new pedagogy of writing as design" (632). The rhetorical principles Hocks defines as operative in digital environments—audience stance, transparency, hybridity—are less important here than her argument that the dual activities of critiquing and producing digital writing constitute a design pedagogy and a return to the rhetorical. Recall here that the turn away from process pedagogy was a turn toward critique and that the turn toward design is a turn away from the critical pedagogies that seemed to thwart the process of student invention by locking expression into the fairly predictable categories of subjectification. I suspect Hocks brings critique together with production with the intention of realizing the fuller implications of design thinking described by Buchanan and outlined by the New London Group. However, the wicked problems of design are wicked precisely because no combination of critique and production can resolve them. To see how this is so, it is vital here to understand Hocks's appeal to critique in the teaching of production as a means of addressing wickedness in design.

Critical attention to the design of Web pages—to the manipulation of audience stance, transparency, and hybridity—is crucial in Hocks's design pedagogy. Her pedagogy begins with critique, but critique is only the beginning: "When we bring an understanding of digital rhetoric to our electronic classrooms, we need to expand our approach not only to rhetorical criticism but also to text production" (644). Critique is an important beginning, according to Hocks, because "students need to learn the 'distanced' process of how to critique the saturated visual and technological landscape that surrounds them as something structured and written in a set of deliberate rhetorical moves. They then need to enact those visual moves on their own" (645). Hocks articulates teaching critical distance with enacting design strategies through discussion of the New London Group's concept of multiliteracies: "This approach to literacy education reinforces the value of teaching students to think of themselves not just as critics but as designers of knowledge" (644). Where critique is an assessment of the present, of what is, design is a fashioning of the future, of what could be. As Hocks puts it, "To establish a balanced rhetorical approach, then, we must offer students experiences both in the analytic process of critique, which scrutinizes conventional expectations and power relations, and in the transformative process of design, which can change power relations by creating a new vision of knowledge" (644–45). Here Hocks is too ambitious. Articulating the immediate challenge of a design problem with changing power relations may require critical distance, but it is a requirement that underestimates the wickedness of designing.

I want to temper Hocks's enthusiasm for the power of critique and the potential for change inherent in design. I do so because claims for teaching students to become more speculative or even activist are not claims for the activity of design as much as they are claims for the benefits of critique. Understood as claims about a stance enabled through student critique, Hocks's hope for student speculation and activism runs afoul of current skepticism in composition research regarding the real impact on students of critical pedagogies. More to the point, design is an activity grounded in responsiveness to the ambiguous immediacy of the artifactual. Design does not begin with critical distance. It does not begin with a measured removal from affective responsiveness. Design begins with the immersion of the designer in responsiveness, responsiveness to artifacts as well as to others as users of artifacts. Expectations and relations do not preexist artifacts, they are the immediate and cumulative experience of interacting with artifacts, and it is these experiences, expectations, and relations that form the conjunction of "signs, things, actions, and thoughts" that is design. Critical reflection on experiences of responsiveness does not create distance, it does not provide a perspective removed from ambiguity. Instead, reflection—not as a beginning, but as an ongoing activity—adds an additional layer of meaning to experience. Any claims for the transformative process of design cannot begin with a desire for distance that does not exist and cannot be had. The wickedness of design rests in the fact that the interactions with and through artifacts of design are always burdened with mutable and multiple interests and sensations not completely available to critical awareness.

As Kress argued, anything short of an immersive engagement with the affective and so synaesthetic experience of objects understands visual elements in digital rhetoric primarily in textual terms, as cognitive appeals and social constructs. Yet Kress and George and even Hocks miss embracing the visceral impact that makes such things as Web pages so rhetorical and so wickedly provocative. Anything short of embracing this wickedness collapses the broader sensory appeals of new media artifacts into the largely disembodied modalities of print. Anything more claims student contact with abstract conditions that overdetermine production and distort the transformative potentials of design activity. Either way, we lose our grasp of design as rhetoric, a wicked problem of responses among actions, words, and objects.

EMBRACING THE WICKED PROBLEMS OF DESIGN

As Kostelnick observed almost twenty years ago, composition studies and design studies shared interest in the prospects of a process paradigm. Since then, as critical theory took hold of academic disciplines across the university, composition studies in particular turned from hope for describing agency within a process paradigm to managing problems of subjectivity, a turn to problems of critically liberating the agency of a composer/designer from structures of social interaction in which, as Kostelnick observed, "collective knowledge of discourse participants 'pre-structures' the communication process, engendering reader expectations that guide text production and processing" (273). One way to view the turn in composition studies from critical theory to design thinking would be to see it as taming the theoretical ambitions of critique, a kind of return, as Hocks suggests, to concern for enabling agency within a design process paradigm that is both practically viable and theoretically robust. My proposal for compositionists is a proposal to tame the ambitions in any appeal to design. It is a proposal to embrace design thinking as a wicked problem, a problem of ambiguity and indeterminacy in audience and purpose, a problem of struggling with our abilities to respond to artifacts, with the capacity in our artifacts to respond to us, as well as the problem of our responsibility we have as designers for the abilities of our artifacts to respond and elicit responses from others.

I want to be clear here. My recommendation for taming the ambitions compositionists might have for their appeal to design is not a suggestion that we turn back from design thinking. As I have argued by drawing from Rittel, design problems are wicked. The wickedness of design is something to be embraced if compositionists are to derive the most from their appeals to the discipline of design thinking. Any attempt to avoid or curtail or solve once and for all the wicked problems of design only blunts the potential incisiveness of design thinking in composition studies.

While they have introduced the vocabularies of design thinking to composition studies, George and Hocks have also not realized the potential to be had in the wickedness of design thinking. Inadvertently reintroducing the privilege of print and critical elaboration as an accounting for visual argumentation, George keeps design from becoming anything more than an extension into other media of the meaning-making activities of print. Hocks similarly fails to fully embrace the wickedness of design thinking by presuming the productive manipulation of design elements requires a command over those elements that is best gained through the discursive articulation of critical distance.

My proposal for embracing the wickedness inherent in design thinking is not a proposal for denying the place of critical discussion or explanation in the composing/designing of a media artifact. Embracing wicked problems of design involves keeping critical discussions and explanations in perspective, retaining them as one among many responses to an artifact. Embracing the wicked problem of design is to embrace the problem of responsiveness. Many models of the wickedness of design are available today in television programs such as *Project Runway* or *Designer's Challenge*. One show in particular that highlights the process of designing as an activity of responding to an artifact is *American Chopper*. In every episode Paul Jr. develops an idea for his motorcycle design through immersion in artifacts of inspiration: jet planes and simulators and talk with pilots for the jet bike, a visit to a firehouse and talk with firefighters for the firefighter bike, and even a visit to a motorcycle museum as inspiration for the heritage bike. The final form of the design takes shape as he puts it together, cutting and welding rims and handlebars and exhaust pipes and gas tanks, placing them together, touching them, looking at them, thinking about them in combination, and talking about them, then developing a response to the artifact, getting a feel for it, changing the pieces around, and beginning the whole process over again.

The wickedness of design is not exhausted by this one example. There are many others. Another good one is *Top Chef* in which the wickedness of design as a problem of responding to artifacts is demonstrated in cooking challenges in which chefs are given a box of disparate ingredients—on one occasion, shrimp, mussels, eggplant, corn flakes, and peanut butter. The chefs must then use all the items as main ingredients to create a single dish. Where the design problem in *American Chopper* is to select and fabricate common elements into a unique theme bike, the problem in *Top Chef* is one of integrating and augmenting a fixed number of elements into a single dish. Both working with a constrained set of design elements and working from a limitless set of design possibilities are manifestations of the wickedness of design thinking. In each case the problem is not one of gaining command over the product or process of design through the acquisition of discursive distance. Instead, the problem is one of cultivating responsiveness through manipulation of artifacts, lots of artifacts. It is also the problem of then finding responsibility for the design. In *American Chopper* the potential design elements may be more open, but the audience for the design, the client for whom the custom bike is being built, is rather narrowly defined, usually one person, and Paul Jr.'s responses to that person informs the choice of themes that helps narrow the choices for usable design elements. In *Top Chef*, while the initial design elements may be predetermined, the audience for the design is far more ambiguous. Not only must the chefs anticipate the responses of the panel of judges, they must also anticipate the responses of their fellow competitors, each of whom has a different cooking background and agenda informing their responses to any of the other contestants' dishes.

From this brief discussion of design thinking represented on television, constraints and options in manipulable design elements, design purposes, and audiences for a design are features of the wickedness embedded in any genuine design task. Learning to design, learning to respond responsibly to any meaningful design task, involves responding to the ambiguity by handling artifacts. In the first-year writing classroom it involves students as designers in the act of shaping their responses to their designs as they shape the artifact of design through their responses to it.

Any number of assignments in the first-year writing classroom may engage students in the wickedness of designing. It matters less whether the elements of a media artifact are more open or more constrained, whether the audience for the artifact is the teacher alone or other writing students or even people who might access the artifact on the Web. What matters most is that the act of designing requires an immersive response to the artifact of design. One assignment I have used to realize the goal of engaging students in responsiveness and the responsibility for responsiveness is what I call the "Taking Advice" assignment. The design task is to create a manipulable media artifact from which other students can take advice about a topic the student designer feels expert in. The task is not to give the advice; it is not for the student to put advice into the artifact. Instead, the task is for the student to create an artifact from which others can take advice. Students are quite familiar with any number of online surveys or quizzes that promise advice on any number of topics from dating to fashion to exercise. What they are less familiar with are the features used in these artifacts, just as they are less aware of how their responses to those features are conditioned. By requiring students to design a media artifact that any member of its audience must respond to, the assignment requires students to work on response at every level and at every step in the design process. Students must manipulate the features of the media artifact to make sure they work, that they do function to actually give advice. They have to think about the responsiveness of advice to the features of the artifact. And they must consider the audience of their artifacts and decide the directions to steer them in terms of the kinds of advice they might find. Students have designed a number of viable artifacts in response to this assignment. As just one example, a student used PowerPoint to design a directed survey in which users click on answers to various questions that lead them to a decision about whether to join the military and which branch of the military they might join. The advice anyone can get from this artifact was not predetermined at the decision point of any single question. So, different people answering the series of questions in different ways can be led down different paths. The images paired with the questions on any given frame contributed to the appeal of the question and the gravity of any decision.

My "Taking Advice" assignment is not particularly revolutionary, and the example of one student's response to it is not even especially exemplary. But the point of embracing the wickedness of designing is not to be either revolutionary or exemplary. Designing is about making artifacts. The wickedness of designing is that it is more than merely the making of an artifact; it is an embrace of ambiguities in our responses to each other with and through our artifacts. For students who complete the "Taking Advice" assignment, learning design is learning a process of responding to others. As compositionists continue the turn to design thinking, it is important to be clear what we mean to do through our appeals to design. The growing number of television programs dedicated to design, as well as the availability of design resources in popular culture in general, indicate just how widespread awareness of design has become. We could worry that design may become too diffuse, that

appeals to design in composition studies become nothing more than an uncritical extension of popular perception. The view I have argued throughout
this essay is that we need to worry instead about invoking the vocabulary of
design without fully embracing the wickedness of problems representable
through that vocabulary. Embracing the wickedness of designing tames our
enthusiasm for our theories. Embracing wickedness, compositionists can not
only articulate flexible paradigms for composing with word and image in
digital media, they can also encourage greater sensitivity to the artifacts we
manipulate to make ourselves who we are with each other.

WORKS CITED

Berlin, James. "Rhetoric and Ideology in the Writing Classroom." *College English*. 50.5 (1988):
   477–94.
Bolter, Jay David, and Richard Grusin. *Remediation: Understanding New Media*. Cambridge: MIT
   Press, 2002.
Buchanan, Richard. "Rhetoric, Humanism, and Design." *Discovering Design: Explorations in Design
   Studies*. Ed. Richard Buchanan and Victor Margolin. Chicago: U of Chicago P, 1995. 23–66.
———. "Wicked Problems in Design Thinking." *The Idea of Design: A* Design Issues *Reader*. Ed.
   Victor Margolin and Richard Buchanan. Cambridge: MIT Press, 2002.
Durst, Russell. *Collision Course: Conflict, Negotiation, and Learning in College Composition*. Urbana:
   National Council of Teachers of English, 1999.
Faigley, Lester. *Fragments of Rationality: Postmodernity and the Subject of Composition*. Pittsburgh: U of
   Pittsburgh P, 1992.
George, Diana. "From Analysis to Design: Visual Communicaion in the Teaching of Writing." *Col-
   lege Composition and Communication* 54.1 (2002): 11–39.
Hansen, Mark. *Embodying Technesis: Technology beyond Writing*. Ann Arbor: U of Michigan P, 2000.
Harris, Joseph. *A Teaching Subject: Composition since 1966*. Upper Saddle River: Prentice Hall, 1997.
Hocks, Mary E. "Understanding Visual Rhetoric in Digital Writing Environments." *College Com-
   position and Communication* 54.4 (2003): 629–56.
Kostelnick, Charles. "Process Paradigms in Design and Composition: Affinities and Directions."
   College Composition and Communication 40.3 (1989): 267–81.
Kress, Gunther. "Design and Transformation: New Theories of Meaning." *Multiliteracies: Literacy
   Learning and the Design of Social Futures*. Ed. Bill Cope and Mary Kalantzis. New York: Rout-
   ledge, 2000. 149–58.
———. "Gains and Losses: New Forms of Texts, Knowledge, and Learning." *Computers and Com-
   position* 22 (2005): 5–22.
Latour, Bruno. *Pandora's Hope: Essays on the Reality of Science Studies*. Cambridge: Harvard UP, 1999.
Mitchell, W. J. T. *Picture Theory: Essays on Verbal and Visual Representation*. Chicago: U of Chicago
   P, 1994.
New London Group. "A Pedagogy of Multiliteracies: Designing Social Futures." *Harvard Education
   Review* 66.1 (1996): 60–92. [See also p. 193 in this volume.]
Petraglia, Joseph. *Reality by Design: The Rhetoric and Technology of Authenticity in Education*. Mah-
   wah: Erlbaum, 1998.
Rittel, Horst W. J., and Melvin M. Webber. "Dilemmas in a General Theory of Planning." *Policy
   Sciences* 4 (1973): 155–69.
Shor, Ira. *When Students Have Power: Negotiating Authority in a Critical Pedagogy*. Chicago: U of Chi-
   cago P, 1996.
Winner, Langdon. "Do Artifacts Have Politics?" *The Whale and the Reactor: A Search for Limits in an
   Age of High Technology*. Chicago: U of Chicago P, 1986.

PART THREE

Making Meaning with Multimodal Composition

Introduction to Part Three

In the beginning of the first decade of the twenty-first century, visual rhetoric became more popular in composition scholarship, thanks to works like Carolyn Handa's *Visual Rhetoric in a Digital World*, Charles A. Hill and Marguerite Helmers's *Defining Visual Rhetorics*, and Mary E. Hocks and Michelle R. Kendrick's *Eloquent Images: Word and Image in the Age of New Media*, to name a few. Some scholars and practitioners called the move toward the visual a revolution due to the rapid increase in new technology and expanded access to multiple modes and media. Others called it an evolution, claiming that new technology was simply a refashioning of old technology and thus reusing old practices in a new way. Regardless of the points of disagreement, these scholars and practitioners challenged the authority, power, and privilege of the printed word and the singular author, arguing that other modes, the image in particular, were also legitimate modes that students and scholars alike could use to compose. Soon, out of this interest in visual rhetoric grew a greater interest in multimodal and multimedia composition, with more scholars and practitioners asking: If we can compose in words and images, why not in other modes too? Although some in the field long ago recognized the value of composing using multiple modes and media—as evidenced by the chapters in this book, particularly in Part One—multimodal composition did not become a matter of serious study or scholarship until recently, as more and more instructors began incorporating multimodal composition into their pedagogy. Yet, even with this turn toward multimodal composition, the field, as a whole, has much to learn.

Composing a text using Microsoft Word or Adobe Acrobat, for example, is different from composing a text using a web-authoring application like Dreamweaver. Composing a text using a wiki or a blog is different from composing a text using Photoshop or MovieMaker. Each technology and each composing practice requires different ways of thinking and knowing and different skills and abilities. If, as instructors, we demand that our students turn in only texts that are produced using Microsoft Word, we should consider what ways of thinking and knowing and what skills and abilities we are privileging and/or excluding from our classrooms. If writing rhetorically means being responsive to the changing technological, economic, social, cultural, and political conditions in a society, then we cannot demand that students only compose in one mode using only one technology. It would be naïve and irresponsible, as well as do little to empower our students. In Part Two, the authors contend that design theory is necessary to composition because it allows for responsiveness and understanding of the changing technological, economic, social, cultural, and political conditions in a society. Here, in Part Three, the authors pick up on this discussion, arguing that decisions about design are also decisions that extend rhetorical principles, such as those that have to do with author, text, audience, and context. They argue that it is time to move beyond the privileged position of the printed word and that design decisions must also take into consideration all possibilities for composing and knowing.

Because we have moved from the book to the screen, Gunther Kress believes that the semiotic changes that result from such a move can be called revolutionary. In the first selection of Part Three, "Gains and Losses: New Forms of Texts, Knowledge, and Learning," Kress outlines what is gained and what is lost because of this revolution and demonstrates the changes that occur when we move from print to the web. He describes gains and losses using examples of time, space, and order. For instance, when we use language, as authors, we construct our words one after another in a particular order to make meaning. In order to understand, readers follow a certain, prescribed path through the work. On the other hand, when we see an image, all elements appear at once in a designated space. Spatial arrangement is what makes meaning, and readers/viewers follow their own path. This is what Kress calls "reading as design," and it challenges the long tradition of author as authority. As he did in "Writing in Multimodal Texts: A Social Semiotic Account for Learning" with Jeff Bezemer (see p. 233 in this volume), Kress advocates for design to be tied to the rhetorical choices we make as communicators. In other words, we need to ask: Which design is most appropriate for a given message, audience, author, and context?

Anne Francis Wysocki's article, "awaywithwords: On the Possibilities in Unavailable Designs," investigates the relationship between the materials (modes and media) and the contextual (place and time) when making communicative choices. She asserts that we can't ignore, for example, our histories, like the histories of places. Wysocki adds to Kress's belief in a rhetorical design, saying it is necessary to think more critically about the materials we use in such a way that we also consider the material's historical, cultural, political, social, and technological constraints. She further argues that students need to think about spaces, how they use those spaces, and how audiences might expect and not expect them to use those spaces in order to be successful multimedia composers.

In "Multimodality, 'Reading,' and 'Writing' for the 21st Century," Carey Jewitt examines the implications for writing and reading on-screen (a remediation of the page according to Bolter and Grusin). The types of text we work with on screen use many modes of representation and communication to make meaning(s). Jewitt analyzes computer games to support his argument that different modes have different realizations for meaning making. For instance, in his analysis he points out that visuals should not be considered just decoration, and therefore lacking argumentative and/or communicative significance, as has often been assumed. Rather, they too have meaning-making capabilities. Multimodal design changes the way we read, he argues, since we need to understand the visual resources of color, texture, and shape as well as understand the path of entry into a text, which can create different meanings for different readers.

The final selection in Part Three is taken from Joddy Murray's book *Non-discursive Rhetoric: Image and Affect in Multimodal Composition,* in which he distinguishes between discursive rhetoric, rhetoric that is centered on the word, and nondiscursive rhetoric, rhetoric that is centered on the image. In this excerpt, "Composing Multimodality," Murray asks us to consider writing as composing an image. He believes that the image should be at the heart of multimodal composition because such an understanding would allow us to "acknowledge and build into our writing processes the importance of emotions in textual production, consumption, and distribution; encourage digital literacy as well as nondigital literacy in textual practice; and develop rhetorical skills that are more closely aligned with the rhetorical methods students experience on a daily basis" (p. 326). Throughout this excerpt and his book, Murray ties his argument to the study of neuroscience in order to show how different and how powerful composing multimodally is compared to composing monomodally with words. Unlike many of the authors in this book, he explains how the brain functions when trying to understand and communicate in multiple modes. For instance, he writes that "[n]on-discursive rhetoric actually makes knowledge *livable* in that it places knowledge in the realm of the senses rather than just in the realm of increasing abstraction" (p. 333). He sees a distinct advantage to nondiscursive rhetoric in that through nondiscursive rhetoric we are able to more fully experience knowledge—through senses, feelings, emotions, and so forth—which has been ignored in the composition classroom, and he advises us to teach our students particular values that are essential to multimodal composition.

Learn we must. Even though multimodal texts such as websites and e-books that combine text, video, and audio became abundant in the last decade, the field of composition has been slow to follow. As evidenced by the selections in this book, a growing number of scholars embrace studying and employing multimodal texts in their own research, and for some, in the classroom as well. However, multimodal composition has not yet become commonplace in our collective pedagogy. The authors in Part Three, however, show us the diverse and expansive meaning that composing in multiple modes can provide the writer.

WORKS CITED

Bolter, Jay David and Richard Grusin. *Remediation: Understanding New Media.* Cambridge: MIT Press, 2000. Print.

Handa, Carolyn. *Visual Rhetoric in a Digital World.* New York: Bedford/St. Martin's, 2004. Print.

Hill, Charles A., and Marguerite Helmers, eds. *Defining Visual Rhetorics.* Mahwah, NJ: Lawrence Erlbaum, 2003. Print.

Hocks, Mary E., and Michelle R. Kendrick, eds. *Eloquent Images: Word and Image in the Age of New Media.* Cambridge, MA: MIT P, 2003. Print.

13 Gains and Losses: New Forms of Texts, Knowledge, and Learning [1]

GUNTHER KRESS

1. FRAMING

Central assumptions of multimodal approaches to representation and communication are (a) that communication is always and inevitably multimodal; and (b) that each of the modes available for representation in a culture provides specific potentials and limitations for communication (Kress & van Leeuwen, 1996). The first assumption requires us to attend to all modes that are active in an instance of communication; the second requires us to attend to the specific meanings carried by the different modes in communicational ensembles (Kress & van Leeuwen, 2001). All this goes together with a kind of common sense, widely shared about public communication, that there has been and continues to be realignment in culturally valued modes. In particular, it seems evident to many commentators that writing is giving way, is being displaced by image in many instances of communication where previously it had held sway.

This realization calls forth a variety of responses, mostly negative, ranging from outright despair, anger, and nostalgia to some still utopian voices on the other end of the spectrum. The response is understandable given the long domination in the West of writing as the culturally most valued form of representation: and more, the long association of the mode of writing with the equally dominant, valued, and powerful medium, namely the book. The fragmentation of the constellation of mode of writing and medium of book has given rise to wide cultural pessimism: responses ranging from the attempts to reimpose the communicational givens of the past, in school curricula for instance, to intemperate outbursts in the various media; with political, social, economic, and cultural decline often all wound up together with this phenomenon in representation and communication.

The issue—given that representation, especially in the linguistic modes of speech and writing, is so closely bound up with social and ethical values— cannot be debated at the level of representation alone. It does, always, have to

From *Computers and Composition* 22 (2005): 5–22.

be seen in the wider framework of economic, political, social, cultural, and technological changes. This is so because on the one hand representation is used as a metaphor for social, cultural, and ethical issues, and because on the other hand representational changes do not happen in isolation. The technologies of representation and those of communication and/or dissemination are everywhere bound up with the larger, wider changes in the (global) economy, in social and political changes, and in accompanying ethnic and cultural changes. Nor can technology by itself be treated as causal. It too ties in with and is rolled up everywhere in this complex. None of this is new. Yet it needs to be reiterated each time the issue is discussed, in mantra-like fashion. Representation and communication are motivated by the social; its effects are outcomes of the economic and the political. To think or act otherwise is to follow phantoms.

2. A REVOLUTION IN THE CONSTELLATION OF MODES AND MEDIA

In this context, the purpose of my talk is to provide essential ways of making sense of the changes in the landscape of communication, provide means of describing and analysing what is going on, and to provide means of navigating between the Scylla of nostalgia and pessimism and the Charybdis of unwarranted optimism. Tools are needed that will allow us to describe what is going on, and theories are needed that can integrate such descriptions into explanatory frameworks. In this context, the emergence of multimodality as a focus in representation, linked for me with a social semiotic theory to account for meaning making, offers the theoretical and descriptive possibility of looking at the issue of changes in representation in a historical perspective, freed from either nostalgia and despair or utopianism. It offers the possibility of a relatively clear assessment of what I call "gains and losses" both representationally and communicationally.

The semiotic changes are vast enough to warrant the term "revolution," of two kinds; of the modes of representation on the one hand, from the centrality of writing to the increasing significance of image; and of the media of dissemination on the other, from the centrality of the medium of the book to the medium of the screen. The fact that these occur as constellations—medium of book with mode of writing and now medium of screen with mode of image—means that the effect has been experienced in an amplified form. The distinct cultural technologies for representation and for dissemination have become conflated—and not only in popular commonsense, so that the decline of the book has been seen as the decline of writing and vice versa.

I use the term "mode" for the culturally and socially produced resources for representation and "medium" as the term for the culturally produced means for distribution of these representations-as-meanings, that is, as messages. These technologies—those of representation, the modes, and those of dissemination, the media—are always both independent of and interdependent with each other. Each has its own quite specific powers and effects. As the constellation of book and writing had been so close and had existed over such long durations, the effects of each separately and of both jointly had not been separated out. It is essential that this should be done: They are distinct, with distinct affordances (for the modes) and distinct facilities (for the media) (Kress, 2003). To give just one, though a central effect of the facilities of the media, we can look at the figure of the author in relation to the medium of the book, especially in its traditional form, compared to the role of the author in relation to the medium of the screen.

What did this author know? As the author, J. W. Simms (1946) knew two things: He knew about his audience and he knew about his subject matter. About his audience he said, in the preface, "The prime instinct of almost any boy will be to make and to create. At seven he will 'wire' the whole house with his telephone system made from empty tins connected with varying lengths of string. . . . His elder brother will improve on this by purchasing a crystal, a telephone receiver, a. . . ." In other words, the author had insight into the life-world of his audience, and it is this that enabled him to assemble the materials that served to meet the second requirement; assembling and presenting the knowledge required for a specific need of the reader in that life-world. The author knew about the reader's world, and that enabled him to work on the reader's behalf to assemble the knowledge that would serve to meet a specific need in this instance. This knowledge was presented in chapters, each a coherent part of an overall body of knowledge presented in orderly fashion in the succession of chapters.

At this point, it is instructive to look at how this knowledge is set out: The chapters are numbered, and the assumption is that there is an apparent building from chapter to chapter: They are not to be read out of order. At the level of chapters, order is fixed. It is also fixed within the chapters and on the page in the reading path that organizes the reader's encounter with the text on the page. We start at the top left corner, move across the page, start at the left of the next line, and so on. Order is firmly coded: the order of chapters, the order pages, of lines and of the line, and, of course, within lines as language, the order of syntax. Within this order, the reader encounters the respective entities to be read: textual, lexical, grammatical and/or syntactic entities— chapters, paragraphs, lines; words, letters, punctuation marks, spaces. So-called proper reading had assumed that the reader adhered to this order; the notions of "reading against the grain" or "resistant reading" are of a much greater recency than this text—first published in 1920 (Kress, 1989).

We might stay with this example for a moment longer to see how reading worked. If order was fixed, as the order given by the author and naturalized by centuries of conventions of reading, then what was the reader's task, and what or where was the reader's freedom to act? My answer is that though order was given, strict, and in many ways fixed, the elements that the reader encountered along the route were quite open. Words are (relatively) empty entities—in a semiotic account they are signifiers to be filled with meaning rather than signs full of meaning, and the task of the reader is to fill these relatively vacant entities with her or his meaning. This is the task we call interpretation, namely interpreting what sign the writer may have intended to make with this signifier. We can easily check this with any text, though we will need to assume a scepsis about words and their meaning and about

FIGURE 13-1   *The Boy Electrician* (content pages and pages of text). (This figure has been reconstructed because reprint rights were not available for the original image. — Bedford Editors)

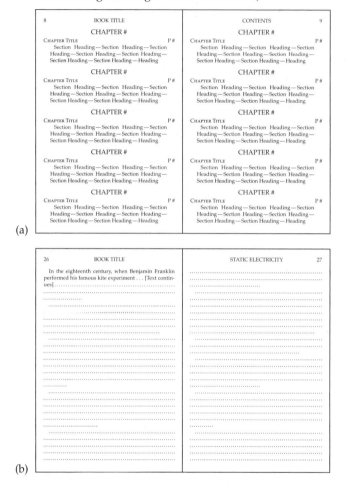

(a)

(b)

words in syntactic arrangements that we have been taught to leave aside when reading. The still existing common sense is that meaning in language is clear and reliable by contrast, with image for instance, which, in that same commonsense, is not solid or clear.

So in [Figure 13-1], we can start on the first line, with the locative and/or spatial preposition "in" and its metaphoric use here in a temporal environment; moving to the definite article "the" that seems so clear, yet is clear only in specific cultural contexts (for example, is what is meant "the" Chinese 18th century? or that of the Mayan calendar?) to the nominal *18th century* the obvious question "When in that century?" — "All throughout the century?" "At the beginning?" "Towards the end?"

Roland Barthes (1977) interestingly addressed this issue of the relative power of author or reader in 1968, in the context of a much wider challenge to power at that time. Theories of reading—as of language more widely—are ready, available, metaphors of the social. In reading the traditional page, the reader has to follow the strict order established by the writer while needing to interpret the word-signifiers, turning them into her or his signs. To illustrate the quantum change, the result of the changes mentioned earlier, here is a contemporary example: As late as 1992, the Institute of Education (IoE), where I now work, represented itself in its prospectus in much the way as *The Boy Electrician*. What was being represented was the structure of the institution, its departments and units, its courses, and the regulations pertaining to them. The order was that of the institution, and the knowledge was that of the institution: why it could do that and why it was similar in its social and/or semiotic principles to those of *The Boy Electrician* is that the assumption—entirely implicitly made and held—was that the structure of the institution and of its knowledge were identical with the needs of the life-worlds of the individuals who might come to it as its students. Readers were assumed to adapt to that order in their reading and then in the manner of their interaction with the institution.

Writing was the dominant mode in the prospectus, though there were some (black and white) images. The current home page is profoundly different. It is not organized following the logic of the traditional written page but following that of the image-based logic of contemporary pages. Tellingly and more significantly, this page has thirteen distinct entry points where the 1992 page had one. We can rightly ask what the significance of that might be. My explanation has to do with the notion of order: The traditional page had one entry point—though being so naturalized by centuries-long convention, it was not even noticeable as a feature. It was an entry point given by convention and used by the author (and the readers), who, remember, knew about the world of the audience. Access to the power of authorship was strictly governed. Here, on the webpage, the presence of thirteen entry points speaks of a very different principle: the author(s) of this page clearly have in mind that visitors will come to this page from quite different cultural and social spaces, in differing ways, and with differing interests, not necessarily known to or knowable by the maker(s) of the page. There is no pregiven, no clearly discernible reading path, either of the home page or of each individual page, or of the site as a whole (the issue of navigation, where maps are relatively unreliable).

The existence of the different entry points speaks of a sense of insecurity about the visitors, a feeling of fragmentation of the audience—who now are no longer just readers but visitors, a quite different action being implied in the change of name.

The organizing principle of this new page is the (assumed) shape of the life-worlds of potential visitors and the interests that arise out of their life-worlds. What the visitors come to find is not knowledge but information; in this new semiotic world, it is the readers who fashion their own knowledge, from information supplied by the makers of the site. That corresponds to a profound change in the situation of authors, readers, and knowledge: "Information is material which [sic] is selected by individuals to be transformed by

FIGURE 13-2   IoE prospectus and IoE home page.

(a)

(b)

them into knowledge to solve a problem in their life-world" (Böck, 2002, 2004). The order of this page and of the whole site is open—I won't even say relatively open, because even though the site and its potentials are constructed and structured and the designers of the site imagine the possibilities of reading, they are not enforced and the possibilities are large.

The principle of design underlying the IoE website is now the semiotically increasingly dominant one: The (imagined) interests of the visitors provide the principles for and of the ordering and/or structuring of the message-entities (it is not clear whether the use of the term page is still useful and apt, or whether it has now become too metaphorical not to be a problem) (Kress, 2003). This is so not only with websites (and their pages) but is increasingly becoming the case with paper-based media—whether newspapers, books and particularly information books (Moss, 2001), magazines but also television screens in differing genres of programming. We might summarize some of the changes in this way:

1929 (publication year of *The Boy Electrician*) and
1992 (publication year of *IoE Prospectus*)

- Given order, order designed by author.
- Page and book with single entry point.
- Knowledge produced by author on behalf of the audience.
- Author knows the life-world of audience and its requirements.
- Reading path fixed (though "naturalized" and hence invisible).
- Author fixes reader's "point of departure."
- Writing dominates the organization of the page.
- Writing is the dominant mode for the presentation of material (image as illustration).
- Use of mode governed by long-established convention: canonical use of modes.

2004

- Open order, order designed by reader.
- "Page" site with multiple entry points.
- Knowledge produced by visitor/reader in accord with the needs of their life-world.
- Page and/or message designers imagine the assumed characteristic of the life-world of their audience.
- Reading path designed by reader and/or visitor.
- Reader designs/selects her/his point of departure.
- Image dominates the organization of the "page."
- Image and writing potentially co-equal for the presentation of material.
- Use of mode governed by "aptness," insecurity about or absence of canonical modes.

There are revealing changes in vocabulary: for instance, from write (and read) to design; from reader to visitor, from page and/or text to message-entity; and others no doubt. And there are equally revealing changes in the principles of representation and organization: from the densely printed (relatively) mono-modal page to the multimodal screen and the new pages; from the conventions of page production to the mode of layout; from writing as dominant to image as dominant.

3. "Affordances": Logics of Modes; Principles of Ordering, and Wording versus Description

In an attempt to gain new insight into possibilities for representing, multimodal descriptions—and multimodal semiotics in particular—have turned away from the enchantment of linguistics with abstraction that had dominated the 20th century. That it had been a response to the prestige and power of the natural sciences and tried to turn linguistic phenomena as near as might be achieved into a resemblance of those that would mirror the phenomena of the natural sciences. By contrast, the emphasis in multimodal work is very much on the materiality of the resources for representation. One consequence is that a concept such as language is itself beginning to lose its plausibility, for at least two reasons: On the one hand, the material differences between speech and writing are so significant as to lead to real differences in the potentials of each for representation, a difference that can hardly be subsumed and accommodated under the one label; on the other hand, speech and writing are themselves composed of such diverse phenomena as to make it difficult to regard each as a unified, homogeneous resource. If we ask, "what do pitch-variation, syntax, vowel quality, energy variations (producing loudness and softness), lexis or textual organization actually share in common features?" then the answer, I take it, is "nothing." These are features—and the same kind of question can be asked of writing—of entirely different nature held together by the device of "grammar," a construct used to clamp together a set of diverse phenomena to produce the complex and diverse resources for representation that we call speech and writing. "Language," a label used to unify such already internally diverse resources, is, in that context, simply an abstraction of doubtful usefulness.

This then leaves the task of finding principles that will show the "affordances," distinct potentials and limitations for representation of the various modes. I use the term logics based on the difference in organization using the possibilities of time and organization using the possibilities of space. Each rests on the material specificity of modes. Speech uses the material of sound— perturbations, changes of pressure, in the air, received and/or interpreted as sound by the ear. This happens in time: alternations in pressure (as well as pitch variation—changes in the frequency of vibration of the vocal cords) take place in temporal succession. One sound happens after another, in language one word after another, one clause after another. Time and sequence in time provide the organizing principle for making meaning. Sequence is used to make meaning; being first has the potential to mean something other than being second or being last.

The meaning attached to first and second and last depends on the culture that has fashioned this resource into syntax and texture. Being first may mean being first in the speaker's attention (the theme of a sentence), or being first in power (the actor in a transitive clause), or being cause of an action, and no doubt many other possibilities. In a sentence such as "Jeremy married Amantha," Jeremy might be occupying first position because he is actor in this action and/or event, or because he is the one who was responsible for this action, or because I am closer to Jeremy as my friend than I am to Amantha; and indeed, he may have been causal in this event. In the two sentences "The sun rose and the mists dissolved" and "The mists dissolved and the sun rose," one clause rather than the other being first has effects on meaning: Not only is a causal relation implied, but there is a suggested shift in worlds: one the everyday world of everyday meteorological events, and the other the mystical world of mystery or fairy tale.

Sequence has effects for authorship and for reading. Hearers (and readers to a somewhat lesser extent) depend on the "unfolding," the revealing of elements one after the other to be able to make sense of the whole. This gives authors a specific power: readers are dependent—at least in their initial hearing and reading—on sequence and on sequential uncovering. It is the author's order, as mentioned earlier, that dominates, initially at least. If the hearer or the reader wishes to reorder what has just been said or what has been written, the recording has to be done on the basis of and against the author's prior ordering.

The logic of space works differently: In the message entity (the image), all elements are simultaneously present—even though they were, of course, in many forms of image—in drawing or in painting, though not in photography—placed there in time and even though the viewer traverses the image-elements in time. And so it is the viewer's action that orders the simultaneously present elements in relation to her or his interest. In spatially organized representation, the elements that are chosen for representation are simultaneously present, and it is their spatial arrangement that is used to make (one kind of) meaning (see Figures 13-1 and 13-2).

In Figure 13-3a Georgia stands on the right hand side of her mother; in Figure 13-3b she stands between her parents. I will not elaborate any more than I did in relation to the linguistic examples. In Figure 13-3b Georgia is the centre both of the representation and of the family (she was then the only child), framed by her parents; in Figure 13-3a she is on the outside of the group, though next to one parent—nearer to her mother and consequently more distant from the other. The relations between the three participants in the two images are structured and represented as being profoundly different. The means for making these meanings are the resources of spatial and simultaneous representation. Georgia has used other affordances of the spatial mode: size for instance. In reality, she was, at that time, taller than she has represented herself here; hence, her size is the representation and/or sign of an affective meaning: affectively she sees her parents as so much bigger. She has also used placement in the framed space, so that her father is, so to speak, lifted off the ground by several inches; in reality he was much shorter than his wife, but Georgia's sign endows him with the same height, though remaining accurate about his actual size. Colour is also affectively used: Her mother is drawn as much brighter, much more colourful than her father, more even than she has drawn herself.

The temporal and sequential logic of speech, and, leaning on speech, of writing, lends itself to the representation of actions and events in time; hence, the ubiquity of forms of narrative in human cultures; hence also the ubiquity of the event and action oriented uses of speech and writing. The question asked by speech, and by writing, is: "what were the salient events and in what (temporal) order did they occur?" The spatial and simultaneous logic of image-representation lends itself equally readily to the representation of salient entities and their (spatially expressed) relations. Display is, in respect to its prominence and significance and ubiquity, the analogue of narrative. The

Figure 13-3   Georgia's family.

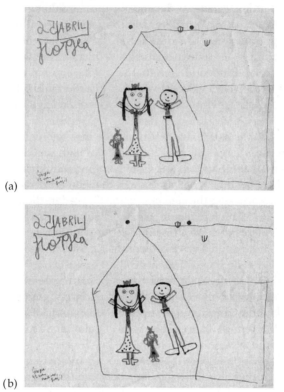

(a)

(b)

question asked by display is: "what were the salient entities in the visually encountered and recollected world, and in what order are they related?"

From these affordances, and from these logics, develop distinct ways of representing the world. In Figure 13-4, this is shown in the visual and verbal representation of a day at the British Museum in London. On the day after the visit by a class of 6-year-olds, the teacher asked the class to "write a story and draw a picture of our visit."

This example is entirely typical of the drawings and stories done by the children in this class. The "story"—a recount—is a chronologically ordered sequence of action-like events, realized here as actional clauses. The day, as recollected in the mode of (speech-like) writing was a day of action-events. The picture, by contrast, shows the salient recollected entities: the façade of the British Museum, as the backdrop to the other salient entities, two mummies, symmetrically arranged. This is not a story, not a recount, but a display: What is being displayed is a selection of elements encountered during the visit to the museum and recollected on the following day. The day, as recollected in the mode of image, was a day of encountering significant objects in a particular space. There is no hint of narration.

FIGURE 13-4   Visit to the British Museum.

The logics supply the raw stuff from which principles of ordering and their meanings are derived. The syntax of speech and of writing are developments from and elaborations of these. Similarly, the arrangements of visual representation, which we can also aptly call syntax, are also developments and elaborations from the logic of spatial display.

Materiality goes beyond the logics of modes: The materiality of sound offers potentials, as mentioned earlier, which different cultures have made use of in their different ways, and still do make use of: similarly with the materiality of graphic representation. We can take, as an instance, the matter of framing and investigate how framing is done in temporal and in spatial representations: in sound by pauses and silences, by lengthening, by intensifying and attenuation; with graphic matter through spaces, lines, spatial separation and connection, through punctuation marks of various kinds, colour bands, and so on. Materiality affects the core of representation: In speech through sounds as vocalic or consonantal conjoined into syllables that, when they become joined with meanings, change their character and function to become morphemes.

Speech and writing are, above all, modes founded on words in order, and image-representation is founded on depictions. The crucial difference is that words are highly conventionalised entities, and only exist in that manner. Otherwise, a sound-sequence—once taken out of the environment in which it was used—becomes difficult to interpret. Consequently, the stock of words in any one culture is always finite at any one moment—though, of course, it is continuously augmented from moment to moment. What is crucial is that if there is no word, then the possibility of representation and communication is ruled out. Only that which is worded can enter into communication; or else, that which is to be represented gets squeezed into the ill-fitting semantic shape of the existing word. Because words rely on convention and on conventional acceptance, words are always general and, therefore, vague. Words being nearly empty of meaning need filling with the hearer and/or reader's meaning. (Semiotically, words are signifiers, not signs: When they are used in representation they become signs—of the maker and of the receiver and/or remaker.)

We treat that as the act of interpretation. With depiction and with images the situation is different: that which I wish to depict I can depict, at the moment at any rate. I can draw whatever I like whenever I like to draw it. Unlike words, depictions are full of meaning; they are always specific. So on the one hand there is a finite stock of words—vague, general, nearly empty of meaning; on the other hand there is an infinitely large potential of depictions—precise, specific, and full of meaning. The former tend to occur in the fixed order of syntax, line, page, text; the latter tend to occur in an open order fixed by the reader and/or viewer's interest. This leads to the paradox of speech and writing as having a finite number of open, relatively vague elements in fixed order, and image or depiction having a possibility of infinitely many full, specific elements in an open order.

At this point, and with these tools, we can begin to ask the question of gains and losses, in the move from one mode and its arrangements to another mode and its different arrangements.

A final point to be made here is that of epistemological commitment. It arises from all that I have indicated. A small example will make the point. If I say, "A plant cell has a nucleus," expressing this bit of knowledge through the mode of writing (or speech) I have to relate the entity "plant cell" with the entity "nucleus" via the verb "have." This expresses a relation of possession, of ownership. In many languages, such as English, or French, or Farsi, or Urdu—languages of the Indo-European family—this is unavoidable. I have to use a word expressing a specific kind of relationship between cell and nucleus. When I draw a cell, say to demonstrate what it might be like, on a whiteboard, I will draw a circle-like entity and place a dot somewhere in that circle. I do not have to express anything about the characteristics of the relation between nucleus and cell—the spatial arrangement does that for me. However, anyone looking at the drawing is entitled to infer that where I have placed the dot is where the nucleus is supposed to be. The mode of depiction forces me into an epistemological commitment, different to that which writing also forced me to make. One is about position in a framed space; the other about a type of (named) relation. One asks questions that point towards causality, agency, power; the other asks questions about position in space, about relations of entities in the (framed pictorial) space. One has elements that are vaguely specified; the other elements that are fully specified. One has a fixed order, given by the author; the other a (relatively) open order established and/or designed by the viewer. One is a world in which causality is just about inescapably there; the other a world in which causality barely figures.

Speech and writing tell the world; depiction shows the world. In the one, the order of the world is that given by the author; in the other, the order of the world is yet to be designed (fully and/or definitively) by the viewer. These are not only different positionings in the world and to the world, with different epistemological positions and commitments, they also bestow different powers on the makers and remakers of representations.

4. BEYOND CRITIQUE TO DESIGN: INTEREST, SUBJECTIVITY, AND RHETORIC

Over the last five decades or so, social framings and attitudes to representation have been transformed in response to or in line with social changes. Whereas, in the 1950s there was a clear sense of convention in relation to representation in speech or in writing, where it appeared under labels such as competence, or mastery, and maybe others, such as elegance, etc. In the late 1960s and in the 1970s that sense was replaced by the term critique. Convention is the result of social power over time, expressed in the form of laws and rules. It takes but little work to uncover the homologies that exist between the social conventions and their appearance as linguistic rules. As language can be described as a natural phenomenon, linguistic rules can be described as natural rules, and these natural rules are used as both metaphors for the social and as means of enforcing the social conventions. Competence is then both social and natural and more potent for seeming the latter rather than the former. Competence expresses a common acceptance and implementation of rules; all those who share the same competence are (naturally and) socially the same.

Critique attempted to unsettle the naturalization of the social and did so particularly through showing the workings of power, whether in representation and communication or elsewhere. However, critique in communication necessarily works on what has been, what is established, and on the agendas of others—it looks back at what has been done by others. It challenges the existing configurations of power and expects that in exposing inequities more equitable social arrangements could be developed. In terms of representation that would amount—at that time when the focus was clearly linguistic—to lessening the effects of power and its realization in linguistic form.

Those who participated in the project of critique in more general terms had the intention of bringing systems and structures into crisis: that was, of course, very much the climate of the times, even though paradoxically it happened when the system had already come into crisis. In retrospect it is clear that aspects of the formerly seemingly fixed social arrangements were already creaking and breaking up. Now, in the early part of the 21st century, there is no need for bringing the social into crisis: It decidedly is. Hence, the project of critique seems somewhat beside the point. In the domain of representation and communication, the crisis manifests itself at every point: genres are insecure; canonical forms of representation have come into question; the dominant modes of representation of speech and writing are being pushed to the margins of representation and replaced at the centre by the mode of image and by others. The once dominant paper-based media—the newspaper and the book above all—are giving way to the screen, or, in as far as they remain as powerful media, are shaped in their appearance, form, and function by the appearances and forms of the newly powerful, the now mythically and increasingly actually dominant medium of the screen.

As one effect of the social and the representational changes, practices of writing and reading have changed and are changing. In a multimodal text, writing may be central, or it may not; on screens writing may not feature in multimodal texts that use sound-effect and the soundtrack of a musical score, use speech, moving and still images of various kinds. Reading has to be rethought given that the commonsense of what reading is was developed in the era of the unquestioned dominance of writing, in constellation with the unquestioned dominance of the medium of the book.

In many ways, it will repay to look once again at the etymology of the English word "read," and its origins in a family where it meant things like advice (the English "-red-" in the name Ethelred or the "-read-" in the epithet "unready"; or the German word "Rat," counsel or advice, but also Rätsel for riddle or mystery). Reading as taking meaning and making meaning from many sources of information, from many different sign-systems, will become the new common sense. But the example of the IoE webpage also shows another crucial change in the meanings of "reading": namely what I have called "reading as design" (Kress, 2004). In relation to message entities (texts?) such as that, the reader finds her or his way around the matter presented on that page, and orders it according to principles, as I suggested, that arise from the reader's life-world. In effect, out of material presented (by an author, designer, and/or design-team?) on a page, the reader designs a coherent complex sign that corresponds to the needs that she or he has. That is a profoundly different notion of reading than that of decoding, the dominant version for many decades and made iconic by the electrical engineering model of Claude Shannon and Warren Weaver (1949).

The new constellation of image and screen—where screen, the contemporary canvas, is dominated by the logic of image—means that the practices of reading becoming dominant are the practices derived from the engagement with image and/or depiction in which the reader designs the meaning from materials made available on the screen—and by transference back to the traditional media—on the new kinds of pages, which are now also organized on these principles and read in line with them.

Where with traditional pages, in the former semiotic landscape, it was the power of the author that ruled, here, it is the interest of the reader, derived from the contingencies and needs of their life-worlds. Of course, this is stating

FIGURE 13-5   The beach at Walberswick from *The Rings of Saturn*.

lower, to the water below them. Whenever they came towards me, fast as bullets, some seemed to vanish right beneath my feet, as if into the very ground. I went to the edge of the cliff and saw that they had dug their nesting holes into the topmost layer of clay, one beside the other. I was thus standing on perforated ground, as it were, which might have given way at any moment. Nevertheless, I laid my head back as far as I could, as I did as a boy for a dare on the flat tin roof of the two-storey apiary, fixed my eyes on the zenith, then lowered my gaze till it met the horizon, and drew it in across the water, to the narrow strip of beach some twenty yards below. As I tried to suppress the mounting sense of dizziness, breathing out and taking a step backwards, I thought I saw something of an odd, pallid colour move on the shoreline. I crouched down and, overcome by a sudden panic, looked over the edge. A couple lay down there, in the bottom of the pit, as I thought: a man stretched full length over another body of which nothing was visible but the legs, spread and angled. In the startled moment when that image went through me, which lasted an eternity, it seemed as if the man's feet twitched like those of one just hanged. Now, though, he lay still, and the woman too was still and motionless. Misshapen, like some great mollusc washed ashore, they lay there, to all appearances a single being, a many-limbed, two-headed monster that had drifted in from far out at sea, the last of a prodigious species, its life ebbing from it with each breath expired through its nostrils. Filled with consternation, I stood up once more, shaking as if it were the first time in my life that I had got to my feet, and left the place, which seemed fear-some to me now, taking the path that descended from the cliff-top

to where the beach spread out on the southerly side. Far off in front of me lay Southwold, a cluster of distant buildings, clumps of trees, and a snow-white lighthouse, beneath a dark sky. Before I reached the town, the first drops of rain were falling. I turned to look back down the deserted stretch I had come by, and could no longer have said whether I had really seen the pale sea monster at the foot of the Covehithe cliffs or whether I had imagined it.

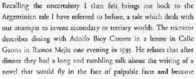

Recalling the uncertainty I then felt brings me back to the Argentinian tale I have referred to before, a tale which deals with our attempts to invent secondary or tertiary worlds. The narrator describes dining with Adolfo Bioy Casares in a house in Calle Gaona in Ramos Mejía one evening in 1935. He relates that after dinner they had a long and rambling talk about the writing of a novel that would fly in the face of palpable facts and become

the matter in extreme form: Traditional pages will continue to exist, for a variety of reasons: For one thing, this revolution is generation-related; for another, it inevitably has a power dimension: The elites will continue to use writing as their preferred mode, and hence, the page in its traditional form. And then there is the fact of affordance; representations that rely on the affordance of the mode of speech and writing can now do so for that reason. Stories will continue to be told, and narratives will continue to be written—because the two modes are apt means for doing so. But it is essential to keep an open mind on this. Figure 13-5 shows a page from W. G. Sebald's (1998) novel *The Rings of Saturn*.

One feature of Sebald's novels is that intensely ordinary, banal images appear on the pages. My hunch is that he used them for the reasons that I have hinted at: different forms of engagement with the world, different modes of reading, different pace—out of the temporal, into the spatial.

If the changed notions of reading are bringing about changes in what readers are, then new modal uses and new media are having equally profound effects on writing and on the notion of author and of authority. The screen offers the facility in ways that the book did not do overtly or concretely offer for the reader to become author, even in the process of reading. I can change the text that comes to me on the screen. My means of disseminating my message are now much like those of other authors. That factor, of course, brings about a radical change to notions of authority: When everyone can be an author authority is severely challenged. The social frames that had supported the figure of the author have disappeared or are disappearing and with that the force of social power that vested authority in the work of the author.

The new media make it possible to use the mode that seems most apt for the purposes of representation and communication: If I need to represent something best done as image I can now do so, similarly with writing. Aptness of mode to the characteristics of that represented is much more a feature now—it is a facility of the new media. Aptness of mode and what is represented is not the only issue: Equally significant now is the aptness of fit between mode and audience. I can now choose the mode according to what I know or might imagine is the preferred mode of the audience I have in mind. This links directly to the crisis in both social framings and in representation: If I can now no longer rely on convention to make my audience take information in modes that are not congenial to them, then questions of my relation to the audience have to become foregrounded, hence the re-emergence over the last two decades of the issue of rhetoric. It is not that rhetorical issues did not exist prior to that, it is that prior to that I could rely on the grooved, habituated forms whether in text-type or in mode or in medium. That certainty is gone; each occasion of representation and communication now becomes one in which the issue of my relation to my audience has to be newly considered and settled on.

The new freedoms for authors and readers bring changes in practices: The question of rhetoric makes my subjectivity in this instance of communication now an issue each time anew. Presenting myself as the appropriate subject for this occasion of communication means that I am each time performing, staging, myself. When there is no stability to authorship or readership that has to be produced each time for this audience, on this occasion. So, whether in choice of genre, in choice of medium or in choice of mode subjectivity is at issue.

Figure 13-6 shows a now entirely usual teaching aid: textbook pages in school science are like that; forty, even thirty years earlier they would have been covered in writing. It is possible to ask the questions I had asked earlier: What does reading mean here? How is this page read? Which mode is dominant? Which mode carries which kind of information? What kinds of information are not focussed on here? What is the reading path—if any? and so on. The question I want to pose here, however, is different: What is the assumed subjectivity of the students to whom not just this aspect of the curriculum but nearly all of science is presented in this manner? And equally, what is the subjectivity of the science teacher who teaches science in this manner? We might imagine an answer by comparing textbook pages of this kind with textbook pages of some forty years ago and ask about implied notions of convention, of competence, of knowledge, and of authority. We would also, of course, need to ask about the subject matter of science itself, when its canonical forms of representation have moved from those of the traditional textbook to those such as here, or equally distinct, to those students now encounter in CD ROMs (Jewitt, 2003).

FIGURE 13-6   The Earth.

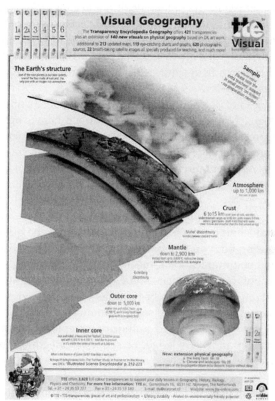

5. APT THEORIES OF MEANING, LEARNING, AND WRITING

It seems clear to me that we cannot continue with existing theories of meaning given the facts of the changes in the social, economic and cultural domain. At the moment, our theories come from the era dominated by notions of conventions and competence, whereas we need theories apt for an era of radical instability. Instead of competence in relation to stable social frames and stable resources for representation, we need the notion of design, which says: In this social and cultural environment, with these demands for communication of these materials, for that audience, with these resources, and given these interests of mine, what is the design that best meets these requirements? Design focuses forward; it assumes that resources are never entirely apt but will need to be transformed in relation to all the contingencies of this environment now and the demands made. The focus on transformation rather than on acquisition makes the designer agentive—in relation to existing socially and culturally made resources, social environments in specific, with the designer's interests in this occasion of design and in relation to that audience (Jewitt & Kress, 2003).

Agency of the individual who has a social history, a present social location, an understanding of the potentials of the resources for communication, and who acts transformationally on the resources environment and, thereby, on self are requirements of communication. Where critique unsettled, design shapes, or has the potential always to shape. It makes individual action central, though always in a field saturated with the past work of others and the present existence of power.

Semiotics does not deal with learning; just as pedagogy or psychology do not deal with signs. However, the process described here is in my view a description of the processes of learning: transformative engagement in the world, transformation constantly of the self in that engagement, transformation of the resources for representation outwardly and inwardly.

6. GAINS AND LOSSES

I have suggested some means for making inroads into the question of gains and losses: focusing both on the material and/or semiotic mean, the modes, and the material communicational means, the media, seeing both necessarily in the context of the larger social and cultural, political, and economic environment. This might enable the beginnings of working descriptively and analytically here—whether around social, communicational, and/or semiotic categories such as authorship and authority, or epistemological categories such as information and knowledge, or semiotic categories such as modes and their affordances, or pedagogic and/or psychological categories such as learning.

Description and analysis is one part of the task. Another, more important part, is the assessment of the social effects of these changes. And even more importantly for me is the question of my own role and my own responsibilities: Do I have a say? Do I have a responsibility not only to describe but also to propose? Do I have the right to oppose? Could I say that these forms that we had—to take a simple example, forms of syntactic complexity such as a complex sentence—are disappearing in this change? But these forms had real effects on what they provided for humans in their engagement with the world, their way of dealing with the world, in terms of conceptual and therefore intellectual power? Could I say that different forms of imagination are fostered and made possible—or some ruled out—by different configurations and uses of modes, and I think that we should strive to be conservatives in some instances and in some respects because these forms of imagination seem one valuable means of being human?

And can I say that depiction is a better means of dealing with much in the world than writing or speech could be? Could I say that the need to be forced into the automatic expression of temporality and causality in speech or writing is something that I not only do not wish but which may be a distortion of the way the world is? Could we have a better physics if image became more dominant? Would the next generation of children actually be much more attuned to truth through the specificity of depiction rather than the vagueness of word? And would it not be a better situation if we could all be authors of apt and accurate representations? And if we took our cue not from conventionally established authority but, equipped with the necessary aesthetic and ethical navigational aids, we were to establish authority and at times even knowledge for ourselves, would that not be a preferable position?

Acknowledgment   I wish to thank Eve Bearn for permission to use the image that forms Figure 13.4, Visit to the British Museum.

NOTE

1. This paper was first presented as one of the featured sessions at the Conference on College Composition and Communication (CCCC) in San Antonio, Texas, on 26 March 2004.

REFERENCES

Barthes, Roland. (1977). The death of the author. In *Image—music—text*. London: Fontana.
Böck, Margit. (2002). Information, wissen und medialer wandel. *Medien Journal, 27*(1), 51–65.
Böck, Margit. (2004). Family snaps: Life worlds and information habitus. *Journal of Visual Communication, 3*(3), 281–293.
Jewitt, Carey. (2003). Computer-mediated learning: The multimodal construction of mathematical entities on screen. In Jewitt Carey & Gunther Kress (Eds.), *Multimodal literacy* (pp. 34–55). New York: Peter Lang.
Kress, Gunther. (1989). *Linguistic processes in sociocultural practices.* Oxford: Oxford University Press.
Kress, Gunther. (2003). *Literacy in the new media age.* London: Routledge.
Kress, Gunther. (2004, March). Gains and losses: New forms of texts, knowledge, and learning. In *Session presented at the Conference on College Composition and Communication.*
Kress, Gunther, & Jewitt, Carey (2003). *Multimodal Literacy.* New York: Peter Lang.
Kress, Gunther, & van Leeuwen, Theo. (1996). *Reading images: The grammar of graphic design.* London: Routledge.
Kress, Gunther, & van Leeuwen, Theo. (2001). *Multimodal discourse: The modes and media of contemporary communication.* London: Edward Arnold.
Moss, Gemma. (2001). Putting the text back into practice: Junior age non-fiction as objects of design. In Jewitt Carey & Gunther Kress (Eds.), *Multimodal literacy* (pp. 73–87). New York: Peter Lang.
Sebald, W. G. (1998). *The rings of Saturn.* London: Vintage.
Shannon, Claude, & Warren, Weaver. (1949). *The mathematical theory of communication.* Urbana, IL: University of Illinois Press.
Simms, J. W. (1946). *The boy electrician.* London: Harrap.

14 awaywithwords: On the Possibilities in Unavailable Designs

ANNE FRANCES WYSOCKI

1. Introduction

You have assigned a research paper in a graduate class you teach. Under what conditions would you accept a paper handwritten in crayon on colored construction paper?

If you can imagine no conditions whatsoever, then for you color of paper and technologies of print typography are like water or stones: things whose natural properties (seem to) necessarily constrain how we can use them. We do not attempt to make soup from stones nor do we imagine early hominids attacking mammoths by throwing water at them. If paper and typography are similar in having such inherent constraints, then it is the neat rows of typographically clean letters on letter-size white paper that are necessary for serious thought.

But.

My claim about the limitations of water, at least, are incorrect, for we can and do use water as weapon, as when police used high-pressure hoses on 1960s Civil Rights marchers in the southern United States. The lesson is that things can be put to many uses, often neither just nor humane. And were we in our classes to study the pressurized water-as-weapon as an example of such use, we would not focus on what it was about water alone that allowed it to be used so against bodies; although one could argue that it was precisely the natural qualities or constraints[1] of water that allow it to be pressurized and so used, were we to talk about this situation only in terms of the water we could rightfully be criticized for acting as though it is ever reasonable to exclude considerations of human life and rights from our work. Instead, in examining this use, we might question what in the context and purposes of the police allowed them to use water in such a way. We might develop an intriguing study into contemporary relations among technologies of water use, law enforcement, and White imaginations about Black bodies. In such a study, we might also learn about the resistances, actions, and particular understand-

From *Computers and Composition* 22 (2005): 55–62.

ings of material things like water that encourage change in relations among people.

In the preceding paragraphs I am, obviously, trying to use water and its varied applications as an analogy for the materials we use in building communications. If our particular uses of water as weapon—or as soup, swimming place, trash receptacle (as the lake on which we live was used in the nineteenth century), energy generator, scarce natural resource—cannot be separated from the relations that hold among people in particular places and times, then how can we believe that whatever we put on paper or the different screens we use—or the paper or screen itself—can be so separated? If how we conceive of water is unseparable from place and time, how can our communication materials, for which we can make no similar claim to naturalness as we can with water, be otherwise?

My desire in this writing, then, is to push at the edges of where Gunther Kress (2005) directs our attentions in many of his writings. I am in happy agreement with him on the need to encourage a rhetorical focus in our teaching—

> In this social and cultural environment, with these demands for communication of these materials, for that audience, with these resources, and given these interests of mine, what is the design which best meets these requirements? (p. 299 in this volume)

—for my experiences working on interdisciplinary software development teams, or with artists working in a range of media, or with people in classes developing instructional materials, have taught me that the question he asks above—entwining context, purpose, audience, and communication strategies (including material choices)—is an approach that helps people working both within and across disciplines or materials to produce effective communication. But there is an addition—or an expansion—that I want to foreground here: I have learned in the process of developing communications that it is always worth asking how our materials have acquired the constraints they have and hence why, often, certain materials and designs are not considered available for certain uses.[2] As with water, constraints of communication materials are often social and historical; to ask after the constraints as we teach or compose can help us understand how material choices in producing communications articulate to social practices we may not otherwise wish to reproduce. That is why, then, I wish to question what becomes unavailable when we think of word and image as Kress has suggested we do, as bound logically and respectively with time and with space.

Did you read my title as "a way with words" or "away with words"? The potential ambiguity, I think, shows how a particular visual space has become natural to how we now read. Space between words has not always been a function of written texts in the West. Our current practices of spacing text on a page developed over hundreds of years, catching on only slowly—as Paul Saenger (1997) has demonstrated through close analysis of manuscripts from throughout Europe—from the seventh through the twelfth centuries and developing out of (Saenger argued) particular practices in Irish monasteries. The development of consistent spacing of words—of a consistent notion of what constitutes a "word" on a page and hence conceptually—seems to have accompanied a shift from the social reading of texts to silent and individual readings. Saenger wanted to argue, also, that it is space between words on a page that—precisely because it allowed or encouraged individual silent reading—gave rise to notions of individuality and so to individual political responsibility (264–276). I am not willing to go that far with him, because his arguments (like those of McLuhan) tend to technological determinism, where it is simply and only the shape of what is on the page or of a book itself that causes immense shifts in human behavior, but Saenger's arguments, like the much simpler example of my title, do ask us to acknowledge that how we use space on pages affects how we read and understand. Saenger's arguments also asked us to acknowledge that space on pages both shapes and grows out of how we understand what words, texts, and reading are: Are they objects and practices embedded (for example) in the shared vocal work of monasteries or in the silence of a far library carrel?

The spaces of pages can also articulate with our larger sense of the spaces within which we read. In a study that entwines captivity narratives from the earliest days of the United States with details of the publication of Emily Dickinson's poetry, Susan Howe (1993), for example, has argued that editing practices that constrain punctuation and unconventional uses of spacing in writing correlate to an American desire to tame space by shaping wilderness into a bright, tight comprehensible regularity—whether wilderness be the dark forest at one's door or the imagined darkness of women's internal lives.[3]

When we speak of the various kinds of space we can use when we shape alphabetic text, then—when we speak of the tops and bottoms of pages, and of the left and right, and the placement of textual elements—we tie into other spatial understandings we have of our embodied worlds, as Kress and Theo van Leeuwen (1996) or Keith A. Smith (1995), for example, have argued that in addition to what I've described above. There is also the front of a book and its back, and all the spatial issues of orientation within a text that so vexed early (and ongoing) developers of hypertext as readers complained that they could not find their ways back to a particular page or could not remember where a text was because on-screen texts did not provide the same learned spatial memory cues as pages in books.

To say then, as Kress does, that what we need to ask when we read is "What are the salient events and in what (temporal) order did they occur?" is not wrong, but I believe—based even on the little I have written about space and words above—it is incomplete. If we are to help people in our classes learn how to compose texts that function as they hope, they need to consider how they use the spaces and not just one time that can be shaped on pages. They also need to question how they have come to understand the spaces of pages so that they can, if need be, use different spaces, potentially powerful spaces that—as Howe, for example, has described—have been rendered unavailable by naturalized, unquestioned practice.

When Kress claims that words are governed by a "temporal and sequential logic," his next move is predictable. Because he has implicitly accepted another logic, that of dichotomous splitting, he must, when he grants certain qualities to words, grant the opposite qualities to what he opposes to words — what he names "image-representations." "Image-representations," therefore, must be governed by a "spatial and simultaneous logic."

There is much to question about using a logic of dichotomies in thinking about the possibilities of multimodalities.

There is, of course, the general questioning of dichotomies and dichotomous thinking that has sparked so much late-twentieth and early twenty-first century writing. There ought to be no need for me to repeat what others have written as they have detailed how, since at least the time of Pythagoras, the engine of dichotomies has driven what many now consider most problematic in western thought.[4]

But for the particular dichotomy with which Kress spends so much time, that of word and image, I think it is probably worth mentioning how W. J. T. Mitchell (1986), for example, has examined the historical dance of word and image in the writings of theorists like Lessing, Locke, and Edmund Burke. Mitchell argued that the separation between these two terms is often the same separation — with all its implications for how we conceive of and so treat each other — that holds between male and female, reason and emotion, civilized and barbarian.[5] To treat the realm of modalities as so divided would seem to me to be inviting us in directions we might otherwise want to question. Instead, we should acknowledge that when we work with what is on pages or other surfaces, alphabetic text is always part of what must be visually arranged and can be designed to call more or less visual attention to itself (with the current academic and literary convention to be that of calling less attention to itself).[6]

It is also worth considering what happens when "image" is used to represent all that is not made exclusively of words. First, even if I were to pretend that the repertoire of communication materials available to us has nothing to do with other practices that shape what we do in the world, I think that "images" — if by that term we mean what many of us implicitly imagine when the term is used, a page-sized or no more than 3" by 3" realistically representational photograph, drawing, or painting — nonetheless exceed logics of space. Such images can appear to be moments pulled out of sequential time because we can apparently see what is in the image all at once, given the angles of vision afforded by our human eyes and, importantly, given the particularly designed compositions of many such objects. In a painted portrait or photograph of a single person or a small group that fills the frame of the image, we see the composition as singular, and then — in looking at the image's elements to understand better how the composition works — we see how the elements relate to each other, what is at top, what is at bottom, what is at left, what is at right: We notice how the elements have been arranged so that we see them in some ordering. What has the composer emphasized for us to see first and what elements are treated so as to retreat into the background to be noticed later, if at all? Notice, then, too, that temporal strategies of composition are very much present even in images that we can apparently perceive all at once. But even visually designed objects that fit the definition I have given of image can more emphatically emphasize how time can be variously present in such objects: think of any painting by Brueghel, such as "Children's Games" or "The Black Death," which are small paintings and yet they give us no way to see what is in them all at once; they require considerable time for separating out the elements and finding compositional structure.

But perhaps more importantly, were we to consider "word" in this same commonsensical way as "image" is here, limiting it to a particular size and to a set of compositional strategies and means of production, it would be as though we were asking people in our classes to go out into the world believing that the only writing everyone everywhere ever does is the academic research essay. We certainly do encounter innumerable visual representations that follow the commonsense definition of image I gave above: We find such images in our wallets, magazines, CD racks, and photo albums, as well as on the walls of our homes and museums and on computer monitors. But it does not take much additional looking to see films, billboards, decorated fingernails, sculptures, typography, the Gilmore Girls, abstract non-representational paintings or animations, the backs of shampoo bottles or the fronts of T-shirts, maps, Amy's or Kristin's tattoos, advertising on the sides of trucks, USA Today's illustrated graphs, the interiors of churches and schools and conference presentation rooms, Carole Maso's repeated use of a Giotto fresco in a novel, any car . . . ; you will undoubtedly have thought of more.

To compare just two of the visually designed objects I listed above, for example a tattoo and a film, is to quickly see that their particular uses of time and space and their social functionings—how different people in different places and times understand what they do—are different. And so to use image to name some class of objects that function in opposition to word is thus either to make an arbitrary cut into the world of designed visual objects or to try to encompass a class so large the encompassing term loses function. To say that all these objects rely on a logic of space is to miss their widely varying compositional potentials.

Like Kress, I too want to understand what is gained and what is lost through any communication practice, especially as computer technologies heighten our awareness of the visuality of texts—but I also want to understand what is possible. If human practices do entwine, as I have been arguing, to the extent that the spacing of lettershapes on a piece of paper reflects and helps continue unquestioned restrictions on behavior or that a habit of understanding words and images as opposites reflects and helps continue beliefs about relations between men and women, then it is possible that trying new spaces on pages or exploring the visuality of alphabetic text can be seeds for changes in such practices and beliefs. But we can only do this if we look beyond what appear to be constraints. As we analyze and produce communications, we need to be asking not only what is expected by a particular audience in a particular context but also what they might not expect, what they might not be prepared to see. It is in the apparently unavailable designs—Emily Dickinson's idiosyncratically punctuated handwriting that has only recently been published as she spaced it on the page or a graduate-level essay composed in crayon on colored paper — that we can see what beliefs and constraints are held within readily available, conventionalized design. By focusing on the human shaping of material, and on the ties of material to human practices, we might be in better positions to ask after the consequences not only of how we use water but also of how we use paper, ink, and pixels to shape — for better or worse — the actions of others.

NOTES

1. I have purposefully avoided using "affordance" here to avoid using the time of this paper to debate or attempt to fix definitions, even though what affordance exists to fix is precisely what is at stake in what I write. What is at stake is the independent life of things — whether those things are water or the shapes of ink on paper: What in any thing is a quality independent of human action and what results from human action and habit? James Gibson's (1979) original discussion of affordance (he said of the term at the time, "I have made it up" [127]) was meant to "impl[y] the complementarity of the animal and the environment" (127), and that "affordances are properties of things taken with reference to an observer but not properties of the experiences of the observer" (137). Gibson acknowledged, "these are slippery terms that should only be used with great care, but if their meanings are pinned down to biological and behavioral facts the danger of confusion can be minimized" (137). Twenty years later, Donald Norman (1999) wrote, "I introduced the term affordance to design in my book 'The Psychology of Everyday Things.' . . . The concept has caught on, but not always with true understanding. Part of the blame lies with me: I should have used the term 'perceived affordance,' for in design we care much more about what the user perceives than what is actually true." Norman went on to differentiate among real and perceived affordances as well as among physical, logical, and cultural constraints (and sometimes he replaced "constraints" with "conventions" when he discussed what develops out of culture); in spite of or perhaps because of these careful delineations, Norman also wrote that "I suspect that none of us know all the affordances of even everyday objects." The slipperiness of "affordance" — as of "biological and behavioral facts" or even of "convention" — results precisely from our inability to fix, with any finality, what the things of our world are capable of doing as we use them within the complex contexts in which we live. And so I have tried with purpose in this paper to use terms like "constraint" and even "convention" that (I hope) are less fixed in our language practices, to hold onto the messiness of how we live with things that both resist and work with us and to hold on, therefore, to considering our communication materials as things whose possibilities we should be trying to open and understand rather than fix.

2. My use of "unavailable designs" rests, obviously and with thanks, on the New London Group's highly useful notion of "available designs." As I understand the term, available designs, the "resources for Design" (p. 194), are what communicators can observe in use around them as they prepare to design new communications; as examples, the New London Group (NLG) mentioned the "'grammars' of various semiotic systems" and "orders of discourse," which include "particular Design conventions" such as "styles, genres, dialects, and voices" (p. 194). As the NLG described the design process, communicators draw on available designs in designing (which also includes "reading, seeing, and listening" [p. 195]), which involves re-presenting and recontextualizing available designs in order to develop the redesigned, which is always a "transformed meaning," "founded in historically and culturally received patterns of meaning" (p. 196). This process can imply certain circularity, with the redesigned then becoming itself an available design for the next go-round. I am curious about how we can break this circle — should we need to — given (as I argue here) how unquestioned, naturalized communication habits can reproduce (another circular process) social practices we might not want. As I argue in this paper, the notion of "unavailable designs" helps get at this by encouraging us to explore unconventional or outsider designs, which might allow of richer transformation — as long as we figure out strategies for helping audiences understand why we do such experimenting. But that is the subject of other writing.

3. For a perspective that focuses on using textual practices to tame social classes rather than genders, see Adrian Johns (1998) (408–428), for a discussion of seventeenth century British attitudes toward — and considerations of how to use reading to control — enthusiasm.

4. Oh heck, let's see: see almost anything by Donna Haraway or by Derrida, for starts.

5. For another perspective on how differing approaches to representation — roughly sketched as the verbal and visual — are historically shaped and situated, see Wendy Steiner (1982).

For other arguments on social consequences of how we have at this time distinguished words from visual work, see Robert Romanyshyn (1989, 1993).

6. For discussion of the development of pages that call little visual attention to themselves, pages in which tightly regulated lettershapes are the bulk of what is visible, see, for example, Kress and van Leeuwen (1996) concerning the work done by ruling classes in the late nineteenth century to preserve their cultural position by claiming the "densely written page" as their own while shaping layout and variety for "'the masses,' or children" (185–186). See also Johanna Drucker (1994) on "unmarked pages" and how such pages develop closely alongside practices of industrialization and standardization; Robin Kinross similarly argued that dreams of neutrality in page layout— dreams of pages whose layout has nothing to do with contemporary ideologies—are tied to specific social structurings.

REFERENCES

Drucker, Johanna. (1994). *The visible word: Experimental typography and modern art, 1909–1923*. Chicago: The University of Chicago Press.
Gibson, James J. (1979). *The ecological approach to visual perception*. Boston: Houghton-Mifflin.
Haraway, Donna. (1991). *Simians, cyborgs, and Women: The reinvention of nature*. New York: Routledge.
Howe, Susan. (1993). *The birth-mark: Unsettling the wilderness in American literary history*. Hanover, NH: Wesleyan UP.
Johns, Adrian. (1998). *The nature of the book: Print and knowledge in the making*. Chicago: University of Chicago Press.
Kinross, Robin. The rhetoric of neutrality. *Design Issues, II*(2), 18–30.
Kress, Gunther. (2005). *Gains and losses: New forms of texts, knowledge, and learning*. Computers and Composition, 22(1).
Kress, Gunther, & van Leeuwen, Theo. (1996). *Reading images: The grammar of visual design*. London: Routledge.
Mitchell, W. J. T. (1986). *Iconology: Image, text, ideology*. Chicago: University of Chicago Press.
Norman, Donald A. *Affordances and design*. Retrieved August 15, 2004, from <http://www.jnd.org/dn.mss/affordances-and-design.html>.
Romanyshn, Robert. (1989). *Technology as symptom and dream*. London: Routledge.
Romanyshn, Robert. (1993). The despotic eye and its shadow: Media image in the age of literacy. In David Michael Levin (Ed.), *Modernity and the hegemony of vision* (pp. 339–360). Berkeley, CA: University of California Press.
Saenger, Paul. (1997). *Space between words: The origins of silent reading*. Stanford, CA: Stanford University Press.
Smith, Keith A. (1995). *Text in the book format*. Rochester, NY: Keith A. Smith Books.
Steiner, Wendy. (1982). *The colors of rhetoric: Problems in the relation between modern literature and painting*. Chicago: University of Chicago Press.
The New London Group. (2000). A pedagogy of multiliteracies: Designing social futures. In Bill Cope & Mary Kalantzis (Eds.), *Multiliteracies: Literacy learning and the design of social futures* (pp. 9–37). London: Routledge.

15

Multimodality, "Reading," and "Writing" for the 21st Century

CAREY JEWITT

As words fly onto the computer screen, revolve, and dissolve, image, sound, and movement enter school classrooms in "new" and significant ways, ways that reconfigure the relationship of image and word. In this paper I discuss these "new" modal configurations and explore how they impact on students' text production and reading in English schools. I look at the changing role of writing on screen, in particular how the visual character of writing and the increasingly dominant role of image unsettle and decentre the predominance of word. Through illustrative examples of ICT applications and students' interaction with these in school English and science (and games in a home context), I explore how they seem to promote image over writing. More generally, I discuss what all of this means for literacy and how readers of school age interpret multimodal texts.

INTRODUCTION

Print- and screen-based technologies make available different modes and semiotic resources in ways that shape processes of making meaning. The particular material and social affordances (Kress & van Leeuwen, 2001; van Leeuwen, 2005) of new technologies and screen, as opposed to page, have led to the reconfiguration of image and writing on screen in ways that are significant for writing and reading. In this paper I describe some of these configurations and explore the design decisions made about when and how writing, speech, and image are used to mediate meaning making. My intention throughout the paper is to challenge the educational foregrounding of the written word and to establish the need for educational research and practice to look beyond the linguistic. In the process I hope to demonstrate how useful multimodal analysis can be in the context of both school literacy and computer applications and gaming (Kress & van Leeuwen, 2001; Kress, et al., 2005; van Leeuwen, 2005).

From *Discourse Studies in the Cultural Politics of Education* 26.3 (2005): 315–31.

Print-based reading and writing are and always have been multimodal. They require the interpretation and design of visual marks, space, colour, font or style, and, increasingly image, and other modes of representation and communication (Kenner, 2004). A multimodal approach enables these semiotic resources to be attended to and moves beyond seeing them as decoration.

I bring together a variety of illustrative examples in order to explore how new technologies remediate reading practices. These examples include computer applications (Microsoft Word), CD ROMs (*Multimedia Science School* [New Media Press, 2001] and *Of Mice and Men* [Penguin Electronics, 1996]) and games (*Kingdom Hearts* [Sony, 2002] and *Ico* [Sony, 2001]). These are selected to show the range of configurations of image and word and to begin to explore how these configurations might be shaped by subject curriculum and different contexts of use.

WRITING IN THE MULTIMODAL ENVIRONMENT OF THE SCREEN

Screen-based texts are complex multimodal ensembles of image, sound, animated movement, and other modes of representation and communication. Writing is one mode in this ensemble and its meaning therefore needs to be understood in relation to the other modes it is nestled alongside. Different modes offer specific resources for meaning making, and the ways in which modes contribute to people's meaning making vary. The representation of a concept (e.g., "cells" or "particles") is realized by the resources of writing in ways which differ from the resources of image, i.e., different criterial aspects are included and excluded from a written or visual representation.

Writing is not always the central meaning making resource in applications for use in school English and science. In some texts writing is dominant, while in others there may be little or no writing. The particular design of image and word relations in a text impacts on its potential shape of meaning. For example, a computer application can be designed to marshal all the representational and communicational "force" of image and word around a single sign; image can be used to reinforce the meaning of what is said, what is written, and so on. In turn, this relationship serves to produce or indicate coherence.

An example of this marshalling of semiotic resources across modes is offered by the PlayStation game *Ico* (Sony, 2001). *Ico* is about a young boy (Ico) who is entombed in a mysterious fortress that he and his rescued companion Yorda must escape. To this end, the two characters travel through the maze-like fortress while defeating shadowy monsters and an elusive sorceress queen. This discussion draws upon video and observational data from a pilot project designed to explore how the game as a multimodal text is realized through the player interaction (Carr & Jewitt, 2005). My discussion is based on multimodal analysis of the game and video data and observation of a game session between three children (aged 8, 15, and 17 years).

In the game *Ico* the ephemeral quality of the central character Yorda is produced through the multimodal design of the modes. This quality is realized by the shared impenetrability of Yorda's speech and its "written transcription." (I discuss this in more detail later in the paper.) It is signalled in the visually ill-defined, changing features and the leaking/blurred boundaries of her form. Her quiet voice, soft, slow ghostly gestures that hesitate and barely finish, along with floating movement, add to this realization of the character. Each of the modes used in the realization of the character Yorda are designed to suggest the same thing: she exists in a liminal space on the boundary between the castle that the game is situated within and the world outside of the castle, to which the player must try and escape.

At other times, image and writing attend to entirely different aspects of meaning in a text. Here I want to turn to some of the "new" configurations of image and writing brought about by the potentials (affordances) of new technologies. In particular, I want to ask how these configurations impact on meaning making, reading, and writing. This discussion needs to be read in the knowledge that sites of display are always socially shaped and located: the "new" always connects with, slips and slides over, the "old" (Levinson, 1999; Manovich, 2002). The ways in which modes of representation and communication appear on the screen are therefore still connected with the page, present and past. Similarly, the page is increasingly shaped and remade by the notion of screen. There are screens that look page-like and pages that look screen-like (e.g., Dorling Kingsley books). Until recently the dominance of image over word was a feature of texts designed for young children. Now, image overshadows word in a variety of texts, on screen and off screen: there are more images on screen and images are increasingly given a designed prominence over written elements.

The prominence of image is typical of many school science applications, such as *Multimedia Science School* (New Media Press, 2004). These examples are drawn from my research on multimodality, learning, and the use of new technologies in school science, mathematics, and English (Jewitt, 2003, 2005). Here I focus on a video recording and observation of the CD ROM *Multimedia Science School* in use in a Year 7 London secondary school classroom.

Where writing does feature on screen, a common function is to name and label elements. In *Multimedia Science School*, for example, the design of image and writing on screen serves to create two distinct areas of the screen: a "frame" and a central "screen within the screen." Multimodal semiotic analysis of the screen design shows that the "frame" attends to the scientific classification and labelling of the scientific phenomenon to be explored. There are a series of "buttons" displayed on the frame. Each "button" has a written "label" on it that relates to the topic areas covered by the CD ROM (e.g., states of matter). These act as written "captions" for what is visually displayed in the central "screen within the screen." The "screen within the screen" on the CD ROM is a multimodal space without any writing at all and it shows the empirical world that is to be investigated. It mediates and provides the evidence that "fills in" the scientific concepts (e.g., "states of matter") labelled by the "frame." In other words, the configuration of writing and image in the CD ROM modally marks these two distinct aspects of school science, i.e., scientific theory and the empirical world. The "frame" relies mainly on writing, layout, and composition. The "screen within a screen" relies on image, colour, and movement.

FIGURE 15-1   Screen from the CD ROM *Of Mice and Men*.

It is not only in school science that image dominates the screen. This is also true of applications used in the English classroom, although, as I will show, the way in which the relationship between word and image is configured is rather different.[1]

The relationship of image and writing in the CD ROM *Of Mice and Men* illustrates several features of the changing relationship between image and writing (Jewitt, 2002). Image takes up more than half the screen in over three-quarters of the "pages" in the CD ROM novel. This serves to decentre writing. Writing is displayed on the screen framed within a white block; this "block" is "placed over" an image that "fills the screen" (Figure 15-1). The full text of the novel *Of Mice and Men* is reproduced on the CD ROM, but the way it is distributed across the screen as opposed to the page differs. The amount of writing per screen is greatly reduced when compared with the page of the novel (so a page consists of three or four paragraphs, whereas each CD ROM screen consists of one paragraph). This "restructuring" "breaks up" the narrative and disconnects ideas that previously ran across one page to fragment the narrative across screens.

The design of writing on screen is connected with the epistemological demands and requirements of a subject area. In school English writing on screen represents the concepts of the curriculum, although in most cases an alternative reading of these concepts is made available through image, movement, and other modes. In school mathematics and science writing appears to be primarily used to name the canonical curriculum entities within the specialized language of the subject.

Writing appears to serve a similar labelling function in computer/PlayStation games. While the multimodal action rolls on, writing is used to name a character or indicate its status, specify a narrative point, or identify a decision. For example, the decision of when and what to represent in writing and/or speech can shape game character and narrative. Writing and speech can be used to give voice and expression to some characters in a game and not others. Watching my daughter (aged 8) and her friends play PlayStation games, I noticed and became interested in how they move through games by using the characters' access to speech as a multimodal clue to their potential to help solve the puzzles and tasks in the game. A character's access to language indicates (was read as a part of) their game value, i.e., their value in achieving the object of the game, to collect resources to move through to the next level of the game. A multimodal semiotic analysis of the game *Kingdom Hearts* (Sony, 2002) shows that some characters have the potential to speak, some respond by written text bubbles when approached by the player/avatar, and others have no language potential at all. The characters that have the most modes of communication are the key to game success.

The design of writing and speech can also subtly shape the identity of a game character. In the game *Ico* (2001), introduced earlier in this paper, the configuration of speech and writing within the multimodal game serves to reference the social function of language as a marker of identity, belonging, and difference. This reference is central to the game narrative and the task of solving the game puzzle and realising its goal, to escape the castle. The "language" spoken by Ico is a kind of global Esperanto, an ungrammatical combination of elements of Japanese, French, and German. Ico's speech is at the same time both universal and inaccessible. His speech is translated into subtitles that run across the bottom strip of the game cut sequences. Yorda's speech, like Ico's, is made up of bits of reworkings of various existing languages, but is "fictional." Her spoken words are translated into a "fictional" pictorial written language. The written language is made up of curling letters that stand somewhere between a Japanese script and Arabic. In other words, neither Yorda's speech nor its written translation is accessible to the player.

The relationship of writing and speech in this game seems to almost defy its essential purpose, to communicate. And yet these incomprehensible languages still mean. In the case of Yorda, writing and speech are pure form. They indicate something of her character by the inaccessibility of her talk. Speech and writing are used to represent Yorda's identity as other-worldly and different. By representing Yorda's "language" as one that can be spoken and written, the game design constructs Yorda as human-like, literate, and sociable. What Yorda "says" cannot be known, but the quiet, soft, and lyrical tone of voice with which she utters her non-understandable statements is an audio sign of her harmless, kind nature (van Leeuwen, 1999). The written script that stands for her words offers a visual echo of the pictorial signs carved on the tomb in which Ico is initially imprisoned. In this way, the written script of the subtitles marks Yorda's connection to the castle. Speech marks her difference from Ico. Writing marks her belonging to the castle; language marks her identity.

The way that writing and speech are used in the game *Ico* is also a part of the construction of the relationship between the characters Yorda and Ico.

Watching the two characters speak and listen to one another, it is clear that Ico cannot understand Yorda's language. (It is unclear whether or not Yorda can understand what Ico says.) The young people we observed playing the game are (like Ico) left to visually interpret the meanings that Yorda struggles to make in gesture, movement, posture, and audibly via her voice. Their interpretation and response to her differs in relation to their game experience and notion of game, which in turn is dependent on the context of play (Carr & Jewitt, 2005). In contrast, the player is offered access to Ico's language, via the written subtitles. The designer's decisions about when and how to use writing and speech mediates the flow of the narrative as a multimodal sequence. Ico's desperate call of Yorda's name is the only talk against the backdrop of action. Ico and Yorda's speech strips away what is said, the content of language, and instead offers the sound, the material form of speech. The material visual form of writing can be highlighted in a similar way. This strips away the content of what is written, like Yorda's fictional written language. This stripping away of the content of writing is what I turn to discuss now: the visualization of word.

The resources of new technologies emphasize the visual potential of writing in ways that bring forth new configurations of image and writing on screen: font, bold, italic, colour, layout, and beyond. The visual character of written texts has always been present to calligraphers, typographers, and others, but the inclusion and recognition of the material and visual qualities of texts is more recent within linguistics (see, for example, Ormerod & Ivanic, 2002; Shortis & Jewitt, 2004).

At times the boundaries between word and image appear entirely permeable and unstable (Chaplin, 1994; Elkins, 1999). The potential of new technologies blur the boundaries between the visual and the written in ways that "recast modes" and the relationships between them. The design of kinetic typography (Lanham, 2001; Maeda, 2000) is an instance of this and one that questions what writing is and can be in the 21st century. This is a question which is further complicated by the changing notion of screen and the development of three-dimensional, flexible, and transparent screens. These changes echo and connect with visual traditions from the past when people's lack of access to writing as a means of communication meant that the parallel visual story was often embedded in ornate visual written texts. Then, as now (although for different reasons), the visual form of writing was not decoration; it was and is designed meaning.

Observing the use of the CD ROM *Of Mice and Men* over a series of school English lessons offers an example of how typography, as a visualization of word, contributes to the ways in which students make meaning of a text. In particular, it offers an insight into the way in which students interpreted the characters' status within the novel as CD ROM. The CD ROM gives information on each of the characters in the form of a "work roster"; a list of character names and roles. Most of the characters' names are written as a list using a font like an old typewriter (Courier-like) and are circled in red. The character names "the boss" and "Curly's wife" are "handwritten" in red ink alongside the list. The different typographic fonts used in the CD ROM mark the connections and disconnections between the characters in the story. Through the contrast of font style, colour, and spatial layout, the two characters, "the boss" and "Curly's wife," are represented as outsiders. The "handwritten" comment "botherin us" written alongside the name "Curly's wife" goes further and positions her as an intruder. The technology encoded in these two fonts mark different social distances between the viewer/reader and the people listed (as well as the list itself). The typewriter font is suggestive of a more distant (cooler) relationship than is the "handwritten" font.

How and when these two different fonts are linked in the CD ROM becomes then a matter of choice, a matter of meaning. For example, the dossier file on "Curly's wife" includes an image of an envelope addressed to "Curly's wife" at Speckled Ranch, the location of the story (Figure 15-2).

When the user clicks on the image on the envelope this activates a hyperlink to a letter from Steinbeck to Clare Luce (the actor who played the character in a theatre production of the book).

FIGURE 15-2   Screen shot of the Curly's wife dossier on the CD ROM *Of Mice and Men*.

FIGURE 15-3   Screen shot of the Curly's wife dossier on the CD ROM *Of Mice and Men* hyperlinked text.

The envelope is produced as "handwritten" using Apple Chancery font while the letter it links to is produced as "typed" using Courier font and scroll bars. This pattern of a "handwritten" font on screen hyperlinked to a text using Courier font occurs throughout the CD ROM. This serves to produce two "distinct" kinds of writing. Apple Chancery font is used to indicate something at the fictional level of the story. Courier font is used to indicate something at the factual level. The fictional narrative of the novel and the descriptions of characters emulate "handwriting" and visually mark the "presence" or "essence" of a human writer. The factual information included in the dossier and hyperlinked texts about the historical places named in the novel use Courier, a font that brings forth the imagery of a machine, the old clunky machine of a typewriter, and suggests the presence of technology as human absence.

Typography is used here to visually express something as belonging to either the personal and potentially fictional or a formal and factual account. These different fonts give the students reading it a visual clue as to the different kinds of work they are expected to engage with. In the case of the handwritten font the work of the student is one of imaginative engagement, while the Courier font suggests that the kind of engagement needed is more distant, more to do with historical fact and evidence. In this way, the qualities of the font used are a key to the textual positioning of the reader.

At times writing on the screen becomes "fully visual." By this I mean that the "content" of the writing is "consumed" by its form. Writing becomes image when it is either too big or too small to relate to the practice of reading. The tiny scrawl of printed words retreats to a textured pattern of lines and it is redefined as a visual representation on screen. When writing moves about the screen, interacting in rhythm with other modes for example, the linguistic meaning of what is written is often illegible and transformed (Jewitt, 2002).

Some think that it is best to separate images and writing in CD ROM versions of books because the images distract students (Graham, 1996). From a multimodal perspective I see the design of image and writing as contributing in different ways to the meaning of a text. From this point of view the spatial relationship between image and writing is a resource for making meaning that can be useful. When writing is separated out and foregrounded to dominate the screen, it can be seen as a kind of "resistance" to the multimodal potential of new technologies and screen. In other words, a large amount of writing on screen is becoming a sign of convention or tradition. Writing on screen functions to reference the values of specialist knowledge, authority, and authenticity associated with print. It signals the literary text and the educated elite or, more prosaically, examination and assessment. It takes a considerable amount of work to maintain writing as the dominant mode on screen. This serves to assert the connection between the old and the new. However, writing is usually one part of a multimodal ensemble of image, music, speech, and moving elements on the screen. It is not only designers and teachers who make decisions about the relationship of image and word in texts. In the next section of this paper I look at an example of how students engaged in these decisions when they made (designed) texts.

STUDENTS' DESIGN OF WRITING AND IMAGE

Students in the classroom (as elsewhere) are engaged in making complex decisions about what mode to use and how best to design multimodal configurations. Here I focus on an example of students' digital design of image and writing in a Year 7 English classroom. This discussion draws on video and observation of a lesson in which the students made a brochure about their secondary school to send to prospective students at local primary schools. The students worked in pairs and each pair designed a double page spread for the brochure using Microsoft Word and digital cameras to produce the pages. Two of the final pages typical of the brochure are shown in Figures 15-4 and 15-5 (the name of the school has been deleted for anonymity).

The technology provided students with access to a range of images, including clip art, borders, word art, imported logos, digital photos, and downloaded images, as well as their own drawings made using Word Draw tools. Each of the spreads in the finished brochure is produced in a different font,

FIGURE 15-4   Page from student-made brochure *Your Basic Day at [School]*.

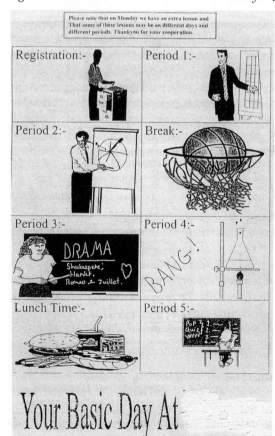

FIGURE 15-5 Page from student-made brochure *IT at [School].*

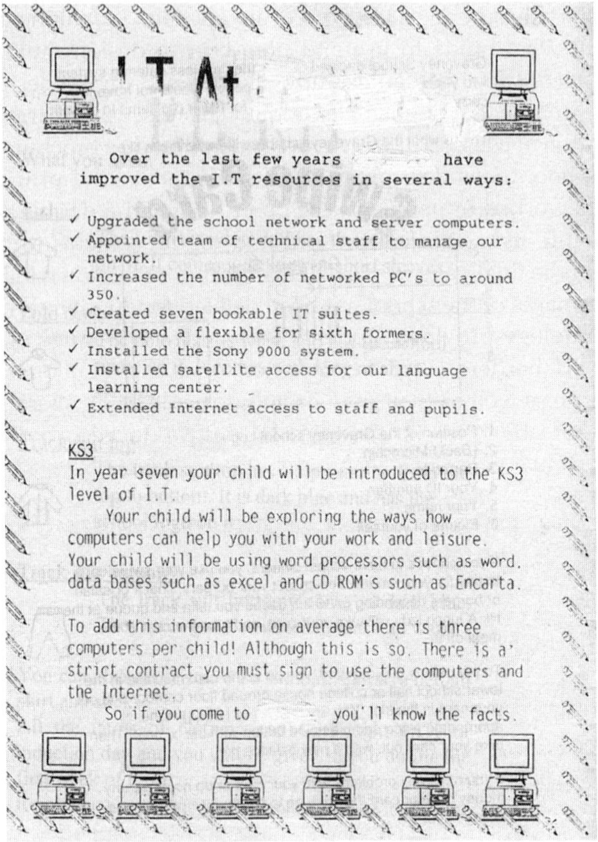

IT At

Over the last few years have improved the I.T resources in several ways:

- ✓ Upgraded the school network and server computers.
- ✓ Appointed team of technical staff to manage our network.
- ✓ Increased the number of networked PC's to around 350.
- ✓ Created seven bookable IT suites.
- ✓ Developed a flexible for sixth formers.
- ✓ Installed the Sony 9000 system.
- ✓ Installed satellite access for our language learning center.
- ✓ Extended Internet access to staff and pupils.

KS3

In year seven your child will be introduced to the KS3 level of I.T.

Your child will be exploring the ways how computers can help you with your work and leisure. Your child will be using word processors such as word, data bases such as excel and CD ROM's such as Encarta.

To add this information on average there is three computers per child! Although this is so. There is a strict contract you must sign to use the computers and the Internet.

So if you come to you'll know the facts.

from plain Courier to "ornate" Apple Chancery. Some students capitalized their written texts, others used bold or italic. Other students chose to use Word Art, complete with shadow and three-dimensional effects. The students appeared to use font as a resource with which to visually mark their individuality within the collective process of making the brochure, rather than the conventional use of font to mark coherence and a sense of audience, in which the individual is masked within the uniform character of the collective.

The facilities of word processing enabled the students to design and redesign their brochure pages, to wrap and unwrap the writing around images, to alter the page setup from landscape to portrait and back again, to change the margins, to move between different font styles and sizes, to import and delete images, and so on. The affordances of Microsoft Word enabled the students to manipulate and design the visual and written elements of their texts with ease. This highlighted the iterative work of design, selection, adaptation, viewing, and so on in which initial commitment was not required. In the process of making the pages the students were engaged in a series of decisions and negotiations. These included whether or not to use a border, what kind of border, whether to import images from "clip art" or to use "Word Art"; decisions about the use of "ready-made" versus "home-made" elements. The students had to compose the writing and decide how to arrange it and the other elements on the page. The students spent considerable time on the layout of their pages.

The students used tables, grids, and other "devices" in their design of the relationship between image and writing on the page. The use of a grid in the "Basic Day" text (Figure 15.4) both organizes the image and writing and provides a visual statement on the organization of time in the school as a regulatory grid for practices. The writing works as a uniform kind of label that equalizes the different periods and produces uniformity focused around time. The layout of the table, its symmetry, and the cells being the same size contribute to the text's representation of the school day as consisting of regularized chunks of time. The images distinguish between the periods by offering visually iconic content. The students used the visual resources that were easily available to them in the classroom, clip art. They adapted some of the images by adding writing. The images they selected from clip art present teaching and school as synonymous with business and a primarily didactic practice. People stand and point at boards. The students' use of images is imaginative and at the same time limited by the provenance of the images within clip art as an Office-based tool.

The students' choice of border in the text "IT at school" (Figure 15.5) is one of pencils poised to write, set around a horizontal border of images of computers that the students made from the clip art image of a computer. They experimented with different borders and settled on this one as they said when asked it is "about writing." In a sense their selection can be seen as a kind of visual classification of "technologies of writing" that realizes their main use of the computer in school to produce word processed texts.

Now I turn to the question of what the reconfiguration of image and word on screen described so far in this paper means for reading.

READING AS A MULTIMODAL PRACTICE

Recognising the multimodal character of texts, whether print-based or digital, impacts on conventional understandings of reading. Texts that rely primarily on writing can still "fit" with the concept of reading as engagement with word. What is ostensibly a monomodal written text offers the reader important visual information which is drawn into the process of reading. Reading is affected by the spatial organization and framing of writing on the page, the directionality, shape, size, and angle of a script (Kenner, 2004). In this way "different scripts can be seen as different modes, giving rise to a variety of potentials for meaning-making" with different "representational principles" underlying each writing system (Kenner & Kress, 2003, 179). In other words, both writing and reading are multimodal activities.

The need to rethink reading (as well as conceptions of text) has not been confined to digital technologies or the screen. As I have mentioned earlier, there is always "slippage" and "connections" between the "old" and the "new." As a consequence, conceptions of reading across a variety of sites of display are in a process of change. The multimodal resources available to readers are central to rethinking what reading is and what it might become in a blended, digital communicational environment. Having said this, the "new" range and configurations of modes that digital technologies make available present different potentials for reading than print texts. These modal reconfigurations almost demand that the multimodal character of reading be attended to.

When comparing the experience of reading a printed novel or a digital text (a "novel as CD ROM" or internet novel) people often talk about what is "best." This comparison is in a sense a false one, as "new" technologies are usually blended with "old" technologies in the classroom; it is rare that a CD ROM actually replaces the original book. Rather than ask "what is best?", the book or the screen, I think it is more useful to ask what is "best" for what purpose. I find Kress's notion of semiotic losses and gains useful for thinking about this (Kress, 2003). This idea can be applied to the difference (the losses and gains) for reading in the shift from one media, the printed book, to another, the digital screen. Elsewhere, I have discussed students' reading of "a novel as CD ROM" and how this enabled the students to engage with the novel as "film," "comic," and "musical" (Jewitt, 2005). Here I discuss how these differences shape the practice of reading using an example of students reading of a CD ROM simulation in school science. The application *Multimedia Science School* is multimodal and, as I have already mentioned, writing is restricted to minimal labelling. The students have to read colour, movement, and image in order to make sense of the concept "particles."

The application *Multimedia Science School* uses image and colour to construct the entities "states of matter" (solid, liquid and gas) and "particles." On the CD ROM images are presented as evidence of the criterial aspects of "particles." The work of the students (in this example Year 7 students in a science classroom) is to "read" the meaning of these in order to construct the notion of particle. In order to "read" the images the students need to be able to understand what it is that they should attend to. They need to know what to select as relevant and important elements from the visual representation. The students that I observed and video recorded using the application were actively engaged with the visual resources of the CD ROM displayed on the screen.

At some points the visual resources of colour, texture, and shape used in the application appeared to stand in conflict with their everyday visual reading of the world. For some students there was a tension between the visual realization of the scientific theory and the everyday as it was shown in the CD ROM. This caused considerable confusion for students' reading and construction of particles. An example of this is the students' reading of the simulation sequence showing the transformation from a solid to a liquid. Image, animated movement, and colour are designed to represent the arrangement of the "particles" in a solid and a liquid. The design is intended to show the animated particles overlaid on the water as an alternative representation of a liquid. During the lesson I noticed that several students interpreted the "particles" in the image as "a part of " a liquid (the water shown in the background). While working with the CD ROM one of the students, Lucy, commented that the particles were "held in the water like jelly." She did not understand the image of the particles as a representation of the water. Lucy did not distinguish between the visual resource of background or foreground (overlay). Instead, her construction of the entity "particle" is of something that "exists within" a liquid, a solid, or a gas rather than the particle as a thing that constitutes a liquid, solid, or gas.

Another problematic visual representation in the CD ROM is the transformation from a liquid to a solid. The use of colour in this sequence was the most problematic for some of the students to "read." The opening screen of the "liquid" to "solid" transformation shows a beaker inside another beaker. The outer one contains ice and the inner one contains water. The water is represented by a pale blue/white colour with reflective qualities. The writing on the "frame" of the screen clearly shows what it is that the students are looking at. Despite this clear label the students are confused about what they are looking at. The students do not "take up" the written information offered to them by the writing on the scientific "frame" of the CD ROM. Instead, they rely solely on image and colour to "read" the transformation. This is one example of the dominance of the visual mode and its impact on student reading. It is as if the conceptual "gap" between the writing on the "frame" and the image on the "screen within the screen" is just too great for the students to be able to make sense of. This difficulty appeared to be a consequence of a difference in the principles that students and the application designers used in relation to the use of the modal resources of colour, texture, and shape. The designers' principles clashed with the students' principles for understanding these resources. Students often privilege one mode over another when they read multimodal texts. In my view it is increasingly the case that readers, especially young readers and computer literate readers, privilege image and colour over writing when reading a multimodal text.

In the example of the transformation from a liquid to a solid the students "read" the visual representation of a liquid to "be a solid." This incident shows how students engage with the modal representations on the screen differently to make sense of a representation. It shows how students sometimes privilege or foreground some modes as being more "reliable" modes in their reading. The multimodal sequence is clearly labelled in writing in the "frame" as being the transformation of "liquid to solid." The "particles" are shown moving more freely and faster at the start of the sequence than they are in the final screen in which the "particles" move slower, "hardly at all," and are compactly arranged. The direction of the line plotted on the graph shows the temperature at the top of the graph as being "higher" than the temperature at the bottom of the graph. In other words, the directionality of the graph represents a decrease in temperature. Even the students' talk demonstrates that they understand the substance is being cooled and the graph is showing a decrease in temperature. Despite all of this information, the students do not read the transformation as being one from a liquid to a solid. The prominence and high value of realism given to resources of image, colour, and texture override everything else that the students know. The designers produced a multimodal text; these students "read" it visually. This highlights the important role of the teacher in mediating the computer applications in the classroom. For example, the teacher could have utilized this reading as a useful point for the discussion of realism and the ways in which school science offers alternative ways of viewing and thinking about the world.

Along with the choice of what mode to "read," the structure of many digital texts opens up options about where to start reading a text—what reading path to take. This question is intrinsically linked to the central focus of this paper, i.e., how the relationship between image and writing changes both the shapes of knowledge and the practices of reading and writing. The design of modes often offers students different points of entry into a text, possible paths through a text and highlights the potential for readers to remake a text via their reading of it. The "reader" is involved in the task of finding and creating reading paths through the multimodal, multidirectional texts on the screen, a fluidity that is beginning to seep out onto the page of printed books (Kress, 2003; Moss, 2001). Writing, image, and other modes combine to convey multiple meanings and encourage the reader to reject a single interpretation and to hold possible multiple readings of a text (Coles & Hall, 2001). The multimodal character of the screen does not indicate a single entry point, a beginning, and an end, rather it indicates that texts are layered and offers multiple entry points. This offers the reader new potentials for reading a text and the design of the text through engagement with it. Reading a written text on a page is usually a linear event in which the author and illustrator guide the eye in a particular direction connected to the reading of a text.

It is certainly the case that multiple reading paths are always a part of the repertoire of an experienced reader (Coles & Hall, 2001). Multimodal texts of the screen redefine the work of the reader who has to work to construct a narrative or assert her or his own meanings via their path through a text. Some have proclaimed that linear narrative is dead and others claim it never lived. I think narratives "live on" in different ways across a range of media. Having said that, I think the facilities of new technologies make non-linear narrative more possible than the printed page does. The design of some children's books (such as *The Jolly Pocket Postman*, Ahlberg & Ahlberg, 1995) and many magazines aimed at young people serves to fragment the notion of linear narrative and to encourage readers to see themselves as writers. In doing so, these texts "undo" the literary forms of closure and narrative. However, the potential for movement and closure through the screen texts is fundamentally different from the majority of classic book-based literary forms and offers the reader the potential to create (however partially) the text being read. The question is not what kind of narrative is best, but what can be done (meant) with the resources that different types of narrative make available. It is a question of what kinds of narrative best fit with the facilities of different media for particular purposes and what role image and writing have in configuring this.

CONCLUDING COMMENTS

Despite the multimodal character of screen-based texts and the process of text design and production, reading educational policy and assessment continue to promote a linguistic view of literacy and a linear view of reading. This fails to connect the kinds of literacy required in the school with the "out-of-school worlds" of most people. The government's National Literacy Strategy (Department for Education and Skills, 1998) for England is one such policy. It is informed by a linguistic and print-based conceptualization of literacy in which the focus is on "word," sentence, and text. At the same time, governments' strategies herald the power of new technologies to change everything. The multimodal character of new technologies produces a tension for traditional conceptions of literacy that maintain written language at their centre.

Traditional forms of assessment continue to place an emphasis on students' handwriting and spelling, skills that the facilities of computers make differently relevant for learning. At the same time, assessment fails to credit the acquisition of new skills that new technologies demand of students, such as finding, selecting, processing, and presenting information from the internet and other sources (Somekh et al., 2001). I want to suggest that the multimodal character and facilities of new technology require that traditional (print-based) concepts of literacy be reshaped. What it means to be literate in the digital era of the 21st century is different than what was needed previously (Gardener, 2000). If school literacy is to be relevant to the demands of the multimodal environment of the larger world it must move away from the reduction of literacy to "a static series of technical skills" or risk "fostering a population of functional illiterates" (McClay, 2002). In short, school literacy needs to be expanded to reflect the semiotic systems that young people use (Unsworth, 2001; Jewitt, 2005).

NOTE

1. This discussion is based on video recordings and observation of the use of the CD ROM *Of Mice and Men* over a series of five Year 9 English lessons in a London school.

REFERENCES

Ahlberg, J., & Alhberg, A. (1995). *The jolly pocket postman*. London: William Heinemann.
Carr, D., & Jewitt, C. (2005). *Multimodality and the playable text*. Paper presented at Computer Assisted Learning Conference, Bristol University, 6 April 2005.
Chaplin, E. (1994). *Sociological and visual representation*. London: Routledge.
Coles, M., & Hall, C. (2001). Breaking the line: New literacies, postmodernism and the teaching of printed texts. *United Kingdom Reading Association, 35*(3), 111–114.
Department for Education and Skills. (1998). The National Literacy Strategy. Retrieved 13 February 2005, from http://www.nc.uk.net.
Elkins, J. (1999). *The domain of images*. New York: Cornell University Press.
Gardener, P. (2000). *Literacy and media texts in secondary English*. London: Cassell Education.
Graham, J. (1996). Trouble for Arthur's teacher: A close look at reading CD-ROMs. In M. Simons (Ed.), *Where we've been: Articles from the English and Media Magazine* (pp. 285–290). London: English and Media Centre.
Jewitt, C. (2002). The move from page to screen: The multimodal reshaping of school English. *Journal of Visual Communication, 1*(2), 171–196.
Jewitt, C. (2003). Reshaping literacy and learning: A multimodal framework for technology mediated learning. Unpublished doctoral dissertation, Institute of Education, London University.

Jewitt, C. (2005). *Technology, literacy, learning.* London: RoutledgeFalmer.
Kenner, C. (2004). *Becoming biliterate: Young children learning different writing systems.* Stoke on Trent: Trentham Books.
Kenner, C., & Kress, G. (2003). The multisemiotic resources of biliterate children. *Journal of Early Childhood Literacy, 3*(2), 179–202.
Kress, G. (2003). *Literacy in the new media age.* London: Routledge.
Kress, G., & van Leeuwen, T. (2001). *Multimodal discourse: The modes and media of contemporary communication.* London: Arnold.
Kress, G., Jewitt, C., Bourne, J., Franks, A., Hardcastle, J., Jones, K., et al. (2005). *Urban classrooms, subject English: Multimodal perspectives on teaching and learning.* London: RoutledgeFalmer.
Lanham, R. (2001). What next for text? *Education, Communication, and Information, 1*(1), 59–74.
Levinson, P. (1999). *Digital McLuhan: A guide to the information millennium.* London: Routledge.
McClay, J. (2002). Intricate complexities. *English in Education, 36*(1), 36–54.
Maeda, J. (2000). *Maeda @ Media.* London: Thames and Hudson.
Manovich, L. (2002). *The language of new media.* Cambridge, MA: MIT Press.
Moss, G. (2001). To work or play? Junior age non-fiction as objects of design. *Reading, Literacy and Language, 35*(3), 106–110.
Ormerod, F., & Ivanic, R. (2002). Materiality in children's meaning making practices. *Visual Communication, 1*(1), 65–91.
Shortis, T., & Jewitt, C. (2004). *The multimodal ecology of texts in A-level examinations.* Paper presented at British Association of Applied Linguistics, Kings College, London, 13 September 2004.
Somekh, B., Barnes, S., Triggs, P., Sutherland, R., Passey, D., Holt, H., et al. (2001). *NGfL Pathfinders: Preliminary report on the roll-out of the NGfL Programme in ten Pathfinder LEAs.* London: Department for Education and Skills.
Unsworth, L. (2001). *Teaching multiliteracies across the curriculum: Changing contexts of text and image in classroom practice.* Buckingham: Open University Press.
van Leeuwen, T. (1999). *Speech, music, sound.* London: Macmillan.
van Leeuwen, T. (2005). *Introducing social semiotics.* London: Routledge.

APPLICATIONS

New Media Press. (2001). *Multimedia science school* (CD ROM). Oxon: New Media Press.
Penguin Electronics. (1996). *Of mice and men* (CD ROM), Steinbeck Series. New York: Penguin Electronics.
Sony. (2001). *Ico.* San Mateo, CA, USA: Sony.
Sony. (2002). *Kingdom hearts.* San Mateo, CA, USA: Sony.

16   *Composing Multimodality*

JODDY MURRAY

Anne Cranny-Francis, in *Multimedia: Texts and Contexts*, reinforces the cultural and spatial aspects of multimodality by describing the landscape of multimedia as the "cartography of contemporary meaning-making" (5). What I like about this description is the locus it creates in space around meaning-making. Creating texts made of several modes and media is nothing new, but thinking of writing and composing as a kind of cartography implies just how much contemporary writing is not simply the alphacentric literacies of verbal language on paper, not just the application of an alphabet on paper. Cartography acknowledges space and the graphical metaphors employed in that space. Cartography acknowledges writing in the recent era of multimodal composition.

. . . I have tried to emphasize how image is at the center of everything we do with our symbol systems: image drives composing just as it provides the mechanisms the brain needs to compose thought. Our sensory systems do many things for us, not the least of which is to provide the input and output for our symbol systems. I realize this metaphor is extremely mechanistic, but it must be remembered that, if we are to teach multimodal composition and multimedia, we must be able to also broaden our notion of writing to the kind of composing done in and among any set of modes and media.[1] No longer can writing remain as merely the enactment of alphacentric literacies because it is no longer the case that monomodal, alphanumeric texts encompass the entirety of textual production. The map itself is made up of sounds, textures, visuals, smells, and tastes—all in increasing combinations, all in increasingly instantaneous delivery. . . . [I]mage and its various sensual constituents are the main compositional element for all textual production because once image is understood as any type of mental formulation based on our available senses in this world, it can become the most important rhetorical tool to any kind of textual production. Instead of breaking rhetoric up into visual rhetoric and

From *Non-Discursive Rhetoric: Image and Affect in Multimodal Composition.* Albany: SUNY P, 2009. 163–88.

aural rhetoric, et cetera (rhetorics based on their modes and media which, ultimately, are usually always already mixed or hybrid), we can talk of discursive rhetoric and non-discursive rhetoric: the former concerned with those modes and media that create discursive meaning; the latter concerned with those modes and media that create non-discursive meaning. Both are used in composition, both become exhibited to one degree or another in most forms of textual production. Because discursive meaning and discursive rhetorics are already, for the most part, well established and exhaustively discussed (partly due to disciplinary boundaries in the academy), . . . [I want] to help establish composing practices for non-discursive texts (or elements) relevant to multisensory texts.[2]

It is now possible to suggest ways that image itself can become important to composing multimodality. This [selection] establishes some basic guidelines for designing text of various modes while emphasizing image as the rhetorical touchstone. . . . [I]t does not directly address invention; rather, the purpose . . . is to help practitioners encourage students to produce multimodal texts: to encourage the process of composition using textual modes that are, themselves, nonverbal: pictures, words, colors, drawings, sounds, et cetera.

Naturally, there may be resistance to this notion of the writing classroom. Some might oppose the goals of such assignments based on image on disciplinary grounds (i.e., we do not teach the visual arts, etc.). But implicit in this [work] is a breaking down of such artificial barriers: asking students to begin composing image is, on the one hand, not too different than what we already ask of students—asking students to write so that they form "clear" sentences so that they might construct a "clear" argument in the hope that it will form "clear" images in the mind of the reader is also a type of composition through image. Many of the pedagogical and process-oriented steps we ask students to undergo in writing traditional, discursive texts are in fact a type of composition that helps the reader form images related to claim-making. To value interdisciplinarity is to value the work of other disciplines, and this includes art. To claim that only art deals directly with the visual is as obviously short-sighted as to claim that only the empiricism of the scientific method is epistemic, or that only the social sciences can effectively research cultures and societies. Writing and rhetoric scholarship has long been interdisciplinary, but the discursive bias among writing teachers may be our most difficult challenge in encouraging multimodality in writing classrooms: too many teachers insist that writing the essay (itself a relatively anomalous textual mode) is the only way to get at critical analysis, close reading, research praxis, cultural criticism, and the principles of rhetoric. Not only can multimodal composition exercise these laudable goals, multimodal composition can do much more: acknowledge and build into our writing processes the importance of emotions in textual production, consumption, and distribution; encourage digital literacy as well as nondigital literacy in textual practice; and develop rhetorical skills that are more closely aligned with the rhetorical methods students experience on a daily basis. As Stuart Selber notes in the Epilogue of *Multiliteracies for a Digital Age*,

> If students are to become agents of positive change, they will need an
> education that is comprehensive and truly relevant to a digital age in
> which much of the instructional agenda seems to be little more than
> indoctrination into the value systems of the dominant computer culture
> [. . . .] such an approach simply replaces one literacy for another; it fails
> to expose students to the wide array of literacies they will need in order
> to participate fully and productively in the technological dimensions of
> their professional and personal lives. (234)

This agency is a goal for all compositionists, and by bringing multiliteracies into
the composition classroom, the full complexity—rather than a reductionism or
simplicity—of writing rhetorically becomes more available to students.[3]

Other than instruction in the mere mechanics of print-based writing,
writing teachers are already suited to ask students to compose rhetorically,
and students must learn to do so using any type of textual symbolization that
is effective for academic, civic, and workplace environments. Anne Frances
Wysocki, in her excellent book *Writing New Media: Theory and Applications for
Expanding the Teaching of Composition*, also makes this point—a point worth
repeating at length here:

> This, then, is why it matters for writing teachers to be doing more with
> new media: writing teachers are already practiced with helping others
> understand how writing—as print-based practice—is embedded among
> the relations of agency and extensive material practices and structures
> that are our lives. Writing teachers help others consider how the choices
> we make in producing a text necessarily situate us (or can try to avoid
> situating us) in the midst of ongoing, concrete, and continually up-for-
> grabs decisions about the shapes of our lives. Writing teachers can fill a
> large gap in current scholarships on new media; they can bring to new
> media texts a humane and thoughtful attention to materiality, produc-
> tion, and consumption, which is currently missing. (7)

Writing and rhetoric teachers are indeed the perfect place for this kind of instruction, as long as they take into account the unavoidable, and powerful,
use of non-discursive text as well. As Cynthia Selfe states in her contribution
to the same book, we must teach new media texts also because "students are
doing so—and their enthusiasm about reading/viewing/interacting with and
composing/designing/authoring such imaginative texts percolates through
the substrata of composition classrooms, in direct contrast to students' *laissez
faire* attitudes toward more conventional texts" (44). Writing teachers are suited
for this kind of work and writing students are excited about this kind of textual production.

THE RHETORICAL IMAGE

There can be no controversy in asserting that photos, typefaces, colors, spaces,
or soundtracks are rhetorical. Each of these could all be experienced by a single
movie trailer advertising the next box office oriented film: the quick succession of scenes and character shots, the exaggerated typefaces with dripping

animations and color, the darkness of the theater and smell of popcorn, the chest-thumping surround sound of the soundtrack and sound effects, et cetera. Each of these is composed, each of these is intended to persuade, each of these are images, each of these (and their collective) is rhetorical.

As implied earlier, image studies is currently gaining ground in composition, though it seems to be doing so without a comprehensive theoretical framework specific to writing or any specific attention to non-discursive text. Steve Westbrook's article, "Visual Rhetoric in a Culture of Fear: Impediments to Multimedia Production" emphasizes just how much rhetoric and composition has seemingly embraced the image without enacting pedagogies that ask students to produce multiliterate texts:

> Ten of the more popular textbooks concerned with visual rhetoric—*Beyond Words* (Ruszkiewicz, Anderson, and Friend); *Seeing and Writing 2* (McQuade and McQuade); *Frames of Mind* (DiYanni and Hoy); *Picturing Texts* (Faigley, George, Palchik, and Selfe); *Practices of Looking* (Sturken and Cartwright); *Ways of Reading Words and Images* (Bartholomae and Petrosky); *Everything's an Argument* (Lunsford and Ruszkiewicz); *Reading Culture* (George and Trimbur); *Writing in a Visual Age* (Odell and Katz); and *Designing Writing* (Palmquist)—contain a total of 2,620 prompts. Of these 2,620 prompts, only 143, or roughly 5 percent, require students to engage in multimedia or visual production [. . . .] Only *Writing in a Visual Age* offers students consistent and flexible opportunities to produce visual texts in the majority of its large-scale assignments. (461–62)

One text not mentioned here, Robert Atwan's *Convergences: Message, Method, and Medium*, takes a more rhetorical look at the relationship between image and word in popular culture by stressing the rhetorical methods involved *and* the various media used. Like Westbrook's comment that many of these new textbooks stress reading over producing, so does this one. But I am not altogether convinced that asking students to become more adept at reading texts of various media is not worthwhile, as long as students also get a chance to produce multimodal texts (which is the case in *Convergences*). What is important here is that rhetoric and composition is changing not so much because we are doing anything very different (we are still teaching rhetoric and textual production); rather, what continues to change most dramatically is the interaction acknowledged between diverse modes of text, both produced and consumed. Even so, we can do more as writing teachers to ask that students produce these diverse and interactive texts all the while remaining centered on the rhetoricity of the image.

There has also been a remarkable increase over the last few years in the number of presentations at CCCC dealing directly with image, or multiliteracies, in addition to a few conferences specifically focused on image and image studies.[4] Journals in the field such as *Computers and Composition* and online journals such as *Enculturation* and *Kairos* both have featured issues dedicated to the visual domain, image and text, and multiliteracies. In addition, there seems to be a recent increase in scholarship on image within the field, especially how image is related to multimodal rhetoric and multimedia.[5]

But what seems lacking in this trend in scholarship is a theory of composing that frames work on the image in a way as to not limit or sacrifice the complexity and inherent legitimacy of non-discursive symbolization for a reduced view of textual production. In the end, one of the most vital roles for images is that they thrive in the domain of the unutterable or unsayable; consequently, composing using discursive text at these moments may actually be more difficult than composing using non-discursive text. Such a view of symbolization would then be capable of accounting for both the discursive and non-discursive aspects of human activity—one that responds to current demands that writing pedagogy include the multisensory, multigenre, and multimedia composition practices.

Specifically, image studies might provide a response to a challenge Lynn Worsham voiced in 1987. Specifically, she calls for a "new" writing experience, one that is limitless and complex:

> A new theory or a new system, or even a meta-system accounting for a multiplicity of theories and systems, at this point of our history, is nothing particularly new. What would be new is an experience of writing, of "literacy," if you will, that brings to pass an awareness of the limits of literacy, an **awareness of the non-discursive elements** in the event of signification. Such writing would tend to contradict or, better yet, seriously complicate, our conventional or stereotypical notions of literacy: It would be the kind of writing that seeks not so much the conceptual and abstract but the sensuous and emotional. It would seek not the truth of propositions but the rigor of possibility and the nuance of the impossible. It would seek not the distance of generalization and objectivity but the nearness of involvement. (236, bold my emphasis)

What Worsham seems to be requesting here is a paradox: she acknowledges that a "new theory" or "new system" would only reproduce the problems of invention experienced to date, while at the same time describing "what would be new" in terms of a theory: one that is "non-discursive": one that is "sensuous and emotional." This [selection] on image attempts to work through this paradox by describing just this kind of nonsystematic theory that captures the "experience of writing," one that points to image and the non-discursive as crucial to the act of writing (and thinking), while, at the same time, authorizing the affective domain as integral to the "sensuous and emotional" aspect and content of the symbols themselves. This [selection], therefore, attempts to answer Worsham's call by uniting image and emotions through non-discursive rhetoric.

In order to write the "nuance of the impossible," as Worsham put it, the first thing we must do is allow the rhetorical image to become the center of our pedagogical practice. *Eloquent Images*, an anthology edited by Mary Hocks and Michelle Kendrick dedicated to the importance of image to writing, weaves together image, new media, and the importance of "design practice" in this way:

> [A]s each chapter in this volume outlines specific forms of design and practice, it delineates part of that complex stratification of functioning

> that constitutes new media's "play" in our digital machines. By looking at new media theories and instances of practice within the stratified, conflicting networks of interpretation, the authors in this volume present important new ways to be nonmodern. Specific instances can move us beyond the merely theoretical to interpret and to create with a fully hybrid eloquence, and the examples offered in the chapters that follow become those everyday practices that enact the verbal and visual complexity of new media. (14)

This effort towards "hybrid eloquence" is reminiscent of Langer's insistence that visual forms are also articulate: eloquence is not a term owned by discursive text, nor is it necessarily monomodal. Eloquence, especially in this anthology, may actually come from the hybridity characteristic of multimodal texts: various media interacting in individually incomplete or incoherent ways that, when taken as a whole, become articulate.[6] Obviously, such a perspective would require the field to stretch its boundaries, a process that has often taken place in the past. In doing so, new knowledge gets integrated while making room for even more. Amy Ione, in *Innovation and Visualization: Trajectories, Strategies, and Myths*, suggests how such stretching works:

> Initial boundaries, I would propose, take form to help us define what is known. Then, as we learn to know more about what we are exploring and what remains unknown, we can once again design a map to bring a tangible quality to emerging information. The beauty of this exercise of stretching our boundaries is that it shows that newly conceived maps can display quantitative and qualitative perspectives, can help shift our understanding of the boundaries and can allow us to bracket information as we inquire—over and over again. Each time we do so we perceive what is "known" and what remains "unknown." Thus the maps are flexible forms. And, as the twentieth-first century unfolds, it is clear that human consciousness has filtered through many maps over the centuries. Our process in effect indicates that boundaries are useful, but they are not static. They also retreat and change location. (154)

Boundaries in discipline identity, boundaries in textual production, boundaries in language and writing: all of these are being stretched by image studies. Like rhetorical theory, it can seem as though "everything is image" in theorizing about non-discursive text, and that may very well be the case. But in stretching these boundaries, vast and newly available areas become apparent: theoretical explorations of new and potentially revolutionary maps shift us into unknown potential. For the rhetorical image to become the center of our pedagogical practice, our current boundaries must stretch.

Another reason image production must become the defining characteristic of what we do as writing teachers is because image . . . is not just a visual object to be perceived by the eye. Not only is image primarily non-discursive, it is also a vehicle for the emotions and a building block of imagination and thought. Ron Burnett's book *How Images Think* underscores the connection image has to neuroscience and to culture:

As more knowledge is gained about the human mind, embodied and holistic, the role of culture and images has changed. Images are no longer just representations or interpreters of human actions. They have become central to every activity that connects humans to each other and to technology—mediators, progenitors, interfaces—as much reference points for information and knowledge as visualizations of human activity [. . . .] In particular, the issues of how images are used to explain biological processes needs to be framed by cultural argument and cultural criticism. (xiv–xv)

Burnett is addressing image both as a methodological tool and image as a rhetorical tool: image may function as a set of topographical representations (as Damasio maintains), but when these images are connected with human behavior, Burnett's book insists that they must be contextualized in culture. This only reinforces the insistence that humanists attend to images even as we compose with them. If we do not, other disciplines will.

In his pivotal work on the changing nature of English studies and the encroachment of electronic texts into the humanities, Richard Lanham's *The Electronic Word: Democracy, Technology, and the Arts* makes the point that new technology demands change in English studies:

So far as I see it, our instinctive posture has been defensive, based on the book and the curricular and professional structures that issue from it. We conceive the humanities as a pickle factory preserving human values too tender and inert for the outside world [. . . .] The harsh world wants to imagine a finer world and we pretend to dwell in it. But our students and the society from which they come will not permit this illusion to continue unchanged; nor will a technology that has volatilized print; nor will our own thinking, our "theory," about what we are and do. All these are asking us to think systemically about literary study, to model it from kindergarten through graduate school [. . . .] We are being asked to explain how the humanities humanize. (25)

The field of rhetoric and composition also seems to suggest its own kind of "pickle factory," one that places printed, discursive text in the center of everything we do. Clearly, students and the world we live in (that includes blogs, podcasts, modular community web spaces, cell phone messaging, and, soon, electronic paper) demand otherwise. We must not only encourage our students to think rhetorically about these new and not-so-new texts, but we must ask them to produce them with deliberate rhetorical aims in mind. Cultural changes, as Lanham suggests, refocus writing theory toward the image: "electronic writing brings a complete renegotiation of the alphabet/icon ratio upon which print-based thought is built," adding "[w]e can detect this foregrounding of images over written words most clearly in the world of business and government communications, but it is happening everywhere" (34).

The emphasis on image and culture requires a kind of non-discursive rhetorical analysis: the parsing and translating of non-discursive textual products and elements into focused claims of argument. For Burnett, this means rhetorical images become "both the outcome and progenitors of vast and interconnected image-worlds" (3). Just as Scharfstein links ambiguity and the ineffable to worlds which are too complex and layered for discursive logic, Burnett admits that "the challenge" with images is converting them into discursive versions of themselves: "to map the experiences of interacting with images into a process that is discursive, intellectual, and emotional so that it can be understood and applied to the viewing process" (7). But as students must interact with these "image-worlds," they must learn how and why images work the way they do: they must learn to read images, sure, but they also must learn how to compose with image, to create their own "image-worlds" that are rhetorical:

> spectators have "evolved" beyond the parameters of viewing in the sense of distance and separation, "the images over there"—to living within the confines of a world where images in the broadest sense intersect with the real at all times. (42)

Burnett also links image to the imagination in that "[t]o be within images is not to be suffocated by them; rather, images are vistas on the brilliance of the human imagination and perhaps this is why images are simultaneously loved, desired, and feared" (42–43). The rhetorical image can become a keystone to all forms of textual production: whether discursive or non-discursive. Image, in short, works at the elemental level of the mind/brain and, as a consequence, at the elemental level of all textual production.

As image and non-discursive rhetoric become applied to more traditional forms, questions about how image can create arguments are inevitable. In truth, no type of text can construct arguments without some knowledge of the targeted audience—whether that text is discursive or non-discursive. Moreover, by virtue of the fact that non-discursive texts are defined as nonlinear and independent on the text that precedes it, argument thought of only as a set of enthymemic or syllogistic propositions is difficult to imagine. But argument is bigger than a set of propositions: images can construct arguments because images carry with them much more than objectified text—emotional connections and connotations pervade image, and given the tendency towards hybridity, image functions well among all textual modes. Because, as Richard Fulkerson suggests, "it is crucial that students learn to participate effectively in argumentation as cooperative, dialectical exchange and a search for mutually acceptable (and contingent) answers," and given enough information about audience and what constitutes "mutually acceptable," image is an ideal conveyor of informal logic, especially in terms of how argumentation relates to digital media and non-discursive texts (17). Locke Carter's article, "Argument in Hypertext: Writing Strategies and the Problem of Order in a Non-sequential World" addresses the problem of order in hypertext, and the problems such a nonlinear structure poses for constructing arguments:

> Syllogisms and analytic rules might be well-suited for certain sciences and pure math, but common sense will show even the most brazen skeptic that the vast majority of arguments are conducted successfully day to

day based on something else. Everyday argument must be based not on the rules of formal logic, but on a kind of informal logic. This reasoning is always dependent on the audience to whom arguments are addressed. (6)

What exactly this "informal logic" is has been variously theorized, but I like how Langer talks about this idea using the term "intuitive logic" . . . —a kind of logic based not entirely on abstract symbols but also on lived experiences. In the end, the term argumentation itself is constantly blurred with exceptions and adaptations that conform more closely to our lived experiences of discourse.

Different modes used in composing multimedia benefit rhetorically from the non-discursive, emotionally charged image. If text could be purely discursive (a questionable notion all by itself, but such text might be said to exist as computer code—though even computer code is eventually translated into machine code which later becomes electronic representations of voltage), then such a text becomes a *doxa* reflective of its programmers rather than an *episteme* tested and validated by the polis. Discursive text must rely on what comes before to construct meaning; non-discursive text is already articulate, creating meaning all at once. I argue here that the rhetorical image is not only a valuable tool in textual production but also the vehicle from which belief becomes lived experience. Image alters our brain, both in the pathways it constructs and the topographical representations it assembles. Non-discursive rhetoric actually makes knowledge *livable* in that it places knowledge in the realm of the senses rather than just in the realm of increasing abstraction. Further, when it comes to make the case of justice and ethical behavior, doxa alone is rarely sufficiently convincing. It is not so much the case that images are more or less imbued with rhetoric to be effective: rather, it may be the case that rhetoric is more or less imbued with image to be effective.

VALUES OF MULTIMODALITY

By no means intended to be exhaustive, this section sets out to derive a few general values of multimodality implied by the five values of non-discursive text. Some values—such as unity, juxtaposition and perspective—seem closely related to discursive practices already well-known and familiar to compositionists. Other values—such as image and layering—are less well-known and are closely related to non-discursive practices. Once established, these five values provide a way for teachers to integrate multimodal composing with their learning objectives.

Though textual production in multimedia is often composed of several modes (i.e., different types of text such as audio, video, print, texture, image, color, etc.), there are some values that become important to an author (or composer) because they hold particular importance and produce various options. These values of multimedia are not principles or rules or dictums or anything very solid or procedural for a very good reason: they produce meaning, but in no way can any particular application of these values produce predictable results. In the end, these elements are "values" because, as authors, we value what they can do for us during textual production. They can be metaphorical, or synecdochical, or simply sensual, but they are only tools from which we carve meaning using many different modes of production. Just as support and elaboration are values of print-based texts because they employ the defining characteristics of discursive text, so too are these five values valuable to non-discursive text.

Though most of these values may seem to be most relevant to visual forms of image and multimodal text, I must emphasize that I intend them here to be relevant to all forms of images: to multisensory textual production. The term "design" has come to mean many things in recent years: from engineering design to sound design to bedroom design. We often think of the word in disciplinary terms, such as graphic design or architectural design. John Heskett's book, *Toothpicks & Logos: Design in Everyday Life,* underscores the difficulty with the term:

> To suggest that design is a serious matter in that sense, however, is problematic. It runs counter to widespread media coverage assigning it to a lightweight, decorative role of little consequence: fun and entertaining—possibly; useful in a marginal manner—maybe; profitable in economic sectors dominated by rapid cycles of modishness and redundancy; but of no real substance in basic questions of existence [. . . .] Design sits uncomfortably between these two extremes. As a word it is common enough, but it is full of incongruities, has innumerable manifestations, and lacks boundaries that give it clarity and definition. As a practice, design generates vast quantities of material, much of it ephemeral, only a small proportion of which has enduring quality. (2–3)

What should be clear by now is that design is just another word for composition. All denotations and connotations aside, design is the act of putting together with intent, and that is exactly what students must do no matter if they are writing the most traditional type of academic essay, or if they are creating a poster for a local event. Heskett says it best:

> Beyond all the confusion created by the froth and bubble of advertising and publicity, beyond the visual pyrotechnics of virtuoso designers seeking stardom, beyond the pronouncements of design gurus and the snake-oil salesmen of lifestyles, lies a simple truth. Design is one of the basic characteristics of what it is to be human, and an essential determinant of the quality of human life. It affects everyone in every detail of every aspect of what they do throughout each day. As such, it matters profoundly. (3–4)

What we are doing as writing teachers is effected by design—it always has been (anyone who has ever taught Modern Language or American Psychological Association formatting guidelines knows this has been the case). Composing, or designing, multimodal texts requires writing teachers to stress design issues that have otherwise been dictated to them by editors, printers, or disciplinary guidelines. Therefore, what follows is a brief list of those values we must teach students if they are to explore non-discursive textual production, and, consequently, become rhetors of multimedia.

Image

As I have suggested already, image is central to textual production. But in terms of composing non-discursive texts, students need to be taught how to use image in their rhetorical practice. Just as any creative writing workshop will necessarily instruct students, by example as well as through specific exercises, the importance and value of constructing images using printed text, so too must multimodal teachers instruct students how to read and write images. Even students, who are long-time camera users and have taken photographs for years, few of these students actually learn to *compose* these photographs, through the lens, darkroom, or image editing software. The composition of a photo is a good place to start talking about image because students need to learn how images are constructed, altered, realtered, and rhetorically invented. Photographs are by no means new to students, but thinking about how they might be used to create an argument probably is new. Web texts, hypermedia, advertisements in newspapers and magazines, icons, even charts and diagrams: visual image as a textual product is ubiquitous. But it is also important to have students think about all the multisensory images that are out there: the smell of a popcorn booth at a carnival, the texture of a glossy magazine, the swell of strings during a romantic scene in a film, the combination of flavors during a meal of fine cuisine. All of these image rhetorics can be persuasive, and the operative rhetoric doing the persuasion is non-discursive. Burke's *identification* is especially at work in such cases:

> You persuade a man only insofar as you can talk his language by speech, gesture, tonality, order, image, attitude, idea, *identifying* your ways with his. Persuasion by flattery is but a special case of persuasion in general. But flattery can safely serve as our paradigm if we systematically widen its meaning, to see behind it the conditions of identification and consubstantiality in general. And you give the "signs" of such consubstantiality by deference to an audience's "opinions." For the orator, following Aristotle and Cicero, will seek to display the appropriate "signs" of character needed to earn the audience's good will. (55–56)

For students to identify with their audience, to build consubstantiality (or rapport) with them, they need to see how images are themselves part of the rhetoric: the clothing and grooming of the speaker, the banner in the background, the elegance of the speakers gesture: all forms of non-discursive text. David Blakesley, in *The Elements of Dramatism*, points out that Burke's, "primary aim of rhetoric is identification":

> Burke believes that in any rhetorical situation there is always a dialectical struggle between the forces of identification and division. People can never be identical or divided in the absolute sense. We have bodies and experiences and a common language, each of which can help us identify with each other. Yet we also have unique experiences that we may interpret differently from others, keeping us divided. (15)

If identification and division are the two forces central to rhetoric, then it is obvious that image may function in either capacity, depending on the rhetor's intent. Each image carries with it a package of emotions, histories, and experiences, and as such, may function for one audience as identification, and for another, division. Either way, images are powerful symbols no matter what sense organs perceive them.

Blakesley also points out how images are themselves, like any type of symbolization, a kind of "terministic screen." In *Language as Symbolic Action*, Burke defines a terministic screen as the use of language to "direct the attention": "Even if any given terminology is a *reflection* of reality, by its very nature as a terminology it must be a *selection* of reality; and to this extent it must function as a *deflection* of reality" (45). Putting aside for a moment the definition or nature of the term "reality," Burke is obviously pointing out the opportunity costs of language: that to notice or attend means that we are also not noticing and not attending the other. Burke uses photography as an example: the same object photographed several times with different filters provides a metaphor for how selection and composition are themselves meaning-making activities. Blakesley suggests this function of image to be an interpretation of reality:

> [A] photograph functions much like a terministic screen. It is a distillation, a selection of the photographer's visual field that may or may not be entirely representative of the whole panorama or of its subject. A photograph can help us see a subject in new ways, but it cannot help us see it in *all* ways [. . . .] An image is a subjective phenomenon, conjured in the interface between the object and the viewer. An image involves an act, in other words. It is common to think of the imagination as that process of mind chiefly responsible for making images out of experience, words, emotions, and even the visual world. An image is the end result of an act of perception, which itself is more than just looking. Perception involves what we believe and know at least as much as it does the physiological process of seeing. Perception also involves language, which provides the grammar and meaning that direct our attention (our "glance") and help us interpret what we see. (109)

Like any type of textual production, working with images means working with student interpretations, and this is why it is so important that students practice reading and interpreting images as they learn to compose with them. Blakesley and Burke are both referring mostly to visual images here, but the need to understand how perception is itself a type of composition must carry over to any of other sensual rhetorics.[7]

It is too tempting for students to consider image (or most textual production for that matter) only in terms of discursive meaning. Too many times I have asked students to include images in their essays, and too many times students interpret that to mean they should illustrate their essays with images that are primarily discursive. For example, students who mention a telephone in their essay often choose to include a cartoonlike drawing of a telephone (usually clip art); if they mention the frustration of a public debate, they might include an image of a stick figure with a question mark over its head. It takes some explanation and practice for students to see how a *composed* image does more than represent or illustrate something in an essay or hypertext; an image can itself be articulate of its own meaning, can persuade on its own merit, and be comprised of complex layers of meaning and emotion as long as it is composed to do so. In other words, students often will choose images that are largely discursive, rather than choose images that are more non-discursive unless prompted to do so.

Another point to emphasize with image is to change the questions students might ask from "What does the text mean?" (in other words, the student wants to translate the text from non-discursive to discursive text) to "How does it feel?" (a more difficult analysis of the emotional content carried by the images involved in the text). The former is a question of denotation, or discursive meaning; the latter is affective and filled with non-discursive meaning. We are not accustomed to asking students how texts make them feel, except occasionally in a writing workshop. In fact, many might consider the question irrelevant. But as textual producers, students need to have some idea of how their audience is going to respond affectively to the images they construct, and so knowing the context and proclivities of their audience is as paramount as ever. Students must consider how a lavender background to a web page effects not only the overall tone of the other textual modes that are there, but also the overall feeling of that web site. Though such a change is only a change of color, it affects the entire image and tone of that particular text.

By far the most important of the values listed here, image is the lexicon, the purveyor of meaning.[8] Printed text might even be considered in this context a remediation of image (one of the oldest), and to the degree printed text itself occludes image is also the degree to which it is "unclear" or without substance. Words become "mere rhetoric" when they do not promise a vision of change or consensus. In the strictest sense, visual images must be composed, and they often must be composed out of several media or modes. Ultimately, students construct rhetoric by inventing, styling, arranging, storing, and delivering images.

Unity

Just as in traditional written composition the thesis provides unity for an essay, multimedia compositions must also use elements to provide unity. Unity can be the second most important element to composing in multimedia because it helps a viewer understand (or interpret) how to focus their attention. Though it is possible to have several unifying factors in a multimedia composition, unity alone can carry significance, social action, or even clarity. This is the concretizing effort of symbolization, or Bakhtin's centrifugal force of language. In the case of multimedia, unity provides *expogesis* by providing coherence, even if it is only applied to one small element. In terms of most printed texts, unity of the design was often a result of monomodality. Alex

White, in *The Elements of Graphic Design*, characterizes the importance of unity this way:

> Because they had very limited resources, the earliest design practitioners achieved visual continuity rather easily: it was *externally* imposed on them by lack of materials. Today, with the abundant resources available as digital information, giving designers the capability to replicate with near exactitude the work of any era, we must exercise *internal* restraint to achieve harmonious, unified design. (51)

Rhetorically, unity indicates many things, not the least of which is coherence between the various elements. Visually, White suggests that proximity, similarity, repetition, and themes with variations all contribute to the overall unity of a design (59). Of course, as will all things, unity can only be achieved if the audience is taken into consideration. Academic audiences, not surprisingly, will expect clear unity just like they expect (usually) a clear thesis; the local music scene in a specific community may not expect much unity at all, preferring a design that functions rhetorically to indicate informality and other possible countercultural denotations and connotations.

Another potential function of unity is the way format might reflect content, or meaning. Asking students to include accompanying reflections or explanations with their multimodal products is one way to emphasize this kind of unity: the reflection should be similar enough to belong to the main product by repeating visual themes, layouts, colors, images, lines, etc. By requiring this, students have to shift from the idea that their product stands alone in space to the idea that their product and their reflection (in itself a rhetorical product) are in dialogue. Asking students to compose more than one product while stressing unity also asks them to explore more of the audiences expectations (such as working with variations to a theme) while maintaining some awareness regarding their overall purpose and goals. For students to value unity, they must also value the way all the various elements of a composition are in dialogue.

Layering

Layers are key to multimodal authoring because these texts are non-discursive. Whereas discursive texts rely on sequence, one utterance elaborating on the previous utterance, non-discursive texts rely on no specific ordering. In many cases, we read these kinds of texts at once, or in any order we choose. As such, non-discursive texts are complex, and this complexity comes from layering during the composing process. Layers provide depth, texture, complexity, nuance, even contradiction: all of which is important in creating multimedia products that move beyond simple representation/illustration. Many software programs designed for image, animation, and/or film must also allow for layers: sound on top of film, effects and filters on top of photos, loops and samples on top of backgrounds and scenes. Layers, in even small numbers, are dialogic.

Like the traditional canon of arrangement, layers produce tensions and resolutions between various elements of a composition. These tensions and resolutions can nourish the will-to-invent; as White has said, the will-to-invent comes from our "never-ending activity of discharging the desiring tension provoked in the organism in the course of its interaction with its environment" (85–86). One way to consider the changes in media over the centuries is in the number of compositional layers these media employ: in fact, when a text is said to *be* a multimedia text, what is often being pointed to are the various levels of layers and the different media that compose it. Layers *define* multimodality and multimedia throughout history, and this is especially true today in large part due to the way the interfaces built into computational software is modeled on the historical metaphors of painting and animation (the latter always previously reliant on layers). Layers can provide tension for the reader, just as juxtaposition can, and this tension is often the driving force of the composition.

Juxtaposition

When we juxtapose two types of text, the dialogue between them can result in the tensions and resolutions mentioned above, or the juxtaposition may simply add complexity and nuance (of tone, voice, design, and/or emotionality). Through the position of various elements, different conversations, or dialogues, are created, thereby providing the possibility of an argument through the spatiality of the elements involved: "Elements on a screen do not exist in isolation, but are interrelated in ways that are meaningful to users. If these interrelations are obscure, then the meanings of a page may also be obscure for many users" (Cranny-Francis 124). Juxtaposition is fundamental to argument, and, therefore, the rhetorical possibilities of multimedia text extend to persuasion. Collage, "the central technique of twentieth-century visual art," is reliant on juxtaposition and scale: two powerful meaning-making tools in multimodal text (Lanham 40).

> To replicate and juxtapose at will, as collage does, is to alter scale, and scaling change is one of the truly enzymatic powers of electronic text. When you click in the zoom box, you make a big decision: you are deciding on the central decorum of a human event, on the boundary-conditions within which that event is to be staged, and hence on the nature of the event itself. (Lanham 41)

That is to say, juxtaposition forms the basis of many other possible functions and affects, and in the hands of a writer, juxtaposition of image can provide a powerful persuasive tool. Consider the image of the smoking aftermath at ground zero on 9/11 juxtaposed with the sound of a busy marketplace in which individual voices can be heard talking about food and clothing purchases. These two images together evoke powerful, affective, and persuasive meaning not possible if presented alone.

Perspective

Spatial considerations are very important, and in creating an architecture of space, multimodal composers must think about providing a vantage point or a point of view. Context is always important, but context can be manipulated with the right vantage point. In the case of visual texts, point of view might establish with whom we sympathize, or it might establish credibility (such as when a camera is focused on a subject from a downward angle, making the subject seem diminutive, trivial; or, conversely, when a camera focuses on a subject from an upward angle, making the subject seem exaggerated, or powerful). Similar to a review of the historical evolution of an idea, perspective in a multimedia composition provides the "outside-view" as well as privileging a particular interpretation.

The architecture of a composition is usually considered to be the manipulation of space, and the value of perspective works with space to help create an experience for the reader. In terms of web authoring and the use of potentially infinite digital space, the writer is often referred to as an architect:

> [Architecture] conveys an understanding of both the complexity of the task, and its combination of art and science. Just as architecture is more than building, so designing a web site is more than translating text into computer language. Architects create the space that is the living environment of a building by manipulating a range of materials and meanings—building materials, shapes, light, colour, intertextual referents, contextual or locational factors. Web site designers do the same. For both architects and designers the major referent must be the social and cultural expectations of users. If users cannot find their way around a space—worse, if they cannot work out how to connect with that space, to include it in their everyday lives—they will simply avoid it. (Cranny-Francis 124)

Multimodal texts—whether a collage, web site, film, etc.—must construct a world in which the reader can reside. This world must be created for a particular audience (just as any rhetorical text is constructed for a particular audience), and the world must have one or more perspective built in. This is not to say that there is no room for multiple perspectives; on the contrary, non-discursive text is ideal for compositions that require multiple perspectives (exactly because they do not rely on sequence). But students must learn about perspective in multimodal composition because there may be a temptation to (1) always adopt their own particular perspective and, therefore, miss the influence of their audience; or (2) design without perspective in mind, sacrificing any sense that the space they build has purpose, or a goal. Writing any type of persuasive text requires imagining perspectives and, often, choosing at least one.[9]

Langer spends a great deal of time talking about space in *Feeling and Form*, becoming perhaps one of the first theorists to talk about virtual environments:

> Architecture creates the semblance of the World which is the counterpart of a Self. It is a total environment made visible. Where the Self is collective,

as in a tribe, its Word is communal [. . .] And as the actual environment of a being is a system of functional relations, so a virtual "environment," the created space of architecture, is a symbol of functional existence [. . . .] Similarly, the human environment, which is the counterpart of any human life, holds the imprint of a functional pattern; it is the complementary organic form. (98–99)

By characterizing the organic nature of function and form in this way, Langer defines the virtual environment as having the "imprint of a functional pattern" worked into the form itself. Form and function work together or not at all. The value of perspective might also be thought of as reflective of the kind of imprint function requires of form. Put in usability terms, perspective ensures usability by integrating the audience into the interface.

Other values of multimodal composition exist, but these I have found are the most important when asking students to employ non-discursive text. Perhaps what is also clear here is that these values, as well as the will-to-invent discussed already, depend heavily on the imagination. Eva Brann, in her ample work *The World of the Imagination: Sum and Substance*, makes clear that the imagination is not to be denied:

What people brusquely deny as logicians and critics, they affirm as human beings in the intimate conversations in which [. . .] works of prose, poetry, painting, plastic art, architecture, and music. Here, on common ground of the imagination, they point out to each other their discoveries: spots of delight and concealed signals and deft devices. Moreover they seem to regard all such communings as belonging within one universe of discourse and reference. (788)

As these values are practiced, as the full benefit of image is willed out of our imagination, we compose as we imagine.[10] It is a rarely perfect, never finished, and always exciting experience to image, and teaching students how to move into this world of composing the multimodal image we will no longer remain biased towards discursive text alone.

CINEMATIC RHETORIC

By [imagining] the future of multimodal composing, this section begins to sketch out where we are headed in rhetoric and composition if the current trends in composing are extended to their logical conclusion. Not only is rhetoric based . . . on multiple modes, it is also the case that we are headed for an intellectual environment that will privilege multiple modes composed *in time*, as in cinema. This not-very-new cinematic rhetoric holds both exciting promise as well as a new set of challenges for teachers of writing, and as we move toward the increased ubiquity of computers and the simultaneous ubiquity of digital products, textual production will move more towards the cinematic and immersive, requiring writing teachers to be better equipped to analyze, instruct, and assess modes of text constructed . . . not only within space, but also constructed within time.

Lev Manovich, in *The Language of New Media*, makes the case that new media in general is moving us to a world that is becoming increasingly cinematic. This seems to be just an extension of the basic premise that as humans, we experience the world within time, and though we can theorize time as an abstraction, it is a very real abstraction for media:

> The printed word tradition that initially dominated the language of cultural interfaces is becoming less important, while the part played by cinematic elements is becoming progressively stronger. This is consistent with a general trend in modern society toward presenting more and more information in the form of time based audiovisual moving image sequences, rather than as [static] text. (78)

What this says about where we are heading in the newest forms of textual production is that texts, as they become more and more dynamic, are also more and more time-based, or experiential. This opens up non-discursive rhetoric beyond the static realm of textual production notable a century ago to textual production that demands being time-based. Web sites are more and more cinematic, with Flash and Shockwave animations, the success of YouTube, and the increasing broadband available to more and more internet users: "As computer culture gradually spatializes all representations and experiences, they are subjected to the camera's particular grammar of data access. Zoom, tilt, pan, and track—we now use these operations to interact with data spaces, models, objects, and bodies" (Manovich 80). Though film and film studies has been around for over a century, technology will do for cinematic text what digital photography has done for photographic text: it will become computable and, at the same time, more and more available to text producers. With the encroachment of cinema on the textual practices of people, corporations, civic groups, governments, and alliances comes the eventual insistence that our students write these texts (just like students are being asked to write web pages today). "Visual culture of a computer age," says Manovich, "is cinematographic in its appearance, digital on the level of its material, and computational (i.e., software driven) in its logic" (180). In short, writing teachers will need to teach the art of cinematic rhetoric, and we will do that the same way we always have: teaching students to understand the rhetorical situation, by helping them imagine and invent texts, and by giving them the tools and skills they need to produce text. The only way this will ever work, however, is if writing teachers understand and practice the way non-discursive text is rhetorical.

Richard Lanham suggests four changes for writing teachers due to the changes in textual production being offered by new technology and electronic literacy, the fourth of which is a similar prediction that writing will become more cinematic.[11] He states that "writing will be taught as a three-dimensional, not a two-dimensional art" (128). Other than the use of hypertext, Lanham points to animation and other 3-D advancements in particular:

> Ever since Greek rhetoric catalogued the basic figures of speech to recreate in a written culture some of the powers of oral speech and gesture,

we have implied patterns—this is what one branch of rhetorical figura-
tion is all about—but we have never let them complete themselves. Now
they can explicate themselves in animations selected by the reader. The
text will move, in three dimensions. Given the current state of digital animation programs, I think we'll come pretty soon to three-dimensional
modeling of basic argumentative patterns. And we add the dimension of
color [. . . .] And with better compression techniques and gigantic memory storage, we can add sound to our reading as well. Word, image, and
sound will be inextricably intertwined in a dynamic and continually
shifting mixture. (128).

Lanham's prescience here is remarkable, given this was written sometime before 1993. We are already witnessing many of these changes, and there are
many new rhetorical products out there in need of analysis. To the extent that
we can apply the "implied patterns" of ancient Greek rhetoric to today's cultural texts, the best result of this gradual movement is its reliance on our understanding of non-discursive text. To the degree a text can evoke emotional
responses, inspire belief, or become articulate through image, that text is exhibiting non-discursive rhetoric.

One of the best ways to get students to experience many of the important
facets of multimodal text is to ask them to create film—documentary film,
especially. Not only is documentary film inherently rhetorical, it immediately
asks students to consider the five multimedia values listed above: students
must string together a collection of moving images; unify the various elements
to convey a thesis, or point; layer transitions, sounds, music, cutaway shots,
and still images to add to the complexity of the documentary; juxtapose a
variety of images to underscore the main points and change the length of
shots and distance of shots; and, finally, choose a perspective from which to
film, interview, oppose, and, perhaps, change from time to time (students often
need to figure out whether they should include themselves in the film as
well). Such a project is challenging, but most computers today come pre-
loaded with software that can help students create their own films, and their
cell phones often have video capture capabilities.

Writing instructors not only need to consider non-discursive text as part
of what they teach students; writing instructors must also be looking ahead to
see what employers, governments, and the culture at large demand from their
textual producers. If what we do for students has any value at all, we must be
ready to adopt the various changes in textual production as they occur, and
that includes the various theories and models we use to develop our curricula
and assess our students' work.

ASSESSING MULTIMODALITY

Teachers who ask students to compose non-discursive texts based in image
must learn to assess this kind of work. Assessment, especially in context of
rhetoric and composition, is never an easy subject: consensus is difficult to
find among members of the discipline, among departments, or even between

instructors teaching the same course. This section deals with the very real possibility that some teachers would loathe to consider assigning multimodal projects to their students for the fear and intimidation of assessing them. By providing some simple techniques for assessment teachers will not have to hesitate assigning multimodal texts.

Obviously, assessing the traditional essay has always been a difficult matter (Baron, White, Lutz, Kamusikiri). Assessing multimodal texts has similar problems (Sorapure). On the other hand, there are at least three areas regarding the assessment of non-discursive text I would like to stress in this [work] as a way, I hope, to encourage writing teachers to assign multimodal texts in their classrooms: the myth of methodical multimodality and the use of reflective self-assessment.

The Myth of Methodical Multimodality

Just as Sharon Crowley and others have worked to dissuade scholars that the "methodical memory" reflected the "quality of authorial minds"—the more logical the writing, the more logical the mind that produced it—so too is there a myth of methodical multimodality. Multimodality (or monomodality, for that matter) does not reflect the "quality of authorial minds": there is no legitimacy to the notion that some of us are "more visual" or "more aural" than others when it comes time to create rhetorically appropriate texts for an audience—only, perhaps, that some of us are more practiced at it. By dispelling this myth, teachers and students cannot claim to "be less visual" or "be more visual" than others (and therefore more or less inclined toward composing multimodal texts). In fact, multimodality is a compositional form that comes from processes based in images which, coincidentally, happens to be closer to the way humans think than the chaining together of concepts as demanded by discursive text.

Part of the difficulty both students and teachers have who are unfamiliar with incorporating multimedia into their rhetorical texts stems from their inexperience in reading such texts. Just as any writing course stresses close reading as a way to improve writing, so must multimodal reading become a method of improving multimodal writing. As teachers of beginning film courses know, it takes some time to get students used to thinking about the intentionality of these texts. This requires practice in what Lanham calls "looking THROUGH" or "looking AT" text:

> We are always looking first AT [the text] and then THROUGH it, and this oscillation creates a different implied ideal of decorum, both stylistic and behavioral. Look THROUGH a text and you are in the familiar world of the Newtonian interlude, where facts were facts, the world was really "out there," folks had sincere central selves, and the best writing style dropped from the writer as "simply and directly as a stone falls to the ground," precisely as Thoreau counseled. Look AT a text, however, and we have deconstructed the Newtonian world into Pirandello's and yearn to "act naturally." (5)

By looking AT a text we are basically revealing it as hypermediation, to use a term from Jay Bolter and Richard Grusin: "Where immediacy suggests a unified visual space, contemporary hypermediacy offers a heterogeneous space, in which representation is conceived of not as a window on the world, but rather as 'windowed' itself—with windows that open on to other representations or other media" (34). In other words, we see the puppeteer's strings, the wizard behind the curtain, and the mic above the head of the actors. The myth of the methodological multimedia student would have us believe that learning to see "AT" rather than "THROUGH" is a mental faculty closer to genetics than pedagogy, and that simply is not the case.

Once students learn how to read and analyze various multimodal texts, they will also begin to build their own will-to-invent. Writing teachers who do not attempt to foster and encourage a student's will-to-invent will wonder what went wrong as they assess the work they assigned. Successful completion of such writing assignments relies on a nonprocedural invention theory; moreover, it also relies on a writing teacher's willingness to challenge their students. Acknowledging non-discursive text, therefore, broadens what is available to writers during text generation. Invention can become a kind of "methodical memory"—a type of "mentalism" which mystifies text generation and, therefore, makes discovery a process of divination (Crowley 13).[12] By allowing students the ability to accept both discursive and non-discursive forms of symbol-making as legitimate in composition, by weighing discursive text and non-discursive text more equally, writers can combat the myth of methodical multimodality. After all, every assignment is a risk, and pedagogues must learn how to adjust their assignments over time to accommodate their particular student populations.

Reflective Self-assessment

Often touted as the panacea of assessment, self-assessment may not be as useful as some writing teachers might think, especially in terms of helping students to see the potential in the writing they do while, simultaneously, helping them to value the dynamic nature of most multimodal writing in new media today. Though reflection is for the most part a valuable exercise, it must be combined with a rigorous method of self-assessment that connects the process elements with the end product in such a way as to discourage any notions of rigidity or finality. As a changing, ever-evolving process, reflective self-assessment only works when practiced with plenty of outside input from the target audience. In the end, the most direct test for a textual product's success is whether or not that product is rhetorically successful, and in the context of the classroom, this audience may not be overtly obvious to some students (and thus unavailable to them through reflective self-assessment). Although I encourage reflection and self-assessment, it is only effective as long as the writing teacher realizes that the reflections they are getting are also rhetorical.

As I mentioned already . . . , assigning a word-based, discursive reflection/narrative/exposition along with the more non-discursive, multimodal text not only asks that students put the two in dialogue (especially if the design of each is reflective of the other), but it also requires that students reveal the way they have willed the text into existence: that there is intent behind what they do. Trial and error or improvisation may work intuitively to get the text invented and made material in the medium in which the student is working, but the final product must be carefully considered and assessed against audience expectations. Like traditional, discursive text, the way the words first get put on the page can vary dramatically and there is no incorrect method; but also like traditional text, non-discursive text that remains and becomes part of the final product should be defensible, justified by what that student thinks the targeted audience requires. This is why reflective self-assessment can work, and this is also why reflective self-assessment is best paired with a rubric, or list of expectations with point values assigned to each element. Any disparity between what their reflection says and what their numeric self-assessment shows might be resolved with a conversation with the student. In the end, however, students who can be honest with themselves and create products with the audience in mind will benefit the most when there is not a writing teacher anywhere to be found.

CONCLUSIONS

I claim three important points about non-discursive rhetoric . . . : first, image, not word, is the basic unit of meaning-making, and image is primarily non-discursive; second, the affective domain need not rely on the false dualism of mind/body, and emotions are as much a part of our capacity to reason as they are part of our healthy mental lives; and, third, despite an obvious bias towards discursive text, we must assign and assess non-discursive text to students if they ever are to understand how image and the affective work together in rhetoric. As Louise Wetherbee Phelps stated in her essay, "Rhythm and Pattern in a Composing Life,"

> I discover [through reflection] how intimately tangled are my composing energies, my work, and my personal growth, daily life, and relationships [. . . .] There is a symbiotic relation between my composing life and the experience that it interprets, because **the power to connect not only feeds on the vitality of life but illuminates and changes its possibilities** [. . . .] The use of language to compose meaning must, like any universal human act, have both great commonalities and incredible idiosyncrasy and individuality. (257, bold my emphasis)

Phelps describes here a non-sequential, nonlinear process full of emotion, intellectual curiosity, and a "generative urge to drive toward form"—an interesting way to put the will-to-symbolize. The integration of selves and the act of composing underscore the importance of non-discursive meaning-making. . . . Phelps brings into focus the composer as a connector, an illuminator, a generator, and a focuser: all images of "construing and constructing" to use Berthoff's terminology. Taken together, the three aforementioned claims . . .

make a case for the scholarship and pedagogy of non-discursive rhetoric, not to replace what we so often need to do with our symbolization (discursive textual production), but to not be ignored or brushed aside any longer by its dominance, either: as Langer puts it, "[the error] is in the very premise from which the doctrine proceeds, namely that all articulate symbolism is discursive" (88).

Multimodality, though nothing new, asks composers to understand and employ non-discursive rhetoric. Though the division between discursive and non-discursive text is—for the convenience of this analysis—somewhat contrived, setting forth any kind of procedural script for students to follow may be more teachable, but would nonetheless also be contrived. The *values* of non-discursive text . . . are intended, therefore, to help students generate connections as they compose multimodal texts. Like a playground stocked with equipment, composers are then free to build their texts (with their intended audience in mind, of course). These texts are wrought with the emotionality of our real, lived experiences; they are willed into existence, willed into composition, and willed into distribution. These multimodal texts are, therefore, images with both discursive and non-discursive elements rhetorically constructed for an audience. By accounting for both types of symbolization, this [selection] provides a writing theory that, as Lynn Worsham put it, can bring forth a world.

NOTES

1. Rodowick, in *Reading the Figural, or, Philosophy after the New Media*, makes a similar point about broadening the term *writing* to include the figural: "What if we were to assume the figural and plastic arts, rather than standing outside of writing, were indeed themselves 'written,' that is, staged on the 'scene of writing,' as Derrida has considered it? First, as I have already pointed out, the symptomatic place that writing now occupies in film theory as a kind of epistemological limit would have to be overturned. Second, it would be necessary to interrogate how the problematic of 'writing' might encounter and redefine, indeed, might be redefined by, the potential intelligibility of figural discourses, including the cinema" (79–80).

2. In *Imagination: A Study in the History of Ideas*, J. M. Cocking seems to imply that even as the Romantic Revolution began to redefine the value of image and imagination to aesthetics, the world of science continued to view epistemology as dependent on the "primary qualities" associated with rationalism. These qualities provided a functional way to categorize the *use* of the imagination and image primarily through the emphasis of one sense—sight—over all others: "The primary qualities were the scientific, quantitative concepts like shapes and mass; the secondary qualities were the *aesthetic* concepts of how things appear to the senses, how they *feel*. The new scientific rationalism was interested in primary qualities; the growing pre-Romantic sensibility in art was interested in secondary qualities; and these belonged, said Addison, to imagination, to the creative part of the mind" (273).

3. Part one of Carolyn Handa's book *Visual Rhetoric in a Digital World: A Critical Sourcebook* emphasizes repeatedly the need to bring multiliteracies—though the book talks mainly of visual literacies—to the pedagogy of the classroom. Craig Stroup, specifically, states that "the practice and teaching of this hybrid literacy will require that those of us in English studies reexamine our customary distinctions and judgments about literacy" (15); Gunther Kress claims that multimodality refashions traditional text into mixed genres, such that "[l]iteracy and communication curricula rethought in this fashion offer an education in which creativity in different domains and at different levels of representation is well understood," making it possible that "[t]he young who experienced that kind of curriculum might feel at ease in a world of incessant change" (54); J. L. Lemke insists that "[w]e certainly cannot afford to continue teaching our students only the literacies of the mid-twentieth century, or even to simply lay before them the most advanced and diverse literacies of today," finally recommending that "[w]e must help this generation learn to use these literacies

wisely, and hope they will succeed better than we have" (91); and Charles Hill suggests that "we should recognize that this purity [of distinct forms of print or visual text] does not exist in the real world, and pedagogical efforts should be aimed toward helping students deal with combinations of picture, word, and symbol" (109).

4. The first Visual Rhetoric Conference was held in Bloomington, Indiana, in 2001 (information may still be found at http://www.uiowa.edu/~commstud/visual_rhetoric). The International Visual Literacy Association (IVLA) has an annual conference and information on their website about other publications relevant to image studies (http://www.ivla.org).

5. David Blakesley and Collin Brooke, as the editors of that special issue of *Enculturation*, state the following about the relationship between "text" and "image": "It is a world where theorists interrogate the no longer obvious or necessary distinction between texts and images, with profound ethical, political, and epistemological implications, as Mitchell and others have shown. We have served witness to the conflation of word and image in the astounding development of media technologies in the late twentieth century. By many measures, we have rediscovered the visual nature of rhetoric. As students and teachers adapt to these new technologies and venues for reading and writing, it will be important to understand the ways that words and images function rhetorically and together in the various forms of media and literature that grab our attention and so delicately direct the intention" (Introduction).

6. See Hocks' "Understanding Visual Rhetoric in Digital Writing Environments" for more on hybridity in digital texts.

7. The website "Encyclo: Olfactory Groups"—at OzMoz.com—is dedicated to fragrances and fragrance composition. Here is how they describe the way fragrances are developed: "A perfume creator composes a story around a central theme just as a writer would. That theme constitutes the main accord of the composition and will determine the family of the perfume, whereas, the secondary accords will indicate its subfamily. There are eight major families: Floral, Chypre, Oriental (Masculine and Feminine), Woody, Aromatic and Hesperide (Masculine and Feminine). Each one of those olfactive families being itself split into several subfamilies." Students, in order to compose fragrances with these images of families, would have to first be able to identify them in a sample, invent, and then produce a fragrance of their own composition.

8. Rudolf Arnheim's book *Visual Thinking* also suggests that the role of image in the mind is elemental: "What we need to acknowledge is that perceptual and pictorial shapes are not only translations of thought products but the very flesh and blood of thinking itself and that an unbroken range of visual interpretation leads from the humble gestures of daily communication to the statements of great art" (134).

9. In the case of Renaissance painters, Michael Ann Holly's book *Past Looking: Historical Imagination and the Rhetoric of the Image* emphasizes the continuing and historical consequences of perspective: "the perspective system originated by Alberti can be construed not only as a painterly device that permits the artist to locate objects spatially in a certain manifest scheme of relationships, but also as a kind of cognitive map for the cultural historian whose directive is to relate events, attitudes, and personalities in a coherent temporal architectonic" (79). Analysis is also affected by perspective: "Analysis is not something that is superimposed on the structure of the work of art; it is instead a continuation of its importance, a playing out of its own expectations of what its ideal viewer should or should not be saying, of where he should come from, of where he should literally take his stand" (80).

10. "Imagining is a mental act that often appears to reveal itself more crucially in its performance than in any particular product it may bring forth" (Casey 40).

11. Lanham's other three changes for composition are (1) "the essay will no longer be the basic unit of writing instruction" (which is also a claim in this book); (2) "we can back off a turn or two on the thumbscrew of spelling instruction"; and (3) "the nature of punctuation surely will change." That Lanham would bother to predict about spelling and punctuation says more about his regard for composition as a discipline than about authentic future changes in the way we teach writing.

12. In Sharon Crowley's book *The Methodical Memory: Invention in Current-Traditional Rhetoric* (1990), invention becomes affected by the dominant faculty psychology of the eighteenth and nineteenth centuries, a movement in rhetoric she labels as "current-traditional" (xii). The result is that invention became a mechanized, institutionalized, repetitive exercise she calls a "form of intellectual poverty" which "shifts discursive authority away from students and onto the academy" (13). The result is a disempowered view of language: "If we grant that cultures are held together by the persuasive potential that exists within language (when they are not held together by the overt use of force, that is), we must grant the importance of rhetoric to such a culture. And we must further grant the importance of invention. When rhetoric is taught as a system of rules for arranging

words, its students may overlook the fact that language, effectively used, can change the way people think and can move them to act [. . . .] Skilled rhetoricians know how to invent culturally effective arguments. Thus they are able to exert noncoercive control over those who don't suspect the power that is in language" (168).

WORKS CITED

Arnheim, Rudolf. *Visual Thinking*. Berkeley: U of California P, 1969.

Atwan, Robert. *Convergences: Message, Method, and Medium*. New York: Bedford/St. Martin's, 2005.

Bakhtin, M. M. *The Dialogic Imagination: Four Essays*. 1981. Ed. Michael Holquist. Trans. Caryl Emerson and Michael Holquist. Austin: U of Texas P, 1998.

Baron, Dennis. "The College Board's New Essay Reverses Decades Toward Literacy." *Chronicle of Higher Education* 51.35 (2005): B14–B15.

Berthoff, Ann E. *Forming, Thinking, Writing*. 2nd ed. with James Stephens. Portsmouth: Boynton/Cook, 1982.

Blakesley, David. *The Elements of Dramatism*. The Elements of Composition Studies Series 11. New York: Longman, 2002.

Blakesley, David, and Collin Brooke. "Introduction: Notes on Visual Rhetoric." *Enculturation* 3.2 (2001).

Bolter, Jay David, and Richard Grusin. *Remediation: Understanding New Media*. Cambridge: MIT P, 1999.

Brann, Eva T. H. *The World of the Imagination: Sum and Substance*. Lanham: Rowman, 1991.

Burke, Kenneth. *A Rhetoric of Motives*. Berkeley: U of California P, 1969.

Burnett, Ron. *How Images Think*. Cambridge: MIT P, 2004.

Locke Carter, Joyce. "Argumentation in Hypertext: Writing Strategies and the Problem of Order in a Nonsequential World." *Computers and Composition* 20 (2003): 3–22.

Casey, Edward S. *Imagining: A Phenomenological Study*. 2nd Ed. Bloomington: Indiana UP, 2000.

Cocking, J. M. *Imagination: A Study in the History of Ideas*. New York: Routledge P, 1991.

Cranny-Francis, Anne. *Multimedia: Texts and Contexts*. London: Sage, 2005.

Crowley, Sharon. *The Methodical Memory: Invention in Current-Traditional Rhetoric*. Carbondale: Southern Illinois UP, 1990.

Damasio, Antonio. *The Feeling of What Happens: Body and Emotion in the Making of Consciousness*. New York: Harcourt, 1995.

———. *Descartes' Error: Emotion, Reason, and the Human Brain*. New York: Putnam's, 1994.

———. *Looking for Spinoza: Joy, Sorrow, and the Feeling Brain*. Orlando: Harcourt, 2003.

———. *Unity of Knowledge: The Convergence of Natural and Human Science*. Annals of the New York Academy of Sciences. Vol. 935. New York: New York Academy of Sciences, 2001.

Derrida, Jacques. *Of Grammatology*. 1967. Trans. Gayatti Chakravorty Spivak. Baltimore: Johns Hopkins UP, 1976.

Handa, Carolyn. *Visual Rhetoric in a Digital World*. New York: Bedford/St. Martin's, 2004.

Heskett, John. *Toothpicks & Logos: Design in Everyday Life*. New York: Oxford University Press, 2003.

Hill, Charles A., and Marguerite Helmers, eds. *Defining Visual Rhetorics*. Mahwah: Erlbaum, 2004.

Hocks, Mary E. "Understanding Visual Rhetoric in Digital Writing Environments." *CCC* 54.4 (2003): 629–56.

Hocks, Mary E., and Michelle R. Kendrick. *Eloquent Images: Word and Image in the Age of New Media*. Cambridge: MIT P, 2003.

Holly, Michael Ann. *Past Looking: Historical Imagination and the Rhetoric of the Image*. Ithaca: Cornell UP, 1996.

Ione, Amy. *Innovation and Visualization: Trajectories, Strategies, and Myths*. Consciousness Literature and the Arts 1. New York: Rodopi, 2005.

Kress, Gunther. *Literacy in the New Media Age*. Literacies 9. New York: Routledge, 2003.

Langer, Susan K. *Feeling and Form: A Theory of Art*. New York: Scribner's, 1953.

Lanham, Richard. *The Electronic Word: Democracy, Technology, and the Arts*. Chicago; U of Chicago P, 1993.

Lemke, J. L. "Metamedia Literacy: Transforming Meanings and Media." *Visual Rhetoric in a Digital World*. Ed. Carolyn Handa. New York: Bedford/St. Martins, 2004. 71–93.

Manovich, Lev. *The Language of New Media*. Cambridge: MIT P, 2001.

Mitchell, W. J. T. *Iconology: Image, Text, Ideology*. Chicago: U of Chicago P, 1986.

———. *Picture Theory: Essays on Verbal and Visual Representation*. Chicago: U of Chicago P, 1994.

———. *The Language of Images*. Chicago: U of Chicago P, 1980.

Phelps, Louise Wetherbee. "Rhythm and Pattern in a Composing Life." *Writers on Writing*. Ed. Tom Waldrep. New York: Random, 1985. 241–57.

Rodowick, D. N. *Reading the Figural, or, Philosophy after the New Media*. Durham: Duke UP, 2001.

Scharfstein, Ben-Ami. *Ineffability: The Failure of Words in Philosophy and Religion*. Albany: State U of New York P, 1993.

Selber, Stuart. *Multiliteracies for a Digital Age*. Studies in Writing and Rhetoric 26. Carbondale: Southern Illinois UP, 2004.

Selfe, Cynthia L. "Students Who Teach Us: A Case Study of a New Media Text Designer." *Writing New Media: Theory and Applications for Expanding the Teaching of Composition*. Ed. Anne Francis Wysocki, et al. Logan: Utah State UP, 2004. 43–99.

Sorapure, Madeleine. "Between Modes: Assessing Students' New Media Compositions." Kairos 10.2 (Spring 2006). 10 Aug. 2006. <http://english.ttu.edu/kairos/10.2/>.

Stroupe, Craig. "Visualizing English: Recognizing the Hybrid Literacy of Visual and Verbal Authorship on the Web." *College English* 62.5 (2000): 607–32.

Westbrook, Steve. "Visual Rhetoric in a Culture of Fear: Impediments to Multimedia Production." *College English* 68.5 (2006): 457–80.

White, Alex. *The Elements of Graphic Design: Space, Unity, Page Architecture, and Type*. New York: Allworth, 2002.

Worsham, Lynn. "The Question Concerning Invention: Hermeneutics and the Genesis of Writing." *PRE/TEXT* 8.3–4 (1987): 197–244.

Wysocki, Anne Frances, Johndan Johnson-Eilola, Cynthia L. Selfe, and Geoffrey Sirc, eds. *Writing New Media: Theory and Applications for Expanding the Teaching of Composition*. Logan: Utah State UP, 2004.

Wysocki, Anne Frances. "Opening New Media To Writing: Opening and Justifications." *Writing New Media: Theory and Applications for Expanding the Teaching of Composition*. Ed. Anne Francis Wysocki, et al. Logan: Utah State UP, 2004. 1–41.

PART FOUR

Assignments and Assessment

Introduction to Part Four

As we continue the century's old debate over what a composition course should be and how to teach such a course, we know one thing for certain: multimodal composition can no longer be ignored. At the heart of this debate exists a tension between those who deem it necessary to drastically change our existing pedagogies to accommodate new technologies and multimodal composition, and those who opt for slowly adapting old or current pedagogies to accommodate new technologies and multimodal composition. Underlying this tension, though, is the need to more closely examine the nature of meaning making in multimodal composition. Understanding how, what, and why knowledge is created during the act of composing multimodally is key to determining the best way to approach our teaching of multimodal composition. The authors in Part Four seek such an understanding.

On the one hand, some of the selections in Part Four demonstrate pedagogical strategies and assignments that may seem familiar to us as they are popular strategies and assignments that have been adopted from traditional composition. Yet, claiming that adapting existing pedagogies would limit our students' understanding of multimodal composition, some of the authors here suggest we cannot simply translate old or current pedagogy into new multimodal composition pedagogy since such a translation would mislead students into believing they can approach working with traditional texts in the same ways they can work with multimodal texts. The authors in Part Four contend that we must approach the composition classroom differently when we incorporate multimodal composition. For example, Daniel Anderson suggests we must conceptualize the composition classroom as a construction site or new media studio so that we may change student perceptions of what is considered composition, effectively breaking from traditional conceptions of the composition classroom and helping them to understand the different ways of knowing that multimodal texts demand readers possess.

Ultimately, the readers of this section need to keep in mind what is at stake when they create multimodal composition assignments, activities, and lesson plans. As we decide what to teach and what not to, we might ask ourselves if we are relying on practices that limit our students. For example, how far away from traditional print pedagogy does multimodal composition pedagogy need to be in order to be successful? Can there be a balance between the traditional and nontraditional assignments, and how do we know when we've achieved it? In borrowing from Kress in the previous section of the book, we may also ask: What do we gain and what do we lose when we implement multimodal composition pedagogy?

Research in multimodality has only recently begun to treat teaching and assessing multimodal composition as a serious undertaking. Jody Shipka, for instance, recently notes the "dearth of scholarship devoted to the assessment of multimodal and new media texts" ("Negotiating" W346). Yet, despite this limited research on implementing multimodal composition curriculum in writing programs, composition instructors are increasingly teaching multimodal assignments, even if only on an individual teacher basis. Though departments are starting to provide teachers with some training and resources to implement multimodal composition pedagogy, these moves are not big enough to provide the support necessary for larger-scale implementation. More resources like Cynthia L. Selfe's *Multimodal Composition: Resources for Teachers* and Cheryl E. Ball and Kristin L. Arola's *Visualizing Composition 2.0: Tutorials for Multimodal Composition*, to name just a few, will make multimodal composition more accessible to a larger number of people, and will serve as justification for investing in the support necessary for larger scale implementation. In the meantime, however, the examples in this section can serve as inspiration for instructors who desire to incorporate multimodal composition into their courses as they highlight ways individuals can do so on their own.

Jody Shipka's web text, "This Was (NOT) an Easy Assignment: Negotiating an Activity-Based Framework for Composing," begins Part Four by presenting a two-year process-based research study that examines the multimodal work of students in a first-year composition course. She offers us her case studies, including three interviews with students, to showcase the tasks and decisions students undertook while composing multimodal texts. She argues that because students were able to utilize a large variety of skills, materials, modes, and technologies, they had more agency in deciding the purposes of their tasks and texts, in challenging traditional understandings of communication, and in producing meaningful texts. In other words, like many authors in this book, Shipka highlights the power multimodal composition can place in the hands of the writer.

In the second reading in Part Four, "Digital Mirrors: Multimodal Reflection in the Composition Classroom," Debra Journet, Tabetha Adkins, Chris Alexander, Patrick Corbett, and Ryan Trauman, present multiple perspectives on the act of reflection, specifically as it is carried out by graduate students who are enrolled in Journet's Digital Media and Composition seminar class. Reflection is more than likely a big part of any composition classroom. However, oftentimes, reflections take the form of written words. Journet asked her students to experiment with assigning their own students other modes and media for reflection. In doing so, her students learned that "modality changed the nature of reflection" because the different modes they used made them think differently about what they were doing as they reflected. In other words, the students became aware of the possibilities/capabilities of different modes. This understanding led them to consider how such reflective practices might impact their own teaching of composition, even as it helped them to understand "the process of teaching and learning with digital media." Those of us who prepare graduate students to teach composition courses can look to Journet and her colleagues as an example of how we might design graduate seminars that critically examine multimodal composition as well as ask graduate students to participate in multimodal composition themselves. As we read this chapter, we might question what strategies or other assignments could help graduate students prepare for teaching multimodal composition, or what texts we may use as examples of what to teach with and assign.

As mentioned above, Daniel Anderson sees the writing classroom as a construction site and new media studio where students participate in activities that develop their practical thinking skills, personal agency, and public participation in civic duties. In "The Low Bridge to High Benefits: Entry-Level Multimedia, Literacies, and Motivation," he explores how we come to know new technologies through experimentation and how these technologies can be utilized in the classroom. He contends that learning multiliteracies leads to personal growth, and he shows us how through examples of what he calls "low-bridge" projects—projects that use new technologies which require minimal technical skill to participate in the act of production. Thus, the composition classroom must be conceptualized as a studio where production is the central activity for hands-on creative work because, like Shipka, Anderson sees a link between being able to produce using multiple modes and media and being able to realize agency, enabling students to fully express themselves.

Much of the debate over whether we should incorporate multimodal composition has to do with how we go about assessing it. How should we assess modes other than print, especially if our training as instructors has largely been on print-based texts? The last two selections in this section attempt to address these questions. Madeleine Sorapure's web text "Between Modes: Assessing Student New Media Compositions" presents a brief overview of the small amount of scholarship on assessing new media texts, and questions whether old means for assessing print-based texts should be adopted, altered, or ignored in terms of assessing nonprint-based texts. Using the tropes of metaphor (substitution) and metonymy (combination/association) as a framework for assessing, Sorapure concludes that it is necessary for instructors to help students examine and work with the relationships between the modes they use to compose their texts. In doing so, instructors and students are better able to see more closely the meaning that arises from combining modes.

Like Sorapure, Elizabeth A. Murray, Hailey A. Sheets, and Nicole A. Williams, in their web text "The New Work of Assessment: Evaluating Multimodal Compositions," demonstrate how to assess multimodal composition without requiring the use of new language as Sorapure suggests. Rather, they use existing department criteria (a grading rubric) to assess work that goes beyond print. Like many instructors, these authors did not have much say in designing a grading rubric for their courses as it was designed by the English department's composition committee. Murray, Sheets, and Williams, like many instructors, made the most of their situation and found ways to use such a rubric to assess the multimodal texts their students were composing in their classrooms. While they do not invent new grading criteria, they do, however, agree with Sorapure that instructors must closely examine the relationships between modes when they are combined in order to understand the meaning of the text. But, unlike Sorapure, they argue for a rhetorical approach that considers both the context for and the affordances (or capabilities) of modes when teaching multimodal texts. Drawing from Cynthia Selfe's sourcebook *Multimodal Composition: Resources for Teachers*, the authors of this piece use research that they gathered from surveys, student work, and observations to show and explain how such an approach can be successfully carried out.

Readers of this section might use these discussions of assessment to think more deeply about the nature of designing multimodal composition assignments. For instance, does using existing grading rubrics originally created for print put students in a position that prevents them from making necessary design decisions? Are we cheating them out of a mind frame or way of thinking, giving them instead a contradictory framework for thinking about composition? Do old ways of assessing limit students' understanding of the meaning-making affordances of different modes? Does translating conventions of print (i.e., must have a thesis, must have correct grammar) to different modes exacerbate a somewhat contorted view of composing with different modes? Possible answers to these questions will help instructors new to multimodal composition develop a more critical eye when designing courses and assessing student work.

WORKS CITED

Ball, Cheryl E., and Kristin L. Arola. *ix: Visualizing Composition 2.0: Tutorials for Multimodal Composition*. Bedford/St. Martin's. 2011. Web. 2012. <http://www.bedfordstmartins.com/Catalog /products/ixvisualizingcomposition20-firstedition-ball>.
Selfe, Cynthia, ed. *Multimodal Composition: Resources for Teachers*. Cresskill: Hampton, 2007. Print.
Shipka, Jody. "Negotiating Rhetorical, Material, Methodological, and Technological Difference: Evaluating Multimodal Designs." *College Composition and Communication* 61.1 (2009): W343–W366. Print.

17

This Was (NOT) an Easy Assignment: Negotiating an Activity-Based Framework for Composing

JODY SHIPKA

Jody Shipka's web text argues that composition students should experiment with modes besides print. As mentioned in the Introduction to Part Four, she investigated students' employment of an activity-based framework and their uses of multiple modes to complete assignments designed specifically to encourage such uses.

Figure 17-1 is a screenshot of a portion of Shipka's introduction as well as an outline of the text, which can be seen on the left side of the image. Readers are encouraged to go online to experience the rest of the web text and to see examples of students' multimodal work. The web address is http://www.bgsu.edu/departments/english/cconline/not_easy

FIGURE 17-1   Shipka's introduction and interface.

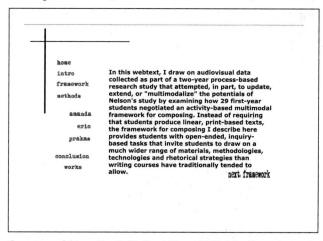

> home
> intro
> framework
> methods
>
> amanda
> eric
> prakas
>
> conclusion
> works
>
> In this webtext, I draw on audiovisual data collected as part of a two-year process-based research study that attempted, in part, to update, extend, or "multimodalize" the potentials of Nelson's study by examining how 29 first-year students negotiated an activity-based multimodal framework for composing. Instead of requiring that students produce linear, print-based texts, the framework for composing I describe here provides students with open-ended, inquiry-based tasks that invite students to draw on a much wider range of materials, methodologies, technologies and rhetorical strategies than writing courses have traditionally tended to allow.
>
> next framework

Source: Computers and Composition Online Special Issue (2007). http://www.bgsu.edu/cconline/not _easy/intro/intro_three.html

From *Computers and Composition Online* Special Issue (2007). http://www.bgsu.edu /cconline/not_easy/

18 Digital Mirrors: Multimodal Reflection in the Composition Classroom

DEBRA JOURNET, TABETHA ADKINS,
CHRIS ALEXANDER, PATRICK CORBETT,
AND RYAN TRAUMAN

The collaboratively written web text "Digital Mirrors: Multimodal Reflection in the Composition Classroom" presents graduate student teachers and their instructor's understanding of what it means to create daily reflections on the teaching of composition using different modes and media. Through their practice with different modes and media, the graduate student teachers (Tabetha Adkins, Chris Alexander, Patrick Corbett, and Ryan Trauman) in Debra Journet's seminar gained experience with technology that they could in turn share with their future composition students. Readers will find the examples of reflections to be particularly useful in imagining the type of work students can do in multiple modes.

This selection includes two screen shots, one of the web text's home page, which provides readers with an understanding of the web text's contents and navigation, and one of the web text's student examples, which includes a link to video text. The rest of the web text can be located at http://www.bgsu.edu/cconline/Digital_Mirrors /index.html

From *Computers and Composition Online* (2008). http://www.bgsu.edu/cconline/Digital _Mirrors/

FIGURE 18-1   Home page and interface.

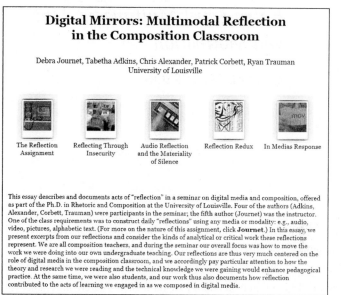

Source: Computers and Composition Online (2008). http://www.bgsu.edu/cconline/Digital_Mirrors/

FIGURE 18-2   Student reflection example.

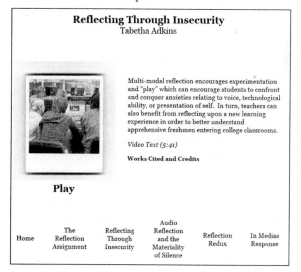

Source: Computers and Composition Online (2008). http://www.bgsu.edu/cconline/Digital_Mirrors /tabetha_adkins_home_01.htm

19 The Low Bridge to High Benefits: Entry-Level Multimedia, Literacies, and Motivation

DANIEL ANDERSON

There is ample evidence that people do not learn anything well unless they are both motivated to learn and believe that they will be able to use and function with what they are learning in some way that is in their interest.

— THE NEW LONDON GROUP

If I worked for 4 hours on biology I would be absolutely miserable, yet I worked for probably 10 on my Tyger collage alone. This is what college classes should be all about, new approaches to things we thought we knew all about. Thanks for letting me think originally again.

— ALEX SHEARER

Alex's assessment of his experience in a first-year writing class clarifies the work of the New London Group (1996), whose call for multiliteracies reflected in part dissatisfaction with alphabetic literacy but in whole a desire to see students as motivated agents of change. The New London Group used the concept of design to show the interconnectedness of a range of literacies, citing five design grammars (linguistic, visual, audio, gestural, and spatial) and a sixth, synthetic category (multimodal) where literacies converge. But the group offered this refined conception of literacies in the service of a larger project, explaining, "literacy educators and students must see themselves as active participants in social change, as learners and students who can be active designers—makers—of social futures" (1996, 65). The group's work offered a helpful corrective to the tendency to link computer literacy to technology-related skills, asking us instead to concentrate on individual engagement and civic opportunities.

But taking the computer out of computer literacies can be equally problematic. Stuart Selber (2004) brought the technological aspects of literacy back into focus by delineating multiliteracies into three categories, one of which is

---

From *Computers and Composition* 25 (2008): 40–60.

a functional literacy concerned with the operation of computers and software. Selber was careful not to limit functional literacy to "the technical aspects of software applications, hardware components, and operating systems" (32–33). Instead, we can critique the cultural dimensions of computers even as we learn to use technologies. Selber suggested that educators make use of computers without falling victim to technical determinism, which yields either false hope based on inevitable technical progress or false hopelessness based on the loss of human agency in a world determined by technologies. The trick is to engage technologies while avoiding lenses through which "both utopian and dystopian visions [of technologies] are exaggerated" (Feenberg, 2002, n.p.). We need a model for computer literacy that emphasizes what Bruno Latour has called "the actors in a technical project" (1996, 162). Following Latour, we can see technologies as nodes on a network that also includes individuals and ideas, each element having an agency.

The final complication arises when we put the network into motion. Technologies are shaped by humans and ideas and in turn reshape human concerns and individuals. According to Latour,

> [technology] is not a human thing, nor is it an inhuman thing. It offers, rather, a continuous passage, a commerce, an *interchange* between what humans inscribe in it and what it prescribes to humans. It translates the one into the other. This thing is the nonhuman version of people, it is the human version of things, twice displaced. What should it be called? Neither object nor subject. An instituted object, quasi object, quasi subject, a thing that possesses body and soul indissolubly. (1996, 213)

Latour offered this interchange metaphor when referring to the microprocessor, and the point was that the microprocessor quickly becomes a hybrid that brings things (both physical things and conceptual matters) and humans together. So, too, computer literacy acts as entity and non-entity, a mediator that continually links converging technologies, concerns, and people. For educators, such a conception allows us to turn computer literacy from a thing into an activity, sloughing off definitions that would fix computer literacy as a set of skills in favor of processes through which multiple literacies can flow, processes like borrowing, mixing, layering, and sharing. Further, seeing that literacies emerge through interchanges of things and people, we can affirm a human agency to counter technical determinism. Concrete technologies and functional skills are put into motion to implement human goals and desires. At the same time, the interchange model gives us permission to concentrate on things, to emphasize skills and emerging technologies. Our understanding of literacies, then, moves continually from concrete tools and skills to conceptual realizations and human goals like a finger tracing both sides of a mobius strip.

But is there more to be gotten from the interplay of people and machines? Why bother to bring composition into the twenty-first century if we can't carry over the ineffable payoff that comes from creation? Why else would Latour (1996) suggest that "there really is love in technologies" or explain that "metaphor means transportation" (282)? Why would Gregory Ulmer (2003) build his electronic literacy, electracy, around the punctuum that stings or assert, "the basic device of aesthetic composition (metaphor to put it in one word), marginalized in literate education, becomes central to electrate learning" (69)? The ultimate value of transforming literacies is to help students discover the ineffable possibilities of the creative process. Ulmer was right to point out how such a process is frequently marginalized in education. My experience is that much of education delivers cold information and boredom. If converging humans and machines not only yield multiple literacies but also hold the potential for delivering body and soul realizations, engagement, educational magic, shouldn't that be our focus when integrating technologies into the composition classroom? The question is rhetorical. The rest of this essay will try to explain why.

1. CONSTRUCTION SITES, PEDAGOGIES, AND PERSONAL MOTIVATION

In *Reassembling the Social*, Latour offered the metaphor of the construction site to call attention to the "making" that goes into any concept or concern, suggesting that construction sites "offer an ideal vantage point to witness the connections between humans and non-humans" (2005, 88). Wandering around such sites, we're likely to experience discoveries unavailable by simply examining a finished product. Latour reported on the experiences of science studies practitioners exploring constructions of facts: "we went back stage; we learned about the skills of practitioners; we saw innovations come into being; we felt how risky it was; and we witnessed the puzzling merger of human activities and non-human entities" (2005, 90). The construction site is intimately concerned with innovations, looking toward technologies as agents that bring people and concerns together. It is also a site of risk and experimentation, a place where "silent implements stop being taken for granted when they are approached by users rendered ignorant and clumsy by *distance*— distance in time as in archaeology, distance in space as in ethnology, distance in skills as in learning" (2005, 80). At such a site, technologies influence activities and people, "objects become mediators," and accidents reveal connections between humans, ideas, and things. Latour's construction site offers a useful model for thinking about integrating new media into the composition classroom. By relying on free, consumer-level (what I call low-bridge) technologies, we can easily create a construction site that emphasizes things used by people (technologies) and people making things (projects). This approach offers practical benefits for instructors and personal benefits for students.

Creating a construction site based on emerging technologies serves as a catalyst for instructors wishing to reconceptualize pedagogies—technical things shed new light on existing paradigms and open possibilities for new methodologies. Reflecting on her experiences teaching with word processors, Patricia Sullivan showed how learning about new technologies can lever conceptual change and create "the possibility, even the probability, that present and future technology may well 'threaten' some aspects of writing theory and pedagogy" (1991, 46). Sullivan's work and early explorations of word processors illuminate one way the discipline of composition comes to know technologies. The process begins with access to new (often soon-to-be-ubiquitous) technologies, enters an experimental phase in which teachers and writers employ the technologies, and then matures into a reflective phase in which theories and pedagogies are layered over activities. Obviously such a model oversimplifies.[1] But, for the purposes of finding practical means of transforming education, the model of technology first, experimentation next, and reflection later offers a direct route to classroom practices through which new literacies can emerge and converge.

I recognize that the claim above raises red flags about technical determinism and the dangers of operating without complete knowledge. I'm loath to delete the section, though, because it will be disingenuous to argue below that students benefit from technical challenges and unfamiliarity without allowing that instructors, too, require skill challenges and will benefit from an ability to experiment with new technologies. Putting technology first promotes opportunities for play and experimentation that can lead to new learning. Albert Rouzie (2005) complained that institutional forces "[blind] most educators to the significance of play already occurring in their classrooms" (27). Margaret Mackey (2002) pointed out that experimentation is "a form of rehearsal [. . . and] an important part of mastering new media" (187). James Paul Gee (2003) made a similar connection with video games, extending the link to critical thinking:

> The game encourages [the gamer] to think of himself as an active problem solver, one who persists in trying to solve problems even after making mistakes; one who, in fact, does not see mistakes as errors but as opportunities for reflection and learning. It encourages him to be the sort of problem solver who, rather than ritualizing the solutions to problems, leaves himself open to undoing former mastery and finding new ways to solve new problems in new situations. (44)

Unknown technical things create ideal situations in which literacy-enriching problem solving activities might play out. Further, entry-level technologies with simplified interfaces, limited feature sets, and broad availability can ease the way towards innovation.[2] Not surprisingly, instructors who jump-start innovation with entry-level software soon find the experience yields pedagogical insights and theorizing that can be layered over practice through reflection, a process often characterized by borrowings and recuperations.

But engaging technical things comes with a bigger payoff. Experimenting with unfamiliar technologies can facilitate a sense of creativity that can lead to motivation. In one of his many studies on creativity and motivation, Mihaly Csikszentmihalyi (2000) pointed out that "one needs to grow, to develop new skills, to take on new challenges to maintain a self-concept as a fully functioning human being" (199). Csikszentmihalyi channeled his discussion of skills and motivation through the concept of flow, or autotelic experience, a state of consciousness associated with creativity and characterized by a sense of intrinsic motivation and pleasure. The results of flow resemble the higher aspirations of critical and media literacies, providing individuals with opportunities for action, a sense of competence and control, heightened awareness of personal identity, avenues for creative self-expression, and a sense of agency. Sadly, Csikszentmihalyi revealed, "our compulsory and uniform educational system is a sure guarantee that many, perhaps a majority in each generation, will spend their youth in meaningless unrewarding tasks" (100). For tasks to have meaning, there must be an optimal correspondence between their degree of difficulty and the skill levels one brings to them. Overly-challenging tasks can limit flow. In most educational situations, though, the opposite holds true. Familiar tasks fail to present a level of challenge that would lead to flow.

Could it be that low-bridge new media technologies provide the right mix of challenge and ease of use for instructors and students to develop a sense of control, creativity, and flow? The entry-level nature of low-bridge technologies ameliorates difficulties that can shut down flow, but the challenge of composing with unfamiliar forms opens pathways to creativity and motivation. Fulfilling Csikszentmihalyi's criteria, low-bridge media technologies "offer a range of 'flow channels' at various levels of skill and commitment" (80). Of course, there is no guarantee that all students will develop this sense of control when faced with skill challenges based on learning new technologies. Still, for those who do respond well to the tasks, the payoffs extend beyond any service-or content-oriented conception of education, since "at the height of their involvement with the activity [people] lose a sense of themselves as separate entities, and feel harmony and even a merging of identity with the environment" (194). The practical benefits of bringing low-bridge technologies into the classroom yield to personal benefits of identity growth and motivation. Why bother with technical skills and things in the composition classroom? Because the making that occurs through the interplay of things and humans yields creative and personal transformations.

2. THE PRACTICAL AND PERSONAL BECOME PUBLIC

Low-bridge media activities offer many opportunities for personal transformations based on engagement, transformations that result in new literacies. But we can also link these multimedia modes of reading and writing to another level of literacy: critical, civic participation and agency. Surveying a range of research, Selber (2004) repeated the call for "an educational system that prepares students to be social critics rather than indoctrinated consumers of material culture" (95). Selber marked this engagement with the term "critical literacies," outlining opportunities for students to develop critiques as they look at design cultures, use contexts, institutional forces, and popular representations of technology. This ability to critique through engagement with technology provides access to (often hidden) cultural discourses (107). But this ability to critique must be more than purely analytical.

Selber sketched possibilities for resistance and change inherent in informed critique, then extended those possibilities through personal agency and rhetorical literacies:

> Students should not be just effective users of computers, nor should they be just informed questioners. Although these two roles are essential, neither one encourages a sufficient level of participation. In order to function most effectively as agents of change, students must also become reflective producers of technology. (182)

Selber had in mind here not student programmers who build their own software (though that is certainly a possible extension of such literacy); instead Selber allowed for this literacy to develop when students are active composers of electronic texts. In discussing literacy development in children, Leslie M. Morrow and Diane H. Tracey (2004) tied agency similarly to multimedia, suggesting that giving students

> the opportunity to make choices about the literacy tasks to participate in offers students responsibility, and empowers them with control over the situation. Choice needs to involve multiple modalities for learning such as more traditional avenues with pencil and paper experiences as well as developing literacy skills through the use of technology, drama, or the visual arts. (477–478)

The design pedagogy advocated by the New London Group (1996) made clear that the connections between literacy, agency, and motivation also extend to cultural critique and possibilities for change: "Designing restores human agency and cultural dynamism to the process of meaning-making . . . [W]orkers, citizens, and community members are ideally creative and responsible makers of meaning. We are, indeed, designers of our social futures" (see p. 208 in this volume). Returning to Csikszentmihalyi, we find that the sense of control and accompanying loss of self derived from the flow experience may offer a "way to cope with problems of personal and societal disintegration . . . by increasing people's control over their own lives" (195). Further, the movement from personal to public through agency leads back to literacy. Cynthia Selfe and Gail E. Hawisher (2004) explained that "people are not simply victims caught in a Web of circumstances" and suggested that "personal motivation and interests, individual actions and decisions . . . can play a substantial role in the development of electronic literacies" (182). The point extends the discussion of literacy and change by reaching back toward the personal and motivation. Motivation becomes not just an effect of integrating low-bridge technologies into the classroom, but a necessary ingredient of conceptions of critical literacy meant to promote agency and change.

The links between motivation, new media, multiliteracies, agency, and civic participation can be readily traced. Less clear, however, are the connections between these items and changes in education. The most compelling advocate for considering personal motivation in terms of transformation in composition is probably Geoffrey Sirc. Sirc doesn't argue for either alphabetic or multimedia literacies but rather advocates that compositionists aim for the expressive *process* of production. Again, we must put things into motion. Sirc (2002) explained, "defining composition, exclusively around the parameters of page or canvas, results in that conventional, academic surface" and instead suggested we think of composition "as a record of tracings, or gestures, a result of a body moving through life" (111). Sirc was looking for a composition that might be "anti-conventional, expressive, discursively hybrid, and technologically innovative" but instead finds in most scholarship a composition that "is all about conventions; which sees its retreat from expressionism in academicism as some sort of progress; which prefers a purified, taxonomized, monophony to hybridity; and consigns discourse on technology to a subrealm of the discipline" (173). Sirc is clear that this over-disciplining of composition bleeds the motivation from students, leading only to "alienation" and "exhaustion" (209). New composing processes feature literacies like juxtaposition, parody, or pastiche and build upon student interests. These remix modes can overcome the boredom and "exhaustion in most writing assignments" (212), making students "architects of their own aesthetics" (132).

Kathleen Tyner (1998) also connected motivation with educational reforms, explaining, "unfortunately, the ideal of citizen democracy is in conflict with the repressive and undemocratic education that students receive daily in the school environment" (229). Tyner saw the liberal arts and media literacies as providing a possible model of reform, hoping that "as communication forms merge in digitized multimedia formats, new relationships between visuals, texts, and graphics [will] call for creative expression . . . ushering in a rich renaissance of artistic expression . . ." (229). Similarly, Csikszentmihalyi suggested, "to test the limits of the mind, the first education should be an artistic one—not in the sense of learning about art or even learning to do art, but in the deeper sense of acquiring an artistic vision" (2000, 205). The recommendations, then, have come full circle—from the practical things and skills of technology to the personal energy of motivation to the public promise of civic change, and now back to the personal power of creative vision, back to the conceptual promise of moving things. If multimedia is linked to motivation, which is linked to literacy, which in turn is linked to critical participation in civil society, then it should come as no surprise that Sirc asked us to integrate new media in our classrooms by beginning with "a theory of textuality that trie[s] to get in touch with the energies in things, to renew people's engagement with the world" (289). The case studies below trace some of those engagements.

3. BUILDING BRIDGES FROM ALPHABETIC LITERACIES USING PLAYLISTS

Kathleen Tyner suggested that even activities calling for multiliteracies can benefit from a healthy grounding in alphabetic literacy, especially for instructors who likely "are secure in their ability to explicate texts with students . . . [and who] can apply familiar principles of alphabetic literacy to further understanding of new genre[s] and media while their tool skills are getting 'up

FIGURE 19-1   Playlists composed by Lindsay Smith and Helen Kearns.

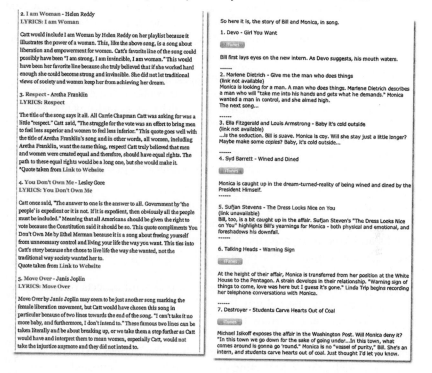

to speed'" (92). Playlist assignments borrow from alphabetic literacies while using the raw materials of music to press toward additional, emerging literacy skills. Students create either a profile or a short narrative by identifying a set of songs that represents the identity of a person or tells a story. The images in Figure 19-1 represent excerpts from two playlists and demonstrate some of the possibilities.

Lindsay Smith's *Carrie Chapman Catt* playlist resembles the familiar research essay in its informational focus. Helen Kearns's *Bill and Monica* playlist represents the affair between Bill Clinton and Monica Lewinski through song. These projects reside very close to traditional conceptions of alphabetic literacy—each writer has excerpted and discussed lyrics from songs much as one might do in an essay. However, new literacies converge with these familiar composing skills. First, a variation of information literacy developed through the playlist projects. Using basic HTML linking, the projects operated on a logic of selecting and borrowing from existing sources. Students determined what amount of a song could responsibly be excerpted, what relevance the excerpted piece had to the profile or story, and what kinds of links could be provided to either lyrics or song samples. The project provided an easy route to thinking about information and remix literacies that were layered over the alphabetic literacies built into the project.

Additionally, the playlist offered a bridge between alphabetic and audio literacies. Students practiced listening literacies as they selected and sequenced the songs that would go into the playlist. Alex Shearer, for instance, created a narrative playlist about a relationship. Discussing the second song in his playlist, he explained,

> all of a sudden the man's attitude changes, and he starts to feel attachment to the woman. This change of attitude comes when the song "Sir Psycho Sexy" transitions from the lyrical phase to an instrumental section which continues until the end of the song. Whereas the first section has a funky, seductive beat, the second section flows freely and is more melodious. Again, the transition in the song mirrors the change in the man's attitude toward the girl he has met. (Shearer, personal communication, November 10, 2006)

A low level of technical effort is required to bring this kind of audio thinking into the composition classroom. While students made links to song samples and Web resources, the basic premise of hearing, selecting, and sequencing songs could have been accomplished using a word processor (or a pencil and a cocktail napkin for that matter).

Finally, playlists expose one of the most powerful aspects of low-bridge multimedia projects: their ability to motivate. The New London Group suggested, "to be relevant, learning processes need to recruit, rather than attempt to ignore and erase, the different *subjectivities*—interests, intentions, commitments, and purposes—students bring to learning" (1996, 71). This engagement is no small matter. Reflecting on his playlist, Alex reported, "I liked the idea of the playlist assignment right from the start. There are certain songs that have always been associated with moods that I have. The trick was blending those moods into a story and then attaching songs whose lyrics made sense in a sequence." Danielle Veal offered a similar reaction:

> I was very excited when I learned that I had to create my own playlist. Music is a huge part of my life. I own over 100 CDs and I have played the violin since the 5th grade. Creating a playlist allowed me to play the role of an executive producer at a record label. I chose the songs that went on the CD and the order in which they were listed. Instead of being random songs, like most CDs, my CD told a story. This playlist tells the story of a young girl named Monica who struggles with obstacles in life. This topic was inspired by close friends of mine and even a little from my own life. (Veal, personal communication, December 7, 2006)

Without exception, students found the ability to bridge their personal and academic interests afforded by the assignment to be highly motivating.

4. BRIDGING FUNCTIONAL AND VISUAL LITERACIES IN COLLAGES

As instructors and students move further away from alphabetic literacies, technical things and skills become more central to the composing process. Composing digital collages, in particular, ratchets up technical difficulties.

FIGURE 19-2   Moriah Halper's "The Tyger" collage.

But there is justification for teaching students to use a digital image editor in the writing classroom.[3] If students are to become visually literate, it helps to spend some time making things with the digital technologies of visual composition. A comparison of two collages can illustrate.

Moriah Halper's collage in Figure 19-2 represents an explication of the poem "The Tyger" by William Blake. The collage integrates images of fire, a tiger, a soldier, an angel, a lamb, and a set of manacles. The elements have corollaries with the imagery of the poem. Additionally, this collage makes use of a snippet of text, a couplet from the poem. The couplet reveals how alphabetic and visual literacies can inform each another. Consider how a reading of the collage might progress if it did not contain the text. Would the imagery alone be enough to make the connection with the poem? In terms of visual literacy, it might be tempting, then, to argue that if the poem can be read through the image without the text, it has succeeded in creating a parallel visual message. Moriah explained:

> I interpreted the poem as if there was a young child questioning God and wondering about all of the evil things in the world . . . I also placed the little girl so that she was looking down upon all of the "evil," as if she was inspecting it and curious about it . . . The red colors in the bottom half of the collage correspond to the fiery imagery in the poem, seen with words like "burning," "fire," and "furnace." (Halper, personal communication, September 23, 2006)

Simple analysis can bring out elements of visual rhetoric like arrangement, balance, contrast, emphasis, shading, color, shape, and line. But, through production of the collage, Moriah applied these visual concepts to the representation of content-area knowledge, here literary interpretation, "plac[ing] the little girl so that she [is] looking down upon all of the evil."

FIGURE 19-3   Kandis Rich's "The Tyger" collage.

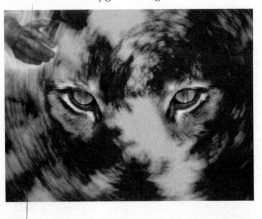

To consider how far such visual arguments can be pushed, examine Figure 19-3 depicting a collage created by Kandis Rich explicating the same poem.

Of Moriah's collage, we asked what would happen if we removed the alphabetic couplet. Let's perform the visual equivalent on Kandis's collage by asking what would happen if we removed the hand of creation from the top-left corner of the image. Would the questions about God inherent in the poem be lost with the removal of the hand? If so, this visual element acts as an explanatory reference, linking the concept of creation to the mixed elements of fire, forest, and tiger in the collage (and poem). To fully read the collage, though, we need to bring technical skills back into our discussion, and we'll need another screenshot (Figure 19-4).

The distortion effect that Kandis has applied to the forest creates a visual twirl that gives the trees a swirled appearance and introduces a sense of motion into the fixed frame of the collage. The Layer Manager palette shows the elements in the image. Note the opacity setting of the forest layer; twirling the forest and then lowering its opacity blends the layer with the image of the tiger underneath. Now, recall that there are no alphabetic cues in this explication, necessitating a new grammar of literary interpretation. Here the twirling combined with the lowered opacity creates a smearing of the kind we might find in the tenor and vehicle of a metaphor; forest and tiger are joined and set into motion, expressing the symmetry and creative energy of the poem through software effects. Image editors call for new skills, grammars, and vocabularies (layering, twirling, cropping, masking, arranging, and so on) through which students can explain elements of the poem. Making things with the software, then, enables students to express the literary through the visual. And, once again, the making leads to motivation.

Kandis reported "this [collage project] was a very interesting and exciting assignment to do. When we learned how to use the program for blending the images, I literally spent hours just trying to figure out how the program worked. I used all kinds of images and manipulated them in so many differ-

FIGURE 19-4   The Twirl Effect and Layer Manager palette.

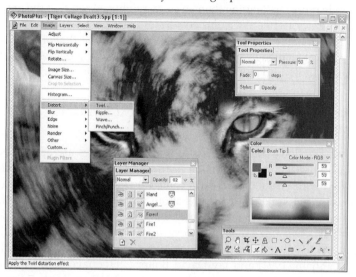

ent ways . . . This assignment gave me a better understanding of the term collage and gave me a whole new way to create a story or describe something in the form of pictures" (Rich, personal communication, December 7, 2006). Not only did the functional literacies developed by "learn[ing] to use the program" translate into visual literacies, this process deepened Kandis's understanding of the collage genre and the poem. The response also reveals flow-like levels of interest and engagement in the project that extend beyond what one might find if Kandis had been asked to turn in a one-to-two page explication of the poem.

Moriah reported similar "addiction" to learning the program and a convergence of literacies:

> The collage was my favorite assignment so far this year. I had a lot of fun playing with the images and tools in PHOTOPLUS. I finished my collages really early because once I started on each collage I would get addicted to working on them and would not be able to move from my computer for hours . . . For some reason, I never feel completely satisfied with my collages. The more I look at them, the more I want to change something around to make them even more perfect . . . In addition to enjoying creating the collages, I also liked conveying the themes and the character analysis through images. It is a lot harder to use images to express how you analyze a work than to simply write a paper. It was interesting and refreshing to take a different approach to analyzing literature.

Moriah's response clearly demonstrates the motivational potential of multimedia projects, as seen in her continual desire to revise and perfect the collages. Other students reported similar fixations on revising these visual compositions. Moriah's response also suggested that a good deal of engagement results from working with unfamiliar modes of expression. That Moriah found the visual mode more challenging than an essay might suggest that the grammars of visual literacy (while difficult because less familiar) may also be difficult because they enable a complexity of expression that rivals that of print. Appropriate technical challenges provide engagement, and the degree of difficulty translates not only into motivation but also into intellectual rigor.

5. BRIDGING TECHNICAL SKILLS AND RHETORICAL LITERACIES THROUGH VIDEO SLIDE SHOWS

The transformations that unfold as alphabetic literacies are applied to new media (as in playlist assignments) or as functional and content-area literacies are blended with visual literacies (in collages) yield high levels of motivation but also raise fundamental questions about what takes place in the composition classroom. At some point we must ask, *as responsible teachers and scholars of composition, how far can we walk from the written word?* To formulate a response to such a question we can think about borrowings and recuperations. Richard Lanham (1993) and Jay David Bolter (1991) have both explored the rhetorical roots of digital spaces. Walter J. Ong (2002), and others after him, leapfrogged print history to recuperate oral traditions that might be applied to aural composition in contemporary media. Hugh Burns (1984) used Aristotle and Kenneth Burke to create invention heuristics for his *Topoi* program. Gail E. Hawisher and Charles Moran (1993) placed e-mail in a tradition reaching back to the Renaissance and through to the middle ages, outlining a rhetoric of e-mail that includes "genres, audiences, voices, uses, and the extent to which any and all of these are influenced by the properties of the medium" (629–630). These borrowings and recuperations serve as bridges over which one can walk further from a constrictive vision that equates composition with the production of alphabetic text. Broadly speaking, these bridges are built from rhetorical concepts that transcend particular literacies: concepts like ethos, pathos, and logos, and the well-worn modes of persuasion. Examining student video slide shows reveals how these broad concepts can be taught through technical experimentation and the making of low-bridge media projects.

The screen shots that follow represent three video slide shows created using Microsoft's MovieMaker software.

Lindsay Smith's *No Better Crop Than Tobacco* slide show (Figure 19-5) documents Lindsay's family farm in rural North Carolina. The video made use of old news clippings and family photographs as well as audio recordings of interviews discussing the history of the farm and of agriculture in North Carolina.

David Berger's *AIDS in Africa* slide show (Figure 19-6) offers information about the plight of orphans living with HIV/AIDS in Sub-Saharan Africa. The video used research sources to provide statistics documenting the issue, and then sequenced these informational screens with images representing the plight of the orphans.

FIGURE 19-5   Lindsay Smith's *No Better Crop Than Tobacco* slide show.

FIGURE 19-6   David Berger's *AIDS in Africa* slide show.

FIGURE 19-7   Katie Lewis's *Beauty* slide show.

Katie Lewis's *Beauty* slide show (Figure 19-7) explores eating disorders among young women. The slide show begins with feelings of low self-esteem represented with text over images, and then contrasts these with images and text representing positive self-esteem in the second half of the video.

Each of the slide shows can be understood in terms of composition concerns familiar to most first-year writing courses. Lindsay's slide show used primary materials to lend an ethos to the piece that matched the personal nature of the project. David's slide show moved from one statistic to another, bringing the problems in Sub-Saharan Africa to light through the build up of information. Interestingly, as David's slide show modified the informational genre with images representing the problem visually, these images added an element of pathos to the video rarely found in research-oriented projects. Katie's video essentially constructed a causal argument by linking low self-esteem with eating disorders. The video layered a proposed solution over the argument as it shifted toward images of positive self-esteem. Taken as a whole, the three videos map familiar territory that ranges from the personal and reflective through the informational and descriptive and toward the persuasive, emphasizing appeals to ethos, pathos, and logos in the process. Of course, this discussion simplifies these rhetorical concerns, but the point is

FIGURE 19-8   Danielle Veal's *The Movement* slide show.

that rhetorical literacies converged with visual and sequential literacies in these slide show projects.

But it would be a missed opportunity if these works merely replicated what have become stale, context-free formulas for composition that multimedia might challenge. Let's look at one more example to consider the concern further.

Danielle Veal's *The Movement* slide show (Figure 19-8) charts the history of the civil rights movement. In some ways the slide show resembles an informational video; it sequences historical information to document a period of history. Unlike David's informational video, however, the bits of historical information come in the form of excerpts from speeches by John F. Kennedy and Martin Luther King, Jr. This composing process can be partially understood by looking at the arrangement of the elements in the composing timeline of the MovieMaker software, as seen in Figure 19-9.

The MovieMaker timeline uses video, audio, and title layers to facilitate composing. The combination of sequential, timeline-based composing and the multiple visual, audio, and textual layers create new possibilities of expression. Danielle frequently employed the title track to layer textual snippets from speeches or credos of equality over images of segregation or racial tension. The process resulted in an ironic juxtaposition that used the image to call into question the conceptual kernel of the alphabetic snippet.

Danielle extended this juxtaposition strategy to the audio track as well, taking excerpts from speeches and sequencing them strategically over the image track. If you look closely at Figure 19-9, however, you'll see that the MovieMaker software provides only a single audio track. To understand the sonic layering process Danielle invoked we need to look at an additional screenshot, an image representing Danielle's work with the audio for the project, as seen in Figure 19-10.

The visible portion of the screenshot contains four tracks. (The audio composition Danielle created actually contained twenty tracks.) Danielle recognized the one-audio-track limitation of the MovieMaker program and decided to learn an alternative piece of software that affords audio layering. Danielle created her layered audio track in the Audacity audio editor, exported it as a single audio track, and then imported this track into MovieMaker, a workaround that surveyed the available means of production and then moved fluidly between software applications and methods of composition.

FIGURE 19-9   The MovieMaker composing timeline.

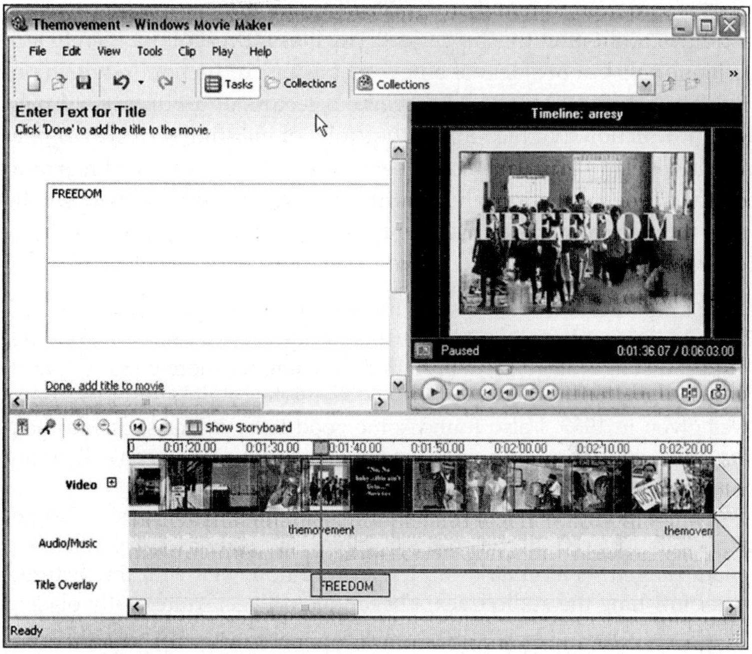

FIGURE 19-10   The Audacity audio editing interface.

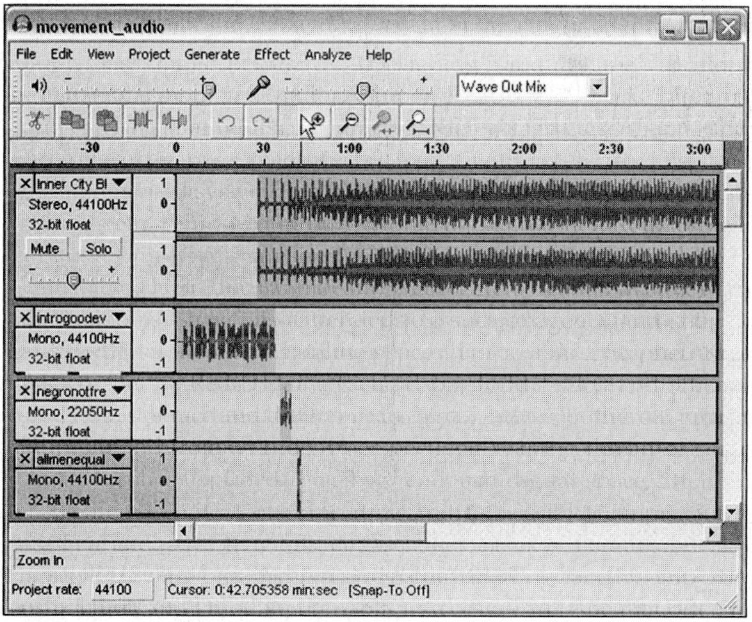

Danielle complemented this fluid multiliteracy with a prolonged process of information gathering and remix literacy, using seventy-eight images and twenty-three audio files for the project. The files represent not merely a collection of materials but artifacts of a new means of production in which notions of originality shift as composers become selectors and remixers of media, a mode of production that recognizes the "folly of insisting on a glut of new materials when there's already so much existing stuff that just need rearranging" (Sirc, 2002, 214). For those who might be quick to dismiss this search-and-combine mode of composition as unoriginal or lacking rigor, I offer Danielle's assessment of the process:

> After listening to the King speech over and over again, I cropped out some important lines and quotes from his speech, still unaware of what my main song was going to be. After searching for more pictures that fit with my theme, I came across John F. Kennedy's civil rights speech that was given in 1963. I also found some good lines in this speech to help my video collage. After doing some brainstorming, and even calling my parents, I found a Marvin Gaye song called "Inner City Blues/Make Me Wanna Holler" that expressed a lot of the same ideas I wanted to get across. So I placed all the cropped quotes and sentences over the song and arranged them in an order that would flow well with the pictures. After finishing the audio track, I began the collage, strategically placing the pictures with the lyrics they matched. I became so addicted to this project that I worked on it day and night, trying to get it to the point of perfection.

Danielle closely studied her materials, brainstormed possibilities, researched to discover new ideas, focused her thinking, refined her project with the help of others, synthesized, drafted, revised, polished, and so on. And she did all of this with the same addictive motivation that marks other multiliteracy projects. Of her work on the video slide show, Danielle said:

> This video collage was the best project I have ever done in my life. I spent so much time on this, and it actually turned out to be an audio collage along with a video collage. I had a vision in my head before I even started the project and I worked at it until it was as perfect as I had seen it in my head. I felt so moved by my own work that I had to extend it.

Clearly, video slide shows like Danielle's serve not only as vehicles for familiar rhetorical concerns but also as transformative projects enabling new modes of composition and literacy including audio, visual, sequential, informational, and remix literacies. But the promise of such projects, as with others discussed here, resides primarily in their ability to create literacy experiences that engage students with learning and allow them into the flow of creativity.

6. THE LOW-BRIDGE STUDIO MODEL OF COMPOSITION

After looking at the case studies above, we might wonder if we have lost track of the initial impetus behind this article—to spell out a philosophy for low-bridge integration of media projects into the writing classroom. The projects display uses of HTML and extensive uses of image, audio, and video editors. But let me reiterate the nature of these projects and the approach discussed here. The playlist projects require little unpacking to see how they might be easily integrated into the classroom. They sit closely aligned with alphabetic literacy and, while the lists above use HTML coding, they require no technology beyond a word processor to compose. The projects do, however, provide an entrée into informational and remix literacies and can also open avenues that bridge audio literacies with composition.

The collages call for a greater investment in technical skill development. The projects, however, have a number of qualities that make them low-bridge paths toward high literacy payoffs. The collages shown here were composed using free image editing software, in this case PHOTOPLUS software available for Windows. In contrast to expensive and sophisticated image editors, a free, minimally featured editor offers an easy-to-transverse path to a composition space that features masking, effects, and layers—key components of digital visual composition. The payoff that comes from such projects is the long-called-for goal of student production of visual compositions, an outcome that promotes convergences of functional, content-area, and visual literacies.[4]

The video slide shows operate with a similar easy-access logic. The key feature of these projects is their basis in remix literacies. Rather than using recorded video, which brings the attendant challenges of locating cameras, learning to film and work with field sound, and locating computers that can download and edit video, these projects collect ready-made materials in the form of images and audio files. They also rely on consumer-level software bundled with the major operating systems. These projects again have a high payoff for the level of investment they require. The learning curve is low for the software, the logistical difficulties are minimized, and the literacies fostered by the projects range from computer literacy to functional software literacy to visual and audio literacy to information literacy to content-area literacy to rhetorical literacy.

It would be misleading, however, to suggest that these projects do not require transformations in the composition classroom. The simplest way to explain these reconfigurations is through a comparison to the studio arts. For years, composition has called for visual and new media projects to be brought into the classroom. The net effect of many of these calls, however, is to foreground analysis of media works, to limit production activities that do take place to the visual, and to offload media production activities to lab environments or dorm rooms.[5] New media is too often an additive, something layered over existing pedagogies and analytical modes. An alternative model, which begins with the notion of production as the central activity of the classroom, is the studio arts. This production, however, is complemented by layers of analysis and theorizing that bubble up from student-created work. The classroom becomes construction site—a site where technical things, created things, and human concerns, flow together. Composition has, to some extent, established this model for alphabetic text, featuring workshopping of student papers. Even these models, though, give short attention to studio-based production—students likely compose their papers on their own, in their dorms or apartments, and then bring them into the classroom for the obligatory review session.

Low-bridge multimedia, in contrast, calls for hands-on time in class for students to work together as they develop technical skills and multiple literacies. The studio classroom acts as Selfe and Hawisher's "technology gateway" because it provides a supportive yet critical environment, a community of peers in which students can "acquire and develop robust sets of digital literacy skills" (2004, 104–105). To create such a context for learning multiliteracies, "teachers [must] become real colearners" (Selber, 2004, 202). This often-lauded decentering is required for "writing as experience-exchange, text as process-action" (Sirc, 2002, 157). Such a space embraces student creativity and pushes for movement from the practical to the personal to the public, knowing that as multimodal projects are moved from the studio to the networked world they will carry forward "the active mobilization of every individual's latent creativity, and then, following on from that, the molding of the society of the future based on the total energy of this individual creativity" (Tisdall, quoted in Sirc, 2004, 157). The studio doesn't shirk from the functional deployment of "skill-based media tools" (Tyner, 156). But always the focus is on "a creative, artistic/aesthetic skill set" because "[w]hile the purpose of technology education may be job readiness, the purpose for arts teachers who use media tools with students is to foster self-expression, creativity, and to find their own 'voice'" (Tyner, 157). Note the pronoun ambiguity in Tyner's recommendation. When it comes to integrating multiliteracies into composition classrooms, those who create environments where writers can experience the personal engagement that will translate into motivation and rich convergences of literacies are few and far between. When it comes to really transforming education with new media, even many compositionists must still find their voice.

NOTES

1. Clearly, these layerings can work the other way, as recognized in the oft-repeated call to "put pedagogy first" when integrating technologies into the classroom. Nancy Kaplan (1991) pointed out that instructors wishing to promote "a social-constructionist pedagogy" found an easy means of doing so in "[o]ff-the-shelf word processing programs, networks, and hypertext tools [that] seem[ed] ready-made to address writing as a social process" (32). There is also a long history of compositionists building specific computer tools upon a foundation of theoretical and pedagogical knowledge. Early technologies such as the Daedalus Integrated Writing Environment developed at the University of Texas or later technologies such as the Writing Studio at Colorado State are just two examples that illustrate a counter-movement to the experiment first, theorize later approach advocated here. Ultimately, classroom implementations of technology often play out with a continual transitioning between technological thing and pedagogical/theoretical idea, a process that twists practice and theory together as continual strands in a technology integration twine.

2. For discussion of the flip-side difficulties that arise when the notion of ease is applied to computers, see Bradley Dilger's "The Ideology of Ease," in which Dilger explains "ease is never free: its gain is matched by a loss in choice, security, privacy, health, or a combination thereof" (2000, n.p.). Dilger showed how students must remain critical even as they reap the benefits of easy-to-use software, ultimately developing a demystified understanding of computing environments and activities. See also Selber's discussion of functional literacies. There is a real danger of failing to recognize the social and political dimensions of technologies, especially off-the-shelf technologies that are frequently seen as neutral tools. Selber pointed out, however, that we are not

condemned to such lack of insight. Following Feenberg and Sherry Turkle, Selber affirms the role of human agency in conceptions of literacy featuring tool metaphors: "As a human extension, the computer is not self-determining in design or operation. The computer, as a tool, depends upon a user, who if skilled enough can use and manipulate its (non-neutral) affordances to help reshape the world in potentially positive ways" (2004, 40). By combining a critical perspective on technologies with an emphasis on human agency, instructors and writers can take off-the-shelf tools and use them in a process through which they further develop computer and critical literacies.

3. Shipka (2005), Wysocki (2004), and Sirc (2002) have demonstrated the value of non-digital multimedia assignments. Shipka's students have created gift boxes and other non-digital projects, allowing them to work with multiple genres and media. Shipka suggested that "a much wider, richer repertoire of semiotic resources, coupled with [student] efforts to purposefully structure the delivery and reception of their work, afford new ways of thinking, acting, and working within and beyond the space of the first-year composition classroom" (279). Wysocki's students have created mixed media maps. Sirc's box logic projects revealed a similar ability to go multimedia without becoming fixated on the digital high-end. The point is not to question these approaches but to sketch out additional literacies that become available through similar digital projects.

4. For the last decade, scholars have frequently pointed out the failure of much of the technology integration efforts in education to move beyond print-centric notions of composition and literacy (Anderson, 2003; George, p. 211; Johnson-Eilola & Wysocki, 1999; Kress, 1998). Anne Wysocki and Johndan Johnson-Eilola go so far as to question the very term literacy for its alphabetic bias. Simultaneously, scholars have begun implementing and theorizing multimodal composition in the classroom, as evidenced by Kathleen Yancey's call for the development of a new curriculum based "not only in words" in her 2004 Chair's address to the annual Conference on College Communication and Composition (p. 62).

5. For more on the status of multimodal composition in writing classes, see Anderson et al.'s "Integrating Multimodality into composition curricula: Survey methodology and results from a CCCC research grant" (2006).

REFERENCES

Anderson, Daniel, Atkins, Anthony, Ball, Cheryl, Millar, Krista H., Selfe, Cynthia, & Selfe, Richard. (2006). Integrating multimodality into composition curricula. *Composition Studies, 34*(2), 59–84.

Anderson, Daniel. (2003). Prosumer approaches to new media composition: Production and consumption in continuum. *Kairos: A Journal of Rhetoric, Technology, and Pedagogy, 8*(1). Retrieved April 30, 2007, from <http://kairos.technorhetoric.net/8.1/index.html>.

Bolter, Jay David. (1991). *Writing space: The computer, hypertext, and the history of writing.* Hillsdale, NJ: Erlbaum.

Burns, Hugh. (1984). Recollections of first generation computer-assisted prewriting. In William Wresch (Ed.), *The computer in composition instruction: A writer's tool.* Urbana, IL: NCTE.

Csikszentmihalyi, Mihaly. (2000). *Beyond boredom and anxiety: Experiencing flow in work and play.* San Francisco: Jossey-Bass.

Dilger, Bradley. (2000). The ideology of ease. *The Journal of Electronic Publishing, 6*(1). Retrieved April 30, 2007, from <http://www.press.umich.edu/jep/06-01/dilger.html>.

Feenberg, Andrew. (2002). Looking backward, looking forward: Reflections on the 20th century. *Dogma.* Retrieved April 30, 2007, from <http://dogma.free.fr/txt/AF Looking-Backward.htm>.

Gee, James Paul. (2003). *What video games have to teach us about learning and literacy.* Gordonsville, VA: Palgrave Macmillan.

George, Diana. (2002). From analysis to design: Visual communication in the teaching of writing. *CCC, 54*(1), 11–39.

Hawisher, Gail E., & Moran, Charles. (1993). Electronic mail and the writing instructor. *College English, 55*(6), 627–643.

Johnson-Eilola, Johndan, & Wysocki, Anne. (1999). Blinded by the letter: Why are we using literacy as a metaphor for everything else? In Hawisher Gail & Selfe Cynthia (Eds.), *Passions, pedagogies, and 21st century technologies.* Logan: Utah State University Press.

Kaplan, Nancy. (1991). Ideology, technology, and the future of writing instruction. In Hawisher, Gail E., & Cynthia Selfe (Eds.), *Evolving perspectives on computers and composition studies: Questions for the 1990s.* Urbana: NCTE.

Kress, Gunther. (1998). Visual and verbal modes of representation in electronically mediated communication: The potentials of new forms of text. In Snyder Ilana (Ed.), *Page to screen: Taking literacy into the electronic age.* London: Routledge.

Lanham, Richard A. (1993). *The electronic word: Democracy, technology, and the arts.* Chicago: University of Chicago Press.

Latour, Bruno. (1996). *Aramis, or the love of technology* (Catherine Porter, Trans.). Cambridge: Harvard University Press.

Latour, Bruno. (2005). *Reassembling the social: An introduction to actor-network theory.* Oxford: Oxford University Press.

Mackey, Margaret. (2002). *Literacies across media: Playing the text.* London: Routledge.

Morrow, Leslie M., & Tracey, Diane H. (2004). Instructional environments for language and learning: Considerations for young children. In James Flood (Ed.), *Handbook of research on teaching literacy through the communicative and visual arts.* Mahwah, NJ: Erlbaum.

New London Group. (1996). A pedagogy of multiliteracies: Designing social futures. *Harvard Educational Review, 66*(1), 60–92. [See also p. 193 in this volume.]

Ong, Walter J. (2002). *Orality and literacy: The technologizing of the word* (2nd ed.). New York: Routledge.

Rouzie, Albert. (2005). *At play in the fields of writing: A serio-ludic rhetoric.* Cresskill, NJ: Hampton Press.

Selber, Stuart. (2004). *Multiliteracies for a digital age.* Carbondale: Southern Illinois University Press.

Selfe, Cynthia, & Hawisher, Gail E. (2004). *Literate lives in the information age: Narratives on literacy from the United States.* Mahwah, NJ: Erlbaum.

Shipka, Jody. (2005). A multimodal task-based framework for composing. *CCC, 57*(2), 277–306.

Sirc, Geoffrey. (2002). *English composition as a happening.* Logan: Utah State University Press.

Sullivan, Patricia. (1991). Taking control of the page: Electronic writing and word publishing. In Gail Hawisher & Cynthia Selfe (Eds.), *Evolving perspectives on computers and composition studies: Questions for the 1990s.* Urbana, IL: NCTE.

Tyner, Kathleen R. (1998). *Literacy in a digital world: Teaching and learning in the age of information.* Mahwah, NJ: Erlbaum.

Ulmer, Greg. (2003). *Internet invention: From literacy to electracy.* New York: Longman.

Wysocki, Anne. (2004). Opening new media to writing: Openings & justifications. In Johndan Johnson-Eilola, Cynthia Selfe, & Geoffrey Sirc (Eds.), *Writing new media: Theory and applications for expanding the teaching of composition.* Logan: Utah State University Press.

Yancey, Kathleen. (2004). Made not only in words: Composition in a new key. *CCC, 56*(2), 297–328.

20   *Between Modes: Assessing Students' New Media Compositions*

MADELEINE SORAPURE

While the first two web texts included in Part Four provide examples of assignments for composing with multiple modes, Madeleine Sorapure reflects on what it means to assess such assignments. In her web text, featured in Kairos's 2006 issue, Sorapure tackles what she calls the "problem with assessment" by offering readers a strategy for understanding the way in which modes combine to make meaning. Such an approach draws on our familiarity with the tropes of metaphor and metonymy, which according to Sorapure, can help us to discuss with our students what it means to be successful multimodal composers. Sorapure's own combination of modes (text, hyperlinks, images, sound, etc.) used to compose her web text argument demonstrates, too, how readers can imagine their own scholarship. Her web text can be accessed at http://kairos.technorhetoric.net/10.2/coverweb/sorapure /betweenmodes.html

FIGURE 20-1 Sorapure discussing assessment.

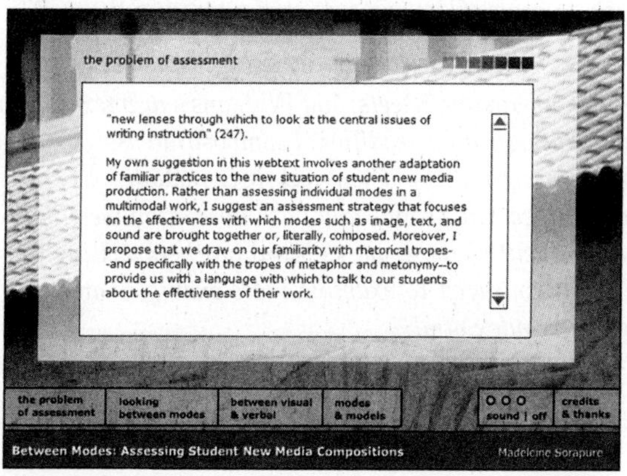

Source: Kairos 10.2 (2006). http://kairos.technorhetoric.net/10.2/coverweb/sorapure/

From *Kairos* 10.2 (2006). http://kairos.technorhetoric.net/10.2/coverweb/sorapure/

21 The New Work of Assessment: Evaluating Multimodal Compositions

ELIZABETH A. MURRAY, HAILEY A. SHEETS,
AND NICOLE A. WILLIAMS

In the preface of "The New Work of Assessment: Evaluating Multimodal Compositions," Elizabeth A. Murray, Hailey A. Sheets, and Nicole A. Williams describe what readers can expect from their web text, stating:

> *You will find that this web text is organized into four distinct sections: The first section situates our argument within the current conversation surrounding multimodal theory and assessment, which shows that multimodal projects are not only important, but that they should be evaluated based upon rhetorical principals. The second section includes survey results which reflect the current assessment practices of composition instructors. The third section explains how compositions instructors can utilize their own Writing Program's rubric to assess a variety of student multimodal compositions, proving that multimodal compositions can be assessed on the basic rhetorical principals used for alphabetic essay evaluation. The final section will demonstrate how composition instructors can assess multimodal compositions with examples from our own students using the traditional rubric that our Writing Program requires.*

One of the goals of Murray, Sheets, and Williams's web text is to help instructors use a grading rubric designed for traditional composition assignments to assess multimodal composition assignments. Their web text includes several students' work, including a video, collage, slide show, and flash animation (see Figure 21-1), as well as the authors' assessment of those works based on their writing program's grading rubric. Readers are encouraged to examine these examples at http://www.bgsu.edu /cconline/murray_etal/index.html

---

From *Computers and Composition Online* (2009). http://www.bgsu.edu/cconline/murray _etal/index.html

FIGURE 21-1   Murray et al. student examples and interface.

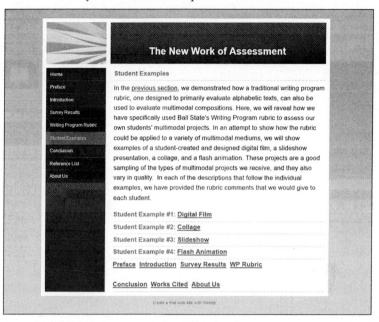

Source: *Computers and Composition Online* (2009). http://www.bgsu.edu/cconline/murray_etal /student-examples.html

Building a Sustainable Environment for Multimodal Composition

Introduction to Part Five

Evolving digital technologies of the past few decades are partly responsible for an increased awareness of multimodal composition. It is hard to ignore technology when many of our students are digital natives, using technology outside of our classrooms on a daily basis. Indeed, technology plays an integral role in the infrastructures needed for successful implementation of multimodal composition pedagogy in our classrooms. Campuses at the forefront of addressing changes in technology and technological practices have created multimedia or multimodal composition studios or centers that help students utilize technology to compose. Yet, Part Five is not just about technology's relationship with multimodal composition. Rather, the authors of this section encourage us to think about every facet of the complex infrastructures in place on our campuses. For instance, they ask us to consider what educators need to invest in—technology, training, facilities, classrooms, tools, supplies, and so on—and weigh these investments against what our institutions value and how those values shape our pedagogy. As we approach the readings in this section, we might ask ourselves if our values as instructors align or contrast with the values of our departments and institutions. What, for instance, would need to change if we were to implement multimodal composition pedagogy? The answer to these questions could help us move forward in providing students a place to practice multimodal composition successfully.

As we examine more closely our campuses' infrastructures and how faculty, administrators, and staff within those infrastructures work or do not work together, we might begin where our teaching takes place, that is, in the classroom. At many universities and colleges, classrooms (even online classrooms) are controlled, designed, organized, and maintained by several administrators and offices that are not necessarily associated with our departments, programs, and fellow instructors. While the classroom (whether consisting of four walls or not) should be at the center of a sustainable learning environment that includes a network of educators and educational resources, it should also be one that is flexible, and therefore able to adapt to the technological, social, and cultural changes that influence our students' literacy practices. In light of this, we might also approach the readings in this section by asking ourselves how instructors can become more involved in the classroom design decisions that take place at the administrative level.

For starters, we might begin by thinking more critically about what instructors do and what our students do inside (and outside) of those classrooms so that we may be better prepared to make decisions about which classroom designs help or hinder those practices. In "The Rhetorical Work of Multimedia Production Practices: It's More Than Just Technical Skill," Jennifer Sheppard begins Part 5 by pointing out why we must pay closer attention to the practices we employ when we create multimedia and multimodal texts. Like many scholars, she argues that we must ask students to be more than simply analyzers of such texts. Students, she contends, should also be producers of these texts because the decisions they make during production are vital to their understanding of rhetoric. Such decisions do not only involve decisions about what technologies to use or what technical skills are needed; rather, Sheppard believes they involve so much more, like negotiating a mode's affordances, for instance. Using her own experience creating a multimedia and multimodal text, she demonstrates just how many decisions a producer has to make. To conclude, she outlines several recommendations that can help us ensure our students have opportunities to engage in the type of decision making needed when producing multimedia and multimodal texts.

A sustainable infrastructure is necessary to carry out and support Sheppard's recommendations. Therefore, Sheppard's selection sets us up for the rest of the chapters in Part Five that talk about the needs associated with building, maintaining, assessing, and negotiating the infrastructures (and the complex relationships among the people, programs, departments, administrators, and technologies within them) on our campuses, whether or not they already allow for multimodal composition. In "Infrastructure and Composing: The *When* of New-Media Writing," Dànielle Nicole DeVoss, Ellen Cushman, and Jeffrey T. Grabill examine more closely the elements of a digital writing environment that help or get in the way of the composing process. Specifically, they are interested in the "when" of new media (the often invisible "institutional and political arrangements") and the decisions that instructors and students have to make when infrastructures break down. They assert that "infrastructures are absolutely necessary for writing teachers and their students to understand if we hope to enact the possibilities offered by new-media composing" (p. 406 in this volume). For example, they write that knowing the "when" puts students in a position to navigate around obstacles that get in the way of composing.

As the authors go on to contend, infrastructures encompass much more than a web of technologies: policies, standards, guidelines, classroom design, and so forth. To DeVoss, Cushman, and Grabill, often the complexities of an infrastructure go ignored or are invisible to students until "breakdowns" occur. Students, they argue, should be familiar with and critical of the infrastructures on their campuses, even before they run into difficulties, and they should conceptualize infrastructures as ever changing. Such an understanding would give students an opportunity to reflect on the possibilities for composing and help them be more attuned to the decision making processes that occur when composing. In other words, the authors argue that students can use this knowledge about infrastructures to then "consider and push at practices and standards in strategic ways" for the purpose of becoming better-informed composers.

Another starting point for investigating infrastructures, Stuart A. Selber suggests, is to think about ways we can be more involved with the institutional computing decisions that are critical to multimodal and multimedia composition. His "Institutional Dimensions of Academic Computing," focuses on the larger contexts in which people and programs are embedded and how a map of those contexts can reveal what an institution values. Drawing from the work of James E. Porter and his colleagues, Selber conceptualizes institutions as rhetorical systems and offers us an overview of "institutional critique and a visual-spatial approach to studying institutional dynamics and interactions" (p. 429). While institutional critique can help expose ambiguity that can, in turn, bring about change, spatial patterns and relationships, he writes, can be studied using postmodern mapping (which examines positioning) and boundary interrogation (which examines power). He presents three institutional maps for academic computing contexts, which include multimedia at Penn State, so that we may think through and reimagine our own maps. The first example visualizes what takes place when composing multimedia and multimodal documents and reveals areas or instances when multimedia and multimodal practices, such as remixing, are devalued. He concludes that his approach for using maps has helped him to see that his institution's values greatly impact pedagogical support for multimedia and multimodal composition.

The final selection in Part Five looks specifically at what it takes to build a multimodal composition program. For instance, Christine Tulley, director of writing at the University of Findlay, demonstrates in her web text, "Taking a Composition Program 'Multimodal': Web 2.0 and Institutional Change at a Small Liberal Arts Institution," the steps she and her fellow colleagues took to create a multimodal composition program. In doing so, she outlines some of the challenges they encountered with faculty, students, and administrators as multimodal composition assignments were incorporated into writing courses. Though every institution is different, her college's program serves as an example of what we might face at our own universities and colleges.

As educators, we have a duty to help students succeed, and that is why it is imperative that we do our best to collaborate with those responsible for building, maintaining, and changing the infrastructures we work within. Such collaboration is crucial in securing the materials, resources, support, technologies, and so forth that students need in order to compose with all the available means necessary for each new composing situation.

22 The Rhetorical Work of Multimedia Production Practices: It's More than Just Technical Skill

JENNIFER SHEPPARD

When I agreed to create a science-based, multimedia web site for kids for a Forest Service Research Lab, I had little idea of what I was actually getting myself into. It quickly became apparent that this project would require far more than just knowledge of relevant software and basic web page creation. Soon, I was meeting with scientists, interviewing local school kids about their web usage, poring over state curricular guidelines, wrangling with a government agency's web standards, navigating the technological constraints of school networks, and much more. What started out as a modest attempt to present local ecological information soon spiraled into a complex, interactive, multimodal web site that took nearly 18 months to complete. Along the way, I became more conscious of the variety of sophisticated literacy and rhetorical practices necessary to create informative and engaging multimedia.

This article chronicles several significant development challenges from my experience as a designer on the Forest Service project as a way of drawing attention to the often-unseen rhetorical dimensions of production in multimedia composition. Rather than viewing development of multimedia as just technical skill, I argue that careful attention to practices of production can demonstrate the critical negotiations writers/designers[1] must undertake as they compose multimedia texts. These development activities build on traditional print-based literacies and rhetorical practices but require additional considerations in order to achieve the desired effects on intended audiences. Beyond established rhetorical concerns such as audience, purpose, and context, designers must also make rhetorical choices specific to the development of multimedia. These technological rhetorical considerations include decisions such as the appropriateness of technologies for a given situation and the selection and integration of media to facilitate reader/user comprehension of the text.

Oftentimes, teaching production of digital texts is viewed by those outside of the computers and composition field as simply a matter of imparting technical skill rather than facilitating development of diverse and significant

From *Computers and Composition* 26 (2009): 122–31.

literacies. Many administrators and colleagues within other areas of English studies do not see the intellectual and practical significance of this work for students and do not recognize the time and intellectual effort necessary to teach and support such composition. This article presents a closer look at the production process of a single multimedia text in order to demonstrate the complex integration of traditional and technological rhetorical practices required for the development of informative, persuasive, and engaging digital texts.

My motivation for writing this piece comes from two distinct yet related sources. First, when I began developing web and multimedia texts for coursework and clients a decade ago, and more recently when I began teaching these practices to my own students, I found a lack of resources bridging practice and theory to support this work. There are hundreds of practical books on the market on how to use software and related technologies, but few of these consider technological rhetorical issues such as how site architecture should be organized to reach target audiences or how integration of video files might impact accessibility for users with different connection speeds to the Internet. Instead, these books are generally concerned with the physical manipulation of applications and provide guidance through step-by-step instructions (e.g., click here, move this there) but do not engage with the contexts in which such technical manipulations are embedded.

On the theory side, the past 15 years have seen increasing calls for the integration of multimedia and multiliteracies into the disciplines of composition and professional communication. Research on multimodal composition has included arguments for expanding our students' range of communicative literacies (Anderson, 2003; Ball & Kalmbach, 2009; Kress & van Leeuwen, 2001; Lemke, 1998; New London Group, see p. 193 in this volume; Selber, 2004; Selfe, 1999, 2004), as well as for better preparing them for academic, professional, and civic expectations through development of greater technological capacity (iText Working Group, 2001; Kress, 2003; Williams, 2001; Yancey, p. 62). While this work has made a compelling case for action, much of it has been theoretically oriented, leading to difficulty translating these ideas into classroom pedagogy and rhetorically purposeful production practices.

My second motivation for writing this piece comes out of my position as an untenured faculty member who is considered *the* technology person for my department. Although I was hired as a specialist in digital media and professional communication, I often find that some colleagues and administrators have little idea of what it is I actually teach, how much time it takes, or why the theoretically informed, project-based approaches I use matter. Some mistakenly see these production-oriented courses as simply a matter of passing on computer skills rather than doing the more valued work of theory, analysis, and argumentation, and they often have little understanding of how this multimedia development work connects to the academic goals of an English department. Although many teachers/scholars in our field have pioneered approaches to teaching with communication and media technologies, they are still often met with similar misperceptions and resistance from colleagues and administrators on their own campuses (Journet, 2007). Such attitudes have repercussions for how faculty are evaluated, for how resources are allocated, and most importantly, for what learning experiences are available to students.

With these motivations in mind, this piece sets out to draw attention to the technological rhetorical work of multimedia production practices through reflection on an extended project. Relying on daily written field notes and analysis of the completed project, I offer three examples of rhetorical issues specific to new media development that are highly relevant to composing practices in the classroom. Following this discussion, I provide several recommended practices for how the lessons learned from this project can be used to shape multimodal assignments in composition and professional communication courses.

1. MULTIMEDIA DEVELOPMENT PROJECT OVERVIEW

The examples and discussion that follow come from reflection on a web-based multimedia project I developed over 18 months for a U.S. Forest Service Research Lab (FSRL). The primary intention of this multimodal piece (called the "Kids' Corner") was to communicate locally related, ecologically and scientifically based information in a way that was appealing and informative to the target audience. We (the Lab's scientific research staff and I, working as a technical communicator and web developer) chose to focus the site's content on students in roughly sixth to eighth grade because research on state curricular science guidelines indicated this age range had the knowledge base to understand relatively sophisticated science methods and ecological concepts relating to the Lab's work. In requesting funds for this project from regional Forest Service administrators, my FSRL colleague and I argued that because children will one day be the primary stakeholders for our forests, it is vital that they learn early on about the environmental value of forests and natural resources. We reasoned that engaging these users in activities that are both educational and fun would help them to build a foundational understanding of how their choices and those of forest managers can impact the environment. We further argued that interactive multimedia technologies would help us to accomplish these goals because content could be created and delivered through multiple modes and media. This would not only allow us to use the rhetorical means most appropriate for a given subject but would also provide options for supporting a greater diversity of learning styles (e.g., Druin & Soloman, 1996; Gee, 2003; Lemke, 1998).

Each of the examples that follow relate to one section of the web site that focuses on the scientific method and its use by lab researchers to study the effects of greenhouse gases on tree growth at the Free Air Carbon-Dioxide Enrichment (FACE) facility in Northern Wisconsin. I chose to reflect on work from this section of the project because it is the richest in terms of both content and my attempts to integrate multimodal elements whenever relevant. As users learn about this 80-acre experiment through text, images, audio, animations, and video clips, they are led through the process of forming a hypothesis, setting up an experiment to test the effects of greenhouse gases on different indicators of tree growth, and analyzing their collected data. The primary goal in creating this module was to provide interactive opportunities that position the site's users as scientists so that they could gain both an understanding of the specific kinds of research these scientists conduct and a more general sense of how the process of scientific inquiry is undertaken.

1.1. Example 1—Negotiating Content: Balancing Approaches to Audience, Communicative Purpose, and Media Affordances

Just as in composing written text, the iterative process of producing multimedia requires a great deal of trying out and revising possibilities. Writers/ designers must continually weigh the suitability of subject matter content, the communicative affordances of various media and modalities, and the appropriate use of various applications for the intended users and their technological capabilities. While negotiation of how best to address these variables happens throughout the development process, the primary approach to any multimedia project should always begin with highlighting the needs, interests, and technical resources of the intended users. Once a clear picture of the audience and the project's communicative goals has been established, *then* writers/designers can begin to consider how multiple media might be employed to help reach the project's goals. As production continues, these ideas should be revisited and revised to ensure that the media and technology choices are meeting the communicative purpose for users and other project stakeholders.

This example illustrates the importance of continual reevaluation of how multimodal components are shaped and integrated into a text's larger rhetorical objectives. By valuing flexibility and an iterative process, designers can produce texts that better acknowledge and accommodate the needs of targeted audiences and the interests of additional (and sometimes unseen) stakeholders.

During development of the scientific method module, the intertwined issues of audience, media choice, and content appropriateness and accuracy were negotiated between the FSRL research ecologists and myself on a frequent basis. As the writer/designer, I was interested primarily in helping target users learn broadly about the process of scientific inquiry, as well as helping them to use this methodology to understand more specifically the kinds of research being undertaken by the FSRL. While the scientists liked this approach in principle, they were also highly concerned with an advanced level of accuracy in the terms and concepts used because this web site would be a public representation of their work (even if the *intended* audience was kids). The scientists and I had many conversations (and occasional disagreements) regarding the complexity of content in this project. As Mary Beth Debs (1991) suggested, such negotiation is always a part of creating technical communication, no matter what mode or medium will result. Inter-group conflict and difficulty in reaching consensus, she wrote, "most often arise[s] from different interpretations of the rhetorical situation, different concepts of the intended audience, and different purposes" (481). As the example below demonstrates, this mismatch in our conceptions of the site's purpose and intended audience(s) was precisely the root of our conflict. While I focused, somewhat idealistically, on the interests and abilities of the sixth-to eighth-grade users we had agreed to target, the scientists were also concerned with a broader audience (and socially situated network of power relations), namely regional administrators in a fairly contentious government agency, as well as professional colleagues in the field of ecology. Although it took some time to uncover their concern for addressing this larger, less obvious audience, it wasn't until I acknowledged their desire to attend to these stakeholders, as well as the students, that we could work productively through our disagreements to reach consensus about the content and media choices we found acceptable.

One example of how this negotiation over audience, content, and media choice played out arose in relation to material on the measurement of leaf area. In general, scientists use leaf area measurements as an indication of the total photosynthetic capacity of a tree. These measurements are a critical means of determining differences between tree growth rates in the test and control groups at the FACE research site and thus are essential to their research activities. However, even with extended explanation, their method for obtaining this information and for putting it to use in their research was still difficult to understand. Because of my own trouble comprehending it, I felt it was important to simplify the concept as much as possible when trying to communicate it to sixth-through eighth-grade students. My concern here for target users, though, conflicted with the ecologists' desire for detailed accuracy and attendance to a larger audience.

During a review meeting with the ecologists to look over initial drafts of the project, I spent a lot of time trying to advocate for a less complex explanation for our users. In observing activities in local science classrooms and reading the state curricular science guidelines, I knew that our target audience would have difficulty with this material and would likely skip over it if it did not make sense. The scientists, though, continued to make choices in their revisions of textual material that focused on detailed correctness at the expense of accessibility for the intended users (e.g., "ozone is harmful to plants vs. ozone is a phytotoxin that damages chloroplasts and a plant's ability to make food") (Field Notes).

As we continued talking, I realized two important things were needed for making our negotiation and completion of this section successful. First, this subject would be a good opportunity to use images and animation to help illustrate the concepts of leaf area measurement by offering a supplement to the written information. Moving images could be used to visualize the ideas and measurement process without having to be quite so detailed. (The accompanying written text could serve the role of explicit explanation and correctness desired by the scientists.) Second, to make this fairly complex information about measuring leaf area accessible and meaningful to users, I would first have to back up and provide greater explication of the concepts underlying the purpose of this activity, namely the process of photosynthesis and the causes and effects of greenhouse gases. It turned out that since these concepts were so implicitly foundational for the scientists (and not directly part of their research), they had little interest in micromanaging this content. This was also an area where I could make use of images and animation to illustrate these concepts more completely than through words alone. Although the resulting revision made the lead-up to interactivity (the part where users actually get to "conduct" some of the experiment) much longer than I had anticipated, it both resulted in a clearer explanation of what the research was seeking to discover and better satisfied the needs of all audiences and project stakeholders.

The process detailed here took time and concessions from both sides, but eventually we were able to reach consensus on a more balanced and age-appropriate approach to teaching this concept without sacrificing specificity and correctness. While our consensus was achieved in part by attending to traditional rhetorical considerations, it would not have been possible without also considering and employing a range of technological rhetorical strategies, such as conveying additional information through images and animation rather than text alone. In this regard, it is important for multimedia designers to attend to traditional rhetorical considerations at the same time as they consider technological rhetorical strategies for addressing particular audiences, stakeholders, and contexts. By employing an iterative process to try out and revise communicative approaches, writers/designers can exploit the full range of modalities to reach their target audience. Exploration of multimodal possibilities should be used as a primary means for navigating rhetorical situations.

1.2. Example 2—Addressing Technological Rhetorical Considerations: Balancing Media Type, Audience Needs, and Contexts of Use

In addition to concerns of content development, visual design, and structural navigation, there are a number of technological rhetorical considerations involved with developing multimedia, particularly web-based multimedia, beyond knowing how to use software. Decisions such as the appropriate use of media for a given message, the size of files and the amount of bandwidth occupied by a project, and the kinds of reception technologies (operating systems, playback applications, hardware capabilities, etc.) typically used by the target audience all factor into how a text is received by intended users. Designers engaged in production practices must negotiate these issues in rhetorically conscious ways in order to create engaging, purposeful, and audience-centered texts. Failure on the part of the designer to navigate these constantly evolving constraints can create not just aesthetic problems but also rhetorical and usability problems. An inability to effectively assess and address the technological rhetorical considerations of production in relation to audience capabilities and intended contexts of use will inevitably lead to users being unable to interact with a multimedia text in the ways intended by the writer/designer.

Perhaps the best illustration from the "Kids' Corner" project of how these technical considerations are rhetorical came on the first day of user alpha testing on the scientific method section. I had shot video for inclusion in the web site of the ecologists gathering data at the FACE research site and analyzing samples in the lab. My intention with this video was to give users an insider's view of the work practices of scientists and to make their research more accessible to the target audience.

During development prior to this early testing, I used the most up-to-date software (at the time) to create content and interactivity. This was particularly significant with regard to the newly released version of Flash I utilized because for the first time it allowed video to be integrated directly into animation authoring files.[2] Initially, I believed the new technological capacity of Flash would be a boon to my design work because all the multimodal components, including the video, could be incorporated into a single interface. I also believed, mistakenly it turns out, the program would further compress video embedded in Flash during publishing, thereby decreasing download time.

To help ensure that my goals were being realized, I viewed the pages regularly during production on both Mac and Windows platforms, using all of the most popular web browsers. Although I would not classify this casual testing as especially rigorous, particularly since I did not account for the fast T1 Internet connections in my lab or the availability of constantly updated software, I did feel that I successfully viewed and used the module on a range of systems and browsers. However, I did not spend much time considering the technologies and connection speeds to which my *intended users*, particularly those in elementary and middle school classrooms and libraries, might have access. I did not really consider the potential implications this lack of attention might hold for the audience and for realizing my rhetorical objectives.

On the first day of alpha testing at a local middle school I found out quickly that most of the computers did not yet have the appropriate version of the necessary Flash plug-in.[3] More astonishing and disheartening to me, though, was the fact that the lab administrator for this school had set up the network to prevent students (or any unauthorized person) from downloading and installing anything on the machines, including plug-ins. Designed in part to restrict access to inappropriate web content and to protect students from potential online predators, this was also a contextual factor common to many schools and libraries which significantly affected the capabilities of my target audience. While students were able to see some content using an older version of the plug-in, this version did not allow them to see the video clips I was testing, causing several users to skim through the accompanying textual explanation without really grasping its importance for the interactivity that followed. Because I did not spend sufficient time researching the contexts of use and technical capabilities of my audience prior to this early draft of the site, I was not able to communicate my ideas to intended users. Although issues such as application version, plug-in availability, and connection speed are in many ways mechanical, they are also rhetorical. Failure to attend to these considerations prevented the target audience from realizing my communicative goal of a site that utilized multimodal elements to help users gain a sense of the scientific method and its application at the FACE site.[4]

As multimedia technologies become increasingly sophisticated, allowing writers/designers to integrate multiple modes and interaction opportunities with greater ease, the need for communicators who can utilize these capabilities in a knowledgeable and practical manner will also continue to grow. It is essential that students learn how to take advantage of these technological capabilities in ways that are appropriate for a given audience and purpose. As a key factor influencing how audiences view, receive, and interact with a text, understanding the technological rhetorical possibilities and limitations for a particular project is a crucial component of successful production practices. Writers/designers who hope to engage their audiences must take ample time to learn about their users and the contexts in which their texts will be used in order to create compelling content, as well as to shape their texts in ways that attend to the needs, interests, and capabilities of users. This example demonstrates that technical considerations for multimedia development are very much rhetorical and that writers/designers need to weigh carefully the pros and cons of their chosen technologies, media, and other production variables to determine what best supports their rhetorical situation and goals.

1.3. Example 3—Being a Multimodal Communicator: The Challenges of Learning to Use Multiple Literacies in Rhetorically Meaningful Ways

Although communicating in multiple modes and media certainly offers numerous opportunities for interacting with an intended audience, it also demands multiple capabilities from the writer/designer for doing so. Some of these capabilities, such as textual writing, come to us more easily because of our lengthy experience with them. For the most part, though, the critical, thoughtful production of other media is far more unfamiliar and demanding.[5] With each new technology, each new medium, we must learn not only how to create with the new form but also how to integrate these new media with others in purposeful, meaningful ways. Perhaps adeptness at multimodal literacies will become less of an issue over time, but currently it is a challenge to take on all of these tasks in a deliberate way as an individual. The following example illustrates one attempt at navigating this less-familiar communicative terrain and how important a willingness to experiment with the possibilities of different modalities can be for the rhetorical effectiveness of the final text.

This example details the complications of trying to integrate sound into the "Kids' Corner" text in a rhetorically purposeful way. I got the idea for adding sound effects to the buttons in the scientific method section from looking at a site suggested by students during a focus group session at a local school. I had asked students what sites they used on a regular basis and several had mentioned *Sports Illustrated for Kids*. I checked it out and two hours later I was still sitting there, hooked by the stories, the games, and, most importantly, the noisy little rollover buttons. I decided that my project had to have something like this.

Adding a sound effect to a button in Flash is a pretty simple technical procedure. More challenging, though, is locating and choosing sounds that are appropriate for one's text. *Arttoday.com,* a subscriber database of images and sounds that I used, had several hundred to select from, all royalty-free and in usable file formats. I picked out about 10 that seemed upbeat and not completely distracting, but I worried they did not seem to completely fit the project. At one point, I wrote in my field notes, "one sounds a bit like a space-ship landing. I like the idea of using the sounds to spice things up like on the *SI Kids* site, but these seem a bit cheesy and without a real purpose" (Field Notes). Still struggling with this issue a month later, I wrote, "They're fun, but I need to think more carefully about the rhetorical purpose and implications of various sounds" (Field Notes). I tried to consider a more rhetorically mean-ingful, less gratuitous use of sound. I thought about searching for or creating sound files that were somehow scientific or representative of sounds that might be heard in the Lab, but I had difficulty coming up with a way to ex-press such abstract activities in an auditory way.

What I came to realize through user testing, though, is that despite the failure to realize my lofty multimodal hopes for the rhetorical value of sound as an expression of meaning, the audience still gained something important from this integration of superfluous sound effects. Student users overwhelm-ingly liked the sound effects as they were because they added an element of play to the experience. That is, something happened on screen (and could hap-pen again and again by mousing over the buttons) besides just static images, animations, and text. In the end, I would argue that while I did not achieve my goal of using sounds to communicate specific meanings, the sound effects did serve a rhetorical purpose by making the text more appealing and fun. This experience was a reminder that while multimedia has the power to com-municate serious information to users through multiple means, it also has the ability to entertain and engage users in novel ways. This more whimsical capability should not be ignored if it has the potential to make a text more attractive and ultimately more persuasive to its target readers/users. This was also a reminder that developing practices necessary to make use of the com-municative capacities of various media is challenging and takes considerable time. It requires exploration and a willingness to embrace alternative ways of reaching rhetorical goals.

2. RECOMMENDATIONS FOR ATTENDING TO PRODUCTION PRACTICES IN MULTIMODAL CLASSROOM PROJECTS

As the preceding examples illustrate, using multimedia to communicate and engage with an audience offers nearly unlimited potential for expression, per-suasion, and representation, and this is a set of practices we must help our stu-dents develop for them to become successful academically, professionally, and civically. However, to realize this promise, we need to assist students in culti-vating awareness of and an appropriate set of responses to the array of tradi-tional and technological rhetorical choices brought about by the circumstances of each new project. Each technical production decision is also rhetorical and has consequences for how a text will be received and used by its intended audience. Although some of these authoring considerations, such as targeting a particular audience and addressing a specific purpose, share much with composition of print-based texts, producing multimedia also requires attention to a number of additional rhetorical concerns. Exploring the communicative affordances of different media and planning their integration with other modes, understanding the technical capabilities and contexts of use for the target audience, and developing an interface and set of interactions that make a text usable and intuitive are just some of the many technological rhetorical considerations specific to successful multimedia production. Writers/designers must learn how to attend to these constraints and possibilities if they want to compose texts that achieve desired communicative outcomes.

Although the project discussed here obviously differs (in terms of project length, setting, stakeholders, content, and more) from possibilities for multimedia composition in the classroom, it nonetheless highlights some important lessons that are relevant to production pedagogy. Based on my own experience and reflection, the following section offers a few broad guidelines for producing multimedia communication in composition and professional communication classrooms. These suggested practices for instructors are not intended as a one-size-fits-all approach, but rather as considerations for shaping multimedia production learning experiences. While many of these guidelines build on traditional, print-based rhetorical practices, they also focus on developing an appreciation for the rhetorical choices specific to the development of new media.

- Recognize and embrace the exploratory and often messy nature of multimedia production. As you shape assignments, keep in mind that much knowledge and expertise with multimedia comes about through trial, error, and troubleshooting, so give students ample room to experiment. Learning how to manipulate image, video, audio, and animation technologies to create multimedia is not an exact science but a matter of trying out and finessing possibilities. Support students in learning to utilize these technologies by providing resources, tutorials, and/or guest presenters, as well as by having realistic expectations for final projects.

- Incorporate opportunities for students to interact with and learn from intended audience members throughout the development process. If possible, have students conduct surveys, focus groups, interviews and/or site visits with target users as they are planning their projects, and have them return to these users with draft versions of their work to seek feedback about content, usability, and appropriateness of chosen media. While the call for audience analysis and input is certainly nothing new, what I am suggesting here is a sustained interaction between writers/designers and readers/users throughout the entire development process. Only by checking their plans and works-in-progress against the needs, interests, and capabilities of their actual users will students be able to revise and refine their multimodal texts so that they effectively achieve their rhetorical intentions.

- Help students interrogate instances of conflict about a project's intended purpose or audience. Most collaborative projects have points of inter-group tension, but pushing students to be explicit about differences of opinion in how they want to approach a project can reveal discrepancies in expectations, intentions, and conceptions of audience. With discussion, these conflicts can become an avenue to producing multimedia that accommodates all writers', stakeholders', and audience members' needs.

- Encourage students to recognize and actively negotiate the relationship between design technologies and capabilities and their influence on the usability of a text's message. Just because something can be done with multimedia does not necessarily mean it should be done. Set up projects to support research into the target population and their technological capabilities in the contexts in which a text will be used. Even with the increasing prevalence of faster connections to the Internet, improved screen resolutions, and greater user access to diverse software and plug-ins, knowing how to use multimedia design tools to minimize obstacles to use and to maximize user interaction is crucial. Students must develop production methods that are attentive to the relationship between technological capabilities and their effect on how a text is used and received by an intended audience.

- Discuss with students what shapes their expectations of academic and/or professional multimedia texts versus those of personal or social texts. While multimedia technologies are ubiquitous and many of our students already engage in development of personal projects, producing texts that integrate various modes and media in a meaningful, rhetorically purposeful way for a specified audience is a complex set of practices that takes time to develop. Each new project requires that writers/designers try out the communicative affordances of a given medium and adapt these to the particular rhetorical demands of a situation. Offering examples and analysis of multimedia texts that demonstrate successful negotiation of the rhetorical considerations specific to new media can provide models for student work, as well as points of reference for helping students and teachers to have shared expectations of the kinds of texts that should be produced.

- Include reflective writing assignments at every stage of the production process so that students are encouraged to be more consciously aware of their own tacit practices. Often, students (and practitioners) get so wrapped up in the activities of development that they fail to recognize the critical and complex work they are actually undertaking. Encourage students to record the media and rhetorical choices they make, as well as the production challenges they face and to discuss the ways in which they negotiate these to complete their projects.

3. MAKING A CASE FOR PRODUCTION OF/IN/WITH MULTILITERACIES

As many scholars in the last decade and a half have argued, constantly evolving technologies for communication provide us with a rich and diverse set of resources for expression beyond written text. In this essay, I have relied on these contentions as they have emerged from the work of Kathleen Blake Yancey (p. 62), Cynthia L. Selfe (1999, 2004), the New London Group (p. 193),

Gunther Kress and Theo van Leeuwen (2001), and others. As these scholars have claimed, multimedia texts hold enormous potential for expanding the range of choices and means we have for communicating with and persuading one another. However, to take full advantage of these new media literacies requires that writers/designers learn to negotiate the rhetorical and the technical situation, as well as to understand how choices in these arenas shape the final product and its reception. Students need support and opportunities to practice composing multimedia texts that not only attend to traditional rhetorical concerns but also account for the rhetorical considerations specific to new media. This includes learning to navigate the potentials and roadblocks that technologies can create for user interaction with a text, as well as the tradeoffs inherent in selecting and integrating various media within a given project. Decisions about these media affordances, technical tools, and contextual circumstances have rhetorical consequences for how a multimedia text will be received and used by its intended audience, so students have to learn to be consciously aware of the rhetorical implications of their choices. This process is necessarily dynamic (as both project contexts and technologies change on a regular basis) and involves flexibility and creativity in navigating the communicative situation, as well as the range of available meaning-making resources. Learning to assess these design and production choices based on the context of a project is challenging, but active engagement with this process offers one of the best ways to understand how multimedia texts work as a powerful means of communication and persuasion.

Further, as so many teachers and scholars in computers and composition have already suggested, we have a responsibility to ensure our students become comfortable and competent with multimodal literacy practices. This must include attention to critical reading and analysis of digital texts, as well as the ability to compose and produce them for others. If we fail to expand our understandings of literacy and rhetorical considerations to incorporate digital composing practices, argued Selfe, "we not only abdicate a professional responsibility . . . but we also run the risk of our curriculum holding declining relevance for students" (2004, 55). Employers, workplaces, and civic engagement all increasingly require participants to possess abilities to communicate effectively through a multitude of digital means. We have an obligation to help students develop rhetorical competencies, particularly with new media, that will prepare them to interact successfully in all of these arenas.

4. CONCLUSION

In *Literacy and Development: Ethnographic Perspectives*, Brian Street argued, "Research, then, I believe, has a task to do in making visible the complexity of local, everyday, community literacy practices and challenging dominant stereotypes and myopia" (2001, 7). Although Street was concerned primarily with accounts of written literacy and culture in developing nations, his description of research that uncovers everyday literacy practices is nonetheless applicable to the project reflected on here. It is precisely stereotypes within the larger field of English studies about the technical, skill-based labor of multimedia production practices that I want to debunk by making visible the traditional and technological rhetorical complexity of this work.

While there is a certain amount of technical knowledge necessary to perform these activities, the production of multimedia is far richer in the ways it shapes meaning than casual observers (including students, colleagues from outside the computers and composition discipline, and administrators) might see. Multimedia production practices are a sophisticated integration of knowing how and when to use appropriate technologies, where to find or how to create the necessary media resources, how to interact with the people involved with a project, and how to prepare the material for the context in which it will be used by its intended audience. Each aspect of this practice is a matter of negotiation, one in which the designer must make decisions that will ultimately impact the meaning and reception of a multimedia text. These are not neutral, value-free skills but rather rhetorical practices in which the choices writers/designers make have consequences. The examples and discussion presented here provide evidence of not just the intellectual demands of multimedia production practices but also a more practical means of integrating the theory and practice of multimodal communication into our classrooms.

If we as teachers/scholars of communication are to play a central role in providing students with the rhetorical and technological capabilities needed to engage fully in academic, professional, and civic life, then we must help both students and colleagues within English studies and our larger institutions understand the role of multimedia production as more than a set of technical tasks. This project illustrates that a pedagogy grounded in a multiplicity of literacies is always about more than simply providing students with the appropriate technological tools and a few skills necessary to use them. Although the complexity and constantly evolving nature of these practices complicate the already difficult job of composition and professional communication educators, they should also be seen as opportunities to further equip students with the literacies and rhetorical tools necessary to interact with the world in thoughtful, informative, and persuasive ways.

NOTES

1. I use the term "writers/designers" throughout this article to call attention to the diverse practices of both form and content development to which multimedia composers must attend.
2. Macromedia, then the maker of Flash, had developed a method for making the frame-per-second (FPS) rate of digital video compatible with the FPS rate for vector-based animation, allowing them to be integrated on the same authoring timeline and at the same playback rate.
3. The Flash 6 Player plug-in is required to view content created in the Flash MX version of the authoring software I used. As a newly released version of the plug-in at the time of testing, the Flash 6 Player did not come as a standard component of web browsers commonly used at that time.
4. In later revision I addressed this issue by removing the video from the Flash movie and linking to each clip separately. This allowed me to use the older plug-in version which came pre-installed with the browser versions used by over 90% of web surfers at the time of this project. This change also significantly reduced download time for the Flash movie.
5. This, of course, is changing as still image and video cameras are integrated into cell phones, as consumer-level production applications such as iMovie are included in software

shipped with computers, and as social networking sites and multimedia blogging become ever more popular. However, despite the fact that many of our students are now coming to our classes with considerable technical expertise and experience (sometimes more than we have) creating their own multimedia rich texts, their work is often missing the major component we *can* bring to the table: rhetorical awareness of how content, technology, and design decisions during production can affect the outcome and reception of such work.

REFERENCES

Anderson, Daniel. (2003). Prosumer approaches to new media composition: Consumption and production in continuum. *Kairos, 8*(1). Retrieved March 3, 2006, from http://kairos.technorhetoric .net/8.1/binder2.html?http://www.hu.mtu.edu/kairos/CoverWeb/anderson/index.html.

Ball, Cheryl, & Kalmbach, James. (Eds.). (2009). *Reading and writing new media.* Cresskill, NJ: Hampton Press for New Dimensions in Computers and Composition series, in press.

Debs, Mary Beth. (1991). Recent research on collaborative writing in industry. *Technical Communication, 38*(4), 476–484.

Druin, Allison, & Solomon, Cynthia. (1996). *Designing multimedia environments for children.* New York: John Wiley.

Gee, James Paul. (2003). *What video games have to teach us about learning and literacy.* New York: Palgrave.

iText Working Group. (2001). iText: Future directions for research on the relationship between information technology and writing. *Journal of Business and Technical Communication, 15*(3), 269–308.

Journet, Debra. (2007). Inventing myself in multimodality: Encouraging senior faculty to use digital media. *Computers and Composition, 24*(2), 107–120.

Kress, Gunther. (2003). *Literacy in the new media age.* New York: Routledge.

Kress, Gunther, & van Leeuwen, Theo. (2001). *Multimodal discourse: The modes and media of contemporary communication.* London: Arnold.

Lemke, J. L. (1998). Metamedia literacy: Transforming meanings and media. In David Reinking, Michael McKenna, Linda Labbo, & Ronald Kieffer (Eds.), *Handbook of literacy and technology: Transformations in a post-typographic world* (pp. 283–298). Mahwah, NJ: Lawrence Erlbaum.

New London Group. (2000). A pedagogy of multiliteracies: Designing social futures. In Bill Cope & Mary Kalantzis (Eds.), *Multiliteracies: Literacy learning and the design of social futures* (pp. 9–37). New York: Routledge.

Selber, Stuart A. (2004). *Multiliteracies for a digital age.* Carbondale, IL: Southern Illinois University Press.

Selfe, Cynthia L. (1999). Technology and literacy: A story about the perils of not paying attention. *College Composition and Communication, 50*(3), 411–436.

Selfe, Cynthia L. (2004). Students who teach us: A case study of a new media text designer. In Anne Wysocki, Johndan Johnson-Eilola, Cynthia L. Selfe, & Geoffrey Sirc (Eds.), *Writing new media: Theory and applications for expanding the teaching of composition* (pp. 43–66). Logan, UT: Utah State University Press.

Street, Brian. (2001). *Literacy and development: Ethnographic perspectives.* London: Routledge.

Williams, Sean D. (2001). Part 1: Thinking out of the pro-verbal box. *Computers and Composition, 18*(1), 21–32.

Yancey, Kathleen Blake. (2004). Made not only in words: Composition in a new key. *College Composition and Communication, 56*(3), 297–320.

23 Infrastructure and Composing: The When of New-Media Writing

DÀNIELLE NICOLE DeVOSS,
ELLEN CUSHMAN, AND JEFFREY T. GRABILL

Rebecca Leibing's digital composition "Sunoco" was created in the beginning weeks of a multimedia writing course; her composition is a digital movie composed from a rather traditional personal narrative essay about her first job at a gas station. Rebecca drew and colored a collection of still images, set them to a digital recording of her reading her paper, and contextualized the combination of images and voice with digital music clips. These media were then tracked together, with the addition of transitions and image pans, using digital video software. To create this piece, she used equipment (software and hardware), technical support, instruction, and different media choices—framed by decisions about color, texture, appeal, and other variables—to fuse what have traditionally been discrete media. Rebecca's composition could be remarked upon as a product in itself—it is funny, smart, and well-written. Certainly, many in the field of composition and rhetoric would choose to focus the analytical lens on this product of new media and for good reasons. However, what is remarkable to us about Rebecca's piece is the story behind its composition, which is revealing of a moment in time, space, institutional relations, and seemingly insurmountable obstacles.

Many researchers pay attention to the what and why of new media without paying attention to the *when* of new-media composing. For example, scholars have done important work that examines the blend of visual and verbal elements in the surfaces and structures of new-media compositions (e.g., Allen; Anson; Bernhardt, "Designing" and "Shape"; DeWitt; George; Handa; Hocks, "Feminist" and "Understanding"; Hocks and Kendrick; Kress "'English'" and "Visual"; Markel; Ruszkiewicz; Sirc; Ulmer; Wysocki and Johnson-Eilola).[1] All of these scholars have in common their focus on new-media writing products, an important topic to be sure. However, few offer frameworks for understanding the spaces for and practices of composing in contemporary, technology-mediated ways. To this growing conversation about new-media composing, we would like to add a focus on the institutional and

From *College Composition and Communication* 57 (2005): 14–44.

political arrangements that—typically invisibly—allow these new-media products to emerge in the first place.

In this essay we focus on the institutional infrastructures and cultural contexts necessary to support teaching students to compose with new media.[2] These often invisible structures make possible and limit, shape and constrain, influence and penetrate all acts of composing new media in writing classes. Although these structural aspects of teaching new media might easily be dismissed as mere inconvenience when they break down or rupture entirely, they are, in fact, deeply embedded in the acts of digital-media composing. We argue that infrastructures are absolutely necessary for writing teachers and their students to understand if we hope to enact the possibilities offered by new-media composing.

Writing within digital spaces occurs within a matrix of local and more global policies, standards, and practices. These variables often emerge as visible and at times invisible statements about what types of work are possible and valuable (encoded, often, in curricula, assessment guidelines, standards, and policies). Some of these issues need the attention of teachers and of program administrators, but we would be miseducating student writers if we didn't teach them that these issues—that which we can too easily dismiss as "constraints"—are indeed deeply embedded in the decision-making processes of writing. If students are to be effective and critical new-media composers, they should be equipped with ways in which they can consider and push at practices and standards in strategic ways.

While the analytical lens that focuses on the *when* of new media keeps in focus the materiality of such media (e.g., the software, wires, and machines), it also brings to light the often invisible issues of policy, definition, and ideology. Indeed, the concept of infrastructure itself demands an integrative analysis of these visible and invisible issues; separations of these issues cannot persist if writing teachers are truly interested in making an impact in both how new media develop and how pedagogies and theories of multimedia composing come into being. We know many people, including ourselves, who have been prevented from working in certain ways as teachers and writers because it was infrastructurally impossible in a given context. Not intellectually impossible. Not even strictly technologically impossible. Something deeper.

Here we adapt Susan Leigh Star and Karen Ruhleder's definition of infrastructure to help us make visible the story behind Rebecca's digital composition. This infrastructural framework allows us to account for any number of "breakdowns" (cognitive, rhetorical, procedural, technical, and so on), to establish the importance of communities of practice, and perhaps most important of all, to focus our attention on the presence and operations of standards and classifications, which lean heavily on all writing practices—and on new-media practices in particular. An infrastructural analysis of the spaces and practices of composing new media gets at some basic and powerful issues with respect to new-media composing: the ways in which new-media writing becomes defined, shaped, accepted, rejected, or some combination of all of these (and more); who gets to do new media; who gets to learn it, where, and how;

and what values get attached to this work (and to its writers and audiences). In these ways, we will show that analyzing the when of new-media composing is as important as analyzing the what and why of new-media composing.

Writing in Digital Environments, Writing with Multiple Sign Systems

We are interested in ways of understanding the contexts of new-media writing because our own experiences suggest that writing with multiple sign systems within technology-mediated environments pushes on systems and established ways of working with a pressure that other ways of writing don't exert.[3] Many of the writing teachers we work with indicate an interest in developing teaching practices that better attend to visual rhetorics and multimedia writing, but these teachers also voice the concern that such teaching is impossible because of the institutional resources currently available to them. This recognition of institutional and technological limitations suggests the need for analytical tools that might help us account for the contexts of new-media writing in ways that enable students and teachers to achieve what they can imagine in and for the composition classroom. But how best to account for the contexts of new-media composing?

Although previous scholars have not adopted the specific language we have here (i.e., "infrastructure"), computers and writing researchers have long paid attention to issues of digital writing environments. Teachers of writing in computer-mediated spaces have been attentive to the spaces in which they teach and to the physical and digital spaces in which students work; for twenty years, composition scholars have published on possibilities and complications related to teaching in computer-mediated settings (for example, in technology classrooms: Bernhardt, "Designing" and "Shape"; Britton and Glynn; Dinan, Gagnon, and Taylor; Gruber; Haas; Kent-Drury; Moran, "Access" and "From"; Palmquist; Palmquist, Kiefer, Hartvigsen, and Godlew; Selfe, *Creating*, "Creating," and "Technology"; with/in electronic spaces like e-mail, bulletin board systems, and MOOs/MUDs: Cooper; Cooper and Selfe; Grigar; Holdstein; Kinkead; LeCourt; Moran and Hawisher; Rouzie; Sanchez; Spooner and Yancey; Thompson; and via distance- and online-education spaces: Buckley; Harris and Wambeam; Webb Peterson and Savenye).

Compositionists have also attended to issues of agency and subjectivity in regard to digital media and online spaces. For instance, Stephen Knadler, Heidi McKee, Teresa Redd, Elaine Richardson, Todd Taylor, and others have addressed issues of race and difference in digital spaces, both from an instructor standpoint and from a student perspective. A strong thread of composition scholarship has explored issues of gender in digital space, attending to the male-centered context of computing and to possible feminist interventions in electronic spaces (e.g., Brady Aschauer; Hocks, "Feminist"; Pagnucci and Mauriello; Rickly; L. Sullivan; Takayoshi, "Building" and "Complicated,"; Takayoshi, Huot, and Huot; Webb; Wolfe). Access — an issue that often manifests itself at intersections of gender, class, and race — has also been addressed as an issue crucial to computers and composition scholarship. Jeffrey Grabill and Alison Regan and John Zuern have targeted issues of access by exploring the movement of computer-mediated composition outside of the classroom and into communities. Lester Faigley, Joseph Janangelo, Charles Moran, and Cynthia Selfe have studied issues of access and traced access across cultural, social, and historical trends.

New technologies have raised questions not only about manifestations of race and gender in the "bodiless" realm of cyberspace and about the real issues of access to machines and networks, but new technologies have also raised speculation about emergent and electronic literacy practices (see, for example, Bolter; Burbules; Heba; Holdstein and Selfe; Joyce; Selfe, "Technology and Literacy"; Tuman). Closely related is scholarship analyzing how specific interfaces potentially shape writing practices and processes (e.g., Condon; Curtis, "Forum"; LeBlanc; McGee and Ericsson; Selfe and Selfe; P. Sullivan; Vernon; Wysocki, "Impossibly" and "Monitoring"; Wysocki and Jasken); certainly, text messaging, blogs, and wikis are shaping research paths related to interfaces of/for writing. Framing all this work are examinations of institutional and political dynamics as they affect writing classrooms via, for example, policies, guidelines, and intellectual property laws (Gurak and Johnson-Eilola; Howard; Johnson-Eilola, "Living"; Kalmbach; Lang, Walker, and Dorwick; Porter, "Liberal" and *Rhetorical Ethics*; Porter, Sullivan, Blythe, Grabill, and Miles; CCCC Committee). These contributions are significant, and help situate composition scholars within emerging—and existing—issues of visual and digital rhetorics and possibilities for new-media production, or at least analysis. Specifically, these contributions help us to better understand the ways that composition researchers have made sense of past and current integrations of technology and writing.

Although the composition scholars mentioned above have noted the increasing prominence given to visual communication, online writing, and digital spaces, and although researchers are paying more attention to the blend of visual and verbal elements, few offer frameworks for understanding the spaces for and practices of composing new media. Issues such as the standards and policies of network use and the institutional locations of new-media curricula still remain invisible—and these issues are integral to understanding and enabling new-media composing. Here we attempt to make visible these and some of the other dynamics of new-media writing. An infrastructural framework helps not only to reveal these dynamics and their consequences, but also to identify access points for discursive agency and change-making within institutions. As an analytical framework, then, an understanding of infrastructure makes strange the taken-for-granted, often invisible, institutional structures implicit in the teaching of new-media composing. In the remainder of the essay, we'll outline this framework and apply it to the new-media writing class in which Rebecca's piece was produced. We demonstrate the utility of an infrastructural framework for writing teachers who hope to uncover the deeply embedded institutional, cultural, and political issues involved in teaching new media.

INFRASTRUCTURE AS ANALYTICAL TOOL

When teachers express frustration with their ability to teach new-media writing, they often point toward specific and often physical infrastructural impediments—computers, software, and networks. An infrastructure of a computer lab certainly would include its server and network system, the machines and their monitors, and the wiring within the room. However, there is something more complex going on in any composing context—both in terms of what frustrates teachers and in terms of how we understand infrastructure itself. If we expand our notion of infrastructure, we would include the policies and standards that regulate the uses of the room. We would also include systems of support for the work that takes place in the room, and the budget and funding (and related decisions) for the material objects in the room. We would include structures for surveillance within the room and within the spaces to which the machines allow access (e.g., the security cameras found in many of the computer labs on our campus; the student tracking function in course-management software that allows teachers to see how often students have accessed a course site and what areas of the course site they have visited). We would consider the tasks and practices that occur within the room—how the material objects are used, to what end, and for what audiences. Our use of the term "infrastructure" reflects the work of Star and Ruhleder, who characterize infrastructure in the following way:

- *Embeddedness.* Infrastructure is "sunk" into, inside of other structures, social arrangements and technologies;

- *Transparency.* Infrastructure is transparent to use, in the sense that it does not have to be reinvented each time or assembled for each task, but it invisibly supports those tasks;

- *Reach or scope.* This may be either spatial or temporal—infrastructure has reach beyond a single event or one-site practice;

- *Learned as part of membership.* The taken-for-grantedness of artifacts and organizational arrangements is a *sine qua non* of membership in a community of practice [. . .]. Strangers and outsiders encounter infrastructure as a target object to be learned about. New participants acquire a naturalized familiarity with its objects as they become members;

- *Links with conventions of practice.* Infrastructure both shapes and is shaped by the conventions of a community of practice; e.g., the ways that cycles of day-night work are affected by and affect electrical power rates and needs. Generations of typists have learned the QWERTY keyboard; its limitations are inherited by the computer keyboard and thence by the design of today's computer furniture [. . .];

- *Embodiment of standards.* Modified by scope and often by conflicting conventions, infrastructure takes on transparency by plugging into other infrastructures and tools in a standardized fashion;

- *Built on an installed base.* Infrastructure does not grow *de novo*; it wrestles with the "inertia of the installed base" and inherits strengths and limitations from that base [. . .];

- *Becomes visible upon breakdown.* The normally invisible quality of working infrastructure becomes visible when it breaks; the server is down, the bridge washes out, there is a power blackout. Even when there are back-up mechanisms or procedures, their existence further highlights the now-visible infrastructure. (113)

If we think of the composing infrastructure on our own campus in these terms, we come up with the following list of infrastructural components:

- computer networks
- network configurations
- operating systems, computer programs, interfaces, and their interrelatedness
- network, server, and storage access rights and privileges
- courses and curricula
- the existence and availability of computer classrooms
- decision-making processes and procedures for who gets access to computer classrooms
- the design and arrangement of computer classrooms
- time periods of classes
- availability of faculty, students, and spaces outside of set and scheduled class times
- writing classifications and standards (e.g., what is writing; what is good writing)
- metaphors of computer programs; metaphors people use to describe programs; metaphors people use to describe their composing processes
- purposes and uses of new-media work
- audiences for new-media work, both inside and outside the university

This list is far from exhaustive, but provides a sense, at least, of the sorts of elements and issues an infrastructural framework can make visible. But there is much more to an infrastructure than what is material or technological. Our list includes standards and classifications—most powerfully what counts as writing, what is permissible in a writing class, and what makes for "good" writing. Infrastructure also entails decision-making processes and the values and power relationships enacted by those processes; and infrastructure is thoroughly penetrated by issues of culture and identity (in ways that space limits prevent us from exploring here). *All* writing activities are contextualized by certain infrastructures; our aim here is to argue for the importance of understanding the distinctive infrastructural dynamics that new-media composing creates as well as the ways that such composing is dependent on infrastructural dynamics that may not be configured to accommodate traditional writing activities.

As an analytical tool, Star and Ruhleder's characteristics of infrastructure have significant scope and heuristic value. However, we don't want the focus of this discussion merely to settle on issues of defining an infrastructure. The most useful question, as Star and Ruhleder assert, may not be *what* an infrastructure is but rather *when* it is. Working from a piece by Yrjö Engeström that asks "When is a tool?" Star and Ruhleder argue that "infrastructure is something that emerges for people in practice, connected to activities and structures" (112). In other words, a tool is not an artifact with "pre-given attributes frozen in time," but rather is given meaning *as* a tool by specific users working on particular problems in specific situations (see also Feenberg; Johnson [Latour]); so too does the meaning and value of an infrastructure emerge. That is, an infrastructure is more than material, is never static, and is always emerging. We want to suggest that writing programs will never adequately come to terms with how to understand and teach new-media composing unless we can come to a productive and activist understanding of infrastructure. For students, understanding infrastructural constraints on new-media composing offers important grounding in the kinds of decisions that influence the possibilities, processes, and final deliverables of their digital writing. Such an understanding will allow students and professors to anticipate and participate in a number of institutional processes that shape infrastructure and so shape how we teach new-media composing.

In what follows, taking Ellen's multimedia writing class as a source of data, we use the notion of infrastructure as a heuristic for reading our local contexts. We focus on when new-media infrastructures emerge and what the dynamics of infrastructure mean for composing in those contexts. Thus, we demonstrate how writing instructors might apply this framework to their classroom and institutional contexts. The material we use here to situate our explanations of an infrastructural approach to writing was collected in a multimedia writing class taught at Michigan State University (MSU). Interested in studying new-media composing processes and the teaching of multimedia writing, Ellen collected student work and also saved the many correspondences to administrators and computing services specialists, the class notes generated on the Blackboard space used for the course, and archives of virtual chats that took place in class.[4] These materials will be excerpted throughout to help us address the larger questions we ponder in this manuscript: What material, technical, discursive, institutional, and cultural conditions prohibit and enable writing with multiple media?[5] How does an infrastructural approach offer a lens through which we can better interpret and understand the multiple conditions at play in our writing classrooms? How can an infrastructural interpretation support and enable new-media writing?

File Management and Standards: Thinking about Products before Processes

Ellen's multimedia writing class allows us to see the structures, technologies, and decisions that teachers and writers navigate. Questions at the forefront of writing with multiple media emerge as soon as the software launches and the interface expands, questions that force writers to consider the material and rhetorical realities in which they will compose and through which their final products will be produced and viewed. For example, before digital video software opens to an interface for composing, a window prompts composers for their project settings. As with writing, the composer must know something about what the final product will be *before* beginning the process. However, in the case of composing a multimedia video product, the writer must also know what kinds of files will be needed and created to meet the demands of the final product—including types of files and media (e.g., chunks of text, images) and specific forms of files and media (e.g., a voice file saved as a .wav, images saved as .jpgs).

The writer, in the case of fairly robust video software like Adobe Premiere, must also have a sense of how the software is installed and runs on the computer and on the networks within which the user composes. Questions the composer must address include: What should the final product look like on screen (e.g., size of viewers' monitors and viewing windows)? What level of sound quality is expected (e.g., mono, stereo, 8 or 16 bits)? How is this product to be delivered (e.g., VHS, CD, online)? How much memory is available and where in the classroom? How much memory is available on the audience's computers? How will the audience members access this project? These questions—and this is but a very short list of the initial considerations a composer of new media must address—work at both the material and the rhetorical level in ways quite different than traditional writing classrooms might (that is, those that rely primarily on text and paper). Addressing these questions before composing even begins not only affects the writing processes of students, but also deeply affects the set-up and delivery of instruction.

In the case of Ellen's multimedia writing' class, answers to these questions began with the file management system on our campus. File-management issues arose before students even entered the class on the first day, and brought to the forefront institutional limitations that influenced the type, quality, and extent of learning that could take place in the class. The general structure of instructional computing on campus works somewhat like this: The campus computing protocol is to load all software from a main server when a user logs on to a campus computer; the rationale for this is related mainly to security and virus-protection measures. Thus little software is installed on and loaded from the local drives of computers—each time students launch a software application, they do so from a remote server. Writing with multiple media and writing within robust multimedia applications like Premiere or Macromedia Director violates this common network structure in various ways. First, because digital video software does not work well when virtual memory is engaged—and virtual memory is always engaged at MSU because individual users do not have the access required to change the control panel settings on the computers—the software will crash. Also, when a student logs off of a machine—or if a machine happens to crash and then reboot while the student is working—all of the students preview files are lost because the files are stored in a folder on the local disk, which is erased from the computer each time a user logs off or the machine restarts. Although the student is relying upon a remotely networked software application, the work students create is actually stored locally (and thus wiped out—deleted—upon restart).

Long before the semester began, Ellen realized that this network structure would influence the work for her class. She thus requested a meeting with the staff member who acts as liaison between instructors and the centralized campus computing facilities. During the meeting, Ellen described her needs for the class and the types of projects students would be composing during the semester (three in all, becoming sequentially more complex, with a final product of a digital portfolio on CD). She described the kinds of files associated with student projects: the project file (command file); the tracked files (e.g., images, voiceovers, music); the preview files (compressed, motion and audio files created when the command file is executed and stored locally); and the final project, typically a 200- to 300-megabyte .mov file. The immediate response of the liaison upon hearing these file types, sizes, and needs was that students absolutely could not write to the local drive of campus machines. She followed up this statement by noting that Ellen would simply have to require fewer assignments and have students produce smaller, nonvideo, projects. She made suggestions that included students working with still rather than motion images. When Ellen balked at having a computer specialist demand certain teaching methods of her, the liaison argued that MSU computing policy clearly states that students cannot write to the local hard drives because there would be no security—anyone could erase their work. It was at this point in the conversation that Ellen realized that the issue wasn't a memory problem at all, but a *policy* problem. The equipment was available for use, but the computers were to be kept clean and safe from the apparently untrustworthy students. At the end of the meeting, Ellen was told that students would absolutely have to save their work to the campus server, that under no circumstances would students be able to save their work to the local computers, and that Ellen would be lucky to get an additional gigabyte of storage space for student projects.

In Ellen's class, the standards for file management established by the university and standards for system operation within the software itself were at odds. The university's standard operating procedure prohibited allowing students to save to local hard disks, but the software standards demanded that files be saved to local hard disks to facilitate the retrieval and compression process among the project file, dependent files, and preview files.

We approach standards from two directions: First, standards can be thought of as the typical approaches that people take as they perform a task; there are "standard" or conventional ways of accessing a network, launching software, and saving files. Second, standards can be thought of as Bowker and Star do: as procedures for how to do things (234). Although these two definitions might seem much the same, and although they do orbit around each other, they are, in fact, quite different. For example, a procedure might dictate an acceptable or appropriate use (e.g., via an "acceptable-use policy" that regulates a particular network); however, the conventions of practice that emerge among users as they work within the system might differ from and even work against established procedures. Users, in this case writers, invent standards as much as they follow them. Clearly, networks—technological and otherwise—are complex systems of interconnected human beings and machines, and because of the complexity of networks, normally transparent issues (e.g., file management, the operation of programs, and so on) become visible when different standards of operation compete.

On our campus, acting through/with/against standards means attending to the local standards of the centralized computer system and its multiple paths of decision-making power and practices, and paying attention to the larger network standards of state-based bodies (i.e., Michnet, the statewide network service upon which MSU's networks are built) and national organizations (the CCCC Position Statement on Teaching, Learning, and Assessing Writing in Digital Environments). Too often, because of institutional and disciplinary trends, writing teachers are absent from the histories and development of standards. On campuses where technology budgets are limited, writing is still often seen as a low-technology subject, and writing classes as low-technology spaces. Although few administrators would argue with the fact that most composing takes place on computers, writing courses and the concerns of writing teachers may not be seen as high-priority items during discussions of standards and policies, and during other decision-making processes. Standards—scripted as policies or regulations—often emerge from technology committees and information-system offices. Participating in and perhaps rescripting standards to support new-media writing is an ongoing process.

Encountering and Rupturing Policies

We will return to this conversation on standards and its infrastructural implications, but first we want to continue to follow the file management pathway—in reality a conflict between local network and more general software standards—to trace how these pathways overdetermine composing practices.

After a writer has addressed the questions we mentioned above related to the production and delivery of a composition, the writer translates the answers to these questions into project settings fixed within the software application being used to compose (see Figure 23-1 for an example from Premiere). The application is then launched, with a menu bar across the top; a project bin in the upper left; monitors next to the project bin; transition; navigator, and history tools on the right; and a timeline across the bottom of the screen (see Figure 23-2, again from Premiere). Although each window merits its own summary, the project bin and the timeline windows are perhaps most dependent on careful file management. These two components of the software are powerful meaning-making tools—the project bin is akin to a file cabinet from which the pieces of the project are drawn as needed; the timeline is akin to a command file (although its graphical interface hides the command language underneath) in which each file from the bin is tracked. The MSU computing policy—an assemblage of classifications, preferences, long-ago-established practices, and standards—hindered not only student access to this composing interface, but the writing they could do within it.

FIGURE 23-1   Screen capture of Adobe Premiere interface.

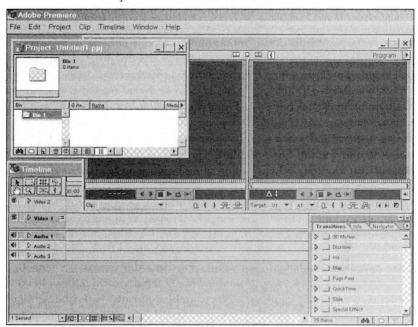

FIGURE 23-2   Screen capture of Adobe Premiere Project Settings interface.

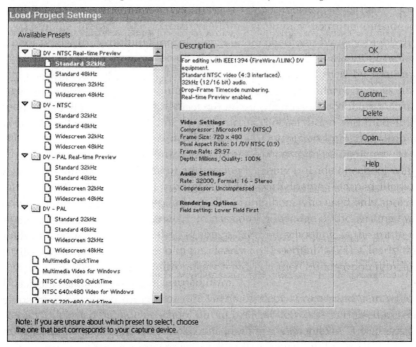

In her conversation with the computing services liaison, Ellen had been told to use specific network space for her class's work; one gig of memory was allocated to this space, for Ellen and for all of the students to share. Ellen's class notes from very early in the semester—January 15, 2002 (the second week of class)—are revealing of the complex routes necessary to access the shared space into which files could be saved:

> Locating your server spaces. The icons on your Mac desktop include your own network space, as well as the "root" space for courses. We'll be using both of these spaces to save files this semester. I want you to visualize where you will be saving your files, so that you can better understand the "save as" windows:
>
> 1. Click twice on the root-space icon to open the folders there.
> 2. Go to MSU or MSU.edu (make sure that you consistently stick with one or the other, although I was told that they're essentially the same thing).
> 3. Go to Course, click twice to open,
> 4. Go to Eng, click twice to open,
> 5. Go to 391, click twice to open. Here we will have one gig of space into which we can save. Each of you will create a folder with your last name on it. We will then save all of our project and preview files here in your respective folders.

Although server space for all of the courses offered at the university can be found by following the process detailed above, the courses—hundreds of them offered each semester—do not exist in one space (as the visual folder metaphor suggests). Instead, the memory devoted to a given course is an articulation of parcels of memory distributed across many pieces of hardware across the campus. From a systems perspective, this is efficient. However, the use to which the one gig of space allotted to the multimedia writing class was put by students pushed not only on the technical structure itself, but also on the assumptions and established standards regulating the use of the technical structure.

Once Ellen was made aware of and began to work through the policies and the technological systems in place—which *are* typically highly functional and efficient—and students began using the systems, the software, and the networks in new ways, they broke down. For example, some students were able to create their folders; five students, however, for reasons never explained or understood by the system administrators, were only able to save to their folders sporadically. Other students were not able to save their work at all on the server space. Further, according to the way in which the systems on campus are set up, once the project files were saved to the server space the actual composing could take place. But this didn't prove to be the case. In some sense, our narrative of what Ellen and her students experienced is a commonplace story of writing teachers and technological breakdown. The impression we wish to avoid, however, is that the case we are presenting is *yet another* story of writing teachers struggling with technology. Yes, this is a story of writing teachers struggling with technology, but that is but one thread of a much larger story.

The types of issues commonplace to new-media writing spaces aren't merely issues to be solved by teachers and administrators before classes begin. They are certainly that, but they are also issues that continue to have an impact on the composing practices of writers as a class begins and unfolds, *and* they are our discipline's attempts to negotiate, adopt, and script writing with multiple media into its practices. Note the various ways that the writers in Ellen's class had to make a number of "nonwriting" decisions related to audience and the technological and rhetorical needs of that audience (e.g., bandwidth, screen size, media form and function). All of these decisions entered them into different orders of discourse, different grammars and conventions of practice, and different areas of knowledge than would typically be entertained in a writing classroom. Note, too, that the discussions Ellen had with campus computing officials made visible the need for writers to negotiate what is—and what isn't—infrastructurally possible.

Networks dictate how and in what ways certain technological resources are available within any infrastructure; in our case, the networks within which Ellen and the students in her course were composing were split across computer classrooms and across buildings. How fast software downloaded from central servers, where students could save their files, and how quickly students could upload material for rendering and previewing often dictated the shape of composing, and the pace of the course itself. In fact, in work and conversations with central computing, it became clear that we understand networks themselves very differently than they do (not merely technically but socially and ideologically as well).

Networks—locally and universally—are core to new-media writing, enacting the old marketing cliché that the network *is* the computer. In fact, as more writing instruction moves to digital spaces and as the majority of students' writing activity takes place in online environments (e.g., instant messaging, blogging), the paths of the transparent streams of bits and bytes merit attention as part of the *when* of infrastructure. This *when* is acutely felt when students are seen as potential threats to the networks as opposed to users; it's felt when course content, file size, and location are prescribed by networking policies and physical structures that support these. Tracing and understanding network paths through wires, cards, ports, and servers and across the policies and standards that shape the design and use of such spaces is often necessary to understand complexities and to negotiate new-media writing.

Structures Become Visible upon Breakdown: Locating Points for Institutional Change

Let's return again to the process of composing new media to show one other way that the infrastructural framework helps reveal places to leverage institutional change: Digital video is composed using timelines. When complete, the timeline is essentially a command file that writes "code" based on the icons of the media tracked and on the project settings. The timeline compiles all the separate media files together into preview files typically housed within the software applications local folder on a computer. Preview files are memory-hungry audio and video files that represent a compilation of just a few seconds of the timeline. Preview files are typically created by keying ENTER after every few seconds of timeline tracked, so that composers can, in effect, replay what they've composed, seeing and hearing the rough cut in the monitor window. When compiled along the way, these files are then collected into one large movie project that itself becomes a file saved with the rest of the media files.

Three weeks into Ellen's multimedia writing course, students were expected to have tracked the basic media components of their project timelines. Students had written and revised their papers, collected the other media they were to integrate and choreograph with their texts, and learned the basics of tracking with the software. As they worked, students began running out of memory to store their files; their computers were crashing frequently due to "type 2" errors. Data transfer was stymied or disallowed completely for files over 10 megabytes—very tiny files in multimedia terms. When students tried to compile their projects, their computers froze, and sometimes crashed completely and wouldn't reboot. More often than not, the freezing and crashing corrupted command files, and hours of work were lost. Tensions in class—and after class, as the constraints of time were felt quite acutely when compiling times were long and class time was relatively short—were high. The class came to a complete stop when the first project was due. For whatever reason, Rebecca Leibing's project was the only one the class was able to preview. Like any other writing project, her work required some revision—in this instance, the music she embedded drowned out her voice in places and she needed more motion across the stills to better provide a sense of flow. Rebecca was able to revise her rough cut to create the project. . . . Two other students eventually completed their files as well, but the rest were not able to complete their projects at all. Because the archive files were completely erased when the computers crashed, students lost their command files—and thus most of their work. Rebecca's project is interesting because it marks the when of infrastructural meltdown; *when* class came to a standstill, *when* her project was anomalously the only one produced, and *when* the typically invisible policy, cultural, and computer system structures became visible upon breakdown.

At this still-early point in the semester, the composing practices of Ellen's students had once again exceeded the technological space of the classroom. Ellen wrote a letter to the vice provost of libraries, computing, and technology (essentially the head of the centralized campus computing systems and the information services director), making a case for additional server/network space for her class and her students' work. She argued for a specific upgrade (from one gig to two gigs), and noted that the class was at an impasse, and that students were prohibited from writing and producing their digital compositions because of the memory limits of the campus network. Ellen implored the vice provost to bend current university policy and to consider allowing students to have continuous access to the hard drives in a folder saved even after a machine crashes and reboots or a student logs off. If students were able to save directly to a fixed local space; they would be able to save their tracking, project, preview, and final movie files. A key portion of the letter Ellen constructed conveyed her awareness of the fact that her course, new to the College of Arts and Letters and unique in the university, would soon no longer be unique — she emphasized the growing importance of writing in digital environments and writing with multiple media.

In response, the vice provost granted nine gigs of additional storage space. Soon afterwards (approximately six weeks into the class), two system managers visited the class to see firsthand the problems students were experiencing. They walked around the room reading error messages, watching students stall the system with file-transfer bottlenecks, and hearing from students about the problems they were experiencing. The students asked questions of the system managers that began to reveal how they were understanding the when of new media. For instance, when one student wondered why users had differential access to server space, she was told that this had to do with an outdated networking hub that bottlenecked when they tried to save. Another student asked how a type 2 error could occur when, upon checking the information on the computer, it appeared to have ample memory capacity for the work. Finally, another student asked where the archives were located when they were creating these pieces. The entire class session the day the two system managers visited consisted of students making apparent their learning about what should have been transparent: the ways in which the system and policies for its use were incompatible with their needs as composers and incompatible with the software's requirements. To their credit, the system managers listened and worked to solve the problems; over the following weekend, they carried out some changes that made the environment more friendly and more usable.

The first change that took place soon after the visit included installing some software applications locally on the computers. As we mentioned earlier, university policy prohibited software from being stored locally, but in the case of the multimedia writing course it was imperative that software be locally accessible. With this installation, software freezes abated. Together Ellen and the students walked through the instructions from the system managers that explained how to copy software off the university's server and onto the local computers. In this case, we — Ellen as instructor, Jeff and Dànielle as program faculty, and students in the course — all gained insight as to how a system might be opened in ways that facilitate local use. Students were also allowed to read and write from their local computers, yet another manipulation of university computing policy. These two changes allowed students to compile their second projects with fewer bottlenecks, freezes, and crashes. In addition, the system administrators turned off virtual memory for all of the computers, so that the video software would work much more smoothly, with fewer type 2 errors. One of the system managers who had visited the class emphasized that Ellen needed to warn students that their folders were not secure—that they would be working on the "honor system" as they wrote to the hard disk.[6] This itself was a significant shift in policy, albeit a temporary and local one. The campus computers were set up so that all student work was erased upon their logout, in part to protect against the spread of viruses, in part so that students could not access one another's files, and in part to protect against the local drives of computers quickly filling with work students stored and never erased. Allowing students to save permanently and locally required that the students adopt conventions regarding privacy and politeness that the campus policy previously restricted students from dealing with and actively participating in.

After these key changes, the technological spaces of the classroom and of student production worked much more smoothly. In the end, Adrienne Brach finished her second project, as did all the other students. The course activities were truncated—because of the need to negotiate and renegotiate and then eventually change the systems in place and the policies governing those systems—so that students produced only two projects. Adrienne's project was in response to a prompt that asked students to select a piece of creative writing and interpret it through a digital composition. Students were asked to show rather than tell their interpretation. Because of the enhanced performance of the software and the new file-management capabilities students had access to, Adrienne was able to take advantage of a variety of media, and a variety of effects.

In her piece, text files—at times multiply layered and scrolling across the screen—appear simultaneously as an image pan moves the view across the still in the opposite direction. Adrienne's piece, "Der Panther," is a gruesomely beautiful interpretation of a German poem in light of *The Dreaded Comparison*, a book that traces similarities between the ideologies implicit in animal cruelty and slavery. Her composition suggests the possibilities of new-media composing when the infrastructure enables them.

The *When* of Infrastructure

Infrastructures can be transparent in that they do in some sense both preexist *and* work, and so even though infrastructures are always already the conditions in and through which we interact, compose, and think, we often *don't* need to think about them. In a sense, however, infrastructure needs to be reinvented each time or assembled for each task. Again, the issue is not what an infrastructure is but *when* it is. When the tasks of composing—including the tasks of thinking, of imagining, of creating—are not consistent with existing standards, practices, and values, infrastructure breaks down, revealing the need to meet the demands of new meaning-making practices. The rupture points, as we've seen from this case, became teachable moments for both the students and Ellen. Both had to learn enough about the interrelations of networks, software, and file management to be able to simply complete assignments. In Ellen's case, a class that had never before been taught at this university introduced new conventions of practice and new forms of meaning making that stressed—in productive ways—the existing infrastructure. The spaces required and composing processes involved *created* a new infrastructure for multimedia writing. It is this time-space-place nexus—the *when* of infrastructure emergence/construction—that we will now explore a bit further.

An infrastructural analysis has helped us understand the composing and learning that took place in Ellen's class and imagine appropriate responses as we rethink courses, writing, and compositions. As Christine Borgman writes, all information infrastructures are "built upon an installed base of telecommunications lines, electrical power grids, and computing technology" (20), and certainly we can read the material aspects of infrastructure in the examples above. Infrastructures are also built upon available "information resources, organizational arrangements, and people's practices in using all these aspects" (20). We also see these elements unfold—and collide—in the writing enabled within Ellen's class. Johndan Johnson-Eilola notes that we live, are composed, and compose "at the nexus connecting an apparently infinite number of social and technological forces of varying weights, strengths, and directions" ("Negative" 17), and certainly the infrastructural dynamics described here create such a nexus.

Within this nexus, students are presented with infrastructural questions as soon as applications like Adobe Premiere are launched. The first few interfaces, shown earlier, demand an understanding of invisible institutional structures and policies, such as those related to permissions to save on networks, file management and architecture, and file size and compression. Before new-media composing can even begin, the software demands that students negotiate an understanding of the deliverables to be produced. These understandings must take into consideration the audiences' system and platform requirements for file formats, memory allocation, and hardware. These infrastructural concerns permeate most networked composing environments including the organizations, workplaces, and institutions where students are likely to find employment. The *when* of new media, in other words, can and should be taught to students as part of and integral to new-media composing.

For teachers and administrators, the question of when an infrastructure for multimedia writing emerges has been answered (i.e., *now*) and will always be delayed (i.e., it continues to emerge). Ellen began her first interventions by breaking existing systems and drawing upon personal, rhetorical, and departmental tactics to save her class and to afford merit—technological and intellectual—to her students' work. We continue to work within emerging infrastructures by tailoring our curriculum, designing our requirements, and adopting different practices and assignments. We also continue this work by building new physical spaces (classrooms), arguing for new virtual spaces (new file-management practices), and pushing for changes in both policies and standards. Some infrastructural interventions require seemingly simple revisions to policies or machines that shape the use of a room, a lab, or a network—revisions that alter who can work there, and when, and produce what. We are attracted to these mundane interventions and will assert, despite the ways in which these assertions often bore our colleagues, that these interventions are powerful and important micropolitical acts of institutional critique, agency, and change (Porter, Sullivan, Blythe, Grabill, and Miles). Infrastructural issues have an impact, literally, on the space of the writing classroom and what happens there—and they do so in ways both visible and invisible.

What this brief discussion reveals to us is how situated new-media composing is—how infrastructures of composing both rupture and create possibilities. Rebecca's piece, being the only successful initial project in a classroom of fifteen students, points to the rupture of an infrastructure. Adrienne's piece suggests the possibilities of new-media writing when an infrastructure works: Her piece grew out of multiple revisions and deeper, fuller uses of the technology made available to her as a result of micropolitical changes in network policy and system use. Our own work with exploring and teaching new-media writing has revealed to us the cultural, political, and institutional contexts of composing—so much so that it is no longer possible for us to look at a product of new media without wondering what kinds of material and social realities made it possible. We also have become aware of the need to reach beyond the frameworks that we typically rely upon to understand composing processes and spaces of composing.

To understand the contexts that make possible and limit, shape and constrain, and facilitate and prevent new-media composing, new-media teachers and students need to be able to account for the complex interrelationships of material, technical, discursive, institutional, and cultural systems. An infrastructural approach reveals the layers and patterns behind the products of new-media composing—patterns that directly affect contemporary writing, writing pedagogy, and writing classrooms. Our claim is that in order to teach and understand new media composing, some understanding of new-media infrastructure is necessary. Without such an understanding, writing teachers and students will fail to anticipate and actively participate in the emergence of such infrastructures, thereby limiting—rhetorically, technically, and institutionally—what is possible for our students to write and learn.

We argued earlier that our field has produced rich work that analyzes the currents of online writing, digital spaces, and media convergence. We also argued, however, that few scholars offer frameworks for understanding the spaces within which such compositions are produced. Here we see that the processes of new media are very much mediated by the dynamics of infrastructures and also that infrastructures might be best thought of as a "when" and not a "what." An infrastructural framework, we hope, creates a tool for composers to navigate the systems within and across which they work, creates a moment for reflection and change within institutional structures, and networks, and creates a framework for understanding writing that moves forward our understandings of how composing and compositions change shape within the complex dynamics of networks.

NOTES

1. This work describes how "writing" has changed to weaving what we might call "traditional" (certainly older) media (like text, graphics, and audio) with and for computer interfaces. Characterizing new media as hybrid, for example, Mary E. Hocks and Michelle R. Kendrick (following the work of Bruno Latour) ask us to move beyond static binaries that separate visual/textual and image/word and to instead create spaces where we can focus on the "complex, interpenetrating relationships between words and images" (5), relationships that are not new but instead remediated with/in today's technologies (see also Bolter and Grusin).

2. We might argue that new media aren't necessarily new: images, motion, sound, video, and other media have existed for decades. What is new, however, are the spaces and interfaces in which and through which these media are woven. What is new is how writing is transformed into composing, requiring the ability to weave together what we might call "traditional" (certainly older) media (like text, graphics, and audio) with and for computer interfaces. What is also new is the access to these media and technologies in our writing classrooms.

3. Consider a traditional writing classroom: Word-processing software is crucial, and a Web browser and Internet access are probably a must. Presentation software might also be used. Students produce primarily text-based documents, which are relatively small in size and can be easily stored, saved, and distributed; these documents are typically designed for print. Compare this classroom to a new-media writing classroom, where robust video-editing and multimedia-production software is in use, where Internet access is necessary to share and stream files, and where files themselves are gigantic—easily filling gigs of hard drives and network space. This is just a thin comparison, but a thick example of the ways in which new-media writing pushes on our established technological systems. From another direction: Consider, also, the assumptions made of writing instruction ten or fifteen years ago. We have each often heard the question, "Why do writing classrooms need computers?" The practices and needs of new-media writing explode this question in multiple directions.

4. Ellen distributed consent forms early in the semester. Most students signed them, thus granting her permission to include their compositions in her research and writing.

5. Although we have taught new-media classes here and at other universities where the courses have run according to plan, this class was chosen for use as a model here because it made visible to us the infrastructural dynamics upon which new-media composing relies. This course also allowed us, because of this visibility, to both critique and alter these infrastructural dynamics.

6. The students knew that they were able to open one another's folders. We agreed to a policy of respecting the privacy of one another's space and of only ever accessing this space with permission. In fact, this "security problem" became an important moment for the class. Students were creating a culture of technology in which they agreed upon practices for use and set a premium on respecting one another's space and work. Students were creating a hospitable environment for learning, an environment that depended upon their shared respect for one another and a shared honoring of an agreement beneficial to everyone. Interestingly, they created this environment inside an infrastructure that doubted their abilities to do so: The computing policy of the classroom that demanded we use remote space as opposed to the local disk space was premised on a belief that students were not honorable—that they would in fact erase the contents of one another's folders if given the chance to do so. What enabled new-media composing here was mutual trust, shared respect, agreement about access, and a culture of technology that ran contrary to the larger computing policy that continued to cripple the progress of the class.

WORKS CITED

Allen, Nancy, ed. *Working with Words and Images: New Steps in an Old Dance.* Stamford, CT: Ablex, 2002.

Anson, Chris M. "Distant Voices: Teaching Writing in a Culture of Technology." *College English* 61.3 (1999): 261–80.

Bernhardt, Stephen A. "Designing a Microcomputer Classroom for Teaching Composition." *Computers and Composition* 7.1 (1989): 93–110.

———. "The Shape of Text to Come: The Texture of Print on Screens." *CCC* 44.2 (1993): 151–75.

Bolter, Jay David. *The Writing Space: The Computer, Hypertext, and the History of Writing.* Hillsdale, NJ: Erlbaum, 1991.

Bolter, Jay David, and Richard Grusin. *Remediation: Understanding New Media.* Cambridge: MIT P, 2000.

Borgman, Christine L. *From Gutenberg to the Global Information Infrastructure: Access to Information in the Networked World.* Cambridge: MIT P, 2000;

Bowker, Geoffrey C., and Susan Leigh Star. *Sorting Things Out: Classification and its Consequences.* Cambridge: MIT P, 1999.

Brady Aschauer, Ann. "Tinkering with Technological Skill: An Examination of the Gendered Uses of Technologies." *Computers and Composition* 16.1 (1999): 7–23.

Britton, Bruce K., and Shawn M. Glynn. *Computer Writing Environments: Theory, Research, and Design.* Hillsdale, NJ: Erlbaum, 1989.

Buckley, Joanne. "The Invisible Audience and the Disembodied Voice: Online Teaching and the Loss of Body Image." *Computers and Composition* 14.2 (1997): 179–87.

Burbules, Nicholas C. "Rhetorics of the Web: Hyperreading and Critical Literacy Practices." Snyder 102–22.

Condon, William. "Selecting Computer Software for Writing Instruction: Some Considerations." *Computers and Composition* 10.1 (1992): 53–56.

Conference on College Composition and Communication (CCCC). "Position Statement on Teaching, Learning, and Assessing Writing in Digital Environments." 2004. 14 June 2005 http://www.ncte.org/groups/cccc/positions/115775.htm.

Conference on College Composition and Communication (CCCC) Committee on Computers and Composition. "Promotion and Tenure Guidelines for Work with Technology." N.d. 14 June 2005 http://www.ncte.org/about/over/positions/level/coll/107658.htm.

Cooper, Marilyn. "Postmodern Pedagogy in Electronic Conversations." Hawisher and Selfe 140–60.

Cooper, Marilyn, and Cynthia L. Selfe. "Computer Conferences and Learning: Authority, Resistance, and Internally Persuasive Discourse." *College English* 52.8 (1990): 847–69.

Curtis, Marcia S. "Windows on Composing: Teaching Revision on Word Processors." *CCC* 39.3 (1988): 337–44.

DeWitt, Scott Lloyd. *Writing Inventions: Identities, Technologies, Pedagogies.* Albany: SUNY P, 2001.

Dinan, John S., Rebecca Gagnon, and Jennifer Taylor. "Integrating Computers into the Writing Classroom: Some Guidelines." *Computers and Composition* 3.2 (1986): 33–39.

Faigley, Lester. "Beyond Imagination: The Internet and Global Digital Literacy." Hawisher and Selfe 129–39.

Feenberg, Andrew. *Critical Theory of Technology.* New York: Oxford UP, 1991.

"Forum: A Conversation about Software, Technology, and Composition Studies." *Computers and Composition* 10.1 (1992): 151–68.

George, Diana. "From Analysis to Design: Visual Communication in the Teaching of Writing." *CCC* 54.1 (2002): 11–39.

Grigar, Dene. "Over the Line, Online, Gender Lines: E-mail and Women in the Classroom." *Feminist Cyberspaces: Mapping Gendered Academic Spaces.* Ed. Kristine Blair and Pamela Takayoshi. Stamford, CT: Ablex, 1999. 257–81.

Gruber, Sibylle. "Re: Ways We Contribute: Students, Instructors, and Pedagogies in the Computer-Mediated Writing Classroom." *Computers and Composition* 12.1 (1995): 61–78.

Gurak, Laura J., and Johndan Johnson-Eilola, eds. *Intellectual Property.* Spec issue of *Computers and Composition* 15.2 (1998).

Haas, Christina. *Writing Technology: Studies on the Materiality of Literacy.* Mahwah, NJ: Erlbaum, 1996.

Handa, Carolyn, ed. *Digital Rhetoric, Digital Literacy, Computers, and Composition.* Spec. issues of *Computers and Composition* 18.1 and 18.2 (2001).

Harris, Leslie D., and Cynthia A. Wambeam. "The Internet-Based Composition Classroom: A Study in Pedagogy." *Computers and Composition* 13.3 (1996): 353–71.

Hawisher, Gail E., and Cynthia L. Selfe, eds. *Passions, Pedagogies and 21st Century Technologies.* Logan: Utah State UP, 1999.

Heba, Gary. "HyperRhetoric: Multimedia, Literacy, and the Future of Composition." *Computers and Composition* 14.1 (1997): 19–44.

Hocks, Mary E. "Feminist Interventions in Electronic Environments." *Computers and Composition* 16.1 (1999): 107–19.

———. "Understanding Visual Rhetoric in Digital Writing Environments." *CCC* 54.4 (2003): 629–56.

Hocks, Mary E., and Michelle R. Kendrick. "Eloquent Images." Introduction. *Eloquent Images: Word and Image in the Age of New Media.* Ed. Hocks and Kendricks. Cambridge: MIT P, 2003. 1–18.

Holdstein, Deborah H. "Interchanges: Power, Genre, and Technology." *CCC* 47.2 (1996): 279–84.

Holdstein, Deborah H., and Cynthia L. Selfe, eds. *Computers and Writing: Theory, Research, Practice.* New York: MLA, 1990.

Howard, Tharon W. *A Rhetoric of Electronic Communities.* Greenwich, CT: Ablex, 1997.

Janangelo, Joseph. "Technopower and Technoppression: Some Abuses of Power and Control in Computer-Assisted Writing Environments." *Computers and Composition* 9.1 (1991): 47–64.

Johnson, Jim [Bruno Latour]. "Mixing Humans and Non-humans Together: The Sociology of a Door-Closer." *Social Problems* 35.3 (1988): 298–310.

Johnson-Eilola, Johndan. "Living on the Surface: Learning in the Age of Global Communication Networks." Snyder 185–210.

——. "Negative Spaces: From Production to Connection in Composition." *Literacy Theory in the Age of the Internet.* Ed. Todd Taylor and Irene Ward. New York: Columbia UP, 1998. 17–33.

Joyce, Michael. "New Stories for New Readers: Contour, Coherence, and Constructive Hypertext." Snyder 163–83.

Kalmbach, James Robert. *The Computer and the Page: The Theory, History and Pedagogy of Publishing, Technology and the Classroom.* Norwood, NJ: Ablex, 1997.

Kent-Drury, Roxanne. "Finding a Place to Stand: Negotiating the Spatial Configuration of the Networked Computer Classroom." *Computers and Composition* 15.3 (1998): 387–407.

Kinkead, Joyce. "Computer Conversations: E-Mail and Writing Instruction." *CCC* 38.3 (1987): 335–41.

Knadler, Stephen. "E-Racing Difference in E-Space: Black Female Subjectivity and the Web-Based Portfolio." *Computers and Composition* 18.3 (2001): 235–55.

Kress, Gunther. "English at the Crossroads: Rethinking Curricula of Communication in the Context of the Turn to the Visual." Hawisher and Selfe 66–88.

——. "Visual and Verbal Modes of Representation in Electronically Mediated Communication: The Potentials of New Forms of Text." Snyder 53–79.

Lang, Susan., Janice R. Walker, and Keith Dorwick, eds. *Tenure 2000.* Spec. issue of *Computers and Composition* 17.1 (2000).

LeBlanc, Paul. *Writing Teachers Writing Software: Creating Our Place in the Electronic Age.* Urbana, IL: NCTE, 1993.

LeCourt, Donna. "Writing (without) the Body: Gender and Power in Networked Discussion Groups." *Feminist Cyberscapes: Mapping Gendered Academic Spaces.* Ed. Kristine Blair and Pamela Takayoshi. Stamford, CT: Ablex, 1999. 153–76.

Markel, Mike. "What Students See: Word Processing and the Perception of Visual Design." *Computers and Composition* 15.3 (1998): 373–86.

McGee, Tim, and Patricia Ericsson. "The Politics of the Program: MS Word as the Invisible Grammarian." *Computers and Composition* 19.4 (2002): 453–70.

McKee, Heidi. " 'YOUR VIEWS SHOWED TRUE IGNORANCE!!!': (Mis)Communication in an Online Interracial Discussion Forum." *Computers and Composition* 19.4 (2002): 411–34.

Moran, Charles. "Access: The A-Word in Technology Studies." Hawisher and Selfe 205–20.

——. "From a High-Tech to a Low-Tech Writing Classroom: 'You Can't Go Home Again.' " *Computers and Composition* 15.1 (1998): 1–10.

Moran, Charles, and Gail E. Hawisher. "The Rhetorics and Languages of Electronic Mail." Snyder 80–101.

Pagnucci, Gian S., and Nicholas Mauriello. "The Masquerade: Gender, Identity, and Writing for the Web." *Computers and Composition* 16.1 (1999): 141–51.

Palmquist, Michael E. "Network-Supported Interaction in Two Writing Classrooms." *Computers and Composition* 10.4 (1993): 25–58.

Palmquist, Mike, Kate Kiefer, James Hartvigsen, and Barbara Godlew. *Transitions: Teaching Writing in Computer-Supported and Traditional Classrooms.* Stamford, CT: Ablex, 1998.

Porter, James E. "Liberal Individualism and Internet Policy: A Communitarian Critique." Hawisher and Selfe 231–48.

——. *Rhetorical Ethics and Internetworked Writing.* Greenwich, CT: Ablex, 1998.

Porter, James E., Patricia Sullivan, Stuart Blythe, Jeffrey T. Grabill, and Libby Miles. "Institutional Critique: A Rhetorical Methodology for Change." *CCC* 51.4 (2000): 610–42.

Redd, Teresa M. " 'Tryin to Make a Dolla outa Fifteen Cent': Teaching Composition with the Internet at an HBCU." *Computers and Composition* 20.4 (2003): 359–73.

Regan, Alison E., and John D. Zuern. "Community-Service Learning and Computer-Mediated Advanced Composition: The Going to Class, Getting Online, and Giving Back Project." *Computers and Composition* 17.2 (2000): 177–95.

Richardson, Elaine B. "African American Women Instructors: In a Net." *Computers and Composition* 14.2 (1997): 279–87.

Rickly, Rebecca. "The Gender Gap in Computers and Composition Research: Must Boys Be Boys?" *Computers and Composition* 16.1 (1999): 121–40.

Rouzie, Albert. "Conversation and Carrying-On: Play, Conflict, and Serio-Ludic Discourse in Synchronous Computer Conferencing." *CCC* 53.2 (2001): 251–99.

Ruszkiewicz, John. "Word and Image: The Next Revolution." *Computers and Composition* 5.3 (1988): 9–16.

Sanchez, Raul. "Our Bodies? Our Selves? Questions about Teaching in the MUD." *Literacy Theory in the Age of the Internet.* Ed. Todd Taylor and Irene Ward. New York: Columbia UP, 1998. 93–108.

Selfe, Cynthia L. *Creating a Computer-Supported Writing Facility: A Blueprint for Action.* Advances in Computers and Composition Studies. Houghton, MI: Computers and Composition P, 1989.

———. "Technology and Literacy: A Story about the Perils of Not Paying Attention." *CCC* 50.3 (1998): 411–36.

Selfe, Cynthia L., and Richard J. Selfe, Jr. "The Politics of the Interface: Power and Its Exercise in Electronic Contact Zones." *CCC* 45.4 (1994): 480–504.

Sirc, Geoffrey. "'What is Composition . . . ?' After Duchamp (Notes toward a General Teleintertext)." Hawisher and Selfe, 178–204.

Snyder, Ilana, ed. *Page to Screen: Taking Literacy into the Electronic Era.* London: Routledge, 1998.

Spooner, Michael, and Kathleen Yancey. "Postings on a Genre of Email." *CCC* 47.2 (1996): 252–78.

Star, Susan Leigh, and Karen Ruhleder. "Steps toward an Ecology Infrastructure: Design and Access for Large Information Spaces." *Information Systems Research* 7.1 (1996): 111–34.

Sullivan, Laura L. "Wired Women Writing: Towards a Feminist Theorization of Hypertext." *Computers and Composition* 16.1 (1999): 25–54.

Sullivan, Patricia. "Desktop Publishing: A Powerful Tool for Advanced Composition Courses." *CCC* 39.3 (1988): 344–47.

Takayoshi, Pamela. "Building New Networks from the Old: Women's Experiences with Electronic Communications." *Computers and Composition* 11.1 (1994): 21–35.

———. "Complicated Women: Examining Methodologies for Understanding the Uses of Technology." *Computers and Composition* 17.2 (2000): 123–38.

Takayoshi, Pamela, Emily Huot, and Meghan Huot. "No Boys Allowed: The World Wide Web as a Clubhouse for Girls." *Computers and Composition* 16.1 (1999): 89–106.

Taylor, Todd. "The Persistence of Difference in Networked Classrooms: Non-negotiable Difference and the African American Student Body." *Computers and Composition* 14.2 (1997): 169–78.

Thompson, Diane. "Electronic Bulletin Boards: A Timeless Place for Collaborative Writing Projects." *Computers and Composition* 7.2 (1990): 43–53.

Tuman, Myron C., ed. *Literacy Online: The Promise (and Peril) of Reading and Writing with Computers.* Pittsburgh: U Pittsburgh P, 1992.

Ulmer, Gregory L. *Heuretics: The Logic of Invention.* Baltimore: Johns Hopkins UP, 1994.

Vernon, Alex. "Computerized Grammar Checkers 2000: Capabilities, Limitations, and Pedagogical Possibilities." *Computers and Composition* 17.3 (2000): 329–49.

Webb, Patricia. "Technologies of Difference: Reading the Virtual Age through Sexual (In)Difference." *Computers and Composition* 20.2 (2003): 151–67.

Webb Peterson, Patricia, and Wilhelmina Savenye. *Distance Education.* Spec. issue of *Computers and Composition* 18.4 (2001).

Wolfe, Joanna L. "Why Do Women Feel Ignored? Gender Differences in Computer-Mediated Classroom Interactions." *Computers and Composition* 16.1 (1999): 153–66.

Wysocki, Anne F. "Impossibly Distinct: On Form/Content and Word/Image in Two Pieces of Computer-Based Interactive Multimedia." *Computers and Composition* 18.2 (2001): 137–62.

———. "Monitoring Order: Visual Desire, the Organization of Web Pages, and Teaching the Rules of Design." *Kairos* 3.2 (1998). 14 June 2005 http://english.ttu.edu/kairos/3.2.

Wysocki, Anne F., and Johndan Johnson-Eilola. "Blinded by the Letter: Why Are We Using Literacy as a Metaphor for Everything Else?" Hawisher and Selfe 349–68.

Wysocki, Anne F., and Julia I. Jasken. "What Should Be an Unforgettable Face . . ." *Computers and Composition* 21.1 (2004): 29–48.

24 Institutional Dimensions of Academic Computing

STUART A. SELBER

My institution was the first to sign an agreement with Napster 2.0, a commercial online music service that replaced the controversial peer-to-peer file-sharing environment developed by an industrious undergraduate student at Northeastern University. Procedurally speaking, the agreement is clear about the terms and conditions of use: Penn State students can stream or download an unlimited number of MP3 song files from the Napster music library. Each student can download song files to up to three different computers, but these files are "tethered" to the system, meaning that they disappear once the computers have been disconnected from the university network. Students can purchase music that they would like to own. Faculty and staff can access the Napster library for a reduced fee and also purchase music. Although there are other rules, this is what the Penn State–Napster agreement generally affords.

Administrators see the deal as part of a larger effort to curb the problem of illegal file sharing over campus networks. In response to pressure from Congress and the Recording Industry Association of America, Penn State has pursued a three-pronged solution: providing sanctioned access to a massive collection of MP3 song files, educating students about copyright law, and taking seriously any and all Digital Millennium Copyright Act (DMCA) notifications, which amount to formal claims of copyright infringement. Investigating DMCA notifications—a move that reduces the risk to Internet service providers of being sued by copyright holders or their representatives—involves various technical measures, including analyzing bandwidth usage patterns and using packet-shaping technologies to prioritize and control network activity. Thus the three-pronged solution employs both technical and educational approaches. At this point, many schools are offering or requiring educational programs on copyright law, some schools are getting tougher when it comes to enforcement, and a few schools (relatively speaking) are providing access to an online music service. To varying degrees and in various combinations,

From *College Composition and Communication* 61 (2009): 10–34.

these are the conventional institutional responses to the heated debate over file sharing.

In certain ways of thinking, the Penn State–Napster agreement is as controversial as the original Napster program. On the surface the agreement appears to be fairly innocuous: Penn State is simply acknowledging the difficulty and undesirability of policing student network activity and offering a legal alternative to illegal file sharing. Proponents lay claim to a progressive stance, one that respects the law and responds to student desire for free and unfettered access to online music. But the agreement does not exist in a vacuum, nor is it void of problems, some of which Penn State administrators recognize. For example, students have complained about the content of the music library: it tends to favor mainstream artists on major labels over independent and nontraditional artists. In addition, the intricate set of firewalls that accompanied the Napster installation discourages—and sometimes outright blocks—legitimate academic uses of peer-to-peer networks. Access is also a problem for people running Macintoshes, open-source operating systems such as Linux, and older Windows computers, for at this point Napster 2.0 only works with Windows 2000 or Windows XP, which make use of special Microsoft security protocols. This matter has especially attracted the attention of students, in part because issues of access often intersect with the economic. Many are under the impression that student access to the Napster music warehouse is free, but this is not exactly true. Full-time Penn State students currently pay an information technology (IT) fee of $202 per semester, and this fee covers the Penn State–Napster agreement. So students who purchase music end up paying twice: first to stream music, which is covered by IT fees, and then to own music (sometimes the same music), which comes at an undiscounted rate of 99¢ a track. Worse yet, and to reiterate, fee-paying students with incompatible computers cannot even access the service. This situation has been exacerbated by administrators who have been unwilling to provide an accounting of IT fee expenditures, including the actual cost of the Penn State–Napster agreement.

As such problems indicate, this agreement, which ostensibly addresses music piracy, is finally about the shaping power of institutional dynamics and forces. Who controls the configuration of academic computing networks? What is the process for developing network policy? Which applications and activities are supported and sanctioned? How do corporate deals and arrangements impact campus computer users? What sorts of assumptions and perspectives inform large-scale technology initiatives? Such questions have been largely ignored in the extensive discussion of the Penn State–Napster agreement, downplaying its implications and larger effects. A discourse of theft dominates the discussion to the exclusion of most other concerns, such as working to understand the culture of file sharing and investigating the support systems required by the changing nature of literacy and learning. The prevailing conversation, which for the most part focuses on the so-called bad behavior of students, ignores numerous intractable technoinstitutional issues.

Students and teachers, however, are inevitably affected by institutional decisions like those represented in the Napster program. No literacy event is an island unto itself: writers depend on such institutional resources as Internet backbones, email servers, library databases, wireless networks, spam filters, and more. Also, there is more to take into account than just hardware devices and software programs. I have argued elsewhere for a considerably broader characterization of what constitutes a computing infrastructure, one that incorporates use contexts (Selber). By this I mean the spaces—physical, pedagogical, organizational—within which computer-based activities are deeply situated. A similar argument has been made by Danielle Nicole DeVoss, Ellen Cushman, and Jeffrey T. Grabill, who encourage teachers to adopt an "infrastructural framework" (see p. 405 in this volume) to understand the ways in which institutional policies and practices shape multimedia composing. According to these more expansive perspectives, the formalized structures of academic computing contain not just wires, silicon chips, and the like, but various agents, values, practices, and forces, all of which have particular histories and tendencies. Such contextual aspects, which can be shaped to some extent through micropolitical action, have a direct effect on a wide range of literacy activities.

Given what is at stake, it is surprising that the field has not engaged itself more energetically in the task of conceptualizing and critiquing the institutional dimensions of academic computing. Although computer specialists have concentrated on a wide range of issues, this work has tended to focus more on students, teachers, classrooms, and programs and less on the larger contexts within which people and programs are embedded. My project focuses on those larger contexts. The first section offers an overview of institutional critique and a visual-spatial approach to studying institutional dynamics and interactions. Using visual-spatial maps for multimedia composing, the next section performs a critique that illustrates the ways in which institutions can mediate literacy activities. Although this discussion is rather descriptive in nature, amounting to a detailed explanation of how to read the maps, it suggests the interests and stakes of academic computing in ways that are meaningful to composition teachers. The conclusion conceptualizes institutional dynamics and interactions as a drama and encourages teachers to involve themselves in the technosocial scenes unfolding on their campuses.

An Overview of Institutional Critique

My approach to institutional critique comes from the work of James E. Porter, Patricia Sullivan, Stuart Blythe, Jeffrey T. Grabill, and Libby Miles. Their essay, "Institutional Critique: A Rhetorical Methodology for Change," outlines important perspectives on structure and agency and provides a cogent basis for not only critical analysis but also productive social action. Institutions are not totalistic, unalterable entities governed by the unilateral actions of an elite few. As Porter et al. explain, "Though institutions are certainly powerful, they are not monoliths; they are rhetorically constructed human designs (whose power is reinforced by buildings, laws, traditions, and knowledge-making practices) and so are changeable" (611). Change is not easy or automatic, but possible if people conceptualize institutions as a rhetorical system, pay attention to its contexts and constituent parts (including operating procedures and working conditions), and acknowledge their own involvements and commitments. The last point here is crucial and bears repeating: Literacy activities are necessarily refracted through institutional prisms; there is no outside territory that provides a neutral ground for analysis or action. This is not so much a criticism as a recognition of the implicated nature of working for/in institutions. In addition, power is understood to be structured and exercised in a particular manner, "through the design of space (both material and discursive)" (621). Spatial patterns and relationships, which are evident in both physical and discourse-based artifacts, reveal important insights about the circulation of power in institutional settings. They also hold a key to making productive social change. Although the field has engaged itself in administrative, classroom, and disciplinary critique, these efforts at social change, while widespread and valuable to academic computing work, tend to serve critical-analytical purposes other than institutional reform and revision.

Spatial patterns and relationships can be studied using various means and methods. Two useful tactics, according to Porter et al., are postmodern mapping and boundary interrogation. Postmodern mapping is a visually oriented critical practice that emphasizes how space is both constructed and inhabited, designed to achieve certain purposes (and not others)" (623). Put in different terms, it aims to denaturalize boundary categories by revealing biases and enabling reclassifications from a different perspective (there is no escaping the influence and partiality of maps, only learning how to become informed consumers and producers of them). Postmodern mapping, then, is not so much about defining but positioning. Researchers who employ its techniques are interested in relative weightings and interpretations.

The second tactic for institutional critique, boundary interrogation, assumes that boundaries—both material and discursive—can reveal the workings and ambitions of cultural power. They can also function as sites within which change can be imagined and initiated. Porter et al. are especially interested in what geographer David Sibley calls "zones of ambiguity," which are "spaces that house change, difference, or a clash of values and meanings" (624). Although never neutral, computer technology is itself inherently ambiguous, providing numerous potential avenues for resistance and transformation. To begin with, the features of software can always be multiply interpreted. There are no universally perfect interfaces without semantic slippage, only idealized representations of literate practice. Despite this reality, some technology designers view ambiguity as a programming bug to be fixed; it is understood to lead to confusion and user errors (Nielsen). Others see it more enthusiastically as a prospective feature of the environment, as something to be exploited and managed, because ambiguity can support multiple learning and working styles and accessibility. William Gaver, Jacob Beaver, and Steve Benford insist that ambiguity is an undervalued resource that can help interface designers construct "intriguing, mysterious, and delightful" systems (233). But no matter the design philosophy, at bottom computer interfaces are contingent texts with intrinsically unstable signifiers.

Zones of ambiguity also exist in the use contexts that help to constitute a technology. It is important to stress that technical features alone do not predetermine the actions of computer users. If they did, a robust vision of institutional critique would hardly be necessary: teachers would simply concentrate their time and energy on strategies for influencing software production. User activity, however, is shaped by many factors and forces, including personal preferences, pedagogical frameworks, and institutional policies. Particularly interesting to scholars in composition are the ways in which language regulates technologically mediated activity. Discourse is, not surprisingly, an unusually potent force, one that sustains or undermines the visions instantiated by designers of computer hardware and software. Of the many types of discourse in technological contexts, Bryan Pfaffenberger singles out myth and ritual as highly compelling forms because they are based on beliefs and attitudes that cannot always be challenged with logical propositions. For example, more than a few teachers on my campus have expressed an inaccurate understanding of copyright law and fair use guidelines. But it is nearly impossible to change the viewpoints of people who have internalized a conservative university stance as the absolute truth. Another example is the link in American culture between technological progress and social progress. For a variety of mythical reasons, this link is perceived by many to be clear and definite rather than ambiguous or indeterminate (Segal).

Responses to the activist call by Porter et al. have been somewhat sporadic and limited in nature. The most direct response came from Marc Bousquet, who remains unconvinced by their lines of attack for encouraging institutional change. He agrees that institutional critique is a needed and worthwhile enterprise, but prefers approaches that use "the organized voice and collective action of composition labor" (494). Such approaches, he argues, have been more effective in historical terms than those that count on managerial insiders attempting to appeal to the bureaucratic logics of institutions.[1] In a published response to Bousquet, Grabill, Porter, Blythe, and Miles question his notion of how change takes place in institutional settings. Their concern is that he "presents an either/or choice, a false and ultimately unproductive binary" (220) between bottom-up and top-down approaches. If Bousquet abandons the latter for the former, dismissing the possibility of making transformations from within managerial-hierarchical systems, Grabill, Porter, Blythe, and Miles seek to draw these approaches together and highlight the liminal spaces created by their interanimations.

The issue here, it seems to me, is a familiar (if complex) one in not only social theory and history but also in third-wave feminist studies (Lorde), African American studies (Gordon and Gordon), and education debates (Giroux). How should subaltern groups respond to dominant power structures? Should the focus be on incremental or wholesale change? Can change be made using the discourses and structures of the powerful, or are alternatives needed? What is the nature of the relationship between accommodation and resistance?

Is it dialectical, antithetical, other? Like Porter et al., my inclination is to see large-scale institutions like educational institutions as situated, overdetermined, and highly conventionalized enterprises replete with contradictions and opportunities that present room for both political engagements and pedagogical maneuverings, which can lead to provisional as well as permanent transformations. Such an inclination does not negate the power and importance of grassroots movements, but takes a systemic approach that recognizes the multiple sources that can contribute to change.

To conclude this section, let me move from discussing the preoccupations and tactics of institutional critique to emphasizing its suitability for technological contexts. Institutional critique concentrates on the thing that has enabled the field to claim a variety of technology domains: ambiguity. A major project for composition has been rearticulating computers as literacy environments (versus computational machines). This project has been assisted by technocultural changes that have pushed out the boundaries of human-computer interaction and expanded the competencies needed to create intelligible interfaces for writing and communication. Also, however, the field has assumed the task of advancing social discourses that make apparent the real and significant linkages between literacy and technology. In some fashion or another, either implicitly or explicitly, these discourses leverage the concept of ambiguity in order to demonstrate disciplinary relevance and contribution—which is to say that they trouble dominant technical orders with reinterpretations foregrounding the shaping power of context and the indeterminate nature of artifact design and use. Making compelling, ongoing connections between literacy and technology will be important to the future status of the field. And that work will require studying, representing, and advancing ambiguity as a disciplinary access point. Institutional critique, and especially the tactic of boundary interrogation, seems uniquely suited to making connections that can open up access to technology.

MAPPING INSTITUTIONAL DIMENSIONS OF ACADEMIC COMPUTING

Now to the pictures. This section presents and discusses three institutional maps from academic computing contexts at Penn State. Recall that these are not meant to illustrate lasting, stable relationships. Nor are they meant to function as representational devices that encode or capture the workings of an institution in a precise manner. These maps, instead, position their elements with and against each other, opening a generative space for thinking through and reimagining the projects of academic computing. In this way, the utility of the maps relates more to enabling than signifying work or activity. The first map returns to the Napster example and considers associations between instruction and production in the framework of multimedia composing. The second map reorients the spatial location of one particular instance of multimedia composing in order to look differently at the institutional connections between pedagogy and technology. The third map reveals my personal positionality and bias, a gesture of transparency that is crucial to institutional critique.

I first want to foreground some of the larger issues at stake in the situations illustrated by the maps. As my discussion of the Penn State–Napster agreement shows, underlying seemingly technical decisions or decisions about seemingly self-contained, discrete matters (like peer-to-peer file sharing) are implications that transcend a single event and ripple through an institution. In the examples that follow, there is a whole series of intersecting questions—some obvious, some not—associated with the organizing schemes for academic computing on my campus. These include, but are not limited to, questions about access (e.g., Is the innovative technology work of graduate students sufficiently supported by the hierarchical priorities and taxonomies of academic computing?), power (e.g., Are there supportive spaces for exploring vernacular practices that might not always be in alignment with institutionalized understandings of literacy?), intellectual property (e.g., Do institutional policies encourage sharing, collaboration, and collective intelligence?), teaching (e.g., Can general-purpose computer classrooms be configured, or reconfigured, in ways that are congruent with the pedagogical objectives of the field, especially those associated with the development of multimodal texts?), and learning (e.g., Do support systems employ pedagogical frameworks that lead to social as well as technical understandings of application software?). The discussion that follows touches on the implications of these questions, which are lurking within the infrastructure of my institution—and within the institutions of other teachers.

Example 1: Composing Multimedia Documents

Figure 24-1 focuses on multimedia composing, writing that involves more than words and that relies on the resources and features of networked computers. The top axis presents a continuum in which to position the institutional value of literacy projects. The bottom axis presents a continuum in which to situate the locus of instruction for those projects. The resulting area creates a space for mapping the relationships between multimedia production and its pedagogy.

At Penn State, original production is a highly valued literacy activity. It is supported by a centralized model of academic computing in which the institution operates the vast majority of computer classrooms on campus. Penn State also develops the documentation and other help systems that support the task of multimedia composing. In contrast, remixed production—the sampling of existing content to create new texts for new contexts—enjoys little (if any) explicit support. One can engage in remixed production, but the institution does not acknowledge it. Notice where I have located the Penn State–Napster agreement in Figure 24-1. There is a great deal of general institutional instruction on how to access and use the Napster music library. In this case, however, "use" is synonymous with listening: there is no discussion of how to sample the library for multimedia production, even under fair-use guidelines.

I have included five other examples to help clarify the dimensions of this map. The Business school asks students to blog about their experiences in

FIGURE 24-1   One institutional landscape for multimedia composing.

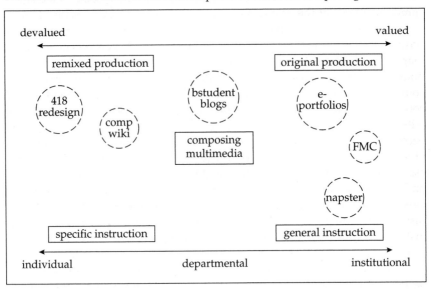

various undergraduate initiatives; it uses these blogs to advertise degree programs to prospective students. The marketing genres here—testimonial and endorsement—tend to value original production, and the expectations and conventions of these genres guide the look and feel of the online spaces. Because Penn State does not offer a blogging platform, the Business school provides the technical and pedagogical support for this occasion of multimedia composing. As of yet, my institution does not operate wikis, either, so the wiki used in the composition program is situated somewhat similarly. The difference is that support for the composition wiki comes from specific instructors, students, and open-source communities, not the department. Also, as its positioning on the map indicates our composition pedagogy values not only original production but also remixed production. My advanced technical writing assignment that asks students to redesign an existing website without creating any new text is, at least in institutional terms, highly devalued: there are no resources that directly support this assignment or its remix pedagogy (see "418 redesign" on the map). The Faculty Multimedia Center (FMC) straddles the line between original production and institutional instruction. The FMC is supposed to be a site where individual teachers learn about multimedia composing, but the instruction is not sensitive to disciplinary concerns. The training and development that happens there is rather generic, organizing around features of hardware devices and software programs. Finally, the e-portfolio system at Penn State is a production platform meant to support over 80,000 undergraduate students. The instructional portions of the system wrap institutional resources around a general process for creating online portfolios. These portions stress originality and attribution more than any other site on the map, probably because a primary audience for e-portfolios is presumed to be potential employers.

What, then, might this map reveal about the nature of multimedia composing in institutional contexts? More specifically, how has working with this map helped me to think about my local setting? Perhaps the most obvious point to make is this: at my school, the pedagogical support for multimedia composing tends to reflect larger institutional values, including a relatively conservative stance toward authorship and intellectual property. This point will come as no great surprise to many academics, for such reflections have become commonplace at colleges and universities, encouraging an atmosphere of legal and ethical uncertainty in which teachers feel constrained to explore assignments that sample and remix multimedia content. In his presentation on key issues in intellectual property at the 2005 CCCC Annual Convention. Lawrence Lessig spoke about the difficulty people often have in sorting out distinctions between what is legally determined, ethically determined, and institutionally determined. Figure 24-1 helps to illuminate the institutional ground of academic computing.

It also helps to illuminate at least two other realities. First, there seems to be an inverse relationship between innovation and support, technical, financial, or otherwise. That is, in many cases, the most innovative instructional activities actually receive the least amount of institutional recognition. At Penn State, graduate students have been responsible for some of the most innovative work in computers and writing, including work associated with the previously discussed composition wiki. Second, Figure 24-1 suggests the potential of institutional forces to exert a shaping influence in technological contexts. Despite the varying positions of the different projects on the map, many of them use the same technologies for production and instruction. These technologies are not neutral, but prone to being integrated into cultures in ways that strengthen rather than defy social and political force.

Example 2: Creating Electronic Portfolios

The next example takes an item from Figure 24-1 and resituates its spatial orientation. As opposed to considering the general landscape of multimedia composing, this example maps one particular endeavor—creating an electronic portfolio—to look more closely at institutional dimensions. Such a move also recasts the relationship between production and instruction., using other conceptual pairings that reveal different sorts of priorities and perspectives.

Figure 24-2 contains two intersecting continua. The horizontal continuum moves from approaches that concentrate on the process of developing an electronic portfolio to those that focus on producing a finished product. The vertical continuum moves from resources that support website development in general to those that specifically support the creation of electronic portfolios. The area created by the interconnection of these axes provides another space for mapping institutional relationships between pedagogies and technologies.[2] Bear in mind that my assumptions about technology expand its scope to

FIGURE 24-2   One institutional landscape for electronic portfolios.

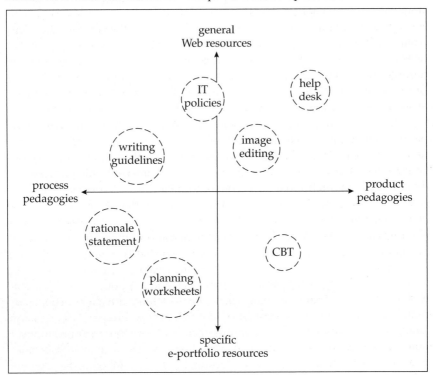

include such things as help resources and computer policies. Also note that my institution has not built or purchased a portfolio system such as Interfolio or Lectora. At Penn State, electronic portfolios occupy the same network space as any other website, and students use a variety of authoring environments to design and edit content.

There are items in all four quadrants of the map, although the landscape attended to by this map is not uniformly populated by institutional elements, as I will talk about later. My discussion begins with the top right-hand quadrant, with general Web resources and product pedagogies, and moves in a clockwise direction, finishing with general Web resources and process pedagogies. This pattern allows me to conclude my explanation of the map with a boundary issue. The most general product support at Penn State is offered by the Help Desk; it fields student queries about computer software and hardware. Helpers could, for example, answer questions about converting files into different formats or backing up files on university servers, but they could not offer advice for developing file naming schemes that are meaningful to portfolio work—and students create and collect countless files that must be managed systematically in a workflow. The same is true for image editing: institutional resources focus on scanning, cropping, resizing, and the like, not on producing effective or ethical images.

Moving to the bottom right-hand corner of the map, CBT stands for computer-based training, and Penn State offers three modules that were specifically developed to support the task of creating an electronic portfolio. Students watch the machine as automated tutorials (or screencasts) run through the technical steps involved in making basic portfolio pages. (These CBT modules, which are not especially helpful or imaginative, were the only items I could find for this portion of the map. There would be other—and better— resources if Penn State had developed or adopted a portfolio system.)

The bottom left-hand corner of Figure 24-2 contains specific resources that can be integrated into a process for creating electronic portfolios. Here there are both student-oriented and teacher-oriented resources. For example, students can access a worksheet that asks them to construct a plan for gathering evidence they will need to support the claims of a portfolio. Teachers can access a research-based rationale for integrating portfolios into their classes as well as worksheets for establishing outcome statements and assessment methods. And there is a rubric that aligns stages of portfolio development with general institutional resources, creating a more specific portal into those resources that foregrounds process.

Staying with process, the examples in the final quadrant include writing guidelines and institutional policies on the development and use of information technologies (IT). The writing guidelines cover drafting and editing a variety of documents: résumés, cover letters, reports, proposals, essays, and more. Although these guidelines are organized in a mode-like fashion and tend to emphasize format, mechanics, and documentation styles, in relative terms they lean toward process more than the CBT modules or general Web resources. IT policies constitute a particularly interesting area to consider. Like most institutions, Penn State has articulated a number of policies on acceptable computer use that govern online writing and communication, including portfolio development. In the main, institutional resources on portfolio development identify a subset of university policies relating to copyright and plagiarism. Teachers certainly need to promote a process approach that is sensitive to legal and ethical issues, and the policies could be integrated into such an approach. But my location of IT policies overlaps product concerns because of the nature of the discourse.

Copyright and plagiarism are treated as if the issues were black and white: students are not encouraged to reason through the full array of concerns associated with portfolio development. These include worries over the law itself, which can limit rather than expand access to online information; over legal and ethical stances of universities, which can have a "chilling effect" on pedagogical innovation and change; and over conventional understandings of originality, creativity, and property, which can value student writing performance over social action or the effects of texts in context. Thus, the policy discourse emphasizes rules and procedures for encouraging students to produce portfolio products that comply with institutional interpretations of copyright and plagiarism. It does not, in other words, attempt to educate students as portfolio developers who can reason rhetorically about legal and ethical matters.

The map in Figure 24-2 is instructive for a few reasons. To begin with, it generates patterns of institutional resource allocation and management. The vast majority of investments—fiscal, instructional, and political—occur in the top two quadrants. This unevenness, which is not really indicated by the map because it is meant to provide examples that illustrate all four quadrants, becomes clear when one plots every portfolio resource, not just a subset for explanatory purposes. The aggregate display indicates that teachers at my institution may need to develop instructional resources that can help students create electronic portfolios that are tailored to specific disciplinary contexts. The map also suggests resources that might impulse toward a greater degree of interpretive flexibility. Those resources crossing boundaries, that inhabit hybrid positions on the map, seem more easily open to recontextualization. On some level, process and product pedagogies always-already exist in dialectical relationship to each other. However, in the case of IT policies, for example, the tensions of this relationship are significant enough to illuminate the "zones of ambiguity" discussed by Porter et al., which, to repeat, constitute institutional interstices with the potential to open spaces for positive action and change. In the abstract, IT policies are typically straightforward and unambiguous: people can and should do these things, not those. But in actual situations of use, interpreting policy can be anything but clear-cut. One need only follow debates over the fair-use clause of U.S. copyright law, especially product-driven debates between the for-profit and nonprofit sectors, to see ambiguity and complexity for IT policies based on strict legal frameworks.

Here is a more concrete example: Teachers at Penn State are expected to host online course activities on institutional servers. The stated reasons for this have to do with protecting student privacy and controlling exposure to commercial appeals. Teachers can vary from this policy only if an activity is not supported by the institution. If off site servers are used, they must afford the same level of privacy and control as institutional servers. More than a few teachers were troubled by the rollout of this policy because they interpreted the rules for variation in technical rather than pedagogical terms. Although Penn State does not currently operate platforms for blogs and wikis, it maintains a course-management system and many other systems and services for both students and teachers. Because my colleagues often feel constrained by the priorities of the course-management system, they tend to use off site servers to support instructional endeavors. Their approaches might indeed be in jeopardy under a technical interpretation of the policy: our computing infrastructure includes relatively comprehensive components for teaching and learning. But its robustness breaks down at the intersections of process and product. For instance, although there are already numerous software programs in place to support both synchronous and asynchronous electronic conversations, these programs are constrained by institutional policies on network authentication. I can invite authors from outside my academic community to participate in an online discussion, to contribute messages that respond to student readings of their writings, but these authors need special accounts that take a week or more to activate and that create work for them. For me, at least, this delay has resulted in losses of instructional momentum and in inabilities to capitalize on teachable moments. These are reasons why I locate outside servers, even though internal servers support several options for managing electronic conversations. As my colleagues demonstrated with their considerable alarm, the IT policy on server use is less than clear about the borders between pedagogy and technology. Those borders, however, are becoming increasingly difficult to delineate, particularly in literacy contexts that involve both process and product concerns. But this vagueness actually functions as a resource: in both general and specific forms, it can encourage interpretive flexibility and reappropriation.

If Figure 24-2 models patterns of resource allocation and suggests resources that might be more susceptible to recontextualization, it also underscores decontextualization practices in institutional contexts that can fragment the relationship between pedagogies and technologies. This fragmentation is frequently a function of various structural divisions that separate the work of academic computing centers from the work of faculty (and vice versa). The CBT modules do not integrate writing instruction, for example, nor does the planning worksheet incorporate advice on using computers for invention purposes. In each site on the map, objects and practices are separated from their contexts, creating situations in which users receive either impoverished technical instruction or impoverished literacy instruction. The map calls attention to this weakness and to the need for institutional interactions that cross administrative boundaries.

Example 3: Mapping My Own Institutional Stances

As a rhetorical methodology, postmodern mapping is keenly interested in how research efforts get defined, framed, and carried out. More than anything else, perhaps, it is a self-critical approach that recognizes the situated nature of each researcher and project. Toward that end, this final example reflects on my own stances toward institutional structures and arrangements, foregrounding personal positionality and bias. Figure 24-3 is a grid for mapping pedagogical tactics in institutional settings. These tactics both accommodate and resist organizational structures in technological contexts, which are characterized on the map in binary terms as centralized or decentralized. Although such organizational structures can coexist to some extent, the grid functions as a heuristic device for conceptualizing available subject positions. Let me first illustrate the positions with examples from different areas of academic computing. I will then discuss what the map suggests in terms of negotiating spatial locations. Note that in my examples no subject position is inherently better than another: they all enable and constrain activity.

One subject position accommodates centralized systems for academic computing. My example here takes up issues associated with computer classroom design and maintenance. As a rule, computer classrooms at Penn State are controlled by central administrators, not academic departments or programs. These administrators take responsibility for every aspect of a computer

FIGURE 24-3   Grid of institutional subject positions.

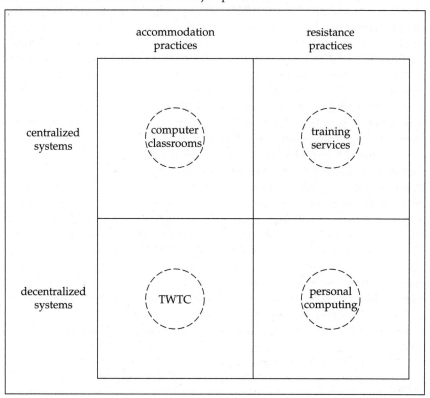

classroom, from designing its configurations—both physical and virtual—to upgrading its machines to troubleshooting everyday problems. There are certainly disadvantages to this approach for composition teachers. Because these classrooms have not been configured as writing classrooms with specialized components, their designs can impede collaboration, especially small-group work, document design (computer classrooms do not typically include scanners and other hardware for manipulating digital images), and many other aspects of writing pedagogy. But there are also advantages to a centralized approach. The English department does not have to budget for computer classrooms, and faculty do not have to maintain and support them. To my mind, the upsides of this situation outweigh the downsides, in large part because faculty would receive little (if any) credit toward tenure and promotion for running a computer classroom. I accommodate centralization in this case because it makes more sense to draw on institutionalized resources than to expend the energy required to create better alternatives.

An inverse subject position resists centralized systems for academic computing. My example here considers institutional training services for software applications. Penn State provides numerous face-to-face courses and online help systems that aim to assist users with computer problems and questions. My students and I have taken courses on editing digital video, creating websites, and developing databases, and we have downloaded tutorials and documentation for many different software programs. These courses and programs tend to support the acquisition of two types of knowledge: descriptive and procedural. Descriptive knowledge consists of concepts and facts about a subject. It is often learned from a textbook or lecture — or, in this case, a written overview of a piece of software. Although descriptive knowledge can be useful, it does not account for the ability to use computers for specific literacy purposes. This is where procedural knowledge (or know-how) fits in. Procedural knowledge underlies skilled action, helping people accomplish things in the world. It is developed in frameworks of meaningful activity that urge users to acquire the knowledge needed to achieve a task at hand. Most technical writers include some combination of descriptive and procedural knowledge in instructional materials, because users benefit from having access to several levels of granularity for understanding computer technologies. The problem is that institutionalized training services cannot possibly account for the diverse frameworks of meaningful activity that exist across a campus. So many of these services end up being overly generic, appealing to no one in particular and failing to capitalize on domain knowledge that could be used to help explain and situate computers. Even procedural materials that employ scenarios come up rather short: the scenarios tend to be underdeveloped in rhetorical terms. For these reasons, I often resist institutionalized training services, opting instead for projects in which students develop help documents that can support computer-based activities in writing courses. I also prepare software tutorials that are tuned specifically to the assignments in my courses.

Sometimes, however, decentralization practices need to be resisted, especially when such practices consolidate control and isolate expertise. At Penn State. I recently became the writing program administrator which is a three-year position that rotates between faculty members in rhetoric and composition. Continually changing this administrative position reduces burnout, enables new ideas, and promotes a sense of shared responsibility for the success of the program. By any measure, these intentions are important to long-term sustainability. But there are also challenges presented by turnover. The one I noticed immediately is infrastructural: How can a writing program capture and exploit expertise as people — administrators, teachers, and students — inevitably come and go? A program can always consult with past participants, and it is certainly true that lived experience provides rich insights into the history of institutional practices. In addition, a writing program can organize and archive its documents. Before computers became widespread, people used folders, filing cabinets, and other physical spaces to support the workflows and interactions of a writing program. But something unexpected happened when faculty started to integrate computers into administrative work: in certain contexts and cases, documents actually became less public and less accessible, dispersing into personal computers with tendencies toward individuation and customization. For the last several years, many of the documents for our composition program have resided in personal email inboxes and on the hard drives of non-university computers. This decentralization fragments institutional memory and continuity, making it difficult to discern what has been done and what needs to be done. It is also wasteful in that the program has had to reconstruct more than a few administrative documents. So we are developing a content management system that can support the workflows and interactions of a document-driven office. Crucial to the system will be an ability to import legacy materials, assign authoring privileges to multiple people, and standardize interface elements that reflect our practices and philosophies. Such a move away from decentralization will help ensure the collection and dissemination of knowledge and expertise.

On the other hand, standardization practices can sometimes produce institutional barriers that are counterproductive in pedagogical terms. Support for this claim is not hard to come across. For example, Penn State presented its academic departments with an opportunity to offer a non-credit teaching with technology certificate for graduate students (labeled TWTC on the map). I was initially skeptical of this opportunity because I could not imagine a standard set of requirements that would be workable for everyone. In part, my skepticism was fueled by the failed attempts of colleges and universities to define universal requirements for certification in the area of computer literacy (Selber). To travel across contexts, these requirements focus on isolated software skills rather than situated literacy events that involve computers, resulting in certification practices that are one-dimensional and impoverished. In reality, however, advisors interpret the requirements for the teaching with technology certificate in diverse ways, localizing them to accommodate various disciplinary concerns and directions. This situation becomes apparent even from a cursory glance at the projects of graduate students who have earned the certificate: they have thought differently about the curricular integration of computer technologies, particularly when it comes to articulating expectations and roles of both teachers and students and using computers for assessment purposes. The ability to decentralize control over this initiative has had certain advantages. On a pragmatic level, the localized instruction is still sanctioned by the institution. Students in the English department enjoy the benefits of certification even as they train to become critics of institutional contexts. On another, no less important, level, the approaches resulting from decentralization dramatize the ways in which computer use shapes—and is shaped by—pedagogical forces: these approaches often rely on incompatible or competing frameworks. So much for the need to convince certificate earners of the non-neutrality of technology.

The absences in maps can be as illuminating as the presences, but not in this particular case: there is no shortage of examples for each location in Figure 24-3. At different times and places, I have accommodated and resisted both centralized and decentralized systems. My pedagogical tactics have been more strategic than anything else, exploiting opportunities to contribute to the rhetorical education of students. But what do the examples suggest about my personal positionality and bias? To begin with, my stances rely on the idea that theory and practice must inform each other in institutional contexts. The dialectical interplay of these two forces opens an especially productive space in which to understand the ways in which institutions can be negotiated. In postmodern fashion, this premise requires teachers to embrace contradictory subject positions that challenge the efficacy of the theory-practice binary. It also blurs distinctions between academic service and research. In my opinion, a sense of praxis drives compelling projects on institutional critique, which combine deep empirical understandings with critical methods specifically designed to support the study of complex rhetorical systems.

Another bias of mine is noticeable in my stance toward the prospects for change. Generally speaking, I prefer to work from within institutional contexts rather than from without, even if change can only be considered to be momentary, fleeting, and partial. Institutions are certainly imperfect, but their structures are not immune to modification. As my examples indicate, I sometimes rely on institutional resources even as I resist conventional practices. This is because computers require a level of support that is unparalleled in the history of instructional technologies. I am sensitive to the fact that institutions can advance—unwittingly or otherwise—oppressive ideas and agendas, and that English departments can be weakly positioned within university structures. But institutions cannot preordain computer use. Nor are they nimble enough to police the micropolitical practices of students and teachers. These realities hold out significant prospects for social change.

Finally, the examples intimate, at least obliquely, the ways in which I understand my responsibilities as a teacher. I see myself as inescapably implicated in the problems of institutions. And so I find myself advocating for a social view of writing that is particularly sensitive to institutional contexts. For me, at least, this has involved a number of pedagogical adjustments—among them, foregrounding the constructed nature of institutions, including the value systems and learning assumptions that organize technological endeavors (my own included); designing assignments that address institutional problems and issues that occupy students; and incorporating spatial approaches as a rhetorical methodology for analyzing writing situations. These adjustments amount to a pedagogy of on-campus service learning that encourages students to involve themselves as conscious social actors. Such encouragement seems to be especially important nowadays, because institutions do not always include students and teachers in decisions that shape academic computing environments.

CONCLUSIONS

Although the discipline certainly imagines computers in contextualized terms, those terms have not always considered institutional dynamics and structures, at least not in a spatial manner. Spatial analyses illuminate patterns and relationships that organize literate activity in academic settings. They also illuminate spaces—intellectual and physical—that might be exploited in the interest of positive change. My examples demonstrate the explanatory potential of institutional critique. As a researcher, teacher, and administrator, postmodern mapping and boundary interrogation have helped me to understand, and respond to, the ways in which my institution mediates academic computing. This mediation is sometimes productive, sometimes unproductive, but always influential, contributing in central ways to the treatment of technology on campus, and thus to the pedagogical possibilities before students and teachers.

More broadly, my examples illustrate an enduring dynamic confronting teachers who plan to concern themselves with institutional critique. This dynamic involves values and their negotiation by both institutions and teachers, which occurs through a variety of contextualizing, decontextualizing, and recontextualizing practices (not necessarily in that order). For example, as the maps demonstrate, teachers can contextualize the relationship between innovation and support in order to understand institutional stances toward intellectual property. Institutions can reinforce this relationship by engaging in decontextualization practices that separate theory and practice through academic or bureaucratic divisions. Teachers, however, can recontextualize the theory-practice binary through pedagogical activities that are sensitive to institutional settings. Here is another example of this dynamic, also from the maps but working in a different direction: Teachers can decontextualize academic computing by turning to non-university servers or systems for pedagogical support. Institutions can contextualize that move (either positively or negatively) through policy documents that articulate acceptable computer use. Teachers, in turn, can recontextualize the boundaries of acceptable computer use by leveraging ambiguity in the distinctions between pedagogy and technology. Such "technological dramas," as Pfaffenberger would call them, develop continuously and in a variety of ways (not always rational), helping to mediate the relationship between pedagogy and technology and helping to define the field of possibilities for action and agency.

A dramatic view is useful here because it suggests unfolding circumstances, actor interdependences, and multiple, often diverging motivations enacting out imperfectly (and sometimes unpredictably) in situated contexts. Kenneth Burke understood communication dramas as an attempt to reconcile goals and contingencies; dramas, from his perspective, are a product of ongoing confrontation between what people desire and what the contexts for those desires make available. As I have attempted to point out, the contexts for technological dramas involve sequences of gestures and counter-gestures—discursive as well as material—that embody interests, needs, and values, which exist in a reciprocal relationship. And they involve social, political, and economic forces that have a bearing on the ways in which pedagogy and technology are understood and represented. Institutional critique translates technological dramas, which are layered, tension-filled, and surprisingly complex, into visible spatial narratives, representing the dynamics of academic computing in a contingent but powerful fashion.

How, then, might teachers become players in the technological dramas unfolding on their campuses? Answers to this question will undoubtedly vary from one institution to another, for they will be a function of the results of particular, localized efforts at postmodern mapping and boundary interrogation. At Penn State, my critique work has suggested several avenues for institutional engagement. My technical writing classes have developed documentation for centralized systems that foregrounds rhetorical dimensions of human-computer interaction. My colleagues and I have contributed to the shape of centralized systems by participating as usability volunteers and by responding to institutional requests for faculty feedback. And in our orientation for new graduate students, we have stressed what is permissible under fair-use guidelines, offering an alternative to the legalistic framework new teachers (and students) confront when registering for university Web server accounts. These interventions—there are many others—have all derived from critique work identifying institutional practices that are either detrimental or insensitive to current composition pedagogy.

If institutional interventions will be various and diverse, there is a constant here that should be emphasized: people in rhetoric and composition are powerfully situated, at least intellectually, to influence academic computing practices, to have a contributing voice on campus that makes a positive and real difference for both students and teachers. As the third map makes plain, teachers can occupy any number of institutional positions over time (and space), both accommodating and resisting the dynamics, interactions, and artifacts of academic computing. However, considering its high-stakes status, composition teachers should attempt to do more than employ approaches that only adopt, reject, redirect, or work around current situations. These are useful approaches, sometimes necessary approaches, and sometimes the only approaches to pursue. But teachers can and should play a key and constitutive role in institutional contexts for technology.

Evidence to substantiate this claim is disclosed by my analyses of the maps. In numerous and different ways, they demonstrate the intellectual value that composition teachers provide their campuses. The various aspects of that value coalesce in a rich social perspective—one that understands academic computing problems as essentially human problems, a perspective that is theoretically sophisticated, empirically informed, and gives preference to access and pedagogical innovation. Such a perspective is nourished not only by rhetorical approaches to professional development and TA education, but by ongoing efforts in the undergraduate classroom to prepare students as producers of multimodal texts. That task invariably puts composition teachers into direct and immediate contact with nearly every dimension of academic computing. In fact, in theory and oftentimes in practice, few other disciplines will know more about how the infrastructure might be employed for productive purposes. It is time to start clarifying that reality for campus colleagues.

Acknowledgments   I want to thank Rebecca Wilson Lundin for her research and for many useful conversations about institutional critique (we puzzled for hours over its meanings and methods). Two anonymous reviewers also made valuable suggestions.

NOTES

1. To summarize one piece of his argument quickly and partially, lower-level administrators such as writing program administrators are too weakly positioned to advocate for substantial, meaningful change. They are, according to Bousquet, "particularly vulnerable, highly individu ated, and easily replaced" (497). He surveys the overall status of composition programs, conclud- ing that the actions of individual administrative workers are all too easily co-opted by the forces that drive increasingly corporate universities. For that reason, an effective intervention requires something closer to social-movement unionism, which leverages the collective power of a mobi- lized workforce in order to improve working conditions and social rights.

2. My first map for electronic portfolios also used interconnected continua and the process- product horizontal axis. The vertical axis, however, moved from activities dealing with formative feedback to those dealing with summative feedback. This configuration provided one way to map out not only pedagogical approaches but also key rhetorical issues for portfolios (e.g., audiences, exigencies, conventions, constraints). Surprisingly, it also tested my assumptions about portfolio development. My impression has been that summative approaches tend to prevail within institu- tional frameworks at Penn State. After all, the online gallery of student examples mostly includes showcase portfolios meant for an audience of employers. In addition, many of the development resources address building career skills. But producing this map encouraged me to realize that my assumptions were not exactly accurate. For example, first-year seminar programs across cam- pus — in the College of Earth and Mineral Sciences, College of Agriculture, College of Communi- cations, and School of Visual Arts — have started to integrate portfolio assignments that can help students plan a course of study and develop learning goals. Such formative approaches are not as visible institutionally because their impetus is decentralized and fragmented, often initiating with individual efforts and then developing unevenly (if at all) in various directions, directions often congruent with either the interests of a faculty member or discipline. What helped me to see these formative practices, which directly challenged my assumptions about literacy activity in my local context, was a method for investigating the relationships between elements in a system. A conven- tional case study method would have left my assumptions intact: in more traditional approaches, institutional cases are bounded by time or activity, not space. In this way, the process of doing in- stitutional critique can be as informative as the resulting analyses themselves.

WORKS CITED

Bousquet, Marc. "Composition as Management Science: Toward a University without a WPA." *Journal of Advanced Composition* 22 (2002): 493–526.

Burke, Kenneth. *A Grammar of Motives.* Berkeley: U of California P, 1969.

DeVoss, Danielle Nicole, Ellen Cushman, and Jeffrey T. Grabill. "Infrastructure and Composing: The *When* of New Media Writing." *College Composition and Communication* 57 (2005): 14–44.

Gaver, William, Jacob Beaver, and Steve Benford. "Ambiguity as a Resource for Design." *Pro- ceedings of the SIGCHI Conference on Human Factors in Computing Systems, Ft. Lauderdale, 5–10 April 2003.* New York: ACM, 2003. 233–40.

Giroux, Henry A. *Teachers as Intellectuals: Toward a Critical Pedagogy of Learning.* New York: Bergin, 1988.

Gordon, Lewis R., and Jane Anna Gordon, eds. *Not Only the Master's Tools: African American Studies in Theory and Practice.* Boulder: Paradigm, 2005.

Grabill, Jeffrey T., James E. Porter, Stuart Blythe, and Libby Miles. "Institutional Critique Revis- ited." *Works and Days* 21 (2003): 219–37.

Lessig, Lawrence. "Intellectual Property: Key Issues." Conference on College Composition and Communication Convention. Moscone Center, San Francisco, CA. 16–19 Mar. 2005.

Lorde, Audre. "The Master's Tools Will Never Dismantle the Master's House." *Sister Outsider: Essays and Speeches by Audre Lorde.* Ed. Audre Lord. Trumansburg: Crossing, 1984. 110–13.

Nielsen, Jakob, ed. *Coordinating User Interfaces for Consistency.* San Diego: Academic Press, 1989.

Pfaffenberger, Bryan. "Technological Dramas." *Science, Technology, and Human Values* 17 (1992): 282–312.

Porter, James E., Patricia Sullivan, Stuart Blythe, Jeffrey T. Grabill, and Libby Miles. "Institutional Critique: A Rhetorical Methodology for Change." *College Composition and Communication* 51 (2000): 610–42.

Segal, Howard P. *Future Imperfect: The Mixed Blessings of Technology in America.* Amherst: U of Massachusetts P, 1994.

Selber, Stuart A. *Multiliteracies for a Digital Age.* Carbondale: Southern Illinois UP, 2004.

Sibley, David. *Geographies of Exclusion: Society and Difference in the West.* London: Routledge, 1995.

25 Taking a Traditional Composition Program "Multimodal": Web 2.0 and Institutional Change at a Small Liberal Arts Institution

CHRISTINE TULLEY

Tulley begins the web text with an interesting look at the development of liberal arts colleges and how they have shaped writing programs. Then, she demonstrates how a composition program can help faculty implement a pedagogy for teaching multimodal assignments. As director of writing at the University of Findlay, Tulley, with the help of other faculty, initiated a plan to change her program's curriculum to give teachers a chance to work with composition students on projects that involved modes besides the printed word. For example, she describes her own classroom strategies and how she asked her students to create a web page using images and sound to construct an argument. Throughout her web text, Tulley explains the types of decisions she and her colleagues had to make as they took the writing program multimodal. The screen shot included in this book is the home page of Tulley's web text. Readers are invited to read the rest of the webtext at http://www.bgsu.edu/departments/english/cconline/Tulley09/

From University of Findlay (nd). http://www.bgsu.edu/cconline/Tulley09/

FIGURE 25-1   "Taking a Composition Program 'Multimodal'" interface and home page.

Source: The University of Findlay (nd). <http://www.bgsu.edu/cconline/Tulley09/>.

The Dynamic Nature of Literacy and Multimodal Composers

Introduction to Part Six

The purpose of Part Six is twofold. First, the selections argue that multimodal composition is powerful because it allows for many voices, including marginalized voices, to be heard, especially in the public domain. As Cynthia Selfe argued in "The Movement of Air, the Breath of Meaning: Aurality and Multimodal Composing" (Part One), asking students to compose in just one mode (mainly the printed word) limits those students who belong to cultures that rely on the use of many different modes. In Part Six, the authors pick up on this argument, showcasing many unique and nontraditional voices that are successful when asked to compose with multiple modes. Because multimodal composition, as characterized by the authors in this book, requires many different literacy skills, it gives many more people opportunities to make meaning.

Second, while there continues to be a growing number of studies investigating multimodal composition, the authors in Part Six call for more scholars and pedagogues to discover the power of multimodal composition through research. They reveal what is at stake if we don't and look at research practices and methodologies that we might use to study different perspectives on multimodal composition, and they suggest multimodal composition as a means of presenting research findings. Thus, the selections in Part Six help us to consider different types of research studies — from analysis to auto-ethnographic studies to case studies — that are useful in identifying the meaning-making processes for multimodal composition. We might use the studies presented here as a way to both create our own, and to question those we have done in the past. While the studies found in Part Six rely heavily on the printed word, they offer other ways for collecting, making sense of, and presenting data through non-text-based modes and media such as images and sound. As many scholars have noted (Cheryl E. Ball and Stuart A. Selber for example), nontraditional scholarship does not typically contribute toward tenure, and thus conducting and presenting research in modes and media other than print is often ignored. But, foregoing non-print modes and media when conducting and presenting research significantly limits our understanding of the research we are doing in significant ways. For example, when presented in a graph or chart, some data is more easily understood or sheds light on patterns that would have otherwise gone undiscovered in traditional paragraph form. Given the vast potential of knowledge acquisition multimodal composition facilitates, we need to ask ourselves how we can best collect and investigate our data and represent our research findings in the multiple modes and media that will be most effective. We need to take full advantage of journals like *Kairos* and *Computers and Composition* that offer a space for such research because doing so will provide a richer understanding of multimodal composition. Finally, as the authors in Part Six do, we need to advocate for more outlets or media like these journals in order to promote and more widely publish our multimodal work.

The first reading focuses on one student's story and demonstrates what is so powerful about multimodal composition, that is, giving a voice to those who are marginalized when only one mode is privileged. As the founders of Digital Underground Story Telling for You(th) (DUSTY), an urban community center that invites participants to create digital stories, Glynda A. Hull and Mark Evan Nelson's analysis study sets out to investigate the "ephemeral yet aesthetically powerful properties of multimodal text design" (see p. 461 in this volume). In "Locating the Semiotic Power of Multimodality," they examine the work of one participant, Randy, in order to characterize these properties. When analyzing Randy's digital story, Hull and Nelson, for instance, deem it necessary to consider the meaning-making affordances of different individual modes and therefore begin their analysis by investigating each mode separately. Yet, like Sorapure and Murray, Sheets, and Williams in Part Four, they also see that investigating the relationships between modes when modes are combined as being just as important. Hull and Nelson conclude that when combined, the modes' relationships to one another provide the viewer with a "qualitatively different" experience. Part Six, therefore, serves to underline the importance of multimodal composition in practice.

Suzanne Kesler Rumsey's study is similar to that of Hull and Nelson's in that she, too, examines the work of a particular culture. In "Heritage Literacy: Adoption, Adaptation, and Alienation of Multimodal Literacy Tools," Rumsey traces her family's Amish roots and discovers that the individuals in her study use a variety of literacy skills. She is particularly interested in heritage literacy, a transferring of literacy knowledge—including the use of practices, tools, and concepts—over generations. Rumsey contends that heritage literacy is multimodal, tying the choice and use of modes to meaning making. She sees a connection between old and new technologies and how each generation must decide which to use and which to ignore. To further examine heritage literacy, Rumsey analyzes the use of quilts as a collaborative and multimodal text that utilizes modes like image, color, pattern, and so forth to make meaning, in this case, to tell family histories. She concludes that the meaning created by the quilts clearly represents an Amish identity. Rumsey's selection, then, can help us question how our own multimodal literacy practices create or represent our identities and how privileging some modes over others can marginalize those identities in the composition classroom.

Steven Fraiberg, in "Composition 2.0: Toward a Multilingual and Multimodal Framework," investigates multilingual and multimodal composition, seeing this type of composition as necessary to twenty-first-century class-rooms and research, particularly because we live in a world that is becoming increasingly globalized. For him, multilingual and multimodal composition is a way to realize the value of all semiotic modes, not just those that are print based. He articulates an understanding of "code mashing," the "complex blending of multimodal and multilingual texts and literacy practices," (p. 498) and uses four analytical perspectives (ecologies, knotworking, remediation, and actant-network theory) as a framework. Through these concepts he looks closely at the processes that shape and are shaped by multilingual and multi-modal composition. Relying on his own experience working for Networld, a technology company in Israel, a society becoming largely networked, he looks at ecologies in which multilingual and multimodal composition practices take place. Composing, he believes, can be conceptualized as knotworking, and composers can be conceptualized as knotworkers who must continually tie and untie languages, tropes, narratives, images, sounds, and ideologies. Fraiberg's work helps us realize how the features of a global world that is highly net-worked and collaborative are instituted on a local level, like in our classrooms. How can such a framework help us see our students as knotworkers situated in a particular ecology? This type of question can help instructors teach mul-timodal composition with greater awareness and predetermined direction that will ultimately result in more successful teaching practices.

The final selection looks at basic writers, an often marginalized, over-looked group in terms of multimodal composition. The authors argue that since basic writers, like first-year writers, are also part of a global digital world, multimodal and digital media assignments have a clear place in the basic writ-ing classroom. In "Remixing Basic Writing: Digital Media Production and the Basic Writing Curriculum," Catherine C. Braun, Ben McCorkle, and Amie C. Wolf give us several examples of how to incorporate such assignments into the basic writing classroom. Their web text presents case studies that describe an assignment and how such an assignment helps basic writers to compose, analyze, and reflect on multimodal composition. Braun's audio essay assign-ment, for instance, builds upon rhetorical principles to investigate meaning making in multiple media. Braun's assignment highlights the responsibility of the composer to make the best decisions about how and what to compose based on the rhetorical situation.

All the assignments shared in this web text demonstrate the need to en-gage students in meaningful composition, even when that requires students to use unfamiliar modes. When working with unfamiliar modes, as McCorkle argues, students are able to better understand the rhetorical principles of composing. Instructors might also find that students who are not engaged in one mode alone may be better suited to compose in another, and thus more successful in the course. Such an approach, therefore, allows students to more thoroughly examine a rhetorical situation, and compose in the modes most appropriate for a given assignment, or most suitable to their individual skills, thus ultimately creating higher-quality texts.

Scholars and pedagogues can use the selections in Part Six to think criti-cally and carefully about how and what we ask our students to compose, especially since our classrooms are becoming increasingly more globalized and diverse. Do we, for example, need to pay more attention to the many cultures our students come from? How do we identify these cultures' literacy practices and then create assignments that draw on them? How is identity constructed through the use of modes? If a student is not particularly successful in one mode, how can we identify a mode that allows for success? The answers to these questions in particular will help guide us in our attempts to more effectively teach, assign, and assess multimodal composition, but they will also guide us in our own research in terms of what we should study, how we should study it, and how we should present what we find.

26   *Locating the Semiotic Power of Multimodality*

GLYNDA A. HULL AND
MARK EVAN NELSON

*A*ll about us, there are unmistakable signs that what counts as a text and what constitutes reading and writing are changing—indeed, have already changed and radically so—in this age of digitally afforded multimodality. To rehearse the obvious, it is possible now to easily integrate words with images, sound, music, and movement to create digital artifacts that do not necessarily privilege linguistic forms of signification but rather that draw on a variety of modalities—speech, writing, image, gesture, and sound—to create different forms of meaning. There are now Web-based scholarly journals that illustrate and explore these possibilities (e.g., *Kairos* and *Born Magazine*[1]), there are community-based media organizations that promote a variety of forms of multimodal composing (Lambert, 2002), and there are beginning to be empirical studies that examine multimodal practices in context (Stein, 2004). And as we will shortly review, of late, helpful theorizing about multimodality has begun (Kress, 2003). Some scholars, it is true, recognized the advent and importance of multimodality as an aspect of literacy a long time ago, taking heed, for example, of the importance of multiple forms of representation (Witte, 1992, 1993). Yet the full import of this sea change in semiotic systems has, for most people, just begun to be felt.

In this article, we want to pay homage to the range of work that is beginning to explore new literacies or multiliteracies (New London Group, see p. 193 in this volume).[2] We hope also to extend this work by making and supporting a still radical claim. We will argue that multimodal composing of the sort to be illustrated here is not simply an additive art whereby images, words, and music, by virtue of being juxtaposed, increase the meaning-making potential of a text. Rather, we plan to demonstrate that through a process of braiding (Mitchell, 2004) or orchestration (Kress & van Leeuwen, 2001), a multimodal text can create a different system of signification, one that transcends the collective contribution of its constituent parts. More simply put, multimodality can afford, not just a new way to make meaning, but a different kind of meaning.

From *Written Communication* 22:2 (2005): 224–61.

Thus, in this article, within the constraints and affordances of a primarily linguistic text, we aim to illustrate and offer an initial framework for analyzing a particular and increasingly popular form of multimodality.

Despite growing interest in, research about, and examples of multimodality, we feel a certain urgency about our project and like-minded work. It is no exaggeration to say that most Western societies remain print dominated, even as pictures push words off the page and even as the Internet and the World Wide Web become more ubiquitous. This is especially true of schools and universities, which are staunchly logocentric, book centered, and essay driven, invested as are most educators in the versions of meaning making whose value they know best and committed as are many educators to sharing the languages and modes of power (Delpit, 1995). Several recent and important policy documents illustrate how easy it is to exclude digital multimodality when addressing issues of literacy and literature and how natural it is to think in terms of print-based, unimodal texts. The National Commission on Writing for America's Families, Schools and Colleges (2003) recently produced a booklet rightly calling on all to recognize anew the importance of writing yet did not make mention of multimodality as a potential type of digital composing and gave just a nod to the mediation of writing via computer technologies. During 2004, a national adult literacy survey was administered in the United States in which participants were asked to perform everyday literacy and numeracy tasks — to fill out forms, to read a paragraph, to calculate sums, and so forth — yet these tasks excluded digital texts, the Internet, and even computers (National Center for Education Statistics, 2003). And recently, the National Endowment for the Arts (NEA, 2004) released the results of a study entitled "Reading at Risk," which decried the significant decline in the consumption of literature among Americans during the past two decades, all within the framework of a traditional canon. The report implied that Americans who are less likely to be avid readers of literature are more likely to engage with other media — television, video, and the Internet — to their detriment and to that of an educated citizenry.[3]

The value of the NEA (2004) report, and other similar calls to action around valued forms of literacy, is that it underscores the importance of developing and maintaining the literacy practice of print-based reading and writing, which, notwithstanding the proliferation of other new media technologies, remains paramount for individual growth and meaningful participation in broader society. However, given the range of semiotic tools available for literate practices at this particular historical moment, we find it worrisome to exclude the new forms of reading and composing from mention, and it concerns us as well to assume a hierarchy of value among them. We believe that the increasingly multiplex ways by which people can make meaning in the world, both productively and receptively, can potentially represent a democratizing force whereby the views and values of more people than ever before can be incorporated into the ever-changing design of our world. We hope to suggest, then, that the new media that afford multimodal composing might helpfully be viewed not as a threat to or impoverishment of the print-based canon or traditional means of composing but rather as an opportunity to contribute a newly invigorated literate tradition and enrich available means of signification.

RELATED LITERATURE

A burgeoning body of theory and research has broadly addressed systems of signification other than the verbal and has explored the interplay between systems, especially visual images and print. The field of visual culture, for example, combines critical and social theory with an analysis of all types of visual media: painting and art, to be sure; the traditional focus of art theory and practice; and television, photography, advertising, and architecture (Mirzoeff, 1999). Visual methods have made their way as well into the social sciences through approaches such as visual anthropology and visual sociology and an ever-increasing interest in documentary research across a range of fields (Coles, 1997; Stanczak, 2004). Literacy studies, on the other hand, have until recently been positioned somewhat peripherally as far as visual things go, mostly eschewing the pictorial in favor of the verbal. This of course is notwithstanding multitudinous examples, historical and modern, of the inclusion of the visual as part of the written: Illuminated manuscripts, such as the *Book of Kells*; illustrated story books for children; experimental novels; scientific treatises that depend heavily on detailed illustration; and everyday workplace documents that juxtapose diagrams, drawings, pictures, and words are a few examples that come to mind (Finnegan, 2002). Yet the commonplace assumption has been, especially in school and university settings, that the affordances of written verbal texts far outstrip what can be offered by or offered in conjunction with other modalities. As we will shortly discuss, such conceptions have begun to shift, and quickly so, in the field of literacy studies, in large part because of the concept of multiliteracies, an idea itself influenced by the increasing prevalence of digital technologies and their potential as a mediational means.

Just as it is possible to look back historically or examine contemporary texts and find various examples of the integration of the verbal and the visual, it is also important to recognize that multimodality also has ancient and deep roots in cultural practices the world over (despite what some would view as its neglect in the West) and that multimodality is in fact what distinguishes human communication. Anthropologist Ruth Finnegan (2002) terms communicating "a multiplex and versatile process" and describes humans' communicative resources as encompassing

> their powers of eye and ear and movement, their embodied interactions in and with the external environment, their capacities to interconnect along auditory, visual, tactile and perhaps olfactory modalities, and their ability to create and manipulate objects in the world. (243)

It is certainly the case that educators regularly rediscover the power that students experience when released to communicate and learn multimodally.

Stein (2004), in fact, on the basis of her work as a language educator and literacy researcher in South Africa, advocates for multimodal pedagogies; these, she writes, "allow for the expression of a much fuller range of human emotion and experience; they acknowledge the limits of language, [and] admit the integrity of silence" (95).

The idea of multiple literacies has a long and helpful tradition in literacy studies (Cole & Scribner, 1981; Cook-Gumperz, 1986; Gee, 1996; Lemke, 1998; Street, 1984). But it was the New London Group (p. 193) that provided an especially useful expansion of literacy through the term *multiliteracies*. This team of scholars from various fields—education, linguistics, and sociology, among others—first met in 1994 in New London, New Hampshire, to discuss the big picture of present and future literacy pedagogy (New London Group), and the group subsequently continued its work in a range of international contexts. In brief, the focus was on "the changing word and the new demands placed on people as makers of meaning in changing workplaces, as citizens in changing public spaces and in the changing dimensions of our community lives—our lifeworlds" (Cope & Kalantzis, 2000, 4). The group's manifesto called for literacy pedagogy to account for the following:

1. "the context of our culturally and linguistically diverse and increasingly globalised societies,"

2. "the multifarious cultures that interrelate and the plurality of texts that circulate," and

3. "the burgeoning variety of text forms associated with information and multimedia technologies" (Cope & Kalantzis, 2000, 9).

At the center of the group's argument for how literacy pedagogy might take into account such issues, and germane to our article as well, is the concept of design. This notion assumes semiotic activity to be a "creative application and combination of conventions that, in the process of design, transforms at the same time that it reproduces these conventions" (New London Group, p. 194, citing Fairclough, 1992, 1995). In the view of the New London Group, it is through an informed, intentional process of design on the part of the individuals, making creative use of available preexisting designs and resources, that meanings, selves, and communities are powerfully made and remade. It is important to note, as does the New London Group, that the process of design in our digital age draws widely on multimodal materials and resources. And in thinking of multimodal texts, it is obvious how useful the notion of design can become as a way to conceptualize the suddenly increased array of choices about semiotic features that an author confronts.

To conceptualize the nature of these choices, we have found the notion of the affordances that are associated with each semiotic modality helpful. Adapting this term from Gibson (1979), who applied it within a scientific, ecological milieu, Kress (1997, 1998, 2003; Kress & van Leeuwen, 1996, 2001) uses it to reference the fit between a semiotic resource, with its inherent properties of organization, and the meaning-making purpose at hand. Pictures, for instance, do not convey meaning in the same way that language does, and as such, their respective meaning-making affordances are different. As Kress (2003) notes, "'the world narrated' is a different world to 'the world depicted and displayed'" (1–4), making the point that although different semiotic modes may seem to encode the same content, they are nonetheless conveyors of qualitatively different kinds of messages. More specifically, the meaning in images is apprehended by the viewer in accordance with an ordering principle that is spatial and simultaneous, whereas language, particularly oral language, is organized and apprehended temporally and sequentially. It is important to note, however, that despite the particular affordances associated with each semiotic mode, the same kind of meaning can in fact be conveyed in quite different modalities, as Kress (1997, 1998, 2003) himself emphasizes. The point is that images, written text, music, and so forth each respectively impart certain kinds of meanings more easily and naturally than others. We believe that this idea is the most crucial conceptual tool that one must bring to bear in understanding the workings and meanings of multimodal texts.

The big challenge yet to be taken up within the study of multimodality is how to locate and define the deeper aesthetic power of multimodal texts. Given what individual modes are and do, how might the unique potential of these modes to aesthetically transcend themselves in multimodal composition be conceptualized and described? This is not to say, of course, that researchers have not offered insights into the effects and implications of acts of multimodal communication. The work of Tufte (1983, 1990, 1997), for example, has been of immense value in understanding how the success or failure of an act of communication often pivots, crucially, on the way in which words, images, and quantitative information are coordinated. Kress (2003, 36) discusses the accordant, complementary processes of transformation and transduction (the reshaping of semiotic resources and the migration of semiotic material across modes, respectively) as the locus of creativity in multimodal communication. However, what has yet to be fully conceived and adequately demonstrated, in our estimation, is an approach to understanding how these processes of transformation and transduction actually play out and to what effect. This is our project: to locate and characterize the ephemeral yet aesthetically powerful properties of multimodal text design.

CONTEXT FOR THE STUDY

Our theorizing about multimodality has not been done just in the abstract; we are fortunate to have been able to study digital multimodal texts created by children and adults and to have these often innovative artifacts push and challenge our conceptualizations. More specifically, for the past 4 years, we have been involved in helping to find, fund, and operate a community technology center located in the urban neighborhood of West Oakland, California, a local bus ride away from the University of California, Berkeley. Called DUSTY, or Digital Underground Storytelling for You(th), this center was conceptualized from the outset as a mechanism for making powerful forms of signification (tools for and practices of digital multimodal composing) available to children and adults who did not otherwise have such access at home or at school.[4] A university and community partnership, it draws professors, undergraduates, and graduate students together with youth and children from the community to study, learn, play, and create. As we have described elsewhere (Hull & James, in press), West Oakland is an isolated community that has fallen on very hard times, with high rates of joblessness and crime, a deteriorating infrastructure, struggling schools, and few of the ordinary resources that most communities take for granted, such as supermarkets, bookstores, restaurants, and banks. Many of its grand old Victorians, once summer homes for the San Francisco wealthy, have been renovated and occupied by outsiders as gentrification intensifies. Yet the West Oakland population, mostly long-time African American residents joined by recent immigrants from Southeast Asia, Mexico, and South America, are finding ways to reclaim its community. With a rich history on which to build, including a significant role during the Civil Rights Movement in the 1960s and a thriving economy related to ship building around midcentury (Rhomberg, 2004), residents are currently alert to and working toward safer, healthier, more equitable, and stable futures. DUSTY is but a small piece in this much larger fabric of community growth and change.

DUSTY started as a center to teach digital storytelling, a form of multimedia composing that consists of images and segments of video combined with background music and a voice-over narrative.[5] Digital stories are, in effect, brief movies distinctive in featuring the digitized voice of the author who narrates a personally composed story and an assemblage of visual artifacts (photographs old and new, images found on the Internet, snippets of video, and anything that one can convert to digital form). In our experience, digital stories have wide appeal among children, youth, and adults, in part simply because they are multimodal and digital, and thereby allow individuals those compositional means and rights that used to be associated just with the world of mass media. They are popular too because they typically privilege a personal voice and allow participants to draw on popular culture and local knowledge. Our youth sometimes create stories that feature their own original digital beats as background music in lieu of commercial hits. Thus, one of the natural expansions of DUSTY has been to teach digital music making, especially because Oakland, California, is known as the birthplace of many famous rappers. At DUSTY, aspiring wordsmiths as young as 9 and 10 can be seen writing their lyrics, practicing their freestyles, and deeply and undistractably engaged in sophisticated software that allows for the creation of digital beats.

A culminating activity at DUSTY is viewing participants' digital stories on the big screen of a local theater or other public venues. On these occasions, we invite authors to answer questions from the audience at the end of the showing. This is one example of how, in the design of our curriculum and participant structures, we attempt to position our digital storytellers as authors, composers, and designers who are expert and powerful communicators, people with things to say that the community and the world should hear.[6]

Given that some DUSTY youth have not always developed this sense of an authorial self in other settings, including school, the opportunity to do so in an alternative educational site becomes all the more important.[7] Thus, DUSTY is organized as an after-school program and a summer camp; in addition, we periodically hold workshops for adults and seniors.

Simultaneous with the creation and operation of DUSTY, we have engaged in research roughly within the tradition of design experiments, whereby program development is intertwined with continual attempts to assess and improve our efforts and document what participants have learned (Design Based Research Collective, 2003; Shavelson, Phillips, & Feuer, 2003). Throughout the years, with our colleagues, we have collected a range of ethnographic and qualitative data, principally field notes from participant observations and interviews. We have also videotaped and audiotaped teaching activities, workshops, and community events, including showings of digital stories. Our data also include pre-post inventories and surveys as we attempt to assess not only what kids and adults learn but also how their notions of self as authors and communicators develop. Of late, especially because of the requirements of the funders, we have begun to collect test scores, attendance records, and grades from school in anticipation of comparative studies that will allow us to estimate whether being in DUSTY appears to affect school-based measures. Last, we archive the digital stories and other artifacts that participants create.

In this article, we feature a digital story created by a young man whose particular mix of talents, interests, and predilections seemed to precisely match the available multimodal mediational means. A musician, rapper, poet, writer, photographer, videographer, and a clear-eyed social critic, Randy joined DUSTY in its first year and has thus far produced half a dozen digital stories, many of them featuring his own music. Below, we analyze what we think is his most impressive work, "Lyfe-N-Rhyme," by attempting to articulate the power it derives from multimodality. After a detailed, fine-grained analysis, we end the article by thinking more globally about the affordances and challenges of multimodal composing.

ANALYZING DIGITAL STORIES

Our first pass at analyzing digital stories was simply to categorize their genres and purposes. By watching the approximately 200 stories created by children, youth, and adults at DUSTY that now reside in our archive, we inductively devised the following broad category scheme:

> Genres: autobiographical narratives; poems and raps; social critique and public service announcements; reenactments or extensions of stories, cartoons, and movies; animations; reports; and biographies and interviews

> Purposes: Offer a tribute to family members or friends; recount or interpret a pivotal moment or key event; represent place, space, or community; preserve history; create art or an artifact; play or fantasize; heal, grieve, or reflect; and reach, inform, or influence a wider audience

Of course, many authors had multiple purposes, and digital storytelling is an internally diverse and necessarily dynamic and evolving genre. We do not make any claims about the relative frequency or stability of the categories; we simply offer this rough cut as a starting description. Although general, this category system has been useful in pointing to directions for more fine-grained analyses. For example, we were initially surprised by the number of stories by children and adults that centered on space, place, and landscape. But as we reflected, we realized first that the visual nature of digital stories invites authors to situate themselves in places; and furthermore, many of our storytellers made strong identity statements through valences of alignment and distancing in relation to particular locales and neighborhoods (Hull & James, in press).

It also became clear through the perusal of the stories in our archive that certain ones stood out as especially evocative not only for us but for the wider audiences with whom they were shared. And thus, we began to puzzle over how to account for or where to locate their power. This was an interesting question for us in a theoretical sense, for it stretched our analytic competencies considerably, but it also has great practical import. If digital storytelling becomes widespread, and certainly if it is incorporated into school-based literacy activities, there will need be a way of saying what is powerful about such compositions. Undoubtedly, images, music, and language are each significant conveyors of meaning and sentiment. However, for especially potent stories, such as Randy's "Lyfe-N-Rhyme," it did not seem to us that any one of these modalities was preponderant over the others. Nor is it satisfying simply to believe that increasing the number of semiotic modalities present in a single composition has an accordant multiplicative effect on the semiotic efficacy of the piece (although this may well be a popular view). The real task, as we saw it, was to understand both the individual and combinatory semiotic contributions made to the synesthetic whole by its material components. To grasp and articulate the emergent qualities of true multimodal design (i.e., design that actually fulfills the promise of expression, which Lemke [1997] describes as multiplicatively powerful), we need to understand the particular logics of organization and respective meaning-making affordances of different modalities. We next describe the methods we devised for this purpose.[8]

Selection of Multimodal Artifact

Given the size of our archive of digital stories and the rich range of multimodal work represented, settling on a story for a fine-grained analysis might have been a complex task. Yet "Lyfe-N-Rhyme" was to us an obvious choice. Of the digital stories from DUSTY that have been viewed by multiple audiences during the past 3 years, Randy's work has received the most acclaim, its expressive power has been regularly commented on, and its emotional and intellectual impact has been frequently noted. The second factor that influenced our choice of text was analyzability. As this was our first attempt at this kind of analysis, we felt it necessary to choose a piece that was not only an exemplar of powerful expression but that also had an economical design (i.e., an artifact that was not so complex as to make it overly difficult to deconstruct). In comparison to many other digital stories produced at DUSTY, "Lyfe-N-Rhyme" is what we might call manageably multimodal. It does not feature any animation or slick transition effects, but rather, it presents a series of different still images that are coordinated with music and the spoken word.

Identification and Representation of Modalities

When choosing a multimodal text, it is necessary to identify which modes, in relation to each other, will be the focus of the analysis. In an ideal world, one would take into account all of the modes—spoken words, images, music, written text, and movement and transitions—but such complexity quickly overwhelms. We chose to focus primarily on the conjunction of images and words and regretfully gave short shrift to music.[9] One could imagine, however, depending on one's analytic rationale and given the particular features and emphases of a multimodal text, different foci and starting points for analysis.

The next step is to visually represent these selected, simultaneously apprehended modes to transcribe the text in such a way as to clearly illustrate the copresence of each focal mode within the boundaries of appropriate units of analysis. Put another way, one must invent a way to graphically depict the words, pictures, and so forth that are copresented in the piece at any given moment. The form that this transcription scheme takes will be dictated to a great extent by the respective materialities and affordances of the focal modes. Consideration must be given to the principles of temporality, segmentability, and so forth respective to each mode, and a common denominator, so to speak, must be found to parse the piece into analyzable multimodal units. This may be the most challenging juncture of the process.

Our solution to this problem was to transcribe "Lyfe-N-Rhyme" in such a way as to make apparent its couplings of images and language. An important semiotic particularity of the variety multimodal texts we are working with is that they unfold in time.[10] Therefore, in examining Randy's "Lyfe-N-Rhyme," we adopted the momentary conjunction of image-spoken language as the basic unit of analysis. The obvious rationale for this choice of minimal unit (this multieme, if you will) is that the independent units into which spoken language and images may each be parsed are fundamentally dissimilar, and as such, they cannot be usefully compared if regarded discretely. However, the trick here was to preserve the temporal relation between the different channels at each moment in the piece but simultaneously set aside the flow of temporality. As a resolution to this problem, we adapted the graphic interface structure used to create the narrative in the first place: a timeline. Adobe Premiere, and virtually every other video editing program like it, entails multiple time-coded tracks in which the various components of the story are rolled out in parallel, so to speak.

With this method of parallel presentation as an inspiration, we conceived of and created a multitracked, horizontal, time-coded transcription format, as

FIGURE 26-1   Transcript format featuring time code and multiple tracks (image, word, and interview notes).

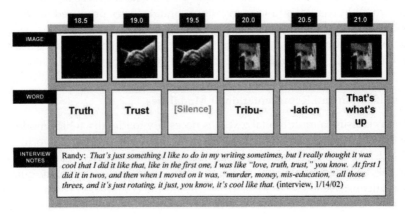

shown in Figure 26-1. Notice that in the specific case of this analysis, the time-line is structured in half-second increments, which was the minimum amount of time that any one image continuously appeared on the screen in "Lyfe-N-Rhyme." In sum, the temporal flow of the piece is frozen into half-second chunks, in accordance with the shortest on-screen duration of any visual image, rendering a minimal analytic unit of a still image and its corresponding half-second of spoken language. Again, it should be emphasized that there is no one formula for transcribing multimodal texts; the timescale (if there is any at all), segmentation scheme, and so on, must be created in direct relation and response to the modes and questions with which one is concerned.

Identification of Semiotic Patterns Across Modes

Once an appropriate transcript format has been decided on and the work of transcription has been completed, the next stage involves carefully examining the transcript for salient patterns, as with any qualitative investigation. What is different and difficult about this kind of examination in relation to multi-modal texts, of course, is that one must not only be cognizant of emerging patterns of various types (thematic, visual, etc.) in each singular mode, but one must also look for identifiable patterns of relation between modes.

In this task, we were aided by two conceptual frameworks, the first help-ing us think about more local multimodal relationships (e.g., the nature of the pairing of word and image) and the other positioning us to think about more global multimodal relationships (e.g., the functioning of one segment of a digital story in relation to another or the whole). For the first, we drew on the distinctions offered by the American pragmatist philosopher C. S. Peirce (1992, 1998) between icon, index, and symbol. For purposes of illustrating these concepts, consider any pictorial image of a donkey. According to Peirce's (1992, 1998) formulation, if this picture were to mimetically stand for the idea of donkey, it would be considered an icon. If the image stood for the concept of stubbornness, for example, the conjunction would constitute an index, where the form does not directly express but rather points to (hence the name) a meaning. Last, in Peircian nomenclature, if the donkey picture represented the concept of the Democratic Party, it would be regarded as a symbol, a strictly social, conventional sign. This system of sign classification not only provides a language to articulate different forms of representation, but it also speaks directly to issues of representational power and effect, as will be illustrated in some detail later. But in brief, we looked to see whether an image, when paired with language and music, functioned as an icon, index, or symbol and whether there were discernable patterns of these functions.

For a framework to aid us in understanding multimodal relationships of meaning on the macrolevel of the organization of the composition as a whole, we drew on Labov's (1997) continuing work on narrative theory, which offers, in effect, a kind of conceptual x-ray device, a way of seeing into and talking about narratives and the connections between their meanings and structure. Thus, in the analysis that follows, we apply Labov's notion of the semantic and structural roles of orientation, abstract, and coda in narratives.[11] Because most of the digital stories in our archive began as narratives of personal experiences, it made conceptual common sense to us to determine whether the dimensions and aspects of narratives identified by linguists, such as Labov (Ochs & Capps, 2001), were present and, if so, how multimodality functioned to amplify meaning and functions.

Rerepresenting Semiotic Patterns

After identifying salient patterns within, between, and among modes, it is useful to return to the drawing board, quite literally, and rerepresent the text in a form that reveals and juxtaposes these patterns (see Appendix C). Further patterning may become evident and a graphic representation of patterns that emerge from the coding of the transcript may make those patterns among patterns more easily discernable. In fact, this kind of richly embedded semiotic patterning may well be the defining feature of powerful multimodal design.

"LYFE-N-RHYME"

Randy's "Lyfe-N-Rhyme" combined poetry with rap and an autobiography with social critique and was situated verbally and visually within local landscapes and neighborhoods, even though it was aimed toward a broad audience.[12] Two minutes and 11 seconds in duration, this digital story presents a simple, coordinated series of mappings between 79 different still images, 4 of which are each repeated once; the lyrics of an original spoken-word poem (see Appendix A); and the fused driving bass line and somber melody of a classic jazz composition by Miles Davis. The video editing software that Randy used to author his piece, Adobe Premiere (Version 6.5), certainly afforded the panoply of pans, zooms, fades, and spins that are characteristic, for instance, of professionally produced content on the order of MTV. Furthermore, Randy could also easily have incorporated video clips, sound effects, and other technological bells and whistles into his project, yet he did not. What he did do, and we believe to a powerfully transformative effect, was achieve an orchestration (Kress & van Leeuwen, 2001) or braiding (Mitchell, 2004) of language, image, and music into a whole. What we hope to demonstrate is that this whole, in the gestalt sense, transcends the collective contributions of its constituent parts. Although it may be taken for granted that something irreducible is brought into existence whenever parts are assembled, we will show how Randy's "Lyfe-N-Rhyme," through an analysis of its design, emerges as a potent symbolic unity, a deeply personal, consequential sign in and of itself.

In his multimedia piece, Randy lays bare intimate, troubling aspects of his life and world, inviting audiences to do the difficult work of reflecting on the intimate concerns they hold for themselves, for those they care about, and for the larger community. Nevertheless, we proceed with the assumption that the story does not tell the whole story. We suggest that it is not only the propositional content of what Randy says and shows that moves us, but it is also the composite form into which these elements are organized. Evident in Randy's "Lyfe-N-Rhyme" is not just a powerful story but also a transcendent synthesis of form and meaning across a variety of semiotic modes. Yes, we are at once touched and disturbed by the words Randy speaks. Yes, the montage of images that he lays out is arranged to an arresting effect: now soothing, now shocking, and so on. And yes, we feel the pulse of the music and verse thump in our chests and minds. Crucially though, we emphasize that the power felt from this piece is not tantamount to the simultaneous, additive experience of the aforementioned effects, as one might suppose. Again, the full import of the semiotic tapestry that Randy crafts is not merely in but also in between the warp and the weft, as we hope in the following paragraphs to demonstrate.

In the sections that follow, we examine the meaning-making affordances of multimodality, and we argue that Randy's composition evidences patterns within and between different modes that together constitute a multimodal whole. In particular, we illustrate respectively how (a) the visual pictorial mode can repurpose the written, linguistic mode; (b) iconic and indexical images can be rendered as symbols; (c) titles, iconic, and indexical images and thematic movement can animate each other cooperatively; and (d) modes can progressively become imbued with the associative meanings of each other. We proceed through the digital story chronologically, beginning with an account of how titles and subtitles function and proceeding with a discussion of the opening sequence of the piece, which serves both an orientation and abstract function, in the sense of Labov discussed above. Next comes a discussion of iterative thematic movement in the piece and its relation to the foregoing titles and abstract and orientation section. Finally, we deal with the ending section, the coda, which is constituted by, builds on, and in fact transcends all of the other sections. Throughout, and most important, we show how it is only in the multimodal laminate that these patterns become evident and that these narrative effects are accomplished. This is to say, each pattern is constituted by and constitutive of others in such a way that what is communicated is distinctive and different from what can be accomplished in one modality alone.

We offer one word to the wise before we begin: It is best to view Randy's "Lyfe-N-Rhyme"[13] and then read the analysis below. We are aware that by attempting to rely primarily on words to explain meaning that is irreducibly multimodal, we are engaging, and are asking readers to join with us, in an uphill task. Please refer to the images and to the schematics provided in Appendices A, B, and C as aids in this process.

Titles as Punctuation

Randy's composition opens with a simple statement of its title. Against a matte black background, about one third of the way down from the upper limit of the screen space, bright scarlet type appears spelling out "Lyfe-N-Rhyme" in all capitals (see Figure 26-2). The contrast of blood red on black is startling; and also striking is the juxtaposition of the perhaps most institutional of font styles, Times New Roman, with radically unconventional orthography. In these contrasts, an intangible tension seems to be set up from the beginning. No words are yet spoken. All we hear as we take in the title are the tones of three simple keyboard chords that overlap slightly at their edges.

In the following section, we analyze how titles and subtitles—or more accurately, their visual features of font, style, and color—function in "Lyfe-N-Rhyme." Our argument will be that multimodality offers opportunities for the expectations set up by conventions of the visual mode to redirect the function of the written linguistic mode. Randy's choice of linguistic symbols (i.e., written language) to bind the beginning of his piece is certainly not unusual. The genre conventions for a story prescribe that a title be given at the start, as the author well knew. However, what is noteworthy about Randy's use of a title is that it is not relegated solely to the beginning of the story. In fact, Randy's story is shot through with titles. At each of six different junctures throughout the piece, he inserts words that function as titles (e.g., "DAMN," "WAIT," and "A PAGE FULL OF RAGE"; see Appendices B and C). Such

FIGURE 26-2   Title frame.

words are not, we would argue, simply word images. In point of fact, Randy does on several occasions use word images in place of a pictorial image; for instance, when he vocally invokes certain abstract concepts, such as justice and worth, he shows images in which these words are featured prominently in written form. What distinguishes the recurrent use of titles in this piece from other word images is a precise parallelism of style. Subtitles are depicted in exactly the same font and red color and with the same black background as the opening title, "Lyfe-N-Rhyme," to which title status indisputably belongs. As a result of this process of partial transduction, we expect that these word images will be functionally title-like.[14]

Again, the dressing of certain word images in a title's clothing, so to speak, creates on some level of consciousness an expectation on the part of the viewer that the word image in question will behave in a title-like way. So in the case of "Lyfe-N-Rhyme," by interspersing title-like word images throughout his composition, Randy effectively delimits what we will call subnarratives within the main text. Thus, when we encounter a title-like image in "Lyfe-N-Rhyme," we are likely to expect that following each subtitle will be a story part that in some respect exhibits the qualities of a fully formed story in and of itself. We may also expect that this story part will end when the next title appears or when the larger story is over (which, by the way, was a defining convention of silent films). In a real sense, then, we see these title-like word images as punctuation of a sort, demarcating both pivotal moments in the larger story and boundaries between its constituent subnarratives. This, we argue, is precisely the kind of emergent structure and meaning about which multimodal communication is uniquely able to bring. We would suggest that here is a case where the influence of the logical organization and meaning-making affordances of the visual (pictorial) mode is serving to repurpose the written linguistic mode in context. The elegance and efficacy of this move are noteworthy, considering the contribution it makes to the power of the composition as a whole, as we hope to show as we proceed with the pieces of our analysis.

A brief methodological aside, we would underscore again the importance of employing the sort of visual transcription described above as an analytic aid. In the case of the subtitles, for example, if one were only to view "Lyfe-N-Rhyme," the connection between these word images—the common visual design features that encode their titleness—might go unnoticed. That is, the word images would be seen in isolation, as they sequentially appeared in the flow of the piece, separated by a myriad of other images and sounds. Thus, the transcription, and more specifically its affordance of the simultaneous visual presentation and apprehension of multiple images in sequence, makes these patterns comparatively much more salient.

Orientation and Abstract

Nearly 4 seconds into the piece, we abruptly first meet the copresence of image and spoken word. Randy lyrically philosophizes as follows: "What's done through life echoes throughout time. It's an infinite chase to become

FIGURE 26-3   The opening sequence of Lyfe-N-Rhyme.

what I was, but what was I? I don't remember. The only thing I know is I've seen it before in the mirrors of my mind."

Concurrently, in the 13-second period during which these four sentences are unhurriedly delivered, a series of five images occupies the visual field. These images, in order of succession, include a photo of a sunlit Sphinx and the Great Pyramid at Giza; a grainy yet photorealistic illustration of Malcolm X, in his characteristic black suit and tie and thick-rimmed glasses; a swirling Dalí-esque painting of hip-hop-culture icon Tupac Shakur; the famous rosy-toned three-quarter-view portrait of Marcus Garvey in full military regalia; and a close-up frontal image of the face of rap artist Biggie Smalls[15] partially obscured in shadow (see Figure 26-3). Also, with the start of this sequence comes a layering of the moody, almost plaintive, trumpet of Miles Davis onto the vibrations of the keyboard chords.

In our analysis, we suggest that each of the multimodal couplings in this 13-second slice of "Lyfe-N-Rhyme," by virtue of their semantic kinship, serve the dual purpose of an orientation section and an abstract section, again to borrow two conceptual tools from Labov's (1997) framework for narrative analysis. First, with these four sentences and five images, Randy orientates or anchors himself and his onlookers in the physical and, most important, cultural time and space of the narrative. His words poetically invite viewers to bear witness to "an infinite chase," his candid examination of society and self. In the imagery, we see a succession of symbols of African American struggles and Black masculinity, with the timelessly monumental accomplishments of ancient Egypt giving way to four Black men who struggled for political, social, and creative self-determination only to be cut down or publicly shamed.[16]

Through examining the conjunctions of images and language in these 13 seconds (i.e., what Randy says and what he shows), a unitary whole emerges. That is, by noticing the categorical thread that runs through this group of five images and by mapping that onto the meanings in the words Randy speaks, these copresent elements become semantically associated, and their linkage contributes to a magnification of the meaning of the whole: a young African American man's search to reconcile personal identity with culture and history. The piece begins with a statement by means of which Randy opens a window onto a universal quality of the human condition. "What's done through life echoes throughout time," he professes. Concomitantly, the image of the Sphinx and pyramid appears on the screen for 3.5 seconds. He next

shifts from stating the universal to relating the personal. Somewhat crypti-
cally, he describes his search for an elusive self that once was but is now lost.
The pictures that accompany this description, the four male figures, add value
and depth in several important ways. They communicate the image of almost
Jungian archetypes, different aspects of possible selves: the thug, the moralist,
the artist, the statesman, the savior, and so forth. They also represent exem-
plars of African American male seekers who arguably may be said to have
fallen short in the end. It is important to notice that these meanings are conveyed without being said as such. There is no direct, iconic, or indexical correspondence between these images and the spoken word; as viewers, it is our
cultural, conventional recognition of these figures that impels us on some
level of consciousness to derive the aforementioned categorical meanings in
the copresence of their portraits.

The semiotic consequence of this recognition is that these images are rendered as authentic symbols and, furthermore, that Randy's personal quest for
a lost self is, through language, implicated and echoed in this symbolic whole.
Still further, it seems significant that the transitions between the sequenced
images of Malcolm X, Tupac, Garvey, and Smalls occur at time intervals that
decrease very regularly. That is, the first image appears for 2.5 seconds, the
second for 2.0 seconds, the third for 1.5, and the fourth for only 1.0. This regularity fortifies the semiotic bond between these images and also signals a
larger level transition to come. In sum, we argue that the resultant multimodal
whole both frames the narrative situation and aligns the respective footings
of author and audience within that situation (Goffman, 1981). That is, it functions as an orientation section, as mentioned above. And perhaps more important, it presents us with the thesis of "Lyfe-N-Rhyme," what Labov (1997)
might call an abstract section.

What is remarkable, moreover, and central to our argument is the irreducible multidimensionality of this sequence. Through each semiotic channel, distinct but related aspects of meaning are imputed to the thesis in such a way
that each mode is doing what it does best while exceeding the comfortable,
conventional limits of its own meaning-making affordances. This is accomplished by virtue of the multimodal orchestration. For example, we would
suggest that the logical simultaneity and semiotic fullness (Kress, 2003) of the
images of Malcolm X and the others flow into and fill in the ambiguities of
Randy's words in such a way as to create emergent meaning, meaning that
makes of each language-image paring an orientation and abstract clause. And
in the abstract section, the whole constitutes the clauses, and the fullness of
the thesis positively reverberates. Randy's infinite search is rendered, in some
sense, finite. His lost self is given a face. His words and his own destiny are
fused with the historicity and aspirations that inhere in those five images,
which is his thesis, not accidentally. This is quite an achievement in 13 seconds.

Again, our argument is that this powerfully organic connection of the
universal themes that those five images symbolically communicate with
Randy's life and personal identity could only have been accomplished within
the multimodal laminate. Furthermore, as we will next argue and explain, the
instances of emergence that we have pointed at in the story features discussed

so far in turn beget additional layers of emergent meaning through higher level forms of multimodal integration.

The Next Level

Thus far, we have discussed two salient patterns in the multimodal design of "Lyfe-N-Rhyme": the title-like word images that meaningfully punctuate the narrative and the 13-second opening section, which, we have asserted, serves both an orientation function and an abstract function with regard to the piece as a whole. The purpose of the next portion of the analysis will be to show how these two components, each itself characterized by emergent meaning derived from effective multimodal integration, fit within the larger organization of the piece and contribute to the further emergence of powerful, irreducible multimodal expression. We will next illustrate how the aforementioned features, by setting up a succession of self-contained yet deeply interconnected subnarratives, help form a consistent tenor and texture throughout the piece. Moreover, we will demonstrate that these subnarratives, individually and in concert, serve to establish and emblematize Randy's message.

Returning to the point in "Lyfe-N-Rhyme" where we stopped our previous discussion, after 16 seconds of running time, the screen goes suddenly, if only momentarily, black. We hear a single clear tone similar to the faint, lingering knell of a temple bell. As the regular decrease in screen time occupied by each of the first five images foretells, we arrive at a new juncture in the piece. The half-second curtain of darkness opens onto a radically different second act and the first of the subnarratives (see Figure 26-4): "Life. Love. Truth. Trust. Tribulation, that's what's up. The older we get, the harder a habit is to kick. Damn."

FIGURE 26-4   Thematic movement from the global to the particular.

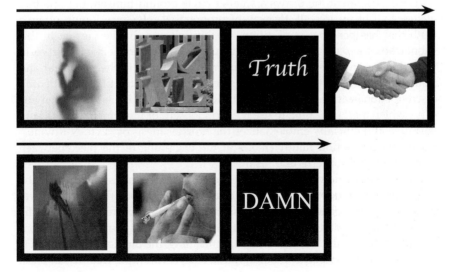

In the nonlinguistic auditory channel, peeling bells and a beseeching trumpet are enjoined by a driving bass-line rhythm, and from this point, the images change precisely in time with the musical beat; the infinite chase is on. The first image, in direct temporal correspondence to the utterance of the word *life*, is a hazy photographic illustration of a dark gray, right-facing silhouette, an androgynous figure represented from the waist up with his or her balled fist held to his or her chin perhaps in a somewhat more upright interpretation of Rodin's "Thinker." Behind the foregrounded figure is a distant green meadow, a cloudless blue sky, and a sweeping, dramatic rainbow that nearly bisects the picture plane diagonally. Five more images follow: a graphic representation of Robert Indiana's ubiquitous pop art sculptural piece "Love," positioned on a white-sand beach; the word *truth* in italicized, violet-colored type on a black background; a photograph of two male Caucasian hands clasped in a handshake against a black field; a photograph of one of New York's World Trade Towers exploding into flames on September 11, 2001; and a photo from the neck up of a well-dressed, middle-aged, bespectacled Black man lighting a cigarette. Significantly, all of these pictorial images evince iconic or indexical associations with the words they are paired with, their linguistic concomitants an important point that we will revisit. Finally, there is the word *damn* spelled out in capital letters in red Times New Roman letters on a black background.[17]

Let us return to the previous argument we offered regarding the boundedness of subnarratives. We see at the outset that Randy invokes universal, almost Kantian categories of human experience: life, love, truth, and trust. Then, he adds an evaluative statement, one that is expressed as truth but not a universal truth. "Tribulation, that's what's up." This statement represents a truth that is necessarily located within the temporal, geographical, historical, and political frames in which the author exists and with which he is concerned. Although, the personal concern at this point is still somewhat implicit. Next, however, he states that "the older we get, the harder a habit is to kick." With this statement, he draws a smaller circle around himself, but one that includes all of us as well. By way of pronominal reference, Randy offers a truth that has personal implications for himself and for the viewer. In this subnarrative, and every other, we argue that he structures a cline in the world view that he presents, a thematic shift from the global to the particular and from the universal to the personal. It is not just the repeated titles that identify discrete subnarratives within "Lyfe-N-Rhyme," but it is also this thematic cline, which marks the plot, to use the term loosely, or movement of each subnarrative and crucially emblematizes the broader thesis of "Lyfe-N-Rhyme." Recall the connection Randy makes at the beginning of the piece between broader cultural concerns and his own.

Here is a hybrid construction of visual boundary signals provided by the titles, iconic and indexical images, and universal-to-personal thematic movement. This construction is iterated throughout this main, middle part of the piece.[18] Indeed, the melding of these features results in a multimodal presentation that echoes itself in both form and meaning, the implication of which is that the message is complementarily broadcast on multiple channels at once.

To once again underscore our central argument, it is vital to recognize that this situation is quite different from one underpinned by the logic of saying and showing is better than saying or showing. Contrary to popular belief, saying and showing do not automatically amount to powerful expression, and when they do, it is often a matter of coincidence. Multimodal communication is powerful to the extent that the constituent modes are integrated in such a way that they each do what they do well and that these strengths are positioned so as to complement one another. As we have tried to demonstrate thus far, this is the kind of integration that "Lyfe-N-Rhyme" exemplifies.

Globalizing the Personal   The last part of our analysis of "Lyfe-N-Rhyme" focuses primarily on the ending sequence of the piece, the last 21 seconds. This may well be the most interesting part of Randy's story and the part that affects viewers the most; although, in these 21 seconds, the only words that are spoken are a restatement of the title of the piece: "This is 'Lyfe-N-Rhyme.'"

There are 10 images that compose this ending (see Figure 26-5), 7 of which make their first appearances and 3 of which are repeated. The sequence begins with an image of Randy wearing a black knit cap and dark bomber jacket and standing against the backdrop of a cream-colored Victorian house that is in a state of slight disrepair, a type of home quite characteristic of West Oakland. He looks in our direction, basically, but above and past us. Next, we see a frontal view of a different West Oakland home, a large white structure with royal blue trim. The windows are boarded up, and there are official City of Oakland orange safety stickers on the boards warning against trespassing. Following this, we see, once again, the image of a broken sidewalk strewn with litter, the photograph that was in a previous subnarrative to index poverty's concrete. Next, there are two other repeated images: a group of young African American men congregating on an Oakland street corner and a hazy view through a rusted chain-link fence onto the blacktop and brown brick buildings of an urban elementary school campus. These images appear earlier in indexical association with the lyrics "capitalism in my veins" (through linguistic implicature indicating that the young men mentioned above are dealing drugs and change, respectively). After this, in moderately rapid succession, several photos appear: images of a bearded olive-skinned man behind the counter of a liquor store, an African American man sitting on a porch,

FIGURE 26-5   Coda or ending sequence.

a trash-filled empty lot surrounded by a chain-link fence, and another abandoned West Oakland Victorian. The final image of the piece is another of Randy. This is a photograph that he took of himself, a view of his face and shoulders from beneath, again wearing a black knit cap, framed by the Corinthian columns and crusty architectural details of the same off-white Victorian house that he stood in front of 20 seconds before. Another salient feature of this final image is the bright rectangle of luminescent sky toward which Randy's head points. This ending sequence of images is markedly different from the preceding two main sections already discussed, but it relates to and builds on them in a profoundly meaningful way.

Before examining the ways that this final section relates to the foregoing two, however, we will specifically discuss three distinctive features of the ending, and the characteristics that we believe warrant discussion, and these 21 seconds as an analyzable whole. First, as mentioned above, no words are spoken throughout the sequence. It is bounded at its beginning by a repetition of the title. Notably, however, the mode of delivery for the repeated words is different. Recall that the only other time the actual title appeared in the piece was at the beginning, where it was typographically shown but not spoken. A further distinction between this section and those preceding it is that this section is bounded by pictures, not words. Instead of title-like word images, we here have two images of the author himself: the first a full-body image, which coincides with his restatement of the title, and the second a skyward head shot, which sees the piece to its end. Last, this part of "Lyfe-N-Rhyme" is distinguished from the other parts in that it does not feature any imagery collected from the Internet or other publicly accessible sources. Rather, all 10 images are photographs taken of a particular West Oakland neighborhood by Randy himself. For the first time, viewers see the undiluted photographic realism of Randy's life world as he sees it.

In interpreting a general pattern evident in these semiotic moves, we might first say that Randy sets up and trades on differences in the logical organization and meaning-making affordances of counterposed semiotic modes. For instance, the fact that he speaks his title and does not represent it in visual type, as was the case earlier, is suggestive of a transformation. It is ostensibly the same information with the same referent, which is the piece itself. Yet, and this is also key, the medium, in the McLuhanesque sense, conveys a message. When one communicates the same idea in different media, one does not say the same thing in each case (McLuhan, 1964). As such, we argue that in introducing this final section of his piece in oral language as well as in bounding the piece with images of himself instead of title-like expressions, Randy is signaling a metamorphosis of meaning.

Evident here is a transformation involving semiotic enrichment. At the start of the sequence, Randy uses voice in lieu of written text to identify the title of his piece. Attending to the basic organizational logics of each mode, the relative semiotic paucity of meaning inherent in written language—again, in the sense that Kress (2003) intends—is replaced with the semiotically fuller oral language. Moreover, in bounding the sequence with images instead of titles, Randy is again opting for a comparatively greater semiotic completeness over the generic reference of language. A crucial point we must make at this juncture, one that must be clearly understood, is that Randy does not avoid language or its expressive power; his piece is in large part a testimony to and celebration of the power of language. In fact, counterintuitive though it at first may seem, it is his powerful use of language and his orchestration of it with image and music that permit, or perhaps even call for, the absence of language in the end.

To facilitate an explanation of this seeming contradiction, let us recapitulate key aspects of the analysis that have already been discussed. At the outset of "Lyfe-N-Rhyme," a sequence of several images appears that symbolically embodies the theme that will be pursued throughout the piece. Out of the multimodal mix emerges a unity of the universal struggles and hopes of the African American male with those of Randy himself. Next comes a series of segments, each delineated by title-like word images and comprising iconic and indexical language-image associations. In theme, the subnarrative within each segment in this body of the piece (to apply an essay metaphor) evinces a slide from the universal to the personal, echoing the thesis that was established in the preceding orientation and abstract section. Finally, then, the ending comprises a sequence of images that we have asserted draws import from the virtual absence of language. So is it our assertion, one might ask, that ultimately, this multimodal composition is at its most powerful when it is at its least multimodal? No, this is certainly not the case. What we would say instead, restating an earlier point, is that it is the multimodality of this piece that affords it, in the end, a transcendent unimodality, of a sort; but this unimodality is illusive. The photographs that appear at the end of "Lyfe-N-Rhyme" are steeped in the associative meanings that went before; therefore, we might say that the mode that is actually present is imbued in a real sense with the copresence of other nonpresent modes.

By way of explanation, consider the three repeated images in the final sequence: the broken sidewalk, the young men on the street corner, and the school yard fence. As was mentioned before, these images were set up within subnarratives in indexical association with "poverty's concrete," "capitalism in my veins," and "change," respectively, language that speaks directly to the main concerns of Randy's thesis. Necessarily, they carry these meanings with them into the final sequence. Also, each of these images is a photograph taken by Randy himself, as are the other images in the final sequence. The image quality and subject matter of these photographs is quite similar. It seems as if they were all taken on a walk through a particular neighborhood on one particular day (and indeed they were). Instinctively, we view these images as a set by virtue of their stylistic and thematic congruence. Accordingly, although only three of the images explicitly carry forth meanings that were previously ascribed, viewers feel those meanings percolate out of the repeated three and saturate the set, in effect.

What happens is that this final section in its turn also takes on a wholeness. It becomes a coda in Labov's (1997) terms, a section that brings us back to the beginning in a sense and speaks thematically to the entire piece. In these simple neighborhood photos, the prior indexical link to language lingers unspoken, and the multilevel thematic cline resonates in its absence. All of these residual meanings coalesce and crystallize within the images in such a way that the global concerns of poverty, crime, desperation, hope, and change are powerfully emblematized. Similar to the portraits of symbolic figures of African American history with which the piece began, Randy's everyday images emerge as profoundly potent symbols in themselves: He conventionalizes the particular and creates a sublime symbolic unity of the global and the personal. And all the while, similar to the solemn rejoinders of a Greek chorus, the jazz trumpet alternately moans, shouts, and weeps.

CONCLUSION

The most striking claim that we want to make on the basis of our analysis is that Randy's "Lyfe-N-Rhyme" represents a different system of signification and a different kind of meaning. As an irreducibly multimodal composition, "Lyfe-N-Rhyme" is not just a good poem whose meaning is enhanced because it has been illustrated and set to music; rather, we would argue that the meaning that a viewer or listener experiences is qualitatively different, transcending what is possible via each mode separately. Through our analysis, we attempted to characterize the relationality between and among modalities and thereby demonstrate some of the semiotic dimensions and strategies that partly accounted for the emergent meaning of Randy's composition. We also believe our analysis and Randy's story offer a strong counterclaim to the argument that digital media simply facilitate the multimodal composing that could and does exist apart from computer technologies. If we are correct, the particular meanings and the experience of viewing and constructing these meanings via this form of multimodality are unique. Believing as we do that a culture and a time's mediational means, our psychological and material tools if you will (Vygotsky, 1978), are intimately connected with our capacities to think, represent, and communicate, it would seem hugely important to widen our definition of writing to include multimodal composing as a newly available means.

Having made this appeal, we are at once intrigued and daunted by the amount and range of research and theorizing that waits to be done. Many scholars have commented on the relationships between old and new technologies, noting for example that new technologies often serve old purposes before they come into their own (McLuhan, 1964) or that new technologies can spawn new literate practices that are not necessarily beneficial (Haas, 1999). One of the issues that our research raises for us is the relationship between multimodality and unimodal texts, such as academic essays. Some have argued that visually dominant meaning systems, such as film, can express all of the meanings that a written text can. For us, the more interesting analytic questions concern the blendings that we notice between new and old textual forms. For example, Randy's "Lyfe-N-Rhyme" and digital stories in general deal in linearity and temporality as their narrative-like compositions unfold on the screen. This makes the multimodality of digital stories closer kin with traditional narrative structure but distant cousins to the more associative potential of new digital forms, such as hypermedia. It may be the case that the power of digital stories for creators and viewers has to do with a happy melding of old and new genres and media. We are led to ask, then, what kinds of meanings do these meldings afford, what power to they have, and what constraints do they offer on what people can know, discover, and express (Bennett, 1991)?

Looking back at our analysis, we are still intrigued by what we did not capture, especially around sound and music and the intersection of these modalities with language and image. To give an instance, we recognize that the layering of a hip hop aesthetic onto a classic jazz substrate simultaneously invokes two pivotal moments in African American history and culture, which very interestingly speaks directly to the theme that Randy sets up in imagery and language at the outset of his piece (recall the images of Egypt, Malcolm X, Tupac Shakur, etc.). This layer of meaning is one we did not take into account. Yet music is pivotal as a means of expression and identification, especially for youth. According to Hudak (1999), "so powerful is the desire to make music with others that one is tempted to conceive of music-making as an emergent, radical engagement with consciousness" (447). Frith (1992) notes how important it is that music is directly experienced through the immediacy of the body. We simply add that the ability to either compose music or merely use music as a layer of meaning in one's composition, to cast a mood around one's story through a musical choice, and to accent, punctuate, or emphasize spoken words through their connection to a beat are some of the pleasures attached to music in a multimodal composition. Music also adds an important emotional element to digital stories, and we believe that some of the satisfaction that viewers and creators experience around this form of multimodality derives from emotionality. Though often ignored, the interplay of emotion, cognition, and learning (for a notable exception, see Dipardo & Schnack, 2004) are what compose Vygotsky's (1934/1986) vision for "a dynamic system of meaning" in which "the affective and the intellectual unite" (10). Perhaps opportunities to create and learn through digital multimodality, such as the personal narratives offered through digital storytelling, could be a step toward that unity.

There are great challenges that accompany the incorporation of digital multimodality into classrooms, challenges that are at once technological, economic, and pedagogic. Nevertheless, we have suggested that there is much to be gained from the effort. We conclude by mentioning one last benefit that has to do with multimodality as a democratizing force, an opening up of what counts as valued communication, and a welcoming of varied channels of expression. It gives us great pleasure that "Lyfe-N-Rhyme," a supremely impressive multimodal composition, was created by a poet of the streets and that Randy's combination of abilities and predilections fit the mediational means of digital storytelling like a hand in a glove. We wonder how many other poets and storytellers there are for whom multimodality would offer unexpectedly powerful affordances.

APPENDIX A

Script for "Lyfe-N-Rhyme"

What's done through life echoes throughout time
It's an infinite chase to become what I was
But what was I? I don't remember
Life, love, truth, trust, tribulation
That's what's up
The only thing I know is I've seen it before in the mirrors of my mind
The older we get, the harder a habit is to kick
Damn! Pleasure, pain, purpose, prison
Justice is a contradiction
Living on a razor, fell into a felony
And handled what was left of me
Life is a lesson
Groove with me
Move like a millipede
Thousands of lands controlled by one hand
Yes, mama's only gun is mama's only son with a guillotine tongue
Murder, money, mis-education
Mill gives an incarceration
Urban voice, heart of the street
Step by step on poverty's concrete
Choice, change, crack cocaine
Capitalism in my veins, yeah, that's what I'm talking about
A page full of rage!
Wait! How does a cage rehabilitate?
Next, America's new war
Billion dollar weapons don't feed the poor
But then again, who cares?
All we do is breathe what they put in the air, yeah
I said it before, I'll say it again
Contradiction, Section 8 living
Society's rival, freedom of speech, who are we to teach
Heart, body, mind, soul
So many different worlds in one planet going on
Youth neglected, expected to listen, born and raised on television
Friction, failure, function, worth
Me and Mom Deuce, family first
Some rules are meant to be broken
Some doors are meant to be opened
And . . . regardless of race
We all mostly come from the same place . . . Love
This is life in rhyme.

APPENDIX B

Global to Personal Thematic Movements in "Lyfe-N-Rhyme"

Represented below is a schematic [Figure 26-6] that illustrates each of the global-to-personal thematic movements in Randy's "Lyfe-N-Rhyme." In each

FIGURE 26-6

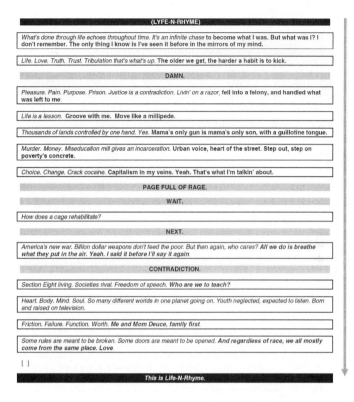

white box, the lyrics from a particular section of the piece are transcribed. Lyrics that appear in italics evidence a meaning that is global or universal in scope, and those that appear in bold type reference more local, personal meanings. The terms that appear in the gray shaded areas in all capital letters are title-like expressions, and those in black shaded areas are statements of the title of the piece. The first title (in black) is displayed only in written language, and the last one is only spoken.

APPENDIX C

An Analysis of Language and Image in "Lyfe-N-Rhyme"

The image below [Figure 26-7] graphically depicts the concurrent unfolding of patterns of spoken language and image presentation throughout Randy's "Lyfe-N-Rhyme." Global-to-personal thematic movements are shown in gray-scale segments. In the two polka-dotted sections, no thematic movement is evident. The checkerboard areas in the image track represent symbolic use of images, and the solid gray areas show images with iconic or indexical significance. Striped bands represent title-like expressions that are both spoken

FIGURE 26-7

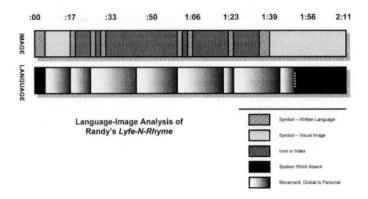

Language-Image Analysis of
Randy's *Lyfe-N-Rhyme*

and seen in written form, and the white bands show statements of the actual title of the piece, which again is first only seen in writing and then, near the end, only spoken.

NOTES

1. *Kairos* can be accessed at www.english.ttu.edu/kairos/index.html, and *Born Magazine* can be accessed at www.bornmagazine.com.

2. There has been a great deal of valuable work on literacy and digital media that would fall under the label of new literacies that we do not review in this article because it is not directly related to the form of multimodality we feature here. In particular, there has been very helpful work on hypertextuality and hypermedia (Bolter, 1991), on uses of the Internet (Hawisher & Selfe, 2000), on critical literacy and new technologies (Knobel & Lankshear, 2002), and on video games as sites for leaning and identity development (Gee, 2003).

3. For instance, the report states, with particular reference to the findings of the 2002 Survey of Public Participation in the Arts,

> that literary readers are nearly 3 times as likely to attend a performing arts event, almost 4 times as likely to visit an art museum, more than 2.5 times as likely to do volunteer or charity work, more than 1.5 times as likely to attend sporting events, and more than 1.5 times as likely to participate in sports activities. (5)

4. DUSTY was cofounded by Glynda Hull and Michael James. We gratefully acknowledge support for DUSTY from the U.S. Department of Education's Community Technology Centers Grants Program, the Community Technology Foundation of California, the University of California's U.C. Links Program, the Robert F. Bowne Foundation, and the City of Oakland's Fund for Children and Youth. We also thank our university and community partners: University of California Berkeley's Graduate School of Education, the Prescott-Joseph Center for Community Enhancement, Allen Temple Baptist Church, Cole Middle School, Castlemont High Schools, and St. Martin de Porres Middle School.

5. Similar to most organizations that offer digital storytelling, DUSTY traces its beginnings to Joe Lambert and Nina Mullen, who founded the Center for Digital Storytelling (CDS) in Berkeley, California. In fact, we began DUSTY with a donation of old computers from CDS (Lambert, 2002).

6. We are partnering with colleagues in India and South Africa to enable youth to exchange digital stories and digital music.

7. For an account of the theoretical framework on identity that underpins the project, see Hull and Katz (2004).

8. Admittedly, the process by which we came to our interpretation of "Lyfe-N-Rhyme" was not quite as systematically predetermined as our account of our methods might imply. We had no clear preexistent model to follow and as such, intuitively felt our way through much of the

analysis. To make it optimally useful and comprehensible to the reader, the procedure described here represents a somewhat cleaned up and pared down explication of the rather more iterative, recursive analytic method we actually applied.

9. By this choice of emphasis, we certainly do not mean to suggest that music and sound are unimportant or semiotically subordinate to the other modes. The musical component of "Lyfe-N-Rhyme" contributes undeniably and importantly to the emergent meaning of the whole, as music almost always does in the most evocative digital stories. It is simply the case that at this point in our own understanding of the entailments and implications of multimodal communication, we find that meaning in music and sound are comparatively more difficult to penetrate than language and image. Nonetheless, woven throughout the following paragraphs is a bit of music-related commentary, and we hope this limited discussion serves to round out our analysis somewhat, lopsided though it is in its privileging of language and image. For an excellent music- and sound-oriented treatment of multimodal communication, see van Leeuwen (1999).

10. There are many forms of digital storytelling, although the distinctions between the varieties are usually not articulated.

11. We used one other conceptual frame. Taking a cue from Saussure (1974), we examined the representational choices made along the paradigmatic axis, referring to the selections of multimodal conjunctions made to fill each half-second semantic slot. Then, we considered how these units operate syntagmatically (i.e., how the individual language-image pairings themselves are interrelated in various ways). Parenthetically, according to this scheme, we might say that this kind of analysis of multiple, copresent modalities requires the addition of a third axis to Saussure's original two, one we might call (only for the sake of preserving parallelism) the emblematic axis, describing the semiotic relationality between sequenced elements in different modal channels. One caveat about our analytic methods is that it is not remotely our intent to offer an example of the full elaboration of the complex frameworks of Saussure, Peirce (1992,1998), or Labov (1997). Rather, we simply and gratefully derive conceptual tools from the work of these scholars for purposes of elucidating only our specific concerns.

12. Randy wanted to reach a wider audience with his work, and in fact, he showed "Lyfe-N-Rhyme" and his other digital stories at a number of public events and forums. One of these was a conference held at the University of California–Berkeley in 2004, the National Council of Teachers of English Research Assembly. At a session featuring work done at DUSTY, Randy premiered a new digital story and answered questions from a rapt audience.

13. "Lyfe-N-Rhyme" can be viewed at http://www.youtube.com/watch?v=yfFg8zNkXZM.

14. The question may arise as to what the semiotic implications are of imputing title-like characteristics to recurrent word images. First and foremost, a title plays an explanatory and referential role in relation to the object with which it is directly associated. The thematic relation between the title and the object may be opaque, as is the case with many examples of work in the plastic arts, and so the referential function is foregrounded. However, the concept of title in the genre of story, the one that primarily concerns us here, calls for a fairly substantial relationality between title and object with regard to both the explanatory and the referential functions. After all, the number of books and popular films we encounter that bear titles wholly unrelated to their narrative content are few indeed. A second critical assumption is that the title refers to only one object. By way of example, if there were a universe in which the films *Jaws* and *Jaws 2* are both naturally called *Jaws*, it would doubtlessly be a confusing place to live. A third assumption, one that is germane only to sequentially organized textual genres, is that the title signals the beginning, that the main content is to follow. One could probably come up with several other postulates for defining titleness, but these three are sufficient to make the present point.

15. Biggie Smalls, also known as Notorious B.I.G., was violently murdered, as was Tupac Shakur. There is popular speculation that the two murders are connected, the product of a personal grudge and a larger East Coast–West Coast rivalry (Smalls was a New York-based artist, and Shakur was based in Los Angeles).

16. Of these four figures, Marcus Garvey was the only one not to be assassinated. He was, however, imprisoned and ultimately deported from the United States after being found guilty of mail fraud. Not long after his deportation, the Universal Negro Improvement Association, a once two-million-strong progressive organization founded by Garvey, virtually collapsed.

17. The "DAMN" presented at the end of the preceding series is one of the title-like word images that, as was previously suggested, segment or punctuate the piece, which begs a brief note of qualification. It may rightly impress the reader that the presentation of this expression at the end of the sequence contradicts the foregoing explanation of the nature of titles: that titles are meant to introduce what follows. So to not be inconsistent, we would remark that the placement of the title at the end of the string above is intended to illustrate and emphasize the boundedness of the

elements between the titles. So to the extent that each of these internal titles forms a boundary between subnarratives, it belongs to both the preceding language-image string and the one that follows. This is not a contradiction but a situational particularization, one might say, of the definition given above.

18. Although there is insufficient space in the text of this article to fully explicate multiple examples of subnarratives, the others are amply illustrated in Appendix B.

REFERENCES

Bennett, A. T. (1991). Discourses of power, the dialectics of understanding, the power of literacy. In C. Mitchell & K. Weiler (Eds.), *Rewriting literacy: Culture and the discourses of the other* (pp. 13–33). New York: Bergin & Garvey.

Bolter, J. (1991). *Writing space: The computer, hypertext, and the history of writing.* Hillsdale, NJ: Lawrence Erlbaum.

Cole, M., & Scribner, S. (1981). *The psychology of literacy.* Cambridge, MA: Harvard University Press.

Coles, R. (1997). *Doing documentary work.* New York: Oxford University Press.

Cook-Gumperz, J. (1986). Literacy and schooling: An unchanging equation? In J. Cook-Gumperz (Ed.), *The social construction of literacy* (pp. 16–44). Cambridge, UK: Cambridge University Press.

Cope, B., & Kalantzis, M. (Eds.). (2000). *Multiliteracies.* London: Routledge.

Delpit, L. (1995). *Other people's children.* New York: The New Press.

Design Based Research Collective. (2003). Design-based research: An emerging paradigm for educational inquiry. *Educational Researcher, 32*(1), 5–8.

Dipardo, A., & Schnack, P. (2004). Expanding the web of meaning: Thought and emotion in an intergenerational reading and writing program. *Reading Research Quarterly, 39*(1), 14–37.

Fairclough, N. (1992). *Discourse and social power.* London: Polity.

Fairclough, N. (1995). *Critical discourse analysis.* London: Longman.

Finnegan, R. (2002). *Communicating: The multiple modes of human interconnection.* London: Routledge.

Frith, S. (1992). The cultural study of popular music. In L. Grossberg, C. Nelson, & P. Treichler (Eds.), *Cultural studies* (pp. 174–186). New York: Routledge.

Gee, J. P. (2003). *What video games have to teach us about learning and literacy.* New York: Palgrave Macmillan.

Gibson, J. (1979). *The ecological approach to visual perception.* Boston: Houghton Mifflin.

Goffman, E. (1981). *Forms of talk.* Oxford, UK: Oxford University Press.

Haas, C. (1999). On the relationship between old and new technologies. *Computers and Composition, 16,* 209–228.

Hawisher, G., & Selfe, C. (Eds.). (2000). *Global literacies and the World-Wide Web.* London: Routledge.

Hudak, G. M. (1999). The "sound" identity: Music-making and schooling. In C. McCarthy, G. Hudak, S. Miklaucic, & P. Saukko (Eds.), *Sound identities: Popular music and the cultural politics of education* (pp. 447–474). New York: Lang.

Hull, G., & James, M. (in press). Geographies of hope: A study of urban landscapes and university-community collaborative. In P. O'Neill (Ed.), *Blurring boundaries: Developing writers, researchers, and teachers: A tribute to William L. Smith.*

Hull, G. A., & Katz, M.-L. (2004). *Crafting an agentive self: Case studies on digital storytelling.* Manuscript submitted for publication.

Knobel, M., & Lankshear, C. (2002, February). *Critical cyberliteracies: What young people can teach us about reading and writing the world.* Keynote address at the National Council of Teachers of English Research Assembly, New York.

Kress, G. (1997). *Before writing: Rethinking paths into literacy.* London: Routledge.

Kress, G. (1998). Visual and verbal modes of representation in electronically mediated communication: The potentials of new forms of text. In I. Snyder & M. Joyce (Eds.), *Page to screen: Taking literacy in the electronic era* (pp. 53–79). Sydney, Australia: Allen and Unwin.

Kress, G. (2003). *Literacy in the new media age.* London: Routledge.

Kress, G., & van Leeuwen, T. (1996). *Reading images: A grammar of visual design.* London: Routledge.

Kress, G., & van Leeuwen, T. (2001). *Multimodal discourse. The modes and media of contemporary communication.* London: Arnold.

Labov, W. (1997). Some further steps in narrative analysis. *Journal of Narrative and Life History, 7* (1–4), 395–415.

Lambert, J. (2002). *Digital storytelling: Capturing lives, creating community.* Berkeley, CA: Digital Diner.

Lemke, J. (1997). Multiplying meaning: Visual and verbal semiotics in scientific text. In J. Martin & R. Veel (Eds.), *Reading science* (pp. 87–113). London: Routledge.

Lemke, J. (1998). Metamedia literacy: Transforming meanings and media. In D. Reinking, M. McKenna, L. Labbo, & R. Kieffer (Eds.), *Handbook of literacy and technology: Transformations in a post-typographic world* (pp. 283–302). Hillsdale, NJ: Lawrence Erlbaum.

McLuhan, M. (1964). *Understanding media: The extensions of man*. New York: McGraw-Hill.

Mirzoeff, N. (1999). *An introduction to visual culture*. New York: Routledge.

Mitchell, W. J. T. (2004, April). *Sounding the idols*. Paper presented at the Conference on Visual Culture, University of California, Berkeley.

National Center for Education Statistics. (2003). *National assessment of adult literacy*. Retrieved September 14, 2004, from http://www.nces.ed.gov/naal/design/about02asp

National Commission on Writing for America's Families, Schools and Colleges. (2003). *The neglected "R": The need for a writing revolution*. Princeton, NJ: The College Board.

National Endowment for the Arts. (2004). *Reading at risk: A survey of literary reading in America*. Retrieved September 10, 2004, from http://www.nea.gov/pub/ReadingAtRisk.pdf

New London Group. (1996). A pedagogy of multiliteracies: Designing social futures. *Harvard Educational Review, 66*, 60–92.

Ochs, E., & Capps, L. (2001). *Living narratives: Creating lives in everyday storytelling*. Cambridge, UK: Cambridge University Press.

Peirce, C. (1992). *Selected philosophical writings, Vol. 1*. Bloomington: Indiana University Press.

Peirce, C. (1998). *Selected philosophical writings, Vol. 2*. Bloomington: Indiana University Press.

Rhomberg, C. (2004). *No there there: Race, class, and political community in Oakland*. Berkeley: University of California Press.

Saussure, F. de. (1974). *Course in general linguistics*. London: Peter Owen.

Shavelson, D. C., Phillips, L. T., & Feuer, M. J. (2003). On the science of education design studies. *Educational Researcher, 32*(1), 25–28.

Stanczak, G. (2004). Visual representation. *American Behavioral Scientist, 47*(12), 1471–1476.

Stein, P. (2004). Representation, rights, and resources: Multimodal pedagogies in the language and literacy classroom. In B. Norton & K. Toohey (Eds.), *Critical pedagogies and language learning* (pp. 95–115). Cambridge, UK: Cambridge University Press.

Street, B. (1984). *Literacy in theory and practice*. Cambridge, UK: Cambridge University Press.

Tufte, E. (1983). *The visual display of quantitative information*. Cheshire, CT: Graphics Press.

Tufte, E. (1990). *Envisioning information*. Cheshire, CT: Graphics Press.

Tufte, E. (1997). *Visual explanations: Images and quantities, evidence and narrative*. Cheshire, CT: Graphics Press.

van Leeuwen, T. (1999). *Speech, music, sound*. London: Macmillan.

Vygotsky, L. (1978). *Mind in society: The development of higher psychological processes*. Cambridge, MA: Harvard University Press.

Vygotsky, L. (1986). *Thought and language*. Cambridge, UK: Cambridge University Press. (Original work published 1934)

Witte, S. (1992). Context, text, intertext: Toward a constructivist semiotic of writing. *Written Communication, 9*, 237–308.

Witte, S. (1993). *Semiotics and writing*. Paper presented at an invited lecture at the University of Wisconsin–Madison.

27 Heritage Literacy: Adoption, Adaptation, and Alienation of Multimodal Literacy Tools

SUZANNE KESLER RUMSEY

My scheduled interview with Mary was on a hot afternoon in July.[1] Her family's property looked typical for Northern Indiana Amish in that it consisted of a white house without shutters or other exterior adornment, a white barn, and several outbuildings. A vegetable garden was visible, and an unhitched buggy was parked near the barn. When I drove into her driveway, I was surprised to find that Mary was mowing her lawn with a bulky, clunky, powered mower of some kind. The Amish I had known before this eschewed all forms of powered machinery.

My family purchases eggs from Mary, so I had asked for an interview some weeks previously. Mary invited me inside her home, which was relatively cooler, and we sat at her dining room table. As we began the interview, Mary's thirteen-year-old daughter, Elaine, joined us. Both women were dressed in plain, darkly colored cotton dresses without pattern or embellishment or even buttons, and they wore white coverings over their pinned up hair.

During the course of our conversation, Elaine interjected comments several times. She was freckled and friendly, and obviously comfortable with me, though I am what the Amish call "English," simply meaning "not Amish." Most Amish children with whom I had had contact during my data collections were shy of me as both an English person and a stranger. I wondered why Elaine was so comfortable with me. As we talked I found out that Elaine and her siblings attend the local public school instead of an Amish parochial school. Mary told me that she sends Elaine and her siblings to public school because "you have to learn to be out with the public too. I mean, if you are just among yourselves . . . you have to be able to communicate with other people too. How can they learn to communicate . . ." Here she stopped with a look of considerable frustration and said, "I can't think what I want to say." I gently teased her and asked if what she wants to say is in Dutch in her head (Pennsylvania Dutch is the German-based language that the Amish speak). She laughed in agreement.

From *College Composition and Communication* 62:1 (2010): 100–26.

At this point I asked Mary's permission to talk with Elaine, and Mary agreed. Elaine told me she is in the sixth grade at the local middle school and has two more years of schooling before she will graduate, as the Amish are only formally educated until the eighth grade. It is not hard to attend public school as an Amish youth, she said, and her friends know that she will finish school in eighth grade. She spoke openly and as articulately as any average sixth grader; her speech was punctuated with the occasional "like," a common filler word of her English peers, which was a marked contrast with her white covering and dark-colored dress.

I was particularly interested in how she adapts to public school as an Amish youth, so I asked her if there are things she does not participate in because she is Amish. She said she cannot participate in after-school activities because "I wouldn't have a way home since we don't drive." Elaine rides the bus to and from school, so she must abide by their scheduling. I asked if she avoids working on computers. Elaine replied, "No, I work on computers along with the other students. I think they are fun. We type papers sometimes and other stuff. I just do what everyone else does." Elaine then told me that she will not miss using a computer when she comes of age and joins the Amish church because "I don't know a lot about them."

Surprised at Elaine using computers, I asked Mary how she feels about computers, as a parent and someone who has joined the Amish church and has lived purposely without such technological innovations. She said, "Well, I don't know. I think maybe sometime they might need to use one for a job or something if they work out. That's why it's important." "Working out" here means to work outside of the Amish farm or home. I asked her if there are other technologies that make her nervous for her children. I note at this point that they have a gas-powered refrigerator and stove, but no electricity in the house, like other Northern Indiana Amish. Mary says. "There's stuff we wouldn't want them to have like a TV or phone. We have a phone booth just down the road that anybody can go use whenever they need it. I think that is enough for us." I note that she does not seem to mind my tape recorder either and is quite comfortable speaking with me during the entire interview.

Heritage Literacy

The anecdote I have described above is part of auto-ethnographic data collected in the summer of 2004 among four generations of my family and the surrounding Amish community. This anecdote describes several "types" of literacy. First, Elaine is engaged in mainstream academic literacy practices. She writes papers and reads texts that her English peers read and write. She has learned how to exist in an English academic setting though her family abides by the traditions of the Amish within her district of Northern Indiana. Second, Elaine is learning computer literacy to some extent. While she claims she does not know very much, she talks about word processing and doing the same activities as other students. And third, Elaine exhibits what Andrea Fishman calls Amish literacy, or the reading and writing of texts particularly associated with the Amish way of life and beliefs within their "immediate community," "larger community," "church community," and "school community" (40). Fishman's work specifically details reading the Bible, nonfiction books, and some fiction, and writing functional texts such as personal correspondence, business communication, labeling, and publication within these four communities. The anecdote implicitly positions Mary and Elaine within those communities; certainly by Fishman's definition, these women exhibit Amish literacy.

However, Elaine also exhibits a type of literacy I have come to call "heritage literacy." Heritage literacy is an explanation of how people transfer literacy knowledge from generation to generation and how certain practices, tools, and concepts are adapted, adopted, or alienated from use, depending on the context. It is lifelong, cross-generational learning and meaning making; it is developmental and recursive; and like all literacies, it builds over time or "accumulates," as Deborah Brandt phrased it in her article "Accumulating Literacy." Heritage literacy, then, describes how literacies and technology uses are accumulated across generations through a decision-making process. As literacy for an individual, community, or group accumulates, contexts, objects, tools, and needs change; in turn, community members adapt to the changes, adopt the changes, or alienate themselves from the changes. And then when these community members pass on their uses of technologies and tools, the next generation must make the same decisions.

This decision-making process is evident in the above anecdote. Mary is in the process of adapting to the idea of computer technologies, a technology and literacy tool traditionally avoided by the Amish, while her daughter Elaine is adopting computer use into her repertoire of literate activities. However, it is important to note that Elaine is not adopting computer literacy without altering it. She is adapting conventional computer usage by engaging with the technology only in limited ways while at school, only until the eighth grade, and only for utilitarian purposes of a job outside of her home in the future. Her use of this literacy tool—one that is becoming imperative to mainstream Americans' day-to-day lives—is mitigated by her religious beliefs and home literacy practices.

Heritage literacy is also multimodal. It accounts for the passage of all sorts of literate practices, not necessarily or exclusively print or alphabetic literacies. For example, Mary and Elaine are both dressed to signify their Amish beliefs and culture. They ascribe to a pattern, a set of signifying symbols, and are "read" as Amish by their choices of clothing, hairstyle, and head coverings. Heritage literacy emphasizes "codified sign systems," such as cuneiform, hieroglyph, or even quilts and manner of dress, as much as it emphasizes more traditional literacies. By emphasizing the multimodality of reading and writing, heritage literacy emphasizes embedded uses of technologies, the decision-making process explained above, and offers depth to our understanding of the impact of computer technologies.

Others within writing studies have offered examples of multimodal literacy practices passed between generations. Ellen Cushman states that bead working is knowledge making. It "codifies tradition, cultural practices, legends, ways of viewing self within world, clan and tribal affiliations, representational styles and so on, depending on its functional and rhetorical purpose" (Cushman, Loom module). Shirley Brice Heath writes that "[p]atterns of using reading and writing in [Roadville and Trackton] are interdependent with ways of using space (having bookshelves, decorating walls, displaying telephone numbers), and using time (bedtime, meal hours, and homework sessions)" (234). And Amish quilts, like Amish clothing, exhibit heritage literacy and multimodality because they are texts that Robert Shaw, an expert on quilts and folk art, says clearly represent "the Amish desire to remain apart from the distracting temptations and complexities of the 'English' world" (172). This desire for separation is seen in the "powerful visual rhythms" in solid-colored rather than printed fabrics and strong geometric patterns (171). These examples of heritage literacy practices show that multimodality need not take place on a computer screen. Instead they show multimodal meaning making quietly being beaded and stitched by hands in places far removed from computer technologies.

Let me unpack the concept of heritage literacy further. Heritage literacy stems from my desire to understand new tools' and technologies' impact on literacy learning and how these literacy practices are passed between generations. Indeed, Brandt's thoughtful explanation of "accumulating literacy" points to the ways that Americans are "having to piece together reading and writing experiences, from more and more spheres, creating new and hybrid forms of literacy" (651). She explains that literacy accumulates "in two directions—vertically (a piling up) and horizontally (a spreading out)" (652) and that "so many generations of literacy, so to speak, now occupy the same social space" (652).

I also desire to understand how cultures maintain traditional practices in the midst of such large-scale technological change. I can see the ways that the four generations of my own family have accumulated literacy, but our accumulation has not been a direct superseding of one form of literacy to another. Further, the concept of accumulation did not seem to explain how and why our Amish neighbors and relatives continue to eschew technological innovation. Essentially, Brandt's timely work offers the "what," and I suggest that heritage literacy offers the "how" and the "why." This article is an effort to explore this how and why of accumulating literacy over time and generations, within a specific population of people. In general, heritage literacy emphasizes not just the "piling up and spreading out" of accumulation; but also the ways that literacy practices pass back and forth between generations; the old inform the new, the new impact the old. Heritage literacy pays careful attention to the choices that individuals and communities make about their literacy development. Finally, heritage literacy, as it incorporates multimodal literacy practices, moves the emphasis of accumulation toward a broad set of sign technologies and systems.

By emphasizing the decision-making process of adoption, adaptation, or alienation from various literacy practices, heritage literacy shows the active involvement each person has with her own literacy development, though she may not even be conscious of that involvement. Choices about literacy and technology use, as noted above, are mitigated by one's community, faith, and family. As Juan Guerra puts it, "the change from an unreflective state of mind to a state of self-awareness is neither linear nor progressive" (26). His concept of "nomadic consciousness" emphasizes that no one ever achieves such a state of consciousness that she has no place else to go; in other words, Guerra points out that our awareness is always changing from critical to naive, or to nostalgic, or to contradictory (30). Generational passage of information and technology use (or consciousness) is not linear or steadfast. If this were the case, I would be suggesting a sort of autonomous or neutral view of literacy where the values, beliefs, and social practices of a culture are passed along without any real construction on the part of the learner. Instead, heritage literacy emphasizes that there is reinterpretation, questioning, and critiquing of literacy practices by each new generation, and that new generations impact older ones in a recursive way.

Heritage literacy builds on nomadic consciousness as it traces the changes and decisions people make about their literacy practices over time. In adopting, adapting, or alienating one's self from a literacy technology, changes also occur in consciousness. The uneven, changing, and negotiated understandings of one's world roughly parallel the ways that that person relates to literacy tools and technologies. For example, if a person moves from a critical consciousness to a nostalgic one where she remembers "the way things were," she may well re-adopt or adapt older forms of literacy technologies as a result. In this way, heritage literacy and Guerra's nomadic consciousness offer a way of conceptualizing reading and writing within cultures as an evolving thing.

Finally, heritage literacy shows interdependence between generations as the new generation depends on the old for their intellectual inheritances, and the old depends on the new for innovations and adaptations, as well as adoptions of literacy traditions. This interdependence is aptly illustrated among the generations of my family and the Amish community members in my research group, but heritage literacy is certainly not restricted to only those with Amish ancestry. Rather, this particular research group offers a unique perspective of multimodality and literacy technology use where one would least expect it to manifest. How much more so, then, are heritage literacy practices evident in different literacy technology uses outside of this community?

ANALYSIS

As a means of exploring heritage literacy further, let me offer another anecdote. This one comes from the four generations of my family who participated in the study. Cora (92) is my great-grandmother; Edna (71) is my grandmother; Lucy (50) is my mother; and Merry (24) is my sister. My great-grandmother was raised Amish and raised her family Amish until she left the church around age 40. My grandmother Edna was about 8 when the family left the Amish church community. The anecdote consists of a series of four images of quilts that exhibit the adoptions, adaptations, and alienations from literacies and technologies in the past generations of my family.

I use quilts as literacy artifacts because I believe that they exemplify multiple modes, which, according to Carey Jewitt and Gunther Kress, include "image, gaze, gesture, movement, music, speech and sound-effect" (1) as well as pattern, texture, and color. Each of these modes is "equally significant for meaning and communication" (2). If literacy, as I noted above, is a "codified sign system," then quilts offer a type of pattern or system of signs that make meaning much as an alphabet, alpha-numeric coding, hieroglyph, or cuneiform might.

Perhaps the easiest way to understand this argument is to look at traditional African American narrative quilts. These quilts used patterns and appliquéd pictures to convey stories, moral lessons, and political stances. Olga Idriss Davis, a researcher of black rhetoric and narrative, writes that the rhetoric in African American quilts "points to the legacy of a people struggling for symbols of expression through pieces of cloth and a myriad of colors. The quilt uncovers the choice of symbols black women used within their community to create a shared, common meaning of self and the world" (67). Davis's quote makes plain that the choices of color, pattern, image, symbol, and even cloth signify and make meaning, just as letters on a page signify and make meaning.

Figure 27-1 is a close-up of my grandmother Edna's quilt. Though I have distinct memories of napping under this quilt as a child and wrestling with my siblings on its surface, currently the quilt hangs in a room of my parents' home that we call "Grammy's Room" because it has been decorated with her in mind. The quilt was pieced by my great-grandmother (Cora) and then

FIGURE 27-1   Edna's quilt.

FIGURE 27-2   Lucy's quilt.

hand quilted by all of my grandmother's aunts, her mother, and her grand-
mothers. The pattern is called "Drunkard's Path," which apparently my grandmother was not very happy about at the time the quilt was made.[2] The pattern
title is also ironic, given that most of the women quilting it were Amish.

Figure 27-2 is of my mother's quilt. It was made around 1975 and pieced
by my great-great-grandmother Katie. All the female family members on that
side of the family helped to quilt it, including my great-grandmother (Cora)
and her sisters, my grandmother (Edna) and her sisters, and many women
from my mother's paternal relatives. My mom told me that she herself put a
few stitches in it. The quilt currently hangs in another room of my parents'
home; however, it has never been used as anything but decoration. My mom
told me that she almost got rid of the quilt many years before my research
began because she did not like the colors. She only kept it because so many of
her family members had helped create it.

These two quilts signify several things. First, the color schemes and patterns connote Amish identity; the Amish use only solid-color fabrics in bold
geometric designs for their own quilts, although they use patterned fabrics
when the quilts are intended for English patrons or friends. The plainness of
the fabrics is a reflection of the Amish desire to remain apart from worldly
things and modern trappings, much as Mary and Elaine's plain clothing signifies their Amish beliefs and culture. There is symmetry in each pattern as
well, perhaps showing the Amish affinity for order. Though no alphabetic
symbols are represented here, the quilt has been "written" by multiple hands
and carries a message.

Adoption of Amish identity and their literacy practice of quilt making has played out strongly between these two quilts. At the time my grandmother's quilt was made, my great-grandmother had left the Amish church, so my grandmother was no longer Amish either. It is interesting that her relatives would make her a quilt signifying Amish identity when she no longer was a part of the community. Similarly, my mother was not Amish, nor had she ever been, but her family ties were enough for the creation of a traditional quilt. Few adaptations in tool use have been made from one quilt to the next. Because both quilts were pieced by Amish women, they were presumably sewn on a treadle sewing machine. Both are hand quilted using needle and thread. While many English quilters have turned to machine quilting to mechanize this process, for the Amish in my study and for the oldest members of my family, to adopt such technologies would violate the basic underpinnings of their identity.

The next quilt in my analysis has images of the 1980s cartoon character Strawberry Shortcake. No one in my family has the blanket, so a description will have to suffice. When my sister and I were young, my mother, grandmother, and great-grandmother made us matching comforters with themed fabric of the Strawberry Shortcake character. A comforter is distinguishable from a quilt because it is "tied" or "knotted" with yarn at six-inch intervals over the surface rather than quilted with tiny hand stitches. Also, a comforter is usually made with a single fabric on its top, instead of a pieced design.

My sister and I were "children of the 1980s," and this is reflected in the appearance of these comforters; we, like many girls, partook of the fad surrounding the red-haired young girl character named Strawberry Shortcake. Instead of purchasing expensive themed bedding, my mother frugally purchased only the themed flat sheets and batting to make into comforters. My sister had the Holly Hobbie character on the back of her comforter, and I had a hand-me-down Star Wars sheet from my older brother on the back.

The adaptations of the Amish literacy practice of quilting are evident in this comforter. First, we had comforters, rather than pieced quilts. Second, those comforters were knotted rather than quilted. Third, instead of solid-colored fabric and geometric designs, we had pop culture cartoon-themed designs. And fourth, any sewing that was needed to create these comforters was done on an electric-powered sewing machine.

What is not as evident is how much of the Amish literacy practice of quilting that we *did* adopt. First, the tradition of creating blankets with layers of fabric and batting is present. Second, the act of gathering together and collaborating to finish a blanket is present as my great-grandmother, grandmother, mother, sister, and I all participated in knotting. Third, the comforter signifies identity, though that identity is no longer Amish per se. My immediate family had no real connection to the Amish culture when I grew up, even though our ancestors and heritage come from the Amish. Hence, the messages constructed within this blanket aligned us more with mainstream culture and ideals.

The final image in Figure 27-3 is a screenshot of a digital movie I created several years ago.[3] I used Adobe Premier to create the piece using still images,

FIGURE 27-3   Screenshot of digital video.

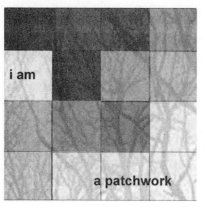

transparency filters, and basic timed transitions to merge image, motion, and text. The piece is silent in an attempt at the "plainness" that Amish strive for. It explores identity, specifically my Amish heritage.

This adaptation shows a quilt that is not at all traditional as it is not a blanket of any sort and lacks the functionality of the previous three examples. In a way, it is an alienation from the traditions of quilt making, albeit with a respectful nod in that direction, because it lacks a blanket's functionality. It shows a further adaptation of quilting-as-literacy practice by using "modern" tools—the computer. There are, however, adoptions of traditional tools and practices present as well. The movie uses layers, much as a quilted blanket is layered. The movie makes meaning with color, pattern, and texture, like any of the blankets. And the movie signifies identity, overtly because of the text and implied in my use of Amish-inspired solid colors.

My point is simply that these four illustrations exhibit heritage literacy "in action" within one family. By viewing them in succession, the decision-making process about which literacies and tools to adopt, adapt, or alienate ourselves from is apparent. However, I chose these four examples knowing that they could help illustrate two other defining features of heritage literacy: multimodality on and off the computer screen and home-based literacy learning.

MULTIMODALITY AND HOME-BASED LITERACY

Even in its current monomodal state, the digital movie screen shot exhibits multimodality. It depicts several media and modes interacting for meaning making: text, pattern, color (media) and visual, image, and spatial modes. In its movie form, sound effect (or the lack thereof), movement, and gesture add to the overall message. However, in a break from current trends in writing studies that focus exclusively on computer-mediated design (see, for example, Jewitt and Kress), I argue that the quilts are equally multimodal. Quilts, like the digital movie, use multiple media and modes such as texture, movement, pattern, and color to make meaning. Note also that both the quilts and the movie are *digital*; both were made with hands and fingers, or *digits*. While no one would argue that a quilt lacks the other defining features of digital writing—e.g., "writing produced on handheld and desktop digital devices and distributed primarily via wireless and wired networks" (DigiRhet 238)— I argue here that a quilt is indeed *multimodal*. Hence, the multimodality of heritage literacy is passed between generations and manifests within a variety of products, from quilts to computer-mediated texts, and each generation makes decisions about which tools and literacies they will use and to what extent.

Indirectly, the above illustration points to the ways that heritage literacy takes place outside of school settings; traditions and literacy practices such as quilting are passed on within family units and often without the direct instruction of a school-like atmosphere. Such a concept is not new, as such researchers as Ann Ruggles Gere and Marcia Farr have explored extracurriculum and *compadrazgo and lirico* respectively; however, heritage literacy sheds new light on those moments of literacy learning and teaching that are embedded in indigenous home-based practices.

Gere's extracurriculum broadens the scope of what is included in a definition of writing instruction outside academe; her work depicts types of writing workshops that "uncouple literacy and schooling" (279). Her examples of the Lansing, Iowa, Writers' Workshop and the Tenderloin Women's Writing Workshop show thoughtful examples of people learning to write outside of school walls. The structure, timing, and focus of the workshops do resemble literacy learning within schools, but they are peer directed and without the state-mandated curriculum of school.

Heritage literacy, like extracurriculum, is literacy learning outside of school walls. In a continuation of Gere's work, heritage literacy highlights those practices that are unstructured and lacking even a modicum of typical school-like learning. The quilting illustrated above is learned by trial and error, in large groups of multigenerational women. Similarly, recipes and cooking are heritage literacy practices learned not by explicit cooking instruction offered to young cooks but by unstructured observation and modeling. Such a means of "instruction" demarcates these events and practices from a school setting and stand in contrast to current composition pedagogies.

Farr offers a similar concept addressing learning outside of school walls called *lirico*. Farr writes that a number of her participants "learned literacy *lirico*; that is, they 'picked it up' informally from others who used only spoken language—not printed materials—to pass on knowledge of the writing system" (470). Farr later states that although "formal schooling is the route to literacy for many people, schooling is clearly not essential" (474). Clearly the concept of heritage literacy mirrors Farr's work; it then builds upon it by exploring multimodal literacies learned *lirico*.

Further, heritage literacy mirrors Farr's concept of *compadrazgo* in which literacy is learned outside of school through social networks and used in religious, commercial, civic, and educational "domains" or contexts. "*Compadrazgo* refers to the Mexican system of godparent-like relationships that function as a reciprocal exchange network to facilitate economic survival and provide emotional and social support" (468). Essentially, *compadrazgo* is an intergenerational network of social and emotional support where surrogate relatives help pass on traditions and values. I believe that *compadrazgo* would be an interesting concept and site of future research in heritage literacy research to explore the generational literacy practices that exist outside of immediate family members or in a wider community base than the one I studied.

Other sites for future research in heritage literacy exist in studying other cultures' or communities' generational literacy traditions. The Amish were a significant community for me to begin with because of my familial connection with them and because they exhibit multimodality where one would least expect to find it; however, heritage literacy applies to all communities and cultures. Finally, heritage literacy, because it offers an alternate understanding of multimodal literacy, suggests that the current trends toward lauding computer-mediated literacy should be put in check. A broader understanding of technological literacy is needed in which there is balance between the new and the old, between modernity and heritage, and between digital and cultural.

NOTES

1. Community participants have been given pseudonyms.
2. The pattern "Drunkard's Path" has been applied to a variety of quilt blocks, many of which look very little like this one.
3. The movie is available for viewing at my website: <http://users.ipfw.edu/rumseys/>.

WORKS CITED

Brandt, Deborah. "Accumulating Literacy: Writing and Leaning to Write in the Twentieth Century." *College English* 57.6 (1995): 649–68.
Cushman, Ellen. "Toward a Rhetoric of New Media: Composing (Me)dia." *Computers and Composition Online* Spring 2004. July 2007 <http://www.msu.edu/~cushmane/newmedia/identity/metis.html>.
Davis, Olga Idriss. "The Rhetoric of Quilting: Creating Identity in African-American Children's Literature." *African American Review* 32 (1998): 67–76.
DigiRhet.org. "Teaching Digital Rhetoric: Community, Critical Engagement, and Application." *Pedagogy* 6.2 (2006): 231–60.
Farr, Marcia. "*En Los Dos Idiomas*: Literacy Practices among Chicago Mexicanos." *Literacy: A Critical Sourcebook*. Ed. Ellen Cushman, Eugene R. Kintgen, Barry M. Kroll, and Mike Rose. Boston: Bedford/St. Martin's, 2001. 467–87.
Fishman, Andrea. *Amish Literacy: What and How It Means*. Portsmouth, NH: Heinemann, 1988.
Gere, Anne Ruggles. "Kitchen Tables and Rented Rooms: The Extracurriculum of Composition." *Literacy: A Critical Sourcebook*. Ed. Ellen Cushman, Eugene R. Kintgen, Barry M. Kroll, and Mike Rose. Boston: Bedford/St. Martin's, 2001. 275–89.
Guerra, Juan. "Putting Literacy in Its Place: Nomadic Consciousness and the Practice of Transcultural Repositioning." *Rebellious Reading: The Dynamic of Chicana/o Cultural Literacy*. Ed. Carl Gutierrez-Jones. Santa Barbara: Center for Chicana/o Studies, U of California, Santa Barbara, 2004. 19–37.
Heath, Shirley Brice. *Ways with Words: Language, Life and Wok in Communities and Classrooms*. Cambridge: U of Cambridge P, 1983.
Jewitt, Carey, and Gunther Kress, eds. *Multimodal Literacy*. New York: Peter Lang, 2003.
Shaw, Robert. "Amish Quilts." *Quilts: A Living Tradition*. Westport, CT: Hugh Lauter Levin, 1995.

28 Composition 2.0: Toward a Multilingual and Multimodal Framework

STEVEN FRAIBERG

I exit my apartment in Tel Aviv and cross Kikar Rabin, the city center where the late prime minister Yitzhak Rabin was shot and the square where endless gatherings and demonstrations take place on what seems to be a weekly basis. As I continue down the street, I see the phrase "know hope" spray-painted on a wall, reflecting the ambiguity and uncertainty of the political situation, one that shifts between "no hope" and "knowing hope." Along the way, I see other evidence of the ways that English is woven into the fabric of everyday life in Israel: graffiti on the walls, storefront signs, printed slogans on T-shirts, and finally the sign of the Internet design company sponsoring my research, Networld, posted above a row of mail boxes.[1] Walking up the three levels to the entrance of this company, I find a converted apartment that houses approximately thirty programmers, graphic designers, and managers. It is a Sunday morning, the beginning of the work week in Israel, and workers at the company are busily engaged in meeting deadlines to complete Web applications and websites for high-tech start-up companies and many of the leading firms in the Israeli high-tech industry. The company itself is bustling with activity and sound, as people wheel in and out of rooms, telling jokes and shouting. Directly across the street is the *shook*, or open market, where one can hear the shouting of vendors yelling *"xamesh shekel le kilo le toot"* ("five shekels for a kilo of strawberries"). Networld, however, is aiming for a very different market. In this article, I wish to examine the mixing of these official and unofficial spaces and the ways English is woven into these contexts. This work is a response to calls in composition for developing a perspective capable of understanding the teaching of English writing within the context of other languages and globalization (Horner and Trimbur). Contributing to this area, scholars have argued for multilingual writing as design (Lu; New London Group, see p. 193 in this volume), code meshing (Canagarajah, "Subversive"), and understanding literacy practices as shaped by and shaping a constellation of historical, economic, social, and ideological factors called "cultural ecologies" (Hawisher and Selfe). In this study, I map out the ways these cultural

From *College Composition and Communication* 62:1 (2010): 100–26.

ecologies operate in situated activities by drawing on examples from six months of ethnographic research in Israeli society. Through the situated study of multilingual and multimodal literacy practices, I argue that this multilingual-multimodal framework is a key for moving our research and teaching into the twenty-first century.

REMIXING COMPOSITION: MASHING MULTILINGUALISM AND MULTIMODALITY

Reimagining writing studies within national and global contexts, Bruce Horner and John Trimbur call for an integration of ESL, composition, and other language instruction. This remixing of the disciplines is key for moving composition and rhetoric into the twenty-first century, in which we find ourselves with an increasingly heterogeneous student body for whom traditional categories of second language do not neatly fit. This is evidenced by the increasing number of generation 1.5 students (Harklau, Losey, and Siegal) who are "in between worlds" (Chiang and Schmida), a phenomenon pointing to the complex, dynamic, heterogeneous, and emergent nature of cultural and linguistic identities. Despite this growing diversity, scholars argue that the field has yet to embrace multilingualism because of a tacit monolingual policy (Horner and Trimbur) and "myth of linguistic homogeneity" (Matsuda, "Myth" 638) that has undergirded much of composition scholarship and teaching. Furthermore, Horner, Trimbur, and Matsuda ("Composition Studies") have traced the historical factors shaping this social formation and the resultant disciplinary split between composition, ESL, and other language instruction. The multilingual and multimodal framework mapped out in this special issue is a move toward bridging this disciplinary divide.

Crossing these disciplinary, linguistic, and geographic boundaries, this work draws on and extends Suresh Canagarajah's essay "The Place of World Englishes in Composition: Pluralization Continued." In this essay, he shifts from code switching and code mixing to what he refers to as code meshing (see also Young). This concept merges world Englishes with African American and Latino rhetorics, bringing together Ben Rampton's notion of *crossing* and Geneva Smitherman's *crossover*, as a strategy for writers to mesh their own native language with the dominant discourse (in this case standard English).[2] Picking up where Canagarajah leaves off, I call for attention to "code mashing," or the complex blending of multimodal and multilingual texts and literacy practices in our teaching and research. This move is aligned with recent shifts in world Englishes by Alastair Pennycook and other scholars (see also Alim, Ibrahim, and Pennycook) who examine global hip-hop to argue for attention to transcultural flows with a focus on *fluidity* and *fixity* or the ways "cultural forms produce new forms of localization, and the use of global Englishes produces new forms of identification" (Pennycook 7). As part of this broader framework, multilingualism is one resource in a more complex semiotic repertoire distributed across local and global contexts. This move furthermore intersects with research on multimodality in which scholars have argued for a broader definition of writing as design (New London Group, p. 193; Kress and Van Leeuwen). Within composition, these calls for a more inclusive framework (Selfe, "Aurality"; Yancey, p. 62) incorporate image (George, p. 211), aurality (Halbritter; Selfe, "Aurality"), gesture (Prior et al.; Wolfe), and even smells and tastes (Shipka). The aim of this broader approach, as Cynthia Selfe articulates, is to increase the bandwidth of semiotic resources for communication in order to make available all means of persuasion.

To date, however, there have been few situated studies of multilingual or multimodal composing. Within digital writing research, for example, a range of scholarship exists on multimodality and technology, yet only recently is there work emerging on the production, distribution, mediation, and reception of multimodal texts (beyond interpretive and hermeneutic analyses). Moving toward a practice-based framework are studies of the ways digital youth *use* new communications technologies (Alexander, "Digital"), text messaging practices in national and international contexts (Lee; Ito; Sun), and in situ observations of multimodal composing (remixing) with attention to jointly mediated activity (Johnson-Eilola; Prior, "Remaking"; Slattery; Spinuzzi; Swarts). In the area of Internet and communication studies, a work by Mizuko Ito, Daisuke Okabe, and Misa Matsuda and another work by Ito et al. further take up an ethnographic approach to examine the ways that social dynamics in spaces such as schools, families, and public transportation are co-constituted by new media. Despite such moves, rich, longitudinal accounts tracing the construction of multimodal texts—mediated by an array of texts, tools, actors, and spaces—remain scarce.

Turning to the area of world Englishes—as well as anthropological linguistics, sociolinguistics, and applied linguistics—the field as a whole remains predominantly focused on talk. Additionally, most of the work on writing focuses on the product as opposed to process. The subset of studies that in fact focuses on process furthermore tends to take a quantitative and cognitive approach as opposed to a situated stance that locates the production, distribution, and reception of texts in wider social, political, cultural, and national contexts. In the area of English as a Second Language, Guadalupe Valdés wrote in 1992 that there were as of yet few studies examining multilingual composing. The same holds true today as Dwight Atkinson and Ulla Connor concur, noting the dearth of studies on situated composing: "Yet it must be admitted that research on multilingual writing development has traditionally been rather limited" (515). Taking up this point, Canagarajah ("Toward") argues that traditional static and bounded models of multilingual writing have focused on the product rather than on the process. Arguing instead for a less bounded and dynamic understanding of language, he proposes a process-oriented approach that conceptualizes the writer as strategically and creatively negotiating or "shuttling between discourses." It is to this issue that I now turn and in so doing argue that the field of rhetoric and composition needs to turn in the twenty-first century.

TOWARD A SITUATED FRAMEWORK OF MULTILINGUAL-MULTIMODAL COMPOSING

As I proceed to map out an alternative theoretical and methodological framework, it is useful to consider how the enterprise of language studies is bound up in the construction of the nation state. As Monica Heller articulates, "If we understand, organize, and draw on those resources as belonging to whole, bounded systems we call 'languages', it is because that notion makes sense in the context of the ways language has been bound up in ideologies of nation and state since the nineteenth century" (2). It is only recently with the onset of globalization and the reorganization of space and time that we are seeing shifts in this bounded philosophy to language studies: "Now that conditions are changing, it is possible to challenge the hegemony of that view, and to offer another one better able to account of the ways speakers are drawing on their resources at a time when boundaries are often deliberately played with" (Heller, 2). In the area of globalization studies, we find a variety of metaphors reflecting this less-bounded approach: global flows or mobilities (Lash and Urry); the global mélange (Pieterse); the network (Castells), and deeply disjunctive scapes (Appadurai). The theoretical and methodological framework articulated in this article offers a way to examine how these flows or scapes are co-constituted in everyday reading, writing, speaking, and design practices. In making this move, this framework "mashes" research in multilingualism and multimodality from North American genre theory, sociocultural studies, activity theory, linguistic anthropology, mediated discourse analysis, new media, and literacy studies. These disciplinary border crossings are key to remixing composition in the context of globalization. Mapping out a less-bounded approach—conceptualizing language as situated, dynamic, heterogeneous, co-constitutive, and contested—this theoretical and methodological framework integrates four analytically separate but deeply interwoven concepts that are described below.

Ecologies

In composition, Kristie Fleckenstein, Clay Spinuzzi, Rebecca Rickly, and Carole Clark Papper have called for an ecological approach for our teaching and research. In this manner, we might understand language as circulating in complex institutional, information, genre, cultural, and global ecologies. Discussing the manner in which literacy practices are deeply situated within complex cultural ecologies, Hawisher and Selfe argue:

> In both global and local contexts the relationships among digital technologies, language, literacy, and an array of opportunities are complexly structured and articulated within a constellation of existing social, cultural, economic, historical, and ideological factors that constitute a cultural ecology of literacy. These ecological systems continually shape, and are shaped by people (Giddens)—at a variety of levels and in a range of ways—as they live out their daily lives in technological and cultural settings. (619)

The study of literacy practices, then, requires attention to the ways they are deeply woven into a constellation of factors. These ecologies are always a "site of contestation between emerging, competing, changing, accumulating, and fading languages and literacies" (629). Within rhetoric and composition, there have been a number of closely related concepts for studying the ways that these constellations of factors shape and are shaped by everyday mundane and routine literate practices. Perhaps most closely aligned is Clay Spinuzzi's concept of genre ecologies.[3] This concept is an extension of genre sets (Devitt), genre systems (Bazerman, "Systems"), and genre repertoires (Orlikowski and Yates). For instance, one might observe the ways classroom activity is jointly coordinated by student laptops, whiteboards, notepads, textbooks, and assignment sheets.[4] While Spinuzzi was referring primarily to durable texts within institutional contexts, we might further examine the ways nondurable and evanescent texts are also part of these genre ecologies, such as the classroom genre Initiation-Respond-Evaluate (IRE), in which the teacher initiates a question, the students respond, and the teacher evaluates. It is important to emphasize that such structures are not conceived of as static or bounded, but as "stabilized for now" (Schryer) or fluid, fuzzy, dynamic, and dialogic. It is within these fluid typifications that we can examine the compound mediation (Spinuzzi) of multilingual texts. By further mapping on Hawisher and Selfe's concept of cultural ecologies, we can complicate this analysis through closer attention to the blending of constellations of wider historical, social, cultural, national, and global factors.

Knotworking

The second concept is the notion of knotworking (Engeström, Engeström, and Vähääho) or the continual tying and untying of genres, objects, texts, and people. This is the process through which ecologies are co-constituted, improvised, shaped, and re-formed. As Fleckenstein et al. argue, the ecological metaphor imagines writing as a web of interlocking social, material, and semiotic relationships and practices conceptualized as clusters or "knots" (394). This framework is key for studying literacy practices as the "*knotty* nature of such interdiscursive complexity is what we must seek to understand" (Irvine, "Commentary" 72; emphasis added). To illustrate with an example from a high-tech workplace, for instance, we might examine how the sketch of a sticky note mediates a conversation in Hebrew and then how this sticky note is passed to a graphic designer who uses it as part of a new "knot" to design an image in conjunction with a graphic design program (with an English interface). These knots, furthermore, shape the fluid and fuzzy pathways shaping the circulation of discourse, the alignments and positioning, participant roles, and topics taken up for discussion. These institutional spheres are furthermore knotted into wider cultural, national, and global spheres in a continual process of tying and untying.

Remediation

The third concept, Jay David Bolter and Richard Grusin's concept of remediation, is key for understanding the ways that texts circulate across the fluid, fuzzy pathways constituted through knotworking.[5] Remediation is the notion that each medium is refashioned from an already existing medium. While Bolter and Grusin's concept is primarily focused on repurposing or transformations across media, Prior et al. argue the concept is applicable to all semiotic modes (gesture, image, gaze, talk, writing) in the context of situated practices. They introduce the term *semiotic remediation*, a concept that moves beyond an understanding of the ways that writing is coordinated with other semiotic systems to a fully dialogic understanding of all semiotic modes. In practice, for instance, one might look at the ways text on a Web page (in English) is taken up in a conversation (in Hebrew), and then how elements of this conversation are remediated into written notes (in English) and finally stretch into longer chains of remediation. Across a range of disciplines, there have been numerous closely related concepts that have been used to capture the key dimensions of this phenomena: reported speech (Voloshinov), double voicing (Bakhtin), antecedent genre (Jamieson), shadow conversations (Irvine, "Shadow"), resemiotization (Iedema), constructed dialogue (Tannen), and entextualization (Duranti and Goodwin).

Actant-Network Theory

The fourth concept, Bruno Latour's actant-network theory, erases the binary between objects and people; together the tools and individuals make up what he calls a third agent, as individuals shape the tools, and in turn the tools shape the individuals. This move expands our notion of conversation; human actors are no longer in dialogue only with one another, but also with other texts and tools. In this manner, we might understand students and teachers as engaged in a (multilingual) dialogue with textbooks, Web pages, assignment sheets, conversations inside and outside classroom, and so forth. Each of these texts and objects is imbued with "affordances" that shape and are shaped by their uptake. Taking a cue from David Russell, who argues for an understanding of objects-as-genres, we might extend genre theory to understand all objects as stabilized-for-now (Schryer) "forms of life" shaping and shaped by everyday interaction. Space, then, is not a static backdrop or stage against which activity takes place, but is co-constituted by the participants and deeply bound up in a process of (re)mediation.

In sum, these four analytic perspectives provide a framework for examining the links between structure and agency (Giddens), or the ways that situated practices shape and are shaped by wider sociocultural contexts. Attending to the process of knotworking, the complex tying and untying of tools (images, symbols, tropes, ideologies, written inscriptions, desks, whiteboards, computer screens, cell phones) and people, we can map out the processes shaping and shaped by the multilingual and multimodal flows (remediation) of discourse (broadly defined) over space and time. This continual tying and untying is an ongoing site of struggle as individuals act on the tools and tools act on the individuals, shaping the alignments and positionings of the actors (or, in Latour's terms, *actants*) in an ongoing negotiation. Multilingual and multimodal literacy practices are deeply bound up in this process. Remixing composition for the twenty-first century requires a shift toward conceptualizing writers as "knotworkers" negotiating complex arrays of languages, texts, tools, objects, symbols, and tropes.[6]

MULTILINGUAL AND MULTIMODAL COMPOSING AT A HIGH-TECH COMPANY

The term *convergence culture* from media theorist Henry Jenkins characterizes how "flow of content across multiple media platforms" collides, intersects, crisscrosses, and interacts "in unpredictable ways" (2). The Israeli high-tech sector is a key site for studying the convergence(s) of semiotic, technological, cultural, national, and global forces.[7] Over the past twenty years in Israel, there has been a rapid growth in the high-tech industry, which currently has more start-up companies (three thousand) than any other place in the world other than the United States (Morgenstern). Resulting from this rapid growth has been a transformation in the economic and social landscape of Israeli society, as it moves from the socialist ideals of the kibbutz to a capitalist system based on globalized high-tech industries. Accompanying these shifts has been a move from Hebrew as the dominant language to a situation in which English is commonplace in many domains. Locating the shifts (from an emic perspective) in a historical context, Israel itself was founded based on the socialist and nineteenth-century Zionist movements to establish the state. Whereas once the kibbutzniks and farmers were pioneers settling the land, it is now high-tech workers who are the "pioneers" and helping to put Israel on the twenty-first-century map. In traditional stories of Israeli history, the trope of David and Goliath is commonly invoked, with a smaller, less-equipped Israeli army overcoming overwhelming forces and odds.[8] Now it is the Israeli high-tech entrepreneurs who are characterized as the national heroes overcoming great economic forces. Whereas once the small, elite commando unit was the symbol of Israeli know-how and capability, it is now the Israeli "high-tech warriors" who are characterized as the units on the front line of the global economy, so to speak. Indeed, to locate the links between high-tech and the military, one does not have to look far. In perhaps one of the most well-known start-up success stories, a software security company called Checkpoint was started by two friends from military intelligence. In the late 1990s, Checkpoint became the highest-traded company on the NASDAQ. Significantly, the name itself not only refers to software security but also indexes the checkpoints set up all along Israel's borders. The linguistic borders in Israeli society are also being infiltrated by English, as indicated by the name of the company, which targets a global market in which English is the lingua franca.

These tropes and national narratives are part of wider cultural ecologies that are deeply "knotted" (converge) into the rhetorics of Israeli high-tech industry as evident on the website at the high-tech design firm Networld.[9] For example, on the Web page is a start-up company depicted as a commando unit. In this representation, however, the instruments of military power have been replaced with a pencil, megaphone, and wrench. A wrench is a particularly telling symbol as it suggests a garage mechanic using "low tech" tools and resonates with stories of Steve Jobs developing the first Apple computer in the back of the family garage. These narratives are deeply bound up in the ethos of the Israeli high-tech community, as is evident at the gatherings of the high-tech technorati located at an industrial center in Holon, Israel, at a group called Garage Geeks. One can also see additional "mashing" in the Hebrew text, and one key term that I wish to foreground in this analysis is the word *megeyes*, which is both the word for the recruitment of employees and the drafting of soldiers for the military. Finally, we can see the ways that English is blended into the Web page with the company slogan and heading "Start Up On Demand" foregrounded at the top of the page similar to the ways that English is foregrounded in the work at these companies. Other English phrases and buzzwords are woven into the text as well, such as "one stop shop," similar to the ways these phrases are often woven into workplace activities.

The fact that Hebrew and English are read from opposite directions might be seen as a "contact zone" (Pratt), and on the website one can see the two languages themselves bumping up against each other. This website further indexes other points of contact as suggested by a national narrative (indexed by the soldiers) that marginalizes Palestinians, Arab Israelis, and other sectors of society. Examining how such multilingual-multimodal assemblages are re-articulated "through fluid, contested, and contingent social forces in local situations" (Johnson-Eilola and Selber) is key to moving composition and rhetoric into the twenty-first century. This "mixing and matching" (Alexander, "Media" 2) challenges the nature of reading and writing and points to the need for rearticulating our teaching, research, and administration. In fact, scholars have recently argued for remix (Johnson-Eilola and Selber; Yancey) as a key metaphor for reimagining the field. Yet such work poses serious challenges for those of us who are not fluent in another language or culture, and indeed my own mastery of Hebrew has been an ongoing struggle. My reading of this website, for instance, includes consultation with two native Hebrew speakers, the academic literature in anthropology and Israeli studies, and triangulation with ethnographic data gathered from field work in the high-tech industry and a range of other contexts. I would argue, however, that this cross-cultural and cross-disciplinary engagement is key to forming new disciplinary "knotworks" necessary for moving our understanding of literacy practices beyond North American contexts. Attention to this process also suggests the need for composition and rhetoric programs to more strongly emphasize learning world languages.

Even without our being fluent in another language, however, there is much that we can do in our own teaching and research to integrate multilingual-multimodal texts and textual practices, including partnering with speakers of other languages in local and global contexts. Forming partnerships also means working closely with multilingual writers in our classrooms. We might, for instance, integrate multilingual-multimodal texts into our assignments by seeking out assistance from native speakers of other languages to perform rhetorical and situated analyses of everything from cereal boxes to street signs. Incorporating our students' multilingualism into the classroom could help move them from deficit positions by (re)locating them as experts in their own language with knowledge and experience that they can share and contribute to the class. This shift also means moving beyond the linguistic signs and attending to the ways that all semiotic modes coordinate literate activity and are dialogic in their own right. In terms of image, for instance, we might move from Bakhtin's concept of "double voicing" to "double vision," by examining the ways that images are always constructed in response to other images and texts, such as the image of the military commando unit on the homepage of Networld in response to wider social, cultural, and national contexts.

In addition to locating multilingual-multimodal texts in broader historical contexts that circulate within cultural ecologies, it is important to examine the production, distribution, and reception of these texts in everyday literacy practices. In order to map out this phenomenon, I sketch out a portrait of the literacy practices of a key informant, Barak, who was one of the owners of the company Networld. Raymond Williams writes that each nation has key words that serve as conceptual metaphors deeply rooted in each individual society. One key word that serves to describe the Israeli character is the metaphor of networking. Israel is a tightly knit society that is based on close networks of people, and this characteristic was evident in Barak's continual cultivation of side projects and connections (including his partnership with me). As he reflected at one of a seemingly endless series of high-tech networking functions, *"ha yisralim yodim* networking" ("the Israelis know how to network"). Indeed, Barak was part of a high-tech community centered around the development of social networking tools. The Web 2.0 community itself was a vast network of meetings, conferences, blogs, presentations, and online sites with events such as Garage Geeks, the Marker Café, the Coils, TWS 2008, Eurekamp, Geek Camp, Media Boom, and more, as the list seemed to continually grow as one site would spin off into another. It is within these dynamic, fluid, and fuzzy networks—composed of an ever changing array of actors, technologies, and spaces—that signs (including English) and symbols were remixed, remediated, re-articulated, and redesigned. Barak was an active agent co-constituting these spaces in a continual process of knotworking as he orchestrated connections, deals, partnerships, and large-scale events through business cards, cell phones, text messages, emails, social networks, and face-to-face interactions in a mixture of Hebrew and English.

As this description suggests, Barak continually sought out strategies to infiltrate high-tech networks, including through attendance at high-tech "mixers" and establishing himself on high-tech social networking sites (these virtual and physical spaces also "mixed"). One of the principle social networking sites of the high-tech community was called the Marker Café, with what seemed the entire community registering for (and converging on) the site soon after it was established. The first time Barak was introduced to the Café occurred in the Networld meeting room at the behest of his marketing consultants (guns for hire). As the team examined the site on a large-screen computer posted on a wall, an instant message popped up from a user inquiring about the company, "*shalom lax . . . oz ma ze bediuyk Networld ba'am*?" ("Greetings . . . so what exactly is Networld Ltd.?"). With a chat ensuing between the online user and a marketing assistant at a wireless keyboard (the formation of a new "knot"), the conversation in the room continued as frames, alignments, and topics switched back and forth between the chat in progress, side conversations, and other marketing issues at hand (the various topics mixing). Broadly, this brief portrait is intended to capture the links between the virtual and physical spaces, as online interactions became woven into the discussions around the meeting room table. These virtual networks were not separate, self-contained spaces apart from the rest of social life but "continuous with and embedded in other social spaces" (8, Miller and Slater qtd. in Ito). Arguing that the digital revolution is a social and cultural one, Heidi McKee further writes, "Merging technologies may create the conditions for convergence to happen, but it is how people integrate these technologies into their lives, how they create cultures and social networks of use that is the real phenomenon at the heart of convergence" (105). This focus demands increased attention to ways that multilingual-multimodal activities are knotted into lived experiences.

Forming a new "knot," Barak quickly registered for the Café and became a manager of an online marketing forum where he posted his own blog as a way to enhance his visibility and status in the community. Shaping these tactical decisions on how to market, position, and represent himself — typically formulated in sessions in the Networld meeting room — were wider institutional, cultural, economic, and global forces. Indexing the widespread influence of America, for instance, it is commonplace to hear Israelis refer to their country as the fifty-first state and on Israeli Independence Day to see American and Israeli flags on cars side by side. These rhetorics naturally filtered into Barak's discourse with frequent references to America, as his alignment with the country was a way to enhance his ethos. For instance, in one blog entry he posted a commentary on presidential candidate Barack Obama's Internet fundraising campaign as an example of the ways that the Internet could be exploited in the upcoming Israeli elections. Embedded in this entry was a picture of Obama standing before the American and Israeli flags. This image echoed the flags found together on Independence Day. In this manner, we can see the ways that images circulated or converged in everyday literacy practices. In this blog entry Barak further characterized the Israeli political candidates as *behind* America (a common trope) with insufficient foresight or time to plan a comprehensive Internet strategy for the upcoming Israeli election cycle.[10] Not insignificantly, he expressed the hope that the Israelis would again prove themselves by displaying their trademark penchant for improvisation, resourcefulness, quick-wittedness, and creativity. Embedded in this narrative were tropes bound up in the construction of national identity echoed on the Networld website (e.g., a small, agile commando unit). These rhetorics furthermore extended to his everyday talk as he frequently dropped the phrase "*yalla* America" or "let's go America" at the completion of activities (such as reviewing a Web text during a meeting) in reference to a famous comedy sketch about the naive and pervasive belief that things were better in America. This code shifting marked not only transitions from one activity to the next but also broader cultural and linguistic transitions in the society. Through such broad-brush analysis we can begin to glimpse the ways wider sociocultural contexts, specifically in this case the influence of the United States, were deeply knotted into activity and dispersed across far-flung literacy networks. In sum, we might understand Barak as continually networking and "knotworking" through the creative and strategic deployment of multilingual-multimodal literacy practices. It is through this process that languages (primarily Hebrew and English), images, tropes, and symbols of all kinds circulated and converged.

Central to such analyses of literacy practices is attention to the ways that cultural ecologies are knotted into text messages, websites, blogs, emails, chats, and an array of other texts or genre ecologies. As a fine-grained example of this process, I return to the meeting room in which much of the activity at Networld took place and a discussion centered on the design of an online social networking tool allowing users to incorporate "enriching" content into their emails, such as quotes, recipes, and so forth. In this meeting, four members of the team (including myself) examined various websites to incorporate into the site as they commented on them, drew on scrap sheets of paper, wrote on a whiteboard, and took written notes on laptops and notepads in a mixture of Hebrew and English. These different objects formed genre ecologies that were often fragile, fleeting, and configured "on the fly." Attention to the tying and untying of these text, tools, and objects — knotworking — is key to the study of the production, distribution, reception, and representation of multilingual-multimodal texts.

The activity itself was centered on evaluating, filtering, aggregating, and remixing (of images, texts, languages, and symbols), or what Johndan Johnson-Eilola refers to as symbolic-analytic work. Central to this activity was the Marantz computer screen on the wall (indicated in the previous section), and as the images and websites on the screen changed, so too did the topics of discussion, positioning, and alignments of the participants. In this setting, the screen oriented the participants (where to look, how to scroll, what content to click on), and the participants oriented the screen in an ongoing negotiation. The screen, furthermore, coordinated activities in conjunction with a range of other texts and tools through compound mediation (Spinuzzi) or textual coordination (Slattery) with English deeply sedimented into these objects.[11]

It is furthermore the complex tying and untying of texts and tools that shaped (and were shaped by) the dynamic pathways through which languages, images, sounds, and symbols circulated. For instance, at one point scanning an image of a recipe from a Betty Crocker website with the logo

spelled out across the top, Barak proceeded to ask, *"mi zot* Betty Crocker?"
("Who is Betty Crocker?"). In this manner, Betty Crocker entered the conversation as it flowed from the screen and into the room. In this sense, the screen
served as a "border crossing" mediating not only the activity in the room but
also the boundaries between local and global contexts as languages, images,
ideologies, and cultural representations converged. Serving as a contextualization cue (Gumperz), the discussion quickly centered on a debate about
what content to import from the Betty Crocker site, how to import it, and even
if the content should be imported at all. Taking the position that it would be
both ethical and legal to use this information, the co-founder of the start-up
Yaniv argued that they would be doing "Betty Crocker" a favor by providing
free marketing through distributing its content on their site, as he argued
"hi trsrixa lehagid otanu toda" (*"she* needs to thank us"). Particularly relevant
is the reference to Betty Crocker as "she." This social construction shaped
the addressivity of the dialogue with "Betty" (as she was often referred to)
literally positioned as a participant in the conversation. On the other side of
the debate, the programmer Hadara expressed an opposing point of view as
she read from a section on the site about copyright entitled "is the Betty
Crocker Content free, and are there any restrictions?" In reading this text
aloud, Hadara was giving voice to (animating) the Betty Crocker site, and in
this way Betty Crocker had a real (embodied) voice in the conversation. In
addition, however, Hadara was accenting the text with her own meaning as
she emphasized the phrase "for your personal use," a move that implied her
own personal position on the issue. In this manner double voicing (Bakhtin)
captures the ways that participants shaped (and were shaped) by the Betty
Crocker site, in an ongoing negotiation. In this scenario, wider struggles related to copyright and ownership (international legal regimes) converged. As
Alexander articulates: "media convergence needs to be understood not only
as a powerful way of manipulating 'texts' to create new meanings, but also a
site of authorial contestation, particularly as more traditional definitions of
composing, authoring, and ownership come under scrutiny, are challenged,
and shift in the production of multimedia texts" ("Media" 4).[12]

In fact this scene launched an extended struggle over the nature of the
site itself in a debate involving several changes in the participants' positions,
both in their theoretical stances and their physical positioning in the room. Indeed these shifts were inextricably intertwined. Woven into these interactions,
Betty Crocker was resemiotized into oral remarks (primarily in Hebrew), a
whiteboard (written as "Betty C"), and Yaniv's written notes (composed in
a mixture of Hebrew and English). The notes (Figure 28-1) formed part of a
"knot" or improvised genre ecology that shaped the remediation of "Betty
Crocker."[13] As the conversation continued, Betty Crocker continued to circulate inside and outside the meeting room across a range of other spaces and
places as it became knotted in new genre ecologies, referred to as "Betty
Crocker," "Betty," and "Betty Crocks." The remediation of Betty Crocker
across texts and talk was bound up in a struggle in which both "Betty" and
the participants were continually repositioned.

FIGURE 28-1   Multilingual notes: Betty Crocker remediated into notepad.

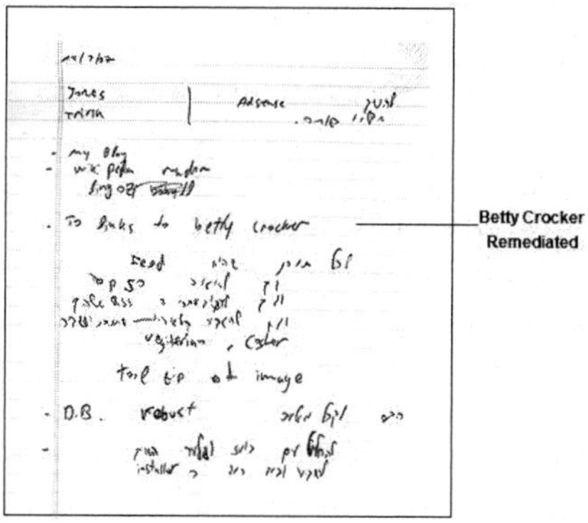

Traditionally, the concept of genre ecology has been used to understand the ways that institutional settings shape (and are shaped by) workplace practices, and this example extends this concept by showing how it can be used in a similar fashion to trace global flows of language and culture (i.e., merged with the concept of cultural ecologies). Such tracing is an argument for a return to writing process studies with close attention to multilingual-multimodal activity. Further a response to post-process critiques (Petraglia), this move calls for attention to the ways that texts position the actors and are knotted into wider social, cultural, national, and global ecologies.[14] In this view technologies such as the Internet—as well as an assemblage of other tools—need to be understood as deeply intertwined in activities as opposed to a domain of "cyberian apartness" (Miller and Slater). Composition studies is uniquely situated for studying these intersections across companies, community, and classroom contexts as it moves toward a twenty-first-century multilingual-multimodal framework.

RE-ARTICULATING COMPOSITION

Overall this analysis suggests a need for a re-articulation, re-assembly, and remixing of teaching, research, and administration. First and foremost this analysis suggests a return to the study of the writing process as bound up in complex cultural and genre ecologies with writers reconceptualized as "knot-workers" engaged in a continual process of tying and untying of languages, texts, tropes, narratives, images, sounds, and ideologies distributed across far-flung networks. Drawing on Foucault's microphysics of power, we might understand these ecologies as structures of distribution, access, and value, or what Jan Blommaert refers to as "literacy regimes." Key to locating the ways actors are co-constituted by these regimes is Bakhtin's notion of authoritative discourse with "knotworkers" continually engaged in negotiating centripetal and centrifugal forces.

Second, this move toward multilingual-multimodal composing calls for attention to "convergence culture" or the point at which global scapes converge in local contexts. Useful for locating these points of convergence is the notion of uptake: "uptake is knowledge of what to take up, how, and when: when and why to use a genre, how to select an appropriate genre in relation to another, how to execute uptakes strategically and when to resist expected uptakes, how some genres explicitly cite other genres in their uptake while some do so only implicitly, and so on" (Bawarshi 653). These uptakes or convergence points are sites of struggle involving durable and symbolic tools sedimented with orientations or tendential forces (Johnson-Eilola).

Third, this shift requires renewed attention to space and place and the ways it is co-constituted by literacy practices. While the examples above have foregrounded work in the high-tech environment, similar analyses can be applied to community contexts or the writing classroom. In an EFL or ESL composition classroom, for instance, we might examine the uptake of Western textbooks in local contexts. As Canagarajah argues, teaching methods and textbooks are not neutral, "but 'constructs' put together by specific social groups for particular ends on the basis of their social practice and interests" ("Resisting" 104). The influence of such constructs is not a case of totalizing *linguistic imperialism* (Phillipson), with the teachers and students wholly adopting its perspective. Instead such curricula are "double voiced" (Bakhtin). This perspective means tracing the ways such objects are taken up, resisted, and transformed. As part of this analysis, it further calls for attending to the ways the uptakes of classroom curriculum are coordinated through a process of "textual coordination" (Slattery) or "compound mediation" (Spinuzzi) with other languages, texts, tools (blackboards, whiteboards, desks), and ideologies.

Fourth, this move means tracing activities beyond bounded and institutional spaces such as companies and classrooms. This less-bounded approach as I have demonstrated in the high-tech sector is part of the "cultural" (Scott and Longo) turn in technical communication away from a "sometimes narrow contextual focus on discrete organizational discourse communities" (3). In workplace contexts, for instance, we need to examine the ways writing is shaped by water cooler conversations, lunch time interactions, and a range of other unofficial practices that filter into workplace activities inside and outside the bounded walls of a company. This understanding necessitates attending to the ways that writing (and design) practices are deeply bound up in polycontextuality and the tracing multilingual and multimodal activity across space and time.

Similarly, in the classroom, we might study how textbooks, blackboards, and classroom conversations become knotted into new genre and cultural ecologies (and vice versa) in libraries, homes, emails, Facebook, Twitter, instant messages, text messages, and more. These shifts necessitate attention to the extracurriculum (Gere) bringing "together the writing outside of school and that inside" (Yancey, p. 72). Within writing studies, we have seen a recent move toward this less bounded approach: Jenn Fishman et al.'s study of student performances; Paul Prior and Jody Shipka's study of the literate activities of writers across school, home, and an array of other contexts distributed across space-time (referred to as "laminated chronotopes"); and Kevin

Roozen's fine-grained case studies tracing the intersections between academic and nonacademic contexts ("From Journals"; "Journalism"; "Math"). Examining hidden literacies (see also Dyson; Finders; Kamberelis and de la Luna) can be extended to the study of multilingual-multimodal literacy practices.[15]

Finally, remixing writing studies in the twenty-first century calls for an expanded definition of writing itself. Johnson-Eilola and Selber argue that remixing is, in fact, a rhetorical act of composing and meaning making. Under this extended definition, we need to conceptualize multilingual-multimodal writers as re-articulating, re-assembling, and redesigning complex genre and cultural ecologies. Making this shift in our classrooms, we might engage students in activities involving juxtaposition, filtering, selection, and recombining. Incorporating multilingualism into these activities, we might ask multilingual speakers or world language learners to use Gloria Anzaldúa's *Borderlands* as one model of multilingual composing. We can also extend Tom Romano's multigenre essay asking writers to incorporate multiple languages and design choices. In doing this work, we might ask native English speakers to collaborate with speakers of world languages to design and remix texts (broadly defined) targeted at a range of local and global audiences. Linked to such work could be reflective papers to articulate (or in Johnson-Eilola's terms *rearticulate*) their linguistic and design decisions. Such activities additionally could offer productive frameworks for collaborations between ESL and composition. We might further seek partnerships with international classrooms and speakers of world languages by having students conduct mini-ethnographies in their own local contexts and cultures and target this research toward international audiences as part of a cross-cultural exchange. Such work would offer students opportunities to imagine global audiences and to receive responses from cross-cultural perspectives. These global partnerships might be developed and sustained through technologies such as online video conferencing. Using technologies, we might furthermore ask our students to study (and implement in our own research designs) multilingual and multimodal composing through the use of screen captures (Geisler and Slattery), digital photos, and digital audio and video recording. In this area, we might follow the lead of Hawisher and Selfe, who are using writing process videos of transnationally connected individuals attempting to record their everyday literate activity (Prior *Writing/Disciplinarity*); their aims are to show how these practices shape—and are shaped by—the global contexts in which they are deployed.

In making such moves, this remixing of composition calls for reconceptualizing teachers, researchers, students, and administrators as "knotworkers" engaged in forming new knots with disciplines, technologies, languages, signs, symbols, spaces, and actors. Critical to this re-assembly is the formation of sustainable global partnerships (Starke-Meyerring, Duin, and Palvetzian) with multilingualism conceptualized as one tool in a writer's wider rhetorical repertoire. Min-Zahn Lu defines composition as boundary work. Tracing multilingual-multimodal literacy practices across official and unofficial spaces necessitates crossing disciplinary, geographic, and linguistic boundaries as composition moves into the twenty-first century.

Acknowledgments   I would like to thank Selin Aviyente, Gail Hawisher, Paul Prior, Kevin Roozen, David Sheridan, and Xiaoye You for their helpful comments and insights on earlier versions of this article. I am also indebted to Kathleen Yancey and the two reviewers for their thoughtful suggestions and comments.

NOTES

   1. The name of the company and the participants in this study have been changed to protect their identities; this study has received Internal Review Board approval.

   2. Min-Zahn Lu also merges research in world Englishes with African American Vernacular English (AAVE) and Native American studies.

   3. Clay Spinuzzi uses genre ecologies to examine micro-, meso-, and macroscopic levels of activity within institutional contexts. In his work, the contradictions at one scope (e.g., macro-institutional policies) are linked to breakdowns at another (e.g., micro-incorrect key stroke). This research extends the application of genre ecologies to show the ways they are linked not only to institutional contexts but also to cultural, national, and global contexts. In addition, this research shows how the concept can be extended to the study of multilingualism and the tracing of linguistic and cultural flows.

   4. This process has been variously referred to by scholars as compound mediation (Spinuzzi), textual coordination (Slattery), and environmental selection and structuring practices (Prior and Shipka).

   5. The term *remediation* is used instead of *circulation*, which may mistakenly imply billiard balls rolling across a table (Agha); remediation points to friction, struggle, and transformation.

   6. I am indebted to David Sheridan for helping to clarify the focus of writers as "knot-workers."

   7. Jonathan Alexander and Heidi McKee extend the application of *convergence*, recently taken up in computers and composition, beyond media to a range of spaces at local, national, and global levels. McKee rightly cautions that the term *convergence* itself is potentially misleading as it may imply a "singularity," and feels it is more accurate to say, "we are living in an age of convergences" (119).

   8. I wish to emphasize that this national narrative is from an emic perspective (how Israelis tell their own history). Indeed, revisionist Israeli historians (Morris) have argued that the Israeli army was in many key ways superior and better organized than the Arab armies in the 1948 War of Independence.

   9. Reading this site as intertext, i.e., a response to a sea of other texts (Bazerman), offers a framework for conceptualizing such objects as complex assemblages of tropes, ideologies, languages, images. Useful for framing such analyses is a description of intertext from Vincent Leitch: "The text is not a unified object, but a set of relations with other texts. Its system of language, its grammar, its lexicon, drag along numerous bits and pieces — traces — of history so that the text resembles a Cultural Salvation Army Outlet with unaccountable collections of incompatible ideas, beliefs, and sources" (qtd. in Porter 59).

   10. This positioning of Israel relative to the United States was a theme that Barak reiterated at other points, such as in another blog post titled *America adeyin lefanenyu* (America Is Still Ahead of Us) about Israeli venture capitalists still having "a lot to learn" about adopting Web 2.0 principles.

   11. While I lack space to fully develop this point, it is important to note that wider national tropes and narratives were orienting the uptake of the tools and technologies. See Ito et. al. ("Personal") for a similar framing to analyze the ways cell phone communication in Japan is bound up in the concept of *keitai*.

   12. Making a similar point, Johnson-Eilola and Selber note that remixing "inhabits a contested terrain of creativity, intellectual property, authorship, corporate ownership, and power" (393).

   13. The fact Yaniv's private notes were in English — and self-talk as he uttered "Fifty links of Betty Crocker" while writing this phrase down — suggests the extent to which English was embedded in his high-tech *habitus*.

   14. Jonathan Alexander ("Digital Youth" 371) similarly argues for attention to both process and ecology.

15. Arguing for attention to unofficial literacy practices that locate writing as one tool in a wider rhetorical repertoire, Cynthia Selfe argues, "We need to better understand the importance that students attach to composing, exchanging, and interpreting new and different kinds of texts that help them make sense of their experience and lives" (642). Within multilingual studies, Canagarajah ("Place") similarly contends: "it is outside the classroom that students seem to develop communicative competence and negotiation of strategies for 'real world' needs of multilingualism" (592).

WORKS CITED

Agha, Asif. *Language and Social Relations.* Cambridge: Cambridge UP, 2007. Print.

Alexander, Jonathan. *Digital Youth.* Cresskill: Hampton Press, 2006. Print.

———. "Media Convergence: Creating Content, Questioning Relationships." *Computers and Composition* 25.1 (2008): 1–8. Print.

Alim, H. Samy, Awad Ibrahim, and Alastair Pennycook, eds. *Global Linguistic Flows.* New York: Routledge, 2009. Print.

Anzaldúa, Gloria. *Borderlands: The New Mestiza=La Frontera.* San Francisco: Aunt Lute Books, 1999. Print.

Appadurai, Arjun. *Modernity at Large: Cultural Dimensions of Globalization.* Public Worlds. Minneapolis: U of Minnesota P, 1996. Print.

Atkinson, Dwight, and Ulla Connor. "Multilingual Writing Development." *Handbook of Research Writing.* Ed. Charles Bazerman. New York: Erlbaum, 2008. 515–32. Print.

Bakhtin, Mikhail M. "Discourse in the Novel." Trans. Caryl Emerson and Michael Holquist. *The Dialogic Imagination.* Ed. Michael Holquist. Austin: U of Texas P, 1981. 259–422. Print.

Bawarshi, Anis. "Taking Up Language Differences in Composition." *College English* 68.6 (2006): 652–56. Print.

Bazerman, Charles. "Intertextuality: How Texts Rely on Other Texts." *What Writing Does and How It Does It: An Introduction to Analyzing Texts and Textual Practices.* Ed. Charles Bazerman and Paul Prior. Mahwah: Erlbaum, 2004. 83–96. Print.

———. "Systems of Genres and the Enactment of Social Intentions." *Genre and the New Rhetoric.* Ed. Aviva Freedman and Peter Medway. London: Taylor and Francis, 1994. 79–101. Print.

Blommaert, Jan. *Grassroots Literacy: Writing, Identity and Voice in Central Africa.* Oxon: Routledge, 2008. Print.

Bolter, Jay David, and Richard Grusin. *Remediation: Understanding New Media.* Cambridge: MIT P, 1998. Print.

Canagarajah, Suresh A. "The Place of World Englishes in Composition: Pluralization Continued." *College Composition and Communication* 57.4 (2006): 586–619. Print.

———. *Resisting Linguistic Imperialism in English Teaching.* Oxford: Oxford UP, 1999. Print.

———. "Subversive Identities, Pedagogical Safe Houses, and Critical Learning." *Critical Pedagogies and Language Learning.* Ed. Bonny Norton and Kelleen Toohey. Cambridge: Cambridge UP, 2004. 116–37. Print.

———. "Toward a Writing Pedagogy of Shuttling between Languages: Learning from Multilingual Writers." *College English* 68.6 (2006): 589–604. Print.

Castells, Manuel. *The Information Age: Economy, Society and Culture. Vol. 1, the Rise of the Network Society (2nd. Ed.).* Oxford: Blackwell, 2000. Print.

Chiang, Yuet-Sim D., and Mary Schmida. "Language Identity and Language Ownership: Linguistic Conflicts of First-Year University Writing Students." Harklau, Losey, and Siegal 85–104. Print.

Devitt, Amy J. "Intertextuality in Tax Accounting: Generic, Referential, and Functional." *Textual Dynamics of the Professions: Historical and Contemporary Studies of Writing in Professional Communities.* Ed. Charles Bazerman and James Paradis. Madison: U of Wisconsin P, 1991. 336–57. Print.

Duranti, Alessandro, and Charles Goodwin. *Rethinking Context: Language as an Interactive Phenomenon.* Cambridge: Cambridge UP, 1992. Print.

Dyson, Anne. *Writing Superheroes: Contemporary Childhood, Popular Culture, and Classroom Literacy.* New York: Teachers College P, 1997. Print.

Engeström, Yrjö, Ritva Engeström, and Tarja Vähääho. "When the Center Does Not Hold: The Importance of Knotworking." *Activity Theory and Social Practice: Cultural-Historical Approaches.* Ed. Seth Chaiklin, Mariane Hedegaard, and Jaal Uffe. Aarhus: Aarhus UP, 1999. 345–74. Print.

Finders, Margaret J. *Just Girls: Hidden Literacies and Life in Junior High.* New York: Teachers College P, 1997. Print.

Fishman, Jenn, Andrea Lunsford, Beth McGregor, and Mark Otuteye. "Performing Writing, Performing Literacy." *College Composition and Communication* 57.2 (2005): 224–52. Print.

Fleckenstein, Kristie S., Clay Spinuzzi, Rebecca J. Rickly, and Carole Clark Papper. "The Importance of Harmony: An Ecological Metaphor for Writing Research." *College Composition and Communication* 60.2 (2008): 388–419. Print.

Geisler, Cheryl, and Shaun Slattery. "Capturing the Activity of Digital Writing: Using, Analyzing, and Supplementing Video Screen Capture." *Digital Writing Research*. Ed. Heidi A. McKee and Danielle N. DeVoss. Cresskill: Hampton P, 2007. Print.

George, Diana. "From Analysis to Design: Visual Communication in the Teaching of Writing." *College Composition and Communication* 54.1 (2002): 11–39. Print.

Gere, Anne Ruggles. "Kitchen Tables and Rented Rooms: The Extracurriculum of Composition." *College Composition and Communication* 45.1 (1994): 75–92. Print.

Giddens, Anthony. *The Constitution of Society: Outline of the Theory of Structuration*. Berkeley: U of California P, 1984. Print.

Gumperz, John J. *Discourse Strategies*. Cambridge: Cambridge UP, 1982. Print.

Halbritter, Scott K. "Sound Arguments: Aural Rhetoric in Multimedia Composing." Diss. U of North Carolina at Chapel Hill, 2004. Print.

Harklau, Linda, Kay M. Losey, and Meryl Siegal. *Generation 1.5 Meets College Composition: Issues in the Teaching of Writing to U.S.-Educated Learners of ESL*. Mahwah: Erlbaum, 1999. Print.

Hawisher, Gail E., and Cynthia L. Selfe, with Yi-Huey Guo and Lu Liu. "Globalization and Agency: Designing and Redesigning the Literacies of Cyberspace." *College English* 68.6 (2006): 619–36. Print.

Heller, Monica. *Bilingualism: A Social Approach*. Basingstoke, UK: Palgrave Macmillan, 2007. Print.

Horner, Bruce, and John Trimbur. "English Only and U.S. College Composition." *College Composition and Communication* 53.4 (2002): 594–630. Print.

Iedema, Rick. *Discourses of Post-Bureaucratic Organization*. Amsterdam: John Benjamins, 2003. Print.

Irvine, Judith T. "Commentary: Knots and Tears in the Interdiscursive Fabric." *Journal of Linguistic Anthropology* 15.1 (2005): 72–80. Print.

———. "Shadow Conversations: The Indeterminacy of Participant Roles." *Natural Histories of Discourse*. Ed. Michael Silverstein and Greg Urban. Chicago: U of Chicago P, 1996. 81–105. Print.

Ito, Mizuko. "Introduction: Personal, Portable, Pedestrian." *Personal, Portable, Pedestrian*. Ed. Mizuko Ito, Daisuke Okabe, and Misa Matsuda. Cambridge: MIT P, 2005. 1–16. Print.

Ito, Mizuko, et al., eds. *Hanging Out, Messing Around, and Geeking Out*. Cambridge: MIT P, 2010. Print.

Ito, Mizuko, Daisuke Okabe, and Misa Matsuda, eds. *Personal, Portable, Pedestrian*. Cambridge: MIT P, 2005. Print.

Jamieson, Kathleen M. "Antecedent Genre as Rhetorical Constraint." *Quarterly Journal of Speech* 61.4 (1975): 406–15. Print.

Jenkins, Henry. *Convergence Culture*. New York: New York UP, 2006. Print.

Johnson-Eilola, Johndan. *Datacloud*. Cresskill: Hampton P, 2005. Print.

Johnson-Eilola, Johndan, and Stuart A. Selber. "Plagiarism, Originality, Assemblage." *Computers and Composition* 24.4 (2007): 375–403. Print.

Kamberelis, George, and Leonora del la Luna. "Children's Writing: How Talk and Text Interact in Situated Practices." *What Writing Does and How It Does It*. Ed. Charles Bazerman and Paul Prior. Mahwah: Erlbaum, 2004. 239–78. Print.

Kress, Gunther, and Theo van Leeuwen. *Reading Images: The Grammar of Visual Design*. London: Routledge, 1996. Print.

Lash, Scott, and John Urry. *Economies of Signs and Space*. London: Sage, 1994. Print.

Latour, Bruno. *Pandora's Hope: Essays on the Reality of Science Studies*. Cambridge: Harvard UP, 1999. Print.

Lee, Carmen K.-M. "Affordances and Text-Making Practices in Online Instant Messaging." *Written Communication* 24.3 (2007): 223. Print.

Lu, Min-Zhan. "An Essay on the Work of Composition: Composing English against the Order of Fast Capitalism." *College Composition and Communication* 56.1 (2004): 16–50. Print.

Matsuda, Paul Kei. "Composition Studies and ESL Writing: A Disciplinary Division of Labor." *College Composition and Communication* 50.4 (1999): 699–721. Print.

———. "The Myth of Linguistic Homogeneity in U.S. Composition." *College English* 68.6 (2006): 637–51. Print.

McKee, Heidi A. "Ethical and Legal Issues for Writing Researchers in an Age of Convergence." *Computers and Composition* 25.1 (2008): 104–22. Print.

Miller, Daniel, and Don Slater. *The Internet: An Ethnographic Approach*. Oxford: Berg, 2000. Print.

Morgenstern, Joseph. "Looking Back on the Israeli Technology Story." *Globes Online*. 22 July 2008. Web. 11 Oct. 2009.

Morris, Benny. *1948: The First Arab-Israeli War*. New Haven: Yale UP, 2008. Print.

New London Group. "A Pedagogy of Multiliteracies: Designing Social Futures." *Designs for Social Futures*. Ed. Bill Cope and Mary Kalantzis. London: Routledge, 2000. 9–38. Print.

Orlikowski, Wanda J., and JoAnne Yates. "Genre Repertoire: The Structuring of Communicative Practices in Organizations." *Administrative Science Quarterly* 39.4 (1994): 541–74. Print.

Pennycook, Alastair. *Global Englishes and Transcultural Flows*. London: Routledge, 2007. Print.

Petraglia, Joseph. "Is There Life after Process? The Role of Scientism in a Changing Discipline." *Post-Process Theory: Beyond the Writing-Process Paradigm*. Ed. Kent, Thomas. Carbondale: Southern Illinois UP, 1999. Print.

Phillipson, Robert. *Linguistic Imperialism*. Oxford: Oxford UP, 1992. Print.

Pieterse, Jan Nederveen. *Globalization and Culture: Global Melange*. Lanham, MD: Rowman and Littlefield, 2003. Print.

Porter, James E. "Intertextuality and the Discourse Community." *Rhetoric Review* 5.1 (1986): 34–47. Print.

Pratt, Mary Louise. "Arts of the Contact Zone." *Profession* 91 (1991): 33–40. Print.

Prior, Paul. "Remaking IO, Remaking Rhetoric: Semiotic Remediation as Situated Rhetorical Practice." *Kairos: A Journal of Rhetoric, Technology, and Pedagogy* 11.3 (2007): n. pag. Web. 11 Oct. 2009.

———. *Writing/Disciplinarity: A Sociohistoric Account of Literate Activity in the Academy*. Mahwah: Erlbaum, 1998. Print.

Prior, Paul, et al. "'I'll Be the Sun': From Reported Speech to Semiotic Remediation Practices." *Text-Interdisciplinary Journal for the Study of Discourse* 26.6 (2006): 733–66. Print.

Prior, Paul, and Jody Shipka. "Chronotopic Lamination: Tracing the Contours of Literate Activity." *Writing Selves, Writing Society: Research from Activity Perspectives*. Ed. Charles Bazerman and David R. Russell. Fort Collins: WAC Clearinghouse, 2003. Print.

Rampton, Ben. *Crossing*. London: Longman, 1995. Print.

Romano, Tom. *Blending Genre, Altering Style: Writing Multigenre Papers*. Portsmouth: Boynton/Cook Heinemann, 2000. Print.

Roozen, Kevin. "From Journals to Journalism: Tracing Trajectories of Literate Development." *College Composition and Communication* 60.3 (2009): 541–73. Print.

———. "Journalism, Poetry, Stand-up Comedy, and Academic Literacy: Mapping the Interplay of Curricular and Extracurricular Literate Activities." *Journal of Basic Writing* 27.1 (2008): 5–34. Print.

———. "Math, the 'Poetry Slam,' and Mathemagicians: Tracing Trajectories of Practice and Person." *Kairos: A Journal of Rhetoric, Technology, and Pedagogy* 11.3 (2007): n. pag. Web. 11 Oct. 2009.

Russell, David R. "Rethinking Genre in School and Society: An Activity Theory Analysis." *Written Communication* 14.4 (1997): 504–54. Print.

Schryer, Catherine. "Records as Genre." *Written Communication* 10.2 (1993): 200–234. Print.

Scott, J. Blake, and Bernadette Longo. "Guest Editors Introduction: Making the Cultural Turn." *Technical Communication Quarterly* 15.1 (2006): 3–7. Print.

Selfe, Cynthia L. "Aurality and Multimodal Composing." *College Composition and Communication* 60.4 (2009): 616–63. Print.

Shipka, Jody. "A Multimodal Task-Based Framework for Composing." *College Composition and Communication* 57.2 (2005): 277–306. Print.

Slattery, Shaun. "Technical Writing as Textual Coordination: An Argument for the Value of Writers' Skill with Information Technology." *Technical Communication Quarterly* 52.3 (2005): 353–60. Print.

Smitherman, Geneva. *Black Talk: Words and Phrases from the Hood to Amen Corner*. Boston: Houghton Mifflin, 1994. Print.

Spinuzzi, Clay. *Tracing Genres through Organizations: A Sociocultural Approach to Information Design*. Cambridge: MIT P, 2003. Print.

Starke-Meyerring, Doreen, Ann Hill Duin, and Talene Palvetzian. "Global Partnerships: Positioning Technical Communication Programs in the Context of Globalization." *Technical Communication Quarterly* 16.2 (2007): 139–74. Print.

Sun, Huatong. "The Triumph of Users: Achieving Cultural Usability Goals with User Localizations." *Technical Communication Quarterly* 15.4 (2006): 457–81. Print.

Swarts, Jason. " Coherent Fragments: The Problem of Mobility and Genred Information." *Written Communication* 23.2 (2006): 173–201. Print.

Tannen, Deborah. *Talking Voices*. New York: Cambridge UP, 1985. Print.

Valdés, Guadalupe. "Bilingual Minorities and Language Issues in Writing: Toward Professionwide Responses to a New Challenge." *Written Communication* 1.9 (1992): 85–136. Print.

Voloshinov, V. N. *Marxism and the Philosophy of Language*. Cambridge: Harvard UP, 1986. Print.

Williams, Raymond. *Keywords: A Vocabulary of Culture and Society*. Oxford: Oxford UP, 1976. Print.

Wolfe, Joanna. "Gesture and Collaborative Planning." *Written Communication* 22.3 (2005): 298–332. Print.

Yancey, Kathleen Blake. "Made Not Only in Words: Composition in a New Key." *College Composition and Communication* 56.2 (2004): 297–328. Print.

———. "Re-Designing Graduate Education in Composition and Rhetoric: The Use of Remix as Concept, Material, and Method." *Computers and Composition* 26.1 (2009): 4–12. Print.

Young, Vershawn A. "Your Average Nigga." *College Composition and Communication* 55.4 (2004): 693–715. Print.

29 Remixing Basic Writing: Digital Media Production and the Basic Writing Curriculum

CATHERINE C. BRAUN, BEN McCORKLE, AND AMIE C. WOLF

Catherine C. Braun, Ben McCorkle, and Amie C. Wolf see basic writing courses that allow students to create using digital media as empowering, especially since basic writers are often positioned as remedial. Providing readers with a rationale for this stance, each author includes an example of an assignment and the types of work students can do using digital media to complete the assignments. Like Murray, Sheets, and Williams in Part Four, they also explain how this work can be assessed, which is a task instructors who lack digital media expertise may struggle with.

The figures of Braun, McCorkle, and Wolf's web text, included here, elaborate on their work's purpose in greater detail. Readers are encouraged to examine each author's approach, which places emphasis on revision and production, to helping basic writers use multiple modes purposively. Braun assigns students an ethnographic assignment in which they are asked to study a community and compose their research findings as an audio essay. One of the several multimodal assignments from McCorkle's basic writing course asks students to work together to compose a short animation that serves as a movie or video game trailer. Finally, Wolf offers up her experience teaching a service-learning basic writing class where students compose audio essays about literacy and education. In the end, the authors highlight how such projects in the basic writing classroom can aid students in becoming critical thinkers.

The rest of the web text can be located in its entirety at http://www.bgsu.edu /cconline/braun/index.htm.

From *Computers and Composition Online* (2007). http://www.bgsu.edu/cconline/braun /index.htm

FIGURE 29-1   Excerpts from Braun, McCorkle, and Wolf's introduction.

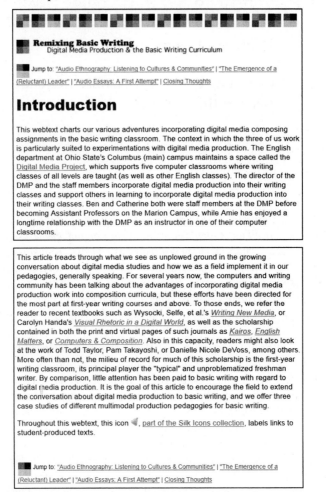

Source: Computers and Composition Online (2007). http://www.bgsu.edu/cconline/braun/intro.html

SUGGESTED FURTHER READING

Readers may find the following texts about multimodal composition helpful. A variety of disciplines and perspectives, such as new media, visual rhetoric, communication, technology, research, among others, are represented.

Alexander, Jonathan. "Technology, Literacy, and Digital Youth." *Digital Youth: Emerging Literacies on the World Wide Web*. Ed. Jonathan Alexander. Cresskill: Hampton, 2006. 33–67. Print.

Anderson, Daniel, et al. "Integrating Multimodality into Composition Curricula: Survey Methodology and Results from a CCCC Research Grant." *Composition Studies* 34 (2006): 59–84. Print.

Ball, Cheryl E., and James Kalmbach, eds. *RAW (Reading and Writing) New Media*. Cresskill: Hampton, 2010. Print.

Ball, Cheryl E., and Ryan M. Moeller. "Converging the ASS[umptions] between U and ME; or How New Media Can Bridge a Scholarly/Creative Split in English Studies." *Computers and Composition Online* (2008). Web. 12 Mar. 2010.

———. "Reinventing the Possibilities: Academic literacy and new media." *Fibreculture Journal* (2007). Web. 12 Mar. 2010.

Baron, Dennis. *A Better Pencil: Readers, Writers, and the Digital Revolution*. New York: Oxford, 2009. Print.

Baron, Naomi B. *Alphabet to Email: How Written English Evolved and Where It's Heading*. New York: Routledge, 2000. Print.

Berry, Patrick W., Gail E. Hawisher, and Cynthia L. Selfe. *Transnational Literate Lives in Digital Times*. Logan: Computers and Composition Digital P/Utah State UP, 2012. Web.

Blair, Kristine, and Christine Tulley. "Remediating the Book Review: Toward Collaboration and Multimodality across the English Curriculum." *Pedagogy: Critical Approaches to Teaching Literature, Language, Composition, and Culture* 9.3 (2009): 441–69. Print.

Bolter, Jay David, and Richard Grusin. *Remediation: Understanding New Media*. Cambridge: MIT P, 2000. Print.

Bridwell-Bowles, Lillian, Karen L. Powell, and Tiffany Walter Choplin. "Not Just Words Any More: Multimodal Communication across the Curriculum." Spec. issue of *Across the Disciplines* 6 (Jan. 2009). Web. 27 Oct. 2010.

Carter, Terry, and Maria A. Clayton, eds. *Writing and the iGeneration: Composition in the Computer-Mediated Classroom*. Southlake: Fountainhead, 2008. Print.

Clark, J. Elizabeth. "The Digital Imperative: Making the Case for a 21st-Century Pedagogy." *Computers and Composition* 27.1 (2010): 27–35. Print.

Coiro, Julie, et al., eds. *Handbook of Research on New Literacies*. New York: Erlbaum, 2008. Print.

Cranny-Francis, Anne. *Multimedia: Texts and Contexts*. London: Sage, 2005.

Dangler, Doug., Ben McCorkle, and Time Barrow. "Expanding Composition Audiences with Podcasting." *Computers and Composition Online* (2007). Web. 22 Mar. 2011.

David, Carol, and Anne R. Richards, eds. *Writing the Visual: A Practical Guide for Teachers of Composition and Communication*. West Lafayette: Parlor, 2008. Print.

Davis, Robert, and Mark Shadle. *Teaching Multiwriting: Researching and Composing with Multiple Genres, Media, Disciplines, and Cultures*. Carbondale: Southern Illinois UP, 2007. Print.

Delagrange, Susan H. *Technologies of Wonder: Rhetorical Practice in a Digital World*. Logan: Computers and Composition Digital P/Utah State UP, 2011. Web.

DeVoss, Dànielle N., Heidi A. McKee, and Richard (Dickie) Selfe, eds. *Technological Ecologies and Sustainability*. Logan: Computers and Composition Digital P/Utah State UP, 2009. *Computers and Composition Digital Press*. Web. 28 Mar. 2012. <http://ccdigitalpress.org/ebooks-and-projects/tes>.

Duffelmeyer, Barb Blakely, and Anthony Ellertson. "Critical Visual Literacy: Multimodal Communication Across the Curriculum." *Across the Disciplines* 3 (Dec. 2005). Web. 10 Sept. 2010.

Fortune, Ron. "'You're Not in Kansas Anymore': Interactions Among Semiotic Modes in Multimodal Texts." *Computers and Composition* 22 (2005): 49–54. Print.

Frost, Alanna, Julie A. Myatt, and Stephen Smith. "Multiple Modes of Production in a College Writing Class." Herrington, Hodgson, and Moran 181–97.

Greenhow, Christine, Beth Robelia, and Joan E. Hughes. "Learning, Teaching, and Scholarship in a Digital Age: Web 2.0 and Classroom Research: What Path Should We Take Now?" *Educational Researcher* 38 (May 2009): 246–59. Print.

Handa, Carolyn. *Visual Rhetoric in a Digital World*. New York: Bedford, 2004. Print.

Hawisher, Gail, and Cynthia Selfe. *Gaming Lives in the Twenty-First Century: Literate Connections*. London: Palgrave Macmillan, 2007. Print.

Herrington, Anne, Kevin Hodgson, and Charles Moran, eds. *Teaching the New Writing: Technology, Change, and Assessment in the 21st-Century Classroom*. New York: Teachers College P, 2009. 181–97. Print.

Hill, Charles A. "Reading the Visual in College Writing Classes." *Intertexts: Reading Pedagogy in College Writing Classrooms*. Ed. Marguerite Helmers. Mahwah: Erlbaum, 2003. 118–43. Print.

Hill, Charles A., and Marguerite Helmers, eds. *Defining Visual Rhetorics*. Mahwah: Erlbaum, 2003. Print.

Hocks, Mary E. "Understanding Visual Rhetoric in Digital Writing Environments." *College Composition and Communication* 54 (2003): 629–56. Print.

Hocks, Mary E., and Michelle R. Kendrick, eds. *Eloquent Images: Word and Image in the Age of New Media*. Cambridge: MIT P, 2003. Print.

Jackson, Brian, and Jon Wallin. "Rediscovering the 'Back-and-Forthness' of Rhetoric in the Age of YouTube." *College Composition and Communication* 61.2 (2009): W374–96. Print.

Jewitt, Carey. *Technology, Literacy, and Learning: A Multimodal Approach*. New York: Routledge, 2006. Print.

Jewitt, Carey, and Gunther R. Kress. *Multimodal Literacy*. New York: Peter Lang, 2003. Print.

Journet, Debra. "Inventing Myself in Multimodality: Encouraging Senior Faculty to Use Digital Media." *Computers and Composition* 24 (2007): 107–20. Print.

Kittle, Peter. "Student Engagement and Multimodality: Collaboration, Schema, Identity." Herrington, Hodgson, and Moran. 164–80.

Klages, Marisa A., and J. Elizabeth Clark. "New Worlds of Errors and Expectations: Basic Writers and Digital Assumptions." *Journal of Basic Writing* 28 (2009): 32–49. Print.

Kress, Gunther R. *Before Writing: Rethinking the Paths to Literacy*. New York: Routledge, 1997. Print.

———. " 'English' at the Crossroads: Rethinking Curricula of Communication in the Context of the Turn to the Visual." *Passions, Pedagogies, and 21st-Century Technologies*. Eds. Gail E. Hawisher and Cynthia L. Selfe. Logan: Utah UP, 1999. 66–88. Print.

———. *Literacy in the New Media Age*. New York: Routledge, 2003. Print.

———. *Multimodality: A Social Semiotic Approach to Contemporary Communication*. London: Routledge, 2010. Print.

————. *Urban Classrooms, Subject English: Multimodal Perspectives on Teaching and Learning*. London: Routledge, 2004. Print.

Kress, Gunther R., and T. van Leeuwen. *Multimodal Discourse: The Modes and Media of Contemporary Communication*. London: Arnold, 2001. Print.

————. *Reading Images: The Grammar of Visual Design*. New York: Routledge, 2006. Print.

LaGrandeur, Kevin. "Digital Images and Classical Persuasion." Hocks and Kendrick 117–36.

Lutkewitte, Claire, ed. *Web 2.0 Applications for Composition Classrooms*. Forthcoming. Southlake: Fountainhead, 2012. Print.

————. "Web 2.0 Technologies in First-Year Writing." *Computers and Composition Online* 26.3 (2009). Web. 2012. (Note: this article best viewed using Internet Explorer)

————. "Writing Students Should Write about Advertisements." *Teaching in the Pop Culture Zone: Using Popular Culture in the Composition Classroom*. Eds. Allison Smith, Michelle Smith, and Rebecca Bobbitt. Boston: Wadsworth, 2008. 135–41. Print.

Maloch, Beth, and Charles Kinzer. "The Impact of Multimedia Cases on Preservice Teachers' Learning About Literacy Teaching: A Follow-Up Study." *The Teacher Educator* 41 (2006): 158–71. Print.

McComiskey, Bruce. "Visual Rhetoric and the New Public Discourse." *JAC* 24.1 (2004): 187–206. Print.

McGrath, Laura, ed. *Collaborative Approaches to the Digital in English Studies*. Logan: Computers and Composition Digital P/Utah State UP, 2011. Computers and Composition Digital Press. Web. 28 Mar. 2012. <http://ccdigitalpress .org/ebooks-and-projects/cad>.

————. "Negotiating Access to New Media." Ball and Kalmbach 305–22.

McKee, Heidi A., and Dànielle Nicole DeVoss. *Digital Writing Research: Technologies, Methodologies, and Ethical Issues*. Cresskill: Hampton, 2007. Print.

McLuhan, Marshall. *Understanding Media: The Extensions of Man*. Boston: MIT P, 1994. Print. [Critical ed. issued by Gingko, 2003]

————, with Quentin Fiore. *The Medium Is the Massage: An Inventory of Effects*. Berkeley: Gingko, 2005. Print.

Morrison, A. "Border Crossings and Multimodal Composition in the Arts." *International Journal of Education and Development Using ICT* (2005, July 30). Web. 10 Oct. 2010.

Nicotra, Jodie. "'Folksonomy' and the Restructuring of Writing Space." *College Composition and Communication* 61 (2009): W259–76. Print.

Prior, Paul. "Moving Multimodality beyond the Binaries: A Response to Gunther Kress' 'Gains and Losses.'" *Computers and Composition* 22 (2005): 23–30. Print.

Prior, Paul, et al. "Re-Situating and Re-Mediating the Canons: A Cultural-Historical Remapping of Rhetorical Activity." *Kairos* 11.3 (2007). Web. 29 May 2007.

Purdy, James P. "When the Tenets of Composition Go Public: A Study of Writing in Wikipedia." *College Composition and Communication* 61.2 (2009): W351–73. Print.

Reid, Alex. "Tuning In: Infusing New Media into Professional Writing Curriculum." *Kairos* 12.2 (2008). Web. 10 Oct. 2010.

———. *The Two Virtuals: New Media and Composition*. Anderson: Parlor, 2008.

Rice, Jeff. *The Rhetoric of Cool: Composition Studies and New Media*. Carbondale: Southern Illinois UP, 2007. Print.

Selber, Stuart. *Multiliteracies for a Digital Age*. Carbondale: Southern Illinois UP, 2004. Print.

Selfe, Cynthia, ed. *Multimodal Composition: Resources for Teachers*. Cresskill: Hampton, 2007. Print.

Selfe, Richard, and Cynthia Selfe. "'Convince me!' Valuing Multimodal Literacies and Composing Public Services Announcements." *Theory into Practice* 47.2 (2008): 83–92. Print.

Sheridan, David M., Jim Rodolfo, and Anthony J. Michel. "The Available Means of Persuasion: Mapping a Theory and Pedagogy of Multimodal Public Rhetoric." *Plugged In: Technology, Rhetoric, and Culture in a Posthuman Age*. Eds. Lynn Worsham and Gary A. Olson. Cresskill: Hampton, 2008. 61–94. Print.

Shipka, Jody. "A Multimodal Task-Based Framework for Composing." *College Composition and Communication* 57 (2005): 277–306. Print.

———. "Negotiating Rhetorical, Material, Methodological, and Technological Difference: Evaluating Multimodal Designs." *College Composition and Communication* 61.1 (2009): W343–66. Print.

———. "On the Many Forms it Took Throughout: Engineering a Multipart, Multiple Site Rhetorical Event." *Exploring Semiotic Remediation as Discourse Practice*. Eds. Paul Prior and Julie Hengst. New York: Palgrave Macmillan, 2010. 52–76. Print.

———. "Sound Engineering: Toward a Rhetoric of Multimodal Soundness." *Computers and Composition* 23 (2006): 355–73. Print.

———. *Toward a Composition Made Whole*. Pittsburgh: U of Pittsburgh P, 2011. Print.

Sirc, Geoffrey. "Box Logic." Wysocki et al. 111–46.

Stein, Pippa. *Multimodal Pedagogies in Diverse Classrooms: Representation, Rights, and Resources*. New York: Routledge, 2008. Print.

Tardy, Christine M. "Expressions of Disciplinarity and Individuality in a Multimodal Genre." *Computers and Composition* 22 (2005): 319–36. Print.

Tufte, Edward. *Envisioning Information*. Cheshire: Graphics Press, 1990. Print.

Ulmer, Gregory L. *Internet Invention: From Literacy to Electracy*. New York: Longman, 2003. Print.

Unsworth, L. *Teaching Multiliteracies Across the Curriculum: Changing Contexts of Text and Image in Classroom Practice*. Buckingham: Open UP, 2001. Print.

Vasudevan, Lalitha, Katherine Schultz, and Jennifer Bateman. "Rethinking Composing in a Digital Age: Authoring Literate Identities through Multimodal Storytelling." *Written Communication* 27 (2010): 442–68. Print.

Vie, Stephanie. "Digital Divide 2.0: 'Generation M' and Online Social Networking Sites in the Composition Classroom." *Computers and Composition* 25 (2008): 9–23. Print.

Welch, Kathleen. *Electronic Rhetoric: Classical Rhetoric, Oralism, and a New Literacy*. Cambridge: MIT P, 1999. Print.

Wesch, Michael. "From Knowledgable to Knowledge-able: Learning in New Media Environments." *Academic Commons* 7 Jan. 2009. Web. 6 Oct. 2010.

Westbrook, Steve. "Visual Rhetoric in a Culture of Fear: Impediments to Multimedia Production." *College English* 68 (2006): 457–80. Print.

Worsham, Lynn and Gary A. Olson, eds. *Plugged In: Technology, Rhetoric, and Culture in a Posthuman Age*. Cresskill: Hampton, 2008. Print.

Wysocki, Anne Francis. "Seeing the Screen: Research into Visual and Digital Writing Practices." *Handbook of Research on Writing: History, Society, School, Individual, Text*. New York: Erlbaum, 2008. Print.

Wysocki, Anne Francis et al., eds. *Writing New Media: Theory and Applications for Expanding the Teaching of Composition*. Logan: Utah State UP, 2004. Print.

Yancey, Kathleen Blake. *Writing in the 21st Century*. Urbana: NCTE, 2009. Web. 2012. <http://www.ncte.org/library/NCTEFiles/Press/Yancey_final.pdf>.

ABOUT THE EDITOR

Claire Lutkewitte, PhD, is an assistant professor of writing at Nova Southeastern University where she teaches a variety of undergraduate and graduate composition courses. She has published and presented on multimodal composition, composition pedagogy, computers and technology, and writing center practice. Her current research interests include investigating the relationships between mobile learning and composition and exploring how new technologies, like mobile technologies, can help or hinder composition instructors and students in and out of the classroom. Her latest work, an edited collection called *Web 2.0 Applications for Composition Classrooms*, examines successful composition assignments that creatively utilize Web 2.0 applications.

ACKNOWLEDGMENTS (*continued from page iv*)

Text Credits

Jonathan Alexander. "Email by Jonathan Alexander." Copyright © 2009 Jonathan Alexander. Reprinted by permission of the author.

Daniel Anderson, et. al, "Figure: Question #114." From *Survey of Multimodal Pedagogies in Writing*. Retrieved from http://www.compositionstudies.tcu.edu/archives/342/cccc-data/index .html. Copyright © 2006 by the National Council of Teachers of English; reprinted by permission.

Reprinted from *Computers and Composition*, Vol. 25/No. 1, Daniel Anderson, "The Low Bridge to High Benefits: Entry-Level Multimedia, Literacies, and Motivation," pp. 40–60. Copyright © 2008 with permission from Elsevier.

Reprinted from *Computers and Composition*, Vol. 21/No. 4, Cheryl E. Ball, "Show, Not Tell: The Value of New Media Scholarship," pp. 403–25. Copyright © 2004 with permission from Elsevier.

Jeff Bezemer and Gunther Kress. "Writing in Multimodal Texts: A Social Semiotic Account of Designs for Learning." From *Written Communication Journal*, April 2008, Vol. 25 no. 2, pp. 166–95. Copyright © 2008 Jeff Bezemer and Gunther Kress. Reprinted by permission of SAGE Publications.

Lisa Bickmore and Ron Christiansen. "'Who Will Be the Inventors? Why Not Us?' Multimodal Composition in the Two-Year College Classroom." From *Teaching English in the Two Year College*, 37. Copyright © 2010 National Council of Teachers of English. Reprinted by permission.

Catherine C. Braun, Ben McCorkle, and Amie C. Wolf. "Remixing Basic Writing: Digital Media Production and the Basic Writing Curriculum." From *Computers and Composition Online*, 2007. Copyright © 2007 by Catherine C. Braun, Ben McCorkle, and Amie C. Wolf. Reprinted by permission.

William Costanzo. "Film As Composition." From *College Composition and Communication*, 37. Copyright © 1986 National Council of Teachers of English. Reprinted by permission.

Dánielle Nicole DeVoss, Ellen Cushman, and Jeffrey T. Grabill. "Infrastructure and Composing: The When of New-Media Writing." From *College Composition and Communication* 57, Copyright © 2005 National Council of Teachers of English. Reprinted by permission.

T. S. Eliot. *Four Quartets*. Copyright © 1936 by Harcourt, Inc. and renewed 1964 by T. S. Eliot. Reprinted by permission of Houghton Mifflin Harcourt Publishing Company. All rights reserved.

T. S. Eliot. *Four Quartets*. Copyright © 1940 by T. S. Eliot and renewed 1968 by Esme Valerie Eliot. Reprinted by permission of Houghton Mifflin Harcourt Publishing Company. All rights reserved.

T. S. Eliot. *Four Quartets*. Copyright © 1942 by T. S. Eliot and renewed 1970 by Esme Valerie Eliot. Reprinted by permission of Houghton Mifflin Harcourt Publishing Company. All rights reserved.

T. S. Eliot. *Four Quartets*. Copyright © 1944 by T. S. Eliot. Reprinted by permission of Faber & Faber Limited.

Steven Fraiberg. "Composition 2.0: Toward a Multilingual and Multimodal Framework." *College Composition and Communication*, 62. Copyright © 2010 National Council of Teachers of English. Reprinted by permission.

Diana George. "From Analysis to Design: Visual Communication in the Teaching of Writing." From *College Composition and Communication*, 54. Copyright © 2002 National Council of Teachers of English. Reprinted by permission.

Bernard Hibbitts. "Making Sense of Metaphor: Visuality, Aurality, and the Reconfiguration of American Legal Discourse" by Bernard Hibbitts from THE CARDOZO LAW REVIEW. Copyright © 2009 Bernard Hibbitts. Reprinted by permission of the author and publisher.

Glynda A. Hull and Mark Evan Nelson. "Locating the Semiotic Power of Multimodality." From *Written Communication*, April 2005, vol. 22 no. 2, pp. 224–61. Copyright © 2005 Glynda A. Hull and Mark Evan Nelson. Reprinted by permission of SAGE Publications.

Jewitt, Carey. "Multimodality, 'Reading' and 'Writing' for the 21st Century." From *Discourse Studies in the Cultural Politics of Education*, 26.3 (2005), pp. 315–31. Reprinted by permission.

Reprinted from *Computers and Composition*, Vol. 22/No. 1, Gunther Kress, "Gains and losses: New Forms of Texts, Knowledge, and Learning" pp. 5–22. Copyright © 2005 with permission from Elsevier.

Reprinted from *Computers and Composition*, Vol. 26/No. 4, Claire Lauer, "Contending with Terms: 'Multimodal' and 'Multimedia' in the Academic and Public Spheres," pp. 225–39. Copyright © 2009 with permission from Elsevier.

William Lutz. "Making Freshman English a Happening." From *College Composition and Communication*, 22:1. Copyright © 1971 National Council of Teachers of English. Reprinted by permission.

Richard Marback. "Embracing Wicked Problems: The Turn to Design in Composition Studies." From *College Composition and Communication*, 61. Copyright © 2009 National Council of Teachers of English. Reprinted by permission.

National Council of Teachers of English. "Position Statement on Multimodal Literacies" by the Multimodal Literacies Issue Management Team of the NCTE Executive Committee. Copyright © 2005 National Council of Teachers of English. Reprinted by permission.

The New London Group. "A Pedagogy of Multiliteracies: Designing Social Futures." From the *Harvard Educational Review*, Volume 66:1. Copyright © 1996 by the President and Fellows of Harvard College. Reprinted by permission of Harvard Education Publishing Group. All rights reserved. For more information, please visit www.harvardeducationalreview.org.

Excerpt from Osmoz.com reprinted with permission from of the Firmenich Corporation.

Penton Media/Sony. Copyright 2012: Penton Media, 93775: FO1012.

Joddy Murray. "Composing Multimodality." From *Non-Discursive Rhetoric: Image and Affect in Multimodal Composition*. Copyright © 2009 by the State University of New York. Reprinted by permission of the State University of New York Press. All rights reserved.

Jeff Rice. "Imagery." From *The Rhetoric of Cool*. Copyright © 2007 Southern Illinois University Press. Reprinted by permission.

Suzanne Kesler Rumsey. "Heritage Literacy: Adoption, Adaptation, and Alienation or Multimodal Literacy Tools." From *College Composition and Communication*, 60. Copyright © 2009 National Council of Teachers of English. Reprinted by permission.

Stuart Selber. "Institutional, Dimensions of Academic Computing." From *College Composition and Communication*, 61. Copyright © 2009 National Council of Teachers of English. Reprinted by permission.

Cynthia Selfe. "The Movement of Air, the Breath of Meaning: Aurality and Multimodal Composing." From *College Composition and Communication*, 60. Copyright © 2009 National Council of Teachers of English. Reprinted by permission.

Reprinted from *Computers and Composition*, Vol. 26/No. 2, Jennifer Sheppard, "The Rhetorical Work of Multimedia Production Practices: It's More than Just Technical Skill," pp. 122–31, Copyright © 2009 with permission from Elsevier.

Geoffrey Sirc. "The Still-Unbuilt Hacienda." From *English as a Happening*. Copyright © 2002 Utah State University Press. Reprinted by permission.

S. L. Star and K. Ruhleder. "Steps Toward an Ecology of Infrastructure: Design and Access for Large Information Spaces." From *Information Systems Research* 7(1). Copyright © 1996 the Institute for Operations Research and the Management Sciences (INFORMS), 7240 Parkway Drive, Suite 300, Hanover, MD 21076 USA. Reprinted by permission.

TechTerms.com. *Definition of Multimedia*. Copyright © 2012 TechTerms.com. Reprinted by permission.

Excerpt from "University of London Postgraduate Certificate in Education." Copyright © 1992 by the Institute of Education at the University of London. Reprinted by permission of the University of London.

Reprinted from *Computers and Composition*, Vol. 22/No. 1, Anne Frances Wysocki, "awaywithwords: On the Possibilities in Unavailable Designs," pp. 55–62, Copyright © 2005 with permission from Elsevier.

Kathleen Blake Yancey. "Made Not Only in Words: Composition in a New Key." From *College Composition and Communication* 56:2. Copyright © 2004 National Council of Teachers of English. Reprinted by permission.

Art Credits

p. 36. "CNET Forum." Copyright © 2012 CBS Interactive. Screenshot is used with the permission of CBS Interactive.

p. 64. Tabula Magellanica qua Tierra del Fuego. Amsterdam: Schenk and Valk, [1709?]. Hand-colored engraving. Geography and Map Division, Title Collection, Chile-Magellan Strait (3). Image courtesy of the Library of Congress.

p. 67. Wassily Kandinsky. "Composition VIII" by Wassily Kandinsky. Copyright © 2012 by the Artists Rights Society (ARS), New York/ADAGP, Paris. Reprinted by permission of the Artists Rights Society (ARS).

p. 68. U. S. Geological Survey. "Map of Tectonic Plates." Image courtesy of the U. S. Geological Survey.

p. 79. U. S. Geological Survey. "Earthquake Map." Image courtesy of the U. S. Geological Survey.

p. 81. Punkvoter.org. Image courtesy of Punkvoter.org.

p. 168. Kathie Gossett, Carrie A. Lamanna, Joseph Squier and Joyce R. Walker. "[Continuing to] Mind the Gap: Teaching Image and Text in New Media Spaces. Kairos: Rhetoric, Technology, Pedagogy." From http://english.ttu.edu/kairos/7.3/binder2.html?coverweb/Gossett/index .html. Screenshot reprinted by permission of Kathie Gossett.

p. 174. Geoffrey Sirc. "Never Mind the Tagmemics: Where's the Sex Pistols?" From *Pre/Text: Electra(lite)* by Geoffrey Sirc. Copyright © 1997 by Pre/Text: A Journal of Rhetorical Theory. Screenshot reprinted by permission of Pre/text Electra(lite).

p. 177. Adrian Miles. "Digital Multiliteracies." From *Violence of Text*. Copyright © 2003 by Adrian Miles. Screenshot reprinted with the permission of the author.

pp. 243 and 248. G. Cole, B. Fraser, K. Grantham, P. Hughes, D. Kent et al. "Measuring Angles." From *Impact Maths 1G*, p. 192. Copyright © 1999 by Heinemann. Reprinted by permission of Pearson Education Limited.

pp. 254 and 255. Carol Chapman and Moira Sheehan. "Total Breakdown." From *Catalyst: A Framework for Success 1—Red Student Book*, p. 8. Copyright © 2003 by Heinemann. Reprinted by permission of Pearson Education Limited.

p. 305. W. D. Sebald. "The Rings of Saturn." by W. D. Sebald and translated by Michael Hulse. Copyright © 1998 by The Harvill Press. Reprinted with the permission of New Directions Publishing Corp.

p. 320. "Steinbeck CD ROM Screenshot." Screenshot used with permission from J. Boylston & Company, Publishers.

p. 323. "Society News Screenshot." Screenshot used with permission from J. Boylston & Company, Publishers.

p. 365. Jody Shipka, "This Was (NOT) an Easy Assignment: Negotiating an Activity-based Framework for Composing." From *Computers and Composition Online* (Special Issue), 2007. Copyright © 2007 by Jody Shipka. Screenshot reprinted by permission of the author.

p. 367. Debra Journet, Tabetha Atkins, Chris Alexander, Patrick Corbett, Ryan Trauman and the University of St. Louis from Bowling Green State University "Digital Mirrors: Multimodal Reflection in the Composition Classroom." Screenshot reprinted by permission of Debra Journet.

p. 381. Lucian Coman. "Poor African Child in the Door." From Shutterstock.com.

p. 381. Petr Kratochvi. "Curious Students." Image courtesy of PublicDomainPictures.net.

p. 381. MitarArt/Shutterstock.com. "Depressed Teenage Girl."

p. 381. Jeff Schultes/Shutterstock.com. "Maasai Children."

p. 382. The Detroit Free Press. "The Intersection of 12th Street and Clairmount Saturday, July 23, 1967." Image courtesy of the Detroit Free Press.

p. 382. Abbie Rowe. "White House Photographs." From *John F. Kennedy Presidential Library and Museum, Boston.*

p. 382. Rowland Scherman. "Martin Luther King March on Washington." 1963. Photo courtesy of the National Archives and records Administration.

p. 382. John Vachon. "Drinking Fountain on the County Courthouse Lawn, Halifax, North Carolina." 1938. Photo courtesy of the Library of Congress.

p. 383. "Audacity Interface." Copyright © 2012 by Audacity®. Screenshot is reprinted by the permission of the Creative Commons License 3.0.

p. 389. Madeleine Sorapure. "Between Modes: Assessing Students' New Media Compositions." From *Kairos* 10.2. Copyright © 2006 Madeleine Sorapure. Screenshot reprinted by permission of the author.

p. 391. Elizabeth A. Murray, Hailey A. Sheets, and Nicole A. Williams. "The New Work of Assessment: Evaluating Multimodal Compositions." Copyright © 2009 Elizabeth A. Murray, Hailey A. Sheets, and Nicole A. Williams. Screenshot reprinted by permission of Hailey A. Sheets.

p. 457. Christine Tulley. "Taking Composition Program 'Multimodal:' Web 2.0 and Institutional Change at a Small Liberal Arts Institution." From <http:::/wwww.bgsu.edu/cconline /Tulley09/>. Screenshot reprinted by permission of the author.

p. 479. David Corio. "Notorious B.I.G." Copyright © David Corio/Redferns 1995. Reprinted by permission of Getty Images.

p. 479. Francis Firth. "The Great Pyramid and the Sphinx [Gazeh, Egypt]." 1862. Photo courtesy of the U. S. Library of Congress.

p. 479. Edmund D. Fountain. "Tupac Shakur Mural." Copyright © Edmund D. Fountain/ZUMA Press/Corbis. Reprinted by permission.

p. 479. "Marcus Garvey, Half-Length Portrait, Facing Left, in Uniform." 1923. Photo courtesy of the Library of Congress.

p. 479. Ray Schatt. "Malcolm X." 1964. Photo courtesy of the Library of Congress.

p. 481. "Building on Fire." Unattributed. 2001.

p. 481. "Lighting Cigarette." Unattributed. Smoking Addiction In People Is Increasing

p. 481. Christian Carollo/Shutterstock.com. "Love."

p. 481. Daniel M. Nagy. "Thinking Man." Daniel M Nagy/Shutterstock.com.

p. 481. "Stock Photo: Handshake" Courtesy of stock.xchng.

INDEX

abilities, different, 20

ADE. *See* Association of Departments of English

Adkins, Tabetha, 354

"Digital Mirrors: Multimodal Reflection in the Composition Classroom" (Journet, Adkins, Alexander, Corbett, and Trauman), 358–59

administration

classroom design decisions, 387–88

negotiating with, for infrastructure, 413

Adobe

Photoshop, 93

Premiere, 412, 415, 467, 493

Systems, 34

advertisements

decoding meaning of, 106

images encountered in everyday life, 306

intention and design, 334

visual rhetoric, 102

African Americans. *See also* American Indians; Hispanic/Latino communities; minorities; Native Americans

civil rights, visual rhetoric, 102

culture, in digital storytelling, 472

historical lack of educational opportunities, 119

images on album covers, 100–105

Traces in the Stream: Literacy and Social Change among African American Women (Royster), 129

AIDS in Africa (Berger; slide show), 372, 373

album covers, as visual rhetoric, 100–105

Alexander, Chris, 354

"Digital Mirrors: Multimodal Reflection in the Composition Classroom" (Journet, Adkins, Alexander, Corbett, and Trauman), 358–59

Alexander, Jonathan, 28

alphabet

exceeding, in multimodal composition, 26

text and conventions of design, 305

ambiguity as a resource, 430–31

American Artistic Handcrafts, Inc., 56

American Indians, aural literature and culture, 120. *See also* Native Americans

American School and University, 99

Amerika, Mark, 55

"Analysis to Design: Visual Communication in the Teaching of Writing, From" (George), 150, 190, 211–32, 258–59

Anderson, Daniel, 25, 26, 28, 32, 39, 150–51, 152, 353, 355

"The Low Bridge to High Benefits: Entry-Level Multimedia, Literacies, and Motivation," 360–80

Anzaldúa, Gloria, 511

architecture, students and presentation, 82–83

argument

"Possibility and Actuality of Visual Arguments" (Blair), 225

photography, used to compose, 335

visual, 225–27

Arnold, Sarah Louise, 211, 219

art, fine. *See also* Modern art

Arttoday.com, 399

composition of Brueghel's paintings, 306

assessment

grading rubric, 382–83

Kairos (online publication), 164, 167, 183, 328, 381, 454, 457

of multimodality, 343–44

student reflection on web-based text, 358–59

web text regarding, 382–83